VIKING FUND PUBLICATIONS IN ANTHROPOLOGY
Edited by Sol Tax

Number Forty

# READINGS IN EARLY ANTHROPOLOGY

# READINGS IN EARLY ANTHROPOLOGY

*edited by*

## J. S. SLOTKIN

ALDINE PUBLISHING COMPANY / CHICAGO

This volume comprises one of a series of publications on research in general anthropology published by the Wenner-Gren Foundation for Anthropological Research,
Incorporated, a foundation created and endowed at the instance of Axel L. Wenner-
Gren for scientific, educational, and charitable purposes. The reports, numbered
consecutively as independent contributions, appear at irregular intervals.

Library of Congress Catalog Card Number 65–16645

*First published 1965 by*
ALDINE PUBLISHING COMPANY
64 East Van Buren Street
Chicago 5, Illinois

*Printed in Japan*

# FOREWORD

JAMES SYDNEY SLOTKIN was a remarkably erudite scholar who was fluent in several languages and was (for an anthropologist) unusually careful and exact in bibliography. He had the habit of noting as he read not only references but also quotations from original source materials. These he classified according to his varying interests, one of which was the history of anthropology. In 1942 he completed a first draft of *Readings in Early Anthropology,* for which, in October, 1946, he wrote the following overly modest Preface.

Some years ago a period of relative leisure permitted considerable reading on the early figures in the development of anthropology. Once in the subject I found myself getting deeper and deeper, but still with the sense of having only scratched the surface. Finally, I typed up the material I had gathered, for future reference.

The circumstances under which the work was done is reflected in the result. It is simply a collection of odds and ends that struck my interest in the course of scattered reading. In no sense is it a history of early anthropology. Some day I hope to write a history of social anthropology, but I would then expect to handle the material quite differently. It seems to me that a real history should give the cultural and social setting of the various theories, and each theory in terms of the frame of reference of the writer who promulgated it. Instead, in this work I have merely collected material in reference to some of my personal interests, with litttle or no regard to its cultural context. Also, there are serious gaps; I need only mention the absence of Vico, for example.

However, some of my colleagues have argued that the material I have thus collected would be interesting to students in the field and that few people would have either the time or the patience to gather the material, even in the haphazard manner that I have done. Therefore, for whatever usefulness it may have, I agreed to allow it to be published in the original form in which it was left some years ago.

From 1946 until his sudden death in 1958 Dr. Slotkin added occasional bits to the manuscript as he encountered relevant items in his reading. After his death (see *American Anthropologist* Vol. 61, No. 5, October, 1958, pp. 844–47), his widow, Elizabeth Cole Slotkin, agreed to prepare the manuscript for publication. It is here presented essentially as it was left in 1946.

In the autumn and winter of 1955–56, Professor Robert Heine-Geldern came to the University of Chicago as part of a Chicago–Frankfort Inter–University Project. This was the occasion for a seminar in "Anthropology as an Integrated Discipline: a Comparison of the Anglo-American and the Continental Traditions," for which Dr. Slotkin prepared a background paper which summarizes the history that he might have written from the source materials which make up the body of this book. It is published for the first time in the pages immediately following.

As Editor of this series, it is a pleasure to present at once a significant chapter in the work of Sydney Slotkin and a collection important for historians of anthropology.

SOL TAX

# WESTERN ANTHROPOLOGY FROM THE TWELFTH
## TO THE EIGHTEENTH CENTURIES

T HE PURPOSE of this paper is to consider the beginnings of anthropology
as a cultural tradition, and to examine how it was developed and transmitted.

The period under consideration has been chosen somewhat arbitrarily. The
paper starts with the twelfth century, when commercial capitalism and extensive
acculturation spread a secular world view among intellectuals. It ends with the
eighteenth century, because most anthropologists are familiar with the subsequent
history of their science.

In summary, I would say that all fields of anthropology were developed by the
end of the eighteenth century. In fact, their bases were established in the sixteenth
and seventeenth centuries. But there was no professionalization in the fields during
the period under discussion; this was a phenomenon which did not occur until
the nineteenth century.

## THE TRANSMISSION AND ACCUMULATION
## OF INFORMATION

Any aspect of culture develops through the transmission and accumulation of
traits. Therefore in a study of anthropological development it seems appropriate
to give some background on how information was transmitted and accumulated
during the period under consideration.

We will begin with a survey of voluntary associations organized for the transmission and accumulation of information.

Universities are institutions for transmitting conventional knowledge. Up to
the twelfth century Western universities were clerical, but from that time on
secular universities were organized to train the secular intellectuals needed by
commercial capitalists. This involved modifying the traditional program of the
seven liberal arts to include new fields of specialization, such as *ars notaria*. But
none of the present anthropological disciplines seems to have been included in
universities—with a few exceptions to be considered later in this paper.

Various groupings of intellectuals were organized to transmit and accumulate
unconventional knowledge. The earliest institution of this sort was the academy,
first formed in the fifteenth century by Florentine humanists under classical Greek

inspiration. The next two centuries saw the foundation of purely scientific societies: the Academia Secretorum Naturae, founded in Naples in 1560 was soon followed by an informal society in London which became Gresham College in 1596. The earliest and most famous of the seventeenth-century scientific academies were the Accademia dei Lincei (Rome, 1603) and the Royal Society (London, 1662). Most academies were national in character.

More directly relevant to anthropological studies were the historiographic organizations founded to give ideological support to the developing national states in the sixteenth century, for these groups often contained sections on "antiquities," including archeology. The earliest known to me is a society for British antiquities (London, 1572–1604). Later examples are L'Académie des Inscriptions et Belles Lettres (Paris, 1663) and the Society of Antiquaries (London, 1717). There were no academies which specialized either in what is now anthropology or in any of its fields. The nearest would be the antiquarian societies, but they combined archeology, topography, early national history, etc.

In addition to national academies, the eighteenth century saw the organization of numerous local learned societies, with broad interests in arts and sciences generally. However, in all the profusion of societies I know of none which specialized in any of the present anthropological fields. In the eighteenth century two other groupings, less formal than the academy and the society, became important: the French salon and the British club.

Discussion of the operation of all these groupings may be postponed until we have considered modes of communication. A good deal of the knowledge in any field is transmitted orally, directly or indirectly; this can be seen in the knowledge differentials between a university trained student and an autodidact, or between an isolated scholar and one in the center of things. One of the most important functions of all the groupings already discussed, therefore, was to provide means for direct and indirect communication between interested persons. An additional purpose explicitly stated by scientific academies was the accumulation of knowledge; this was achieved by the moral and financial encouragement of research.

Writing was the only significant kind of mediated communication. Scholarly writing took two forms: quasi-personal letters and public treatises. Scholars corresponded with one another. If a letter contained important information the recipient would send copies of it to his other correspondents, and so on. After the popularization of printing such letters were often printed and circulated by the sender himself. In this connection, another function of the academy was to make this form of communication simpler and more efficient. A research worker would send a single letter to the Secretary of the Royal Society, let us say; his letter would then be read at a meeting of the Society and published in its transactions.

In the early period, public treatises were hand written and therefore scarce and expensive; but printing was sufficiently well developed by the sixteenth century to permit relatively cheap and widespread distribution of scholarly reports. These published works were owned and loaned by the scholars themselves to one another. (The secular libraries played a relatively unimportant role in scientific development, though they included the Biblioteca Mediceo-Laurenziana of Florence,

1571, and the Oxford University Library, founded in 1603).

An important advance was the development of the learned periodical, for this operated as a medium for the general communication of short reports in all fields of scholarship. The first of these magazines was the French *Journal des scavans* established in 1665; this was soon followed in the same year by the English *Philosophical Transactions* of the Royal Society. Later, and more international in character, was the Latin *Acta eruditorum* founded in 1682.

In some respects, communication was easier than it is at present. First, Latin was the international language of scholars, until national states increased the social value of mother tongues in the seventeenth century. Second, scholars formed an international fraternity, and did not allow wars or other forms of opposition between countries to interfere with their communication, until the rise of nationalism in the nineteenth century.

So far we have examined the transmission and accumulation of information from the twelfth to eighteenth centuries. Now let us turn to the development of the anthropological disciplines themselves.


## PHYSICAL ANTHROPOLOGY

Physical anthropology will be taken to consist of human paleontology and human biology.

Two factors have contributed to the development of human paleontology. One is inductive—the finding of hominid fossils. The other is deductive, based upon a consideration of the relation between man and other organisms.

I know of no texts dealing with hominid fossils recognized as such until the eighteenth century. At that time the anatomist and physician John Hunter stated that some human fossils were "many thousand centuries old," and developed a rudimentary theory of organic evolution. But no one seems to have built on his theories.

Throughout the period under consideration there were many who believed in materialism, which, in combination with the concept of the chain of being, leads to an evolutionary theory (as in Lucretius). However, no early texts on the subject exist, probably because anyone who was known to be against the origin myths in Genesis was severely punished. Biologists interested in the animals of the world were led to systematize their knowledge by means of taxonomies, but man was almost invariably excluded, as a being distinct from other animals. The few taxonomists who did include man always considered him separately from the other primates, like Joannes Johnstonus in 1632; Linnaeus, in 1735, was an early exception. Amateur philosophers occasionally used this taxonomic material to develop an evolutionary theory, but their attempts were sporadic and isolated. The earliest text known to me on organic evolution based upon comparative considerations is that of Lucilio Vanini in 1616. The most ambitious effort in this direction was Monboddo's *Origin and Progress of Language* (1773–92); he was labeled an eccentric and became an international joke for believing that man was descended from apes.

Racial biology followed from an awareness of race differences. The latter was always present, but became more obvious as explorers extended Western knowledge of the races of the world.

Descriptive racial biology was developed by university anatomists who included exotic peoples among their subjects as these became available for study; Vesalius noticed the relation between shape of skull and race in 1543 and Camper wrote on the relation between facial angle and race in 1791. However, racial anatomy never became a subject of any particular interest in medical schools. Meanwhile, travellers, including physicians on exploring expeditions, paid attention to the racial differences they encountered and applied the current taxonomic principles to human beings. The first racial classification was that of the traveller François Bernier, published in 1684. He divided mankind into Europeans, Africans, Asiatics, and Lapps. His taxonomy laid the groundwork for the eighteenth-century classifications by the naturalists Linnaeus and Blumenbach, which are the basis of modern racial classification.

The awareness of racial differences led to a debate over monogenesis as against polygenesis. The controversy was not so much between scientists as between what we would now call fundamentalists and advanced thinkers. Monogenesis (i.e., that all mankind is descended from Adam and Eve) was the orthodox position, being based upon the official origin myths found in Genesis. But monogenesists had the problem of accounting for racial differences. Their favorite naturalistic explanation was geographic (based upon the inheritance of acquired characteristics), though Leonardo da Vinci and others pointed out the inadequacy of such an hypothesis. Polygenesis is first mentioned as a possibility by Gillaume de Conches in the twelfth century. The position is maintained, with little elaboration, by Paracelsus and Giordano Bruno in the sixteenth century. Polygenesis finally became a popular theory as a result of Isaac de La Peyrere's exposition published in 1655.

## ARCHEOLOGY

In the early period, paleolithic and neolithic tools were discussed by mineralogists; most of them accepted Pliny's explanation of them as thunderbolts. It was not until the sixteenth century that Michele Mercati stated that these stones were the tools of a primitive people unacquainted with metals. This idea was accepted by a few antiquarians in the next century, such as Anselm Boèce de Boodt and William Dugdale; it became more widespread in the eighteenth century.

The prevailing archeology, however, was historic rather than prehistoric. The earliest professional antiquarians are found in Italy, where their function was twofold: to discover a glorious past for the city states and thus give them ideological reinforcement, and to support humanistic secularization by examples drawn from Greek and Roman cultures. The most important early professionls were Niccolo Niccoli, Ciriaco de' Pizzicolli and Flavio Biondi, all of whom were active in the fifteenth century.

The development of national states in northern Europe led to great activity in historic archeology, for the first of the two reasons given above. In each country were a few professional, and many amateur, antiquarians, who met frequently and wrote voluminously. The first formal organization of antiquarians was founded in London in 1572, beginning a type of voluntary association which has persisted to the present in all Western society.

The present distinction between dirt archeologists and historical theorists also existed in the period we are discussing. On the one hand were the antiquarians already considered; their writings tend to be purely descriptive. On the other hand were amateurs in various walks of life who were interested in what was called social philosophy or moral science; these people often enunciated grand theories of prehistoric development.

In general these theories fall into two classes, those of social degradation and those of social progress. Conservatives who were dismayed by rapid social and cultural change accepted the idea of the decay of nature, which implied a theory of social degeneration. From an original golden age, man had passed through silver and bronze ages and was now in the final iron age (the selection of metals was more figurative than literal.) The advocates of social and cultural change were intellectuals who supported the overthrow of feudalism; they adopted theories of social evolution. In this regard, the earliest text known to me is by Boccaccio in the fourteenth century; its elaboration (presumably on a Lucretian basis) was by the humanist Juan Luis Vives in 1531. He developed a point of view which was to persist until the end of the nineteenth century—a concept of unilinear evolution, employing data from children and so-called primitives to fill in the theoretical gaps for early societies, using rationalism in prehistoric reconstructions, etc. This theory of social and cultural evolution became a commonplace among eighteenth-century liberals. But we will postpone further discussion of the matter to the section on social anthropology.


## ETHNOGRAPHY

Throughout this period ethnographers were usually travellers. Some idea of the background of these people can be obtained from the following thirteenth-century accounts: Jacobus de Vitriaco was a crusader who wrote on the customs of the peoples in the middle East; he gives valuable information on acculturation. Giovanni di Plano Carpini and Willem van Ruysbroek were displomats sent to the Mongols, Johannes de Monte Corvino was an Asiatic missionary, and Marco Polo was an Asiatic merchant.

The mercantile explorers of Africa provided much new material, beginning with Antonio Malfante in the fifteenth century. And, of course, we have descriptions of the Americas from Christopher Columbus on.

Expeditions began to have ethnographic specialists who gathered data for administrative, economic or missionary purposes. The earliest seems to have been Ramon Pan, who was ethnographer in one of Columbus' expeditions. Sixteenth-century accounts of organized ethnographic activity can be found in the missionary work undertaken by Matteo Ricci among the Chinese or by Bernardino de Sahagùn among the Aztecs.

Innumerable travel accounts were written from the fifteenth to the eighteenth centuries, so that by the end of the period all the major culture areas were known to Western scholars. At an early date attempts were made to compile this ethnographic data into usuable form. The Ebstorf *mappamundi* is an ethnographic map of the thirteenth century. There were many compilations; the earliest based on some first hand observation were fourteenth-century works, namely, that by William Adam and the anonymous *Libro del Conoscimiento*.

As the number of travel accounts increased, they began to be published in collections. An important sixteenth-century example was edited by Giovanni Battista Ramusio. This was followed by a long series of collections in various languages; the most famous in English is that of the Hakluyts.

Most accounts were written by travellers who successively visited a number of societies and wrote sketchily upon many cultures. An eighteenth-century classic example of this genre is the series of publications resulting from James Cook's expeditions. A few travellers, especially missionaries, remained in one society for years and wrote in some detail upon a single culture. Usually they give brief accounts, such as the *Annual Letters* of the Jesuit missionaries; a more extended report is Martin Dobrizhoffer's monograph on the Abipones published in 1783.


## LINGUISTICS

Universalistic Christianity required missionaries, and if these were to be effective they had to speak the language of the people they were trying to convert. Thus some missionaries became linguistic specialists, beginning with Arabic in the thirteenth century. At that time, the first professorships in language (Arabic) were established in the clerical universities. Religious debates with Islamic scholars necessitated better comprehension of the original Biblical texts, so by the next century there were also professorships in Hebrew, Aramaic and Greek. The study of the latter languages spread to the secular universities in the sixteenth-century, because secular, Catholic humanist, and Protestant intellectuals needed similar information in their struggle with fundamentalist Catholics.

Meanwhile, the increasing use of vernaculars—first by literary men and later by scholars—led to study of their own language. Thus, in his apology for the use of Italian as a literary language, Dante in the fourteenth century discussed the function of speech. He accepted the myth that Hebrew was the first language and that linguistic diversity in "idioms" began with the destruction of Babel. However, he was aware of linguistic change and dialect geography, and argued that each idiom itself has become diversified into various vernaculars because of isolation through time. He believed that the original idiom could be reconstructed from its various vernaculars by means of the age-area hypothesis.

The study of linguistic processes was also continued by monogenesists. They had the problem of explaining linguistic diversity, and did so by examining contemporary processes which seemed to produce the phenomenon. Thus Kenelm Digby and Thomas White durng the seventeenth century discussed linguistic change and dialect geography in general terms. More precise formulations were given in the eighteenth century when James Parsons demonstrated phonetic shifts between some Indo-European languages and William Marsden did the same for Malayo-Polynesian.

Some antiquaries were interested in early historical documents and thus were led to a study of the languages involved. For instance, François Hotman in the sixteenth century and Edward Lhuyd in the seventeenth, studied Celtic; Franciscus Junius and George Hicks investigated Germanic in the seventeenth century.

Meanwhile, widespread travel resulted in an increasing interest in exotic languages. Thus, Andrew Boorde, *ca.* 1547, gave linguistic texts for each country he visited. Linguistic compilations began in the same century with Konrad Gesner; his *Mithridates* contains vocabularies and texts in a number of languages.

Thus there was developed a substantial body of knowledge about languages and linguistic processes. This information was then used by scholars to classify languages—and we have the foundations of the comparative method. The philologist Joseph Juste Scaliger classified European languages in the sixteenth century. He divided them into eleven unrelated "mother tongues," of which four are relatively important and seven unimportant. The former were classified, on the basis of their word for "god," into Latin *(deus)*/ Greek *(theos)*/ Teutonic *(godt)*/ and Slavonic *(boge)*. The seven minor "mother tongues" are Epirotic, Tartaric, Hungarian, Finnish, Irish, Britannic, and Basque. In 1643, Claude de Saumaise demonstrated that Scaliger's Latin, Greek, Teutonic and also Persian, were related. Another great advance took place in the eighteenth century when William Jones showed that Sanskrit was an Indo-European language.

## ETHNOLOGY

Ethnology is here taken to mean a study of the historical relations between cultures.

There were no students of ethnology as such. There were amateurs who focused their attention on one basic problem—monogenesis or polygenesis. The polygenesists pointed to the great diversity of cultures as evidence for their position. The monogenesists attempted to show similarities among cultures, and the universal diffusion of all other cultures from a single original—usually Egyptian or Hebrew. Perhaps the most important contribution was made by the lawyer, Hugo Grotius, in 1642. While arguing that the American Indians are the lost tribes of Israel, he set down the basic methodological criteria for discriminatng between independent invention and diffusion. Another work of contemporary methodological interest is the 1760 study by Charles de Brosses on the relation between the ancient Egyptian and modern African religions.

## SOCIAL ANTHROPOLOGY

If we consider social anthropology to be the comparative study of cultures, it does not begin until the sixteenth century, when a substantial body of travel accounts became available.

It is possible to call Machiavelli's method comparative, because he explicitly generalizes from Roman and Italian data; but one has the feeling his examples are really *ex post facto*. It is quite different with Montaigne. Here we have a humanist, sceptic and man of affairs, who is an amateur student of mankind. He is aware of the diversity of customs from his own travel and by reading many travel accounts, though he believes in the psychic unity of mankind. He delights in demonstrating that personality is subject to social and cultural influences, so that man is irrationally ethnocentric.

The French administrator Jean Bodin also used a rudimentary comparative method. The expanding French state found it difficult to impose its laws upon newly conquered peoples, and Bodin tried to explain the trouble. He employed travel accounts to show a relation between culture and geography, and argued that laws suitable to a people living in the French climate were not suitable to peoples living in different climates.

During the seventeenth century the comparative method was elaborated explicitly. Some explanation of the rationale behind this is in order. Western culture has adopted from the Romans a concept of natural law. Briefly, every kind of thing in the universe, including man, at the time of its creation was given certain characteristics; these constitute the law of its nature. However, natural laws are general principles, which have to be specifically applied according to the particular situations confronting one; in the case of man, these are the customs of one's society, which are its civil law. Now, Cicero stated that it is a simple matter to differentiate between natural and civil law: whatever is done universally is part of the law of nature, and whatever is peculiar to one or some societies belongs to civil law. The seventeenth-century procedure, therefore, was to compare accounts of customs from different points in space and time, and to generalize their common features as part of the law of nature. This comparative method was applied to many aspects of culture; the most popular were the fields of law and religion.

The innumerable wars of the rising national states injured mercantile capitalists to such an extent that the lawyer, Grotius, tried to put international law on an incontrovertible basis. In *De jure belli ac pacis* published in 1625, he attempted empirically to derive international law from the law of nature by means of the comparative method, and the introduction to the volume is still a classic of that method.

Edward Herbert of Cherbury was an amateur who studied religion. By applying the comparative method he discovered "five undeniable Propositions. . . . which not only we, but all Mankind in general, must needs acknowledge:

    I. That there is one Supreme God.

    II. That he ought to be worshipped.

    III. That Virtue and Piety are the chief Parts of Divine Worship.

    IV. That we ought to be sorry for our Sins, and repent of them.

    V. That Divine Goodness doth dispense Rewards and Punishments both in this life, and after it."

The revolutionary social conditions during the eighteenth century produced a shift in social anthropological interests. A theory of social and cultural evolution was elaborated by liberal intellectuals to give ideological support to the revolu-tionary interests, and their theories dominated social anthropology until the end of the nineteenth century.

These theories developed in two main centers: the clubs of Edinburgh and Glasgow, to which belonged those whom I call the Scottish evolutional school (Smith, Monboddo, Ferguson, Kames, etc.), and the Parisian salons to which Turgot and Condorcet belonged. Both groups had organized means of transmitting their ideas, in addition to their own publications. Men like Smith and Ferguson were professors of moral philosophy and related subjects in Scotch universities, while in France *L' Encyclopédie* gave authoritative sanction to the theory of social progress.

Essentially their theory was as follows: Assuming unilinear evolution, a taxonomy of cultures is established in terms of a theory of social progress—for example, primitive, savage and civilized. Known cultures are then classified in terms of that taxonomy, and the ethnographic data about culture in each category are used to establish generalizations about the nature of each cultural category. Theories of cultural change are used to explain how some cultures evolve from one category to the next while others remain fixed. Whenever possible, these theories of cultural change are supported by historical evidence; gaps are filled by rational conjectures. The whole method was subjected to critical analysis, and a sophis-ticated methodology was worked out. However, the ethnographic data were not themselves subjected to critical consideration; the use of the historical method in social anthropology is a product of the twentieth century.

# TABLE OF CONTENTS

# I

# TO THE END OF THE FOURTEENTH CENTURY

ON THE BASIS of the material presented in this chapter, it may be stated that, during the first fourteen centuries in western Europe, social phenomena were considered to be supernaturally caused. The whole universe was created and is ruled by a god, and any understanding of it that man can achieve must be based upon divine revelation as recorded in the Old and the New Testament, for "All Scripture is given by inspiration of God."[1]

Because they accepted Genesis as true, most writers of the period had a static view of man and society. In physical anthropology, man was thought of as made by a god in his own image, on the sixth day of the creation of the universe, and with a soul which distinguished him from all other animals. Archeology seems to have been virtually nonexistent, and historical linguistics was perforce limited to tracing contemporary languages back to Hebrew, the language of Adam. Social evolution was limited to comparisons between the culture of man in the Garden of Eden and after the fall.

As a result of the creation and rule of the universe by a god, it is completely organized and animated by him. And, since what is true of a whole is equally true of its parts, this also applied to man and society. Therefore, the universe was taken as the prototype of man and his society, and comparisons were made between the macrocosm and the microcosm. This conception of the universe, society, and man as each a system, plus the organic analogy applied to society, gave the scholars of the period a valuable sense of the interdependence between the parts of society and culture.

Since a god created the universe, he established it according to the rules of his will and/or reason. The laws of god are those proceeding from his will; the laws of nature, those inherent in the universe, including man as one of its parts. The relation between these two types of law was an important consideration to the scholastic philosophers. According to William of Ockham, the law of nature proceeded from the will of god and was therefore synonymous with the law of god. On the other hand, for Hugo of St. Victor the law of nature was derived from the reason inherent in the god's being, and unalterable even if he himself were to will it. An intermediate position was held by Thomas Aquinas, who maintained that, though the law of nature was derived from god's reason, it is sanctioned by his will.

1

## PHYSICAL ANTHROPOLOGY

### Paul of Tarsus

Paul of Tarsus (d. *ca*. 67) accepted the Old Testament version of the creation of the universe[2] and man[3] by a god. Also, every species of inanimate and animate thing was created materially different.

God . . . giveth to every seed his own body. All flesh is not the same flesh: but there is one kind of flesh of men, another flesh of beasts, another of fishes, and another of birds. There are also celestial bodies, and bodies terrestrial.[4]

. . . if you belong to Christ, then you are true[5] descendants of Abraham and his heirs under the promise.

. . . physical cravings are against the Spirit, and[6] the cravings of the Spirit are against the physical; the two are in opposition, so that you cannot do anything you please.

However, he insisted upon the equality of man in the Christian church.

There is no distinction between Jew and Greek, for they all have the same Lord, and he is generous to all who call upon him.[7]

There is neither Jew nor Greek, there is neither bond nor free, there is neither male nor female: for ye are all one in Christ Jesus.[8]

### Later New Testament Writers

The authors of Luke-Acts (*ca*. 90),[9] Hebrews (*ca*. 95), the Gospel of John (*ca*. 110),[10] and II Peter (*ca*. 190)[11] believed in the creation of the universe as given by Genesis, and of course the narrative on the creation of man was also accepted by the later New Testament writers.

. . . from the beginning of the creation God made them male and female.[12]

For Adam was first formed, then Eve.[13]

Jude states in his Epistle (*ca*. 125) that subhuman animals have only instinctive knowledge, while man learns as well.

But these speak evil of things which they know not: but what they know naturally, as brute beasts, in those things they corrupt themselves.[14]

The author of Luke-Acts asserts that all mankind is derived from a common ancestor.

(God) hath made of one blood all nations of men for to dwell on all the face of the earth, and hath determined the times before appointed, and the bounds of their habitation.[15]

### Augustine

Aurelius Augustinus (350–430) followed the Old Testament account of man's origin.

God created only one single man . . . And woman . . . was . . . created . . . out of man.[16]

. . . whoever is anywhere born a man, that is, a rational, mortal animal, no matter what unusual appearance he presents in color, movement, sound, nor how peculiar he is in some power, part, or quality of his nature, no Christian can doubt that he springs from that one protoplast . . . if they are human, they are descended from Adam.[17]

. . . reckoning by the sacred writings, we find that not 6000 years have yet passed (since man was created).[18]

Augustine also viewed man in relation to other beings.

. . . man ('s) . . . nature was to be a mean between the angelic and bestial.[19]

God . . . made man a rational animal consisting of soul and body . . . [and] has given to the good and to the evil, being in common with stones, vegetable life in common with trees, sensuous life in common with brutes, intellectual life in common with angels alone.[20]

## Isidorus of Seville

To Isidorus of Seville (d. 636), racial differences are the result of geographic factors.

In accordance with diversity of climate, the appearance of men and their color and bodily size vary and diversities of mind appear. Thence we see that the Romans are dignified, the Greeks unstable, the Africans crafty, the Gauls fierce by nature and somewhat headlong in their disposition which the character of the climates bring about.[21]

Ethiopia is so called from the color of its people, who are scorched by the nearness of the sun. The color of the people betrays the sun's intensity, for there is never-ending heat there.[22]

## Thomas Aquinas

Thomas Aquinas (1225–1274) concurred in the creation story as given in Genesis.

Nothing except God can be eternal.[23]

God is the Creator of the world: hence . . . the world began.[24]

. . . every being in any way existing is from God.[25]

He also accepted the Old Testament account of the creation and history of man.

The first formation of the human body . . . was immediately from God.[26]

. . . the body of man is said to have been formed from the slime of the earth.[27]

. . . in man there is some likeness to God, copied from God as from an exemplar; yet this likeness is not one of equality, for such an exemplar infinitely excels its copy.[28]

It was necessary for woman to be made, as the Scripture says, as a *helper* to man . . . in the work of generation.[29]

God alone could produce . . . a woman from the rib of man.[30]

God made man outside of paradise, and afterwards placed him there to live there during the whole of his animal life; and, having attained to the spiritual life, to be transferred thence to heaven.[31]

It was fitting that it [i.e., the Garden of Eden] should be in the east; for it is to be believed that it was situated in the most excellent part of the earth.[32]

Thomas examined man's relation to other types of beings and put him midway between angels and lower animals.

Nature passes from one extreme to another through the medium.[33]

In this way we are able to perceive the wondrous connection of things. For we always find the lowest in the highest genus touching the highest of the lower genus: thus some of the lowest of the animal kind scarcely surpass the life of plants, such as oysters which are immovable, have only the sense of touch, and are fixed to the earth like plants.[34]

. . . life appears through various operations in different degrees of living things.[35]

[Let us] consider the distinction of corporeal and spiritual creatures: firstly, the purely spiritual creature which in Holy Scripture is called angel; secondly, the creature wholly corporeal; thirdly, the composite creature, corporeal and spiritual, which is man.[36]

The different grades of life which are found in different living creatures can be discovered from the various ways in which the Scripture speaks of them, as Basil says. The life of plants, for instance, is very imperfect and difficult to discover, . . . only in generation is a vital act observed in them . . . But amongst animals, those that live on land are, generally speaking, more perfect than birds and fishes, not because the fish is devoid of memory, . . . but because their limbs are more distinct and their generation of a higher order, (yet some imperfect animals, such as bees and ants, are more intelligent in certain ways) . . . fishes are merely bodies having in them something of a soul, whilst land animals, from the higher perfection of their life, are, as it were, living souls with bodies subject to them. But the life of man . . . [is] the most perfect grade.[37]

But we must observe that the nobler a form is, the more it rises above corporeal matter, the less it is merged in matter, and the more it excels matter by its power and its operation; hence we find that the form of a mixed body has another operation not caused by its elemental qualities. And the higher we advance in the nobility of forms, the more we find that the power of the form excels the elementary matter; as the vegetative soul excels the form of the metal, and the sensitive soul excels the vegetative soul. Now, the human soul is the highest and noblest of forms. Wherefore, it excels corporeal matter in its power by the fact that it has an operation and a power in which corporeal matter has no share whatever. This power is called the intellect.*[39]

[He anticipated Descartes by enunciating a mechanical theory of animal behavior]; choice is not in irrational animals.[40]

The degree of " nobility " of a form depends upon the powers of its soul.

The Philosopheer [i.e., Aristotle] says (De anima, 2. 3) The powers are the vegetative, the sensitive, the appetitive, the locomotive, and the intellectual.

. . . There are five genera of powers of the soul, as above numbered. Of these, three are called souls, and four are called modes of living. The reason of this diversity lies in the various souls being distinguished according as the operation of the soul transcends the operation of the corporeal nature in various ways; for the whole corporeal nature is subject to the soul, and is related to it as its matter and instrument. There exists, therefore, an operation of the soul which so far exceeds the corporeal nature that it is not even performed by any corporeal organ; and such is the operation of the rational soul. Below this, there is another operation of the soul, which is indeed performed through a corporeal organ, but not through a corporeal quality, and this is the operation of the sensitive soul . . . The lowest of the operations of the soul is that which is performed by a corporeal organ, by virtue of a corporeal quality . . . Such is the operation of the vegetative soul.[41]

* " . . . the difference which constitutes man is rational, which is applied to man on account of his intellectual principle. Therefore the intellectual principle is the form of man . . . the proper operation of man as man is to understand ; because he thereby surpasses all other animals."[38]

. . . the powers of the nutritive soul are prior by way of generation to the powers of the sensitive soul; for which, therefore, they prepare the body. The same is to be said of the sensitive powers with regard to the intellectual.[42]

Then follows an analysis of man from the viewpoint of comparative anatomy.

The sense of touch, which is the foundation of the other senses, is more perfect in man than in any other animal; and for this reason man must have the most equable temperament of all animals. Moreover man excels all other animals in the interior sensitive powers, as is clear from what we have said above [in *Summa* i. 78. 4]. But by a kind of necessity, man falls short of the other animals in some of the exterior senses; thus of all animals he has the least sense of smell. For man of all animals needs the largest brain as compared to the body; both for his greater freedom of action in the interior powers required for the intellectual operations . . . and in order that the low temperature of the brain may modify the heat of the heart, which has to be considerable in man for him to be able to stand up erect. So that the size of the brain, by reason of its humidity, is an impediment to the smell, which requires dryness. . . .

Horns and claws, which are the weapons of some animals, and toughness of hide and quantity of hair or feathers, which are the clothing of animals, are signs of an abundance of the earthly element; which does not agree with the equability and softness of the human temperament. Therefore such things do not suit the nature of man. Instead of these, he has reason and hands whereby he can make himself arms and clothes, and other necessaries of life, of infinite variety. Wherefore the hand is called by Aristotle (*De anima*, 3, 8), *the organ of organs*. Moreover this was more becoming to the rational nature, which is capable of conceiving an infinite number of things, so as to make for itself an infinite number of instruments.

. . . An upright stature was becoming to man for four reasons. First, because the senses are given to man, not only for the purpose of procuring the necessaries of life, for which they are bestowed on other animals, but also for the purpose of knowledge. Hence, whereas the other animals take delight in the objects of the senses only as ordered to food and sex, man alone takes pleasure in the beauty of sensible objects for its own sake. Therefore, as the senses are situated chiefly in the face, other animals have the face turned to the ground, as it were for the purpose of seeking food and procuring a livelihood; whereas man has his face erect, in order that by the senses, and chiefly by sight, which is more subtle and penetrates further into the differences of things, he may freely survey the sensible objects around him, both heavenly and earthly, so as to gather intelligible truth from all things. Secondly, for the greater freedom of the acts of the interior powers; the brain, wherein these actions are, in a way, performed, not being low down, but lifted up above other parts of the body. Thirdly, because if man's stature were prone to the ground he would need to use his hands as fore-feet; and thus their utility for other purposes would cease. Fourthly, because if man's stature were prone on the ground, and he used his hands as fore-feet, he would be obliged to take hold of his food with his mouth. Thus he would have a protruding mouth, with thick and hard lips, and also a hard tongue, so as to keep it from being hurt by exterior things; as we see in other animals. Moreover, such an attitude would quite hinder speech, which is reason's proper operation.

## William of Conches

The existence of different races raised the question of monogenesis *versus* polygenesis; the latter, as a heretical opinion, was touched upon only gingerly by William of Conches (1080-*ca.* 1150).[43]

. . . and this is what the divine page says: *That God made woman out of Adam's side* (Gen. 2 : 21). However, we do not wish to take literally, that God made the first man from a rib. But some might say, that for the same reason many men and women could have been created at that time, and now also. We say that this is true, if that is the divine will.[44]

## ARCHEOLOGY

### Saxo Grammaticus

The archeology of the period is exemplified by the following excerpt from Saxo Grammaticus (1150–1206) on the megalithic remains in Denmark:

That the country of Denmark was once cultivated and worked by giants, is attested by the enormous stones attached to the barrows and caves of the ancients. Should any man question that this is accomplished by superhuman force, let him look up at the tops of certain mountains and say, if he knows how, what man hath carried such immense boulders up to their crests. For anyone considering this marvel will mark that it is inconceivable how a mass, hardly at all or but with difficulty movable upon a level, could have been raised to so mighty a peak of so lofty a mountain by mere human effort, or by the ordinary exertion of human strength.[45]

## HISTORY AND ETHNOGRAPHY

In western Europe itself perhaps the earliest social history was the *Chroniche Fiorentine*[46] of Giovanni Villani (d. 1348).

The earliest information on other cultures that was gathered by travelers was that of pilgrims who visited Palestine and then wrote descriptions of the Holy Land. However, they were religious people primarily interested in what related to the Christian church, and there is usually little mention of the customs of non-Christians; indeed, one went so far as to write:

Now I have spoken of the abbeys and monasteries of Jerusalem, those without and within Jerusalem, and the Latin streets; but I have not named the monasteries and churches of the Syrians, nor of the Greeks, Jacobins, Boamins, Nestorians, nor Armenians, nor of the other people who render no obeisance to Rome, of whom were many abbeys and churches in the city. For I did not wish to say anything of those people I have named who do not render obeisance to Rome.[47]

The earliest account of interest is the *Peregrinatio Aetheriae* (*ca.* 385),[48] which, though it has very little on non-Christians, contains a good description of the rituals of the Christian church at Jerusalem. Others of importance are Antoninus (sixth century), *Itinerarium* (*ca.* 565),[49] which has some information on the Jews; an anonymous account of *ca.* 1199;[50] Burchardus de Monte Sion (thirteenth century), *Descriptio terrae sanctae* (1280);[51] Wilhelm von Boldensele (fl. 1336), *Hopoeporicon ad terram sanctam* (1336);[52] and Ludolfus de Suchem (fourteenth century), who writes in his *De itinere terrae sanctae* (1350):[53]

I have . . . long desired to write an account of the position of those countries, their condition, their villages, strong places, cities, castles, men, manners, places of prayer and wonders.[54]

Few early traders wrote accounts of their travels; the best is that of Cosmas

Indicopleustes (sixth century), *Christiana topographia* (*ca.* 547).[55]

Numerous compilations were produced, mainly distinguished by a lack of veracity. Some of those which were most widely circulated were the productions of Isidorus of Seville (d. 636),[56] Ravennas Anonymous (seventh century),[57] Gervasius of Tilbury (fl. 1211),[58] Lambert of St. Omer (fl. 1100),[59] Honorius Solitarius (fl. 1100),[60] Guido di Ravenna (fl. 1119),[61] the *Lucidarius* (*ca.* 1190),[62] Gossuin de Metz (thirteenth century),[63] and the fictitious but amusing *Travels of Sir John Mandeville* (fourteenth century).[64]

Ethnographic data was used by Roger Bacon (1214?–94) in his *Opus maius* (1267);[65] in fact, he himself states that he wrote his description of various peoples "in accordance with the experience of writers on nature and of travelers respecting the places and races of the habitable world."[66]

The Crusades which began in 1097 resulted in large-scale contact with Near Eastern and North African cultures.

The Crusades contributed more than any great series of events between the time of Claudius Ptolemy and the middle of the thirteenth century to the broadening of man's geographic horizon, and, with it, the broadening of the whole range of human activity . . . But the Crusades did more than give the people a wider knowledge of places: they brought them into contact with new customs, new religions, new ideals and modes of life. . . . All this tended to displace men from habitual and local modes of thought; Europe became more cosmopolitan, and the way was prepared for that profound change in man's entire attitude towards life which we now call the Renaissance.[67]

Many crusaders wrote accounts of their experiences, and these works constitute the first important body of intimate and authentic information of foreign cultures that was available to the western European.[68] Some of the more important are those by Guilelmus of Tyre (1130?–90?),[69] Robert de Clari (fl. 1220–1216),[70] Geoffroi de Villehardouin (d. *ca.* 1212),[71] Jacobus de Vitriaco (d. 1240),[72] and Jean Joinville (1224?–1317?).[73]

[Before 1245], although the thriving merchants of Venice and Genoa and Pisa grew rich upon the Eastern trade, they knew it only at its termini, the ports of the Levant. . . . Islam, the hereditary foe of Christendom, lay like a wall between Europe and all the trade routes to the East. . . . The century lying between 1245 and 1345 is of unique importance in the history of medieval travel, because for a brief period it brought into contact the East and the West. . . . this was the result of the conquests of . . . the Tartars.

The Tartar conquests began at the beginning of the thirteenth century, when Chinghiz Khan and his hordes came down from Mongolia and attacked the Chinese Empire, taking Peking in 1214 and by degrees, in the course of the next fifty years, extending their sway until they ruled almost the whole of Eastern Asia. . . .

[In the middle of the thirteenth century the Tartars conquered the caliphates of Bagdad and Syria]. For this reason . . . [the Europeans] saw in the Tartars . . . a possible ally against a common enemy [Islam], . . . Gradually there took shape and dream of converting the Tartars to Christianity and then forming a great Tartar-Christian alliance which should smite Islam hip and thigh, reconquer Palestine and Egypt, and succeed where crusades from the West alone had failed. . . . But the fair hopes of the Christian missions were slain by the final conversion of the Ilkhans to Islam in 1316, and though a great missionary effort took place between 1318 and 1336, and Catholic bishoprics continued to be founded in these parts and maintained a wonderful vitality, we hear little of them after about 1340.[74]

The narratives of many of the diplomats contain valuable ethnographic data. Some of the more important are Giovanni di Plano Carpini (d. 1252), *Historia Mongalorum* (1247);[75] Willem van Rrysbroek (thirteenth century), *Itinerarium* (*ca.* 1256);[76] and Hethum (*ca.* 1235–*ca.* 1314), *Journey to Batu and Mangu Khans* (post 1255).[77]

Among the reports of traders there is the famous *Book* (1299)[78] of Marco Polo (1254–1323), and the less valuable work by Francesco Balducci Pegolotti (fourteenth century), *Libro di divisamenti di Paesi* (*ca.* 1340).[79] Other accounts by travelers are Ramon Lull's (1235–1315) novel *Blanquerna* (*ca.* 1284),[80] part of which is based upon his own travels;[81] and *El libro del conoscimiento* (*ca.* 1355).[82]

Finally, there are the missionaries. They include Ricoldo da Monte Croce (1242–1320),[83] Giovanni da Monte Corvino (fl. 1305),[84] Jordanus Catalani (fl. 1330),[85] Andrew of Perugia (fl. 1326),[86] Odorico da Pordenone (1286–1331),[87] John de Cora (fl. 1330),[88] Pascal of Vittoria (fl. 1338),[89] and Giovanni dei Marignolli (fourteenth century).[90]

## LINGUISTICS

On the basis of the narrative in Genesis, it was usually assumed that Hebrew was the first language and that all others were derived from it.[91]

### Isidorus of Seville

Isidorus of Seville (d. 636) represents the earlier school of thought on historical linguistics.

The diversity of languages arose after the flood, at the building of the tower; for before that proud undertaking divided human society among different languages there was one tongue for all people, which is called Hebrew. . . . At first there were as many languages as peoples, then more peoples than languages, because many peoples sprang from one language.[92]

There are three sacred languages, Hebrew, Greek, and Latin, and they are supreme through all the world.[93]

What sort of language God spoke at the beginning of the world when he said "Let there be light," it is difficult to discover. For there were no languages yet. Likewise it is hard to learn in what tongue he spoke later to man's external ear, especially when he spoke to the first man or to the prophets, or when God's voice sounded corporeally as when he said, "Thou art my beloved son," where it is believed by certain authorities that he used that one and single language that existed before there was a diversity of languages.[94]

. . . nations have arisen from tongues, not tongues from nations.[95]

### Dante

Dante Alighieri (1265–1321) illustrates the ideas on linguistics that existed at a later period, when a knowledge of the phenomena of linguistic change and dialect geography tended to produce a more sophisticated conception of the subject.

. . . we do not find that any one before us has treated of the science of the vernacular language, while in fact we see that this language is highly necessary for all. . . . But because the business of every science is not to prove but to explain its subject, in order that men may know what that is with which the science is concerned, we say (to come quickly to the point) that what we call the vernacular speech is that to which children are accustomed by those who are about them when they first begin to distinguish words; or to put it more shortly, we say that the vernacular speech is that which we acquire without any rule, by imitating our nurses. There further springs from this another secondary speech, which the Romans called grammar. And this secondary speech the Greeks also have, as well as others, but not all. Few, however, acquire the use of this speech, because we can only be guided and instructed in it by the expenditure of much time, and by assiduous study. Of these two kinds of speech also, the vernacular is the nobler, as well because it was the first employed by the human race, as because the whole world makes use of it, though it has been divided into forms differing in pronunciation and vocabulary. It is also the nobler as being natural to us, whereas the other is rather of an artificial kind; and it is of this our nobler speech that we intend to treat.

This then is our true first speech. I do not, however, say "our" as implying that any other kind of speech exists beside man's; for to man alone of all existing beings was speech given, because for him alone was it necessary. Speech was not necessary for the angels or for the lower animals, but would have been given to them in vain, which nature, as we know, shrinks from doing. For if we clearly consider what our intention is when we speak, we shall find that it is nothing else but to unfold to others the thoughts of our own mind. Since, then, the angels have, for the purpose of manifesting their glorious thoughts, a most ready and indeed ineffable sufficiency of intellect, by which one of them is known in all respects to another, either of himself, or at least by means of that most brilliant mirror in which all of them are represented in the fulness of their beauty, and into which they all most eagerly gaze, they do not seem to have required the outward indications of speech. . . .

The lower animals also, being guided by natural instinct alone, did not need to be provided with the power of speech, for all those of the same species have the same actions and passions; and so they are enabled by their own actions and passions to know those of others. But among those of different species not only was speech unnecessary, but it would have been altogether harmful, since there would have been no friendly intercourse between them. . . . And if any one should rejoin that . . . magpies and other birds speak, we say that it is false, because such action is not speaking, but a kind of imitation of the sound of our voice, or in other words, we say that they try to imitate us in so far as we utter sounds, but not in so far as we speak. . . .

And so it is evident that speech has been given to man alone. But let us briefly endeavour to explain why this was necessary for him.

Since, then, man is not moved by natural instinct but by reason, and reason itself differs in individuals in respect of discernment, judgement, and choice, so that each one of us appears almost to rejoice in his own species, we are of the opinion that no one has knowledge of another by means of his own actions or passions, as a brute beast; nor does it happen that one man can enter into another by spiritual insight, like an angel, since the human spirit is held back by the grossness and opacity of its mortal body. It was therefore necessary that the human race should have some sign, at once rational and sensible, for the inter-communication of its thoughts, because the sign, having to receive something from the reason of one and to convey it to the reason of another, had to be rational; and since nothing can be conveyed from one reason to another except through a medium of sense, it had to be sensible; for, were it only rational, it could not pass from the reason of one to that of another; and were it only sensible it would neither have been able to take from the reason of one nor to deposit in that of another.

Now this sign is that noble subject itself of which we are speaking; for in so far as it is sound, it is sensible, but in so far as it appears to carry some meaning according to the pleasure of the speaker it is rational.

Speech was given to man alone, as is plain from what has been said above. And now I think we ought also to investigate to whom of mankind speech was first given, and what was the first thing he said, and to whom, where, and when he said it; and also in what language this first speech came forth. Now, according to what we read in the beginning of Genesis, where the most sacred Scripture is treating of the origin of the world, we find that a woman spoke before all others; I mean that most presumptuous Eve, when in answer to the inquiry of the devil she said, "We eat of the fruit of the trees which are in Paradise, but of the fruit of the tree which is in the midst of Paradise God has commanded us not to eat, nor to touch it, lest peradventure we die." But though we find it written that the woman spoke first, it is, however, reasonable for us to suppose that the man spoke first; and it is unseemly to think that so excellent an act of the human race proceeded even earlier from woman than from man. We therefore reasonably believe that speech was given to Adam first by him who had just formed him.

Now I have no doubt that it is obvious to a man of sound mind that the first thing the voice of the first speaker uttered was the equivalent of God, namely *El*,* whether in the way of a question or in the way of an answer. It seems absurd and repugnant to reason that anything should have been named by man before God, since man had been made by him and for him. . . . also we can fully determine the place where our first speech was uttered; for if man was inspired with life outside Paradise, he first spoke outside; but if within, . . . the place of his first speech was within.

Since human affairs are carried on in very many different languages, so that many men are not understood by many with words any better than without words, it is meet for us to make investigation concerning the language which that man who had no mother, who was never suckled, who never saw either childhood or youth, is believed to have spoken. . . . we say that a certain form of speech was created by God together with the first soul. And I say "a form," both in respect of words and their construction and of the utterance of this construction; and this form every tongue of speaking men would use, if it had not been dissipated by the fault of man's presumption, as shall be shown further on.

In this form of speech Adam spoke; in this form of speech all his descendants spoke until the building of the Tower of Babel, which is by interpretation the tower of confusion; and this form of speech was inherited by the sons of Heber, who after him were called Hebrews. With them alone did it remain after the confusion. . . . Therefore Hebrew was the language which the lips of the first speaker formed. . . . †

. . . almost the whole human race had come together [to construct the Tower of

---

* In a later work he had Adam say: "Ere I descended to the infernal anguish, *J* was the name on earth of that supreme good whence cometh the gladness that doth swathe me; *El* was he called thereafter."[96]
† Dante later gave a different version, for in the *Paradiso* Adam says: "The tongue I spoke was all quenched long ere the work that ne'er might be completed was undertaken by the folk of Nimrod."[97]

Babel]. . . . when they were struck by such confusion from heaven, that all those who were attending to the work, using one and the same language, left off the work on being estranged by many different languages and never again came together in the same intercourse. For the same language remained to those alone who were engaged together in the same kind of work; for instance, one language remained to all the architects, another to those rolling down blocks of stone, another to those preparing the stone; and so it happened to each group of workers. And the human race was accordingly then divided into as many different languages as there were different branches of the work; and the higher the branch of work the men were engaged in, the ruder and more barbarous was the language they afterwards spoke.

But those to whom the hallowed language remained were neither present, nor countenanced the work; but utterly hating it, they mocked the folly of those engaged in it. But these, a small minority, were of the seed of Shem (as I conjecture), who was the third son of Noah; and from them sprang the people of Israel, who made use of the most ancient language until their dispersion.

On account of the confusion of tongues related above we have no slight reason for thinking that men were at that time first scattered through all the climes of the world, and the habitable regions and corners of those climes. And as the original root of the human race was planted in the regions of the East, and our race also spread out from there on both sides by a manifold diffusion of shoots, and finally reached the boundaries of the West, it was then perhaps that rational throats first drank of the rivers of the whole of Europe, or at least some of them. But whether these men then first arrived as strangers, or whether they came back to Europe as natives, they brought a threefold language with them, and of those who brought it some allotted to themselves the southern, others the northern part of Europe, while the third body, whom we now call Greeks, seized partly on Europe and partly on Asia.

Afterwards, from one and the same idiom received at the avenging confusion, various vernaculars drew their origin, as we shall show farther on. For one idiom alone prevailed in all the country which from the mouths of the Danube, or marshes of Maeotis to the western boundary of England, is bounded by the frontiers of Italy and France and by the ocean; though afterwards through the Sclavonians, Hungarians, Teutons, Saxons, English, and many other nations it was drawn off into various vernaculars, this alone remaining to almost all of them as a sign of their common origin, that nearly all the above-named answer in affirmation *io*.

Starting from this idiom, that is to say, eastward from the Hungarian frontier, another language prevailed over all the territory in that direction comprised in Europe, and even extended beyond. But a third idiom prevailed in all that part of Europe which remains from the other two, though it now appears in a threefold form. For of those who speak it, some say in affirmation *oc,* other *oil,* and other *si,* namely the Spaniards, the French, and the Italians. Now the proof that the vernaculars of these nations proceed from one and the same idiom is obvious, because we see that they call many things by the same names, as *Deum, celum,* . . . and almost all other things. . . .

We must now put whatever reason we possess to the proof, since it is our purpose to investigate matters in which we are supported by the authority of none, namely, the change which has passed over a language which was originally of one and the same form. . . . Let us now inquire why it is that this language has varied into three chief forms, and why each of these variations varies in itself; why, for instance, the speech of the right side of Italy varies from that of the left (for the Paduans speak in one way and the Pisans in another); and also why those who live nearer together still vary in their speech, as the Milanese and Veronese, the Romans and the Florentines, and even those who have the same national designation, as the Neapolitans and the people of Gaeta, those of Ravenna and those of Faenza, and what is stranger still, the inhabitants of the same city, like the Bolognese of the Borgo S. Felice and the Bolognese of the Strada Maggiore.[98] One and the same reason will explain why all these differences and varieties of speech occur.

We say, therefore, that no effect as such goes beyond its cause, because nothing can bring about that which itself is not. Since therefore every language of ours, except that created by God with the first man, has been restored at our pleasure after the confusion, which was nothing else but forgetfulness of the former language, and since man is a most unstable and changeable animal, no human language can be lasting and continuous, but must needs vary like other properties of ours, as for instance our manners and our dress, according to distance of time and place. And so far am I from thinking that there is room for doubt as to the truth of our remark that speech varies "according to difference of time," that we are of opinion that this is rather to be held as certain. For, if we consider our other actions, we seem to differ much more from our fellow-countrymen in very distant times than from our contemporaries very remote in place. Wherefore we boldly affirm that if the ancient Pavians were to rise from the dead they would talk in a language varying or differing from that of the modern Pavians. Nor should what we are saying appear more wonderful than to observe that a young man is grown up whom we have not seen growing. For the motion of those things which move gradually is not considered by us at all; and the longer the time required for perceiving the variation of a thing, the more stable we suppose that thing to be. Let us not therefore be surprised if the opinions of men who are but little removed from the brutes suppose that the citizens of the same town have always carried on their intercourse with an unchangeable speech, because the change in the speech of the same town comes about gradually, not without a very long succession of time, whilst the life of man is in its nature extremely short.

If, therefore, the speech of the same people varies (as has been said) successively in course of time, and cannot in any wise stand still, the speech of people living apart and removed from one another must needs vary in different ways; just as manners and dress vary in different ways, since they are not rendered stable either by nature or by intercourse, but arise according to men's inclinations and local fitness.[99]

Dante was also aware of linguistic diffusion.

. . . the people of Bologna . . . receive into their own dialect something borrowed from their neighbours of Imola, Ferrara, and Modena, just as we conjecture that all borrow from their neighbours.[100]

He attempted to reconstruct the original Italian language from its various dialects by means of the age-area hypothesis.

Now the supreme standards of those activities which are generically Italian are not peculiar to any one town in Italy, but are common to all.[101]


## SOCIAL ANTHROPOLOGY

**Paul of Tarsus**

Paul of Tarsus ' (d. 67?) conception of the nature of man is a fusion of the

Eastern ascetic world view which was then current in the Mediterranean area, the late Hebrew, and the neo-Platonic.

His analysis of man is based upon a dichotomy between body and soul.

There is a natural body, and there is a spiritual body.[102]

Man has a "mortal body,"[103] but the soul is immortal. And only the desires of the soul are good; those of the "vile body"[104] are bad.

So then with the mind I myself serve the law of God; but with the flesh the law of sin.[105]

For I know that in me (that is, in my flesh), dwelleth no good thing.[106]

His moral masochism reached its heights in his advocacy of chastity.[107]

Throughout life there is a struggle between the body and soul for domination over man.

Walk in the Spirit, and ye shall not fulfil the lust of the flesh. For the flesh lusteth against the Spirit, and the Spirit against the flesh: and these are contrary the one to the other; so that ye cannot do the things ye would.[108]

Let not sin therefore reign in your mortal body, that ye should obey it in the lusts thereof.[109]

Man is egocentric; "For all seek their own."[110]

The supernatural, in the person of a single god, is the cause of all; "For of him, and through him, and to him are all things.[111] However, the devil also has a finger in the pie.

Wherefore we would have come unto you, even I Paul, once and again; but Satan hindered us.[112]

Paul's conception of social phenomena's being supernaturally caused was the foundation of the theological interpretation of history which Augustine systematically developed later.

For by him were all things created, that are in heaven, and that are in earth, visible and invisible, whether they be thrones, or dominions, or principalities, or powers: all things were created by him, and for him.[113]

What if God, willing to shew his wrath, and to make his power known, endured with much longsuffering the vessels of wrath fitted to destruction: And that he might make known the riches of his glory on the vessels of mercy, which he had afore prepared unto glory?[114]

Have they [i.e., the Jews] stumbled that they should fall? God forbid: but rather through their fall salvation is come unto the Gentiles, for to provoke them to jealousy.[115]

For it is God who worketh in you both to will and to do of his good pleasure.[116]

Later writers like Augustine and Otto of Friesingen were particularly impressed by his idea of the judgment day and made it the framework of their interpretation of history. To Paul, the history of mankind was composed of the strivings between the forces of good and evil in the individual and the group, and at the day of judgment each man will receive his final reckoning.

Be not deceived; God is not mocked: for whatsoever a man soweth, that shall he also reap. For he that soweth to his flesh shall of the flesh reap corruption; but he that soweth to the Spirit shall of the Spirit reap life everlasting.[117]

He distinguished between three kinds of law: the law of nature, to which all mankind was subject because it was inherent in man's nature; the law of Moses, given to the Jews by god through divine revelation; and the law of Jesus, supernaturally revealed to the Christians.

For as many as have sinned without law shall also perish without law: and as many as have sinned in the law shall be judged by the law; (For not the hearers of the law are justified before God, but the doers of the law shall be justified. For when the Gentiles, which have not the law, do by nature the things contained in the law, these, having not the law, are a law unto themselves: Which shew the work of the law written in their hearts, their conscience also bearing witness, and their thoughts the mean while accusing or else excusing one another).[118]

And unto the Jews I became as a Jew, that I might gain the Jews: to them that are under the law, as under the law, that I might gain them that are under the law; To them that are without law, as without law (being not without law to God, but under the law to Christ), that I might gain them that are without law.[119]

But before the faith came, we were kept under the law, shut up unto the faith which should afterwards be revealed.[120]

He reveals his ethnocentrism by attributing local customs to the law of nature.

Doth not even nature itself teach you, that, if a man have long hair, it is a shame unto him? But if a woman have long hair, it is a glory to her: for her hair is given her for a covering.[121]

Paul used the organic analogy in illustrating social differentiation and interdependence.[122]

## Later New Testament Writers

All the later New Testament writers concurred in the division of man into body and soul,[123] of which the former is mortal, the latter immortal[124] and leaves the body after death.[125] Life is a continual struggle[126] between the evil desires of the body and the good desires of the soul.[127] Man is naturally egocentric,[128] but the writer of Timothy (*ca.* 150) also mentions the existence of "natural affection."[129]

All events are supernaturally caused; as the writer of Matthew (*ca.* 80) says of the sparrows, "and one of them shall not fall on the ground without your Father."[130] Of course, social phenomena were included in the conception of supernatural causality.

Submit yourselves to every ordinance of man for the Lord's sake: Whether it be to the king, as supreme; Or unto governors, as unto them that are sent by him for the punishment of evil doers, and for the praise of them that do well.[131]

. . . angels and authorities and powers . . . [are] made subject unto him.[132]

A man can receive nothing, except it be given him from heaven.[133]

However, in one place the writer of Timothy gave a cultural explanation of social phenomena.

For the love of money is the root of all evil: which, while some coveted after, they have erred from the faith, and pierced themselves through with many sorrows.[134]

Paul's conception of history as a struggle between the forces of good and evil, with a final reckoning at the day of judgment, was elaborated upon by the later writers of the New Testament.[135] The Revelation (*ca.* 95) of John of Ephesus symbolized the two opposing forces in terms of Jerusalem and Babylon, the cities of god and the devil, respectively,[136] an allegory that became the basis of history to Otto of Friesingen.

The author of Luke-Acts (*ca.* 90) differentiated between the laws of Moses and Jesus.

The law and the prophets were until John: since that time the kingdom of God is preached, and every man presseth into it. And it is easier for heaven and earth to pass, than one tittle of the law to fail.[137]

In Hebrews (*ca.* 95) a distinction is made between the " carnal " law of Moses and the spiritual law of Jesus, and the latter seems to have become part of the law of nature, since it is impressed upon man's nature.

[Jesus] is made, not after the law of a carnal commandment, but after the power of an endless life.[138]

This is the covenant that I will make with them after those days, saith the Lord; I will put my laws into their hearts, and in their minds will I write them.[139]

To the writer of Timothy, law originated when men became evil.

But we know that the law is good, if a man use it lawfully; Knowing this, that the law is not made for a righteous man, but for the lawless and disobedient, for the ungodly and for sinners, for unholy and profane, for murderers of fathers and murderers of mothers, for manslayers, for whoremongers, for them that defile themselves with man-kind, for menstealers, for liars, for perjured persons, and if there be any other thing that is contrary to sound doctrine.[140]

Finally, the author of Ephesians (*ca.* 93) included Paul's organic analogy in the letter.[141]

## Christian Church Fathers

Scattered statements of interest to social scientists are to be found in the writings of the early Christian church fathers.

Tertullian (160?–230?) distinguished between the laws of god and nature.

The argument for Christian practices becomes all the stronger, when also nature, which is the first rule of all, supports them. . . everything which is against nature deserves to be branded as monstrous among men; but with us it is to be condemned also as sacrilege against God, the Lord and Creator of nature.

Demanding then a law of God, you have that common one prevailing all over the world, engraven on the natural tablets to which the apostle too is wont to appeal, as when in respect of the woman's veil he says, "Does not even Nature teach you?" [I Cor. 11: 14]—as when to the Romans, affirming that the heathen do by nature those things which the law requires [Rom. 2:14], he suggests both natural law and a law-revealing nature.*[143]

He also discussed the growth of population and social progress.

. . . the human race has progressed with a gradual growth of population, either oc-

* "These testimonies of the soul are simple as true, commonplace as simple, universal as commonplace, natural as universal, divine as natural."[142]

cupying different portions of the earth as aborigines, or as nomad tribes, or as exiles, or as conquerors . . ., or by the more ordinary methods of emigration, which they call ἀποικίαι or *colonies,* for the purpose of throwing off redundant population, disgorging into other abodes their overcrowded masses. The aborigines remain still in their old settlements, and have also enriched other districts with loans of even larger populations. Surely it is obvious enough, if one looks at the whole world, that it is becoming daily better cultivated and more fully peopled than anciently. All places are now accessible, all are well known, all open to commerce; most pleasant farms have obliterated all traces of what were once dreary and dangerous wastes; cultivated fields have subdued forests; flocks and birds have expelled wild beasts; sandy deserts are sown; rocks are planted; marshes are drained; and where once were hardly solitary cottages, there are now large cities. No longer are savage islands dreaded, nor their rocky shores feared; everywhere are houses, and inhabitants, and settled government, and civilised life. What most frequently meets our view (and occasions complaints), is our teeming population; our numbers are burdensome to the world, which can hardly supply us its natural elements; our wants grow more and more keen, and our complaints more bitter in all mouths, whilst Nature fails in affording us her usual sustenance. In very deed, pestilence, and famine, and wars, and earthquakes have to be regarded as a remedy for nations, as the means of pruning the luxuriousness of the human race.[144]

Origen (185?–254?) analyzed the nature of law.

What law do you mean to say, good sir, is "king of all things?" If you mean those which exist in the various cities, then such an assertion is not true. For all men are not governed by the same law. You ought to have said that "laws are kings of all men," for in every nation some law is king of all. But if you mean that which is law in the proper sense, then it is this which is by nature "king of all things;" although there are some individuals who, having like robbers abandoned the law, deny its validity, and live lies of violence and injustice. We Christians, then, who have come to the knowledge of the law which is by nature "king of all things," and which is the same with the law of God, endeavor to regulate our lives by its prescriptions, having bidden a long farewell to those of an unholy kind.[145]

Other church fathers reiterated the equality of man.

. . . you come into this world of ours and depart from it after a time with equal rights.[146]

. . . all men are begotten alike, with a capacity and ability of reasoning and feeling, without preference of age, sex, or dignity. Nor do they obtain wisdom by fortune, but have it implanted by nature.[147]

God, who produces and gives breath to men, willed that all should be equal, that is, equally matched. He has imposed on all the same condition of living; He has produced all to wisdom; He has promised immortality to all; no one is cut off from His heavenly benefits. For as he distributes to all alike, His one light, sends forth His fountains to all, supplies food, and gives the most pleasant rest of sleep; so He bestows on all equity and virtue. In His sight no one is a slave, no one a master; for if all have the same Father, by an equal right we are all children.[148]

Ambrose (340?–397) used the organism as an argument by analogy to prove the interdependence of the members of society, following Paul of Tarsus.

If . . . any one wishes to please all, he must strive in every thing to do, not what is

useful for himself, but what is useful for many. . . . Hence humanity is called a particular
.and innate virtue in man, for it assists its partner.

The very form of thy body and the use of thy limbs teach thee this. Can one limb claim
the duties of another? Can the eye claim for itself the duties of the ear; or the mouth the
duties of the eye; or the hand the service of the feet; or the feet that of the hands? Nay,
the hands themselves, both right and left, have different duties to do, so that if one were
to change the use of either, one would act contrary to nature. . . .

Imagine for a moment, and give to the eye the power to withdraw the understanding
from the head, the sense of hearing from the ears, the power of thought from the minds,
the sense of smell from the nose, the sense of taste from the mouth, and then assume
them itself, would it not at once destroy the whole course of nature? . . . So then we
are all one body, though with many members, all necessary to the body. . . . And if one
member suffers, all the members suffer with it.

So we see how grave a matter it is to deprive another, with whom we ought rather to
suffer, of any thing, or to act unfairly or injuriously towards one to whom we ought to
give a share in our services. This is a true law of nature, which binds us to show all kindly
feeling, so that we should all of us in turn help one another, as parts of one body, and
should never think of depriving another of anything, seeing it is against the law of nature
even to abstain from giving help. We are born in such a way that limb combines with limb,
and one works with another, and all assist each other in mutual service. But if one fails
its duty, the rest are hindered. If, for instance, the hand tears out the eye, has it not
hindered the use of its work? If it were to wound the foot, how many actions would it not
prevent? But how much worse is it for the whole man to be drawn aside from his duty
than for one of the members only. If the whole body is injured in one member, so also
is the whole community of the human race disturbed in one man. The nature of mankind
is injured, as also is the society of the holy Church, which rises in one united body, bound
together in oneness of faith and love.[149]

Ambrosiaster (fl. *ca.* 375) was perhaps the first to make explicit the doctrine
of the supernatural origin of kings.

The king has the image of god, as the bishop has that of Christ.[150]

. . . the king should be adored on earth as the vicar of god.[151]

## Augustine

It was Aurelius Augustinus (354–430) who first developed a systematic body
of social thought in accordance with the Christian viewpoint. His *De civitate dei*
(413–26) is essentially a theological interpretation of history.

The occasion of this work is significant:

. . . it was my first endeavor to reply to those who attribute the wars by which the
world is being devastated, and especially the recent sack of Rome by the barbarians, to
the religion of Christ, which prohibits the offering of abominable sacrifices. . . . Then
out of this there arose the question, why wicked and ungrateful men were permitted to
share in these benefits [i.e., those of God]; and why, too, the hardships and calamities
of war were inflicted on the godly as well as on the ungodly.[152]

He developed his argument from the premise of supernatural causality.

God supreme and true, with His Word and Holy Spirit (which three are one), one God
omnipotent, creator and maker of every soul and of every body; . . . from whom is

every mode, every species, every order; from whom are measure, number, weight; from whom is everything which has an existence in nature, of whatever kind it be, and of whatever value . . .—that God can never be believed to have left the kingdoms of men, their dominations and servitudes, outside of the laws of His providence.[153]

Therefore that God, the author and giver of felicity, because He alone is the true God, Himself gives earthly kingdoms both to good and bad. Neither does He do this rashly, and, as it were, fortuitously,—because He is God not fortune,—but according to the order of things and times, which is hidden from us, but thoroughly known to Himself.[154]

Wherefore, when the kingdoms of the East had been illustrious for a long time, it pleased God that there should also arise a Western empire, which, though later in time, should be more illustrious in extent and greatness. And, in order that it might overcome the grievous evils which existed among other nations, He purposely granted it to such men as, for the sake of honor, and praise, and glory, consulted well for their country, in whose glory they sought their own, and whose safety they did not hesitate to prefer to their own, suppressing the desire of wealth and many other vices for this one vice, namely, the love of praise.[155]

And, therefore, it was not only for the sake of recompensing the citizens of Rome that her empire and glory had been so signally extended, but also that the citizens of that eternal city, during their pilgrimage here [on earth], might diligently and soberly contemplate these examples, and see what a love they owe to the supernal country on account of life eternal, if the terrestrial country was so much beloved by its citizens on account of human glory.[156]

Therefore, also, we see, in the light of that truth which, veiled in the Old Testament, is revealed in the New, namely, that it is not in view of terrestrial and temporal benefits, which divine providence grants promiscuously to good and evil, that God is to be worshipped, but in view of eternal life, everlasting gifts, and of the society of the heavenly city itself;—in the light of this truth we see that the Jews were most righteously given as a trophy to the glory of the Romans; for we see that these Romans, who rested on earthly glory, and sought to obtain it by virtues, such as they were, conquered those who, in their great depravity, slew and rejected the giver of true glory, and of the eternal city.[157]

And now . . . God . . . having determined to chastise the corruption of men, which was worthy of far heavier chastisement than the irruption of the barbarians, tempered His indignation with such mildness as, in the first instance, to cause that the king of the Goths should be conquered in a wonderful manner, lest glory should accrue to demons, whom he was known to be supplicating, and thus the minds of the weak should be overthrown; and then, afterwards, to cause that, when Rome was to be taken, it should be taken by those barbarians who, contrary to any custom of all former wars, protected, through reverence for the Christian religion, those who fled for refuge to the sacred places, and who so opposed the demons themselves, and the rites of impious sacrifices, that they seemed to be carrying on a far more terrible war with them than with men. Thus did the true Lord and Governor of things both scourge the Romans mercifully, and, by the marvellous defeat of the worshippers of demons, show that those sacrifices were not necessary even for the safety of present things; so that, by those who do not obstinately hold out, but prudently consider the matter, true religion may not be deserted on account of the urgencies of the present time, but may be more clung to in most confident expectation of eternal life.[158]

Augustine emphasized man's sociality.

. . . as to the other animals, He created some solitary, and naturally seeking lonely places,—as the eagles, kites, lions, wolves, and such like; others gregarious, which herd together, and prefer to live in company,—as pigeons, starlings, stags, and little fallow deer, and the like: but neither class did He cause to be propagated from individuals, but called into being several at once. Man, on the other hand, [is one] whose nature was to be a mean between the angelic and bestial. . . . And therefore God created only one single man, not, certainly, that he might be a solitary, bereft of all society, but that by this means the unity of society and the bond of concord might be more effectually commended to him, men being bound together not only by similarity of nature, but by family affection. And indeed He did not even create the woman that was to be given him as his wife, as he created the man, but created her out of the man, that the whole human race might derive from one man.[159]

All men are equal: "by nature, as God first created us, no one is the slave either of man or of sin.[160]

Following Paul of Tarsus, he distinguished between natural, Jewish, and Christian law.

There are three laws. One is that of the Hebrews, which the apostle calls the law of sin and death [Rom. 8:2]. The second is that of the Gentiles, which he calls the law of nature [Rom. 2:14–15]. . . . The third law is the truth of which the apostle speaks when he says, "The law of the spirit of life in Christ Jesus hath made me free from the law of sin and death" [Rom. 8:2].[161]

He had a sense of the dynamics of culture.

But woe unto thee, thou stream of human custom! Who shall stay thy course? How long shall it be before thou art dried up?[162]

They rise and set; and by rising, they begin as it were to be; and they grow, that they may become perfect; and when perfect, they wax old and perish; and all wax not old, but all perish. Therefore when they rise and tend to be, the more rapidly they grow that they may be, so much more they hasten not to be. This is the way of them.[163]

He also conceived of social progress.

The education of the human race, represented by the people of God, has advanced, like that of an individual, through certain epochs, or, as it were, ages, so that it might gradually rise from earthly to heavenly things, and from the visible to the invisible.[164]

. . . if we count the ages as days, in accordance with the periods of time defined in Scripture. . . . The first age, as the first day, extends from Adam to the deluge; the second from the deluge to Abraham, equalling the first, not in length of time, but in the number of generations, here being ten in each. From Abraham to the advent of Christ there are, as the evangelist Matthew calculates, three periods, in each of which are fourteen generations,—one period from Abraham to David, a second from David to the captivity, a third from the captivity to the birth of Christ in the flesh. There are thus five ages in all. The sixth is now passing, and cannot be measured by any number of generations. . . . After this period God shall rest as on the seventh day, when He shall give us (who shall be the seventh day) rest in Himself. . . . There we shall rest and see, see and love, love and praise. This is what shall be the end without end.[165]

## Orosius

Paulus Orosius (fl. 418), a disciple of Augustine, continued the work of his master in the *Historiarum adversum paganos* (418).[166]

You [i.e., Augustine] bade me reply to the empty chatter and perversity of those who, aliens to the City of God, are called "pagans" because they come from the countryside and the crossroads of the rural districts, or "heathen" because of their wisdom in earthly matters. Although these people do not seek out the future and moreover either forget or know nothing of the past, nevertheless they charge that the present times are unusually beset with calamities for the sole reason that men believe in Christ and worship God while idols are increasingly neglected. You bade me, therefore, discover from all the available data of histories and annals whatever instances past ages have afforded of the burdens of war, the ravages of disease, the horrors of famine, of terrible earthquakes, extraordinary floods, dreadful eruptions of fire, thunderbolts and hailstorms, and also instances of cruel miseries caused by parricides and disgusting crimes. I was to set these forth systematically and briefly in the course of my book.[167]

He then proceeds to develop his thesis in terms of supernatural causality.

There is no man living today, I think, who does not acknowledge that God created man in this world.[168]

God is the sole ruler of all the ages, kingdoms, and regions.[169]

In the first place, we hold that if the world and man are directed by a Divine Providence that is as good as it is just, and if man is both weak and stubborn on account of the changeableness of his nature and his freedom of choice, then it is necessary for man to be guided in the spirit of filial affection when he has need of help; but when he abuses his freedom, he must be reproved in a spirit of strict justice. Everyone who sees mankind reflected through himself and in himself perceives that this world has been disciplined since the creation of man by alternating periods of good and bad times. Next we are taught that sin and its punishment began with the very first man. Furthermore, even our opponents, who begin with the middle period and make no mention of the ages preceding, have described nothing but wars and calamities. What else are these wars but evils which befall one side or the other? Those evils which existed then, as to a certain extent they exist now, were doubtless either palpable sins or the hidden punishments for sin.[170]

He was aware of the succession of civilizations.

. . .four main kingdoms were preeminent in successive stages at the four cardinal points of the world, to wit, the Babylonian kingdom in the East, the Carthaginian in the South, the Macedonian in the North, and the Roman in the West.[171]

. . .one God has directed the course of history, in the beginning for the Babylonians, and in the end for the Romans.[172]

## Isidorus of Seville

Isidorus of Seville (d. 636) summed up the knowledge of his day in the encyclopedic *Etymologiae*.

He defines history and gives its function in the following passages:

History is the story of what has been done, and by its means what has taken place in the past is revealed.[173]

Histories of the heathen do no harm to their readers where they tell what is useful. For many wise men have put past deeds into their histories for the instruction of the present.

Besides, in history the total reckoning of past times and years is embraced and many necessary matters are examined in the light of the succession of consuls and kings.[174]

There are two basic types of law, divine and human, with a number of subdivisions of the latter.

All laws are either human or divine. Divine laws depend on nature, human laws on customs; and so the latter differ, since different laws please different people. Divine law is *fas;* human law is *jus.*[175]

*Jus* is the general term and *lex* is a kind of *jus. Jus* is so-called because it is just (*justum*). All *jus* is made up of laws and customs.

*Lex* is the written ordinance. *Mos* is custom approved by its antiquity, or unwritten *lex.* For *lex* is derived from *legere* (to read) because it is written.

*Mos* is old custom and is drawn merely from *mores. Consuetudo* (custom) is a sort of *jus* established by *mores;* which is taken instead of *lex* when *lex* fails. And it makes no difference whether it depends on writing or reason, since reason commends written law also.

Moreover if *lex* is in accordance with reason, all that is in accordance with reason will be *lex,* as far as it agrees with religion, is in harmony with knowledge, and is beneficial for salvation. And *consuetudo* is so-called because it is in common use.[176]

*Jus* is either natural, or civil, or universal.[177]

[1.] *Jus naturale* [law of nature] is what is common to all peoples, and what is observed everywhere by the instinct of nature rather than by any ordinance, as the marriage of man and woman, the begetting and rearing of children, the common possession of all, the one freedom of all, the acquisition of those things that are taken in the air or sea or on the land.[178]

[2.] *Jus civile* [civil law] is what each people or state has enacted as its own law, for human and divine reasons.[179]

[3.] *Jus gentium* [universal law or law of nations] is the seizing, building, and fortifying of settlements, wars, captivitites, servitudes, postliminies, treaties, peaces, truces, the obligation not to violate an ambassador, the prohibition of intermarriage with aliens. And it is called *jus gentium* because nearly all nations observe it.[180]

Laws were made in order that the boldness of men may be checked by fear of them, and innocence be safe among the wicked, and the power of harm bridled among the wicked by the dread of punishment.[181]

## Otto of Friesingen

Otto Friesingensis (d. 1158) carried on the tradition of the theological interpretation of history. Following the Revelation of John of Ephesus, he divided mankind into two groups, the inhabitants of Babylon, the city of the devil, and Jerusalem, the city of God, and viewed history as the progressive triumph of the latter over the former.

. . . we are privileged to understand clearly that God does not neglect His world, as some claim, but rather that by His omnipotent majesty He created things that were not, by His all-wise providence guides His creatures and by His most kindly grace preserves what He guides and controls.[182]

He abandoned so many ages of the past, not by forcing them into sin but by not giving them what was His own—with this purpose, that by the example of those that had gone before He might reveal to future generations what must be avoided by them, that they might render thanks unto their Saviour.[183]

Now it was in the East, as can be gathered from the book of Genesis, in the Land of Eden, that Paradise is believed to have been established. While the first man dwelt therein, he became disobedient to the word of God, and so by a righteous judgement of God he was cast out into this pilgrimage; he began, first in Asia, to till the ground that had been cursed. And he begat sons, the first citizens of the two cities [Babylon and Jerusalem] of which I have undertaken to treat. The elder, incited by envy of the other's good works, murdered his brother and was the first to build a city in this vale of tears. After Abel was slain, another son was born to Adam, named Seth, who is a figure of the resurrection; from him the people of God was afterwards begotten.[184]

After the Flood, when Noah planted a vineyard, he drank of the wine and was drunken, and because of his drunkenness he stripped himself naked. One of his sons seeing him thus mocked him; the other covered him. Accordingly these two brothers were, after the Flood, the first citizens of the two cities which constitute the theme of my book.[185]

For it is our intention to set forth . . .a history in which on the one hand the varying experiences of the citizens of Babylon* and their sufferings, and, on the other hand, the progress and achievements of the citizens of Christ, their progress through and beyond those sufferings, shall be interwoven.[187]

[Before the time of Jesus] you will find few who, because of their words or their deeds, deserved to be counted among the approved citizens of Jerusalem.[188]

For heretofore [i.e., before Jesus], though I had at my command much regarding the citizens of the world, I was in a position to say but little about the citizens of Christ, because from the time of the first man to Christ almost the whole world (except a few of the Israelitish race), led astray by error, given over to empty superstitions, ensnared by the mocking devices of demons, and caught in the toils of the world, is found to have fought under the leadership of the devil, the prince of this world. "But when the fulness of the time came, God sent forth his Son" into the world to lead back into the highway mortal men, who were wandering like the brutes through trackless and devious places.[189]

[The city of Jerusalem is equivalent to the Christian church after the time of Constantine. The holy city] made progress, first by remaining hidden in the other until the coming of Christ, after that by advancing gradually to the time of Constantine. But after Constantine, . . .since not only all the people but also the emperors (except a few) were orthodox Catholics, I seem to myself to have composed a history not of two cities but virtually of one only, which I call the Church. For although the elect and the reprobate are in one household, yet I cannot call these cities two as I did above; I must call them properly but one—composite, however, as the grain is mixed with the chaff.[190]

This work of ours, which we have entitled THE TWO CITIES, is, plainly, divided into three parts. For, whereas the City of Christ, or the Kingdom of Christ with reference to its presence or its future status, is called the Church, it exists in one form so long as it is seen to hold the good and the bad in one embrace; it will exist in another at that time when it shall cherish only the good in the glory of the heavenly embrace; it existed in yet another while it lived subject to the princes of the heathen before "the fulness of the Gentiles" was come. . . .

The evil city likewise, we find, has three states or stages. Of these the first was before the time of grace, the second was and is during the time of grace, the third will be after this present life.[191]

* " . . . that well-known Babylon, a figure of that city of which all they are citizens who insolently attempt to resist the ordinances of God."[186]

And so, when both the cities shall have been presented before the throne of His majesty —the one set at the right hand (that is, the better part), the other at the left—the cause of each shall be decided by a most righteous judgement[192]

Antichrist shall be smitten and the earthly city shall be utterly destroyed. But the City of Christ shall be magnified and exalted and shall be brought to a glorious consummation to reign with Him forever.[193]

## John of Salisbury

One of the earliest and most important theories of political organization was developed by John of Salisbury (1120?–80) in his *Policraticus* (1159).[194]

The law of God is fundamental.

Law is the gift of god, the model of equity, a standard of justice, a likeness of the divine will, the guardian of well-being, a bond of union and solidarity between peoples, a rule defining duties, a barrier against the vices and the destroyer thereof, a punishment of violence and all wrongdoing.[195]

Now there are certain precepts of the law which have a perpetual necessity, having the force of law among all nations and which absolutely cannot be broken with impunity.[196]

Political organization is a consequence of the fall of man.

. . .if iniquity and injustice, banishing charity, had not brought about tyranny, . . . perhaps . . . there would be no kingdoms at all, since it is clear from the ancient historians that in the beginning these were founded by iniquity as presumptuous encroachments against the Lord, or else were extorted from him.[197]

For the earliest fathers and patriarchs followed nature, the best guide of life. They were succeeded by leaders, beginning with Moyses, who followed the law, and judges who ruled the people by authority of the law; and we read that the latter were priests. At last in the anger of the Lord they were given kings, some good, but many bad.* For Samuel had grown old, and when his sons did not walk in his ways, but followed after avarice and uncleanness, the people, who perchance had deserved that such priests should be in authority over them, forced God, whom they had despised, to give them a king.[194]

Perhaps John's most important contribution was his introduction of the organic analogy, which he states he had adopted from Plutarch's *Institutio Trajani*, a work otherwise unknown.

A commonwealth, according to Plutarch, is a certain body which is endowed with life by the benefit of divine favor, which acts at the prompting of the highest equity, and is ruled by what may be called the moderating power of reason. Those things which establish and implant in us the practice of religion, and transmit to us the worship of God (here I do not follow Plutarch, who says "of the Gods") fill the place of the soul in the body of the commonwealth. . . . The place of the head in the body of the commonwealth is filled by the prince, who is subject only to God and to those who exercise His office and represent Him on earth, even as in the human body the head is quickened and governed by the soul. The place of the heart is filled by the Senate, from which proceeds the initiation of good works and ill. The duties of eyes, ears, and tongue are claimed by the judges and governors of provinces. Officials and soldiers correspond to the hands. Those who always attend upon the prince are likened to the sides. Financial officers and keepers

* " . . . princely authority . . . was instituted by the Lord to banish wrongs."[198]

(I speak now not of those who are in charge of prisons, but of those who are keepers of the privy chest) may be compared with the stomach and intestines, which, if they become congested through excessive avidity, and retain too tenaciously their accumulations, generate innumerable and incurable diseases, so that through their ailment the whole body is threatened with destruction. The husbandmen correspond to the feet, which always cleave to the soil, the need the more especially the care and foresight of the head, since while they walk upon the earth doing service with their bodies, they meet the more often with stones of stumbling, and therefore deserve aid and protection all the more justly since it is they who raise, sustain, and move forward the weight of the entire body. . . . Our author after his fashion lays down many things of this kind, which he elaborates at great pains and with a treatment which is rather diffuse.[200]

This organic analogy gave him a sense of the interdependence of the members of a society.

. . . each and all are members one of another.[201]

Office is the duty of doing the acts which laws or morals enjoin upon a given individual. Its function is to bring different acts into harmony by allotting them to the different individuals to whom they are appropriate.[202]

Then and then only will the health of the commonwealth be sound and flourishing when . . . each and all are as it were members one of another by a sort of reciprocity, and each regards his own interest as best served by that which he knows to be most advantageous for the others.[203]

## Thomas Aquinas

Thomas Aquinas (1225?–74?) noted man's lack of instincts and general immaturity at birth[204] and emphasized his sociality.

Now, man has an end to which his whole life and all his actions are ordered; for man is an intelligent agent, and it is clearly the part of an intelligent agent to act in view of an end. Men, however, adopt different methods in proceeding towards their proposed end, as the diversity of man's pursuits and actions clearly indicates. Consequently man needs some directive principle to guide him towards his end.

But the light of reason is placed by nature in every man, to guide him in his acts towards his end. Were man intended to live alone, as many animals do, he would require no other guide to his end. Then would each man be a king unto himself, under God, the highest King, inasmuch as he would direct himself in his acts by the light of reason given him from on high.

However, it is natural for man to be a social and political animal, to live in a group, even more so than all other animals, as the very needs of his nature indicate. For all other animals nature has prepared food, hair as a covering, teeth, horns, claws as means of defence, or at least speed in flight. Man, on the other hand, was created without any natural provision for these things. But, instead of them all he was endowed with reason, by the use of which he could procure all these things for himself by the work of his hands. But one man alone is not able to procure them all for himself; for one man could not sufficiently provide for life, unassisted. It is, therefore, natural that man should live in company with his fellows.

Moreover, all other animals are able to discern by inborn skill what is useful and what is injurious; just as the sheep naturally recognizes the wolf as his enemy. Some animals even recognize by natural instinct certain medicinal herbs and other things necessary for their life. Man, however, has a natural knowledge of the things which are essential for his life only in a general fashion, inasmuch as he has power of attaining knowledge of the particular things necessary for human life by reasoning from universal principles. But it is not possible for one man to arrive at a knowledge of all these things by his own individual reason. It is, therefore, necessary for man to live in a group so that each one may assist his fellows, and different men may be occupied in seeking by their reason to make different discoveries, one, for example, in medicine, one in this and another in that.

This point is, further, most plainly evidenced by the fact that the use of speech is a prerogative proper to man. By this means one man is able fully to express his conceptions to others. Other animals, it is true, express their feelings to one another in a general way, as a dog may express anger by barking and other animals may give vent to their feelings in various manners. So man communicates with his kind more completely than any other animal known to be gregarious, such as the crane, the ant and the bee.[205]

He argued for the psychic unity of mankind on the basis of monogenesis.

. . . all men born of Adam may be considered as one man, insamuch as they have one common nature, which they received from their first parents.[206]

As to the development of society and political organization, he reasoned as follows:

If, therefore, it is natural for man to live in the society of many, it is necessary that there exist among men some means by which the group may be governed. For where there are many men together, and each one is looking after his own interest, the group would be broken up and scattered unless there were also someone to take care of what appertains to the common weal. . . . Therefore, in every group there must be some governing power.[207]

. . . by nature all men are equal.[208]

[However,] in the primitive state [i.e., in the Garden of Eden], which was most proper and orderly, inequality would have existed.

. . . We must needs admit that in the primitive state there would have been some inequality, at least as regards sex, because generation depends upon diversity of sex; and likewise as regards age; for some would have been born of others; nor would sexual union have been sterile.

Moreover, as regards the soul, there would have been some in equality as to righteousness and knowledge. For man worked not of necessity, but of his own free-will, by virtue of which man can apply himself, more or less, to action, desire, or knowledge; hence some would have made a greater advance in virtue and knowledge than others.*

There might also have been bodily disparity. For the human body was not entirely exempt from the laws of nature, so as not to receive from exterior sources more or less advantage and help: since indeed it was dependent on food wherewith to sustain life.[210]

Therefore it was not beneath the dignity of the state of innocence that one man should be subject to another. . . . Mastership has a twofold meaning. First, as opposed to slavery, in which sense a master means one to whom another is subject as a slave. In other sense mastership is referred in a general sense to any kind of subject; and in this sense even he who has the office of governing and directing free man, can be called a

---

* "For those who excel in intelligence, are naturally rulers; whereas those who are less intelligent, but strong in body, seem made by nature for service."[209]

master. In the state of innocence man could have been a master of men, not in the former but in the latter sense. . . .

But a man is the master of a free subject, by directing him either towards his proper welfare, or to the common good. Such a kind of mastership would have existed in the state of innocence between man and man, for two reasons. First, because man is naturally a social being, and so in the state of innocence would have led a social life. Now a social life cannot exist among a number of people unless under the presidency of one to look after the common good; for many, as such, seek many things, whereas one attends only to one.\*. . . Secondly, if one man surpassed another in knowledge and virtue, this would not have been fitting unless these gifts conduced to the benefit of others.[212]

Evidently Thomas thought that the king was established by means of a social contract, for in a discussion of the deposition of tyrants he stated:

. . . it seems, that to proceed against the cruelty of tyrants is an action to be undertaken, not through the private presumption of a few, but by public authority. First of all, if to provide itself with a king belongs to the right of any multitude, it is not unjust that the king set up by that multitude be destroyed or his power restricted, if he tyrannically abuse the royal power. It must not be thought that such a multitude is acting unfaithfully in deposing the tyrant, even though it had previously subjected itself to him in perpetuity; because he himself has deserved that the covenant with his subjects should not be kept, since, in ruling the multitude, he did not act faithfully as the office of a king demands.[213]

In his consideration of the nature of society, he argued from the relationship between the macrocosm and the microcosm and used the organic analogy.

. . . the best kingly administration will be one which is patterned after the regime of nature. In things of nature, however, there is found to be both a universal and a particular rulership; universal, by the fact that every thing is embraced under the rulership of God, who governs all things by His providence. The particular rulership which is found in man is most like the Divine rulership. For this reason man is called a smaller world, since in him there is found the form of universal rulership. For, just as the universe of corporeal creatures and all spiritual powers come under the Divine government, in like manner are the members of the body and the other powers of the soul controlled by reason, and thus, in a certain proportionate manner, reason is to man what God is to the world. Since man is by nature a social animal living in a group, . . . a likeness of the Divine rulership is found in him, not only in this, that a single man is ruled by his reason, but also in that a multitude is governed through the reason of one man. . . . Therefore let the king recognize that such is the office which he undertakes, namely, that he is in the kingdom what the soul is in the body, and what God is in the world.[214]

His fundamental interpretation of history was theological, since "He governs all the acts and movements that are to be found in each single creature."[215] However, when dealing with practical matters, he sometimes used a geographic interpretation.[216]

Thomas' discussion of law is classic: "Law is a rule and measure of acts, whereby man is induced to act or is restrained from acting."[217] The following is his classification and description of the various types of law:

[1. Law of god, communicated to man by divine revelation;] a law is nothing else but a dictate of practical reason emanating from the ruler who governs a perfect community.

\* " . . . the best kind of government is government by one."[211]

Now it is evident, granted that the world is ruled by Divine Providence, . . . that the whole community of the universe is governed by Divine Reason. Wherefore the very Idea of the government of things in God the Ruler of the universe, has the nature of a law. And since the Divine Reason's conception of things is not subject to time but is eternal, . . . therefore it is that this kind of law must be called eternal. . . . Accordingly the eternal concept of the Divine law bears the character of an eternal law, in so far as it is ordained by God to the government of things foreknown to Him.[218]

. . . the Divine law is twofold, namely, the Old [Testament] Law and the New [Testament] Law. . . . As the father of a family issues different commands to the children and to the adults, so also the one King, God, in His one kingdom, gave one law to men, while they were yet imperfect, and another more perfect law, when, by the preceding law, they had been led to a greater capacity for Divine things.[219]

[2. Law of nature, implanted by god into man's nature;] since all things subject to Divine providence are ruled and measured by the eternal law, as was stated above; it is evident that all things partake somewhat of the eternal law, in so far as, namely, from its being imprinted on them, they derive their respective inclinations to their proper acts and ends. Now among all others, the rational creature is subject to Divine providence in the most excellent way, in so far as it partakes of a share of providence, by being provident both for itself and for others. Wherefore it has a share of the Eternal Reason, whereby it has a natural inclination to its proper act and end: and this participation of the eternal law in the rational creature is called the natural law. . . . the light of natural reason, whereby we discern what is good and what is evil which is the function of the natural law, is nothing else than an imprint on us of the Divine light. It is therefore evident that the natural law is nothing else than the rational creature's participation of the eternal law.[220]

The natural law is promulgated by the very fact that God instilled it into man's mind so as to be known by him naturally.[221]

By the natural law the eternal law is participated proportionately to the capacity of human nature.[222]

[3. Human law;] from the precepts of the natural law, as from general and indemonstrable principles, . . . the human reason needs to proceed to the more particular determination of certain matters. These particular determinations, devised by human reason, are called human laws, provided the other essential conditions of law be observed. . . . The human reason cannot have a full participation of the dictate of the Divine Reason, but according to its own mode, and imperfectly. Consequently, as on the part of the speculative reason, there is in us the knowledge of certain general principles, but not the proper knowledge of each single truth, such as that contained in the Divine Wisdom; so too, on the part of the practical reason, man has a natural participation of the eternal law, according to certain general principles, but not as regards the particular determinations of individual cases, which are, however, contained in the eternal law. Hence the need for human reason to proceed further to sanction them by law.[223]

But it must be noted that something may be derived from the natural law in two ways: first, as a conclusion from premises, secondly, by way of determination of certain generalities. . . . Some things are therefore derived from the general principles of the natural law, by way of conclusions; e.g., that *one must not kill* may be derived as a conclusion from the principle that *one should do harm to no man*: while some are derived therefrom by way of determination; e.g., the law of nature has it that the evil-doer should be punished; but that he be punished in this or that way, is a determination of the law of nature.

Accordingly both modes of derivation are found in human law. But those things which are derived in the first way, are contained in human law not as emanating therefore exclusively, but have some force from the natural law also. But those things which are derived in the second way, have no other force than that of human law.[224]

. . . positive law is divided into the *law of nations* and *civil law,* according to the two ways in which something may be derived from the law of nature, as stated above. Because to the law of nations belong those things which are derived from the law of nature, as conclusions from premises, *e.g.,* just buyings and sellings, and the like, without which men cannot live together, which is a point of the law of nature, since man is by nature a social animal. . . . But those things which are derived from the law of nature by way of particular determination, belong to the civil law, according as each state decides on what is best for itself.[225]

[*a.* Law of nations.] The law of nations is indeed, in some way, natural to man, in so far as he is a reasonable being, because it is derived from the natural law by way of a conclusion that is not very remote from its premises. Wherefore men easily agree thereto. Nevertheless it is distinct from the natural law, especially from the natural law which is common to all animals.*[227]

[*b.* Civil law.] A law, properly speaking, regards first and foremost the order to the common good. Now to order any thing to the common good, belongs either to the whole people, or to someone who is the viceregent of the whole people. And therefore the making of a law belongs either to the whole people or to a public personage who has care of the whole people: since in all other matters the directing of anything to the end concerns him to whom the end belongs.[228]

The general principles of the natural law cannot be applied to all men in the same way on account of the great variety of human affairs: and hence arises the diversity of positive laws among various peoples.[229]

Human law has the nature of law in so far as it partakes of righ reason; and it is clear that, in this respect, it is derived from the eternal law. But in so far as it deviates from reason, it is called an unjust law, and has the nature, not of law but of violence.[230]

## Dante

Dante Alighieri (1265–1321) did not have a very optimistic view of man's nature.

O thou our human nature, ever prone to sin! O thou, full of iniquity from the first and ever afterwards without cessation![231]

He treated of society in relation to the macrocosm and the microcosm.

. . . the relation of the partial order to the total order is the same as the relation of the part to the whole. Now the part is related to the whole as to its end and supreme good; wherefore also the order in the part is related to the order in the whole as to its end and supreme good. Whence we learn that the excellence of the partial order does not transcend the excellence of the total order, but rather the other way. Since, then, we may discover a twofold order in things, to wit the order of the parts with reference to each other, and their order with reference to some unity which is not itself a part (for instance the order

* " . . . the right of nations is distinct from natural right. . . . Now, it belongs not only to man but also to other animals to apprehend a thing absolutely; wherefore the right which we call natural, is common to us and other animals . . . But the right of nations falls short of natural right in this sense . . . because *the latter is common to all animals, while the former is common to men only.*"[226]

of the parts of an army with reference to each other, and their order with reference to the general), the order of the parts with reference to that unity is the superior order, as being the end of the other; for the other exists for its sake, and not conversely. Wherefore if the essential principle of this order is to be found even in the parts of the human multiplicity, much more may we look to find it in that multiplicity or totality itself, by virtue of the previous syllogism; since that order, or essential principle of order, is the superior. But we find it in all the parts of the human multiplicity. . . . Therefore it is found, or ought to be found, in the totality itself. And thus all the parts. . . subordinate to kingdoms, together with the kingdoms themselves, should be ordered with reference to a single prince or princedom, that is the monarch or monarchy.

Further, the totality of men is a whole relatively to certain parts, and it is likewise a part relatively to a certain whole. That is, it is a whole relatively to special kingdoms and nations, as shown above; and it is a part relatively to the whole universe, as is self-evident. Therefore, what we consider a proper correspondence of the components of the totality of men to that totality itself, we should also consider a proper correspondence of the totality of men to that whole of which it, in its turn, is a component. Now its parts properly correspond to it by means of having each one single principle only, as may easily be gathered from what has gone before. Wherefore it is true that it, in its turn, properly corresponds with the universe, or with its prince (who is God, and monarch in the unqualified sense), by means of having one single principle only, to wit the sole prince. Whence it follows that the monarchy is necessary to the world for its well-being.[232]

In one place he gives a geographic interpretation of cultural phenomena.

. . . nations, kingdoms, and cities have their special conditions which ought to be regulated by different laws. For a law is a rule to direct life. And naturally the Scythians who live outside the seventh clima, and experience great inequality of days and nights, and are oppressed by an almost intolerable chill of frost, must needs be regulated in a different way from the Garamante who live under the equinoctial circle and always have the light of day equal in length to the darkness of night, and because of the excessive heat of the air cannot endure to be covered with a superfluity of garments.[233]

## Oresme

Nicolas Oresme (d. 1382) announced a generalization on money (usually known as Gresham's law) which is interesting as one of the earliest social laws discovered in western Europe.

The rate of exchange and the price of moneys must be for the kingdom as a law and a firm ordinance which in no way must alter exchange. . . . gold and silver, by such mutations and changes, shrink and diminish in a kingdom, and in spite of all vigilance and prohibition that may be taken, they go abroad where they are accorded a higher value for, by adventure, men carry more voluntarily their moneys to the places where they know these have a greater value.[234]

## Chaucer

Geoffrey Chaucer (1340?–1400) derived the origin of religion from fear, thus anticipating almost all later theorizers on the evolution of religion. In *Troilus and Criseyde* (*ca.* 1380)[235] he says:

Eek drede fond first goddes, I suppose.[236]

## Ball

John Ball (d. 1381) was the ideological leader of the unsuccessful English revolution of 1381. His ideas were summarized in the Blackheath sermon (1381), which has come down only in the highly colored versions found in writers identified with the ruling class. The text of the sermon was a popular couplet:

> Whan Adam dalf, and Eve span,
> Wo was thanne a gentilman?[237]

My good friends, things cannot go on well in England, nor ever will until everything shall be in common; when there shall neither be vassal nor lord, and all distinctions levelled; when the lords shall be no more masters than ourselves. How ill they have used us! and for what reason do they thus hold us in bondage? Are we not all descended from the same parents, Adam and Eve? and what can they show, or what reasons give, why they should be more masters than ourselves? except, perhaps, in making us labor and work for them to spend. They are clothed in velvets and rich stuffs, ornamented with ermine and other furs, while we are forced to wear poor cloth. They have wines, spices, and fine bread, when we have only rye and the refuse of the straw; and, if we drink, it must be water. They have handsome seats and manors, when we must brave the wind and rain in our labors in the field; but it is from our labor they have wherewith to support their pomp. We are called slaves; and, if we do not perform our services, we are beaten, and we have not any sovereign to whom we can complain, or who wishes to hear us and do us justice. Let us go to the king [Richard II], who is young, and remonstrate with him on our servitude, telling him we must have it otherwise, or that we shall find a remedy for it ourselves. If we wait on him in a body, all those who come under the appelation of slaves, or are held in bondage, will follow us, in the hopes of being free. When the king shall see us, we shall obtain a favorable answer, or we must then seek ourselves to amend our condition.[238]

Three earlier letters by Ball remain, written to his followers.

John Schep, some tyme Seynt Marie prest of Yorke, and nowe of Colchestre, greteth welle Johan Nameles, and Johan the Mullere, and Johan Cartere, and biddeth hem that thei ware of gyle in borugh, and stondeth togiddir in Goddis name, and biddeth Peres Ploughman go to his werke, and chastise welle Hobbe the robber [i.e., Sir Robert Hales, Treasurer], and taketh with you Johan Trewman, and alle his felaws, and no mo, and loke scharpe you to one heued [i.e., head], and no mo.

> Johan the Muller hath ygrownde smal, smal, smal;
> The kyngis sone of hevene shalle pay for alle.
> Be ware or ye be wo,
> Knoweth your frende fro your foo,
> Haveth ynowe, and seythe 'Hoo:'
> And do welle and bettre, and flethe synne,
> And seketh pees, and holde therynne.
> And so biddeth Johan Trewman and alle his felawes.[239]

Jon Balle greteth yow wele alle and doth yowe to understande, he hath rungen youre belle. Nowe right and myght, wylle and skylle. God spede every ydele. Nowe is tyme Lady helpe to Ihesu thi sone, and thi sone to his fadur, to make a gode ende, in the name of the Trinite of that is begunne amen, amene, pur charite, amen.[240]

John Balle seynte Marye prist gretes wele alle maner men and byddes hem in the name of the Trinity, Fadur, and Sone and Holy Gost stonde manlyche togedyr in trewthe, and helpez trewthe, and trewthe schal helpe yowe. Now regneth pride in pris, [//] and covetys is hold wys, [//] and leccherye withouten shame [//] and glotonye withouten blame. [//] Envye regnith with tresone, [//] and slouthe is take in grete seson. [//] God do bote, for now is tyme amen.[241]

## CHURCH VERSUS STATE

In the field of social thought, the major point of dispute during the period under consideration was the relation between the church and the state. The object of the argument was to determine whether the former or the latter was to be predominant. Of course most of the clergy championed the supremacy of the church. On the other side, few spirits were hardy enough to argue from the dominance of the state; most of them merely advocated coequal power.[242]

### Gelasius I

At an early date Pope Gelasius I (d. 496) had maintained the superiority of the church over the state.

The authority of the emperor is derived from the divine authority.[243]

Before the coming of Christ there were some who were justly and legitimately both kings and priests, such as Melchizedek; and Satan imitated this among the unbelievers, hence it was that the pagan emperors held the office of Pontifex Maximus. The true and perfect king and priest was Christ Himself, and in that sense in which His people are partakers of His nature they may be said to be a royal and priestly race. But Christ, knowing the weakness of human nature, and careful for the welfare of His people, separated the two offices, giving to each its peculiar functions and duties. Thus the Christian emperor needs the ecclesiastic for the attainment of eternal life, and the ecclesiastic depends upon the government of the emperor in temporal things. There are, then, two authorites by which chiefly the world is ruled, the sacred authority of the prelates and the royal power; but the burden laid upon the priests is the heavier, for they will have to give account in the divine judgement, even for the kings of men: thus it is that the emperor looks to them for the means of his salvation, and submits to them and to their judgement in sacred matters. The authority of the emperor is derived from the divine order, and the rulers of religion obey his laws: he should therefore the more zealously obey them.[244]

### Gregory VII

Pope Gregory VII (1020?–85) ardently upheld the supremacy of the church.

If the Holy Apostolic See, through the princely power divinely bestowed upon it, has jurisdiction over spiritual things, why not also over temporal things?[245]

. . . are they [i. e., kings] not of the sheep which the Son of God committed to St. Peter?. . . .

Does any one doubt that the priests of Christ are to be considered as fathers and masters of kings and princes and of all believers?[246]

The *Dictatus pape* (1075),[247] written under the influence of Gregory VII, had as one of its dicta:

That he [the pope] has the power to depose emperors.[248]

This authority was exercised by Gregory VII when he excommunicated Henry IV.

. . . through my power and authority, I deprive King Henry . . . of the government over the whole kingdom of Germany and Italy, and I release all Christian men from the allegiance which they have sworn or may swear to him, and I forbid any one to serve him as king.[249]

I . . . did not reinstate him in the royal power from which I had deposed him in a Roman Synod . . .

I take from him all royal power and state . . . . as Henry is justly cast down from the royal dignity for his insolence, his disobedience and his deceit, so Rudolf, for his humility, his obedience and his truthfulness is granted the power and dignity of kingship.

And now, most holy fathers and princes [of the Roman Synod], I pray you to take such action that the whole world may know and understand that if you are able to bind and loose in Heaven, you are able also on earth to grant and to take away from every one according to his deserts empires, kingdoms, principalities, dukedoms, marquisates, earldoms and the property of all men.[250]

Gregory VII usually acknowledged the supernatural origin of kings and wrote to them as those "whom God has placed at the summit of human affairs."[251] But when crossed, he developed a more secular hypothesis as to the origin of kings:

Who does not know that kings and princes derive their origin from men ignorant of God who raised themselves above their fellows by pride, plunder, treachery, murder— in short, by every kind of crime—at the instigation of the Devil, the prince of this world, men blind with greed and intolerable in their audacity.[252]

## Bernard of Clairvaux

Bernard of Clairvaux (1091–1153) was a more moderate proponent of church supremacy.

[He wrote to the pope that the administration of justice concerns temporal governors rather than bishops;] apostolic man though you are, you usurp a mean office unworthy of you, and descend to the level of those who are of less account . . . . Which seems to you the greater dignity and power, that of forgiving sins, or that of dividing estates? The truth is that there is no comparison between them. These lower earthly things have their own judges, the kings and princes of the earth. Why trespass on another man's province? Why put your sickle in another man's harvest? Not that men in your position are unworthy, but because to devote yourselves to such matters when you have enough to do with better is unworthy of you.[253]

. . . set about . . . with the word, not with the sword. Why should you again try to use the sword, which you were once for all bidden to put into its sheath? Yet if any one should deny that you have the sword, he does not seem to me to have paid sufficient attention to his Lord's word, "Put back thy sword into the sheath." [John,, 18:10–11] To you, then, the sword belongs, and it should be unsheathed, it may be with your consent, though not by your hand. Otherwise, if it no way belonged to you, when the apostles said, "Lo, here are two swords" [Luke, 22:38], the Lord would not have replied, "It is enough"; He would have said, "They are too many." Both swords belong to the Church, the spiritual and the material; the one is to be used to defend the Church, but the other must ever be banished from the Church; the one is wielded by the priest, the other by the soldier, but of course with your consent, and at the command of the Emperor.[254]

[And to King Conrad:] Never more sweetly, more harmoniously, or more closely could kingship and priesthood have been united or planted together than when they both alike met in the person of the Lord, since He was made for us out of both tribes according to the flesh, at once High Priest and King. And not only so, but he has also mingled them and united them in His Body. . . . Therefore. what God hath joined let not man put asunder. What Divine authority has sanctioned let man's will be the more diligent to fulfill, and let those whom precepts have united be united in their minds. Let them help each other, defend each other, bear each other's burdens . . . . May my soul never come into the counsel of those who say that either the peace and liberty of the Churches is injurious to the Empire, or that the prosperity and exaltation of the Empire are harmful to the Churches. For God, the Founder of both, has not joined them for destruction, but for edification.

If you know this, how long do you continue to pass over their common reproach, their common wrongs [i.e., the revolt of the Roman people against the pope]? Is not Rome at once the Apostolic See and the capital of the Empire?. . . . Therefore gird thee with thy sword upon thy thigh, O, most mighty, and let Caesar restore to himself the things which are Caesar's, and to God the things which are God's. It is well known that both are in the charge of Caesar, viz., to guard his own crown and to defend the Church. One befits the King; the other the defender of the Church.[255]

Bernard believed in the supernatural origin of kings.[256] Finally, in one letter he used the organic analogy.[257]

### John of Salisbury

John of Salisbury also considered kings to have been divinely appointed,[258] but subordinate to the church.

God's ministers are they that have been called by the divine governance to procure the salvation of themselves and others by rooting out and correcting vices, or by implanting and increasing the virtues. But those who minister to Him in the sphere of human law are as much inferior to those who minister in divine law as things human are below things divine.[259]

### Innocent III

Pope Innocent III (1160–1261) argued in terms of the following analogy:

As God, the creator of the universe, set two great lights in the firmament of heaven, the greater light to rule the day, and the lesser light to rule the night [Gen. 1:15-16], so He set two great dignities in the firmament of the universal church, . . . the greater to rule the day, that is, souls, and the lesser to rule the night, that is, bodies. These dignities are the papal authority and the royal power. And just as the moon gets her light from the sun, and is inferior to the sun in quality, quantity, position, and effect, so the royal power gets the splendor of its dignity from the papal authority.[260]

### Thomas Aquinas

Thomas Aquinas argued for the subordination of the state to the church.

. . . it is not the ultimate end of an assembled multitude to live virtuously, but through virtuous living to attain to the possession of God. Furthermore, if it could attain this end by the power of human nature, then the duty of a king would have to include the direction of men to this end. . . . But, because a man does not attain his end which is the possession of God, by human power, but by Divine power, . . . the task of leading him to that end does not pertain to human government but to divine. . . . [And] in order that spiritual things might be distinguished from earthly things, the ministry of this kingdom has been entrusted not to earthly kings, but to priests, and in the highest degree to the chief priest, the successor of S. Peter, the Vicar of Christ, the Roman Pontiff, to whom all the kings of Christian peoples are to be subject as to our Lord Jesus Christ Himself. For those to whom pertains the care of intermediate ends should be subject to him to whom pertains the care of the ultimate end, and be directed by his rule.[261]

[Therefore] the king ought to be subject to the dominion and government administered by the office of priesthood.*[263]

## Boniface VIII

The bull *Unum sanctam* (1302)[264] of Pope Boniface VIII (1228–1303) is the most positive statement made on behalf of the dominance of the church over the state.

By our faith, we are forced to believe and maintain one holy Catholic and Apostolic Church. . . . Of this one and only Church . . . there is only one body and one head, not two heads as if it were a monster, and that one head is Christ and the vicar of Christ, Peter, and his successors. . . . We must then understand that all were committed to him. . . . In the power of this Church, so we are told in the Gospel, are two swords, the spiritual and the temporal. For when the apostles said, "Here are two swords," we must understand that, as Apostles were speaking, there was a question of the Church, and remember that the Lord did not reply that there were too many, but that they were enough. He who would deny that the temporal sword is in Peter's power, but ill takes note of the Lord's words: "Put up again thy sword into its place" [Matt. 26:52]. Both swords, then, belong to the Church, the spiritual and the material, the latter to be used for the Church, the former by it. The former, too, is in the priest's own hands, the latter in those of Kings and soldiers to be employed under the direction of the priest. Sword must be under sword, and the temporal authority under the spiritual. For when the Apostle said, "There is on power but from God; and those that are, are ordained of God" [Rom. 13:1], they would not be so ordained were not sword subject to sword, and the material one, as the inferior, raised to high places by the spiritual one. . . . Now, that the spiritual power excels the temporal in dignity and nobility, is as clear as that things spiritual excel things temporal. . . . The voice of truth tells us that it is the business of the spiritual power to institute, to establish, the temporal power; and, if it is not in order, to judge it.[265]

## Dante

The most famous defense of the independence of the state from the authority of the church is the *De monarchia* (*ca.* 1310) of Dante Alighieri. He developed his argument in the following manner:

. . . in the first place we may inquire and examine whether it [i.e., monarchy] is needful for the well-being of the world; in the second, whether the Roman people rightfully assumed to itself the function of monarchy; and in the third, whether the authority of the monarchy depends immediately upon God, or upon some other minister or vicar of God.[266]

[1.] . . . we must consider what is the goal of human civilisation as a whole.[267]

. . . the work proper to the human race, taken as a whole, is to keep the whole capa-

* "The secular power is subject to the spiritual, even as the body is subject to the soul."[262]

city of potential intellect constantly actualised, primarily for speculation, and secondarily (by extension, and for the sake of the other) for action.

And . . . it is evident that in the quiet or tranquillity of peace the human race is most freely and favourably disposed towards the work proper to it.[268]

All concord depends on unity in wills. The human race when best disposed is a concord. . . . Therefore the human race when best disposed depends upon a unity in wills. But this unity cannot be unless there is one will dominating and ruling all the rest to oneness. . . Nor can that one will exist unless there be a single prince of all, whose will may be the mistress and ruler of all others. Now if all the above deductions are sound, which they are, it is necessary for the best disposition of the human race that there should be a monarch in the world, and therefore for the well-being of the world that there should be a monarchy.[269]

[2.]. . . the Roman people acquired to itself the empire of the world by right.[270]

[3.] The present question . . .concerning which we are to make inquiry, lies between two great lights, to wit the Roman pontiff and the Roman prince; and we are to ask whether the authority of the Roman monarch, who is monarch of the world by right, as proved in the second book, is immediately dependent upon God; or rather on some vicar or minister of God, by whom I understand the successor of Peter, who in very truth bears the keys of the kingdom of heaven.[271]

. . . the authority of the empire is not caused by the authority of the supreme pontiff.[272]

. . . the said authority depends immediately upon the summit of all being, which is God.[273]

. . . unutterable providence. . . has set two ends before man to be contemplated by him; the blessedness, to wit, of this life, which consists in the exercise of his proper power and is figured by the terrestrial paradise, and the blessedness of eternal life, which consists in the fruition of the divine aspect, to which his proper power may not ascend unless assisted by the divine light. And this blessedness is given to be understood by the celestial paradise. . . .

Wherefore man had need of a twofold directive power according to his twofold end, to wit, the supreme pontiff, to lead the human race, in accordance with things revealed, to eternal life; and the emperor, to direct the human race to temporal felicity in accordance with the teachings of philosophy.[274]

## Marsiglio

Neither the Bible nor the church fathers had discussed the formation of political organization to any extent, and in the struggle for domination between the church and state, the implications of the question became important. The first systematic hypothesis to gain any degree of currency was that of social contract. Though Leo VIII (7. 965)[275] and Manegold of Lauthenbach* (fl. 1090)[277] had considered

* "[First use of social contract theory]. No man can make himself king or emperor, and so the people set some one man over them, that he may govern and rule them by reason of his righteous authority, that he may render to each his own, encourage the just, supress the unjust, in a word, do justice to all men. But if at any time he infringes the compact by which he was set up, and breaks forth into disquieting and confounding and destroying what he was set up to keep in order, then, on the ground of right reason, he absolves the people from the allegiance which bound them in fealty to one another, since he himself has first broken faith. Besides, the people do not by any means bind themselves by oath to obey all his mad whims, nor does the compulsion of their allegiance force them to follow wherever fury and madness may drive him."[276]

this hypothesis, it received its most important early expression in the work of Marsilius of Padua (d. 1342).

As the object of the state is that men may live and live well, we must first treat of living, and of its modes; for the state is necessary for everything undertaken by the community of men comprising the state.[278]

But concerning living and living well . . . for fulfilling that life a civil community is necessary; for perfect life cannot be attained otherwise. . . . Although observation and experience may teach us this truth, nevertheless we wish to point out more distinctly its cause, showing that, since man is innately composed of contrary elements, something of his substance is being continually wasted because of the conflicting actions and passions of these elements. Moreover, since man is born unprotected from his environment, and thus is liable to suffering and destruction, he needs arts of diverse sorts whereby he may ward off noxious things. And since such arts cannot be employed save by a number of men, nor preserved save through their communication from age to age, it is necessary for men to congregate in order to acquire what is useful and to escape what is injurious.[279]

Among men thus congregated contention arises naturally, which, if not regulated by the rule of justice, leads to division and strife, and finally to the dissolution of the community. It is, therefore, necessary to introduce into the community the rule of justice and to set up a guardian, or protector. Since it is the function of the guardian to restrain dangerous transgressors and others who are agitators or who seek to harass the community from within or without, the state must have within itself the means of repression. Moreover, the community has other needs for convenience and security—certain things in time of peace, others in time of war; it is, therefore, necessary that there shall be in the community those who will provide these things, in order that the common demands can be supplied whenever expedient or imperative.[280]

Men are associated together for the sake of living sufficiently—that is, to obtain the things which are necessary to themselves and to transmit such things from generation to generation. This congregation in its perfected form, containing the limit of sufficiency in itself, is called the state. The various things needed by those desiring to live well cannot be procured by men of a single rank or office. It is necessary that there be diverse ranks or offices among the members of the community, each rank or office contributing something which man needs for the sufficiency of life. These various orders or offices constitute the multiplicity and diversity of the parts of the state.[281]

Men have come together into a civil association for the sake of convenience and the resulting sufficiency of life, and in order to escape the opposite conditions.[282]

According to truth and the opinion of Aristotle (*Politica* 3. 6) the legislator—that is, the effective and peculiar creator of law, is the people,—or the majority of them—acting through election, or more directly through vote in general assembly of the citizens, commanding that something be done or omitted in the field of human social conduct, under pain of temporal punishment.[283]

. . . human legislative authority pertains to the whole body, or majority, of citizens.[284]

## THE DECAY OF THE WORLD

### Apocrypha and Pseudepigrapha
Some of the extra-canonical Hebrew writings of the first two centuries C.E.

contained a pessimistic doctrine about the decay of the world which later influenced the theory of social degradation in the post-Renaissance period.

For the youth of the world is past, and the strength of the creation already exhausted.[285]

They that be born in the strength of youth are of one fashion, and they that are born in the time of age, when the womb faileth, are otherwise. Consider therefore thou also, how that ye are less of stature than those that were before you. And so are they that come after you less than ye, as born of the creature which now beginneth to be old. and is past the strength of youth.[286]

For the world hath lost its youth, and the times begin to wax old.[287]

## Cyprian

The doctrine of the world's decay was taken over by Cyprian (*ca.* 210–58) and thus passed into Christian tradition.

. . . now . . . the world is collapsing and is oppressed with the tempests of mischievous ills. . . . Lo, the world is changing and passing away, and witnesses to its ruin not now by its age, but by the end of things.[288]

. . . the world has now grown old, and does not abide in that strength in which it formerly stood; nor has it that vigour and force which it formerly possessed.[289]

## Bernard of Chartres

Bernard of Chartres (d. *ca.* 1130)[290] employed a simile that was to become a favorite in later times:

Bernard of Chartres used to say that we, like dwarfs on the shoulders of giants, can see more and farther not because we are keener and taller, but because of the greatness by which we are carried and exalted.[291]

## Spenser

Edmund Spenser (1552?–99) gave poetical expression to the theory of the decay of the world.

>          antique age yet in the infancie
> Of time, did live then like an innocent.[292]
> But when the world woxe old, it woxe warre old.[293]
> Ne wonder; for the heavens revolution
> Is wandered farre from where it first was pight,
> And so doe make a contrarie constitution
> Of all this lower world toward his dissolution.[294]
> And all this world with them amisse doe move,
> And all his creatures from their course astray,
> Till they arrive at their last ruinous decay.[295]

## Castiglione

Baldassare Castiglione (1478–1529) protested against the theory of social degradation by arguing that the ancients were not innately superior to the moderns.[296]

# II

# THE FIFTEENTH AND SIXTEENTH CENTURIES

T HE FIFTEENTH and sixteenth centuries constitute the era of the rise of commercial capitalism. One of its products was the Renaissance, which in the fields under discussion was characterized by a naturalistic empiricism opposed to the theological and authoritarian world view of the preceding epoch. Also, the great number of accounts written by the explorers of the time exhibited a diversity of customs which struck the attention of many scholars. This resulted in two other important developments in the contemporary social anthropology: a cosmopolitan outlook and the use of the comparative method in the development of generalizations about social phenomena.

In physical anthropology the breakdown of the theological point of view permitted human dissections and the drawing of comparisons between man and other animals, while the newly discovered races forced a re-examination of the problem of monogenesis versus polygenesis. And as far back as 1463, a Jew by the name of Samuel Sarsa (d. 1463) had been burned at the stake for heresy "because he asserted the great antiquity of the world."[1]

## PHYSICAL ANTHROPOLOGY

### Leonardo da Vinci

Leonardo da Vinci (1452–1519) was as remarkable in this field as in all the others which claimed his attention; one is tempted to exclaim with Delacroix, "He discovered everything."[2]

He appreciated the relations between man and other animals, and made important contributions to comparative anatomy.

It is an easy matter for whoever knows how to represent man to afterwards acquire . . . universality, for all the animals which live upon the earth resemble each other in their limbs, that is in the muscles, sinews and bones, and they do not vary at all, except in length or thickness as will be shown in the Anatomy.[3]

Show a man on tiptoe so that you may compare a man better with other animals.
Represent the knee of a man bent like that of the horse.
To compare the bone structure of the horse with that of the man you must show the man on tiptoe in representing the legs.
Of the relationship that exists between the arrangement of the bones and muscles of the animals and that of the bones and muscles of the man.[4]

. . . represent the legs of frogs, for these have a great resemblance to the legs of the man, both in the bones and in the muscles.[5]

Man. The description of man, in which is contained those who are almost of the same species just as the baboon, the ape and others like these which are many.[6]

Write of the varieties of the intestines of the human species, apes and such like.[7]

In fact man does not vary from the animals except in what is accidental, and it is in this that he shows himself to be a divine thing; for where nature finishes producing its species there man begins with natural things to make with the aid of this nature an infinite number of species; and as these are not necessary to those who govern themselves rightly as do the other animals it is not in their disposition to seek after them.[8]

His remark on race shows insight:

The black races in Ethiopia are not the product of the sun; for if black gets black with child in Scythia, the offspring is black; but if a black gets a white woman with child the offspring is grey. And this shows that the seed of the mother has power in the embryo equally with that of the father.[9]

He even tried his hand at historical reconstruction.

How the first picture was nothing but a line which surrounded the shadow of a man made by the sun upon a wall.[10]

## Dürer

In order to discover the ideal proportions of the human figure, Albrecht Dürer (1471–1528) made a painstaking study of the proportions of the human figure and facial angles.[11]

## Gesner

It was customary for early writers on animals to exclude man as a creature apart. Thus, Conrad Gesner (1516–65) has no place for man in his *Historia animalium*.[12] In this work the various animals are listed alphabetically; the lower primates and some fantastic creatures thought to be related to them are described.[13]

## Wotton

A notable exception to this omission of man from discussions of animals is to be found in a work by Edward Wotton (1492–1555). In fact, he devotes a whole book of his *De differentiis animalium*[14] to man.[15]

## Pereira

Gomez Pereira (fl. 1554) anticipated Descartes by asserting that the difference between man and other animals lay in the fact that, while man has reason, beasts are mere machines.[16]

## Rorario

Girolamo Rorario (1485–1556), on the other hand, formulated the paradoxical thesis that "beasts often reason better than man."[17]

## Vesalius

The great Vesalius in the beginning of the sixteenth century, was the first that taught physicians to study nature in dissecting human bodies; which was then considered by the church as a kind of sacrilege.[18]

Andreas Vesalius (1514–64), as the founder of modern anatomy,[19] placed physical anthropology on a precise basis. Besides, he made tentative beginnings in comparative anatomy[20] and noticed the relationship between the shape of the skull and race.

It seems that certain nations have something peculiar in the shape of their head. The heads of Genoese, and more particularly of Greeks and Turks, almost exhibit a round shape. To this also (which not a few of them think elegant and consider to be well adapted to the turbans which they use in various ways) the midwives sometimes contribute at the urgent request of the mother. The Germans, indeed, have a very flattened occiput and a broad head, because the boys always lie on their backs in their cradles. . . . More oblong heads are reserved to the Belgians . . . because' their mothers permit their little boys to sleep turned over in their beds, and as much as possible on their sides.[21]

### Belon

Pierre Belon (1517–64) investigated the comparative anatomy of man and bird.[22]

### Montaigne

Michel Eyquem de Montaigne (1533–92) was not sure of man's relations with other animals.

As to that cousinship between the animals and ourselves, I do not take much account of it.[23]

But when, among the most moderate opinions, I meet with arguments which endeavour to demonstrate the close resemblance between us and the animals, and to show how large a share they have in our greatest privileges, and with how much reason they have been likened to us, truly, I abate a great deal of our presumption, and willingly renounce that imaginary kingship which we are supposed to have over the other creatures.[24]

If we are to believe Pliny and Herodotus, there are, in certain regions, species of men who have very little resemblnce to our kind.

And there are hybrid and ambiguous forms between the human and brute nature.[25]

However, he applied his relativisitc standards to the whole animal kingdom and therefore refused to make man predominant.

Let him explain to me, by the force of his reason, on what foundation he has built those great advantages he thinks he has over the other creatures. What has induced him to believe that wonderful motion of the heavenly vault, the eternal light of those torches rolling so proudly over his head, the awe-inspiring agitations of that infinite sea, were established, and endured through so many centuries, for his service and convenience.[26]

With this same vanity of imagination he makes himself the equal of God, assumes to himself divine qualities, selects and separates himself from among the multitude of other creatures, carves out their shares to each of his fellows and comrades, the animals, and allots to them their portion of faculties and powers according as it seems good to him. How can he know, by the force of his understanding, the secret and internal motions of the animals? By what comparison between them and himself does he suppose them to be as stupid as he thinks?

When I play with my cat, who knows but that she regards me more as a plaything than I do her?[27]

In short, whatever is not as we are, is not worth a rap. And God himself, to be any good, must be like us. . . . From which it is clear that it is not upon any true ground of reason, but from a foolish arrogance and stubbornness, that we put ourselves before the other animals, and remove ourselves from their condition and fellowship.[28]

[1. Other animals have intelligence like man.] Why do we deny them a soul, and life and reason? Have we discovered in them any stubborn, senseless stupidity, we who have no concern with them but to obey them? Shall we say that we have seen no other creature but man in possession of a reasoning mind?[29]

[a. Other animals exhibit intelligence[30] and imagination.*] After all, which of our arts do we not see in the activities of animals? Is there any organization regulated with more order, with a better distribution of charges and functions, and more consistently maintained, than that of the bees? Can we imagine that so well-ordered a disposition of activities and occupations could be carried on without reason and foresight?[32]

We may see well enough, in most of their works, how much the animals surpass us, and how much we fall short in the art of imitating them. And yet, in our ruder performances, we are sensible of what faculties we employ, and we know that our mind applies to them its utmost powers; why do we not conclude the same of the animals? Why do we ascribe to I know not what slavish instinct of nature those works that excel anything we can do by nature or art?[33]

I say then . . . that there is no reason to imagine that the beasts do, through a natural and enforced instinct, the same things that we do by choice and skill. From like results we must infer like faculties; and we must consequently confess that the same reason, the same method, that we employ in working are also employed by the animals.[34]

[b. Man's "inborn reason"[35] has many flaws.[36]] We have strangely overrated this precious reason we so much glory in, this faculty of knowing and judging.[37]

[Even if one were to assume that animal activity is "instinctive," similar phenomena can be found in man;] we make many movements which are not the effect of will. . . . A man who is falling shoots out his arms in front of him, by a natural impulse which makes our limbs lend each other their services, and stirs them quite apart from our reason.[38]

We possess by a natural instinct and teaching the skill to fortify our bodies and protect them by acquired means.[39]

[2. Animals have means of communication as well as man.[40]] That defect which hinders communication between us and them, why may it not as well be in ourselves as in them? It is a matter of conjecture with whom the fault lies that we do not understand one another; for we understand them no more than they do us. By the same reasoning they may regard us as beasts, as we do them. . . .

We must observe the parity there is between us. We have some halfway understanding of their meaning, as the animals have of ours, in about the same degree. They cajole us, they threaten us, they entreat us, as we do them. Moreover, it is very evident to us that they are able fully and completely to communicate with one another, that they understand one another, and not only those of the same species, but also those of different species.[41]

[He comes to the following conclusion:] I have said all this to establish the resemblance to human conditions, and to bring us back and join us to the majority. We are neither superior nor inferior to the rest. All that is under heaven, says the sage [in Ecclesiastes],

* "Even animals are like ourselves subject to the force of imagination, witness those dogs that die of grief for the loss of their masters. We see them bark and tremble in their dreams, and horses will neigh and kick.[31]

is subject to one law and one fate. . . . Some difference there is; there are orders and degrees, but under the aspect of one same Nature. . . .

Man must be forced and lined up within the barriers of this organization. The poor wretch has no mind really to step over them. He is shackled and entangled, he is subjected to the same obligation as the other creatures of his order, and is of a very mediocre condition, without any real and essential prerogative and pre-eminence.[42]

## Bellarmine

Roberto Francesco Romolo Bellarmine (15421–1621) wrote on the chain of being.[43]

## Paracelsus

Paracelsus, i.e., Theophrastus Bombastus von Hohenheim (1493–1541), was particularly preoccupied with the problem of monogenesis versus polygenesis. Though he accepted the biblical version of man's creation,[44] the newly discovered races inclined him in favor of polygenesis.

[He argues against the thesis] that all people came from one father, though from one god who gives the soul to all. The same god, who gives and has given everything, and who is known by philosophy, did not allow such forms and so many kinds of people to come from one father but from many, and neither did he order anything unnatural or monstrous, but given all an equal soul, though not similar forms, for quite manifold forms have been born through the father. It might also seem proper . . . to tell who was the first father of the bipeds, if we could calculate back; however, this is not philosophical, but would be an amusing joke. In order to know the first father from whom all children are born, we must have been there; therefore, what philosopy will tell us how he was born?[45]

However this may be, we are all descended from Adam, and we are all those that ought to be called men, and our first father was made by god with his hands. . . . That is the creation of man. But still another thing has to be considered, namely, that the children of Adam did not inhabit the whole world. That is why some hidden countries have not been populated by Adam's children, but through another creature, created like men outside of Adam's creation. For god did not intend to leave them empty, but has populated the miraculously hidden countries with other men . . . that is why it is not necessary to prove that the people in the hidden countries are descended from Adam.*[48]

An anonymous follower of Paracelsus was even more heretical, doubting the creation narrative itself, as given in the Old Testament.

Moses understood no physics, but writes particularly as a theologian . . . therefore he had the gift of understanding the creation in a particular way, and not entirely, as the necessity of the case required it to be described. Perhaps he did not know any better . . . for he was not a physicist from youth on. . . . Therefore his description is quite

* " . . . we are all descended from Adam. And I cannot refrain from making a brief mention of those who have been found in hidden islands and are still little known. To believe that they have descended from Adam is difficult to conceive—that Adam's children have gone to the hidden islands. But one should well consider, that these people are from a different Adam. It will be difficult to maintain, that they are related on the basis of flesh and blood."[46]

"It cannot be believed that such newly found people in the islands are of Adam's blood."[47]

unintelligible to laymen. For it would be a weak ground for a physicist, if he were to give credence to the text on creation according to Moses.[49]

## Bruno

Giordano Bruno (1548–1600) also had a polygenetic theory of man.

> For of many colors
> Are the species of men, and the black race
> Of the Ethiopians, and the yellow offspring of America,
> And that which lies hidden in the caves of Neptune,
> And the Pygmies always shut up in the hills,
> Inhabitants of the veins of the earth, and custodians
> Of the mines, and the Gigantic monsters of the South,
> Cannot be traced to the same descent, nor are they sprung
> From the generative force of a single progenitor.
> Every island everywhere can give a beginning to things,
> Although the same form is not preserved everywhere the same,
> For one species flourishes in one place, another in another.[50]

It is said in the prophets, and is well known among the same people [i.e., the Jews[, that all races of men are to be traced to one first father, or to three, as we learn and firmly believe from the Hebrew remains, of which some trace the only superior race, that is, the Jews, to one protoplast, and the other races to the two first, which were created two days before. The religion of the recently discovered Chinese enumerate three differently named protoplasts, twenty thousand years ago. No one of sound judgement can refer the Ethiopian race to that protoplast.[51]

> The regions of the heavens are three; three of air; the water
> Is divided into three; the earth is divided into three parts.
> And the three races had three Patriarchs,
> When mother Earth produced animals, first
> Enoch, Leviathan, and the third of which is Adam;
> According to the belief of most of the Jews,
> From whom alone was descended the sacred race.[52]

## Bodin

Jean Bodin (1530–96) attempted to classify mankind.

. . . the people of the South are of a contrarie humour and disposition to them of the North: these are great and strong, they are little and weak: they of the north hot and moyst, the others cold and dry; the one hath a big voyce and greene eyes, the other hath a weake voyce and black eyes; the one hath a flaxen haire and a faire skin, the other hath both haire and skin black; the one feareth cold, and the other heate.[53]

It was difficult for him to explain these differences.

[It would not do] to observe the climate alone, for we see in climates that be alike and of the same elevation foure notable differences of people in colour, without speaking of other qualities, for that the West Indians are generallie of a duskish colour like unto a roasted quinze, unless it be a handfull of men that are black, whom the tempest carried from the coast of Affrike: and in Sivill of Spaine the men are white, at Cape Bonne Esperance black, at the river of Plate of a chestnut colour, all being in like latitude, and like climates, as we reade in the histories of the Indies which the Spaniards have left in writing: the cause may be the change from one countrie to another, and that the Sunne in Capricorne is neerer unto the earth by all the eccentricall latitude, the which are above foure hundred thousand leagues.[54]

## ARCHEOLOGY

The Renaissance humanists derived their inspiration from ancient Greece and Rome, and particularly in Italy the archeological remains were studied by fifteenth- and sixteenth-century scholars.[55] One of the earliest classical archeologists was Ciriaco de' Pizzicolli (1391–1457?), who avidly, though carelessly, recorded and collected much material.[56]

Paleolithic and neolithic artefacts found scattered throughout western Europe had puzzled scholars for centuries, and even in the sixteenth century they were a problem. Ulisse Aldrovandi (1522–1605?) said that they were natural accretions developed by geological processes;[57] Conrad Gesner (1516–65), that they were thunderbolts.[58] Stone projectile points were usually called "elf arrows" or "thunderbolts" by laymen, the latter interpretation still has contemporary currency.[59] However, Michele Mercati (1541–93), in his *Metallotheca vaticana,*[60] stated that these stones were the weapons of a primitive people unacquainted with the use of metals.[61]

Interest in more recent archeological remains increased, and solid works of scholarship were produced, such as William Camden's (1551–1623) *Britannia* (1586).[62]

## HISTORY AND ETHNOGRAPHY

The first genetic history in western Europe was the *Mémoires (ca.* 1498)[63] of Philippe de Comines (1445–1509). In the sixteenth century the genetic tradition was carried on by Thomas More (1478–1535), *The History of King Richard the Thirde (ca.* 1513),[64] and Michel de Castelnau (1520?–92), *Les mémoires.*[65]

Some attention was paid to the customs of western European countries, particularly folklore; a good example of the work of the period is that by William Camden (1551–1623).[66]

The humanists were interested in the depiction of the Greek and Roman cultures and the tracing of western European customs from those of Greece and Rome.[67]

Reports on the exotic cultures appeared in the accounts of pilgrims,[68] diplomats,[69] and traders,[70] but their importance was overshadowed by a new source of information, that of the maritime explorers.

The Mediterranean Sea was the main sea route of international trade before the fifteenth century. Italian merchants were . . . the chief tradesmen of the Mediterranean. At one time they defeated all their rivals but already in the fourteenth century the importance of Italian trade was on the wane. In the middle of the fourteenth century the Italian merchants suffered a heavy blow—the Turks, already in possession of Asia Minor, occupied Constantinople and the Black Sea. These conquests of the Turks finally cut off Italian towns from those of the Near East. But the worst of it was that the Turks made even more difficult all travel to far-away India. Formerly trading caravans found it difficult to penetrate to this distant land. Meanwhile India appeared to European merchants as a land of fabulous and innumerable riches. This was partly true; but even more was added by the phantastic tales of merchants returning from India. To check the truth of these legends was very difficult, and travel took much time; to go there and back one had to spend several years.

Such were the causes for the hunt for new, shorter and less dangerous routes to India.

In the twelfth to fifteenth centuries European ships made more and more distant voyages. Voyages from the Baltic and North Sea around the European coast to the Mediterranean became more frequent and ships passed through the Strait of Gibralter to the Atlantic Ocean.

Several groups of islands in the eastern part of the Atlantic were discovered, and some galleys travelled far to the south along the African coast.

All these travels widened the geographical outlook of the sea travellers and prepared the ground for the great geographical discoveries of the fifteenth to sixteenth centuries.[71]

There is little ethnographic information in the reports on the Canary Islands.[72] In the latter half of the fifteenth century a fair amount of material began to appear on Africa, such as that by Gomez Eannes de Azurara (fifteenth century),[73] Diogo Gomes (b. *ca.* 1420),[74] and on the explorations of Vasco da Gama.[75] But with the discoveries of Christopher Columbus (1446?–1506)[76] a new era began.[77] Some conception of the wealth of data which then became available can be had from examining such contemporary collections as those edited by Giovanni Battista Ramusio (1485–1557),[78] Richard Eden (1521?–76),[79] and Richard Hakluyt (1552–1616).[80]

An attempt was made to digest this mass of material through compendia. At first the interest was mainly geographic, but later more emphasis was given to ethnography. Thus, one of the earliest books, the *Cosmographicus*[81] of Petrus Apianus (1495–1552), is primarily concerned with astronomy, astronomical instruments, geography, etc., and only a few pages are devoted to anything resembling ethnographic information.[82] But later works show more interest in anthropological data, e.g., Benedetto Bordone (fl. 1528) *Libro (Isolario)*;[83] Sebastian Franck (1499–1542), *Weltbuch;*[84] Sebastian Münster (1489–1552), *Cosmographiae universalis* (1544);[85] and Giovanni Botero (1540–1617), *Le relationi universali* (1591).[86]

## Hotman

Francois Hotman (1524–90) was interested in the origin of the French.

. . . the Nation of the *Franks* first came into *Gallia* . . . from the marshy Country which lies upon the *Ocean,* between the Rivers *Elb* and *Rhine.*[87]

## LINGUISTICS

Andrew Boorde (1490?–1549), in *The Fyrst Boke of the Introduction of Knowledge* (*ca.* 1547), gave linguistic texts for each country he visited and illustrates the interest which had begun to develop in the languages of the world. Konrad Gesner's (1516–65), *Mithridates*[88] contains vocabularies and texts in a number of languages. Somewhat later, Hieronymous Megiser (*ca.* 1553–1618) also produced a *Thesaurus polyglottus* (1592),[89] followed by *Specimen quinquaginte diversarium atque inter se differentium linguarum, & dialectorum,*[90] which primarily consists of the Lord's Prayer in various languages.

## Montaigne

Michel Eyquem de Montaigne (1533–92) was aware of the phenomenon of linguistic change.

Seeing the continual changes that have taken place in our tongue to this day, who can expect that fifty years hence it will be used in its present form? Every day it slips from our hands, and during my lifetime it has altered by one half.[91]

He also realized the affinity between the Romance languages.

When in Italy, I suggested to somebody who was at great pains to learn Italian, that, provided he only sought to make himself understood, without being particularly ambitious to excel, he should simply use the first words that came to his tongue, Latin, French, Spanish, or Gascon, and that by adding the Italian terminations, he would never fail to hit upon some dialect of the country, either Tuscan, or Roman, or Venetian, or Piedmontese, or Neapolitan, and so lay hold of some one of the many different forms.[92]

It is a pity that he did not elaborate this remark, because of its important implications.

## Hotman

Francois Hotman (1524–90) attempted to discover the linguistic affiliations of the ancient and modern French people.

. . . the *Ancient Gauls* had a peculiar Language of their own, not much differing from the British. . . . The Language which we at present make use of, may easily be known to be a Compound of the several Tongues of divers Nations: And . . . may be divided into four parts. One half of it we have from the *Romans.* . . . The other half of it may be subdivided thus, One third of it we hold from the *Ancient Gauls,* another from the *Franks,* and the last from the *Greek* Language.[93]

## SOCIAL ANTHROPOLOGY

### Fortescue

John Fortescue (1394?–1476?) was particularly interested in the nature of law.

The human race, from the time when it went out from Paradise, even until the people of Israel received by the hand of Moses at Mount Sinai the law written by the Lord, was governed by the law of Nature.[94]

What else . . . can the Law of Nature be but this . . . *the Truth of Justice, which is capable of being by right reason revealed?*[95]

. . . we have proved that law to be eternal, and, while man's state has changed, to be wholly unchanged itself.[96]

For, as the philosopher [Aristotle] says, in the fifth of his *Ethics,* "The Law of Nature is the same, and has the same force all the world over."[97]

This Law of Nature all the laws of the Old and New Testament approved, diminishing nothing therefrom. . . . And whatever other laws there are, called human, they are either by this law established, or by its authority, as supplementing it, they subsist.[98]

. . . all human laws are either the Law of Nature, Customs, or States.[99]

To Fortescue, political organization first resulted from conquest, but later developed through social contract.

Ther bith ij kyndes off kyngdomes, of the wich that on is a lordship callid in laten *dominium regale* [absolute monarchy], and that other is callid *dominium politicum et regale* [limited monarchy]. And thai diversen in that the first kynge mey rule his peple bi suche lawes as he makyth hym self. And therfore he mey sett uppon thaim tayles and other imposicions, such as he wol hym self, with owt thair assent. The secounde kynge may not rule his people bi other lawes than such as thai assenten unto. And therfore he mey sett upon thaim non imposicions withowt thair owne assent.[100]

Whan Nembroth [i.e., Nimrod] be myght for his owne glorie made and incorperate the first realme, and subdued it to hymself bi tyrannye, he wolde not have it governyd bi any other rule or lawe, but bi his owne wille; bi wich and for the accomplisshment therof he made it. . . . And thus I suppose first began in Realmes *dominium tantum regale*. But aftirwarde, whan mankynde was more mansuete, and bettir disposid to vertu, grete comunaltes, as was the felowshippe that came in to this lande with Brute, willynge to be unite and made a body pollitike callid a reawme, havynge an hed to governe it; —as aftir the saynge of the philisopher [Aristotle], every comunalte unyed of mony parties must nedis have an hed;—than they chese the same Brute to be ther hed and kynge. And thai and he upon this incorperacion, institucion, and onynge of him self into a reaume, ordenyd the same reaume to be ruled and justified by suche lawes as thai all wolde assent unto; wich lawe therfore is callid *polliticum,* and bi cause it is ministrid bi a kynge, it is callid *regale*.[101]

## More

Thomas More's (1478–1535) *Utopia* (1516)[102] is noteworthy for its explanation of cultural facts in terms of empirical social phenomena, rather than supernaturally. The most important analysis in the book is that on the causes of crime.

" . . . a simple theft is not so great an offence, that it ought to be punished with death. Neither is there any punishment so horrible, that it can keep them from stealing, who have no other craft, whereby to get their living. Therefore in this point, not you only, but also the most part of the world, be like evil schoolmasters, which be readier to beat, than to teach their scholars. For great and horrible punishments be appointed for thieves, whereas much rather provision should have been made, that there were some means, whereby they might get their living, so that no man should be driven to this extreme necessity, first to steal, and then to die." "Yes," quoth he, "this matter is well enough provided for already. There be handicrafts, there is husbandry to get their living by, if they would not willingly be nought." "Nay," qoth I, "you shall not escape so: for first of all, I will speake nothing of them, that come home out of war, maimed and lame, as not long ago, out of Blackheath Field, and a little before that, out of the wars in France: such, I say, as put their lives in jeopardy for the weal public's or the king's sake, and by reason of weakness and lameness be not able to occupy their old crafts, and be too aged to learn new: of them I will speak nothing, because war like the tide ebbs and flows. But let us consider those things that chance daily before our eyes.

"First there is a great number of gentlemen, which cannot be content to live idle themselves, like drones, of that which others have labored for: their tenants I mean, whom they poll and shave to the quick by raising their rents (for this only point of frugality do they use, men else through their lavish and prodigal spending, able to bring themselves to very beggary), these gentlemen, I say, do not only live in idleness themselves, but also carry about with them at their tails a great flock or train of idle and loitering serving-men, which never learned any craft whereby to get their livings. These men as soon as their master is dead, or be sick themselves, be incontinent thrust out of doors. For gentlemen had rather keep idle persons, than sick men, and many times the dead man's heir is not able to maintain so great a house, and keep so many serving-men as his father did. Then in the mean season they that be thus destitute of service, either starve for hunger, or manfully play the thieves. For what would you have them do? When they have wandered abroad so long, until they have worn threadbare their apparel, and also impaired their health, then gentlemen because of their pale and sick faces, and patched coats, will not take them into service. And husbandmen dare not set them to work, knowing well enough that he is nothing meet to do true and faithful service to a poor man with a spade and mattock for small wages and hard fare, which being daintily and tenderly pampered up in idleness and pleasure, was wont with a sword and a buckler by his side to strut through the street with a bragging look, and to think himself too good to be any man's mate. . . .

"But yet this is not the only necessary cause of stealing. There is another, which, as I suppose, is proper and peculiar to you Englishmen alone." "What is that?" quoth the Cardinal. "Forsooth," quoth I, "your sheep that were wont to be so meek and tame, and so small eaters, now, as I hear say, be become so great devourers and so wild, that they eat up, and swallow down the very men themselves. They consume, destroy, and devour whole fields, houses, and cities. For look in what parts of the realm doth grow the finest and therefore dearest wool, there noblemen and gentlemen, yea and certain abbots, holy men god wot, not contenting themselves with the yearly revenues and profits, that were wont to grow to their forefathers and predecessors of their lands, nor being content that they live in rest and pleasure nothing profiting, yea much annoying the weal public, leave no ground for tillage, they inclose all in pastures; they throw down houses; they pluck down towns, and leave nothing standing, but only the church to make of it a sheep-house. And as though you lost no small quantity of ground by forests, chases, lawns, and parks, those good holy men turn all dwelling-places and all glebeland into desolation and wilderness.

"Therefore that one covetous and insatiable cormorant and very plague of his native country may compass about and inclose many thousand acres of ground together within one pale or hedge, the husbandmen be thrust out of their own, or else either by cunning and fraud, or by violent oppression they be put besides it, or by wrongs and injuries they be so wearied, that they be compelled to sell all: by one means therefore or by other, either by hook or crook they must needs depart away, poor, silly, wretched souls, men women, husbands, wives, fatherless children, widows, woeful mothers, with their young babes, and their whole household small in substance and much in number, as husbandry requireth many hands. Away they trudge, I say, out of their known and accustomed houses, finding no place to rest in. All their household stuff, which is very little worth, though it might well abide the sale; yet being suddenly thrust out, they be constrained to sell it for a thing of nought. And when they have, wandering, soon spent that, what can they else do but steal, and then justly, god wot, be hanged, or else go about abegging. And yet then also they be cast in prison as vagabonds, because they go about and work not: whom no man will set awork, though they never so willingly offer themselves therto. For one shepherd or herdsman is enough to eat up that ground with cattle, to the occupying whereof about husbandry many hands were requisite.

"And this is also the cause that victuals be now in many places dearer. Yea, besides this the price of wool is so risen, that poor folks, which were wont to work it and make cloth of it, be now able to buy none at all. And by this means very many be fain to forsake work, and to give themselves to idleness. For after that so much ground was inclosed for pasture, an infinite multitude of sheep died of the rot, such vengeance God took of their inordinate and insatiable covetousness, sending among the sheep that pestiferous murrain, which much more justly should have fallen on the sheepmasters' own heads. And though the number of sheep increase never so fast, yet the price falleth not one mite, because there be so few sellers. For they be almost all come into a few rich men's hands, whom no need forceth to sell before they lust, and they lust not before they may sell as dear as they lust. Now the same cause bringeth in like dearth of the other kinds of cattle, yea and that so much the more, because that after farms plucked down and husbandry decayed, there is no man that passeth for the breeding of young store. For these rich men bring not up the young ones of great cattle as they do lambs. But first they buy them abroad very cheap and afterward, when they be fatted in their pastures, they sell them again exceeding dear. And therefore (as I suppose) the whole incommodity hereof is not yet felt. For yet they make dearth only in those places where they sell. But when they shall fetch them away from thence where they be bred faster than they can be brought up: then shall there also be felt great dearth, when store beginneth to fail there where the ware is bought.

"Thus the unreasonable covetousness of a few hath turned that thing to the utter undoing of your island, in which thing the chief felicity of your realm did consist. For this great dearth of victuals causeth every man to keep as little houses and as small hospitality as he possibly may, and to put away their servants: whether, I pray you, but abegging; or else (which these gentle bloods and stout stomachs will sooner set their minds unto) astealing? . . . Doubtless unless you find a remedy for these enormities, you shall in vain advance yourselves of executing justice upon felons."[103]

For who knoweth not, that fraud, theft, rapine, brawling, quarrelling, brabling, strife, chiding, contention, murder, treason, poisoning, which by daily punishments are rather revenged than refrained, do die when money dieth? And also that fear, grief, care, labours and watchings do perish even the very same moment that money perisheth? Yea poverty itself, which only seemed to lack money, if money were gone, it also would decrease and vanish away.[104]

More believed in the social contract.

. . . the commonalty chooseth their king for their own sake and not for his sake: for this intent, that through his labour and study they might all live wealthily safe from wrongs and injuries: and . . . therefore the king ought to take more care for the wealth of his people, than for his own wealth, even as the office and duty of a shepherd is in that he is a shepherd, to feed his sheep rather than himself.[105]

However, he also assumed sociality as fundamental to man's nature.

For to what purpose serve leagues? say they. As though nature had not set sufficient love between man and man.[106]

## Vives

Juan Luis Vives (1492–1540) was another scholar who limited himself to naturalist explanations of social phenomena.

I have produced my reasons from Nature, not out of divine oracles, so that I should not leap across from philosophy to theology.[107]

He too gave a social explanation of crime.

For when the general bounty has been exhausted, some, since they have not the means of subsistence, are driven to robbery in the city and on the high-roads; others stealthily commit burglary; the women, who are of suitable age, casting aside modesty, are not able to keep their chasity, but put it on sale for a trifle, nor can they be persuaded to abandon this vicious practice; the old women straightway take to pandering, and sorcery as a furtherance to pandering; the little children of the poor are most viciously taught; the poor themselves with their children, cast down before the sanctuaries or wandering from place to place begging, do not participate in the sacraments and hear no sermons, and we know not according to what law or by what conventions they live, nor what are their religious beliefs . . . . . it is much more important for the magistrates to devote their energy to the producing of good citizens than to the punishment and restraint of evil-doers. For how much less need would there be to punish if these matters were rightly looked after beforehand![108]

*Fewer thefts, acts of violence, robberies, murders, capital offences, will be committed; less frequent will be pandering and sorcery.* Seeing that poverty will be alleviated, which drives men first into vices and bad habits, and then encourages and provokes such crimes as these.[109]

But most remarkable is Vives' theory of cultural evolution.

We men are born for society, and cannot live thoroughly without it. Nature has wisely made provision for this, both so that the arrogance of the haughtiest animal should be repressed when he sees that he has need of so many things, and also when he recognises the necessity for the winning of mutual love, which increases by intercourse and exchange of thoughts. . . . For the exercise of the social instinct, speech has been given to men, how otherwise could society exist, since our minds are hidden away in so dense a body? How completely dead and torpid would the mind be if it only found expression in the look of the eyes, if we could only express our manifold thoughts by mute nods![110]

First of all, the love of self-preservation which nature planted in man, stimulated him to pay attention to the fact, that he could not subsist even for a moment if the nourishment of life was wanting; therefore before all else, he had to attend to those things which he must have in order to nourish and sustain himself; of course in matters of eating and drinking, he had to underatand how to distinguish the beneficial from the harmful foods, and how to prepare and preserve them. And, since the body was liable to many diseases, and, as it were, to an ever recurring tyranny, he sought means to fortify himself against disease, so that it should not attack him, and that he might drive it out if it did attack him. Then he reflected that his tender body, exposed as it was to injury from the weather and the sun, was harmfully affected by these vicissitudes, and he invented a means of protecting himself from the violence of cold and heat, from winter and storms. So, first, covering was applied to the body. Then, since clothes afforded too little protection against the greater forces of Nature, man heaped up things impenetrable to those dangers, stones, mud, fragments of rock, wood, hard substances, with which to protect himself. But since even then men were not sufficiently secure from wild beasts, who might make an attack upon them while they were careless and unaware, or weighed down by sleep, they sought means of sheltering themselves, so that their rest might be more secure.  Since, through his great helplessness and need of so many and such varied things, no one was sufficient for himself, at first, many people lived together in the same cave: then as affection narrowed its bounds, a man and his wife seceded with their children; they came out of the caves, and built for themselves huts and tents of small pieces of wood, and covered the roofs with small twigs of trees. At first these huts were built here and there as if spots widely spread over the open plain; just as now, cities and towans are built. But soon, because affection exhorted those who wished each other well not to go farther away, and because need of mutual help urged them, certain persons brought their own huts together into a kind of village. But, however much simplicity flourished among them, yet, in men exposed to, and suspicious of, injury, some complaints existed. Naturally they all referred these to the oldest man, just as sons to their father, and he, since man's nature at this time was less corrupt, obtained power over the rest, because he was older; and for that reason, he was believed to surpass every one else in experience and wisdom. But when they discovered that there were not want-ing some to whom white hair and wrinkles did not bring much goodness of mind and heart, and others whose cunning increased with years, they sought out someone who was the wisest and best. In this also they made mistakes; for a decision cannot be made as to who is wise except by a wise man. If for any reason they reverenced greatly a particular man, to him they submitted themselves; of course it was for that reason which seemed to them most powerful in human affairs; to some this was money, to others, beauty; to others, strength of body and mind; to others, eloquence; to others, birth; to others, knowledge; to others, the reputation of justice. But since there were many who strove for that honour, and the worse claimants would not yield to those who were better, because pride persuaded each that he was the best, then there arose parties in the multitude who did not act by the dictates of reason, but with excited passions, and to settle the discord, one was elected by common agreement to be judge; or at any rate after conflict one was proclaimed the victorious claimant. In those primitive times it was sufficient to state what ought not to be done; the ruler's word restrained both the hands and the wills of the people; so great among them was respect for right and justice. Contumacy grew; then laws were passed, and penalties were attached to their violation, since now it was not sufficient to forbid; punishment was threatened for the terror of all, lest insolence should spread itself abroad. The wish to do evil seized not only one or two persons, but multitudes of men, and whole peoples: so that the general animosities sought to glut themselves in general bloodshed. To ward off these sudden risings, those who were united by community of interests, surrounded them selves with walls, and sought weapons with which to repulse hostile attacks. Changes in these conditions were brought about in the course of time according to opportunities; daily business brought men together, and speech bound them to move as closely as possible amongst one another in an indivisible, perpetual society. By help of speech, their minds, which had been hidden by concentration on bodily needs, began to reveal themselves; single words were at-tended to, then phrases and modes of speaking, as they were appropriate for use, i.e. as they were marked by public agreement of opinion, which is, as it were, what a mint is to current coin . . .

When men had duly provided for the necessities of life, the human mind passed from necessities to conveniences, so that having acquired them, man might not only have some-thing by which to protect himself from such great and constant danger, but something pleasant in which he might delight now that the sense of want had been driven away. For while the whole of man's nature was oppressed by the vast power and uncertainty of necessity, everything had been changed into an enemy; nor could man think of any-thing except of raising this blockade.

But when everything seemed quiet and peacable, bodily pleasure and mental pride showed themselves, and they sought, and, as it were, claimed the greatest portion of sovereignty over man. Men became slaves of pleasure, and planned many delights; they became the slaves of pride, and made many inventions to serve as vain ornaments, whereby was gained a reputation for superiority. Then those remedies against necessity, and the devices for convenience, were either transferred to the service of pleasure, or dragged over to the most bitter tyranny of pride, so that they might either delight the body, or perform as it were a play on the stage before the eyes of the beholders. For man's needs it was enough to have few things, and such as could easily be produced. Luxury added more, and pleasure and pride united, found no bound or limit. Man's mind, freed from anxiety for the needs of the present, began to live again, and to contemplate leisurely, as it were, this theatre, in which man was placed by God; to examine separate objects, which were in the heavens and in the elements, earth and water: namely constellations, living being, plants, gems, metals, stones, and the contents of his own mind. Curiosity led him forward, and when he thought he had made a discovery, he felt great joy as if from a victory. That pleasure was constantly increasing, since some things seemed to follow from the finding of others, just as when the beginning of a thread is secured, it is found to be connected with another set of things quite different from those which were being examined. Then, in showing his inventions as if they were children born from himself, he derived pleasure by no means small in imparting them to others. From the admiration of others for him, he felt at first great joy, but when all eyes were turned towards him, an idea of superiority and pride grew in him. A violent desire for display exciting greater admiration, increased to such a degree, that some persons neglected all duties of life, so as to devote and give themselves up entirely to investigation; and then if anyone contradicted them, there arose strife, fashions and sects. This desire impelled others to know what no one else knew;—what was going to happen, or what was buried or hidden in great darkness. Then came men, who through desire for money, or the possession of the pleasures which they coveted, ventured most impiously to learn from an evil spirit those secrets which they could not learn from a mortal.[111]

In the beginning first one, then another experience, through wonder at its novelty, was noted down for use in life; from a number of separate experiments the mind gathered a universal law, which after it was further supported and confirmed by many experiments, was considered certain, and established. Then it was handed down to posterity. Other men added subject-matter which tended to the same use and end. This material, collected by men of great and distinguished intellect, constituted the branches of knowledge, or the arts, to use the general name. . . .

Now, this unbridled eagerness for knowledge had been carried very far, when, in the midst of the course, that on-rush of mental energy began to be checked by the most capable minds, while they considered what at length was to be the goal of such a wide and anxious course, what was to be the reward of such continuous labour . . . because the human mind, provided with its small lamp, is not able to attain to the conception of that ultimate end, unless it has been enlightened by the end itself; as happens to those who go into dark places by help of a light. Therefore, there was need of God, not only to teach us how to come to Him, but also to lead us by the hand, since we are weak, and constantly liable to fall. This is the function of religion, which we receive from God Himself, a ray from His Light, strength from His Omnipotence. This alone brings us back to the course from which we came, and towards which we are going.[112]

## Rabelais

As an ardent humanist, François Rabelais (1483?–1553) was opposed to the scholastics,[113] clergy,[114] and royalty[115] of his day; some other remarks scattered through his writings are of particular interest to the social scientist.

On the origin of man, he referred to

. . . the beginning of the world, (I speak of a long time, it is above forty quarantaines, or fourty times fourty nights, according to the supputation of the ancient Druids) a little after that Abel was killed by his brother Cain.[116]

Nature . . . created Man naked, tender, and frail, without either offensive or defensive Arms; and that in the Estate of Innocence, in the first Age of all, which was the Golden Season; not as a Plant, but living Creature, born for Peace, not War.[117]

"Men are born to relieve and assist one another,"[118] but they are also egocentric; "Philauty, or Self-love, is that which blinds your judgement, and deceiveth you."[119]

Nature made us equal: But Fortune has exalted some, and other some has depressed.[120]

He believed in the existence of the law of nature.

. . . if . . . black do signifie grief, by good reason then should white import joy. Nor is this signification instituted by humane imposition, but by the universal consent of the world received, which Philosophers call Jus Gentium, the Law of Nations, or an uncontrolable right of force in all countreyes whatsoever: for you know well enough, that all people, and all languages and nations, (except the ancient Syracusans, and certain Argives, who had crosse and thwarting soules) when they mean outwardly to give evidence of their sorrow, go in black; and all mourning is done with black, which general consent is not without some argument, and reason in nature, the wich every man may by himself very suddenly comprehend, without the instruction of any; and this we call the Law of nature: By vertue of the same natural instinct, we know that by white all the world hath understood joy, gladnesse, mirth, pleasure, and delight.*[123]

Rabelais mentioned the succession of civilizations.

. . . the transport and revolution of Kingdomes and Empires, from the Assyrians to the Medes, from the Medes to the Persions, from the Persions to the Macedonians, from the Macedonians to the Romans, from the Romans to the Greeks, from the Greeks to the French, etc.[124]

He was skeptical of wild rumors about exotic peoples.

. . . we found a diminutive, monstrous, mishapen, old Fellow, call'd Hear-say. . . . About him stood an innumerable number of Men and Women. . . .

Among the rest, they descanted with great Prolixity on the Pyramids and Hieroglyphics of Egypt, of the Nile, of Babylon, of the Troglodytes, the Himantopodes or Crump-footed Nation, the Blaemiae People that wear their Heads in the middle of their Breats, the Pygmies, the Cannibals, the Hyperborei and their Mountains, the Aegipanes with their Goat's-feet, and the Devill and all of others: every individual word of it by Hear-say.

I am much mistaken if I did not see among them Herodotus, Pliny, Solinus, Berosus, Philostratus, Pomponius Mela, Strabo, and God knows how many other Antiquaries.[125]

[In another place he complained of the French:] And so inquisitive they are, that

* In narrating the story of a murder, Pantagruel says: "the Cause of the Murther seemed to be so natural, as to be grounded upon the Law of Nations, and the rational Instinct of all the People of the World."[121]
" . . . by Natural Equity, by the Law of Nations."[122]

they will be stark staring mad at those who come out of strange countries, unless they bring a whole budget full of strange stories, calling them dolts, blockheads, ninny-hammers, and silly oufs.[126]

## Bruno

Giordano Bruno (1548–1600) was an early expositor of the theory of social progress.

*Prudenzio:* I do not wish to give up the opinion of the ancients, because as the wise man says [Job 12 : 12,] in antiquity lies wisdom.

*Teofilo:* And he adds: prudence lies in many years. If you entirely comprehend what you are saying, you will see that, on your basis, the contrary of what you are thinking is to be inferred. I maintain that we are older and have lived longer than our predecessors: I mean in respect to certain opinions, as in the matter under discussion [i.e., astronomy]. The judgement of Eudoxus could not have been as mature as that of Calippus, who lived thirty years after the death of Alexander the Great, for the former lived slightly after the renascense of astronomy—unless he had been reborn and could have added observations to observations in the same way as he added years to years. For the same reason, Hipparchus must have known more than Calippus, because he saw the changes which took place up to one hundred and ninety-six years after the death of Alexander. It is reasonable to assume that Menelaus, the Roman geometer, knew more than Hipparchus, inasmuch as he saw various changes four hundred and sixty-two years after Alexander's death. Macometto Aracense must have seen more, one thousand two hundred and two years after that; Copernicus saw more of it, almost until our time, one thousand eight hundred and forty-nine years after the same event. But some among these, who have come later, have not been wiser than those who went before. The bulk of those living in our time have not more judgement, however; this occurs because the former have not lived, and the latter do not live, other people's years; and what is worse, the former exist as dead, and the latter, in terms of their own years of life.[127]

## Montaigne

Michel Eyquem de Montaigne (1533–92) is the cosmopolitan skeptic par excellence and man of the world.

Not because Socrates has said it, but because it is really in my nature, and perhaps a little more than it should be, I look upon all men as my fellow-citizens, and would embrace a Pole as I would a Frenchman, subordinating this national tie to the common and universal one.[128]

No propositions astonish me, no belief offends me, however much opposed to my own.[129]

The confusion we see in the ways of the world has had this good effect upon me, that the difference between my conduct of life and ideas and those of the world is to me instructive rather than displeasing.[130]

His *Essais* (1580) are the fruit of "my studies, whose subject is Man."[131] "The governments, customs, and languages of distant countries are my delight,"[132] and there were few things that pleased him more than travel.

. . . travel appears to me a profitable exercise; the mind is continually exercised by observing new and unknown things. And I know no better school, as I have often said, for modelling one's life, in that it containually brings us face to face with so many other lives, ideas, and customs, and gives us a relish for human nature in so perpetual a variety of forms.[133]

The different customs I find in one nation after another please me by their very diversity; each custom has its reason. Whether the plates be of tin, of wood, or of earthenware, whether the meat be boiled or roast; whether they give me butter or oil, whether nut-oil or olive-oil; whether dishes be hot or cold, it is all one to me . . ..

When I have been outside of France, and people have asked me, out of politeness, whether I would like to be served with French dishes, I laughed at the idea; and I always sought the tables that were most thick with foreigners.

I am ashamed when I see my countrymen steeped in that silly prejudice which makes them fight shy of any customs that differ from their own; when they are out of their village, they seem to be out of their element.[134]

Montaigne was greatly influenced by the contemporary explorations.[135] His cosmopolitanism resulted from his awareness of the diversity of custom produced by his reading and travels.

How the ideas of men diverge![136]

There is nothing in which the world varies so much as in customs and laws. Many a thing is abominable here that is commended elsewhere.[137]

Not only every country, but every city and every profession has its particular form of civility.[138]

In short, every nation has many habits and customs which to any other nation are not only strange but amazing and barbarous![139]

I believe that no fancy, however crazy, can enter into the human imagination, of which we do not find an example in some popular usage, and which consequently is not founded on and supported by our reason. There are countries where the people are accustomed to turn their backs on those they salute, and never look at the man they intend to honour. In one nation, when the king spits, the most favoured of the ladies of the court stretches out her hand, and in another the most eminent about him stoop to collect his ordure in a linen cloth.[140]

Being accustomed to a thing blinds the eye of judgement. Barbarians are in no way more wonderful to us than we are to them, nor with more reason, as every one would allow if, after going over those newly discovered examples, he could reflect upon his own and sanely compare them. Human reason is a tincture infused, about equal measure, into all our opinions and manners, whatever form they may take, infinite in matter, infinite in diversity.*[143]

But the effects of custom are far better discovered in the strange impressions she makes on our minds, where she meets with less resistance. What can she not impose on our judgements and beliefs? Is there any opinion so fantastic (I I leave aside the gross impostures of religions, by which so many great nations and so many worthy persons have been besotted; for, they being beyond the reach of our human reason, to go astray in them is more excusable in such as are not extraordinarily illuminated by divine favour— but, of other opinions, is there any too extravagant for her to implant and establish by laws, in whatever regions she pleases?[144]

*" . . . every man's tastes are regulated by habit or the usages of his village."[141]

"Here [at Kempton] was proof of what M. de Montaigne said elsewhere: that if these people neglect the use of what we use, it is because they despise it; for, though they have great abundance of pewter plate, scoured as at Montaigne, they gave us only wooden plates, well polished indeed and very handsome."[142]

To sum up, in my opinion there is nothing that custom does not or cannot do, and with reason does Pindar, as I have been told, call her the "Queen and Empress of the world."[145]

This cultural diversity led him to deny ethnocentrism.

. . .from what I have heard of that nation [i.e., Brazil], I can see nothing barbarous or uncivilized about it, except that we all call barbarism that which does not fit in with our usages. And indeed we have no other level of truth and reason but the example and model of the opinions and usages of the country we live in. There we always see the perfect religion, the perfect government, the perfect and accomplished manner of doing all things.[146]

He saw that the customs of his own culture were no more rational than those of others.

Having once had occasion to justify one of our observances, and one that was accepted with absolute authority in the far-outlying districts surrounding us, and not content, as most men are, to find it established merely by force of laws and examples, but searching still further into its origin, I found that it was built on so weak a foundation, that I, who had to encourage it in others, was all but disgusted.[147]

He who would rid himself of this violent prejudice of custom will find that many things are accepted with undoubting resolve, which have no support but in the hoary beard and wrinkles of the usage which attends them.[148]

I would willingly excuse my countrymen for having no other rule and pattern of perfection but their own manners and usages, for it is a common weakness, not of the vulgar only but of practically all men, not to look beyond the ways they have been born to. I could understand the ordinary man, should he see Fabricius or Laelius, regarding their looks and bearing as barbarous, since they are neither clothed nor fashioned according to our mode. But I do complain of his particular unwisdom in being so completely blinded and deluded by the authority of the fashion of the day as to be capable of altering his mind and opinion every month, if custom requires it, and of judging himself so diversely.[149]

He even unfavorably compared customs in western Europe with those of other cultures.

Many of our laws and customs are barbarous and monstrous.[150]

I should like to hear somebody justify by reason those laws of honour which so often contradict and collide with the laws of reason [particularly in respect to duelling].[151]

The savages who roast and eat the bodies of their dead do no scandalize me as much as they who persecute and torture the living.[152]

We may therefore well call those people [i.e., the Brazilians] barbarians in respect to the rules of reason, but not in respect to ourselves, who surpass them in every kind of barbarity.[153]

Compare our ways with those of a Mohammedan or pagan; you will always fall short of them.[154]

He emphasized the constraint of the culture of a group upon the individuals reared in that group.

. . . the principal effect of the force of custom is to seize and grip us so firmly, that we are scarce able to escape from its grasp, and to regain possession of ourselves sufficiently to discuss and reason out its commands. In truth, since we imbibe them with our mother's milk, and the world shows the same face to our infant eyes, we seem to be born to follow this same path; and the common ideas that we find current around us, and infused into our souls with the seed of our fathers, appear to be general and natural. Whence it comes that what is off the hinges of custom we believe to be off the hinges of reason: God knows how unreasonably for the most part.[155]

Therefore "custom dulls the senses"[156] and "hides from us the true aspect of things."[157]

Whatever I may be aiming at, I am obliged to force some barrier of custom: so carefully has she barred all our approaches.[158]

We are all convention; conventions carry us away, and we neglect the substance of things.[159]

. . . most commonly we consult custom and example rather than reason.[160]

Almost all the opinions we hold are taken on authority and trust.[161]

It is not by our reasoning or our understanding that we have received our religion, but by outside authority and command.[162]

. . . we only receive our religion after our own fashion, and at our own hands,and no otherwise than the other religions are received. Either we happen to have been born in a country where it is practised, or we regard its antiquity or the authority of the men who have upheld it, or we fear the menaces which attach to unbelief, or are attracted by its promises. These considerations ought to weigh in our belief, but as subsidiaries only; they are human ties. A different region, other witnesses, the like promises and threats, might in the same way imprint upon us a contrary belief.

We are Christians by the same title as we are natives of Perigord or Germany.[163]

Montaigne seems to have been the first western European to realize that conscience is the internalization of the mores of the group.

The laws of conscience, which we say are born of Nature, are born of custom: as every man holds in inward veneration the opinions and manners received and approved around him, he is unable to let go his hold on them without remorse,or to cling to them without approval.[164]

His cosmopolitanism led to skepticism.

I think my opinions are good and sound; but who does not think the same of his?[165]

What kind of goodness can that be that was yesterday held in honour, and will cease to be so tomorrow, and which the mere crossing of a river turns into a crime?

What kind of truth can that be that is bounded by these mountains,and that becomes a lie to the people on the other side?[166]

What do I know?[167]

He reflected the empiricism of his day and rebelled against authoritarianisn.

. . . the truth is not to be decided by the authority, nor accepted on the testimony, of another.[168]

And yet . . . men's opinions are accepted in obedience to ancient beliefs, by authority and upon trust, as if they were religion and law. . . . This truth, with all its elaborate scaffolding of arguments and proofs, is received as if it were a firm, solid, and unshakable body, never more to be doubted. On the contrary, all strive in emulation to plaster up and corroborate their accepted belief, with all the power of their reason, which is a supple tool, pliant and adaptable to any figure. Thus is the world filled with, and steeped in, nonsense and lies. . . .

The god of scholastic knowledge is Aristotle; to question his laws is as profane as it was to question those of Lycurgus at Sparta. We accept his teaching as if it were mages-terial law, when it is perhaps as wrong as any other . . .

No part of it may be discussed with a view to doubt, but only to defend the founder of the school from foreign objections; his authority is the end and aim, beyond which no inquiry is to be tolerated.[169]

Before the principles which Aristotle introduced were in repute, other principles satisfied human reason, as his statisfy us at this moment. What letters-patent, what special privilege have these, that the course of our discoveries should stop at them, and that they should for all time to come possess our belief? They are no more exempt from being thrust out of doors than their forerunners.[170]

And as some have said of Virtue that it is no greater for being of long standing, so I hold of the Truth that it is no wiser for being older.[171]

His empiricism found expression both in the goal and in the method of his social studies. He was interested in natural laws[172] that would aid man in adjusting to his environment.

We call contrary to Nature what happens contrary to what is customary; there is noth-ing whatsoever that is contrary to Nature. This universal and natural reason should dispel from our minds the errors and the wonder caused by what is new and strange.[173]

It is one same Nature that rolls its course. If we could form a sufficient esimate of its present state, we might safely infer the whole of its future and the whole of its past.[174]

But, when all is said, it is difficult in human actions to lay down a rule so exact by the discourse of reason that Fortune will not assert her right.[175]

The inference we try to draw from the likeness of events is uncertain, because they are always unlike. No quality is so universal, in the appearance of things, as diversity and variety.[176]

All things hold together by some similarity or other; every example limps, and the connexion that is drawn from experience is always faulty and imperfect. And yet com-parisons join at some corner or other.[177]

Montaigne was skeptical of supernatural causation of phenomena;[178] his method was naturalistic.

I would rather believe facts than reasons.[179]

Who has ever gained any intelligence from Logic?[180]

Others form man; I describe him.[181]

Medicine is built up on examples and experience; so is my theory.[182]

The historians . . . are entertaining and easy, and at the same time man in general, whom I seek to know, appears there more alive and entire than anywhere else; there we see the diversity and truth of his inward nature, in the gross and in detail, the variety of the means by which he is knit together, and the accidents which threaten him.[183]

In his consideration of man's nature, Montaigne premised the existence of both body and soul.

He has a body, he has a soul; he is impelled by his senses, stirred by his mind.[184]

. . .we are built up of two principal and essential parts, the separation of which is the death and destruction of our being.[185]

. . . the soul . . . is sole and sovereign mistress of our condition and conduct. The body has, saving in greater or less proportion, but one course and one bent. The soul is variable in all manner of forms, and subjects to herself and to her empire, whether it be great or small, the feelings of the body and all other accidents . . . .The beasts, that keep the mind under control, leave to their body their sensations, free and natural, and consequently almost one and the same in each species, as appears in the conformity of their movements.[186]

His conception of the soul and its relation to the body was very different from that held by orthodox Christians. He professed ignorance as to the nature of the soul[187] and considered it to be mortal.[188] There is a "close affinity between mind and body"[189]; the soul affects the body,[190] and the body affects the soul.[191]

The shocks and agitations that our soul receives through the bodily passions have a great influence upon her; but still more have her own feelings, which have so strong a hold upon her, that it is perhaps tenable that she is only moved and propelled by the breath of her own winds, and that, unless stirred by them, she would remain inactive.[192]

He refused to acknowledge that the bodily desires were evil and ought to be suppressed in favor of the desires of the soul.[193] And, though the soul is important, he was primarily interested in the natural aspects of man.

It is, after all, man with whom we have to do, whose condition is wonderfully corporeal.[194]

Life is a material and corporeal movement.[195]

Man is egocentric.

It must be noted that to every creature nothing is dearer and of more account than its own existence.[196]

Nature has implanted in animals an instinct to look after themselves and keep out of harm's way.[197]

But sociality is an important part of man's nature, too.

There is nothing to which Nature seems so much to have inclined us as to society.[198]

He who does not live in some degree for others, hardly lives for himself.[199]

. . . human society will hold and keep together at whatsoever cost. In whatever position you place human beings, they will shake up and arrange themselves in stacks and heaps, just as uneven bodies, bundled into a sack without any order, will themselves find the means of uniting and settling down together, often better than they could have been arranged by art.

King Philip made a collection of the most wicked and incorrigible men he could find, and settled them all in a city which he had built for them, and which took its name from them [Poneropolis, "Rogues' City"]. I imagine that out of their very vices they established among themselves a civil constitution, a regular and decent society . . .

Necessity reconciles men and brings them together. This accidental union afterwards taken shape in laws.[200]

However, Montaigne was too much of a realist not to appreciate "man's inhumanity to man."

Nature herself, I fear, has fastened on man a certain instinct to inhumanity.[201]

There is nothing so unsociable and so sociable as man: the one by his vice, the other by his nature.[202]

Man's virtues are often the product of his vices—a proposition taken up by the ascetic moralists of the seventeenth century and elaborated by Mandeville in the eighteenth.

Compassion acts as a spur to clemency; and the wisdom to preserve and govern our lives is aroused by our fear. How many fine actions are due to ambition! how many to presumption! In short, no conspicuous and gallant valour but is caused by some unruly emotion.[203]

It is evident to me that we do not willingly lend to devotion any other services but those that gratify our passions. There is no hostility that surpasses that of the Christian. Our zeal works wonders when it seconds our propensity to hatred, cruelty, ambition, avarice, detraction, rebellion. Against the grain, towards kindness, good-will, moderation, it will neither walk nor fly, unless borne, as by a miracle, by some uncommon disposition.[204]

He was also aware of the fact that intimate social relations are necessary for the development of affection.

If there be a real law of Nature, that is to say any instinct that is universally and permanently rooted in animals and men (which is not beyond dispute), I may say that, in my opinion, next to the anxiety for self-preservation and avoiding what is harmful, which is possessed by every animal, the affection which the begetter has for his offspring takes the second place. And,because Nature seems to have recommended to us this affection, looking to the extension and advance of the successive parts of this her machine, it is not to be wondered at if the love of children towards their parents, since it goes backwards, is not so great.[205]

. . . animals . . . know their young only as long as they hang on to their teats.

Moreover it is easily seen by experience that this natural affection, to which we give so much authority, has very slender roots. For a very small gain mothers every day allow their children to be torn from their arms, in order to take charge of ours; we make them abandon their own to some wretched nurse to whom we are not willing to commit ours, or to some goat, forbidding them not only to suckle their own, whatever danger these may thereby incur, but even to give any care to them, that they may devote themselves entirely to the service of ours. And in most of them we soon see, begotten by habit, a bastard affection more vehement than the natural, and a greater solicitude for the preservation of the foster-children than of their own. . . . Animals change and bastardize their natural affection as readily as we.[206]

Man is irrational.

How variously our passions react upon our thoughts and reasoning faculties, and change our ideas to their very opposites![207]

Passion rules us much more strongly than reason.[208]

Man's nature is plastic at birth, and personality is a product of habit.

The young of bears and dogs show their natural disposition, but men, being very soon influenced by customs, opinions, and laws, easily change or disguise their nature.[209]

Habit . . . can not only mould us into any shape she pleases . . ., but also teach us to change and vary.[210]

Let us also call the habits and conditions of each one of us, Nature; let us rate and treat ourselves by this standard; let us stretch our appurtenances and our calculations thus far. For thus far, it seems to me, we have some excuse. Habit is a second Nature, and no less powerful. What my habit lacks, I seem to lack myself.[211]

[However, in the following passage he gives more weight to innate tendencies:] Natural inclinations are assisted and strengthened by education, but they seldom change and are seldom mastered. In my time a thousand natures have escaped towards virtue, or towards vice, in spite of a contrary training. . . . These original qualities are not to be extirpated; they may be covered and concealed. . . . Just see what our own experience teaches. There is no man, if he listen to himself, who will not discover in himself a particular nature, a dominant nature, that struggled against his education and against the tempestuous passions that oppose it.[212]

Montaigne believed in the psychic unity of mankind.

I take men to be pretty much all alike.[213]

. . . for men are all of one species, and are provided, more or less, with the like tools and instruments for judging and understandng.[214]

He used a geographic interpretation for personality types.

. . . the form of our being depends on the atmosphere, the climate and the soil on which we are born, and not only our complexion, our stature, our constitution and countenance, but also the faculties of our mind . . . so that, as fruits and animals are born differing from one another, men are born more or less warlike, just, temperate and docile; here given to wine, elsewhere to theft and lechery; here inclined to superstition, elsewhere to unbelief; here to freedom, there to slavery; capable of one science or one art; dull or clever; obedient or rebellious; good or bad, according as the place where they live inclines them; and assume a new disposition if they change from one place to another, like the trees.[215]

He observed that culture was an interdependent system.

It is much to be doubted whether the manifest advantage of changing an established law, be it ever so bad, outweighs the evil involved in the removing of it, inasmuch as a government is a structure of various parts so closely joined together, that it is impossible to shake one part without the whole body feeling the concussion.[216]

He appreciated the importance of communication in the organization of society, and inveighed aginst lying on that basis—thus anticipating an argument of some eighteenth century moralists.

Lying is indeed an accursed vice.[217]

As speech is the only means that men have of understanding one another, the man who violates it is a traitor to society. It is the only instrument for communicating our wishes and thoughts; it is the interpreter of our soul. If it fails us we can no longer hold together, we shall cease to know one another. If it deceives us, it breaks off all our intercourse and dissolves all the ties of our government.[218]

Montaigne was in a dilemma when dealing with the law of nature, i.e., "the laws of reason that Nature has imprinted in us."[219] On the one hand, contemporary tradition postulated their existence; on the other, he was impressed by the diversity of custom. He was somewhat skeptical of the existence of such laws.

If there be a real law of Nature, that is to say any instinct that is universally and permanently rooted in animals and man (which is not beyond dispute).[220]

. . . those people amuse me who, to give some certainty to laws, say that there are some that are fixed, perpetual and immutable, which they call laws of Nature, and which by the very condition of their being, are imprinted in humankind. And of these some say they are three, some four, some more, some less; a sign that it is a mark as doubtful as the rest. Now, they are in such a hapless case (for what else can I call it but haplessness, that out of an infinite number of laws there does not happen to be one at least that has been permited by Fortune and the heedlessness of chance to be universally accepted by the consent of all nations?), they are, I say, so unhappy, that of those three or four selected laws there is not one that is not rejected and disowned, not by one nation, but by many.[221]

However, he seemed to think that laws of nature probably existed, though modified by man's intelligence.

I can quite believe that there are laws of Nature, such as we may observe in other creatures; but in us they have vanished, this fine human reason of ours thrusting itself into everything, commanding and domineering, confusing and distorting the face of things, in its vanity and inconsistency.[222]

Since it has pleased God to endow us with some capacity for reason, in order that we may not, like the beasts, be slavishly subject to the common laws, but rather that we should adapt ourselves to them by exercising our judgement and free will, we ought indeed to yield a little to the simple authority of Nature, without being tyrannically carried away by her; reason alone should guide our inclination.*[226]

The laws that Nature gives us are always happier than those we give ourselves. Witness the Golden Age as depicted by the poets, and the condition in which we see those nations to be living which have no other laws.[227]

Following his preference for the law of nature, he gave idealized descriptions of some of the New World cultures[228] which foreshadow Rousseau's conception of the noble savage and the back-to-nature movement, and nineteenth century romanticism.

These people are wild in the sense in which we call wild the fruits that Nature has produced by herself and in her ordinary progress; whereas in truth it is those we have altered artificially and diverted from the common order, that we should rather call wild. In the first we still see, in full life and vigour, the genuine and most natural and useful virtues and properties, which we have bastardized in the latter, and only adapted to please our corrupt taste. And yet in some of the uncultivated fruits of those countries there is a delicacy of flavour that is excellent even to our taste, and rivals even our own. It is not reasonable that art should gain the point of honor over our great and powerful mother Nature. We have so overburdened the beauty and richness of her works with our inventions, that we have quite smothered her. And yet, wherever she shines in her purity, she marvelously puts to shame our vain and trivial efforts. . . .

Those nations, then, appear to me so far barbarous in this sense, that their minds have been formed to a very slight degree, and that they are still very close to their original simplicity. They are still ruled by the laws of Nature, and very little corrupted by ours; . . . they are still in . . . a state of purity.[229]

Nature, to show that there is nothing barbarous in her conduct of affairs, will often,

---

* "True justice, which is natural and universal, is otherwise regulated, and more nobly, than that other special, national justice, which is restricted by the necessities of our governments."[223]

The sanction of the law of nature is inherent in it: "Shall we force the universal law of Nature, which is seen in every living thing under heaven, and which ordains that we tremble under pain?"[224]

"In this universe of things I allow myself to be ignorantly and carelessly guided by the general law of the world. I shall know it well enough when I feel it."[225]

in nations least cultivated by art, engender production of the mind that will vie with the most artistic productions.[230]

The popular and purely natural poetry has a charm and artlessness, in which it may compare in its principal beauty with poetry perfected by art.[231]

He appreciated "the continual variation in human things"[232] and saw history as an irregular progression and regression.

We do not move forwards; we rather prowl about, turning this way and that. We retrace our steps.[233]

He often bewailed the fact that his was "so feeble an age."[234]

The corruption of the times is made up of the individual contributions of each one of us; some contribute treachery, others injustice, irreligion, tyranny, avarice, cruelty, according as they are more or less influential; the weaker sort bring to it folly, vanity, idleness.[235]

He used the organic analogy when contemplating the rise and fall of societies.

There is a wonderful relation and correspondence in that general scheme of the works of Nature, which clearly proves that it is neither accidental nor carried out by divers masters. The diseases and conditions of our body are reflected in states and governments; kingdoms, republics are born, flourish and decay with old age, as we do. We are subject to a useless and harmful superabundance of humours. . . .

We may observe that States are often sick of a like superabundance, and it has been the custom to purge them in different ways. Sometimes a large number of families are allowed to leave a country for its relief, and seek settlements in other regions at the expense of strangers. . . . At times too they purposely fomented war with some of their enemies, not only to keep their soldiers in breath, lest idleness, the mother of corruption, should bring worse evils upon them . . . but also to bleed their Commonwealth, to vent a little the too exuberant heat of their young men, and to prune and thin out the branches of that too lustily growing stock.[236]

At one point he offered a hypothesis as to the evolution of political organization.

It is probable that this [i.e., valor] was the first virtue that manifested itself in man, and gave to one man an advantage over another, enabling the strongest and bravest to become master of the weaker, and acquire a particular rank and reputation; wherefore it was dignified in speech with that honourable name. Or perhaps it was that among the very warlike nations the prize and most worthy appellation was given to the quality that was most familiar to them.[237]

Montaigne was puzzled by the similarity of customs in different parts of the world.

I have often marvelled to see, divided by great distances of time and place, so many coincidences in popular, fabulous ideas, so many uncivilized customs and beliefs, which, from whatever side we may look at them, seem to have no connection with our inborn reason. The human mind is a great worker of miracles. But in this correspondence there is a something much more anomalous which I am unable to define.[238] [He then gives a list of Middle American customs which are similar to those of western Europe.[239]]

## Bellarmine

Roberto Francesco Romolo Bellarmine (1542–1621) was in favor of the gregarious theory of society.

. . . the nature of man is such that he is a social animal; for indeed brutes are so endowed by nature that each is sufficient to himself, but man needs so many things that he can in no way live alone. . . . man is born without clothing, without a home, without food, lacking all necessities, and although he has hands, and reason, by which he can prepare all instruments, nevertheless each one needs a long time to develop, and so long that it is impossible for one man to be sufficient to himself for all necessities, especially since we are born unskilled, and the arts are learned rather by instruction than by experience; therefore it is necessary that we should live in society, and that one should aid the other.

Besides, even were each one sufficient to himself for the necessities of life, yet he would never, unaided, be able to protect himself from the attacks of wild beasts and robbers, but for this purpose it is necessary for men to assemble and to ward off attacks with their combined strength.[240]

He argued against the social contract theory.

. . . the statement is false which Cicero makes [*De inventione* 1], namely, that there was formerly a time when men wandered about in the manner of beasts, then, through the eloquence of some wise orator, they were induced to assemble, and to live together. . . . But that state of affairs never existed, nor could it have existed at any time. For Adam was a very wise man, and without doubt did not allow men to wander about like beasts, and Cain, his son, even built a material city; before Cain and Adam, man did not exist.[241]

. . . even if servile subjection began after the sin of Adam, nevertheless there would have been political government even while man was in the state of innocence.[242]

. . . political power . . . comes directly from God alone.[243]

He made the usual distinction between the law of nature and the law of nations.

. . . the natural law is not sufficient, for it gives only general principles, and does not come down to particular cases.[244]

. . . the law of nations is a sort of conclusion drawn from the natural law by human reason.[245]

## Gentili

Alberico Gentili (1552–1608) places sociality at the basis of human society.

. . . defence for honour's sake . . . is undertaken without any fear of danger to ourselves, through no need of our own, with no eye to our advantage, but merely for the sake of others. And it rests upon the fundamental principle, that nature has established among men kinship, love kindliness, and a bond of fellowship (as Marcus Tullius [Cicero] says); and that the law of nations is based upon this association of the human race. . . . All this universe which you see, in which things divine and human are included, is one, and we are members of a great body. . . . Moreover, nature has made us all kindred, since we have the same origin and the same abode. She has implanted in us love for one another and made us inclined to union.[246]

. . . man was born for fellowship, and it is his duty to aid others, not to live for himself alone.[247]

. . . society cannot be maintained except by the love and protection of those who compose it.[248]

For on these two things, a consciousness of weakness and the fear of punishment, are based nearly all the laws of mankind by which society is held together; as Lactantius says.[249]

He was interested in objective rather than normative generalizations in his study of international law.

Let the theologians keep silence about a matter which is outside of their province.[250]

In discovering the law of nations, he anticipated Grotius to some extent in the use of the comparative method.

. . . the law of nations is that which is in use among all the nations of men, which native reason has established among all human beings, and which is equally observed by all mankind. Such a law is natural law.* . .

This statement, however, must not be understood to mean that all nations actually came together at a given time, and that thus the law of nations was established . . . and it is not necessary to understand the word *omnes* in such a way that when one speaks of the usage of all nations it should be considered to mean absolutely every nation; since countless numbers of these, in regions widely separated from us, utterly different in their customs, and of different tongues, remain unknown. . . . for if the Romans, Greeks, Jews, and barbarians, in short, all known peoples, have made use of a certain code of laws, it may be assumed that all men have made use of that same code. It is from the known that we learn the unknown. In fact, as the rule of a state and the making of its laws are in the hands of a majority of its citizens, just so is the rule of the world in the hands of the aggregation of the greater part of the world. Moreover, this is especially true of the unwritten law; for a custom is binding upon all the members of a state and is called the custom of the entire state, even if every citizen has not agreed to it, but haply some have opposed it.[252]

Besides this inductive approach he also used the deductive.

But there is another more elegant definition of the law of nations . . . namely, that there are everywhere certain unwritten laws, not enacted by men (since all men could not all assemble in one place, nor were they all of one speech), but given to them by God.† For example, the one which takes first place with all men, that one should worship God;‡ and the second, that one should honour father and mother. Such laws are not written, but inborn; we have not learned, received, and read them, but we have wrested, drawn, and forced them out of nature herself. We have not received them through instruction, but have acquired them at birth; we have gained them, not by training, but by instinct.

Nevertheless, this definition also permits us to ask the question, what this natural reason is, or how it is made manifest. To this question the following reply must be made: that natural reason is evident of itself and therefore those who rely on it are content merely to say: "This is perfectly clear from nature itself.§[256]

The law of nature, the law of nations, and civil law are analogous in their origin.

. . . not only is the civil law an agreement and a bond of union among citizens, but the same is true of the law of nations as regards nations, ‖ and the law of nature as regards mankind.[258]

* " . . . what is natural to men is common to all men."[251]
† " . . . international law is a portion of the divine law, which God left with us after our sin."[253]
‡ "Religion is a part of the law of nature."[254]
§ "International law is based on natural principles which have been implanted in all by nature, and which are so well known that they need neither argument nor art to establish them."[255]
‖ " . . . the law of nations is founded upon the consent of nations.[257]

. . . although the civil law is not of necessity the law of nations, yet the law which belongs to the nations ought also to apply to their citizens. It is true that the civil law does not correspond to the law of nature and of nations in all respects; but yet it is not wholly unlike the law of nature or that of nations. And that it does not correspond in all respects is due to the common nature of all states or to the individual nature of some of them.[259]

The laws of nature and of nations are eternal.

The statement of some, that the law of nature and of nations may be changed in any part, is false.*[261]

In fact, these laws are immutable, since they are based upon truth, which is immutable, just as other laws are based upon opinion.[262]

## POLITICAL PRAGMATISTS

When Renaissance empiricism was applied to the realm of governmental affairs, the pragmatic school of political science was born. Thus was produced the first empirical social science in western Europe. The men who belonged to this group obseved society in order to develop general principles useful in governing; some, like Comines, based their generalizations on analyses of one or two instances that they themselves had witnessed; others, like Machiavelli, used Greek, Roman, and Italian history to furnish their material; and, finally, a comparative method was developed which utilized data from all cultures, of which Bodin was the most distinguished exponent.

### Sansovino
The purpose of the works produced by the pragmatic school was well expressed by Francesco Sansovino (1521–86).

. . . my intent was, when I tooke this matter first in hand, drawing the substance (the finall end of this studie) foorth of histories, therby to take away from others, the length, tediousnes of reading and toyling themselves.[263]

. . . this worke . . . will be of great helpe and aide to those that be studious, for that I imagine, it will enriche the privat discourses, and the publicke actions of those that shall chaunce at any time to use and handle these conceits in humain actions, which almost have been ever the self-same in all times and amongst all men: and for that in the working and negotiating of affaires, as wel in publick as in privat, they will minister unto them many conditions and partes, the which conceits although they be somewhat generall, yet neverthelesse they will give no small light partitie: how to knowe the partes and conditions of greatest advauntage in particular things, as well of publicke actions, as of private affaires.[264]

. . . there is nothing more necessary for a Prince in this world then Histories, for so much as being the mirrours & maisters of our life: they shew and teach us what the government of a cittie and Province ought to be, what lawes we ought to institute & cause our subjects to observe, in what manner to increase & maintain divine worships, in what sort to exercise morall vertues, and how to reape benefit of counsell in our affaires of importance.[265]

* " . . . the law . . . of nature . . . cannot be annulled."[260]

## Comines

Philippe de Comines (1445–1509) was the founder of the pragmatic school.

He is the first modern writer . . . who in any degree has displayed sagacity in reasoning on the characters of men, and the consequences of their actions, or who has been able to generalize his observations by comparison and reflection.[266]

In Comines' own words:

. . . one of the greatest means to make a man wise is to have studied the histories of ancient times, and to have learned to frame and proportion our councils and undertakings according to the model and example of our ancestors: for our life is but of short duration, and not sufficient to give us experience of so many things.[267]

## Machiavelli

Niccolo Machiavelli (1469–1527) was the greatest of the political pragmatists. To him the purpose of history was to provide the data for generalizations to be used in the efficient control of political affairs.

He will . . . learn from the lessons of . . . history how an empire should be organized properly.[268]

. . . if any lesson is useful to citizens who govern republics, it is that which demonstrates the causes of the hatreds and dissensions in the republic, so that, having learned wisdom from the perils experienced by others, they may maintain themselves united.[269]

Such generalizations are possible because of the uniformity of nature, which in the realm of social phenomena produces a constancy in human nature.

Whoever considers the past and the present will readily observe that all cities and all peoples are and ever have been animated by the same desires and the same passions; so that it is easy, by diligent study of the past, to foresee what is likely to happen in the future in any republic, and to apply those remedies that were used by the ancient, or, not finding any that were employed by them, to devise new ones from the similarity of events.[270]

Wise men say, and not without reason, that whoever wishes to foresee the future must consult the past; for human events ever resemble those of preceding times. This arises from the fact that they are produced by men who have been, and ever will be, animated by the same passions, and thus they must necessarily have the same results. It is true that men are more or less virtuous in one country or another, according to the nature of the education by which their manners and hahits of life have been formed. It also facilitates a judgement of the future by the past, to observe nations preserve for a long time the same character; ever exhibiting the same disposition to avarice, or bad faith, or to some other special vice or virtue.[271]

The precepts are to be used in everyday life and must therefore be empirical, based upon man's acutal behavior rather than in terms of some theoretically desirable morality. This objective approach to social phenomena is Machiavelli's great contribution to the development of social science in western Europe.

Machiavelli pronounces no judgement on the moral value of individual deeds, but on their practical effect as political actions . . . he has quite the aspect of a physiologist making experiments in vivisection, and using his anatomical knife to dissect the different organs and ascertain their functions.[272]

All those who have written upon civil institutions demonstrate (and history is full of examples to support them) that whoever desires to found a state and give it laws, must start with assuming that all men are bad and ever ready to display their vicious nature, whenever they may find occasion for it. If their evil disposition remains concealed for a time, it must be attributed to some unknown reason; and we must assume that it lacked occasion to show itself; but time, which has been said to be the father of all truth, does not fail to bring it to light . . . . men act right only upon compulsion; but from the moment they have the option and liberty to commit wrong with impunity, then they never fail to carry confusion and disorder everywhere. It is this that has caused it to be said that poverty and hunger make men industrious, and that the law makes men good; and if fortunate circumstances cause good to be done without constraint, the law may be dispensed with. But when such happy influence is lacking, then the law immediately becomes necessary.[273]

. . . as my aim is to write something that may be useful to him for whom it is intended, it seems to me proper to pursue the real truth of the matter, rather than to indulge in mere speculation on the same; for many have imagined republics and principalities such as have never been known to exist in reality. For the manner in which men live is so different from the way in which they ought to live, that he who leaves the common course for that which he ought to follow will find that it leads him to ruin rather than to safety. For a man who, in all respects, will carry out only his professions of good, will be apt to be ruined amongst so many who are evil. A prince therefore who desires to maintain himself must learn to be not always good, but to be so or not as necessity may require. . . . I am well aware that it would be most praiseworthy for a prince to possess all of the . . . qualities that are esteemed good; but as he cannot have them all, nor entirely observe them, because of his human nature which does not permit it, he should at least be prudent enough to know how to avoid the infamy of those vices that would rob him of his state; and if possible also to guard against such as are likely to endanger it. But if that be not possible, then he may with less hesitation follow his natural inclinations. Nor need he care about incurring censure for such vices, without which the preservation of his state may be difficult. For, all things considered, it will be found that some things that seem like virtue will lead you to ruin if you follow them; whilst others, that apparently are vices, will, if followed, result in your safety and well-being.[274]

## He appreciated the role of society in the development of personality.

It seems that not only do cities differ from each other by their manners and institutions producing either men of harsh or gentle character, but such differences are oservable also between families of the same city. The proof of this may be found in every city; and we read of many instances of it in Rome. For we find that the men of the family of Manlius were severe and inflexible; the Publicoli were affable and lovers of the people, whilst the Apii were ambitious and hostile to the people; and so on, each family having its own distinctive characteristics. This cannot be attributed only to the blood, for that is necessarily modified by marriage; but must be the result of the difference of education in the several families. For it is of great importance whether a youth in his tender years hears any act praised or censured; this necessarily makes a lasting impression upon his mind, and becomes afterwards the rule of his life for all time.[275]

## Machiavelli was also a precursor of Malthus.

. . . that . . . inundations, pestilences, and famines occur cannot be doubted, both because all history is full of accounts of them, and because we see the effects of them in the oblivion of things, and also because it seems reasonable that they should occur. For in nature as in simple bodies, when there is an accumulation of superfluous matter, a spontaneous purgation takes place, which preserves the health of that body. And so it is with that compound body, the human race; when countries become overpopulated and there is no longer any room for all the inhabitants to live, nor any other places for them to go to, these being likewise all fully occupied,—and when human cunning and wickedness have gone as far as they can go,—then of necessity the world must relieve itself of this excess of population by one of those three causes; so that mankind, having been chastised and reduced in numbers, may become better and live with more convenience.[276]

He had a cyclical theory of culture change.

. . . human affairs being in a state of perpetual movement, always either ascending or declining.[277]

. . . as all human things are kept in a perpetual movement, and can never remain stable, states naturally either rise or decline.[278]

There is nothing more true than that all the things of this world have a limit to their existence; but those only run the entire course ordained for them by Heaven that do not allow their body to become disorganized, but keep it unchanged in the manner ordained, or if they change it, so do it that it shall be for their advantage, and not to their injury. . . And those are the best-constituted bodies, and have the longest existence, which possess the intrinsic means of frequently renewing themselves, or such as obtain their renovation in consequence of some extrinsic accidents. And it is a truth clearer than light that, without such renovation, these bodies cannot continue to exist; and the means of renewing them is to bring them back to their original principles.[279]

The general course of changes that occur in states is from a condition of order to one of disorder, and from the latter they pass again to one of order. For as it is not the fate of mundane affairs to remain stationary, so when they have attained their highest state of perfection, beyond which they cannot go, they of necessity decline. And thus again, when they have descended to the lowest, and by their disorders have reached the very depth of debasement, they must of necessity rise again, inasmuch as they cannot go lower.[280]

He used this cyclical theory as an argument against the superiority of the ancients over the moderns.[281]

Class struggle, in republics at least, is the fundamental disorganizing factor.

The causes of nearly all the evils that afflict republics are to be found in the great and natural enmities that exist between the people and the nobles, and which result from the dispositon of the one to command, and the indisposition of the other to obey.[282]

He also made an observation on the succession of civilizations.

. . . all the virtues that first found a place in Assyria were thence transferred to Media, and afterwards passed to Persia, and from there they came into Italy and Rome. And if after the fall of the Roman Empire none other sprung up that endured for any length of time, and where the aggregate virtues of the world were kept together, we nevertheless see them scattered amongst many nations, as, for instance, in the kingdom of France, the Turkish empire, or that of the Sultan of Egypt, and nowadays the people of Germany, and before them those famous Saracens, who achieved such great things and conquered so great a part of the world, after having destroyed the Roman Empire of the East.[283]

Finally, Machiavelli was interested in the evolution of society and political organization.

The little security which the natives found in living dispersed; the impossiblity for each to resist isolated, either because of the situation or because of their small number, the attacks of any enemy that might present itself; the difficulty of uniting in time for defence at his approach, and the necessity of abandoning the greater number of their retreats, which quickly became a prize to the assailant,—such were the motives that caused the first inhabitants of a country to build cities for the purpose of escaping these dangers. They resolved, of their own accord, or by the advice of some one who had most authority amongst them, to live together in some place of their selection that might offer them greater conveniences and greater facility of defense. . . . Chance has given birth to . . . different kinds of government amongst men; for at the beginning of the world the inhabitants were few in number, and lived for a time dispersed, like beasts. As the human race increased, the necessity for uniting themselves for defence made itself felt; the better to attain this object, they chose the strongest and most courageous from amongst themselves and placed him at their head, promising to obey him. Thence they began to know the good and honest, and to distinguish them from the bad and vicious; for seeing a man injure his benefactor aroused at once two sentiments in every heart. They blamed the first, and on the contrary honoured those the more who showed themselves grateful, for each felt that he in turn might be subject to a like wrong; and to prevent similar evils, they set to work to make laws, and to institute punishments for those who contravened them. Such was the origin of justice. This caused them, when they had afterwards to choose a prince, neither to look to the strongest nor bravest, but to the wisest and most just. But when they began to make sovereignty hereditary and non-elective, the children quickly degenerated from their fathers.[284]

## Bodin

Jean Bodin (1530–96) also had a theory of the formation of society.

. . . before there was either Citie or citisen, or any forme of a Commonweale amongst men, everie master of a familie was a maister in his owne house, having power of life and death over his wife and children: but after that force, violence, ambition, covetousnesse, and desire of revenge had armed one against another, the issues of warres and combats giving victorie unto the one side, made the other to come unto them slaves: and amongst them that overcame, he that was chosen cheefe and captaine, under whose conduct and leading they had obtained the victorie, kept them also in his power and commaund as his faithfull and obedient subjects, and the other as his slaves. Then that full and entire liberty by nature given to every man, to live as himselfe best pleased, was altogether taken from the vanquished, and in the vanquishers themselves in some measure also diminished, in regard of the conquerour; for that now it concerned everie man in privat to yeeld his obedience unto his chiefe soveraigne; and he that would not abate any thing of his libertie, to live under the lawes and commaundement of another, lost all. So the word of *Lord* and *Servant,* of *Prince* and *Subject,* before unknowne unto the world, were first brought into use. Yea Reason, and the verie light of nature, leadeth us to beleeve very force and violence to have given course and beginning unto Commonweals.[285]

However, Bodin is best known for his geographic interpretation of history.

Hitherto we have treated of that which concernes the generall Estate of Commonweales; Let us now shew what may be particular to some, through the diversitie of peoples humors, to the end that wee may accommodat the publicke weale to the nature of the place; and the ordinances of man to the laws of nature, wherof many have had small regard: but striving to make nature obedient to their edicts, have oftentimes troubled, yea ruined great estates. . . . For even as we see a great varietie in all sorts of beasts, and in every some notable alteration for the diversitie of regions: in like sort we may say, that there is in a manner as great difference in the nature and disposition of men, as there is of countries.[286]

Therefore a wise governour of any Commonweale must know their humours, before he attempt any thing in the alteration of the state and lawes. For one of the greatest, and it may be the chiefest foundation of a Commonweale, is to accommodat the estate to the humor of the citisens; and the lawes and ordinances to the nature of the place, persons, and time.[287]

For which cause wee must varie the estate of the Commonweale to the diversitie of places; like unto a good Architect, which doth fit his building according to the stuffe hee finds upon the place: So should a wise Polititian doe. . . . Let us first speake of the nature of the people of the North and South, and then of the East, and West, and the difference betwixt the mountainers & those that live in vallies, or in moorish places, or that are subject to violent winds: then will we shew how much discipline may change the nature and disposition of men, rejecting the opinions of *Polybius,* and *Galen,* who held, That the countrey and nature of the place did rule necessarily in the manners of men.[288]

He did not distinguish between direct climatological influences upon individual temperament and indirect geographic effects on personality as a result of a direct influence upon culture.

And even as they which live at the extremities of the Poles, are Flegmatike, and at the South melancholie; even so they which are thirtie degrees on this side the Pole, are cholerike; and then drawing towards the South, more sanguin and melancholike.[289]

. . . the people of the South are of a contrarie humour and disposition to them of the North: these are great and strong, they are little and weak: they of the north hot and moyst, the others cold and dry; the one hath a big voyce and greene eyes, the other hath a weake voyce and black eyes; the one hath a flaxen haire and a faire skin, the other hath both haire and skin black; the one feareth cold, and the other heate; the one is joyfull and pleasant, the other sad; the one is fearefull and peaceable, the other is hardie and mutinous; the one is sociable, the other solitarie; the one is given to drinke, the other sober; the one rude and grosse witted, the other advised and ceremonious; the one is prodigall and greedie, the other is covetous and holds fast; the one is a souldier, the other a philosopher; the one fit for armes and labour, the other for knowledge and rest.[290]

. . . the barrennesse of the soyle . . . makes townes more populous: for an enemie affects not a barren countrey, and the inhabitants living in safetie doe multiplie, and are forced to traffique or to labour. . . . But those that dwell in vallies become soft and slothfull through the richnesse of the soyle. And as they that lie upon the sea for their traffique, and those of barren countries for their sobrietie, are industrious: in like sort those which make the frontiers of two estates beeing enemies, are more fierce and warlike than the rest, for that they are continually in warre, which makes men barbarous, mutinous, and cruell; as peace makes men quiet, courteous, and tractable.[291]

But I am not of their opinions, who draw their arguments of civilitie and barbarisme from the effects of heate and cold, finding every day by common experience, that the Southerne people go beyond all other nations in quicknes of wit, whereas barbarisme and rude behaviour proceede from ignorance and want of education.[292]

But he that would see what force education, lawes, and customes, have to chaunge nature, let him looke into the people of Germanie, who in the time of *Tacitus* the Proconsull, had neither lawes, religion, knowledge, nor any forme of a Commonweale; whereas now they seeme to exceed other nations in goodly cities, and well peopled, in armes, varietie of artes, and civill discipline.[293]

The government of every Citie is of great force in the alteration of the peoples natures and dispositions: if they be oppressed with tyrannie and servitude, they grow faintharted and dejected: they which live in popular estates and enjoy their liberties, must of necessitie be more bold and warlike, wherein not only the nature of the heavens and regions in generall are to be considered, but also the particularities of the regions. What may grow in the minds of men from the ayre, water, winds, hills and vallies, what from religion, lawes, customes, discipline, and from the state of every commonweale, and not to observe the climate alone, for we see in climates that be alike and of the same elevation foure notable differences of people in colour, without speaking of other qualities, for that the West Indians are generallie of a duskish colour like unto a roasted quinze, unlesse it be a handfull of men that are black, whom the tempest carried from the coast of Affrike: and in Sivill of Spaine the men are white, at Cape Bonne Esperance black, at the river of Plate of a chestnut colour, all being in like latitude, and like climates, as we reade in the histories of the Indies which the Spaniards have left in writing: the cause may be the change from one countrie to another, and that the Sunne in Capricorne is neerer unto the earth by all the eccentricall latitude, the which are above foure hundred thousand leagues. The transportation of Collonies works a great difference in men, but the nature of the heavens, winds, waters and earth, are of more force. The Colonie of the Saxons which *Charlemaine* brought into Flanders, differed much from all the French, but by little and little they were so changed as they retaine nothing of the Saxon but the language, the which is much altered, pronouncing their aspirations more lightly, and interlacing the vowels with the consonants: as the Saxon when he calles a horse Pferd, the Flemings say Perd, and so of many others.[294]

It is most certaine that if lawes and customes be not well maintained and kept, the people will soone returne to their naturall dispositions.[295]

Bodin developed an empirical theory of the cause of revolutions, a phenomenon of great concern to the political pragmatists.

Among all the causes of seditions and changes of Commonweales there is none greater than the excessive wealth of some few subjects, and the extreme povertie of the greatest part.[296]

## Ayala

Baltasar Ayala (1548–84) was a pragmatist.

I have thought it a work worth doing, so far as my legal studies and historical reading enabled me, to describe how . . . great military glory was gained, as regards the men and methods employed and the kind of discipline resorted to. The result will show that men's qualities are the same now as formerly and that the chances and occurrences which befall us from day to day are the same as befell men formerly; so that it will not be difficult for one who ponders with diligence on things of old and examines them with judicial deliberation to employ the past—appropriate task for a wise man—in judging the present, in foretelling the future, and in educing from old examples remedies fit (because of the similarity of the circumstances) for modern ills.[297]

For instance, he gives

some propositions relating to war and cautions for commanders, affirmed by the examples of men of old.[298]

He gave the usual description of cultural evolution.

. . . liberty is an institution of the law of nature, in that before the development of *jus gentium* all men were born free and were reckoned each other's peers and equals . . . But the *jus gentium,* which has its basis in natural reason, introduced war and slavery. For, as man's wickedness increased, right natural reason—and there is nothing diviner than it; it is in virtue of it that we are superior to the beasts, taught that this wickedness of man ought to be restrained by war and captivity and slavery.

In the same way, under the law of nature, in that primitive time which pagans used to call the Golden Age, all things were in common and nothing belonged to any individual, but in following ages it was found that community of goods was not adapted to man's debased nature, and so the *jus gentium,* under the guidance of natural reason, developed the system of private ownership and all the differences incidental to it.[299]

## Botero

Considering the problem of how to get people to live in cities, Giovanni Botero (1540–1617) developed urban sociology in *Delle cause della grandezza e magnificenza deele citta* (1588).[300]

A Citie, is called an Assembly of Men, brought together to live happily: and, Greatnesse of a Citie, is tearmed not the spaciousnesse of scituation, or compasse of Walls; but the multitude of Inhabitants, and their power. Now, men are drawn together, moved thereunto, eyther by authority, force, pleasure, or utilitie, which may arise.[301]

Now, supposing Utilitie be the same; whence, as from a primarie cause, the greatnesse of a Citie proceedeth: because this Utilitie is not simple, and of its owne nature, but consisting of divers formes, and manners; it resteth, wee see what sort of profit, or commoditie, best agreeth with our present purpose. Let us conclude then; That to make a Citie great, conveniencie of Scituation, fertilitie of Land, facilitie of Passage, are most requisite.[302]

Let us now enquire, what things those are, which may move the multitude (of their owne nature indifferent, to stay here, or abide there) to come rather to one place, than another; and how Trade of Merchandize may be brought rather hither, than thither.[303]

[1.] Religion, and the honour of God, is a matter so necessarie, and of such importance, that undoubtedly it inviteth the greater number of men, and Negotiation: And the Cities which in this kinde have super-eminence; and reputation above the rest, doe also excell in Greatnesse.[304]

[2.] The commoditie of Studies, is an effectuall meanes to allure people, and especially young men, to the Citie.[305]

[3.] Cities where Royall Audiences are, Senates, Parliaments, or any sort of supreme Tribunall Seats, necessarily are frequented.[306]

[4.] There is not any thing more importeth to encrease a Citie, and to make it plentifull in Inhabitants, and abundant in all things, than the Industrie of Man, and multitude of Arts.[307]

[5.] People, in these our dayes, are so taxed by their Princes; induced thereunto, partly by Avarice; partly by Necessitie: that wheresoever any the least hope is discovered them, of Freedome, or Immunitie; thither they greedily repaire.[308]

[6.] To have some great Trade in hand, will also very much availe, to attract people to a Citie[309]

[7.] A most important thing to purchase Greatnesse to a Place, is Dominion: For this implyeth, dependence; dependence, concourse; and concourse, Greatnesse.[310]

[8.] . . . the abode of Noblemen in Cities, illustrates them, and maketh them more populous; not onely, because their Persons and Families remaine there: but besides, for that a man of Qualitie spendeth more largely, and liberally, for the concurrence, and emulation of others, in Cities, where hee seeth, and is dayly seene of Honourable Persons.[311]

[9.] . . . the Residence of a Prince infinitely availeth, to enlarge and make great a Citie, to the greatnesse of whose Empire, it proportionably encreaseth. Because, where the Prince resideth, there are Parliaments, or Senates, (tearme them which you will) kept; the Supreme Tribunals of Justice, the Privie Councels, and of State: There, concurre all the Affaires of importance. [etc,][312]

Let no man beleeve, the foresaid meanes, or any other, which may bee found out, can make a Citie encrease infinitely. It is assuredly a matter worthie consideration, from whence it cometh, that Cities arrived to a certaine height of magnitude, and power, can passe no further, but either firmely abide therein, or else fall back againe.[313]

The greatnesse of Cities, ordinarily, is fixed in this, how they may commodiously be preserved; but greatnesse, which dependeth on causes remote, or ill disposed meanes, little lasteth: For, everie one seeketh for conveniencie, and facilitie. There may be added also to the former; That great Cities are much more subject to Dearth, than little; because they need a greater quantitie of Victuals: They are also subject to the Plague; for the infection more easily fasteneth there, and with greater mortalitie; finally, they are subject to all the difficulties [in getting supplies] repeated by us, because they stand in need of more.[314]

It remaineth onely, that having brought our Citie to the Greatnesse, which the condition, and other circumstances of Scituation, remembered before in our Discourse, can afford; Diligence may be used, in the conservation and maintenance thereof: to which, Peace, Justice, and Plentie, are helpfull; for, Justice secureth every one in his owne; by Peace, Tillage, Trade, and Arts flourish; by Plentie of Victuals, the sustenation of life is made easie; and nothing retaineth the people more merry, and chearefull, than the cheapnesse of Bread. Finally, all those things which cause Greatnesse, are likewise the aptest meanes to preserve it: For the Causes of the production of things, and conservation of them, are assuredly the same.[315]

## FINANCIAL PRAGMATISTS

### Copernicus

The monetary generalization first formulated by Oresme was rediscovered a number of times in the sixteenth century. The first was by Nicolaus Copernicus (1473–1543):

If it does not do to introduce a new and good money, while the old is bad and continues to circulate, a much greater error is committed by introducing alongside of an old currency, a new currency of less value; this latter does not merely depreciate the old, it drives it away, so to speak, by main force.[316]

### Discourse of the Common Weal

Besides Oresme's law,[317] *A Discourse of the Common Weal of This Realm of England* (1549) enunciated the law of supply and demand.

. . . yt is the rarietie and plentie therof that maketh the price therof base or higher.[318]

It also presented a picture of the evolution of media of exchange.

. . . use exchange, ware for ware, without coine, as it was before coine was found, as I rede, in the time of homer. Also the Civill Lawe doth the same affirme. Which thinge weare verie cumbersome, and would Require muche cariadge of wares up and downe, wheare now by the benefite of coine a man maie by those tokens fetch the ware he lacketh a far of, with owt anie great trowble of Cariadge; and hard weare it readiely to find all wares, that the one hath, might paie the other of equal valew.[319]

## Agricola

George Agricola (1494–1555) discussed the evolution of money, too.

When ingenious and clever men considered carefully the system of barter, which ignorant men of old employed and which even today is used by certain uncivilised and barbarous races, it appeared to them so troublesome and laborious that they invented money. Indeed, nothing more useful could have been devised, because a small amount of gold and silver is of as great value as things cumbersome and heavy; and so peoples far distant from one another can, by the use of money, trade very easily in those things which civilised life can scarcely do without.[320]

## Gresham

Finally, there is the well-known version of Oresme's law by Thomas Gresham (1519–79).

Ytt may pleasse your majesty to understande, thatt the firste occasion off the fall of the exchange did growe by the Kinges majesty, your latte ffather, in abasinge his quoyne ffrome vi ounces fine too iii ounces fine. Wheruppon the exchainge fell fforme xxvi*s*. viii*d*. to xiii*s*. iv*d*. which was the occasion thatt all your ffine goold was convayd ought of this your realme.[321]

## EVOLUTION OF POLITICAL ORGANIZATION

In the fifteenth century the struggle between church and state continued. The people's attitude is reflected in a caricature[322] which proved to be so popular that it was reproduced a number of times.[323]

In the sixteenth century a debate was renewed which lasted for three hundred years—a dispute on the origin of political organization. The argument was a reflection of the social conflicts of the time. In the first place, there was the struggle of the rising capitalist and middle classes against the aristocracy; second, the fight of minority religious groups against the political system which oppressed them, particularly on the part of Protestants in Catholic countries and vice versa.[324]

Favorite arguments in defense of the status quo were the patriarchal and conquest theories, which, for example, Bodin upheld; for by virtue of the right of parenthood or conquest the king was master and the people must perforce obey.

On the other hand, those who wishd to change the existing order usually subscribed to the social contract theory. If sovereignty is the result of a contract entered into between a group and an individual for the sake of upholding the interests of the former, when the king oppresses the people he breaks his part of the bargain, the contract is broken, and the people may set up whatever new government they see fit.

## Ponet

John Ponet (1514?–56) argued:

. . . for a great long time, that is, untill after the generall flood, there was no civill or politike power, and . . . it was then first ordained by God himself . . . to maintaine justice.[325]

Kings, Princes and Governours have their authority of the people, as all laws, usages, and policies, do declare and testifie.[326]

All laws do agree, that men may revoke their Proxies, and letters of Atturney, when it pleaseth them: much more, when they see their Proctours and Atturneys abuse it.[327]

## Hotman

François Hotman (1524–90) wrote of ancient Gaul:

But concerning all these Kingdoms, one thing is remarkable, and must not lightly be past by; which is, That *they were not hereditary,* but *conferr'd* by the *People* upon such as had the reputation of being just Men. Secondly, That they had no *arbitrary* or *unlimited Authority,* but were bound and *circumscribed* by *Laws;* so that they were no less accountable to, and subject to the Power of the People; than, the People was to theirs; insomuch that those *Kingdoms* seem'd nothing else but *Magistracies for life.*[328]

He then attempted to show that the people's rights had continued down through history.

One passage can be found on the decline of nations.

. . . even as Humane Bodies decay and perish, either from some outward Violence, or some inward Corruption of Humours, or lastly thro' Old Age: so Commonwealths are brought to their Period, sometimes by Foreign Force, sometimes by Civil Dissentions, at other Times by being worn out and neglected.[329]

## Buchanan

George Buchanan (1506–82) took a similar position.

*B.*    . . . there is a mutual compact of the king with the citizens.

*M.*    It seems so.

*B.*    Does not he who first breaks the compact, and does anything contrary to his pact, nullify the pact and break the agreement?

*M.*    He does.

*B.*    Therefore, if the bond is broken which attached the king to the people, are not all his rights derived from the pact, which he nullified, forfeited?
*M.*    They are forfeited.[330]

## Vindiciae contra tyrannos

The *Vindiciae contra tyrannos* (1579)[331] contains the best analysis of this point of view.

The princes exceed their bounds, not contenting themselves with that authority which the almighty and good God hath given them, but seek to usurp that sovereignty, which he hath reserved to himself over all men, being not content to command the bodies and goods of their subjects at their pleasure, but assume licence to themselves to enforce the consciences, which appertains chiefly to Jesus Christ.[332]

It then belongs to princes to know how far they may extend their authority, and to subjects in what they may obey them, lest the one encroaching on that jurisdiction, which in no way belongs to them, and the others obeying him which commandeth further than he ought, they be both chastised, when they shall give an account thereof before another judge.[333]

The question is, If it be lawful to resist a prince violating the law of God, or ruinating the church, or hindering the restoring of it?[334]

Briefly, he, whosoever he is, who has received authority from a company, is inferior to that whole company, although he be superior to any of the particular members of it.[335]

. . . we say that the people establish kings, puts the sceptre into their hands, and who with their suffrages, approves the election.[336]

Briefly, for so much as none were ever born with crowns on their heads, and sceptres in their hands, and that no man can be a king by himself, nor reign without people, whereas on the contrary, the people may subsist of themselves, and were, long before they had any kings, it must of necessity follow, that kings were at the first constituted by the people; and although the sons and dependants of such kings, inheriting their fathers' virtues, may in a sort seem to have rendered their kingdoms hereditary to their offsprings, and that in some kingdoms and countries, the right of free election seems in a sort buried; yet, notwithstanding, in all well-ordered kingdoms, this custom is yet remaining.[337]

. . . men by nature loving liberty, and hating servitude, born rather to command, than obey, have not willingly admitted to be governed by another, and renounced as it were the privilege of nature, by sumbitting themselves to the commands of others, but for some special and great profit that they expected from it.[338]

Let us then conclude, that they are established in this place to maintain by justice, and to defend by force of arms, both the public state, and particular persons from all damages and outrages.[339]

When, therefore, that these words of mine and thine entered into the world, and that differences fell amongst fellow citizens, touching the propriety of goods, and wars amongst neighbouring people about the right of their confines, the people bethought themselves to have recourse to some one who both could and should take order that the poor were not oppressed by the rich, nor the patriots wronged by strangers.

Nor as wars and suits increased, they chose someone, in whose wisdom and valour they reposed most confidence. See, then, wherefore kings were created in the first ages; to wit, to administer justice at home, and to be leaders in the wars abroad, and not only to repulse the incursions of the enemy, but also to repress and hinder the devastation and spoiling of the subjects and their goods at home; but above all, to expel and drive away all devices and debauchments far from their dominions.[340]

Seeing then that kings are ordained by God, and established by the people, to procure and provide for the good of those who are committed unto them, and that this good or profit be principally expressed in two things, to wit, in the administration of justice to their subjects, and in the managing of armies for the repulsing their enemies: certainly, we must infer and conclude from this, that the prince who applied himself to nothing but his peculiar profits and pleasures, or to those ends which most readily conduce thereunto, who contemns and perverts all laws, who uses his subjects more cruelly than the barbarous enemy would do, he may truly and really be called a tyrant, and that those who in this manner govern their kingdoms, be they of never so large an extent, are more properly unjust pillagers and free-booters, than lawful governors.[341]

There is ever, and in all places, a mutual and reciprocal obligation between the people and the prince; the one promises to be a good and wise prince, the other to obey faithfully, provided he govern justly. The people therefore are obliged to the prince under condition, the prince to the people simply and purely. Therefore, if the prince fail in his promise, the people are exempt from obedience, the contract is made void, the right of obligation of no force. Then the king if he govern unjustly is perjured, and the people likewise forsworn if they obey not his lawful commands. But that people are truly acquit from all perfidiousness, who publicly renounce the unjust dominion of a tyrant, or he, striving unjustly by strong hand to continue the possession, do constantly endeavour to expulse him by force of arms.[342]

## Hooker

Richard Hooker (1553?–1600) also accepted the theory of social contract, but he turned it in favor of royalty.

Things casual do vary, and that which a man doth but chance to think well of cannot still have the like hap. Wherefore although we know not the cause, yet thus much we may know; that some necessary cause there is, whensoever the judgements of all men generally or for the most part run one and the same way, especially in matters of natural discourse. . . . For that which all men have at all times learned, Nature herself must needs have taught.[343]

. . . nature itself teacheth laws and statutes to live by. The laws which have hitherto been mentioned [i.e., "Laws of Reason or Nature"] do bind men absolutely even as they are men, although they have never any settled fellowship, never any solemn agreement amongst themselves what to do or not to do. But forasmuch as we are not by ourselves sufficient to furnish ourselves with competent store of things needful for such a life as our nature doth desire, a life fit for the dignity of man; therefore to supply those defects and imperfections which are in us living single and solely by ourselves, we are naturally induced to seek communion and fellowship with others. This was the cause of men's uniting themselves in the first politic Societies, which societies could not be without Government, nor Government without a distinct kind of Law from that which hath been already declared. Two foundations there are which bear up public societies; the one, a natural inclination, whereby all men desire sociable life and fellowship; the other, an order expressly or secretly agreed upon touching the manner of their union in living together. The latter is that which we call the Law of a Commonweal, the very soul of a politic body, the parts whereof are by law animated, held together, and set on work in such actions, as the common good requireth.[344]

All men desire to lead in this world a happy life.[345]

And because the greatest part of men are such as prefer their own private good before all things.[346]

If therefore when there was but as yet one only family in the world, no means of instruction human or divine could prevent effusion of blood [between Cain and Abel]; how could it be chosen but that when families were multiplied and increased upon earth, after separation each providing for itself, envy, strife, contention and violence must grow amongst them?[347]

To take away all . . . mutual grievances, injuries, and wrongs, there was no way but only by growing unto composition and agreement amongst themselves, by ordaining some kind of government public, and by yielding themselves subject thereunto; that unto whom they granted authority to rule and govern, by them the peace, tranquility, and happy estate of the rest might be procured.[348]

## La Boétie

Etienne de La Boétie (1530–63) wrote the most interesting work defending the democratic position.

. . . freedom is our natural state.[349]

. . . nature, handmaiden of God, governess of men, has cast us all in the same mold in order that we may behold in one another companions, or rather brothers.* If in distributing her gifts nature has favored some more than others with respect to body or spirit, she has nevertheless not planned to place us within this world as if it were a field of battle, and has not endowed the stronger or the cleverer in order that they may act like armed brigands in a forest and attack the weaker. One should rather conclude that in distributing larger shares to some and smaller shares to others, nature has intended to give occasion for brotherly love to become manifest, some of us having the strength to give help to others who are in need of it. Hence, since this kind mother had given us the whole world as a dwelling place, has lodged us in the same house, has fashioned us according to the same model so that in beholding one another we might also recognize ourselves; since she has bestowed upon us all the great gift of voice and speech for fraternal relationship, thus achieving by the common and mutual statement of our thoughts a communion of wills; and since she has tried in every way to narrow and tighten the bonds of our union and kinship; since she has revealed in every possible manner her intention, not so much to associate us as to make us one organic whole, there can be no further doubt that we are all naturally free, inasmuch as we are all comrades.[351]

There are three kinds of tyrants; some receive their proud position through election by the people, others by force of arms, others by inheritance.[352]

It is true that in the beginning men submit under constraint and by force; but those who come after them obey without regret and perform willingly what their predecessors had done because they had to.[353]

But why all this? Certainly not because I believe that the land or region has anything to do with it, for in any place and in any climate subjection is bitter and to be free is pleasant.[354]

Instead of the geographic interpretation, he gives social reasons.

One never pines for what he has never known; longing comes only after enjoyment and constitutes, amidst the experience of sorrow, the memory of past joy. It is truly the nature of man to be free and to wish to be so, yet his character is such that he instinctively follows the tendencies that his training gives him.†

Let us therefore admit that all those things to which he is trained and accustomed seem natural to man and that only that is truly native to him which he receives with his primitive, untrained individuality. Thus custom becomes the first reason for voluntary servitude.[356]

. . . the essential reason why men take orders willingly is that they are born serfs and are reared as such. From this cause there follows another result, namely that people easily become cowardly and submissive under tyrants.[357]

---

* "Ournature is such that the common duties of human relationship occupy a great part of the course of our life.[350]

† "It cannot be denied that nature is influencial in shaping us to her will and making us reveal our rich or meager endowment; yet it must be admitted that she has less power over us than custom, for the reason that native endowment, no matter how good, is dissipated unless encouraged, whereas environment always shapes us in its own way, whatever that may be, in spite of nature's gifts. The good seed that nature plants in us is so slight and so slippery that it cannot withstand the least harm from wrong nourishment; it flourishes less easily, becomes spoiled, withers, and comes to nothing."[355]

# III

# THE SEVENTEENTH CENTURY

A NTHROPOLOGY did not make the great strides in the seventeenth century that marked the history of so many other sciences. The influence of the Old Testament account of man's history still handicapped substantial progress in physical anthropology and linguistics. However, it was during this period that the scientific foundations of ethnography and ethnology were laid. In social anthropology, the rationalistic a priori world view of the seventeenth century produced a lot of fruitless discussion, particularly on the subjects of natural religion and the law of nature, but, on the other hand, in the same fields the inductive comparative approach of some scholars marked the beginning of the comparative science of culture.

## PHYSICAL ANTHROPOLOGY

The recently discovered races of men still perplexed scholars, and many cautiously expressed their disbelief in Genesis.

**Bacon**
Thus, Francis Bacon (1561–1626) stated:

If you consider well, of the People of the *West Indies,* it is very probable, that they are a Newer, or a Younger People, then the People of the Old World.[1]

**Vanini**
Lucilio Vanini (1585—1619) put the following words into the mouth of one of the speakers in a dialogue:

Others have dreamed that the first man has taken his origin from mud, putrified by the corruption of certain monkeys, swine, and frogs, and thence (they say) proceeds the great resemblance there is betwixt our flesh and propensions, and that of those creatures. Other athiests, more mild, have thought that none but the Ethipians are produced from a race of monkeys, because the same degree of heat is found in both. . . . Athiests cry out to us continually, that the first men went upon all four as other beasts, and 'tis by education only they have changed this custom, which, nevertheless, in their old age, returns to them.[2]

**Campanella**
Tommaso Campanella (1568–1639) conceived of a plurality of worlds, with men on each.

If the inhabitants which may be in other stars are men, they did not originate from Adam and are not infected by his sin.[3]

But all these worlds were created.

. . . it is very doubtful whether the world was made from nothing, or from the ruins of other worlds, or from chaos, but . . . [I] certainly think that it was made, and did not exist from eternity.[4]

## La Peyrère

A book on polygenesis which caused much stir in its day is the *Praeadamitae*[5] of Isac de La Peyrère (1594–1676).

It is a natural suspition that the beginning of the world is not to be receiv'd according to that common beginning which is pitched in *Adam,* inherent in all men, who have but an ordinary knowledge in things: For that beginning seems enquirable, at a far greater distance, and from ages past very long before; both by the most ancient accounts of the *Chaldaeans,* as also by the most ancient Records of the *Aegyptians, Aethiopians* and *Scythians,* and by parts of the frame of the world newly discovered, as also from those unknown Countries, to which the *Hollanders* have sayled of late, the men of which, as is probable, did not descend from *Adam.*

I had this suspition also being a Child, when I heard or read the History of *Genesis:* Where *Cain* goes forth; where he kills his brother when they were in the field; doing it warily, like a thief, least it should be discovered by any: Where he flies, where he fears punishment for the death of his Brother: Lastly, where he married a wife far from his Ancestors, and builds a City. Yet, although I had this doubt in my mind, yet durst I not speak any thing of it, which did not rellish of that received opinion, concerning *Adam* created first of all men; till I met with the 12, 13, 14 verses of the 5 ch. of the Epist. of St. *Paul* to the *Rom.* which I have in hand, and consider of now twenty years, or there-abouts. And as he who goes upon Ice, goes warily where he cracks it, being not well frozen, or tender; but where he finds it frozen, and well hardned, walks boldly: So I dreaded first, least this doubtfull dispute might either cut my soles, or throw me head-long into some deep Heresie, if I should insist upon it. But so soon as I knew by these verses of the Apostle, that sin was in the world before it was imputed; and when I knew, and that certainly, that sin began from *Adam* to be imputed, I took heart, and found all this dispute so solid, that I pass'd through it with lesse fear.[6]

He gave the following evidence for the existence of men before Adam:

[1. Indirect biblical testimony.[7] Therefore] from this Tenet, which asserts Men to have been before *Adam,* the History of *Genesis* appears much clearer, and agrees with it self.[8]

[2. The traditions of the Gentiles.] Moreover, from this Tenet, which asserts Men to have been before Adam, the History of *Genesis* . . . is wonderfully reconciled with all prophane Records whether ancient or new, to wit, those of the *Caldeans, Egyptians, Scythians,* and *Chinensians;* that most ancient Creation which is set down in the first of *Genesis* is reconciled to those of *Mexico,* not long ago discovered by *Columbus;* It is likewise reconciled to those Northern and Southern Nations which are not known, All whom, as likewise those of the first and most ancient creation were, its probable, created with the Earth it self in all parts thereof, and not propagated from *Adam.*[9]

[3. The lapse of time necessary for the development of the sciences among the most ancient cultures known, for] it is an inconsistent time which is reckon'd from *Adam* to

*Abraham* the *Chaldaean,* or to *Moses* the *Egyptian,* and it is unadvisedly set down to be sufficient to gain the knowledge of those arts which *Arbraham* and *Moses* were exact in. But certainly the time 'twixt *Noahs* flood and *Abraham* would be likewise a great deal more incompetent, if according to the same inconsideratenesse, it should be proportioned as sufficient for the attainment of the forementioned disciplines; especially Astronomy, Theology, and Magick.[10]

[4. The Old Testament is a secondary source edited at a comparatively late date; therefore the fact that pre-Adamites are not mentioned specifically is not a conclusive argument against their existence.[11]]

[*a.*] . . . either I believe that the originals of them [i.e., the books of the Old Testament] were dictated to holy authors, or taken out and copied from the Originals.[12]

[*b.*] Truly I think that *Moses,* whose end it was to write chiefly his own History, and the History of the times wherin he liv'd, wrote very briefly all the things which were before his own time; especially such things as concern'd the first creation.[13]

[5.] There is a great errour in reading the Scripture many times, when that is taken more generally, which ought to be particularly understood: as that of *Adam,* whome Moses made first Father of the Jews, and whom we hyperbolically call the first Father of all men.[14]

[6. An argument from the concept of eternity, since] the creation of the world, which is said from eternity, by the authority of both Testaments, could by no means be understood since *Adam* was made, according to the definition of both ages. Whether you call eternity, which is reckoned from many ages, and times. Or whether you understand it indefinitely or undeterminatly. For it is known that the time betwixt us and *Adam* is within account. For the times from *Adam* are of a known period, without the account of ages. Besides, there is a great deal of difference betwixt those things that preceeded the beginning of all things, and those things which were before *Adam.*[15]

[7. The lack of positive historical testimony is due to the destruction of the earliest data.[16]]

[He then summarizes:] We have seen that the Gentiles in their kind, and affection to their kind were opposite to the Jewes, were begotten of another stock than the Jews; and also call'd and esteem'd strangers by the Jews themselves. We have seen the Gentiles, the first men that were, *Gen,* Chap. 1. created with the Sun and Moon, which determinate beginning is unknown to all men.

On the other side we have seen *Adam,* from whom the Nation of the Jews is deriv'd, created apart from those first men created in the first Chapter, and from the men of the first creation.[17]

## Two Essays

In 1695 an anonymous writer published another polygenetic theory.

The *West-Indies,* and the vast Regions lately discovered towards the South, abound with such Variety of Inhabitants, and new Animals, not known, or ever seen in *Asia, Africa,* or *Europe,* that the Origin of them doth not appear so clear as some late Writers pretend; especially seeing there are no Records or Monuments of their Transmigrations out of *Asia,* or any other known Parts of the World, either before, or after the Flood; and their Differences from all the rest of the Globe, in Manners, Languages, Habits, Religions, Diet, Arts, and Customs, as well as in their Quadrupeds, Birds, Serpents, and Insects, render their Derivation very obscure, and their Origin uncertain, especially in the common Way, and according to the vulgar Opinions of planting all the Earth from one little spot.

The great Zeal to maintain a *Jewish* Tradition, put many learned Christians upon the Rack to make it out. Every Corner is searched to find out a Word, a Rite, or a Custom, in order to derive from thence many Millions of different People. . . . All Nations agree in some Words, and in some Customs; therefore a Resemblance in a few of them is no Proof.[18]

He gave the following arguments in favor of polygenesis: (1) The cultural differences between the Old and New Worlds.[19] (2) The geographic difficulties of migration.[20] (3) The differences in flora and fauna* between the Old and New Worlds.[22] On the basis of these propositions he stated:

I can see no Way at present to solve this new Face of Nature, by old Arguments fetched from Eastern Rubbish, or Rabinical Weeds, unless some new Philosopher starts up with a fresh System; in the mean Time let them all [i.e., flora and fauna of the New World] be *Aborigines.*[23]

He concluded that the flora and fauna of the New World originated independently through spontaneous generation.[24]

The writer also struggled with the problem of the causes of racial differences.

As many Difficulties lie against the *Mosaick* System of confining all Species of living terrestrial Creatures within the *Asiatick* or *Primaeval Paradise,* and afterwards to *Noah's* Ark; so more seem to arise against the Propagation of all Mankind out of one single Male and Female, unless all Posterity, both Blacks and Whites, separated by vast Seas, were all included actually in Form within *Adam* and *Eve.*

The Origin of Negroes lies very obscure; for Time out of Mind there hath been Blacks with a wooly Substance on their Bodies instead of Hair; because they are mentioned in the most ancient Records now extant in the World. 'Tis plain, their Colour and Wool are innate, or seminal from their first Beginning, and seems to be a specifick Character, which neither the Sun, nor any Curse from *Cham* could imprint upon them.

Not the first, because many other Nations, living under the same Climates and Heats, are never black; as the *Abyssines,* the *Siamites,* the *Brasilians, Peruvians,* &c. neither will any White every become a Black, in *Guinea, Congo,* or *Angola,* though born there; neither will any Negroes produce Whites in *Virginia,* or *New England.* The Textures of their Skins and Blood differ from those of Whites. .

Not the latter; for what Curse is Change of Colour, that being only accidental to Beauty, which consists wholly in Proportion and Symmetry? The old Statues in black Marble, are as much, if not more, valued than those in white. Besides, the Curse upon *Cham's* Account must have turn'd many of the *Asiaticks,* and all the *Egyptians,* into Negroes; for they were curs'd more peculiarly then the western remote Coasts of *Africa.*

This Colour (which appears to be as ingenite, and as original as that in Whites) could not proceed from any Accident; because, when Animals are accidentally black, they do not procreate constantly black ones, (as the Negroes do) as in Dogs, Cows, Sheep, and in some Birds; accidental Colours vary in the same numerical Subject by Changes of Season, of Diet, of Culture, &c. but a Negroe will always be a Negroe, carry him to *Greenland,* give him Chalk, feed and manage him never so many Ways.[25]

* " . . . the Animals of the new World . . . differ in Specie from those of the old."[21]

## Hale

These ideas, opposed as they were to the teachings of the Bible, did not pass unchallenged. Matthew Hale (1609–76) wrote a large (and often dull) tome to prove:

1. That Mankind had an Original of his Being *ex non genitis*.
2. That this Origination of Mankind was neither casual, nor meerly natural.
3. That the Efficient of Man's Origination, was and is an Intelligent Efficient of an incomparable Wisdom and Power.[26]

In that short yet admirable History of the Creation delivered by *Moses* in the first Chapter of *Genesis,* he gives us an exact Account of the Origination both of Mankind and of the whole World.[27]

He viewed man's relation to other animals in terms of a modified version of the scholastic doctrine of the powers of the soul.

There are several Ranks of Being in this inferior World, which have various specifical Degrees or Ranks of Perfection one above another.

The first division of them is into things Inanimate, and things Animate; wherein the latter have another, and a nobler Form, or (if that Word be disliked) Nature than the former.

Of things Animate there are three distinct natures, the latter exceeding still not only in degree but in kind, perfection, and excellence of nature the former; namely, things vegetable, that have simply Life, with those operations incident to Life. The second sensible, that have not only a Life of vegetation, but a Life of sense, and faculties, and operations corresponding to it. The third rational or intellectual, that hath not only a Life of vegetation and sense, but an intellectual Life, and faculties and operations subservient and suitable to that Life.[28]

## Burnet

Thomas Burnet (1635–1715) also argued from the authority of the Bible.

'Tis the Sacred Writings of Scripture that are the best Monuments of Antiquity, and to those we are chiefly beholden for the History of the first Ages, whether Natural History or Civil.[29]

We are assur'd by Divine Authority, that the Earth and Mankind had a beginning.[30]

We say all these Things arose and had their first Existence or Production not six thousand Years ago.[31]

. . . there are many particular Marks and Arguments, that the Generations of Men have not been from Everlasting. All History, and all Monuments of Antiquity, of what kind soever, are but of a few Thousand of Years date; we have still the Memory of the Golden Age, of the first State of Nature, and how Mortals lived then in Innocency and Simplicity. The Invention of Arts, even those that are necessary or useful to Human Life, hath been within the Knowledge of Men.[32]

All the Artificial and Mechanical World is in a manner new; and what you may call the *Civil* World too is in a great Measure so. What related to Government, and Laws; to Wars and Discipline; we can trace these things to their Origin, or very near it.[33]

Man had different characteristics than at present during "the first State of Nature."

Men's Lives were much longer before the Flood, and next after it, than . . . now.[34]

We might add . . . that they were greater as well as longerliv'd, than they are at present.[35]

He too took a stab at explaining racial differences.

We see the *Blacks* do not quit their Complexion immediately, by removing into another Climate, but their Posterity changeth by little and little, and after some Generations they become altogether like the People of the Country where they are.[36]

## Descartes

René Descartes (1696–50) at an early age developed the theory that animals are machines.

From the very perfection of animal actions we suspect that they do not have a free will.[37]

Later, he tentatively applied the same idea to man.[38]

Man is distinguished from other animals by the possession of reason.

. . . the difference that exists between men and brutes . . . [is based upon the fact that] not merely . . . [do] the brutes have less reason than men, but . . . they have none at all.[39]

As a result, only man has speech.

. . . we ought not to confound speech with the natural movements which betray passions and may be imitated by machines as well as manifested by animals; nor must we think, as did some of the ancients, that brutes talk, although we do not understand their language.[40]

## Cyrano de Bergerac

Cyrano de Bergerac (1619–55) believed in naturalism.

Since the wise man sees nothing in the world which he does not understand or which he considers incapable of being understood, he ought to abominate all these expressions like miracles, prodigies, supernatural events, invented by the stupid to excuse the weakness of their minds.[41]

In fact, he was an agnostic[42] and skeptical of the biblical version of creation;[43] he even had a vague evolutionary theory.[44]

As a follower of Gassendi,[45] he opposed Descartes and advocated the close relationship between man and the oher animals. He stated that "birds reason"[46] and have a language.[47]

. . . although birds imitate your words they do not understand them; but when you in turn imitate the barking of a dog or the song of a nightingale you do not understand what the dog or the nightingale means. From that you may deduce that neither birds nor men are any the less reasonable on this account.[48]

He satirized the Cartesian tenets of the absence of reason and language in other animals in his stories of the four-footed men on the moon[49] and the birds on the sun.[50] In short, he deprecated not only ethnocentrism* but anthropocentrism as well, that is,

* " . . . the opinions we have sucked in with our milk always appear to us the most reasonable."[51]

the intolerable pride of human beings, who are convinced that Nature was made for them alone.[52]

## Cordemoy
Géraud de Cordemoy (1620–84) applied the Cartesian thesis to the vocalization of animals.

[He argued] that *Brutes* need no soul to cry, or to be moved by Voyces, or even to imitate the sound of our words; and that if the cry of those, that are of the same *species,* disposeth them to approach one another, and maketh those that are of a different kind, to retire; the cause of *that* is to be sought no where else but in their Bodies and the different construction of their Organs. But at the same time I find, that in Men, the motion of the parts, which serve for the Voyce, or of those that are moved by it, is ever accompanied with some *thoughts;* and that in *Speech* there are always two things, *viz.* the *Formation* of the *Voyce,* which cannot proceed but from the *Body;* and the *Signification* or the *Idea,* that is joyn'd therewith, which cannot come but from the Soul.[53]

## Bayle
Pierre Bayle (1647–1706) disagreed with both the Cartesians and the anti-Cartesians, stating that the differences between animals are the result of differences in biological organization rather than in the nature of their souls.

. . . if it [i.e., "the soul of beasts"] doth not produce acts so noble as those of our soul, it is not it's fault, or because it is of a nature less perfect than the soul of man; it is only because the organs it animates do not resemble ours* . . . unite it to a well chosen human body; it will become the soul of a man of parts, and be no more that of a beast.

You may see therefore that it is impossible for the School-Philosophers to prove, that the souls of men, and those of beasts, are of a different nature.[55]

Respecting the relationship between man and the other animals, throughout the whole period covered in this work the dominant conception was that of the "chain of being," i.e., the gradation of fixed species.

One of the consequences of the dominant theology was what has been termed the principle of plenitude.

. . . the principle of plenitude . . . cover[s] . . . the thesis that the universe is a *plenum formarum* in which the range of conceivable diversity of *kinds* of living things is exhaustively exemplified, but also any other deductions from the assumption that no genuine potentiality of being can remain unfulfilled, that the extent and abundance of the creation must be as great as the possibility of existence and commensurate with the productive capacity of a "perfect" and inexhaustible Source, and that the world is the better, the more things it contains.[56]

[As a corollary, there developed a] conception of the plan and structure of the world which, through the Middle Ages and down to the late eighteenth century, many philosophers, most men of science, and, indeed, most educated men, were to accept without question—the conception of the universe as a "Great Chain of Being," composed of an immense, or—by the strict but seldom rigorously applied logic of the principle of continuity—of an infinite, number of links ranging in hierarchical order from the meagerest kind of existents, which barely escape non-existence, through "every possible" grade

* " . . . the Creator of all things has fixed every soul to a certain train of thoughts, by making it depend on the motions of certain bodies."[54]

up to the *ens perfectissimum*—or, in a somewhat more orthodox version, to the highest possible kind of creatures, between which and the Absolute Being the disparity was assumed to be infinite—every one of them differing from that immediately above and that immediately below it by the "least possible" degree of difference.[57]

This thesis was based upon a static conception of eternally fixed species and did not involve the idea of the higher orders of being developing from the lower.

## Charron

Pierre Charron (1541–1603) subscribed to the chain of being.

. . . the Order and Constitution of the Universe is not vastly unequal; There are no great Irregularities, nor large void Spaces in it; nor such Unlikeness and wide Disproportion between the several Parts that go into this Composition, as some People may imagine. The Excellencies of the several Species rise and fall gradually; And those, whom Nature hath placed near, or close to one another, have all of them a mutual Resemblance; tho' some have more, and some have less of it. And thus we may observe a near Neighbourhood, and close Affinity between Mankind and other Animals. They are a-kin in many Things, and several Properties are alike and common to both. Several Things indeed there are, wherein they differ; but these are not so vastly disproportionate and distant, but that they still are next adjoyning Links, twisted within one another, in the great Chain of the Universe.[58]

The *Body* of Man hath several very particular and distinguishing Qualities, which are Excellencies peculiar to himself, and such as Beasts have no Share at all in. The first and most remarkable seem to be these that follow: *Speech,* and *Erect Stature*. . . . The *Hand,* which is a Prodigy in Nature, and no other Creature, not even the Ape it self, hath any thing comparable to it; the natural *Nakedness* and *Smoothness* of our *Skin; Laughing* and *Crying;* the *Sense* of being *Tickled;* the *Eye-Lash* upon the lower Lid of the *Eye;* a visible *Navel;* the *Point* of the Heart inclining toward the Left-Side; the *Knee,* which is said to stand forward in no other Creature whatsoever; the *Palpitation* of the *Heart; Bleeding* at the Nose, which you will think very odd, when you recollect that Men carry their Head upright, and Beasts hang theirs down toward the Ground; *Blushing* for *Shame; Looking Pale* for *Fear; Multiplying* at all times indifferently; not moving their *Ears,* which in other Animals is a Signification of their inward Passions: But These are sufficiently discover'd in Manking by looking *Red* or *Pale;* and particular Motions of the *Eyes* and *Nose.*

Others, tho' they are not altogether his own, and incommunicable, yet may be styl'd Peculiar, in respect of the Degree and the Advantage he hath above others which partake of them: Such are the Number of his *Muscles,* and vast Quantity of Hair upon his Head; the Nimbleness and wonderful Variety of *Motions* in his *Limbs* and *Joints;* the great *Abundance* of the *Brain;* the *Largeness* of his *Bladder;* the *Form* of the *Foot,* so very long forward, and so short a Heel behind; the vast *Quantity,* the *Clearness* and the *Fineness* of the *Blood;* the *Easiness* and *Agility* of the *Tongue;* the *Multitude* and unspeakable *Variety* of his *Dreams,* so extreamly above all other Animals, that Man alone deserves the Name of a *Dreaming Creature;* the *Faculty* of *Sneezing:* And, to be short, the innumerable different *Motions* of his *Eyes,* and *Nose,* and *Lips.*[59]

## Petty

William Petty (1623–87) constructed "Scales of animate being."

I make two Scales of animate being, that is to say, of beings which act by souls. The one whose top is Man, and whose bottom is the smallest and the simplest animall that man can discern; and of the other scale, the maker of the . . . visible world is the top and Man the bottome. Nor do I presume to offer a third scale, but stop here and say *Abyssus abyssum invocat,* or quit it to the sublimer thoughts of others. . . .

Placing Man on the top of the lower scale, I make many sorts or species of Comparisons between him and his Inferior animalls, downe to the lowest, and presume to infer the like gradations to be in the upper scale. . . .

I doe not only compare man with the Inferior Creatures of the small scale, but I doe also compare the highest emprovements of mankind in his masse, with the rudest condition that man was ever in; thereby inferring that if man hath improved soe much in the severall past Centuries and ages of the world, how far he might proceed in six thousand yeares more, or in any other number of ages, that is to say how farr he might advance from the bottome (where he now is) towards the top of the great scale.[60]

## Man is similar to other animals in his reflexes.

Young Whelps, and all new borne Creatures, as soon as ever they are borne repaire to the dugge, and fight or strive one against another for the better dugge, before they can learne by any experience that there is either milke in the dugge, or that such strivings will availe to the procurement of the fuller teat.[61]

Man and other animalls Scratch where it itches, naturally.[62]

## Man differs from other animals in a number of ways..

*A.* . . . tell me wherein differs from all other Animalls. . . .

*B.* (1) A man hath speech* which exceedingly advantageth his reason.

(2) Man only consulteth about eternal happiness after death.

(3) Man only enquires into the next causes of effects, and into the causes of these causes, and so forwards (to the 3rd, 4th, 5th, &c. causes) according to the strength and reach of his imagination; and careth not only for his daily food, sleep, lust, &c., but for and untill the end of his life and also for many generations to come; and will expose himself to the danger of present death and wounds for these remote matters.

(4) A man doth differ from all other animals in use of the female, and generation. By using the same without designe or desire of generation, and when generation is needlesse or impossible. In making such rules and lawes concerning the same, as no other animall doth; and all this while making all the acts and instruments thereof ridiculous, shamefull, and filthy, so as not to bee seen or spoken of in the company and presence of others without laughter.[64]

He then gives a more particular description of the "lesser scale of animate being."

As to the description of the lesser Scale (whereof man is the topp and the smallest Magott the bottom) wee say as follows:—

1. Man being the first or Topp of this Scale, the question is what Animall shall bee next. Unto which question, because no certain Answer can bee given, wee shal substitute probable Hypothesis instead of them. . . . I therefore propound an Elephant for the next Creature in dignity to a Man, not because of his great strength (which is equall to the strength of Man assisted by Levers & Sences and Wheels) but rather because of his wonderfull Dexterity ariseing from the various & multiform use & Application of

* "*A.* What do you call Speech?

"*B.* Sounds articulate called Words, composable out of lesser sounds called Letters; by which words all things, qualities, sensations, and thoughts may bee represented to the mind by the eare; as if the eyes, nose &c. had originally represented the same. And the other animals besides Man have it not, but in a very low degree, in what concerns their food sleep and lust."[63]

his probossis, which in many cases equalls, & in some exceeds those of a man's hand.

2. I give him the 2d. place for his Memory & understanding, which I have heard extende to the greatest use of the Language of those Men with whom he converses, being a faculty not soe eminent in any other Animall. Moreover since Longevity, or living till 80 or 90 years of age, doth accompany the dexterity, memory & intellect above mentioned, it seems to mee that the said Qualifications together with his great strength for Execution, doth give him a fair pretence to the next place in the Scale after Man.

3. In the Opinion of most men, the Ape or rather the Drill (which is the largest & most manlike species of Apes) should claim the 2d. place unto which we have preferred the Elephant, 1st. because his shape is far neerer to that of Man, than any other Animall's is, and for that his Actions as they have been reported by those who pretend to know them do in many points resemble those of a Man. Nevertheless since it be true that an Elephant can understand the language better then a Drill, and that the *Mens* of an Elephant doth come neerer to the *Mens* of a man, although the shape of a Drill comes neerer the shape of a man, I shall choose (as I have done) to give preference unto the Elephant.

Speech is more peculiar unto, and copious in a Man than in any other Animall, and consequently wee might in that respect give the 2d. place to Parrots, or that species of them, in which the formation of Articular sounds and the imitation of Man's Speech is most conspicuous. Nor is an Ape so considerable to mee for imitating the externall & visible motion of the parts & Organs of a Man, as speaking Birds are for imitating, by a sort of reason and internall sence, the motion of the hidden and unseen instruments of speech, which are the Muscells of the Lungs & Larynx. But it is plain that although Parrotts do pronounce words, that they do it but as sounds, and not like men, as the signs of things, Actions & Notions; & consequently this faculty of speaking birds extending onely to sounds & not to the Conceptions of the Mind, I think it not sufficient for degrading the Elephant from the second place in the Scale, & serves onely to give the Parrott a pretence to contest with the Ape for precedency.

4. Haveing admitted the Parrott to a right or Competition, I will not exclude the Bee. . . . I say that if what is reported concerning the pollicy and Government of Bees, be true,—considering how little while they live, and either how much knowledge is conjoint with them, or how much they learn in a Small time, as also what Art is visible in the Makeing of their honycombe,—I say their Souls seem as like the Souls of men as their bodies are unlike.[65]

He goes on to consider the races of man.

. . . of man itself there seems to be severall species,* To say nothing of Gyants & Pigmyes or of that sort of small men who have little speech and feed cheifly upon Fish called Uries. For of these sorts of men, I venture to say nothing, but that 'tis very possible there may be Races and generations of such; since wee know that there are men of 7 foot high & others but four foote, that is to say, the one a foote and a half above, & the other a foot and a halfe below the middle stature of mankind which I take to bee 5 foot & a half. I say there may bee Races and generations of such Men, whereof wee know the individualls; as wee see vast differences in the Magnitude of severall other Animalls which bear the same name,—as between the Irish wolf Dogg and the Bullonian Tumbler

* "Whether many species of Man were made at or about the same time, and when and where was each made?"[66]

"If mankind bee as old as the rest of the world, it cannot have been made longer than the time wherein one paire of mankind breeding might have multiplied themselves to the number we find now upon the surface of the earth, which is between 3 and 4 hundred millions. Which agreeth with what Moses relateth thereof."[67]

& the Iceland Shock; [etc.]. . . . And what difference is between the Bulke of one Man & another, seemes to mee, to bee also in their Memories, Witts, Judgements & withall in their externall Sences. . . .

Besides those differences between Man & man, there bee others more considerable, that is, between the Guiny Negros and the Middle Europeans; & of Negros between those of Guiny and those who live about the Cape of Good Hope, which last are the Most beastlike of all the Souls of Men with whom our Travellers are well acquainted. I say that the Europeans do not onely differ from the aforementioned Africans in Collour, which is as much as white differs from black, but also in their Haire which differs as much as a straight line differs from a Circle; but they differ also in the shape of their Noses, Lipps and cheek bones, as also in the very outline of their faces & the Mould of their skulls. They differ also in their Naturall Manners, & in the internall Qualities of their Minds.[68]

## Leibniz

On the basis of his Law of Continuity,* Gottfried Wilhelm von Leibniz (1646–1716)[70] was led to the conception of gradation in organic life.

Men are connected with the animals, these with the plants, and these again with the fossils, which will be united in their turn with bodies which the senses and the imagination represent to us as perfectly dead and shapeless. Now since the law of continuity demands that *when the essential determinations of a being approach those of another so that likewise accordingly all the properties of the first must gradually approach those of the last,* it is necessary that all the orders of natural beings form only one chain, in which the different classes, like so many links, connect so closely the one to the other, that it is impossible for the senses and the imagination to fix the precise point where any one begins or ends: all the species which border on or which occupy, so to speak, the regions of inflection and retrogression being obliged to be equivocal and endowed with characters which can refer to the neighboring species equally. Thus the existence of Zoophytes for example, or, as Buddeus calls them, *Plant-Animals,* is nowise monstrous, but it is indeed agreeable to the order of Nature that there are some. And such is the force of the principle of continuity with me that, not only should I not be astonished to learn that beings had been found which as regards many properties, for example, those of maintaining and multiplying themselves, might pass for vegetables with as good right as for animals, and which would reverse the ordinary rules, based upon the supposition of a perfect and absolute separation of the different orders of simultaneous beings which fill the universe; I should be so little astonished, I say, that I am indeed convinced that there must be such, that Natural History will perhaps some day succeed in knowing them, when it shall have studied more this infinite number of living beings, whose minuteness hides them from ordinary observation and which are found concealed in the bowels of the earth and the depths of the water.[71]

. . . there may be intermediate creatures between those which are far apart. . . . Birds, so different from man in other things, approach him in speech; but if monkeys could speak like parrots, they would go farther.† The *law of continuity* declares that nature

* "Nothing is accomplished all at once, and it is one of my great maxims, and one of the most verified, that *nature makes no leaps*: a maxim which I called the *Law of Continuity*. . . . This law declares that we pass always from the small to the great; and the reverse, through the medium, in degree as in parts."[69]

† "As for *organs* [of speech], monkeys have them apparently as suitable as ours for the formation of words, but they do not take the least step in this direction. Thus it must be that they lack an invisible something."[72]

leaves no gap in the order she follows; but every form or species is not the whole order.[73]

All organisms, or at least all animals, have souls.

It seems to me . . . certain, that if there are corporeal substances, man in not the only one, and it appears probable that beasts have souls although they lack consciousness.[74]

And I know not whether we have sufficient reason for rejecting the *vegetative souls*, since persons of much experience and judgement recognize a great analogy between plants and animals, and you, sir [i.e., Locke], have appeared to admit animal souls.*[76]

If we are to give the name of Soul to everything which has perceptions and desires in the general sense which I have explained, then all simple substances or created Monads might be called souls; but as feeling is something more than a bare perception, I think it right that the general name of Monads or Entelechies should suffice for simple substances which have perception only, and that the name of *Souls* should be given only to those in which perception is more distinct, and is accompanied by memory.[77]

All organisms also have perception.

. . . life . . . must always be accompanied by perception in the souls.†[79]

I am inclined to the belief that there is some perception and appetition also in the plants, because of the great analogy which exists between plants and animals; and if, as is commonly supposed, there is a vegetable soul, it of necessity has perception. Yet I do not cease to attribute to mechanism all that takes place in the bodies of plants and animals, except their first formation. Thus I agree that the movement of the plant called sensitive arises from mechanism, and I do not approve of having recourse to the soul when the question is that of explaining the detail of the phenomena of plants and animals.[80]

However, different kinds of organisms perceive differently.
1. Mere living beings perceive unconsciously.‡
2. Lower animals have simple perception, i.e., they are conscious.

. . . animals have perception, and . . . it is not necessary that they have thought, that is to say, that they have reflection or what may be its object.[82]

3. Man has "apperception," i.e., he is self-conscious.

. . . in man's case, his perceptions are accompanied with the power of reflection.[83]

The soul of man . . . always knows itself and continues to exist with self-consciousness.[84]

These differences are summed up in the following passage:

. . . when the Monad has organs so arranged that they give prominence and sharpness to the impressions they receive, and consequently to the perceptions which represent these (as, for instance, when, by means of the form of the eye's humours, the rays of light are concentrated and act with more force), this may lead to *feeling*, that is to say, to a perception accompanied by *memory*, in other words, a perception of which a certain echo long remains, so as to make itself heard on occasions. Such a living being is called

---

* "I dare not maintain that plants have no souls, nor life, nor any substantial form."[75]

† "I thought you could avail yourself of a more general term than that of *thought*, viz.: that of *perception*, attributing thought only to minds, while perception belong to all the entelechies."[78]

‡ [He sometimes limited perception to only two types, simple perception and apperception; e.g.,] there are two kinds of perception, one simple and the other accompanied by the reflections which are the origin of the sciences and of reasoning."[81]

an *animal,* as its Monad is called a *soul.* And when this soul is raised to *reason,* it is something more sublime and is reckoned among spirits, as will presently be explained. It is true that animals are sometimes in the condition of mere living beings and their souls in the condition of mere Monads, namely, when their perceptions are not sufficiently sharp to be remembered, as happens in a deep dreamless sleep or in a swoon. But perceptions which have become completely confused are sure to be developed again in animals. . . . Thus it is well to make distinction between *perception,* which is the inner state of the Monad representing outer things, and *apperception,* which is *consciousness* or the reflective knowledge of this inner state, and which is not given to all souls nor to the same soul at all times.[85]

Animals do have association of ideas.

Memory provides the soul with a kind of *consecutiveness,* which resembles reason, but which is to be distinguished from it.[86]

Man differs from other animals in the possession of reason, the product of "apperception" and memory.

. . . we distinguish the man from the beast by the faculty of reason.[87]

. . . man is the only rational animal.[88]

. . . the reasoning soul . . . is . . . entirely different from the other souls which we know because it is capable or reflection.[89]

Sense is perception which contains something distinct and is combined with attention and memory. . . . Besides the lowest degree of perception, which also occurs in those who are stunned, and the intermediate degree, which we call sense . . . there is a certain higher degree which we call thought. Now thought is perception combined with reason.[90]

I understand . . . the distinction . . . between the reasoning of men and the consecutions of animals, which are a shadow of the reasoning of men.[91]

For minds are not like souls, without reason, empirics, having knowledge only of facts and relations; minds have knowledge of the necessity of eternal truths, are able to understand the reason of facts, and can imitate the architecture of God.[92]

It is also through the knowledge of necessary truths, and through their abstract expression, that we rise to *acts of reflexion,* which makes us think of what is called *I,* and observe that this or that is within us: and thus, thinking of ourselves, we think of being, of substance, of the simple and the compound, of the immaterial, and of God Himself, conceiving that what is limited in us is in Him without limits. And these acts of reflexion furnish the chief objects of our reasonings.[93]

But the Law of Continuity even operates in the gap between association of ideas and reasoning.

There is a connexion among the perceptions of animals which has some likeness to reason; but it is based only on the memory of *facts* or effects, and not at all on the knowledge of *causes.* . . . But *genuine reasoning* depends upon necessary or eternal truths . . . which produce an indubitable connexion of ideas and infallible inferences. The animals in which these inferences do not appear are called the *lower animals;* but those which know these necessary truths are properly those which are called *rational animals,* and their souls are called *minds.* These souls have the power to perform acts of reflexion and to observe that which is called ego, substance, soul, mind, in a word, immaterial things and truths. And this it is which makes science or demonstrative knowledge possible to us.[94]

. . . man as well as the animal is inclined to put together in his memory and imagination what he has observed united in his perceptions and experience. It is in this that all the reasoning, if so it may be called, of animals consists, and often that of men, so far as they are empirical and govern themselves only by the senses and examples, without examining whether the same reason still has force.[95]

We perceive many things within and without us, which we do not understand, and we *understand* them, when we have distinct ideas of them, together with the power of reflection and of drawing from them necessary truths. Animals therefore have no understanding, at least in this sense. . . . Thus in my view the *understanding* corresponds to what among the Latins is called *intellectus,* and the exercise of this faculty is called *intellection,* which is a distinct perception united with the faculty of reflection, which is not in animals. Every perception united with this faculty is a thought, which I do not accord to the animals any more than understanding, so that we may say there is intellection when thought is distinct. For the rest, the perception of the signification of signs does not deserve to be distinguished here from the perception of the ideas signified.[96]

In so far as the concatenation of their perceptions is due to the principle of memory alone, men act like the lower animals. . . . Indeed, in three-fourths of our actions we are nothing but empirics.[97]

### Ray and Willughby

The seventeenth century produced many compendia on the animals of the world, but man was almost invariably excluded. Discussions of primates, excluding man, are found in Franz Wolfgang (1564–1628),[98] as well as in John Ray (1627–1705)[99] and Francis Willughby (1635–72).[100]

Willughby, under Ray's direction, was one of the first to develop a natural classification of animals. Though he excluded man, his description of lower primates is interesting.

BEASTS: Viviparous, Clawed, Not Rapacious

Man-like; having *faces* and *ears* somewhat resembling those of *Men,* with only four broad
    *incisores,* or cutting teeth, and two short eye-teeth, not longer then the other, their
    *fore-feet* being generally like *hands,* with *thumbs,* going upon their *heels;* whether
    the
    *Bigger kind;* either that which hath a *short tail:* or that which hath *no tail.*
       1.  BABOON, *Drill.*      APE- *Jackanapes.*
    *Lesser kind;* having a *long tail* . . .
       2.  MONKEY, *Marmosit.*     SLOTH, *Haut,* Ay.[101]

Ray's classification was based upon the digits and teeth.[102]

### Jonstonus

Though Joannes Jonstonus (1603–75) did include man in his *Thaumatographia naturalis,*[103] he considered him separately from the other primates.[104]

### Fabricius ab Aquapendente

Hieronymus Fabricius ab Aquapendente (1533–1619) made an important comparative study of the vocal organs of,[105] and the sounds produced by,[106] lower animals and man. In the latter investigation he came to the conclusion that the lower animals do have a language but that man's speech is more complex, the lips and tongue are used in its production, and it has clearer and more distinct articulation. Man's speech varies from group to group, while that of animals within the same species is more uniform. The animals communicate to express emotions and employ the following means: look, gesture, sound, voice, and language. The lower animals chiefly use the throat in vocal communication, while man employs the throat only for the production of the vocal sounds, which are then articulated by the lips and tongue.

### Casserio

At about the same time, Giulio Casserio (1561–1616) also published on the comparative anatomy and physiology of the vocal and auditory organs.[107]

### Willis

Thomas Willis (1621–75) wrote on the comparative anatomy and physiology of the nervous system.[108] As to the difference between man and other animals, he wrote:

. . . the Soul of the Brute . . . is different from the Rational Soul and also . . . is much inferiour and Material.[109]

### Tyson

The scientific foundation of the comparative anatomy of primates was laid by Edward Tyson (1650–1708) in his careful report on the dissection of a chimpanzee.

I have made a *Comparative* Survey of this *Animal,* with a *Monkey,* an *Ape,* and a Man. By viewing the same Parts of all of these together, we may the better observe *Nature's Gradation* in the Formation of *Animal* Bodies, and the Transitions made from one to another.[110]

For tho' I own it to be of the *Ape* kind, yet . . . in the *Organization* of abundance of its Parts, it more approaches to the Structure of the same in *Men:* But where it differs from a *Man,* there it resembles plainly the Common *Ape,* more than any other Animal.[111]

. . . our *Pygmie* is no *Man,* nor yet the *Common Ape;* but a sort of *Animal* between both; and tho' a *Biped,* yet of the *Quadrumanus-kind.*[112]

### Bernier

A respectable classification of the races of man was given by François Bernier (1620–88).

Although in the exterior form of their body, and especially in their faces, men are almost all different one from the other, according to the different districts of the earth which they inhabit, . . . still I have remarked that there are four or five species or races of men in particular whose difference is so remarkable that it may be properly made use of as the foundation for a new division of the earth.

I comprehend under the first species . . . all Europe, except a part of Muscovy. To this may be added a small part of [North] Africa . . . and also a good part of [Western and Southern] Asia. . . . For although the Egyptians, for instance, and the [East] Indians are very black, or rather copper-coloured, that colour is only an accident in them, and comes because they are constantly exposed to the sun; and for those indidividuals who take care of themselves, and who are not obliged to expose themselves so often as the lower class, are not darker than many Spaniards. It is true that most Indians have something very different from us in the shape of their face, and in their colour which often comes very near to yellow; but that does not seem enough to make them a species apart, or else it would be necessary to make one of the Spaniards, another of the Germans, and so on with several other nations of Europe.

Under the second species I put the whole of Africa, except the coasts I have spoken of. What induces me to make a different species of the Africans, are, 1. Their thick lips and squab noses, there being very few among them who have aquiline noses or lips of moderate thickness. 2. The blackness which is peculiar to them, and which is not caused by the sun, as many think; for if a black African pair be transported to a cold country, their children are just as black, and so are all their descendants until they come to marry with white women. The cause must be sought for in the peculiar texture of their bodies, or in the seed, or in the blood—which last are, however, of the same colour as everywhere else. 3. Their skin, which is oily, smooth, and polished, excepting the places which are burnt with the sun. 4. The three or four hairs of beard. 5. Their hair, which is not properly hair, but rather a species of wool, which comes near to the hairs of some of our dogs; and, finally, their teeth whiter than the finest ivory, their tongue and all the interior of their mouth and their lips as red as coral.

The third species comprehends [the rest of Asia]. . . . The people of all those countries are truly white; but they have broad shoulders, a flat face, a small squab nose, little pig's-eyes long and deep set, and three hairs of beard.

The Lapps make the fourth species. They are little stunted creatures with thick legs, large shoulders; short neck, and a face elongated immensely; very ugly and partaking much of the bear. . . .

As to the Americans, they are in truth most of them olive-coloured, and have their faces modelled in a different way from ours. Still I do not find the difference sufficiently great to make of them a peculiar species different from ours. Besides, as in our Europe, the stature, turn of the face, the colour and the hair are generally very different, as we have said, so it is the same in other parts of the world; as for example, the blacks of the Cape of Good Hope seem to be of a different species to those from the rest of Africa. They are small, thin, dry, ugly, quick in running.[113]

Then, as might be expected from a Frenchman, he proceeds to consider the relative beauty of the women of each of these races.[114]

## ARCHEOLOGY

Stone Age artefacts were still thought to be thunderstones by Joannes de Laet (1593–1649),[115] Lodovico Moscardo (fl. 1656),[116] and Robert Sibbald (1641–1722);[117] but others agreed with Mercati, such as Anselm Boèce de Boodt (1550?–1632)[118] and William Dugdale (1605–86). The latter stated in his description of Oldbury :

On the North part of this Fort, have been found, by plowing, divers Flint stones, about four inches and a half in length, curiously wrought by grinding, or some such way, into the form here exprest [and an illustration is given]; the one end shaped much like the edge of an Pole-Axe, which makes me conjecture, that, considering there is no flint in all this part of the Countrie, nor within more than *xl.* miles from hence, they being at first so made by the native Britans, and put into a hole, boared through the side of a staff, were made use of for weapons, inasmuch as they had not then attained to the knowledge of working iron or brass to such uses.[119]

So extensive was the interest in archeology in the seventeenth century that antiquarian societies were formed, and the Academie des Inscriptions et Belles-Lettres of Paris began publication of its *Histoire et mémoires* in 1666.[120]

### Selden

John Selden (1584–1654) wrote a valuable epigraphical treatise.[121]

## HISTORY, ETHNOGRAPHY, AND ETHNOLOGY

In the field of European history, François Eudes de Mézeray (1610–83) wrote a chronology of the kings of France which included headings on "Manners and Customs" and "Church," under which he considered all aspects of culture.[122]

The *Memoires*[123] of Jacques de Saulx, Comte de Tavannes (1620–83) was in the genetic tradition of Comines.

Some antiquaries were interested in the history of the customs of their own culture; John Aubrey (1626–97) investigated the surviavls of paganism in his *Remaines of Gentilisme and Judaisme* (1686–87).[124] John Selden (1584–1654) wrote erudite treatises on European,[125] Hebrew,[126] and Syrian[127] antiquities. Much work was done during this period on the Greek and Roman cultures.[128]

A great deal of exploration took place in the seventeenth century;[129] Samuel Purchas' (1575–1626) *Purchas His Pilgrimes* (1625)[130] is a contemporary collection of reports on some of these discoveries. Joannes de Laet (1593–1649) compiled a series of books on various countries for the Elzevir publishing house from 1624 to 1630; some of the more interesting are the *Nieuwe Wereldt*[131] and *De imperio magni mogolis*.[132] In 1673 appeared the first ethnographic monograph in western Europe, *Lapponia*[133] by Johannes Scheffer (1621–79).

Cosmographies which were primarily ethnographic in character are to be found during this period, such as those by Philill Clüver (1580–1622)[134] and Peter Heylyn (1599–1662).[135] Pierre d'Avity (1573–1635) gave some idea of the procedures developed in these works.

. . . the Science or Knowledge of the world . . . is gotten by the conversation of many, by divers discourses and reports, either by word or writing, by the managing of affaires, conference with straungers, voyages into divers places, the knowledge of divers humors, and in a word, by the judicious consideration of the manners and life of one and other . . . a good part of this knowledge is comprehended in the discourse of this Booke, where you may see all sorts of persons and nations lively and naturally described, and represented with their manners and customes, as curiously as might be.[136]

To many contemporary scholars the crucial instance in deciding between monogenesis and polygenesis was the American Indian, and the adherents of the biblical account attempted to prove that New World man had migrated from the Old World, while their opponents tried to prove the opposite contention. Others were struck by a similarity of customs and then attempted to trace their diffusion from a common center.

## Brerewood

Edward Brerwood (1565?–1613) argued that the American Indian had probably migrated to the New World from Siberia by way of Alaska.

. . . what if the innumerable people of so many Nations, as are knowne to inhabite & overspread the huge continent of *America,* be also of the same [i.e., Tartar] off spring? Certainely, if I be not greatly deceived, they are no other. For first that their originall must be derived from *Asia* is apparent, because, (as he that readeth the relations and histories of those Countries of *America* may easily observe) they have no rellish nor resemblance at all, of the Artes, or learning or civility of *Europe*: And their colour testifieth, they are not of the *Africans* progeny (there being not found in all that large continent, any blacke men, except a few about the River of S. *Martha,* in a small Countrey called *Quarequa:* which by force and violence of some tempest, are supposed to have beene transported thither, from the parts of *Guiny* or *Aethipia.*) Therefore it seemeth, that they had their originall from *Asia.* Which yet, will appeare more credible, if it be observed, which by the *Spaniards* discoveries is well known to be true, namely, that the West side of *America* respecting *Asia,* is exceeding much better peopled than the opposite or East side, that respecteth toward *Europe.* And, as for these reasons it is very likely, that *America* received her first inhabitants, from the East border of *Asia:* So is it altogether unlike, that it received them from any other part of all that border, save from *Tartary.* Because in *America* there is not to be discerned, any token or indication at all, of the arts or industry of *China,* or *India,* or *Cataia,* or any other civill region, along all that border of *Asia.* But in their grosse ignorance of letters, and of arts, in their idolatry, and the specialties of it, in their incivility, and many barbarous properties,[137] they resemble the old and rude *Tartars,* above all the Nations of the earth. Which opinion of mine touching the *Americans* descending from the *Tartars,* rather than from any others Nation in that border of *Asia,* after the neere vicinity of *Asia* to *America,* this reason above all other, may best establish and perswade: because it is certaine, that the Northeast part of *Asia* possessed by the *Tartars,* is if not continent with the West side of *America,* which yet remayneth somewhat doubtfull: yet certainely, and without all doubt, it is the least disjoyned by sea, of all that coast of Asia.[138]

## Purchas

Samuel Purchas (1577?–1626) had a simple solution to the problem of the diversity of cultures.

Confusion [i.e., at the Tower of Babel] caused division of Nations, Regions and Religions.[139]

## Grotius

Hugo Grotius (1538–1645) had a rather farfetched theory of migration, though he used the methodological criteria for determining between diffusion and independent invention.

I am of the opinion that almost all those tribes who are on this side the Isthmus of Panama are of Norse descent, being led to it by the following considerations. That Iceland was inhabited by Norsemen, the monuments of both peoples, their traditions, language, and the most ancient rule of Norway over the Icelanders clearly show. Now many are believed to have migrated there before the year 1000, when the religion of Norway was still heathen. From Iceland they went into Greenland, which some consider an island, others a part of the continent of America. There, likewise, the language is the same; formerly the government was the same. Frisland is near to it, on which the commentary of the Zenos of Venice exists, unless, perhaps, it is a part of either Iceland or Greenland. Next to this is Estotiland, a part of the American continent, to which fishermen from Frisland resorted two centuries before the Spaniard came into the New World. All these words have the same ending, the sound denoting the country in the language of the Germans, of whom the Norsemen were formerly a part, as appears from Pliny, Tacitus, nay, from the language itself and from their manners. So, also, the lands which stretch from this point to the Isthmus of Panama have names similar in sound, Cimatlan, Coatlan, Guecoslan, [etc.] . . . , in all which words the pronunciation of the Spaniards has dropped the last letter. The Mexicans and their neighbours, as soon as the Spaniards came there, said that they were not natives, but that their ancestors had come from the north. The district in which they first settled after Estotilandia now, likewise, retains the name of its origin, for it is called Norimbega, which is nothing else than Norway, it being softened in sound by the Spaniards, who are accustomed to place B for W. And towards California there is a people possessed of the same language and customs with that of Mexico, and there is the people of Alavardus, that is Langobardus. The Spaniards call it New Mexico, when in truth it is Old Mexico, from whence they came into the other, as they say, 800 years before. Words are added, many of which were German, that is, Norwegian, but there are a few which in their course have come to our knowledge. Teut, the god of Germany, is the same also among those nations, Ba-god, the lesser, an imaginary god; Guaira, Waiert, the lash; Top-hos, the covering of the head; Lame, Lam, the lamb. Places situated besides streams end in Peke, for Beke, which is stream among the Germans. Whoever has a mind to inquire into these things will discover more resemblances. Their customs likewise afford no slight mark of their origin. Their judges are twelve in number, as there were formerly among the Goths and other nations of Sandinavia; and their neighbours, the Saxons, whence the number was introduced into England. They spent their life in hunting, as the Mexicans used to say of their ancestors. The reckoning of time by nights, the washing of newly-born infants in running water, their belief in dice, even to the loss of liberty— all these you will learn from Tacitus and the German writers, were customs of Germany. A man was permitted to have only one wife, with the exception of a few of the nobles, an ordinance which the same Tacitus attributes to the Germans, so that this mark distinguishes them from the other barbarians. . . . Marriage is permissible to their women, as to the Germans, only once. Posts in Florida have been set up for the ascertainment of the maximum heat, such as Pliny informs us the Cauchi had. From time immemorial they believed that the soul survived the body, a doctrine which Lucan despises as Arctic. Criminals were severely punished in their persons. You have the same practice also alluded to by Tacitus respecting the Germans. . . . There was a chair and a table for every individual by the hearth; sons were the heirs of sisters, their bodies were almost naked, unless where modesty forbids it, and there were other customs similar to those which Tacitus has described regarding the Germans. Now, these having been found in the places of which we are treating, indicate, it is clear, a German . . . origin. Even to sacrificing men to the Gods is a German custom, upon which as the savageness became more developed, there supervened the practice of feeding upon human flesh. Now, in what I have just said as to these tribes on this side the Isthmus of Panama being almost all of Norwegian origin, I have not spoken in vain.[140]

In the same way he traced the Yucatecans from Ethiopia,[141] the Peruvians from China,[142] and the rest of the inhabitants of Latin America from Melanesia.[143]

## Hale

In his advocacy of monogenesis, Matthew Hale (1609–76) was faced with the problem of the American Indian.

The late Discovery of the vast Continent of *America* and Islands adjacent, which appears to be as populous with Men, and as well stored with Cattel almost as any part of *Europe, Asia,* or *Africa,* hath occasioned some difficulty and dispute touching the Traduction of all Mankind from the two common Parents supposed of all Mankind, namely *Adam* and *Eve.*[144]

Touching the Traduction of Mankind into *America,* I do suppose these things following:
1. That the Origination of the common Parents of the Humane Nature hapned in some part of *Asia.*
2. That though the Origination of the common Parents of Mankind were in *Asia,* yet some of their Descendents did come into *America.*
3. That such Migration into *America* by the Descendents from *Adam,* was not only possibly, but fairly probable, notwithstanding all the objected Difficulties.
4. That the Migrations of the Descendents of *Adam* and *Noah* into *America,* was successive, and interpolated.
5. That although we cannot certainly define the Time or Manner of all these Migrations, yet many of them were long since, or, as we may reasonably conjecture, some Thousands of Years since; but yet after the Universal Deluge.
The Means of Transmigration of the Children or Descendents of *Adam* and *Noah* from *Asia* into *America* must be either by Land or by Sea, or by both; and if by Sea, then it must be designed, and *ex proposito,* or casually.
I think it probable it may be all of these ways, but especially by Sea.[145]

And it is not yet certainly discovered, though conjectured, that there is any Neck of Ground, or passage by Land from any part of *Europe* or *Asia* into any part of the Continent of *America.*

There remains therefore nothing that I can reasonably conjecture to accommodate the difficulty, but to suppose what I have formerly intimated; That although it should be granted that there is now no such Land-passage extant, yet within the compass of 4000 Years elapsed since the Flood there have been some such Junctures of Land-passages between the Northern parts of *Asia* or *Europe,* and some Northern parts of the Continent of *America,* or between the South-east parts of *China* or the *Philippine* Islands, and the Southern Continent (though lately there be discovered an interposition of Sea between the Island *del Fuogo* and that Southern Continent) whereby either from *Asia* to *Groenland* in the North, or from *China* to *Terra australis incognita* on the South a Land-passage might be from *Asia* to *America* for Men and Brutes, though for some Ages past either by the violence of the Water, or by Floods or Earthquakes, which hath made great alterations in the Globe of the Earth and Seas, that Bridge or Line of Communication be now broken and obliterated. And truly he that observes the infinite company of Islands lying between the Continent of *China* and *Nova Guinea,* almost contiguous to each other, hath probable reason to believe that these were all formerly one Continent joyning *China* and *Nova Guinea* together, though now by the irruption of the Sea crumbled into many small Islands.[146]

. . . it may seem reasonable to conclude, 1. That the *Americans* had their Original from the Inhabitants of *Europe, Asia* and *Africa,* that transmigrated into that Continent either intentionally, or casually, or both. 2. That those Migrations were not of any one single Nation or People, but from many or divers Nations. 3. That these Migrations were not altogether, or at one time, but successively in several Ages; some earlier, some later. 4. That therefore it is impossible to determin the Time or first *Epocha* of such Migrations, but only that they were all since the Universal Deluge, which is now above 4000 Years since. . . . 5. That if we should admit that the first Migration thither were above 2000 Years since, of an hundred Pairs they might easily propagate a number competent enough to people all that vast Continent. 6. That it seems that since the last of these ancient Migrations, suppose that of *Madoc* and his *Britons,* until our late Migrations by the *Spaniards, French, English, Dutch* and *Scotch,* there probably interceded an interval of at least four or five hundred Years, in all which interval the Commerce and Communication between *Europe* or *Asia,* and *America,* hath as it were slept, and been forgotten both by them and us. 7. That in that interval of 500 Years or thereabouts in all Parts, but in some Parts far greater, there must in all probability happen a great forgetfulness of their Original, a great degeneration from the Primtive Civility, Religion and Customs of those places from whence they were first derived; a ferine and necessitous kind of Life, a conversation with those that having been long there were faln into a more barbarous habit of Life and Manners, would easily assimilate at least the next Generation to Barbarism and Ferineness.[147]

## Hooke

Robert Hooke (1635–1703) neatly posed the problem of the origin of the American Indian from an ethnological point of view, in a discussion on the wheel,

An Invention of so great Use, that it seems impossible ever to be lost by Mankind, after it be once known: Which Consideration makes me very much wonder whence those Men came, that inhabited *America,* before the *Spaniards* overrunning and conquering of it; since it seems probable, that if they, or their Ancestors, had sprung from any People here, on this Side of the World, *viz.* from *Europe, Asia* or *Africa,* they must needs have carried along with them the useful Invention of the *Wheel*; but it has been observed, that they knew nothing at all concerning it, nor any the least Use of it, throughout all *America,* before the *Europeans* came among them. So that we must conclude, either that they were made Inhabitants before the Invention of the Wheels was found, or that they never had any Origination from any Generation of Men in those Parts of the World, at least not from the *Tartars,* who, of all People, do most frequently use them.[148]

## Rycaut

Paul Rycaut (1628–1700) expressed a point of view similar to that of Brerewood.

Various have been the opinions amongst Historians concerning the Original of this People; of which the most probable, as I conceive, is, that they proceeded from the Race of the Northern Tartar, whom they resemble in the shape and air of their features, and in their barbarous way of living; but then we must fansie, as some Geographers do, that the West side of *America* is Continent with *Tartary,* or at least disjoyned from thence by some narrow strait; of which I am well persuaded we have no certain Knowledge.[149]

## Temple

To William Temple (1628–99), all civilization had diffused from India.

From these famous Indians, it seems to be most probable, that Pythagoras learned and transported into Greece and Italy the greatest part of his natural and moral philosophy, rather than from the Egyptians, as is commonly supposed; for I have not observed any mention of the transmigration of souls, held among the Egyptians, more ancient than the time of Pythagoras. . . .

Nor does it seem unlikely that the Egyptians themselves might have drawn much of their learning from the Indians; for they are observed, in some authors, to have done it from the Aethiopians; and chronologers, I think, agree, that these were a colony that came anciently from the river Indus, and planted themselves upon that part of Africa, which from the name was afterwards called Aethiopia, and in all probability brought their learning and their customs with them. The Phoenicians are likewise said to have been anciently a colony that came from the Red Sea, and planted themselves upon the Mediterranean; and from thence spread so far the fame of their learning and their navigations.

To strengthen this conjecture, of much learning being derived from such remote and ancient fountains as the Indies, and perhaps China; it may be asserted with great evidence, that though we know little of the antiquities of India, beyond Alexander's time, yet those of China are the oldest that any where pretend to any fair records; for these are agreed, by the missionary Jesuits, to extend . . . far above four thousand years.[150]

For my own part, I am much inclined to believe that, in these remote regions, not only Pythagoras learned the first principles, both of his natural and moral philosophy; but that those of Democritus (who travelled into Egypt, Chaldea, and India, and whose doctrines were improved by Epicurus) might have been derived from the same fountain; and that, long before them both, Lycurgus, who likewise travelled into India, brought from thence also the chief principles of his laws and politics, so much renowned in the world.

For whoever observes the account already given of the ancient Indian and Chinese learning and opinions,[151] will easily find among them the seeds of all these Grecian productions and institutions: as the transmigration of souls, and the four cardinal virtues; the long silence enjoined his scholars, and propagation of their doctrines by tradition, rather than letters, and the abstinence from all meats that had animal life, introduced by Pythagoras: the eternity of matter, with perpetual changes of form, the indolence of body, and tranquillity of mind, by Epicurus: and among those of Lycurgus, the care of education from the birth of children, the austere temperance of diet, the patient endurance of toil and pain, the neglect or contempt of life, the use of gold and silver only in their temples, the defence of commerce with strangers, and several others by him established among the Spartans, seem all to be wholly Indian, and different from any race or vein of thought or imagination, that have ever appeared in Greece, either in that age, or any since.[152]

## Hobbes

Thomas Hobbes (1588–1679), on the other hand, considered Greece to have been the center of diffusion.

The Graecians, by their Colonies and Conquests, communicated their Language and Writings into Asia, Egypt, and Italy; and therein, by necessary consequence their *Daemonology* . . . : And by that meanes, the contagion was derived also to the Jewes, both of *Judaea,* and *Alexandria,* and other parts, whereinto they were dispersed.[153]

## LINGUISTICS

### Scaliger

Joseph Juste Scaliger (1540–1609) classified the European languages.[154] He divided them into eleven unrelated "mother tongues," of which four are relatively important, and seven unimportant. The former were classified on the basis of their word for "god" into Latin (*deus*), Greek (*theos*), Teutonic (*godt*), and Slavonic (*boge*). The seven minor mother tongues are Epirotic, Tartaric, Hungarian, Finnish, Irish, Britannic, and Basque.

### Brerewood

Edward Brerewood (1565?–1613) modified Scaliger's classification.

. . . there are at this day, fourteene mother tongues in *Europe* (beside the *Latine*) . . . And those are the 1 *Irish,* spoken in *Ireland,* & a good part of *Scotland:* the 2 *Brittish* in *Wales, Cornewaile,* and *Brittaine* in *France:* the 3 *Cantabrian* neere the Ocean, about the *Pyrene* hils, both in *France,* and *Spaine:* the 4 *Arabique,* in the steepy mountaines of *Granata,* named *Alpuxarras:* the 5 *Finnique,* in *Finland,* and *Lapland:* the 6 *Dutch,* in *Germany, Belgia, Denmarke, Norwey,* and *Suedia:* the old 7 *Cauchian,* (I take it to be that, for in that part the *Cauchi* inhabited) in East *Frisland,* for although to strangers they speake *Dutch,* yet among themselves they use a peculiar language of their owne: the 8 *Slavonish,* in *Polonia, Bohemia, Moscovia, Russia,* and many other regions, . . . although with notable difference of dialect, as also the *British, Dutch,* in countries mentioned have: the old 9 *Illyrian,* in the Ile of *Veggia,* on the East side of *Istria* in the bay of *Liburnia:* the 10 *Greeke,* in *Greece,* and the Ilands about it, and parts of *Macedon,* and of *Thrace:* the old 11 *Epirotique* in the mountaine of *Epirus:* the 12 *Hungarian* in the greatest part of that Kingdome: the 13 *Iazygian* in the North side of *Hungaria* betwixt *Danubius,* & *Tibiscus,* utterly differing from the *Hungarian* language: And lastly, the 14 *Tartarian,* of the *Precopenses,* betweene the river of *Tanais,* and *Borysthenes,* neere *Maeotis,* & the *Euxine* sea, for, of the *English, Italian, Spanish,* and *French,* as being derivations, or rather degenerations, the first of the *Dutch,* and the other three of the *Latine,* seeing I now speake onely of originall or mother languages, I must be silent.[155]

He also made some mention of the North African languages.

. . . the *Punique* tongue seemeth to me out of question, to have bin the *Canaanitish* or old *Hebrew* language.[156]

. . . the language of the *Canaanites,* was eyther the very same or exceedingly neere the *Hebrew.* And certainly touching the difference that was betweene the *Hebrew* and the *Punique,* I make not doubt but the great distance from their primitive habitation, and their conversation with strangers, among whom they were planted, and together with both, the length of time which is wont to bring alteration to all the languages in the world were the causes of it.[157]

### Saumaise

Claude de Saumaise (1588–1653?) showed that a relationship exists between Latin, "Teutonic," Greek, and Persian[158]; his most striking arguments were based on the names of numerals[159] and kinship terms.[160]

## Petty

William Petty (1623–87) was particularly interested in the languages of Great Britain.

The Language of *Ireland* is like that of the *North* of *Scotland,* in many things like the *Welch* and *Manques;* but in *Ireland* the *Fingallians* speak neither *English, Irish,* nor *Welch;* and the People about *Wexford,* tho they agree in a Language differing from *English, Welch,* and *Irish,* yet 'tis not the same with that of the *Fingalians* near *Dublin.* . . .

The *Irish* Language, and the *Welch,* as also all Languages that have not been the Languages of flourishing Empires, wherein were many Things, many Notions and Fancies, both Poetical and Philosophical, hath but few words;* and all the names of Artificial things brought into use, since the Empire of these Linguists ceased, are now expressed in the language of their Conquerors, by altering the Termination and Accents only.[162]

## Digby and White

Discussing the confusion of tongues after the destruction of the Tower of Babel, Kenelm Digby (1603–65) and Thomas White (1593–1676) were led to an analysis of the factors that produce linguistic change.

But hence, perhaps, some may ground their belief, that 'Tis not easie to imagine whence *Languages* should have been *divided* amongst mankind, and have grown into so many kinds. To which we reply, that, whoever shall but observe what is usuall in his own City or Countrey, will easily discern how so great a variety of Dialects has grown into the world. For, 'tis evident, the perfection of a Language consists among the Betterbred; and the *rude People* corrupt the lesse usuall words, those that speak *fast* cut them short, the *Countrey folks* likewise make a speciall pronunciation of their own. Adde to these, that divers Cities and Provinces have form'd Dialects of their own; which yet, ther's no doubt, are contain'd all under one Idiome.

Consider, then, the minglings of distinct languages; a Country sometimes being subdu'd by a Nation of a different Idiome; sometimes, by the frequent Travels of single persons, the words of one Idiome being deriv'd to another.

Lastly, let's reflect on the originall *root* of *diversity:* Which consists in this, That, words are compos'd of *Vowels* and *Consonants;* and the differences of *Vowels* rise from a wider or a more form'd and regular opening both of the Mouth and Throat; but, that of *Consonants* proceeds from an interception of the Breath going out through the diverse organs of the Teeth, Lips, Tongue; from its allision to them and the Palate of the mouth; with some help of the Nostrills and the shutting up of the Throat.

Now, 'tis evident, these members and instruments of *Voice* are compos'd of the *Elements;* and consequently, from their temperament, are more dispos'd to one motion then to another; and, which follows, that, from the *Site* of the Regions where men live, they are more inclin'd to some *Vowels* or *Consonants* then to others: whence it comes to passe, that, without any farther pains, *Vowels* and *Consonants* are chang'd by little and little, and ther's such a diversity made, that they can no longer understand one another.

And, that the difference of *Idioms* grew after this manner, from the very beginning; it may be conjectur'd, because the *Chaldaick, Syriack, Arabick* Tongues discover a manifest derivation from and affinity with the *Hebrew.* And, that the *Aegyptian,* too, of old sprung from it, seems . . . conjecturable . . . .

* " . . . the languages of the most flourishing Empires was ever the most copious and elegant, and that of mountainous Cantons the contrary."[161]

To conclude, it seems naturall to the Originall Tongue to be very short, *viz.* if *Mono-syllables* only, as much as concerns the *primitive* words: and the primitive words, of necessity, are of a determinate number, since, we scarce find more than seven first-Consonants; for the rest are varied either in a greater or lesse *aspiration,* or by the *composition* of more together; whence, 'twould be no hard thing to find the number of all the *primitive* words: wherefore, 'tis clear, there cannot be many originall Idioms, whose primitive words should be Monosyllables.[163]

### Wilkins

To an orthodox person like John Wilkins (1614–72), all such considerations were wasted effort.

There is scarce any subject that hath been more thoroughly scanned and debated amongst Learned men, than the *Original* of *Languages* and *Letters.* . . . But to us, who have the revelation of Scripture . . . 'tis evident enough that the first Language was *con-created* with our first Parents, they immediately understanding the voice of God speaking to them in the Garden. And how Languages came to be *multiplyed,* is likewise manifested in the Story of the *Confusion of Babel.*[164]

### Junius, Hickes, etc.

Nevertheless, a number of scholars approached particular languages from an empirical point of view. Franciscus Junius (1589–1677) investigated the relations between the Germanic languages in his *Etymologicum anglicum*[165] and made a comparative study of the Gothic, Runic, and Anglo-Saxon alphabets.[166] George Hickes (1642–1715) was another who made the Germanic languages his specialty.[167]

An influential grammar of the time was that in the Port Royal series,[168] written by Antoine Arnauld (1612–94) and Claude Lancelot (1615?–95).

## SOCIAL ANTHROPOLOGY

### Descartes

The philosophy of René Descartes (1596–1650) was based upon cosmopolitan skepticism.

It is good to know something of the customs of different people in order to judge more sanely of our own, and not to think that everything of a fashion not ours is absurd and contrary to reason, as do those who have seen nothing.[169]

. . . in seeing many things which, although they seem to us very extravagant and ridiculous, were yet commonly received and approved by other great nations, I learned to believe nothing too certainly of which I had only been convinced by example and custom.[170]

I had been taught, even in my College days, that there is nothing imaginable so strange or so little credible that it has not been maintained by one philosopher or other, and I further recognised in the course of my travels that all those whose sentiments are very contrary to ours are yet not necessarily barbarians or savages, but may be possessed of reason in as great or even a greater degree than ourselves. I also considered how very different the self-same man, identical in mind and spirit, may become, according as he is brought up from childhood amongst the French or Germans, or has passed his whole life amongst Chinese or cannibals. I likewise noticed how even in the fashions of one's clothing the same thing that pleased us ten years ago, and which will perhaps please us once again before ten years are passed, seems at the present time extravagant and ridiculous. I thus concluded that it is much more custom and example that persuade us than any certain knowledge.[171]

Descartes's great contribution to the science of man was his application of the mechanistic philosophy to biological organisms. By considering all animals, including man, as machines,[172] he showed that cause and effect operate in man as in the rest of nature, and that therefore man can be subjected to scientific investigation.

Starting from the assumption that animals behaved simply as machines, he regarded every activity of the organism as a *necessary* reaction to some external stimulus, the connection between the stimulus and the response being made through a definite nervous path: and this connection, he stated, was the fundamental purpose of the nervous structure in the animal body. This was the basis on which the study of the nervous system was firmly established.[173]

To him, customs are developed in two ways, either slowly and unconsciously or by fiat.

. . . those people who were once half-savage, and who have become civilized only by slow degrees, merely forming their laws as the disagreeable necessities of their crimes and quarrels constrained them, could not succeed in establishing so good a system of government as those who, from the time they first came together as communities, carried into effect the constitution laid down by some prudent legislator.[174]

## Bossuet

However, it should not be assumed that the supernatural explanation of social phenomena was ignored. Jacques Bénigne Bossuet (1627–1704) was the foremost exponent of the theological interpretation of history in the seventeenth century.

. . . that long Chain of *particular* Causes, which make and unmake Empires, depend upon the secret Orders and Decrees of the *Divine* Providence. God, that sitteth in the highest Heavens, holds the Reins of all the Kingdoms.[175]

Thus it is that *God* reigneth over all People. Let us no longer talk of *Chance* or *Fortune,* or speak of it only as a Name wherewith we conceal our Ignorance. That, which is *Chance* in respect of our uncertain Councils, is a concerted Design in a higher Council.*[177]

. . . the Empires of the world have ministred to *Religion,* and the Preservation of the People of *God.*[178]

Thus have all the great Empires, which we have seen upon the Earth, concurred by several ways and means to the good of *Religion,* and the *glory of God,* as God himself hath declared by his Prophets.[179]

God hath also decreed that the course of human things should have its Issues and its Proportions; I mean, that Men and Nations have had Qualities commensurate to the Advancements to which they have been design'd; and that, excepting some certain extraordinary Strokes, wherein God hath been willing to manifest his *own* Hand in particular, there are no very great Changes happen, but what may deduce their Causes from precedent Ages.

And as, in all Affairs, there is that, which prepares them; that, which determines to undertake them; and, lastly, that, which makes them have success: So the true Science

* "[Thus] you will be the better able to refer things to the order of that *eternal Wisdom* on which they depend."[176]

of History is to observe, in every time, those secret Dispositions, which have prepar'd and made way for great Changes, and the important Conjunctures, which have brought them to pass.

Indeed it is not sufficient to look only just before one, that is to say, to consider those great Events, which all on a sudden do decide the Fortune of Empires. He, that would gain a deep and thorough Knowledge of human things, ought to take them at their first Head and Spring; and he must observe the Inclinations, and the Tempers; or, so to speak all in one word, the *Character,* as well of the People governing in general, as of the Princes in particular; or, if you please, of all the extraordinary Men, who by the Importance of the Part they have in the World, have contributed, either well or ill, to the change of States, and to the publick Fortune.[180]

## Barclay

John Barclay (1582–1621) was the first to make an extensive investigation of the ethos of cultures.

. . . there is no diversity, which is more worthy of wonder, then this, that men borne to liberty . . . should also serve; their owne dispositions, the fate of the times, wherein they live, forcing them, as it were, into certaine affections, and rules of living. For every age of the world has a certaine Genius, which over-ruleth the mindes of men, and turneth them to some desires. Some ages breath nothing but martiall discipline; and within few yeares, all are againe composed to peace and quietnesse; Sometimes Common-wealths, and sometimes Monarchies are affected by the people, Some Nations, that seemed (as it were) to be borne to barbarisme, in processe of time, are brought to perfect civility: and in some few ages, are perverted againe to their old barbarisme. So the world in generall, did oft flourish with great abilities, and after a while, industry slackening, hath beene covered (as it were) with a cloud, and lost.[181]

. . . the changeable Geniuses of the ages . . . proceeded . . . from a certaine force, which I may almost call Fate, swaying the hearts of men to those ends that are ordayned for them.[182]

[After discussing the advances of the Renaissance, he continues:] Nor can this change proceede from any thing but the Genuis, as it were, of this age. Whose excellency, when after an approynted time it shall expire, will give up the world, as it may be feared, unto another, and ruder Genius; and after the expiration of certaine yeares, returne againe.[183]

So that we may distinguish the difference of the ages, not more perfectly by the motions of the starres, then by the deflexion of mankinde into divers dispositions, and abilities.[184]

But there is another force, that ravisheth away the mindes of men, and maketh them addicted to certaine affections. Namely, that spirit which being appropriate to every region, infuseth into men, as soone as they are borne, the habit, and affections of their owne country. For, as the same meats according to the various manners of dressing, may be changed in tast, but the inward quality of nourishing or hurting, can by no qualification be altogether lost: so in every Nation, among all the tides of succeeding ages, which alter the manners and mindes of men, one certaine quality remaines never to be shaken off; which the Fates have distributed to every man, according to the condition of the place wherein hee was borne. From thence come those ancient vices, which still endure, as proper to the climate, which in histories have commended or branded whole Nations: as here, the poeple are naturally light, unconstant, & wavering in their resolutions:

there, the grosser and graver mindes are naturally swelled with a melancholy pride, under the shew of hidden wisdome.[185]

[He seemed to think that "Genius" was the result of innate racial differences as well as those of geography, for in the New World] naked barbarisme, abhorred by mankinde, is used by the wild people, whom no lawes nor industry has tempered. . . . The Natures of those rude people are incapable of our civility.[186]

[He then proceeds] to examine the inhabitants and Genius of our owne worlde; the habit of each countrey, the condition of the soyle, the temper of the ayre, or distemper in either kinde.[187]

[Analyses are given of France; Great Britain; Germany and Belgium; Italy; Spain; Hungary, Poland, Russia, and Scandinavia; Turkey and Judaism.[188]]

[The Jews] have every where mixed their manners, and to their owne disposition (in which with greatest obstinacy they continue) they adde the Genuis of the place where they are borne.[189]

Nature hath granted, beside the Genius of their native Countrey, something proper to every man.[190]

[Then follows a classification of "humane dispositions."[191]]

But it is not enough to finds out this diversity of humane mindes, as nature onely hath stamped it. There is another thing besides, that may either perfect or change a disposition: namely, their estate of life.[192]

There are not onely in Courts, but in all kinds of life, different dispositions of rich and poore men.[193]

## Campanella

Tommaso Campanella (1568–1639) wrote in the tradition of More and, like him, gave a social explanation of cultural phenomena in *The City of the Sun* (1623).

They say that all private property is acquired and improved for the reason that each one of us by himself has his own home and wife and children. From this self-love springs. For when we raise a son to riches and dignities, and leave an heir to much wealth, we become either ready to grasp at the property of the state, if in any case fear should be removed from the power which belongs to riches and rank: or avaricious, crafty, and hypocritical, if anyone is of slender purse, little strength, and mean ancestry. But when we have taken away self-love, there remains only love for the state.[194]

And they consider him the more noble and renowned who has dedicated himself to the study of the most arts and knows how to practice them wisely. Wherefore they laugh at us in that we consider our workmen ignoble, and hold those to be noble who have mastered no pursuit; but live in ease, and are so many slaves given over to their own pleasure and lasciviousness; and thus as it were from a school of vices so many idle and wicked fellows go forth for the ruin of the state.[195]

In Naples there exist seventy thousand souls, and out of these scarcely ten or fifteen thousand do any work, and they are always lean from overwork and are getting weaker every day. The rest become a prey to idleness, avarice, ill-health, lasciviousness, usury, and other vices, and contaminate and corrupt very many families by holding them in servitude for their own use, by keeping them in poverty and slavishness, and by imparting to them their own vices. . . .moreover, . . . grinding poverty renders men worthless, cunning, sulky, thievish, insidious, vagabonds, liars, false witnesses, etc.; and . . .

wealth makes them insolent, proud, ignorant, traitors, assumers of what they know not, deceivers, boasters, wanting in affection, slanderers, etc.[196]

In one place he anticipated the eugenecists.

[In the City of the Sun] men and women are so joined together, that they bring forth the best offspring. Indeed, they laugh at us who exhibit a studious care for our breed of horses and dogs, but neglect the breeding of human beings.[197]

## La Peyrère

Isaac de La Peyrère (1594–1676) had a theory of the evolution of religion and magic.

The Priests and Philosophers amongst the Gentiles, who knew not God the Father, and the Creator, observ'd several Spirits and Gods, whom they determined governours of several ranks and degrees, and whom they plac'd either in the heaven, or in the stars, or in the fire, or in the air, or in the water, or in the earth, or under the earth, and whose shapes they did not deny might be called up by several wayes of sacrifice and inchantment; For certainly they considered a certain affinitie, and fellow-suffering of those Spirits with all things created, on whom, by their sympathie and similitude they had an influence. They thought that all animals and vegetables, from trees, to metals and stones, were mov'd and led by those Spirits. . . .

Who will wonder then, that men being left by God, after their creation, in their own power, and turn'd over to so many Spirits, Gods, and Lords, who set them a work, did appoint and worship so many several sorts of Gods, under so many divers shapes of things created.[198]

Besides, the Theologie of the Gentiles begot their Magick; and those which were the Priests of their Gods, were also their Magicians. The Antients thought there were hidden vertues in all things terrestrial, either by a divine ray, or a vertue so disposing them, or infus'd by intelligences, by way of mediate, or impress'd in them in the creation by primitive copies. . . . Therefore with such efficacious things they were thought to work wonders. . . . For, as the vertue operative from things occult produced things manifest, so these Magicians, by the help of things manifest, seem'd to produce hidden effects by the influxions of stars, and things natural sympathizing with the celestial. And imagin'd, that the celestial influxions, mix'd with the power of things natural, produc'd effects admirable here on earth, though the causes of them were in heaven.

Hence it is that they relate that the shapes of stars and gods have by enchantments been call'd down, and the Gods themselves forc'd by their charms, by sacrifice, consecrations, incense, invocations, and imprecations.[199]

From those inchantments all witchcrafts and Philtres took their beginnings, by which men were either bewitched to love or hatred, or made well or ill. To this adde the impressions either of good or bad vertues, in those Images, which they call *Talismanical,* by characters, adjuration, lights, sounds, numbers, words, and names. For they thought that Nature express'd hidden effects in like shapes, as it were by sympathie, and that the Gods express'd the truth of Ideas by manifest Images.[200]

## Burnet

To orthodox scholars there was no such thing as cultural evolution, but merely the social differences that existed before and after the fall of man. Historical reconstruction was then used by them to determine the sort of culture man had when he was in the Garden of Eden, and, after the expulsion, how that culture degenerated to its present state. A good example of this approach is given by Thomas Burnet (1635?–1715).

The World hath not stood so long but we can still run it up to those artless Ages, when Mortals lived by plain Nature; when there was but one Trade in the World, one Calling, to look to their Flocks; and afterwards to till the Ground, when Nature grew less liberal.[201]

[The methodological criterion used in reconstruction was the usual evolutionary one of development from the simple to the complex.] 'Tis natural to the Mind of Man to consider that which is compound, as having been once more simple.[202]

. . . we should now take a Prospect of the moral World of that Time, or of the civil and artificial World.[203]

Trades . . . were in a Manner needless, or at least in such Plainness and Simplicity, that every Man might be his own Workman. Tents and Bowers would keep them from all Incommodities of the Air and Weather. . . . They had little need of merchandizing then, Nature supply'd them at Home with all Necessaries, which were few, and they were not so greedy of Superfluities as we are. . . . Men were not carnivorous in those Ages of the World, or did not feed upon Flesh, but only upon Fruits and Herbs. . . . And of this natural diet they would be provided to their Hands, without further Preparation, as the Birds and Beasts are.[204]

This is a short and general Scheme of the primaeval World, compared with the modern; yet these Things did not equally run thro' all the Parts and Ages of it; there was a Declension and Degeneracy, both natural and moral, by Degrees, and especially towards the latter End; but the principal Form of Nature remaining till the Deluge and the Dissolution of the Heavens and Earth, till then also this civil Frame of Things would stand in a great Measure.[205]

## Hale

Matthew Hale (1609–76) investigated the growth of population.

I shall now search out what may be those Correctives, that may be applicable to the Reduction of the Generations of Mankind to an Equability, or at least to keep it within such bounds as may keep it from surcharging the World; whereby if in the Period of 2, or 3, or 4000 Years it may grow too luxuriant, yet it may in probability be so far abated, as may allow it an Increase of the like number of Years to attain its former proportion. So that by these Prunings there may be a consistency of the Numbers of Mankind, with an eternal succession of Individuals.

Those Reductions that may be supposed effectual for these Ends, and such as the course of Mankind seem to have had great Experiences of, are 1. Plagues and Epidemical Diseases: 2. Famines: 3. Wars and Internecions: 4. Floods and Inundations: 5. Conflagration.[206]

## Temple

William Temple (1628–99) believed in the psychic unity of mankind and explained variations geographically and culturally. In the following passages a geographic interpretation predominates.

The nature of man seems to be the same in all times and places, but varied, like their statures, complexions, and features, by the force and influence of the several climates where they are born and bred; which produce in them, by a different mixture of the humours, and operations of the air, a different and unequal course of imaginations and passions, and consequently of discourses and actions.

These differences incline men to several customs, educations, opinions, and laws, which form and govern the several nations of the world, where they are not interrupted by the violence of some force from without, or some faction within, which, like a great blow, or a great disease, may either change or destroy the very frame of a body; though, if it lives to recover strength and vigour, it commonly returns in time to its natural constitution, or something near it.

(I speak not of those changes and revolutions of State, or institutions of government, that are made by the more immediate and evident operation of divine will and providence; being the themes of divines, and not of common men; and the subjects of our faith, not of reason.)

This may be the cause that the same countries have generally in all times been used to forms of government much of a sort; the same nature ever continuing under the same climate, and making returns into its old channel, though sometimes led out of it by persuasions, and sometimes beaten out by force.

Thus the more northern and southern nations (extremes, as they say, still agreeing) have ever lived under single and arbitrary dominions; as all the regions of Tartary and Muscovy on the one side, and of Afric and India on the other: while those under the more temperate climates, especially in Europe, have ever been used to more moderate governments, running anciently much into commonwealths, and of later ages into principalities bounded by laws which differ less in nature than in name.[207]

It may be said further, that, in the more intemperate climates, the spirits, either exhaled by heat, or compressed by cold, are rendered faint and sluggish; and by that reason the men grow tamer, and fitter for servitude. That, in more temperate regions, the spirits are stronger, and more active, whereby men become bolder in the defence or recovery of their liberties.[208]

He also had a geographic interpretation for cultural phenomena.

In countries safe from foreign invasions either by seas or rivers, by mountains and passes, or great tracts of rough, barren, and uninhabited lands, people lived generally in scattered dwellings, or small villages: but, where invasion is easy, and passage open, and bordering nations are great and valiant; men crowd together, and seek their safety from numbers better united, and from walls and other fortifications, the use whereof is to make the few a match for the many, so as they may fight or treat on equal terms. And this is the original of cities; but the greatness and riches of them increase according to the commodiousness of their situation, in fertile countries, or upon rivers and havens, surpass the greatest fertility of any soil, in furnishing plenty of all things necessary to life or luxury.[209]

However, he often gave a social explanation of cultural and psychological differences.

. . . all manners are [learned], by the conversation we use.[210]

Since the ground of trade cannot be deduced from havens, or native commodities (as may well be concluded from the survey of Holland, which has the least and the worst; and of Ireland, which has the most and the best, of both) it were not amiss to consider, from what other source it may be more naturally and certainly derived: for, if we talk of industry, we are still as much to seek, what it is that makes people industrious in one country, and idle in another. I conceive the true original and ground of trade to be, great multitude of people crowded into small compass of land, whereby all things

necessary to life become dear, and all men, who have possessions, are induced to parsimony; but those, who have none, are forced to industry and labour, or else to want.
Bodies, that are vigorous, fall to labour; such, as are not, supply that defect by some sort
of inventions or ingenuity. These customs arise first from necessity, but increase by
imitation, and grow in time to be habitual in a country; and wherever they are so, if it
lies upon the sea, they naturally break out into trade, both because whatever they want
of their own, that is necessary to so many men's lives, must be supplied from abroad;
and because, by the multitude of people, and smallness of country, land grows so dear,
that the improvement of money that way is inconsiderable, and so turns to sea, where
the greatness of the profit makes amends for the venture.

This cannot be better illustrated, than by its contrary, which appears no where more
than in Ireland; were, by the largeness and plenty of the food, and a scarcity of people,
all things necessary to life are so cheap, that an industrious man, by two days labour, may
gain enough to feed him the rest of the week; which I take to be a very plain ground of
the laziness attributed to the people: for men naturally prefer ease before labour, and will
not take pains, if they can live idle: though when, by necessaity, they have been inured
to it, they cannot leave it, being grown a custom necessary to their health, and to their
very entertainment: nor perhaps is the change harder, from constant ease to labour, than
from constant labour to ease.[211]

[Previously he had spoken of] wit being sharpened by commerce and conversation
of the cities.[212]

In one passage he hinted at a "great man" theory of history.

But after all, I do not know whether the high flights of wit and knowledge, like those
of power and of empire in the world, may not have been made by the pure native force
of spirit or genius, in some single men, rather than by any derived strength among them,
however increased by succession; and whether they may not have been the atchievements
of nature, rather than the improvements of art.[213]

Temple developed a cyclical theory of cultural dynamics, as did Vico a century
later.

. . . knowledge and ignorance, as well as civility and barbarism, may succeed each
other in the several countries of the world.[214]

Science and arts have run their circles, and had their periods in the several parts of the
world: they are generally agreed to have held their course from East to West, to have
begun in Chaldea and Egypt, to have been transplanted from thence to Greece, from
Greece to Rome; to have sunk there, and, after many ages, to have revived from those
ashes, and to have sprung up again both in Italy and other more western provinces of
Europe. When Chaldea and Egypt were learned and civil, Greece and Rome were as
rude and barbarous as all Egypt and Syria now are, and have been long. When Greece
and Rome were at their heights in arts and sciences, Gaul, Germany, Britain, were
as ignorant and barbarous, as many parts of Greece or Turkey can be now.

These, and greater changes, are made in the several countries of the world, and courses
of time, by the revolutions of empire, the devastations of armies, the cruelties of conquering and the calamities of enslaved nations; by the violent inundations of water in
some countries, and the cruel ravages of plagues in others.[215]

It is very true and just, all that is said of the mighty progress that learning and knowledge have made in these western parts of Europe, within these hundred and fifty years;
but that does not conclude, it must be at a greater height than it had been in other

countries, where it was growing much longer periods of time; it argues more how low it was then amongst us, rather than how high it is now.

Upon the fall of the Roman empire, almost all learning was buried in its ruins: the Northern nations that conquered, or rather overwhelmed it by their numbers, were too barbarous to preserve the remains of learning or civility, more carefully than they did those of statuary or architecture, which fell before their brutish rage.[216]

It were too great a mortification to think, that the same fate [as that in repect of the arts] has happened to us, even in our modern learning; as if the growth of that, as well as of natural bodies, had some short periods, beyond which it could not reach, and after which it must begin to decay. It falls in one country or one age, and rises again in others, but never beyond a certain pitch. One man, or one country, at a certain time runs a great length in some certain kinds of knowledge, but loses as much ground in others, that were perhaps as useful and as valuable. There is a certain degree of capacity in the greatest vessel, and, when it is full, if you pour in still, it must run out some way or other; and the more it runs out on one side, the less runs out at the other. So the greatest memory, after a certain degree, as it learns or retains more of some things or words, loses and forgets as much of others. The largest and deepest reach of thought, the more it pursues some certain subjects, the more it neglects others.[217]

He had a wider perspective than most historians of his day, for he was impressed by contemporary ethnographic material.

These four great monarchies [i.e., Crete, Egypt, Greece, and Rome], with the smaller kingdoms, principalities, and states, that were swallowed up by their conquests and extent, make the subject of what is called ancient story. . . . The orders and institutions of these several governments, their progress and duration, their successes or decays, their events and revolutions, make the common themes of schools and colleges the study of learned and the conversation of idle men, the arguments of histories, poems, and romances. . . .

Yet the stage of all these empires, and revolutions of all these heroic actions, and these famous constitutions (how great or how wise soever any of them are esteemed), is but a limited compass of earth, that leaves out many vast regions of the world, the which, though accounted barbarous, and little taken notice of in story, or by any celebrated authors, yet have a right to come in for their voice, in agreeing upon the laws of nature and nations (for aught I know) as well as the rest, that have arrogated it wholly to themselves; and besides, in my opinion, there are some of them that, upon enquiry, will be found to have equalled or exceeded all the others, in the wisdom of their constitutions, the extent of their conquests, and the duration of their empires or states.[218]

Now, because the first scene is such a beaten road, and this so little known or traced, I am content to take a short survey of our four great schemes of government or empire, that have sprung and grown to mighty heights, lived very long, and flourished much in these remote (and, as we will have it, more ignoble) regions of the world: whereof one is at the farthest degree of our eastern longitude, being the kingdom of China. The next is at the farthest western, which is that of Peru. The third is the outmost of our northern latitude, which is Scythia or Tartary. And the fourth is Arabia, which lies very far upon the southern.[219]

[After a description of these four cultures,[220] he concludes:] it must, I think, be allowed, that human nature is the same in these remote, as well as the other more known and celebrated parts of the world: that the different governments of it are framed and cultivated by as great reaches and strength of reason and of wisdom, as any of ours;

and some of their frames less subject to be shaken by the passions, factions, and other corruptions to which those in the middle scene of Europe and Asia have been so often and so much exposed: that the same causes produce every where the same effects; and that the same honours and obedience are in all places but consequences or tributes paid to the same heroic virtue or transcendent genius, in what parts soever, or under what climates of the world, it fortunes to appear.[221]

He developed theories on the evolution of various aspects of culture.

In the first and most simple ages of each country, the conditions and lives of men seem to have been very near of kin with the rest of the creatures: they lived by the hour, or by the day, and satisfied their appetite with what they could get from the herbs, the fruits, the springs they met with when they were hungry or dry; then, with what fish, fowl, or beasts they could kill, by swiftness or strength, by craft or contrivance, by their hands, or such instruments as wit helped or necessity forced them to invent.[222]

He had a euhemeristic theory of the origin of religion.

Among the simpler ages or generations of men, in several countries, those who were the first inventors of arts generally received and applauded as most necessary or useful in human life, were honoured alive; and, after death, worshipped as gods. And so were those who had been the first authors of any good and well instituted civil government in any country. . . .

From these sources, I believe, may be deduced all or most of the theology or idolatry of all the ancient Pagan countries.[223]

Temple conceived of the evolution of political organization in terms of a combined patriarchal and social contract theory.

. . . if we deduce the several races of mankind in the several parts of the world from generation, we must imagine the first numbers of them, who in any place agree upon any civil constitutions, to assemble not as so many single heads, but as so many heads of families, whom they represent, in the framing any compact or common accords;* and consequently, as persons who have already an authority over such numbers as their families are composed of.

For if we consider a man multiplying his kind by the birth of many children, and his cares by providing even necessary food for them till they are able to do it for themselves (which happens much later to the generations of men, and makes a much longer dependence of children upon parents, than we can observe among any other creatures): if we consider not only the cares, but the industry he is forced to, for the necessary sustenance of his helpless brood, either in gathering the natural fruits, or raising those which are purchased with labour and toil; if he be forced for supply of this stock to catch the tamer creatures, and hunt the wilder, sometimes to exercise his courage in defending his little family, and fighting with the strong and savage beasts (that would prey upon him as he does upon the weak and the mild): if we suppose him disposing with discretion and order whatever he gets among his children, according to each of their hunger or need, sometimes laying up for to-morrow what was more than enough for to-day, at other times pinching himself, rather than suffering any of them should want; and as each of them grows up, and able to share in the common support, teaching him both by lesson and example, what he is now to do as son of this family, and what hereafter as the father of another; instructing them all, what qualities are good, and what are ill, for their health

* " . . . laws serve to keep men in order when they are first well agreed and instituted, and afterwards continue to be well executed."[224]

and life, or common society (which will certainly comprehend whatever is generally esteemed virtue or vice among men), cherishing and encouraging dispositions to the good; disfavoring and punishing those to the ill; and lastly, among the various accidents of his life, lifting up his eyes to Heaven, when the earth affords him no relief; and having recourse to a higher and greater nature, whenever he finds the frailty of his own; we must needs conclude, that the children of this man cannot fail of being bred up with a great opinion of his wisdom, his goodness, his valour, and his piety. And if they see constant plenty in the family, they believe well of his fortune too.

And from all this must naturally arise a great paternal authority, which disposes his children (at least till the age when they grow fathers themselves) to believe what he teaches, to follow what he advises, and obey what he commands.

Thus the father, by a natural right as well as authority, becomes a governor in this little State; and if his life be long, and his generations many (as well as those of his children), he grows the governor or King of a nation, and is indeed a *pater patriae*. . . .

These seem to have been the natural and original governments of the world, springing from a tacit deference of many to the authority of one single person. Under him (if the father of the family or nation) the elder of his children comes to acquire a degree of authority among the younger, by the same means the father did among them; and to share with him in the consultation and conduct of their common affairs. And this, together with an opinion of wisdom from experience, may have brought in the authority of the elders so often mentioned among the Jews; and in general of aged men, not only in Sparta and Rome, but all other places in some degree, both civil and barbarous. . . .

Thus a family seems to become a little kingdom, and a kingdom to be but a great family.

Nor is it unlikely that this paternal jurisdiction in its successions, and with the help of accidents, may have branched out into the several heads of government commonly received in the schools. For a family, governed with order, will fall naturally to the several trades of husbandry, which are tillage, gardening, and pasturage (the product whereof was the original riches). For the managing of these and their increase, and the assistance of one man, who perhaps is to feed twenty, it may be a hundred children (since it is not easily told how far the generations may extend with the arbitrary choice and numbers of women, practised anciently in most countries) the use of servants comes to be necessary. These are gained by victory and captives, or by fugitives out of some worse governed family, where either they cannot or like not to live, and so sell their liberty to be assured of what is necessary to life; or else by the debased nature of some of the children who seem born to drudgery, or who are content to increase their pains that they may lessen their cares, and upon such terms become servants to some of their brothers whom they most esteem or choose soonest to live with.[225]

## MAN'S NATURE

The seventeenth century witnessed a resurgence of self-castigation, which was particularly encouraged by Protestant divines who applied the contemporary world view and knowledge to the problem of extirpating the evil in man which he has by virtue of the original sin. Some valuable nuggets are to be found in the arid wastes of these theological harangues, for the dour examination of man's innate visciousness unearthed some valuable information on his nature.

## Charron

Montaigne's follower, Pierre Charron (1541–1603), joined the former's point of view to the religious outlook of the time. The basis of his approach is found in long discussions of a cosmopolitan nature, some of which are taken directly from Montaigne.

. . . there is nothing so confidently asserted, and believed in one place, but is as generally received, as peremptorily maintained, nay, as fiercely contradicted and condemned in another.[226]

Nothing so extravagant, nothing so absurd, but hath found its Assertors and Abettors. And this not only in the fanciful Conceits of Private Persons, but in the more general Sense and Agreement of large Societies and Communities. Thus *History* tells us, that what is detested as Impious, Unjust, and Unnatural in one Country, has been receiv'd with Veneration, and practis'd as highly Decent, and a Duty, nay, even esteem'd an Act of Religion in another. And there are not many Laws, or Customs, or Opinions, which we can say, have univerally obtain'd, or have been every where rejected. The *Marriages of near Relations,* Some condemn as Incestuous; but Others have not only allow'd, but recommended, may, in some Cases even enjoyn'd them. The *Murdering of Infants,* and *of Parents, when old and decrepid,* and the *having Wives in common* [also].[227]

He emphasized the constraint of culture upon the individual.

How few are there of those Opinions, which we profess to entertain, that, when look'd into, are not at last resolv'd into Authority, and taken upon Trust? We believe and act, we live and die upon Credit and Consent; and our great Business is to conform our selves to Custom, and to think and do like the rest of the World, and according to what They, not our own Reason, esteems most adviseable. Thus *Fashions,* and not *Judgement,* govern Mankind.[228]

. . . that *Universal Infection of common and popular Opinions entertain'd in the World;* With which the Mind is tinctur'd early, and these take Possession, and usually keep it obstinately. Or, which is yet worse, sometimes wild and fantastical Delusions have been drunk in, and with these the Mind is so strongly season'd, so grossly cheated, that They are not only not dismiss'd, but made the Rule of our Judgements, and the Measure of Truth in other Cases.[229]

Now that which renders such Instruction so marvellously powerful, is, that they are taken in very easily, and as hardly lost again: For that which comes first, takes absolute Possession; and carries all the Authority you can desire; there being no Antecedent Notions to dispute the Title, or call the Truth of it in Question. While therefore the Soul is fresh and clear, a fair and perfect Blank, flexible and tender, there can be no Difficulty in making it what you please; for this Condition disposes it to receive any manner of Impression, and to be moulded into any manner of Form.[230]

His analysis of the nature of man is in terms of the following outline:

### FIVE CONSIDERATIONS OF MAN
#### and the Condition of Human Nature

I. Natural, consisting of the Parts whereof he is compounded, with their several Appurtenances.

II. Natural and Moral; by stating the Comparison between Him and Brutes.

III. By giving a Summary Account of his Life.

| IV. A Moral Description of his Qualities and Defects, under Five Heads. | 1. Vanity.<br>2. Weakness.<br>3. Inconstancy.<br>4. Misery.<br>5. Presumption |
|---|---|
| V. Mix'd or Natural and Moral; resulting from the differences between some Men and others, in | 1. Their Temper.<br>2. Their Minds and Accomplishments.<br>3. Their Stations and Degrees of Quality.<br>4. Their Professions and Circumstances.<br>5. Their Advantages and Disadvantages; Natural, Acquired, and Accidental.[231] |

[I. He accepts the Biblical account of the origin and history of man.[232]
II. Comparative anatomy and physiology; see under "Physical Anthropology."
III. A moral exhortation merely.
IV. Ditto.
V. This section deals with the factors in personality development and proceeds as follows:]

Now the last Part of our Understanding for attaining to a right Knowledge of Man, must consist of the Distinctions and Differences observable in Him: And These are of several sorts, according to the different Parts of which Humane Nature is compounded, and the different Methods and Capacities in which Men may be consider'd, and compar'd with one another. At present we will instance in Five, which seem to be the Principal; and of so large Extent, that all the rest may be reduc'd to them. For, generally speaking, all that is in Man is either Body or Spirit, Natural or Acquired, Publick or Private, Apparent or Secret; and accordingly this fifth and Last Consideration shall branch it self into Five Particulars, which shall be so many Capital Distinctions between Man and Man.

The First of these is *Natural, Essential,* and *Universal;* in which the whole Man, both Body and Mind, are concern'd.

The Second is principally *Natural* and *Essential;* but in some measure *Artificial* and acquir'd too; and this concerns the Strength and Capacity of the Mind.

The Third is *Accidental,* and depends upon Men's Conditions and their Duties respectively; the Ground of all which is taken from the Circumstance of Superiour or Inferiour.

The Fourth is likewise *Accidental,* and relates to Men's particular Professions, and different ways of Living.

The Fifth and Last considers them with regard to the *Advantages* and *Disadvantages,* by which either Nature or Fortune hath distinguished them.[233]

[1.] the First, most remarkable, and universal Distinction between some Men and Others, is That which regards the whole Person, the Mind and Body both, and all the Parts whereof Man consists. And This is deriv'd from the different Situation of Countries, and Divisions of the World; In proportion to which there necessarily follows a Difference in the Aspects and Influences of the Heavens, the Distance of the Sun, the Temperament of the Air, and the Nature of the Soil: And from hence Men receive different Complexions, and Statures, and Countenances; nay, different Manners and Dispositions; and different Faculties of the Soul too. . . . As the Nature of the Fruits, and of other Animals, is very different, according to the Regions where they spring and are bred; so Men likewise owe their Temper to their Country; and upon this account bring into the World with them Dispositions Greater or Less, to War, Courage, Justice, Temperance, Docility, Religion, Chastity, Wit, Goodness, Obedience, Beauty, Health, and Strength.[234]

God . . . produces Men of different Understandings and Parts, according to the Constitution of their Parents, and the Concurrence of other Natural Causes; nay, even according to the different Climate, and the Country, and Air they are born in. For *Greece* and *Italy* have ever been observ'd to produce Men of quicker and clearer Wit than *Muscovy* and *Tartary*. . . . Now the Brain is properly the Instrument of the Reasonable Soul, and therefore upon the due Temperament of This, a great deal must needs, indeed the Whole in a manner, will depend.[235]

. . . the Principal *Temperaments,* which serve, assist, and set the Reasonable Soul on working, and which distinguish the Excellencies of the Mind, according to its Faculties, are *Three.*[236]

The *Temperament* proper for *Understanding* is a Predominance of Dry. . . . Thus . . . Those of Southerly Countries excel in Wisdom, from the Drought of their Brain, and their inward Heat being moderated by that of a violent Sun without, which exhales it.

The *Temperament* best accommodated to the *Memory* is *Moist* . . . hence . . . the Inhabitants of the *Northern* Climates have the strongest Memories, for these are under a moister Air, by means of their great Distance from the Sun. . . .

The *Temperament fittest* for the *Imagination,* is *Hot.* . . . [Therefore in] more moderate Climates, between the *North* and the *South,* . . . Men are observ'd to excel in those Arts and Sciences, which are deriv'd from the Strength and Sprightliness of Fancy.[237]

[2.] This Second Distinction, which concerns the Minds of Men, and their inward Accomplishments, is by no means so manifest as the former. . . . According to this Distinction, there are . . . Three sorts of Men, which divide them into Three Classes or Degrees of Souls.

In the First and lowest of these Ranks we may place those of weak and mean Souls, which are almost of a Level with Body and Matter; of slender and narrow Capacities; almost perfectly passive, and such as Nature seems to have made on purpose to Endure and Obey. . . .

In the Second and middle Row, are Those of a tolerable Judgement and Understanding, and such as make some Pretensions to Wit and Learning, Management and Address: These Men know Something, but they are not sufficiently acquainted with Themselves. . . .

In the Third and Highest Order, are the Men blest with a lively, clear, and penetrating Wit.[238]

[3.] This *Accidental Distinction,* which regards the State of Life wherein Men are placed, the Offices they execute, and the Relations they mutually bear to one another, is grounded upon the Two great Principles, and Fundamental Supports of all Humane Society, which are, Commanding and Obeying, Power and Subjection, a Superior and an Inferior Station.[239]

[4.] We now . . . take another Difference between Some Men and Others, into Consideration; which depends upon their different Professions, Conditions, and Ways of Life, Some follow a Life of Business and Company; Others avoid This, and make their Escape out of the World, by running into Solitude. Some are fond of Arms and a Camp; Others hate and abhor them, [etc.][240]

[5.] This Last Distinction is abundantly notorious, and visible to every Eye; It hath indeed several Branches and Considerations included under it; but all I think may be conveniently enough reduced to Two General Heads; which, according to the vulgar way of Expression, may be termed, Happiness and Unhappiness; being High or Low in the World. To that of Happiness or Greatness, belong Health, Beauty, and other Qualifications and Advantages of Body and Person, Liberty, Nobility, Honour, Authority, Learning, Riches, Reputation, Friends. In Unhappiness or Meanness of Condition are comprehended the Contraries of all These . . . Now these Particulars are the occasion of infinite variety in Men's Circumstances and Conditions of Life.[241]

Charron gave his views on the evolution of culture.

Upon the Supposition, that Men had from the Beginning been all accustom'd to Clothes, it is not easy to conceive how any Number of them should ever take up a Fancy of throwing them aside again, and going Naked; both because a Regard to their Health, which must needs have suffer'd extreamly by so disadvantageous an Exchange, and a Regard to Modesty and Shame too, must in all reason have persuaded the contrary. And yet we see, this is still the Fashion in several Nations, which is a great Presumption of its having once been the Fashion of all Mankind naturally.[242]

I shou'd make no doubt but the Contrivances of Hutts and Houses, and other Shelters against the Violence of the Seasons, and the Assaults of Men, was a much more ancient Institution than that of Cloathing; and there seems to have been more of Nature and Universal Practice in it; for we see that Beasts and Birds do the same thing.[243]

## Dyke

Daniel Dyke's (d. 1614) *The Mystery of Selfe-Deceiving*[244] is virtually an encyclopedia of deceit, based upon a detailed taxonomy of the varieties of the besetting sin. Some idea of the exhaustiveness of the treatment can be gathered from the major classification:

I thinke . . . that all the deceitfulnes of the heart . . . may be reduced to these two heads: First, the deceitfulness whereby we deceive *others* onely; Secondly, that whereby also we deceive *our selves*.[245]

[I.] First, the deceitfulnes whereby we deceive *others*.[246]

[II.] . . . *selfe-deceit* . . . may be considered either in the minde or affections *joyntly together,* or in the affections *separately,* and *by themselves*.[247]

[A.] The former decitfulnesse shewes it selfe specially in foure things: 1. in *judging:* 2. in *perswading:* 3. in *promising:* 4. in *practising*.[248]

[B.] Hitherto we have spoken of that deceitfulnesse of heart, which is *joyntly* in the minde, and affections: it remaineth now, that we speake of that deceitfulnesse of the affections, *by themselves.* Where first, wee will speake of their deceit in *generall,* and then secondly in *speciall,* of the deceit of some speciall affections.[249]

Some of the statements in the book differ from psychoanalytic propositions only in the terminology employed. Narcissism is fundamental in the individual.

. . . pride and selfe pleasing . . . naturally is in us all.[250]

Man's emotions influence his activity.

. . . though it may seem that judgement belongs properly to the mind, yet because here the affections interpose themselves, . . . the erroneous judgement of the minde commonly receiveth its tincture from the affections.[251]

The unconscious plays an important role.

Man knoweth his inward thoughts, purposes, and desires, but the frame and disposition of his heart hee knowes not, nor yet alwaies the qualities of those thoughts, whither they tend, what secret deceit lyes and lurkes in them.[252]

As it fareth with the eye, which seeing other things, sees not it selfe, nor the face wherein it standeth, so it is with our hearts, knowing other things, yet ignorante of themselves, strangers at home: We know not what we are in present, much lesse what wee shall be hereafter, in tryall and temptation.[253]

Nothing more easie then for a man to deceive himselfe; for the heart by reason of the great wickednesse thereof, is a bottom-lesse and unsearchable gulfe of guile; in somuch as none can know, not onely anothers, but not his owne heart.[254]

Man rationalizes in order to placate the superego.

The hearts deceitfulnes in hiding that evill which she purposeth to doe, or is in doing, is to make faire even of the quite contrary. And therefore in her witty wickednes, she inventeth some colourable pretence to shadow her malice and mischief.[255]

## Esprit

Jacques Esprit's (1611–78) thesis was that all man's actions are fundamentally egocentric.

I have often resolv'd in my Mind, what might be the Cause, that humane Virtues have always been, and are still so undeservedly approv'd; and I cou'd find none, but an erroneous Opinion, that those Actions which seem Reasonable, Just, Good, and Generous, proceed from Reason, Justice, Goodness, and Generosity.[256]

. . . since Self-love is become the Master and Tyrant of Man, it suffers in him no Virtue or good Action, but what is useful to it, and . . . it employs them all to compass its different aims and views. So that it is only with reference to the ends of Self-love, that Reason induces Men to have a respect for their Parents, to assist the Poor, and to observe the Laws of Justice. Thus they do not commonly perform all these Duties, but when they are acted by Self-love. . . . ev'ry body owns that they commonly act by Interest, or Vanity.[257]

## Pascal

Blaise Pascal (1632–62) made the most moving analysis of human nature. Basic is man's egocentrism.

The nature of self-love and of this human Ego is to love self only and consider self only.[258]

All men naturally hate one another. They employ lust as far as possible in the service of the public weal. But this is only a pretence and a false image of love; for at bottom it is only hate.

To pity the unfortunate is not contrary to lust. On the contrary, we can quite well give such evidence of friendship, and acquire the reputation of kindly feeling, without giving anything.

From lust men have found and extracted excellent rules of policy, morality, and justice; but in reality this vile root of man, the *figmentum malum,* is only covered, it is not taken away.

*Injustice.*—They have not found any other means of satisfying lust without doing injury to others.[259]

But there is also a desire for the approbation of others.

We have a fountain of self-love which represents us to ourselves as being able to fill several places outside of ourselves; this is what makes us happy to be loved.[260]

Man differs from the other animals in that he possesses reason, while they have instinct.

I cannot conceive man without thought; he would be a stone or a brute.[261]

Instinct and reason, marks of two natures.[262]

However, man is not rational.

*Nature corrupted.*—Man does not act by reason, which consitutes his being.

The corruption of reason is shown by the existence of so many different and extravagant customs.[263]

All our reasoning reduces itself to yielding to feeling.[264]

. . . the perception of reason is bounded by passion.[265]

Habit and custom are great forces.

Custom is our nature.[266]

. . . education produces natural intuitions, and natural intuitions are erased by education.[267]

What are our natural principles but principles of custom? In children they are those which they have received from the habits of their fathers, as hunting in animals. A different custom will cause different natural principles. This is seen in experience; and if there are some natural principles ineradicable by custom, there are also some customs opposed to nature, ineradicable by nature, or by a second custom. This depends on disposition.[268]

Parents fear lest the natural love of their children may fade away. What kind of nature is that which is subject to decay? Custom is a second nature which destroys the former. But what is nature? For is custom not natural? I am much afraid that nature is itself only a first custom, as custom is a second nature.[269]

The most important affair in life is the choice of a calling; chance decides it. Custom makes men masons, soldiers, slaters. "He is a good slater," says one, and, speaking of soldiers, remarks, "They are perfect fools." But others affirm, "There is nothing great but war, the rest of men are good for nothing." We choose our calling according as we hear this or that praised or despised in our childhood, for we naturally love truth and hate folly. These words move us; the only error is in their application. So great is the force of custom that out of those whom nature has only made men, are created all conditions of men. For some districts are full of masons, others of soldiers, etc. Certainly nature is not so uniform. It is custom then which does this, for it constrains nature. But sometimes nature gains the ascendancy, and preserves man's instinct, in spite of all custom, good or bad.[270]

Custom is the source of our strongest and most believed proofs. . . . it is custom that makes so many men Christians; custom that makes them Turks, heathens, artisans, soldiers, etc.[271]

Fashion even and country often regulate what is called beauty. It is a strange thing that custom should mingle so strongly with our passions.[272]

As custom determines what is agreeable, so also does it determine justice.[273]

He believed in social progress; speaking of exaggerated respect for antiquity, he asked:

Is not this to treat unworthily the reason of man and to put it in a level with the instinct of animals, since we take away the principle difference between them, which is that the effects of reason accumulate without ceasing, whilst instinct remains always in the same state? The cells of the bees were as correctly measured a thousand years ago as to-day, and each formed a hexagon as exactly the first time as the last. It is the same with all that the animals produce by this occult impulse. Nature instructs them in proportion as necessity impels them; but this fragile science is lost with the wants which give it birth: as they received it without study, they have not the happiness of preserving it; and every time it is given to them it is new to them, since nature having for her object nothing but the maintenance of animals in a limited order of perfection, she inspires them with this necessary science, always the same, lest they may fall into decay, and does not permit them to add to it, lest they should exceed the limits that she has prescribed to them. It is not the same with man, who is formed only for infinity. He is ignorant at the earliest age of his life; but he is instructed unceasingly in his progress; for he derives advantage, not only from his own experience, but also from that of his predecessors; since he always retains in his memory the knowledge which he himself has once acquired, and since he has that of the ancients ever present in the books which they have bequeathed to him. And as he preserves this knowledge, he can also add to it easily; so that men are at the present day in some sort in the same condition in which those ancient philosophers would have been found, could they have survived till the present time, adding to the knowledge which they possessed that which their studies would have acquired by the aid of so many centuries. Thence it is that by an especial prerogative, not only does each man advance from day to day in the sciences, but all mankind together make continual progress in proportion as the world grows older, since the same thing happens in the succession of men as in the different ages of single individuals. So that the whole succession of men, during the course of many ages, should be considered as a single man who subsists forever and learns continually, whence we see with what injustice we respect antiquity in philosophers; for as old age is that period of life most remote from infancy, who does not see that old age in this universal man ought not to be sought in the times nearest his birth, but in those the most remote from it? Those whom we call ancient were really new in all things, and properly constituted the infancy; and as we have joined to their knowledge the experience of the centuries which have followed them, it is in ourselves that we should find this antiquity that we revere in others.[274]

[However, he later made some qualification:] Man's nature is not always to advance; it has its advances and retreats. . . .

The discoveries of men from age to age turn out the same.[275]

He was impressed by the role of chance in history.

The least movement affects all nature; the entire sea changes because of a rock.[276]

Cleopatra's nose: had it been shorter, the whole aspect of the world would have been altered.[277]

Cromwell was about to ravage all Christendom; the royal family was undone, and his own for ever established, save for a little grain of sand which formed in his ureter. Rome herself was trembling under him; but this small piece of gravel having formed there, he is dead, his family cast down, all is peaceful, and the king is restored.[278]

[In an imaginary discourse to a young nobleman:] it is . . . an accident by which you find yourself master of the wealth you possess . . . not only do you find yourself the son of a duke, but also do you find yourself in the world at all, only through an infinity of chances. Your birth depends on a marriage, or rather on the marriages of all those from whom you descend. But upon what do these marriages depend? A visit made by chance, an idle word, a thousand unforseen occasions.

You hold, you say, your wealth from your ancestors; but was it not by a thousand accidents that your ancestors acquired it and that they preserved it?[279]

To Pascal, the origin of political organization lay in conquest.

The cords which bind the respect of men to each other are in general cords of necessity; for there must be different degrees, all men wishing to rule, and not all being able to do so, but some being able.

Let us then imagine we see society in the process of formation. Men will doubtless fight till the stronger party overcomes the weaker, and a dominant party is established. But when this is once determined, the masters, who do not desire the continuation of strife, then decree that the power which is in their hands shall be transmitted as they please. Some place it in election by the people, others in hereditary succession, etc.

And this is the point where imagination begins to play its part. Till now power makes fact; now power is sustained by imagination in a certain party, in France in the nobility, in Switzerland in the burgesses, etc.

These cords which bind the respect of men to such and such an individual are therefore the cords of imagination.[280]

## Glanvill

Joseph Glanvill (1636–80) believed in the importance of self-love.

. . . every man is naturally *Narcissus,* and each *passion* in us, no other but *self-love* sweetened by milder Epithets.[281]

He emphasized the constraint of culture.

. . . the almost insuperable *prejudice* of *Custome,* and *Education:* by which our minds are encumber'd, and the most are held in *Fatal Ignorance* . . . though . . . the *Soul* were a pure ἄγραφον γραμματεῖον; yet *custom* and *education* will so blot and scrible on't, as almost to incapacitate it for after-impressions. Thus we judge all things by our *anticipations;* and condemn or applaud them, as they agree or differ from our *education-prepossessions.* One Countrey laughs at the *Laws, Customs,* and *Opinions* of another, as absurd and ridiculous; and the other is as charitable to them, in its conceit of theirs. This confirms the most sottish *Idolaters* in their accustomed adorations, beyond the conviction of any thing, but *Dooms-day.* The impressions of a barbarous *education* are stronger in them, than *nature;* when in their cruel *worships* they launce themselves with knifes, and expose their harmless *Infants* to the *flames* as a Sacrifice to their *Idols.* . . . There is nothing so *monstrous,* to which *education* cannot form our ductile *minority;* it can lick us into shapes beyond the *monstrosities* of those of *Affrica.* . . . For our initial age is like the melted wax to the prepared Seal, capable of any impression from the documents of our Teachers.* The *half-moon* or *Cross,* are indifferent to its reception; and we may with equal facility write on this *rasa Tabula,* Turk, or Christian. We came into the world like the unformed *Cub;* 'tis *education* is our *Plastick:* we are baptized into our opinions by our Juvenile nurture, and our growing years confirm those unexamined Principles. For our first task is to learn the *Creed* of our Countrey; and our next to maintain it. We seldom examine our Receptions, more then Children their *Catechisms;* For *Implicit* faith is a vertue, where

* . . . easie Youth in its *first addresses* to Learning, is perfectly *passive* to the *Discipline* and *Instructions* of its *Teachers,* whose *Documents* are *promiscuously* received with ready submission of Understandings, that *implicitely* depend on *their Authority.* We suck in the first Rudiments as we *do* the *common Air* . . . without *discrimination* or *election,* of which indeed our tender and unexercised minds are not capable."[282]

*Orthodoxie* is the object. Some will not be at the trouble of a Tryal: others are scar'd from attempting it. . . . We are bound to our Countreys opinions, as to its laws: and an accustomed assent is *tantamount* to an infallible conclusion. He that offers to dissent, shall be out-law'd in his reputation. . . . Thus *Custom* conciliates our esteem to things, no otherwise deserving it: what is in *fashion,* is handsom and pleasant; though never so uncouth to an unconcern'd beholder. . . . On the other hand we start and boggle at what is *unusual.* . . . we thus mistake the infusions of *education,* for the *principles* of universal *nature.*[283]

However, he ascribed some influence to the natural environment.

. . . as some Regions have their proper Vices, not so generally found in others; so have they their mental depravities, which are drawn in with the common air of the Countrey. And I take this for one of the most consierable causes of the diversity of *Laws, Customes, Religions, natural* and *moral* doctrines, which is to be found in the divided Regions of the inhabited Earth.[284]

Glanvill was opposed to the theory of social degradation.

. . . as the Noble Lord *Verulam* hath noted, we have a mistaken apprehension of *Antiquity*; calling that so, which in truth is the worlds Nonage. . . . Upon a true account, the *present age* is the worlds *Grandaevity*; and if we must to *Antiquity,* let multitude of days speak.[285]

. . . the sole Instances of those illustrious Heroes, *Cartes, Gassendus, Galilaeo, Tycho, Harvey, More, Digby;* will strike dead the opinion of the worlds decay, and conclude it, in its *Prime.*[286]

[However, in another context he wrote:] the . . . *Earth* . . . [is] now in its exhausted and decrepit *Age.*[287]

## La Rochefoucauld

In the same way, "self love" was fundamental to François La Rochefoucauld (1613–80).

Self love is the love of oneself and of all other things for one's own sake; it makes men idolize themselves and would cause them to tyrannize over their neighbours, had they the opportunity: it never rests outside itself, and if it dwells at all on external objects, it is only to extract nourishment from them, as bees do from flowers. Nothing equals the impetuosity of its desires, the depth of its schemes, or the ingenuity of its methods; its agility is unrivalled, its transformations find no parallel in the *Metamorphoses,* its subtleties none in the art of chemistry. It is impossible to fathom the depths or pierce the gloom of the abyss in which it dwells. There it remains, sheltered from the keenest sight; there it comes and goes, all unperceived, often invisible even to itself. There it conceives, breeds, and rears, unknowingly, a vast number of appetites and dislikes—some of so monstrous a shape that it fails to recognize them when exposed to the light of day, or cannot bring itself to own them. Out of the night that covers it are born the absurd ideas it entertains of itself; thence come its errors, its ignorance, its clumsiness, and its fatuous beliefs about itself—its notion that its feelings are dead when they are but asleep, that it has lost its activity when once it is at rest, and that it has got rid of the appetites it has for the moment appeased. But the dense gloom that hides it from itself does not prevent it from seeing outside objects; wherein it resembles the eyes, which perceive everything except themselves. Nay, where it is chiefly concerned, and in its weightiest affairs to which the violence of its desires compels its whole attention, there is nothing which it cannot see, feel, hear, imagine, suspect, detect, or divine; so much so that one is tempted to believe that each of its passions possesses a magic all its own. Nothing can surpass the intimacy and strength of its attachments, which it vainly attempts to sever when menaced by dire calamities. Nevertheless it sometimes contrives to do, quickly and easily, what had defied its whole effort for years, and from this it may reasonably be inferred that its desires are kindled, not by the beauty and worth of their objects, but by its own imagination; that its own appetite lends them value and glamour; that it is its own quarry, and that it pursues its own pleasure when it pursues the things that please it. It is compounded of opposites; it is imperious and servile, honest and deceitful, merciful and cruel, timid and bold. Its tastes vary as do the temperaments which guide it and cause it to seek now fame, now wealth, and now pleasure. It changes with every change in our age, fortune, or experience; but it cares not whether it has several aims or only one, for it can distribute its devotion among several or centrate it on one as and how it pleases. It is fickle, and putting aside such changes as are due to outside causes, there are numberless others which spring from itself and its own resources. It is fickle out of sheer fickleness, or out of frivolity, passion, love of novelty, weariness, or disgust. It is capricious, and may sometimes be observed to labour with the utmost zeal and incredible industry to obtain things which are in no way profitable to it, nay, even harmful, but which it insists on pursuing because it wants them. It is unaccountable and often devotes its entire energies to the most frivolous pursuits, taking the keenest pleasure in those that are most insipid and the greatest pride in those that are most contemptible. It is to be found in all ages and conditions of life; it exists everywhere and on everything; it even exists on nothing, and can make use of things and of their absence alike. It even joins forces with those who attack it, takes parts in their schemes, and, marvellous though it may appear, shares their hatred of itself, conspires for its own defeat, and labours for its own ruin; in a word, it cares only to exist, and, provided it exists, is content to be its own enemy. It should therefore cause us no surprise if it occasionally allies itself with the most rigid austerity and treats boldly with its ally for its destruction, for at the very moment when it destroys itself at one point, it regains its ascendancy at another. When it appears to abandon its own pleasure, it is only having a respite or pursuing it in a new shape, and when it is beaten, and we think we have done with it, we find it rising in triumph from its own defeat. That is a portrait of self love, whose whole life is ceaseless activity. In the physical world it may be compared to the sea, in the ceaseless ebb and flow of whose waves it finds a true emblem of the perpetual turmoil of its thoughts and of its eternal unrest.[288]

And like Pascal, he remarked upon man's irrationality.

The heart always outwits the head.[289]

We fail to realize how much our actions are influenced by passion.[290]

The importance of the unconscious did not escape him.

We are far from comprehending the full extent of our desires.[291]

Man is a social animal.

It would be useless to speak of how necessary society is to men: all desire it, and all search for it, but few secure the means of rendering it agreeable and of making it last. Each one wishes to find his pleasure and his advantages at the expense of others; one always prefers himself to those with whom he proposes to live, and one almost always makes them feel this preference; it is this which troubles and which destroys society. It would be necessary at least to know how to conceal this desire or preference, since it is too natural in us for us to have the power to undo it; it would be necessary to make one's pleasure that of others, to spare their self love, and never injure it.[292]

He anticipated Mandeville's "private vices, public benefits."

Our virtues are, more often than not, vices in disguise.[293]

Those who would describe victory by reference to its causes might be tempted to call it the daughter of Heaven, as poets do; since its origin is not to be found on earth. For it is born of countless deeds, each of which, so far from being designed to attain it, is referable solely to the personal aims of its author. It is, in fact, the great collective achievement of an army of individuals, each of whom seeks his own honour and promotion.[294]

He realized the effect of culture upon personality.

The accent of our native land dwells in our hearts and minds just as it cleaves to our tongues.[295]

And in considering the role of the individual in history, La Rochefoucauld stressed the social factors involved.

Be nature never so lavish with her gifts, she requires fortune's help to make a hero.[296]

Merit is the gift of nature, but fortune provides occasions for its display.[297]

Finally, he was interested in cultural decline.

Luxury and excessive refinement are sure signs of national decadence, since when individuals are too devoted to their private interests they neglect the common welfare.[298]

## Bayle

The theme of Pierre Bayle (1647–1706) was, "How do Men deceive themselves!"[299] One reason for this is the constraint of culture.

. . . there's nothing strange in an Error's becoming universal, considering the little care Men take to consult their Reason, when they give in to what they hear others say, and the little use made of the Occasions offer'd of undeceiving 'em.[300]

Very few make it their business to examine whether common Opinions be true or false: Isn't it enough, say they, our Fathers believ'd it?*[302]

He made a point of the irrationality of man.

. . . the Mind of Man being subject to infinite Caprice and Variety, no Rule can be laid down concerning it, not liable to a thousand Exceptions. The safest is that which is for the most part true, to wit, That Man is not determin'd in his Actions by general Notices, or Views of his Understanding, but by the present reigning Passion of his Heart.[303]

You may call Man a reasonable Creature, as long as you please: still it's true, he hardly ever acts by fixt Principles.[304]

. . . speculative Opinions are not the true Springs of our Actions.[305]

He almost always follows the reigning Passion of his Soul, the Bias of his Constitution, the Force of inveterate Habits, and his Taste and Tenderness for some Objects more than others.†[307]

* " . . . none, except a few Philosophical Minds, ever dream of examining whether what they see allow'd on all hands be true or no. This every one supposes done long since, and that the Ancients have clear'd the Coast of all Error; and therefore delivers in his Turn to Posterity as infallible."[301]

† " . . . the Pleasure, and the cheapness of the Pleasure, is what makes some Vices more common than others, and not our Opinions upon the Turpitude of 'em in the degrees of more or less."[306]

How comes it, pray Sir, tho there's so prodigious a Diversity of Opinions concerning the manner of serving God, and the Forms of Civil Life; yet one finds the same Passions reign eternally in all Countrys, and in all Ages? That Ambition, Avarice, Envy, Lust, Revenge, are so rife all the World over. That the Jew and Mahometan, Turk, and Moor, the Christian and Infidel, Tartar and Indian, the Inhabitants on the Continent and those of the Isles, the Nobleman and Yeoman, all kinds of Men, who differ in almost all things else, except the general Notion of Humanity, shou'd so exactly agree with regard to these Passions, one wou'd think they copy'd one from t'other? Whence can this proceed, but from hence, That the true Principle of Man's Actions (I except those in whom the Grace of the Holy Spirit operates efficaciously) is nothing else then the Complexion, the natural Inclination for Pleasure, a tast for particular Objects, a desire of pleasing others, the Turn given us by conversing with one set of Acquaintance, or some other Disposition resulting from the Ground of our corrupt Nature, whatever Country we are born, or whatever Principles bred in?[308]

He mentioned "the particular Genius of each Nation."[309]

When applied to history, his skepticism led him to the formulation of principles of historical criticism.[310]

## POLITICAL PRAGMATISTS

### Bacon

Francis Bacon (1561–1626) wrote in the tradition of the pragmatic political scientists of the sixteenth century; "*Histories* make Men Wise."[311] A good example of his approach is to be found in "Of seditions and troubles."

*Shepheards* of *People,* had need know the *Kalenders* of *Tempests* in *State;* which are commonly greatest, when Things grow to Equality As Natural Tempests are greatest about the *Aequinoctia.* And as there are certaine hollow Blasts of Winde, and secret Swellings of Seas, before a Tempest, so are there in States . . .

Libels, and licentious Discourses against the State, when they are frequent and open; And in like sort, false Newes, often running up and downe, to the disadvantage of the State, and hastily embraced; are amongst the Signes of *Troubles.* . . .

Also, when Discords, and Quarrells, and Factions, are carried openly, and audaciously; it is a Signe, the Reverence of Government is lost. . . .

So when any of the foure Pillars of Government, are mainly shaken, or weakned (which are *Religion, Justice, Counsell,* and *Treasure,*) Men had need to pray for Faire Weather.
. . .

The *Matter* of *Seditions* is of two kindes; *Much Poverty,* and *Much Discontentment.* . . .

The *Causes* and *Motives* of *Seditions* are; *Innovation* in *Religion; Taxes; Alteration of Lawes and Customes; Breaking of Priviledges; Generall Oppression; Advancement of unworthy persons; Strangers; Dearths; Disbanded Souldiers; Factions growne desperate;* And whatsoever in offending People, joyneth and knitteth them, in a Common Cause.[312]

He was a realist, interested in what actually occurred rather than in what ought to be; "to speake Truth, in Base Times, Active Men are of more use, then Vertuous."[313]

Men are irrational in their acts.

There is in Humane Nature, generally, more of the Foole, then of the Wise; And therefore those faculties, by which the Foolish part of Mens Mindes is taken, are most potent.[314]

[It is a mistake] to imagine People to be too reasonable.[315]

This is increased by "the Raigne or Tyrannie of Custome."[316]

The *Indians* (I meane the Sect of their Wise Men) lay Themselves quietly upon a Stacke of Woode, and so Sacrifice themselves by Fire. Nay the Wives strive to be burned with the Corpses of their Husbands. . . . Many Examples may be put, of the Force of *Custome,* both upon Minde, and Body.[317]

Man is egocentric.

For there is no such *Flatterer,* as is a Mans Self.[318]

However, he is also social by nature.

. . . man in the first stage of his existence is a naked and defenceless thing, slow to help himself, and full of wants.[319]

. . . a Naturall and Secret Hatred, and Aversation towards *Society,* in any Man, hath somewhat of the Savage Beast.[320]

There is in Mans Nature, a secret Inclination, and Motion, towards *love* of others; which, if it be not spent, upon some one, or a few, doth naturally spread it selfe, towards many; and maketh men become Humane and Charitable; As it is seene sometime in Friars.*[322]

Bacon had a conception of the growth and decline of society as correlated with certain cultural developments.

In the *Youth* of a *State,* Armes doe flourish; In the *Middle Age* of a *State, Learning;* And then both of them together for a time: In the *Declining Age* of a *State, Mechanicall Arts* and *Merchandize.*[323]

He believed in social progress.

The antiquity of ages is the youth of the world.[324]

As for antiquity, the opinion touching it which men entertain is quite a negligent one, and scarcely consonant with the word itself. For the old age of the world is to be accounted the true antiquity; and this is the attribute of our own times, not of that earlier age of the world in which the ancients lived; and which, though in respect of us it was the elder, yet in respect of the world it was the younger. And truly as we look for greater knowledge of human things and a riper judgement in the old man than in the young, because of his experience and of the number and variety of the things which he has seen and heard and thought of; so in like manner from our age, if it but knew its own strength and chose to essay and exert it, much more might fairly be expected than from the ancient times, inasmuch as it is a more advanced age of the world, and stored and stocked with infinite experiments and observations.[325]

He was partial to a geographic interpretation of culture.

. . . the *Northern Tract* of the World, is in Nature the more Martiall Region; Be it, in respect of the Stars of that Hemisphere; Or of the great Continents that are upon the *North,* whereas the *South Part,* for ought that is knowne, is almost all Sea; Or (which is most apparent) of the Cold of the *Northern* Parts, which is that, which without Aid of Discipline, doth make the Bodies hardest, and the Courages warmest.[326]

His generalization on population took into consideration the cultural factor of the standard of living.

---

* "Divinitie maketh the Love of our Selves the Patterne; The Love of our Neighbours but the Portraiture."[321]

Generally, it is to be foreseene, that the Population of a Kingdome, (especially if it be not mowen downe by warrs) doe not exceed, the Stock of the Kingdome, which should maintaine them. Neither is the Population, to be reckoned, onely by number: For a smaller Number, that spend more, and earne less, doe weare out an Estate, sooner then a greater Number, that live lower, and gather more.[327]

He anticipated the mercantilist doctrine of the necessity for a favorable balance of trade.

. . . the increase of any Estate, must be upon the Forrainer, (for whatsoever is some where gotten, is some where lost).[328]

## Naudé

Gabriel Naudé (1600–53) was a less interesting political pragmatist.[329]

## Seckendorf

In the seventeeth and eighteenth centuries Germany developed its own school of political pragmatism, the Cameralists. Veit Ludwig von Seckendorf (1626–92) was its most distinguished exponent in the period under discussion.

When first, at the request of the sovereign, I described the condition of a certain sovereignty, in the same way and manner as in this work, I was asked to continue the description and to arrange it in such a way that it could be applied to other countries and sovereignties.[330]

I did not want to take as a model a sovereignty that is too high and general, nor too small and narrow, but as much as possible I took the middle road, which at the same time is best known to me. However, I believe that it is not difficult to make the transposition or application on a larger or smaller scale, and according to the directions which I have given to take care of the particular circumstances of each individual case . . . I hope that the general cases and regulations, according to which individual institutions are regulated, are indicated in this treatise.[331]

He was skeptical of the existence of national characteristics.

The origin, nature and sentiments, virtues and vices, of the inhabitants of a country, are made quite a lot of by old and new writers, although they are made without basis on uncertain assumptions, and they are too easily generalized from the example of a few people to whole nations and peoples.

That is why . . . he who wants to describe the inhabitants of his country in a useful way should not waste his time with such dubious matters. And just as experience shows that in all places there can be found good and bad, skilled and unskilled, diligent and lazy, pugnacious and cowardly, tricky and simple, people; so one can grasp in a small district the difference that in some of its regions more or less of the above mentioned types can be found which cannot be ascribed to the innate nature of those people, but to their education and subsistence. If, however, one find through long range observation that in a country the majority of its inhabitants are disposed to this or that skill, trade, and virtue, or, on the contrary, vice and deficiency, one should take notice of that very carefully, just as it should not remain unknown to what religion or faith the inhabitants of a country belong.[332]

He was greatly interested in the social organization of countries.

It is necessary to know the difference between people in a country by their status. There is known, according to the general usage of the German countries, how nearly everywhere, beside people of high estate and sovereignty, there can be found three different estates; that there are some noblemen, some burghers, and some peasants.[333]

In some countries and sovereignties the highest sovereign has below him prelates, counts, and gentlemen.[334]

In the *Christen-Stat*[335] he considered the problem of population.

When . . . one undertakes to speak of the common means of support and the freedom of citizens, and of the measures necessary for improving their condition in these respects, a considerable difference must be taken into account between countries: for the situation is of one sort in the case of those which derive their ordinary support from agriculture, and of another sort with those that are devoted to trade and commerce, particularly to navigation. Because less of the latter exists in Germany, than in other regions, we have the more occasion to speak of the other sort. We must know, therefore, that under ordinary circumstances *each region can properly maintain only so many people from its own resources as can get their means of support from its yield.* For example, if we consider a village which has only arable land enough for the cultivation of ten plows, no more than that number of peasants or teamsters can profitably live there, but the others must get their living by artisanship, or get a chance to work outside the boundaries of the locality. If this does not occur, each hinders the others, or there is a scarcity of support. There can also be no more handworkers in the locality than these peasants need, etc.[336]

## Harrington

James Harrington (1611–77) was particularly interested in the development of an empirical political science for purposes of social reform.

No man can be a Polititian, except he be first an Historian or a Traveller; for except he can see what Must be, or what May be, he is no Polititian: Now if he have no knowledge in story, he cannot tell what hath been; and if he hath not been a Traveller, he cannot tell what is: but he that neither knoweth what hath been, nor what is; can never tell what must be, or what may be.[337]

. . . that the Politicks can be master'd without study, or that the people can have leisure to study, is a vain imagination; and what kind of *Aristocracy,* Divines and Lawyers would make, let their incurable run upon their own narrow bias; and their perpetuall invectives against Machiavill (though in some places justly reproveable, yet the only Polititian, and incomparable Patron of the people[338]) serve for instruction. I will stand no more unto the Judgement of Lawyers and Divines in this work, then unto that of so many other Tradesmen.*[340]

Neither HIPPOCRATES nor MACHIAVEL introduc'd diseases into man's body, nor corruption into government, which were before their times; and seeing they do but discover them it must be confest that so much as they have don tends not to the increase but the cure of them, which is the truth of these two authors.[341]

He believed in the irrationality of society.

The people cannot see, but they can feel.[342]

The major part of mankind gives itself up in the matter of religion to the public leading.[343]

* " . . . there is not any public person, not any magistrat, that has written in the politics worth a button. All they that have bin excellent in this way, have bin privat men . . . There is *Plato,* there is *Aristotle,* there is *Livy,* there is *Machiavel.*"[339]

In one place he explained culture by means of the "Genius" of each society.

. . . the Fame of *Mahomet* and his *Prudence* is especially founded in this, That whereas the *Roman Monarchy,* (except that of *Israel*) was the most imperfect, the *Turkish* is the most *perfect* that ever was. Which happened in that the *Roman* (as the *Israelitish* of the *Sanhedrim* and the *Congregation*) had a mixture of the *Senate* and the *people;* and the *Turkish* is *pure:* and that this was pure, and the other mixed, happened not through the wisdome of the *Legislators,* but the different *Genius* of the *Nations;* the people of the *Eastern parts,* except the *Israelites,* (which is to be attributed to their *Agrarian*) having been such as scarce ever knew any other condition than that of *Slavery.* And these of the *Western* having ever had such a Relish of liberty, as through what despair soever could never be brought to stand still, while the Yoke was putting on their Necks, but by being fed with some hopes of reserving unto themselves some part of their *Freedome.*[344]

However, he gave a social explanation of some cultural phenomena; for example,

. . . the Tillage bringing up a good Souldiery, bringeth up a good Common-Wealth . . . for where the owner of the Plough comes to have the Sword too, he will use it in defence of his own.[345]

His study of the relations between economy and political organization attain the proportions of an institutional analysis.[346]

Riches, in regard that men are hung upon these, not of choice . . . but of necessity and by the teeth:* for as much as he who wanteth bread, is his servant that will feed him: if a man thus feed an whole people, they are under his Empire.

Empire is of two kinds, *Domestick* and *National,* or *Forrain* and *Provinciall.*

*Domestick Empire* is founded upon *Dominion.*

Dominion is Propriety reall or personall, that is to say, in Lands, or in money and goods.

Lands, or the parts and parcels of a Territory, are held by the Proprietor or Proprietors, Lord or Lords of it, in some proportion; and such (except it be in a City that hath little or no Land, and whose revenue is in Trade) as is the proportion or ballance of dominion or property in Land, such is the nature of the *Empire.*

If one man be sole Landlord of a Territory, or overballance the people, for example, three parts in four, he is Grand Signior: for so that Turk is called from his *Property;* and his *Empire* is absolute *Monarchy.*

If the Few or a Nobility, or a Nobility with the Clergy be Landlords, or overballance the people unto the like proportion, it makes the *Gothick* ballance . . . and the *Empire* is mixed *Monarchy,* as that of *Spain.* . . .

And if the whole people be Landlords, or hold the Lands so divided among them, that no one man, or number of men, within the compasse of the *Few* or *Aristocracy,* overballance them, the *Empire* (without the interposition of force) is a *Common-wealth.*[348]

For Dominion personal or in money, it may now and then stir up a *Melius* or a *Manlius,* which if the *Common-wealth* be not provided with some kind of *Dictatorian* power, may be dangerous, though it have been seldom or never successfull: because unto propriety producing Empires, it is required that it should have some certain root or foot-hold, which, except in Land, it cannot have, being otherwise as it were upon the wing.

Neverthelesse, in such Cities as subsist most by Trade, and have little or no Land as *Holland* and *Genoa;* the ballance of Treasure may be equal unto that of Land in the cases mentioned.[349]

* "*Agriculture* is the Bread of the Nation, we are hung upon it by the teeth."[347]

> . . . *where there is inequality of Estates, there must be inequality of Power; and where there is inequality of Power, there can be no Common-wealth.*[350]

> . . . *where there is equality of estates, there must be equality of power; and where there is equality of power, there can be no Monarchy.*[351]

He maintained that certain aspects of culture are necessary to a society.

> As not this language, nor that language, but some language; so not this religion, nor that religion, yet som religion is natural to every nation.[352]

Harrington supported the partiarchal theory of political evolution.

> . . . it is with all Polititians past dispute, that paternal power is in the right of nature; and this is no other than the derivation of power from the Fathers of Families, as the naturall Root of a Common-wealth; and for Experience, if it be otherwise in that of *Holland,* I know no other Example of like kind. In *Israel,* the Sovereign power came clearly from this natural root, the Elders of the whole people, and *Rome* was born *Comitiis Curiatis* in her Parochial Congregations, out of which *Romulus* raised her *Senate,* then all the rest of the Orders of that Common-wealth, which rose so high: For the depth of a Common-wealth is the just height of it.[353]

In addition, he believed in a "naturall Aristocracy."

> . . . *twenty men* (if they be not all *ideots,* perhaps if they be) can never come so together, but there will be such difference in them, that about a *third* will be *wiser,* or at least *lesse foolish* then all the rest; these upon acquaintance though it be but small, will be discovered, and (as Stags that have the largest heads) lead the herd; for while the *six* discoursing and arguing one with another, shew the eminence of their parts, the *fourteen* discover things that they never thought on; or are cleared in divers truths which had formerly perplexed them: wherefore in matter of common concernment, difficulty or danger, they hang upon their lips as *children* upon their *fathers,* and the *influence* thus acquired by the *six,* the eminence of whose parts, is found to be a stay and comfort to the *fourteen,* is (*Authoritas patrum*) the *authority of the Fathers.* Wherefore this can be no other than a *naturall Aristocracy* diffused by *God* throughout the whole body of *mankind,* to this end and purpose; and therefore such, as the *people,* have not only a natural, but a positive obligation to make use of as their *guides.*[354]

## MERCANTILISTS

With the increased development of commercial capitalism, a practical interest arose in economic laws that would be useful to the traders. Thus was produced the first pragmatic school in economic science, mercantillism.

### Mun

The classic generalization of the mercantilists was to the effect that the prosperity of a country depends upon its favorable balance of trade. Thomas Mun (1571–1641) formulated it in this manner:

> The trade of Merchandize, is not onely that laudable practize wherby the entercourse of Nations is so worthily performed, but also (as I may terme it) the verie *Touchstone* of a kingdomes prosperitie, when therein some certen rules shall be diligently observed.*

* " . . . it were to be wished, that this mysterie of Merchandising might be left only to them, who have had an education thereunto; and not to be undertaken by such, who leaving their proper vocations, doe for want of skill in this, both overthrow themselves and others who are better practised."[355]

For, as in the estates of private persons, wee may accompt that man to prosper and growe rich, who being possessed of revenues more or lesse, doth accordingly proportion his expences; whereby he may yearlie advance some maintenance for his posteritie. So doth it come to passe in those Kingdomes, which with great care and wariness doe ever vent out more of their home commodities, then they import and use of forren wares; for so undoubtedly the remainder must returne to them in treasure. But where a contrarie course is taken, through wantonnesse and riot; to over waste both forren and domestike wares; there must the money of necessitie be exported, as the meanes to helpe to furnish such excesse, and so by the corruption of mens conditions and manners, manie rich countries are made exceeding poore, whilest the people thereof, too much affecting their owne enormities, doe lay the fault in something else.[356]

## Child

As matter-of-fact businessmen, the mercantilists usually limited their search for cause and effect in cultural phenomena to the social sphere. A good example of this is to be found in Josiah Child's (1630–99) arguments for a decrease in the rate of interest.

. . . the abatement of interest is the cause of the increase of the riches of any kingdom.[357]

[Decrease in the rate of interest] inclines a nation to thriftiness. . . .

The frugal Italians of old, and the provident Dutch of later times, I think have given the world sufficient proof of this theorem; and if any shall tell me, it is the nature of those people to be thrifty, I answer, all men by nature are alike; it is only laws, custom, and education that differ men; their nature and disposition, and the disposition of all people in the world, proceed from their laws; the French peasantry are a slavish, cowardly people, because the laws of their country have made them slaves; the French gentry, a noble, valiant people, because free by law, birth, and education: in England we are all free subjects by our laws, and therefore our people prove generally courageous; the Dutch and Italians are both frugal nations, though their climates and governments differ as much as any, because the laws of both nations incline them to thriftiness; other nations I could name, are generally vain and prodigal, not by nature, nor for want of a good country, but because their laws, &c. dispose them so to be.*[359]

[A decrease in the interest rate also] encreases the people of a nation; this . . . necessary follows the encrease of trade and improvement of lands, not that it causes married men to get more children.

But 1st, a trading country affording comfortable subsistences to more families than a country destitute of trade, is the reason that many do marry, who otherwise must be

---

* "[Child argued in favor of the naturalization of Jews, for] that they would reside with us, is proved from the known principles of nature, viz.

"Principle 1. All men are by nature alike, as I have before demonstrated, and Mr. Hobbs has truly asserted, how erroneous soever he may be in other things.

"Principle 2. Fear is the cause of hatred, and hatred of separation from, as well as evil deeds to, the parties or government hated, when opporunity is offered: this by the way shews the difference between a bare connivence at dissenters in matters of religion, and a toleration by law: the former keeps them continually in fear, and consequently apt to sedition and rebellion, when any probable occasion of success presents; the latter disarms cunning ambitious-minded men, who wanting a popular discontented party to work upon, can affect little or nothing to the prejudice of the government. And this methinks discovers clearly the cause why the Lutherans in Germany, Calvinists in France, Greeks in Turky, and sectaries in Holland, are such quiet peaceable-minded men, while our Non-conformists in England are said to be inclinable to strife, war, and bloodshed; take away the cause, and the effect will cease."[358]

forced to live single; which may be one reason why fewer people of either sex are to be seen unmarried in Holland at 25 years of age, than may be found in England at 40 years old.

2dly, Where there is much employment, and good pay, if we want hands of our own, we shall draw them from others. . . .

3dly, We shall keep our own people at home, which otherwise for want of employment would be forced to leave us, and serve other nations, as too many of our seamen, shipwrights, and others have done.

4thly, Our lands and trade being improved, will render us capable not only of employing, but feeding, a far greater number of people as is manifest in that instance of the land of Palestine.[360]

## Petty

William Petty (1623–87) was interested in the discovery of social laws* because of "the vanity and fruitlessness of making Civil Positive Laws against the Laws of Nature,"[362] and, as will be seen later, he developed "political arithmetick" to give him precise quantitative generalizations. He insisted upon careful social surveys to get the kind of data he wanted, and studied all aspects of the life of the people he himself observed.†

Petty was interested in urban sociology. In the first place, he saw the relationship between urbanization and division of labor.

I say, that a Thousand Acres, that can feed 1000 Souls, is better than 10000 Acres of no more effect, for the following reason, *viz*.

1. Suppose that some great Fabrick were in Building by a Thousand Men, shall not much more time be spared if they lived all upon a Thousand Acres, then if they were forced to live upon ten times as large a Scope of Land.

2. The charge of the cure of their Souls, and the Ministry would be far greater in one case than in the other; as also of mutual defence in case of Invasion, and even of Thieves and Robbers: Moreover the charge of the administration of Justice would be much easier, where Witnesses and Parties may be easily Summoned, Attendance less

---

* "[One of 'the Causes of irregular Taxing' is] An Opinion, that certainty of Rules is impossible, and but an idle Notion."[362]

† Some idea of the extent to which he went beyond the usual investigations of the time, can be gathered from the Table of Contents of his Irish study:

"Of the Lands of *Ireland*, with the present distribution and Values of the same.

"Of the People, Houses and Smokes; their Number, Differences and Values.

"Of the Church and Benefices.

"Concerning the late Rebellion and its effects.

"Of the future Settlement of *Ireland*, Prevention of Rebellions, and its Union with *England*.

"Of the Government of *Ireland*, Apparent and Internal.

"Of the Militia and Defence of *Ireland*.

"Of the *Caelum, Solum, and Fruges;* or the Air, Soil and Products of *Ireland*.

"Of the Rate which the Lands in *Ireland* do bear to each other, with the History of the several Valuations of the same.

"Of the Money of *Ireland*, and the Causes of its Decrease, with the Remedy for the same.

"Of the Trade of *Ireland*, and its Impediments; the Commodities, and aptitude for Traffick, and incidently of the Cloaths and Dyet of the People: Of Sumptuary Laws, Absentees, *&c.*

'Of the Religion, Language, Manners, and Interest of the present Inhabitants of *Ireland;* as also of the Present and Ancient Divisions and Names of the Lands.

"Some Miscellany Remarques and Intimations concerning *Ireland*, and the several matters aforementioned."[363]

expensive, when Mens Action would be better known, when wrongs and injuries could not be covered, as in this peopled places they are.

Lastly, those who live in Solitary places, must be their own Soldiers, Divines, Physicians, and Lawyers;* and must have their Houses stored with necessary Provisions (like a Ship going upon a long Voyage,) to the great wast, and needless expence of such Provisions.[365]

Second, he understood the importance of means of communication and transportation in the growth of cities.

I think 'tis certain, that while ever there are people in *England,* the greatest cohabitation of them will be about the place which is now *London,* the *Thames* being the most commodious River of this Island, and the seat of *London* the most commodious part of the *Thames;* so much doth the means of facilitating Carriage greaten a City.[366]

Third he was aware of the ecological distribution of various urban phenomena.

. . . in the Quarterly Bills, we reduce the Diseases to Three Heads, *viz.* Contagious, Acute, and Chronical; applying this distinction to Parishes, in order to know how the different Scituation, Soil, and way of living in each Parish, doth dispose Men to each of the said Three Species.[367]

And most surprising, he gave an analysis of ecological succession in urban areas.

. . . what . . . is the true effect of forbidding to build upon new foundations? I answer to keep and fasten the City to its old seat and ground-plot, the which encouragement for new Buildings will remove, as it comes to pass almost in all great Cities, though insensibly, and not under many years progression.

The reason whereof is, because men are unwilling to build new houses at the charge of pulling down their old, where both the old house it self, and the ground it stand upon to make a much dearer ground-plot for a new house, and yet far less free and convenient; wherefore men build upon new free foundations, and cobble up old houses, until they become fundamentally irreparable, at which time they become either the dwelling of the Rascality, or in the process of time return to waste and Gardens again, examples whereof are many even about *London.*

Now if great Cities are naturally apt to remove their Seats, I ask which way? I say, in the case of *London,* it must be Westward, because the Windes blowing near 3/4 of the year from the West, the dwellings of the West end are so much the more free from the fumes, steams, and stinks of the whole Easterly Pyle; which where Seacoal is burnt is a great matter. Now if it follow from hence, that the Pallaces of the greatest men will remove Westward, it will also naturally follow, that the dwellings of others who depend upon them will creep after them. This we see in *London,* where the Noblemens ancient houses are now become Halls for Companies, or turned into Tenements, and all the Pallaces are gotten Westward; Insomuch, as I do not doubt but that five hundred years hence, the King's Pallace will be near *Chelsey,* and the old building of *Whitehall* converted to uses more answerable to their quality.[368]

He knew that the size of a population depended upon its food supply.

The Extreme Number of people that any Land can well and comodiously maintayn is so many as what the said [husbandry] can furnish milk, cream, fresh butter, new

---

* "Cloth must be cheaper made, when one Cards, another Spins, another Weaves, another Draws, another Dresses, another Presses and Packs; than when all the Operations above-mentioned, were clumsily performed by the same hand."[364]

laid eggs, fresh meat, fish and fowl, Sallett, fruits, gardens of pleasure, meal for Sadle and Coachorses, & which number is unnecessary here to Determine.[369]

But, also, that this is modified by other factors.

. . . if the People are not in the same proportion as the Land, the same must be attributed to the Scituation of the Land, and to the Trade and Policy of the People superstructured thereupon.[370]

He gave social explanations of various traits.

. . . difference in Land and People, arises principally from their Situation, Trade, and Policy.[371]

. . . difference of Improvement in Wealth and Strength, arises from the Situation, Trade, and Policy of the places respectively; and in particular from Conveniences for Shipping and Water Carriage.[372]

As for the Manners of the *Irish,* I deduce them from their Original Constitutions of Body, and from the Air; next from their ordinary Food; next from their Condition of Estate and Liberty, and from the Influence of their Governours and Teachers; and lastly, from their Ancient Customs, which affect as well their Consciences as their Nature. For their Shape, Stature, Colour, and Complexion, I see nothing in them inferior to any other People, nor any enormous predominancy of any humour.

Their Lazing seems to me to proceed rather from want of Imployment and Encouragement to Work, than from the natural abundance of Flegm in their Bowels and Blood. . . .

They are accused also of much Treachery, Falseness, and Thievery; none of all which, I conceive, is natural to them; for as to Treachery, they are made believe, that they all shall flourish again, after some time; wherefore they will not readily submit to those whom they hope to have their Servants; nor will they declare so much, but say the contrary, for their present ease, which is all the Treachery I have observed; for they have in their hearts, not only a grudging to see their old Proprieties enjoyed by Foreigners, but a persuasion they shall be shortly restor'd. As for Thievery, it is affixt to all thin-peopled Countries, such as *Ireland* is, where there cannot be many Eyes to prevent such Crimes; and where what is stolen, is easily hidden and eaten, and where 'tis easy to burn the House, or violate the Persons of those who prosecute these Crimes, and where thin-peopled Countries are govern'd by the Laws that were made and first fitted to thick-peopled Countries; and where matter of small moment and value must by try'd, with all the formalities which belong to the highest Causes. In this case there must be thieving, where is withal, neither encouragement, nor method, nor means for Labouring, nor Provision for Impotents.[373]

As for *Thieves,* they are for the most part begotten from the same Cause [as paupers, namely, unemployment]; For it is against Nature, that any Man should venture his Life, Limb, or Liberty, for a wretched Livelyhood, whereas moderate Labour will produce a better. But of this see Sir *Thomas Moor,* in the first part of his *Utopia.*[374]

. . . an excessive Taxe, causes excessive and insuperable want, even of natural necessities, and that on a sudden, so as ignorant particular persons, cannot finde out what may to subsist by; and this, by the law of Nature, must cause sudden effects to relieve it self, that is, Rapines, Frauds.[375]

Petty anticipated Max Weber on the relationship between capitalism and Protestantism.

Liberty of Conscience, Registry of Conveyances, small Customs, Banks, Lumbards, and Law Merchant, rise all from the same Spring, and tend to the same Sea.[376]

I now come to the first Policy of the *Dutch, viz*. Liberty of Conscience; which I conceive they grant upon these Grounds. (But keeping up always a Force to maintain the Common Peace,) 1. They themselves broke with *Spain,* to avoid the imposition of the Clergy. 2. Dissenters of this kind, are for the most part, thinking, sober, and patient Men, and such as believe that Labour and Industry is their Duty towards God. (How erroneous soever their Opinions be.) 3. These People believing the Justice of God, and seeing the most Licentious persons, to enjoy most of the World, and its best things, will never venture to be of the same Religion and Profession with Voluptuaries, and Men of extreme Wealth and Power, who they think have their Portion in this World.

4. They cannot but know, That no Man can believe what himself pleases, and to force Men to say that they believe what they do not, is vain, absurd, and without Honor to God.

5. The *Hollanders* knowing themselves not to be an Infallible Church, and that others had the same Scripture for Guides as themselves, and withal the same interest to save their Souls, did not think fit to make this matter their business; not more than to take Bonds of the Seamen they employ, not to cast away their own Ships and Lives.

6. The *Hollanders* observe that in *France* and *Spain,* (especially the latter) the Churchmen are about one hundred to one, to what they use or need; the principal care of whom is to preserve Uniformity, and this they take to be a superfluous charge. . . .

9. . . . Moreover it is to be observed that Trade doth not (as some think) best flourish under Popular Governments, but rather that Trade is most vigorously carried on, in every State and Government, by the Heterodox part of the same, and such as profess Opinions different from what are publickly established.[377]

He gave a social explanation of revolutions.

The causes of Civil Wars here in *Europe* proceed very much from Religion, *viz*. the punishing of Believers heterodox from the authorized way, in publicke and open places, before great multitudes of ignorant people, with loss of life, liberty, and limbs. . . .

Civil Wars are likewise caused by peoples fansying that their own uneasie condition may be best remedied by an universal confusion. . . .

Moreover, the peoples believing that Forms of Government shall in a few years produce any considerable alteration as to the wealth of the Subject; that the Form which is most ancient and present is not the best for the place, that any established family or person is not better then any new pretended, or even then the best Election that can be made; that Sovereignty is invisible, and that it is not certainly annexed unto some certain person or persons.

Causes of Civil War are also, that the Wealth of the Nation is in too few mens hands, and that no certain means are provided to keep all men from a necessity either to beg, or steal, or be Souldiers.

Moreover, the allowing Luxury in some, whilst others needlesly starve.

The dispensing of benefits upon casual and uncertain Motives; the giving vast Emoluments to persons and parties of no certain visible merit.[378]

Finally, Petty had a conception of the rise and fall of cultures, and their succession.

The People of England come from France; Those of France from Greece; Those of Greece from Asia Minor; and those from the Native Lands of our first and comon Parents.[379]

. . . why should we trouble our selves what shall be five hundred years hence, not knowing what a day may bring forth; and since 'tis not unlikely, but that before that time we may be all transplanted from hence into *America,* these countreys being over-run with Turks, and made waste, as the Seats of the famous Eastern Empires at this day are.[380]

## Barbon

Nicholas Barbon (1640?–98), as did Petty, went beyond the narrow economic considerations usual to the mercantilists and considered broader problems. For instance, he spoke of the evolution of political organization.

There was never any part of Mankind so wild and barbarous, but they had Difference and Degree of Men amongst them, and invented some things to shew that Distinction.[381]

In the Infancy of the World, Governments began with little Families and Colonies of Men; so that, when ever any Government arrived to greater Height than the rest, either by the great Wisdom or Courage of the Governor, they afterwards grew a pace.[382]

An analysis is given of man's needs.

The Use of Things, are to supply the Wants and Necessities of Man: There are Two General Wants that Mankind is born with; the Wants of the Body, and the Wants of the Mind.

Wares, useful to supply the Wants of the Body, are all things necessary to support Life, such are in Common Estimation; all those Goods which are useful to supply the Three General Necessities of Man, Food, Clothes and Lodging. . . .

Wares, that have their Value from supplying the Wants of the Mind, are all such things that can satisfie Desire. . . .

Amongst the great Variety of things to satisfy the Wants of the Mind, those that adorn Mans Body, and advance the Pomp of Life, have the most general Use, and in all Ages, and amongst all sort of Mankind, have been of Value.[383]

He reflected the cosmopolitanism of the age of discovery.

. . . it's only Use and Custom by which Habits become Grave and Decent, and not any particular Conveniency in the shape; for if Conveniency were the Rule of Commendation, there would arise a Question not Easily to be Determined, Whether the *Spanish* Garb made strait to the Body, or the loose Habit of the *Turks,* were to be Chosen?[384]

Barbon differed from most mercantilists in his geographical interpretation of culture.

[In] *England.* . . . The Inhabitants are naturally Couragious, as appear from the Effects of the Climate, in the Game Cocks, and Mastiff Dogs, being no where else so stout.[385]

## North

In all, social laws were searched for and used wherever possible by the mercantilists. Thus Dudley North (1641–91) spoke of "the Universal Maxim I have built upon, *viz.* That Plenty of any thing makes it cheap.[386]

## STATISTICIANS

Reflecting the metrical tendency in contemporary physical science, the pragmatists became interested in the quantification of social data.

## Seckendorf

As early as 1655, Seckendorf discussed the necessity of, and a program for, social statistics for administrative purposes.

[Contemporary authorities had stated that errors are to be found in books on political matters, which] either because of their age do not fit our times any more, or that they are incomplete and many necessary and important pieces of information have been omitted, or that they are based on uncertain reports and general hearsay rather than on the true basic facts, nay, one will even find that completely false, wrong, and matters detrimental to the country, are produced, of which one could give many examples.

That is why in a sovereign administration it becomes very useful and advantageous, nay, even necessary, that a thorough description be made, which is grounded upon inspection and the concrete condition of the things themselves, of the country and sovereignty, of its administration . . . as well as of its external condition, a description of which the sovereign and all classes of civil servants can make use, as far as it is necessary and possible.[387]

[He then gives] a general model, according to which the material description of each particular country could be arranged.[388]

The information desired was to be presented in tabular or cartographic form wherever possible, and under the following headings:

1.  The name, origin, and circumstances of a sovereignty and country; including the derivation of its name, the origin of the sovereignty, and the geographical situation and boundaries of the country.[389]

2.  The subdivisions and dependencies of a country; according to its natural and artificial boundaries, including administative and judicial districts, and other information such as on the streets, bridges, and passes of the various subdivisions.[390]

3.  The quality and fertility of the country.[391]

4.  The people and inhabitants of the country; the strata of the population and the characteristics of each.[392]

## Graunt

In the *Natural and Poltical Observations. . . Upon the Bills of Mortality* (1662),[393] John Graunt (1620-74)[394] was the first to discover the statistical regularity of social phenomena.

. . . among the several *Casualties* some bear a constant proportion unto the whole number of *Burials;* such are *Chronical* Diseases, and the Diseases whereunto the City is most subject; as for Example, *Consumptions, Dropsies, Jaundice, Gout, Stone, Palsie, Scurvy, Rising of the Lights* or *Mother, Rickets, Aged, Agues, Fevers, Bloody Flux* and *Scowring;* nay, some Accidents, as *Grief, Drowning, Men's making away themselves,* and being *Kill'd by several Accidents, &c.* do the like; whereas *Epidemical* and *Malignant* Diseases, as the *Plague, Purples, Spotted Fever, Small Pox* and *Measles* do not keep that equality: so as in some Years, or Months, there died ten times as many as in others.[395]

. . . the numbers of those that have been *Drowned, Killed by falls from Scaffolds,* or by *Carts running over them, &c* . . . depends upon the casual Trade and Employment of men.[396]

The Diseases, which beside the *Plague* make years unhealthful in this City, are *Spotted-Fevers, Small-Pox, Dysentery,* called by some *The Plague in the Guts,* and the unhealthful Season is the *Autumn.*[397]

. . . although in the Country the *Christenings* exceed the *Burials,* yet in *London* they do not.[398]

There are more *Males* than *Females;* we say next, That the one exceed the other by about a thirteenth part. So that although more Men die violent deaths than Women, that is, more are *slain* in *Wars, killed* by *Mischance, drowned* at *Sea,* and die by the *Hand of Justice;* moreover, more Men go to *Colonies,* and travel into forein parts, than Women; and lastly, more remain unmarried than of Women, as *Fellows* of *Colleges,* and *Apprentices* above eighteen, *&c.* yet the said thirteenth part difference bringeth the business but to such a pass, that every Woman may have an Husband, without the allowance of Polygamy.[399]

[He therefore draws this conclusion:] *Christian Religion,* prohibiting *Polygamy, is more* agreeable to the *Law of Nature,* that is, the *Law of God,* then *Mahumetism,* and others, that allow it: for one Man his having many Women, or Wives, by Law, signifies nothing, unless there were many Women to one Man in Nature also.[400]

## Petty

Petty was the greatest exponent of social statistics in the seventeenth century. In the words of a contemporary:

The excellent Author . . . has . . . made it appear that Mathematical Reasoning, is not only applicable to Lines and Numbers, but affords the best means of Judging in all the concerns of humane Life.[401]

Petty was impressed by Graunt's observations; he spoke

of Wonderful Conclusions drawn out of the Bills of Mortality, which no man medled withall in 70 years before the Author undertook it; and no man since hath either confuted, or added any more unto, those conclusions.[402]

The Observations upon the *London-Bills of Mortality* have been a new Light to the World; and the like Observation upon those of *Dublin* [by Petty], may serve as Snuffers to make the same Candle burn clearer.[403]

He developed a methodology for his "political arithmetick" based upon Francis Bacon's inductive principles.[404]

The Method I take . . . is not yet very usual; for instead of using only comparative and superlative Words, and intellectual Arguments, I have taken the course (as a Specimen of the Political Arithmetick I have long aimed at) to express my self in Terms of *Number, Weight,* or *Measure;** to use only Arguments of Sense, and to consider only such Causes, as have visible Foundations in Nature; leaving those that depend upon the mutable Minds, Opinions, Appetites, and Passions of particular Men, to the Consideration of others; Really professing my self as unable to speak satisfactorily upon those Grounds (if they may be call'd Grounds), as to foretel the cast of a Dye; to play well at

---

* "When I find out puzling and perplext Matters, that may be brought to Terms of Number, Weight and Measure, and consequently be made demonstrable; And when I find Things of vast and general Concernment, which may be discuss'd in a few Words: I willingly ingage upon such Undertakings."[405]

"The words *considerably bigger* having been used in some things, that were read [at the Royal Society], Sir *William Petty* cautioned, that no word might be used but what marks either number, weight, or measure."[406]

Tennis, Billiards, or Bowles, (without long practice,) by virtue of the most elaborate Conceptions that ever have been written *De Projectilibus & Missilibus,* or of the Angles of Incidence and Reflection.

Now the Observations or Positions expressed by *Number, Weight,* and *Measure,* upon which I bottom the ensuing Discourses, are either true, or not apparently false, and which is they are not already true, certain, and evident, yet may be made so by the Sovereign Power, *Nam id certum est quod certum reddi potest,* and if they are false, not so false as to destroy the Argument they are brought for; but at worst are sufficient as Suppositions to shew the way to that Knowledge I aim at.[407]

Against all this will be objected, that these computations are very hard if not impossible to make; to which I answer onely this, that they are so, especially if none will trouble their hands or heads to make them, or give authority for so doing: But withall, I say, that until this be done, Trade will be too conjectural a work for any man to employ his thoughts about; for it will be the same wisdom in order to win with fair Dice, to spend much time in considering how to hold them, how much to shake them, and how hard to throw them, and on what angles they should hit the side of the Tables, as to consider how to advance the Trade of this Nation; where at present particular men get from their neighbours (not from the earth and sea) rather by hit then wit, and by the false opinions of others, rather then by their own judgements.[408]

Sir *Francis Bacon,* in his *Advancement of Learning,* hath made a judicious *Parallel* in many particulars, between the *Body Natural,* and *Body Politick,* and between the Arts of preserving both in Health and Strength: And it is as reasonable, that as *Anatomy* is the best foundation of one, so also of the other; and that to practice upon the Politick, without knowing the *Symmetry, Fabrick,* and *Proportion* of it, is as *casual* as the practice of Old-women and Empyricks.

Now, because *Anatomy* is not only necessary in Physicians, but laudable in every Philosophical person whatsoever; I therefore, who profess no Politicks, have, for my curiosity, at large attempted *the first Essay of Political Anatomy.*

Furthermore, as Students in Medicine, practice their inquiries upon cheap and common *Animals,* and such whose actions they are best acquainted with, and where there is the least confusion and perplexure of Parts; I have chosen *Ireland* as such a Political *Animal,* who is scarce Twenty years old [i.e., since the " Act for the Settling of Ireland" (1652)]; where the *Intrigue* of *State* is not very complicate, and with which I have been conversant from an *Embrion;* and in which, if I have done amiss, the fault may be easily mended by another.

'Tis true, that curious *Dissections* cannot be made without variety of proper Instruments; whereas I have had only a commin *Knife* and a *Clout,* instead of the many more helps which such a Work requires: However, my rude appraoches being enough to find whereabout the Liver and Spleen, and Lungs lye, tho' not to discern the Lymphatick Vessels, the *Plexus Choroidus,* the *Volvuli* of vessels within the Testicles; yet not knowing, than even what I have here readily done, was much considered, or indeed thought useful by others, I have ventur'd to *begin* a *new* Work, which, when Corrected and Enlarged by better Hands and Helps, I believe will tend to the Peace and Plenty of my Country; besides which, I have no other end.[409]

## King and Davenant

Some of Petty's followers were Gregory King (1648–1712)[410] and Charles Davenant (1656–1714). The latter was a popularizer of social statistics.

By Political Arithmetic, we mean the art of reasoning by figures, upon things relating to government.[411]

A great statesman, by consulting all sorts of men, and by contemplating the universal posture of the nation, its power, strength, trade, wealth and revenues, in any counsel he is to offer, by summing up the difficulties on either side, and by computing upon the whole, shall be able to form a sound judgement, and to give a right advice: and this is what we mean by Political Arithmetic.[412]

## Halley

Edmund Halley (1656–1742) made an important contribution to statistics in his calculation of mortality rates;[413] his figures were used by life insurance companies for almost two centuries. In these investigations he had occasion to mention some of the factors which influence size of population.

. . . the Growth and Encrease of Mankind is not so much stinted by any thing in the Nature of the *Species,* as it is from the cautious difficulty most People make to adventure on the state of *Marriage,* from the prospect of the Trouble and Charge of providing for a Family.[414]

## DEGRADATION VERSUS PROGRESS

In the post-Renaissance period a controversy arose in the sciences between the advocates of authority and empirical observation. One of the forms this took was an argument as to the relative superiority of the ancients and moderns respectively. And this in turn was often based on the debate between the supporters of the rival theories of degradation (usually called "the decay of the world") and progress. Some of the men who took part in the controversy have already been discussed: Montaigne, Spenser, and Temple, who were "Ancients"; and Bacon, Bruno, Castiglione, Machiavelli, and Pascal, who were "Moderns."

## Purchas

Samuel Purchas (1577?–1626) spoke of "the olde and decrepit Age of the World."[415]

## Hakewill

George Hakewill (1578–1649) wrote the most important confutation of the theory of the decay of the world,

. . . to demonstrate the *providence of God* in the *preservation of the World,* and to prove that it doth not *universally* & *perpetually decline.*[416]

For a false and fond similitude it is of some, which they take up as a most witty and proper one, that wee being compared to the Ancients, are as Dwarfes upon the shoulders of Giants: it is not so, neither are we Dwarfes, nor they Giantes, but wee are all of one stature, save that wee are lifted up somewhat higher by their meanes, conditionally there be found in us the same studiousnesse, watchfulnesse and love of truth, as was in them: which if they bee wanting, then are we not dwarfes, nor set on the shoulders of giants, but men of a competent stature groveling on the earth.[417]

However, instead of a theory of progress he employed a cyclical theory.

. . . as the Heavens remaine unchangeable, so doth the Church triumphant in Heaven, and as all things under the cope of heaven vary and change, so doth the militant heere on earth; it hath its times and turnes, sometimes flowing and againe ebbing with the *sea,* sometimes waxing, and againe waning with the *Moone.* . . .

And if the *Moone* thus change, and all things under the *Moone,* why should we wonder at the change of *Monarchies* and *Kingdomes?* much lesse petty states & private families: they rise, and fall, and rise againe, and fall againe. . . . what was lost to one part, was gained to another; and what was lost in one time, was to the same part recovered in an other; and so the ballance by the divine providence over-ruling all, kept upright.[418]

There is (it seemes) both in *wits* and *Arts,* as in all things besides, a kinde of *circular progresse*: they have their *birth,* their *growth,* their *flourishing,* their *fayling,* their *fading,* and within a while after their *resurrection,* and *reflourishing* againe.[419]

But as I cannot easily grant, that men *alwayes,* and in all places waxe worse and worse; so I doe not believe that alwayes, & in all places they waxe better and better, or that they stand at a stay: But as in the *Arts* & *Sciences,* so likewise in matter of *manners,* there is *a vicissitude,* an *alternation* & *revolution,* as before hath beene touched in part. The world is sometimes better & sometimes worse, according to the times of warre or peace, the conditions of Princes and Lawes, and the execution of them. Sometimes *vertue* increaseth in one kingdome, and decreaseth in another; and againe in the same kingdome *one vice* growes up, and another withers, at least wise for a time.[420]

### Wilkins

John Wilkins (1614–1672) echoed Francis Bacon.

Antiquity does consist in the Old Age of the World, not in the Youth of it. In such Learning as may be increased by fresh Experiments and new Discoveries; 'tis we are the Fathers, and of more Authority than former Ages; because we have the advantage of more Time than they had, & Truth (we say) is the Daughter of Time.[421]

### Milton

John Milton (1608–74) wrote a poem to prove "That Nature Submits Not to the Decay of Old Age."

The Father Omnipotent, setting the stars on strong foundations, has taken thought for the sum total of things, and with weights inerrant has poised in perfect balance the scales of the Fates, and has bidden each thing in all the mighty array to keep unceasingly the tenor of its way.[422]

But neither do you, Earth, lack that old-time vigor of a far-off age.[423]

So, in a word, the righteous series of all things will go on into endless time, until the final fires shall lay waste the wide compass of the lands, embracing the poles, and the peaks of the vast skies at their highest, and the enginery of the universe shall burn on a giant pyre.[424]

### Dryden

John Dryden (1631–1700), in defending the literature of his time, also argued against the theory of degradation.

For good sense is the same in all or most ages; and course of time rather improves Nature, than impairs her. What has been, may be again: another Homer, and another Virgil, may possibly arise from those very causes which produced the first; though it would be impudence to affirm, that any such have yet appeared.[425]

## Wotton

William Wotton (1666–1727) wrote a refutation of Temple.

Mankind has always been of the same Make.[426]

. . . the World has gone on, from Age to Age, Improving; and consequently . . . it is at present much more Knowing than it ever was since the earliest Times to which History can carry us.[427]

To prove this point, he wrote what was in effect a history of post-Renaissance science.

## LAW OF NATURE

The rationalistic and empirical world views of the seventeenth century, and the ethnographic data gathered since the beginning of the age of discovery, were applied to the old concept of the law of nature. The rationalists used a deductive approach; the empiricists, an inductive. Usually an analysis was first made of the nature of man, an then the conclusions were applied to a consideration of the law of nature, particularly in regard to law and religion.

## Herbert

Edward Herbert of Cherbury (1583–1648) was one of the first rationalists to tackle the problem.

If, throught the elements, minerals, plants and animals in an identical form according to the variety of species, it [i.e., "Natural Instinct"] promotes precisely similar functions [with self-preservation as the goal], why should it not manifest itself in ourselves?[428]

I pass now to the definition of Natural Instinct. I may preface it by saying that it has two aspects; in one aspect it is the faculty which conforms; in the other it is the state of conformity itself, that is to say, it is expressed in apprehension. So far as it is a faculty it is the immediate instrument of divine Providence, some measure of which is imprinted on our mind. In the second aspect *natural instincts are expressions of those faculties which are found in every normal man, through which the Common Notions touching the internal conformity of things . . . are brought into conformity independently of discursive thought.*[429]

Common Notions . . . form that part of knowledge with which we were endowed in the primeval plan of Nature*[431]

Accordingly if there is a Common Notion that Nature does nothing in vain, we must hold that it is the very voice of Nature which asserts it. If there is a Common Notion which tells us not to do to another what you would not have done to yourself, we must conclude that the universe itself is governed according to this maxim.[432]

Common Notions above all tend towards the preservation of individuals, species, general classes and the Universe itself. Unless a law inwardly demanded and drawn from the universal wisdom of nature did not avert the mutual destruction of things, they would all conflict with such violence that they would instantly fall into ruins.[433]

I take the chief criterion of Natural Instinct to be universal consent (putting aside persons who are out of their minds or mentally incapable).[434]

* "God . . . has bestowed Common Notions upon men in all ages as media of His divine universal Providence."[430]

Whatever principles, then, make the same impression on us and are universally received is the same way, must be assumed to be Common Notions.[435]

All races require law, that is to say the Common Notions possessed by them arranged in due order.* Yet different versions of this law have been given by different lawgivers. But while among legal codes differences exist on many points, there is the closest agreement concerning religion or civil and political justice as such. I hold, therefore, that this universal consent is the teaching of Nature Instinct and is essentially due to Divine Providence.[437]

Religion is a Common Notion; no period or nation is without religion. We have, then, to search for what is by universal consent acknowledged in religion and compare these universal principles with each other; and what is universally acclaimed as religious truths must be recognized as Common Notions. . . . In addition, Law is a Common Notion. Accordingly we must proceed in the same way and admit only those laws as sound which are approved of by the whole world.[438]

But I do not find this Universal Consent only in laws, religions, philosophies and written expositions; I hold that certain inner faculties are inscribed in our minds by which these truths are brought into conformity.[439]

Added impetus to the search for a natural religion was provided by the fact that the numerous Christian sects which flourished at the time, each insisting that its dogma was the absolute truth and that all others were false, produced such confusion[440] that some men tried to find a basis for religion which would not be shaken by the conflicting creeds. Herbert thought he had discovered it.

Five undeniable Propositions [exist] . . . which not only we, but all Mankind in general, must needs acknowledge:

I. *That there is one Supreme God.*
II. *That he ought to be worshipped.*
III. *That Vertue and Piety are the Chief Parts of Divine Worship.*
IV. *That we ought to be sorry for our Sins, and repent of them.*
V. *That Divine Goodness doth dispense Rewards and Punishments both in this Life, and after it.*[441]

Thus it appears that the *Heathens* did not only agree with us Christians in worshipping the *Supream God,* but also in the same most principal and essential kind of Worship.[442]

. . . their Religious Worship or Rites . . . [are] the Invention of the Priests only; wherefore this Crime ought solely to be imputed to their Great Men, and not to the Populace, who were only passive in the matter. I suppose none will deny but that Priests have introduced Superstition and Idolatry, as well as sown Quarrels and Dissentions where-ever they came . . . . the Laity['s] . . . .great Defection from the Pure Worship of the *Supreme God* being justly to be attributed to the Sacerdotal Order.[443]

Herbert used the comparative method to prove his "undeniable Propositions";[444] while many other authors wrote on the known religions of the world in order to justify Christianity.[445]

## Leibniz

Gottfried Wilhelm von Leibniz (1646–1716) defended Herbert's doctrine of innate ideas against Locke.

* "Such are the principles that there are some actions which we ought to perform, and others which we ought to shun. Among the duties they command are piety and gratitude to our benefactors and particularly towards God."[436]

I admit that to think of these innate truths and to unravel them discernment is necessary; but they do not on that account cease to be innate.[446]

I do not ground the certainty of innate principles upon universal consent.[447]

Innate ideas and truths cannot be effaced, but they are obscured in all men (as they
are now) by their inclination towards the needs of the body, and oftener still be the occurrence of bad customs. There characteristics of the internal light would always be
shining in the understanding and would give fervor to the will, if the confused perceptions
of sense did not engross our attention.[448]

I am . . . persuaded that a great many opinions pass for truths which are only the
effects of custom and credulity, and that there are many such opinions, too, which certain
philosophers would fain account for as matters of prejudice, which are, however,
grounded in right reason and in nature.[449]

That which has not been attained without reason, and was not attained by reasoning
alone, should be referred in part to the natural instincts.[450]

Man instinctively lives according to the law of nature, and the sanctions of that
law are inherent in the acts themselves.

There can be *natural rewards and penalties* without a legislator; intemperance, for example, is punished by disease.[451]

. . . it is not so much the pain of a law, as a natural pain which the act draws upon
itself.[452]

In addition, man has an instinctive sense of virtue.

It is true that the name of virtue depends upon the opinion of those who give it to
different habits or actions, according as they deem them good or bad and use their
reason; but all are sufficiently agreed as to the notion of virtue in general, although they
differ in its application.[453]

Sociality is also an instinct.

I . . . [am] averse to the view of Hobbes, who did not admit that man was made for
society, conceiving that he has been forced into it by necessity and by the wickedness
of those of his species. But he did not consider that the best men, free from all wickedness, united themselves the better to obtain their purposes, as the birds flock together
the better to travel in company, and the beavers unite in large numbers to make great
dams, in which work a small number of these animals could not succeed; and these
dams are necessary to them, to provide reservoirs of water or little lakes, in which they
build their huts and catch the fish upon which they feed. This then is the foundation
of the society of the animals which are adapted to it, and nowise the fear of their kind,
which is rarely found among animals.[454]

Now nature gives to man and also to most of the animals affectionate and tender
feelings for those of their species. . . . Besides this general instinct of *society*, which
may be called *philanthropy* in man, there are some more particular forms of it, as the
affection between the male and the female, the love which father and mother bear toward
the children, . . . and other similar inclinations which make this natural law, or this
image of law rather, which, according to Roman jurisconsults, nature had taught the
animals. But in man in particular there is found a certain regard for dignity, for propriety,
which leads him to conceal the things which lower us, to be sparing of shame, to have
repugnance for incests, to bury dead bodies, not to eat men at all, nor living animals.
One is led further to be careful of his reputation, even beyond need, and of life; to be

subject to remorse of conscience, and to feel those *laniatus et ictus,* these tortures and torments of which Tacitus, following Plato, speaks; besides the fear of a future and of a supreme power which arises, moreover, naturally enough.[455]

As a consequence of this instinctive sociality, man is benevolent and capable of disinterested love.

Benevolence. . . . is not an act, but a *habit* or strong inclination of the mind, which we have acquired either by the fortune of birth, or by a special gift of God, or by repeated practice.[456]

Benevolence is the habit of love.
To love anyone is to delight in his happiness.[457]

There are two ways of desiring the good of others, the one when we desire it on account of our own good, the other when we desire it as if it were our own good. The first is the way of him who esteems, the second of him who loves; the first is the feeling of a master to his servant, the second that of a father to his son; the first is the feeling of a man towards the tool he requires, the second that of a friend to a friend; in the first case the good of others is sought for the sake of something else, in the second for its own sake.[458]

When one loves a person sincerely one does not seek one's own advantage or a pleasure severed from that of the beloved person, but one seeks one's pleasure in the contentment and in the felicity of this person. And if this felicity did not please in itself, but merely because of an advantage resulting therefrom to us, this would no longer be pure and sincere love. It must be then that pleasure is immediately found in this felicity, and that grief is found in the unhappiness of the beloved person. For whatever produces pleasure immediately through itself is also desired for itself, as constituting (at least in part) the end of our wishes, and as something which enters into our own felicity and gives us satisfaction.

This serves to reconcile two truths which appear incompatible; for we do all for our own good, and it is impossible for us to have other feelings whatever we may say. Nevertheless we do not yet love altogether purely, when we seek the good of the beloved object not for itself and because it itself pleases us, but because of an advantage we foresee from it. But it is apparent from the notion of love which we have just given that we seek at the same time our good for ourselves and the good of the beloved object for itself, when the good of this object is immediately, finally (*ultimato*) and through itself our end, our pleasure, and our good; as happens in regard to all the things wished for because they are pleasing in themselves, and are consequently good of themselves, even if one should have no regard to consequences; these are ends and not means.*[460]

Leibniz believed in a natural aristocracy.

As the order of States is established on the authority of those who govern them and on the dependence of their peoples, nature which destines men for civil life endows them at birth with different qualities, some for commanding, others for obeying, in order that the power of the sovereign in a monarchy and the inequality between those who command and those who obey in a republic, be no less founded on nature than on law, on virtue than on fortune. So princes ought to be above their subjects by their virtue and

* "[There exists] the difficult problem, . . . how there can be a disinterested love apart from hope and fear and every consideration of advantage; the solution being that the happiness of those in whose happiness we take pleasure becomes a part of our own happiness, for things which give us pleasure are desired for their own sake."[459]

their natural qualities, as they are above them by the authority which the laws give them, in order to reign both by natural right and by civil right, like the first kings in the world, who having been raised to the government of their peoples by their virtue and their intellectual gifts, commanded as much by nature as by law, by merit as by fortune.[461]

He put children and "savages" on a par, like the nineteenth-century English evolutionists.

It is true that children and savages have the mind less altered by customs.[462]

The following was his view of the function of history:

The use of history consists principally in the pleasure there is in knowing origins, in the justice rendered to the men who have deserved well of other men, in the establishment of historical criticism, and especially of sacred history, which supports the foundations of revelations, and (putting also aside the geneologies and laws of princes and powers) in the useful teachings which the examples furnish us. I do not despise the thorough examination of antiquities, even to the smallest trifles; for sometimes the knowledge which the critics draw from them may be of use in more important matters. . . . But I wish there might be some persons who would devote themselves preferably to drawing from history that which is more useful, as the extraordinary examples of virtue, remarks upon the convenience of life, stratagems of politics and of war. . . . I wish also that an infinite number of things of this nature, by which we might profit, might be drawn from books of travel, and be arranged according to the order of the subjects.[463]

## Grotius

The customary code of Europe, in military and maritime questions, as well as in some others, to which no state could apply its particular jurisprudence with any hope of reciprocity, grew up by degrees to be administered, if not upon solid principles, yet with some uniformity. The civil jurists, as being conversant with a system more widely diffused, and of which the equity was more generally recognized than any other, took into their hands the adjudication of all these cases. In the fifteenth and sixteenth centuries, the progress of international relations, and, we may add, the frequency of wars, though it did not at once create a common standard, showed how much it was required.[464]

Therefore, in the seventeenth century an attempt was made to put international law on an incontrovertible basis by subjecting the old concept of the law of nations derived from the law of nature to a re-examination, in order to determine which laws were of universal validity. Utilizing the inductive comparative method, Hugo Grotius (1583–1645) was the great figure in this field.

The municipal law of Rome and of other states has been treated by many, who have undertaken to elucidate it by means of commentaries or to reduce it to a convenient digest. That body of law, however, which is concerned with the mutual relations among states or rulers, whether derived from nature, or established by divine ordinances, or having its origin in custom and tacit agreement, few have touched upon. Up to the present time no one has treated it in a comprehensive and systematic manner; yet the welfare of mankind demands that this task be accomplished.[465]

Fully convinced . . . that there is a common law among nations, which is valid alike for war and in war, I have had many and weighty reasons for undertaking to write upon this subject. Throughout the Christian world I observed a lack of restraint in relation to war, such as even barbarous races should be ashamed of; I observed that men rush to arms for slight causes, or no cause at all, and that when arms have once been taken up there is no longer any respect for law, divine or human; it is as if, in accordance with a general decree, frenzy had openly been let loose for the committing of all crimes.[466]

[But] such a result cannot be accomplished unless—a point which until now has not been sufficiently kept in view—those elements which come from positive law are properly separated from those which arise from nature. For the principles of the law of nature, since they are always the same, can easily be brought into a systematic form; but the elements of positive law, since they often undergo change and are different in different places, are outside the domain of systematic treatment, just as other notions of particular things are.[467]

The methodology involved is then considered.

In two ways men are wont to prove that something is according to the law of nature, from that which is antecedent and from that which is consequent. Of the two lines of proof the former is more subtle, the latter more familiar.

Proof *a priori* consists in demonstrating the necessary agreement or disagreement of anything with a rational and social nature; proof *a posteriori,* in concluding, if not with absolute assurance, at least with every probability, that that is according to the law of nature which is believed to be such among all nations, or among all those that are more advanced in civilization. For an effect that is universal demands a universal cause; and the cause of such an opinion can hardly be anything else than the feeling which is called the common sense of mankind.[468]

First of all, I have made it my concern to refer the proofs of things touching the law of nature to certain fundamental conceptions which are beyond question, so that no one can deny them without doing violence to himself. For the principles of that law, if only you pay strict heed to them, are in themselves manifest and clear, almost as evident as those things which we perceive by the external senses. . . .

In order to prove the existence of this law of nature, I have, furthermore, availed myself of the testimony of philosophers, historians, poets, finally also of orators. Not that confidence is to be reposed in them without discrimination; for they were accustomed to serve the interests of their sect, their subject, or their cause. But when many at different times, and in different places, affirm the same thing as certain, that ought to be referred to a universal cause; and this cause, in the lines of inquiry which we are following, must be either a correct conclusion drawn from the principle of nature, or common consent. The former points to the law of nature; the latter, to the law of nations.

The distinction between these kinds of law is not to be drawn from the testimonies themselves (for writers everywhere confuse the terms law of nature and law of nations),* but from the character of the matter. For whatever cannot be deduced from certain principles by a sure process of reasoning, and yet is clearly observed everywhere, must have its origin in the free will of man.[470]

History in relation to our subject is useful in two ways: it supplies both illustrations and judgements. The illustrations have greater weight in proportion as they are taken from better times and better peoples; thus we have preferred ancient examples, Greek and Roman, to the rest. And judgements are not to be slighted, especially when they are in agreement with one another; for by such statements the existence of the law of nature, as we have said, is in a measure proved, and by no other means, in fact, is it possible to establish the law of nations.[471]

* "[The Roman jurists,] no less than the others, often confuse these terms, frequently calling that the law of nations which is only the law of certain peoples, and that, too, not as established by assent, but perchance taken over through imitation of others or by pure accident."[469]

The following analysis is given of the kinds of law.

[I.] The law of nature is a dictate of right reason, which points out that an act, according as it is or is not in conformity with rational nature, has in it a quality of moral baseness or moral necessity; and that, in consequence, such an act is either forbidden or enjoined by the author of nature, God.

The acts in regard to which such a dictate exists are, in themselves, either obligatory or not permissible, and so it is understood that necessarily they are enjoined or forbidden by God. In this characteristic the law of nature differs not only from human law, but also from volitional divine law; for volitional divine law does not enjoin or forbid those things which in themselves and by their own nature are obligatory or not permissible, but by forbidding things it makes them unlawful, and by commanding things it makes them obligatory.[472]

The law of nature, again, is unchangeable—even in this sense that it cannot be changed by God.[473]

But many things, which were permitted by nature, universal customary law, by a kind of common understanding, has been able to prohibit.[474]

. . . the very nature of man, which even if we had no lack of anything would lead us into the mutual relations of society, is the mother of the law of nature. . . .

The law of nature nevertheless has the reinforcement of expediency; for the Author of nature willed that as individuals we should be weak, and should lack many things needed in order to live properly, to the end that we might be the more constrained to cultivate the social life.[475]

Man is, to be sure, an animal, but an animal of a superior kind, much farther removed from all other animals than the different kinds of animals are from one another; evidence on this point may be found in the many traits peculiar to the human species. But among the traits characteristic of man is an impelling desire for society, that is, for the social life—not of any and every sort, but peaceful, and organized according to the measure of his intelligence, with those who are of his own kind; this social trend the Stoics called "sociableness." Stated as a universal truth, therefore, the assertion that every animal is impelled by nature to seek only its own good cannot be conceded.*

Some of the other animals, in fact, do in a way restrain the appetency for that which is good for themselves alone, to the advantage, now of their offspring, now of other animals of the same species. This aspect of their behaviour has its origin, we believe, in some extrinsic intelligent principle, because with regard to other actions, which involve no more difficulty than those referred to, a like degree of intelligence is not manifest in them. The same thing must be said of children. In children, even before their training has begun, some disposition to do good to others appears, as Plutarch sagely observed; thus sympathy for others comes out spontaneously at that age. The mature man in fact has knowledge which prompts him to similar actions under similar conditions, together

---

* "Wherefore, in general, it is by no means true that
> You must confess that laws were framed
> From fear of the unjust,
a thought which in Plato some one explains thus, that laws were invented from fear of receiving injury, and that men are constrained by a kind of force to cultivate justice. For that relates only to the institutions and laws which have been devised to facilitate the enforcement of right; as when many persons in themselves weak, in order that they might not be overwhelmed by the more powerful, leagued themselves together in order to establish tribunals and by combined force to maintain these, that as a united whole they might prevail against those with whom as individuals they could not cope."[476]

with an impelling desire for society, for the gratification of which he alone among ani-mals possesses a special instrument, speech. He has also been endowed with the faculty of knowing and of acting in accordance with general principles. Whatever accords with that faculty is not common to all animals, but peculiar to the nature of man.*

This maintenance of the social order, which we have roughly sketched, and which is consonant with human intelligence, is the source of law properly so called. To this sphere of law belong the abstaining from that which is another's, the restoration to another of anything of his which we may have, together with any gain which we may have received from it; the obligation to fulfil promises, the making good of a loss incurred through our fault, and the inflicting of penalties upon men according to their deserts.

From this signification of the word law there has flowed another and more extended meaning. Since over other animals man has the advantage of possessing not only a strong bent towards social life, but also a power of discrimination which enables him to decide what things are agreeable or harmful (as to both things present and things to come), and what can lead to either alternative: in such things it is meet for the nature of man, within the limitations of human intelligence, to follow the direction of a well-tempered judge-ment, being neither led astray by fear or the allurement of immediate pleasure, nor carried away by rash impulse. Whatever is clearly at variance with such judgement is understood to be contrary also to the law of nature, that is, to the nature of man.[478]

[II.] . . . another kind of law is volitional law, which has its origin in the will. Volitional law is either human or divine.[479]

[A.] We begin with human law, because that is familiar to the greater number. Human law, then, is either municipal law, or broader in scope than municipal law, or more re-stricted than municipal law.[480]

[1.] Municipal law is that which emanates from the civil power. The civil power is that which bears sway over the state. The state is a complete association of free men, joined together for the enjoyment of rights and for their common interest.[481]

. . . the mother of municipal law is that obligation which arises from mutual con-sent; and since this obligation derives its force from the law of nature, nature may be considered, so to say, the great-grandmother of municipal law†. . . . But expediency afforded an opportunity also for municipal law, since that kind of association of which we have spoken, and subjection to authority, have their roots in expediency.[483]

[2.] The law which is narrower in scope than municipal law, and does not come from the civil power, although subject to it, is of a varied character. It comprises the commands of a father, of a master, and all other commands of a similar character.[484]

[3.] The law which is broader in scope than municipal law is the law of nations; that is the law which has received its obligatory from the will of all nations, or of many nations. I added "of many nations" for the reason that, outside of the sphere of the law of nature, which is also frequently called the law of nations, there is hardly any law com-

* "But sacred history, besides enjoining rules of conduct, in no slight degree reinforces man's inclina-tion towards sociableness by teaching that all men are sprung from the same first parents."[477]

† " . . . since it is a rule of the law of nature to abide by pacts (for it was necessary that among men there be some method of obligating themselves one to another, and no other natural method can be imagined), out of this sorce the bodies of municipal law have arisen. For those who had associated themselves with some group, or had subjected themselves to a man or to men, had either expressly promised, or from the nature of the transaction must be understood impliedly to have promised, that they would conform to that which should have been determined, in the one case by the majority, in the other by those upon whom authority had been conferred."[482]

mon to all nations. Not infrequently, in fact, in one part of the world there is a law of nations which is not such elsewhere.[485]

. . . just as the laws of each state have in view the advantage of that state, so by mutual consent it has become possible that certain laws should originate as between all states, or a great many states; and it is apparent that the laws thus originating had in view the advantage, not of particular states, but of the great society of states. And this is what is called the law of nations, whenever we distinguish that term from the law of nature.[486]

The proof for the law of nations is similar to that for unwritten municipal law; it is found in unbroken custom and the testimony of those who are skilled in it. The law of nations, in fact, as Dio Chrusostom well observes, "is the creation of time and custom." And for the study of it the illustrious writers of history are of the greatest value to us.[487]

[B.] What volitional divine law is we may well understand from the meaning of the words. It is, of course, that law which has its origin in the divine will; and by this origin it is distinguished from the law of nature, which also, as we have said, may be called divine. . . .

This law, moreover, was given either to the human race, or to a single people.*[489]

[1.] To the human race we find that the law was thrice given by God: immediately after the creation of man, a second time in the renewal of human kind after the Flood, lastly in the more exalted renewal through Christ.[490]

[2.] Among all peoples there is one to which God vouchsafed to give laws in a special manner; that is the Jewish people.[491]

A final point of anthropological interest is his long discussion on the evolution of property.[492]

## Pufendorf

Samuel Pufendorf (1632–94) followed Grotius but substituted a rationalistic approach. Man's sociality, and the fact that he had always lived in society, were the fundamental premises of his deductive system.

I have made the basis of all natural law the social life of man. . . . For the nature of man has ever been determined by God for social life in general, but it was left to the choice of men to establish and enter particular societies under the guidance of reason, which fact does in no way make the law of nature arbitrary. What, furthermore, is more obvious than this? That the nature of man, in so far as it was made by the Creator a social one, is the norm and foundation of that law which must be followed by any society, whether it be universal or particular.†[495]

---

* "[There] is another source of law besides the source in nature, that is, the free will of God, to which beyond all cavil our reason tells us we must render obedience. But the law of nature of which we have spoken, comprising alike that which relates to the social life of man and that which is so called in a larger sense, proceeding as it does from the essential traits implanted in man, can nevertheless rightly be attributed to God, because of His having willed that such traits exist in us."[488]

† One of his arguments in favor of man's sociality was based upon the nature of language. "This one fact alone might be sufficient proof that man was intended by nature for a social life, namely, that he of all creatures has been given the ability to express his thoughts to others by means of articulate sounds, which faculty can be of no logical use to men, unless they lead a social life . . . the weakness which is the lot of individual men can be removed most conveniently by the aid of others, and . . . another man cannot gird himself to bring me aid unless he first knows my needs, which knowledge can be gained most promptly by signs, and best of all by articulate words."[493]

By the natural state of man we do not understand that condition which nature intended should be most perfect and for his greatest good, but that condition for which man is understood to be constituted, by the mere fact of his birth, all inventions and institutions, either of man or suggested to him from above, being disregarded, since they give a very different aspect to the life of man. By them we understand not only the different forms and general culture of the life of man, but especially civil societies, at the formation of which a suitable order was introduced into mankind's existence.*[497]

Now in order that we may form some conception of this natural state, as it would have been without any aid or invention coming from the hand of man or given by God, we must imagine man as dropped from somewhere into this world and left entirely to his own resources, with no help from his fellows after birth, and, furthermore, endowed with no more gifts of body and mind than are now generally discovered in men without previous culture, nor aided by any special attention from God. Such a condition must be regarded as most miserable, whether you imagine man to have come from the beyond as a babe, or as a man already endowed with his full stature and strength. As an infant he must certainly have perished, unless by some miracle an animal had given the poor babe nourishment from its own body, but this association with brutes would certainly have given their foster-child much of their own savagery. Were he a full-grown man, we would have to imagine him naked, able to make only inarticulate sounds, devoid of all knowledge and customs of men, in constant fear.[498]

Now the rights attendant on this natural state of man can be easily gathered, in the first place, from the desire common to all animals, whereby they cannot but use every means to preserve their body and life, and to avert every thing that would destroy them, and, in the second place, from the fact that those who enjoy this state are subject to no man's orders. For it follows from the first consideration that men, constituted in a natural state, may use and enjoy everything that is open to them, and may secure and do every thing that will lead to their preservation, in so far as no injury is done to the right of others. And from the second, that they may use their own judgement and decision, provided, of course, that it is framed on this natural law, just as they use their own strength, to secure their own defence and preservation. And in this respect also the state of nature has come to be described as a natural liberty, since every man, antecedent to any act of man, is understood to be under his own right and power, and to be subject to the power of no other man. And so every man is considered equal to every other man, since neither is the subject of the other.[499]

But we maintain that the race of men never did live at one and the same time in a simple state of nature, and never could have, since we believe on the authority of the Holy Writ, that the origin of all men came from the marriage of a single pair. Now Eve was subject to Adam by the right of the husband, *Genesis,* iii. 16, and their offspring were, immediately after birth, under the father's power and the control of the family. . . .

Therefore, a state of nature never actually existed, except in some altered form, or only in part, as when, indeed, some men gathered together with others into a civil state, or

"But it is clear that the power which words have of bearing this or that meaning, that is, of giving rise to a certain idea in the mind, is theirs not by nature, or any intrinsic necessity, but arises from the mere judgement and institution of men. For otherwise no reason could be shown for the same thing being expressed in different languages by different words. This is also true of the different forms and outlines of letters."[494]

* He appreciated the powerful constraint of culture: "to have been brought up from infacy on some one idea is so powerful an influence that, even though the idea be fallacious, the thought of questioning it scarcely ever occurs to a man, certainly if he has no more wit than the common run of humanity."[496]

some such body, but retained a natural liberty against the rest of mankind; although the smaller their membership, the nearer it must have approached a pure state of nature. So when at the first mankind separated into different family groups, and now have divided into states, such groups live in a mutual state of nature, in so far as no one group obeys another, and all the members have no common master.*[501]

It is a question of greater importance whether a natural state, as it concerns other men, bears the character of war or peace; or, what amounts to the same thing, whether those who live in a natural state, that is, who have no common master, and neither obey nor command one another, should be considered as mutual enemies, or, indeed, as peaceable people and friends.[502]

. . . the main argument for the opposite [i.e., the latter] opinion is the origin of the human race, as the infallible authority of the Sacred Scriptures teaches us, for they show that the natural state of men was one of peace rather than war, and that men were more like friends to one another than enemies. To the first man, made by the hand of God from clay, there was united a mate whose substance was drawn from man himself, so that he might cherish her forthwith in a tender love, since she was of his own flesh and bone. And God joined her to him by a further and most holy bond. Since from this pair all mankind is descended, the human race is related by no mere general tie of friendship, such as may come from similarity of appearance, . . . but by the tie which comes from common ancestry and blood, and which is marked by a kindly affection for one's own. A memory of this relationship has practically vanished among those who are far removed from the parent stock, and yet, when a man disregards it, and adopts an attitude of hostility towards others, it is proper to feel that he has departed from his primitive and natural state.

. . . Furthermore, since the first men lived in a state which was by no means one of hostility, but was charged with pure friendship, and since the rest of men have sprung from such a state, it is clear that, if men really want to bear in mind their first beginning, they should be regarded not as enemies but as friends. In fact, societies were at the beginning introduced among mankind, not with the purpose of avoiding a natural state, but because the human race could not be increased and preserved without them. And a natural state grew out of this condition, because as men multiplied they could no longer be embraced in one society. And so there is no point in asserting that, had there been no social state, men in the beginning of things would have lived at enmity with one another, unless you wish to imagine that, in the beginning, a multitude of men, in no way related to one another, suddenly sprang into being.[503]

We conclude from all this that the natural state of men, even when considered apart from commonwealths, is not one of war, but of peace; a peace founded on the following laws: A man shall not harm one who is not injuring him; he shall allow every one to enjoy his own possessions; he shall faithfully perform whatever has been agreed upon; and he shall willingly advance the interests of others, so far as he is not bound by more pressing obligations. For since a natural state presupposes the use of reason, any obligation which reason points out cannot, and must not, be separated from it; and since every man is able of himself to appreciate that it is for his advantage to conduct himself in such a way as to profit from the friendly attitude of men rather than incur their anger, he can easily judge, from the similarity of nature, that other men feel the same way.[504]

* "But it is not proper to oppose a state of nature to a social life, since even those who live in a state of nature can, and should, and frequently do, lead a mutually social life."[500]

The evolution of political organization took place by means of a modified type of social contract.

But it must be confessed that this natural peace is but a weak and untrustworthy thing, and therefore that it is, without other safeguards, but a poor custodian of man's safety.[505]

Therefore, the real and principal reason why the fathers of families left their natural liberty and undertook to establish states, was in order that they could surround themselves with defences against the evils which threaten man from his fellow man.[506]

. . . the many who come together for this end must agree on applying the means suittable for that end. For no matter how great the number of them be, nothing will be accomplished unless they agree on the best way in which that common defence should be established, and prevent each and every man from desiring to direct his strength as he sees fit. For they will be but a hindrance to each other, torn by conflicting opinions and working to opposite ends.[507]

The number and the nature of those pacts by the intervention of which a state is built up are discovered in the following manner. If we imagine to ourselves a multitude of men endowed with natural liberty and equality, who voluntarily set about to establish a new state, it is necessary for the future citizens, as the first step, to enter into an agreement, every individual with every other one, that they are desirous of entering into a single and perpetual group, and of administrating the considerations of their safety and security by common council and leadership. . . .

But after such a group, already taking on the rudiments and beginnings of a state, has been formed by the pact mentioned, it is yet further necessary for a decree to be passed upon the form of government that shall be introduced. For until this decision is reached, it will be impossible to take consistent action on matter concerning the common safety. . . .

After the decree upon the form of government, a new pact will be necessary when the individual or body is constituted that receives the government of the group, by which pact the rulers bind themselves to the care of the common security and safety, and the rest to render them obedience, and in which there is that subjection and union of wills, by reason of which a state is looked upon as a single person. From this pact there finally comes a finished state. . . .

What we have said thus far on the two pacts and one decree, can be illustrated by what Dionysius of Halicarnassus, Bk. II, at the outset of his history, recounts of the founding of the Roman state. . . .

Now we would not have it thought that these remarks on the pacts which give rise to a state, are a creation of our imagination, because the origins of most states are unknown, or at least it is not entirely certain that they were established in that manner. For one thing is sure, namely, that every state had at some time its beginnings. And yet it was necessary that those who compose a state be not held together before its establishment by the same bond as they are afterwards; and that they be not subject to the same persons to whom they are afterwards. Yet since it is impossible to understand that union and subjection without the above-mentioned pacts, they must have interposed, tacitly at least, in the formation of states. Nor is there anything to prevent men from being able to reason out the origin of a thing, despite the fact that there remain no written records upon them.[508]

And yet it does not follow from the desire to live together, that a man is led to civil government, since that love can be satisfied by less developed societies and intimate associations with others, which can be conceived of without states.[509]

He likewise treats the subject of the evolution of property.

. . . before any conventions of men existed there was a community of all things, not, indeed, such as we have called positive, but a negative one, that is, that all things lay open to all men, and belonged no more to one than to another. But since things are of no use to men unless at least their fruits may be appropriated, and this is impossible if others as well can take what we have already by our own act selected for our uses, it follows that the first convention between men was about these very concerns, to the effect that whatever one of these things which were left open to all, and of their fruits, a man had laid his hands upon, with intent to turn it to his uses, could not be taken from him by another.[510]

Now men left this original negative community of things and by a pact established separate dominions over things, not, indeed, all at once and for all time, but successively, and as the state of things, or the nature and number of men, seemed to require.[511]

## Cumberland

Richard Cumberland (1631–1718) was another who made a deductive analysis of the law of nature.

*The Laws of Nature* are the only solid Foundations of all Morality and Civil Polity. . . .

These Laws (like most other Conclusions discoverable by the Light of Nature) are investigated, traced out and demonstrated, by the one or other of these two Ways, either,

*First,* By such manifest Effects as follow from these Laws themselves, which, in other Words, is the Demonstration of *Causes by their Effects.* Or, Secondly, By those evident Causes from whence these Laws themselves originally take their Source and Rise: And this is no other than demonstrating *Effects from their Causes.*

According to the first Method, the *Laws of Nature* are considered as Causes necessarily producing Effects. According to the second Method, the *Laws of Nature* are looked upon as necessary Effects resulting from such and such natural Causes.

The Foundation of our Enquiry is laid in the second Method of Reasoning.

The Reality and Force of these Laws themselves; the Demonstration of them, according to the first Method of Reasoning; their actual Existence, and the binding Obligation of them, are Points well pursued and handled by *Hugo Grotius,* and by his Brother *William Grotius,* . . . as also by . . . *Robert Sharrock.* . . . [and] *John Selden.*[512]

Various factors are important in the development of human personality.

. . . we must say something concerning the various Customs and Manners of several Nations, and, I had almost said, of Mankind in general.

Now, the various different Habits are acquired and superinduced, partly from a Diversity of Disposition, or of a natural Propensity, tending to such and such Manners and Behaviour; partly from the Temperature of Constitution, Climate, Country, Education, Religion, Fortune, and those several Employments, in the Discharge of which Mankind are severally engaged.

From Manners and Behaviour thus acquired, there is, if we may so say, almost another Nature, as it were, superinduced upon man.[513]

Like Pufendorf, Cumberland refuted Hobbes by insisting that man is a social animal.

. . . the Soul is naturally adapted to enter into Society the most extensive; and . . . unless the human Soul does submit to enter into such a Society, it neglects its principal Use and Employment, and lets go the best Advantages of its own natural Disposition.[514]

We must . . . make some few Remarks upon the Energy and strong Propensity of the human Mind, in the Invention of Words, written Marks, and other arbitrary Signs; by Help of which the Mind is both able to recollect universal and particular Notions, and also signify or communicate them to others. And this so distinguishing, specific a Characteristic of Man above all other Animals, is of mighty Consequence in establishing first, and then preserving Civil Society.[515]

What is more, all social animals are "benevolent."

I chose to enquire into the true Causes of that Benevolence, which Animals of the same Species exert towards each other;—a Benevolence so very remarkable, between Brute-creatures of the same Kind. For I have determined and settled it in my own Mind, as a Point of the clearest Evidence, That all these Causes, with many more of much higher Importance, are discoverable in Mankind. And—consequently, that the whole human Species, is, from these and such like Causes as these, at least, to say no more, naturally fitter for such an Association, for such an Intercourse as this;—an Intercourse which, beyond all Question, beyond all manner of Doubt, is, generally speaking, very friendly.[516]

[He observes] That, since every Child of Man continues longer helpless than other Animals, and requires, for a longer Period, the Care and Assistance of Parents; that therefore, from so continued an Use, from so habitual an Exercise of Parental Love, the Affection grows so predominant and powerful, that Parents, with great Anxiety and Dread, fear for them every Evil, but, above all, the Evil of Death. And, *this Anxiety, this Dread, this Love rises, increases proportionably, in a compounded Ratio of the Time multiplied into the Care employed in rearing and educating them.* . . . And, this is the effectual Motive, the efficient Cause, why Parents, with more than ordinary Care and Diligence, labour this one Point: And, that they daily, more and more, betray fuller Proofs of this Στοργη, of this natural Affection, than ever yet could be discovered in any other Animals whatsoever. . . . into this single *Principle, Cause* or *Source* is ultimately resolvable also all the reciprocal Love, the reflected-back Affection of Children towards their Parents: and likewise, all the mutual, benevolent Love of Relations by Blood; and—this Progress and flowing of Affection will, at last, naturally lead us into a Love for all Mankind . . . which fully prove, that Man is fitly and peculiarly made to discharge the Duties and Offices of a friendly Society.[517]

. . . the Powers and Capacities of Men, even supposing them to be nearly equal, furnish us with Arguments in favour of *reciprocal Benevolence* and *Good-will,* rather than with Arguments to favour the Attempts of *mutual death* and *Destruction.*[518]

Besides, the interests of the individual and his group are identical.

[The end of society] most certainly, is the public, common Good of the Whole; which Good implies in it some certain Happiness, the several Parts and Portions of which are dispensed to the good Members of the Community; and, by Consequence, are the natural Rewards of Obedience: Not to mention those Punishments which these same Laws denounce and threaten.[519]

For there is no Method which directs any one single Person to his own Happiness, which does not equally direct *all* to the common united Happiness of *All.*[520]

Animals, the very Moment they consult and provide for their own Preservation and Safety, at the very same Moment they consult and provide for the Continuance of their Species; and, in the necessary Consequence of Things, they, at the very same Moment, promote the Good and Happiness of All.[521]

By the Terms *Common* or *Public Good,* I would be understood to signify and mean, *The whole Aggregate or Sum-total of all* those various and several Kinds of *Good,* fromwhich all Individual Rational Beings, collectively considered, can be benefited and receive an additional Happiness or Advantage by our Abilities, Means, Powers, and Interposition.[522]

[As a result of] the *Sanction of these Laws* . . . it is necessarily implied and understood, That, *the Law of Nature* always, under all given Circumstances, demonstrates, that *Acts* promoting *the public, universal Good,* are the *only Acts* which, in themselves, sufficiently and powerfully can promote the full, compleat private Happiness of each and every Individual.[523]

Neither do we, with less Difficulty, learn, from Experience, the Truth of the following Propositions.

Prop. 1. *It is necessary to the Common Good that there should be a Division, a Distribution of Things and mutual Assistances.*

Prop. 2. *Such a Division or Distribution must be maintained inviolable, by acting both towards others, and towards ourselves, according to such a Measure as the Preservation of Nations, of Civil Societies, of Families, (in all which Relations we ourselves stand) requires from us.* From these two Propositions, all the Laws of Nature, and all the moral Virtues flow: And, this *Connection* we learn to be as necessary in Morality as we find it necessary to the Life and Health of an animated Body, *viz.* That, Nourishment must be distributed thro' all the several Parts and Members of it: And, that, a Distribution, thus laid and established in Nature, must be preserved by the Offices, Duties and Employments of all the Members mutually relative both to one and all: That, by such united Influences, the principal Parts, in the first Place, and the less-principal Parts, in the second Place, may be eased of Obstructions and also repaired, (whenever, at any Time, there happens a Consumption, a Loss,) in order to strengthen and increase the Energies, Powers, Operations and Measures of them, as settled and prescribed by Nature.[524]

The following is Cumberland's analysis of the law of nature.

. . . the Law of Nature is a Proposition arising from the Nature of Things.[525]

. . . certain Practical Propositions of unchangeable Truth . . . are necessarily impressed upon our Minds from the Nature of Things.[526]

We are here to understand by Laws of Nature, such Laws as are to direct the Behaviour of all Civil instituted Societies, and of all Individuals towards all, let these Civil Societies be modelled into any and what Form soever: Or, even supposing that these Forms are not as yet reduced into any Establishments.[527]

By Laws of Nature, we understand some Propositions of unchangeable Truth and Certainty, which are to direct and govern the voluntary Motions of rational free Agents, in the Election of Good, and in the avoiding of Evil: Which Laws lay Obligations upon all outward Acts of Behaviour, even in a State of Nature, prior and antecedent to all Laws of human Imposition whatsoever: And are clearly distinct from every Consideration of all such Compacts and Agreements as constitute civil Government.[528]

The Law of Nature . . . is a Proposition, which, with an Evidence sufficiently clear from the Nature of Things, is impressed by the Will of the first Cause, upon the human Mind; declaring, What Agency (or Method of free Action) answers best to the common Happiness of all Rational Beings:—From which PROPOSITION or LAW, if steadily pursued, sufficient Rewards necessarily follow; and, from which PROPOSITION or LAW, if neglected, sufficient Punishments do as necessarily arise: And BOTH (that is, the Rewards and the Punishments) flow essentially from the Nature of Rational Agents.[529]

He used a patriarchal theory of the evolution of political organization.

. . . the Human-kind, and, by consequence, all Societies and Families, sprang from the matrimonial Union of one *Man* with one *Woman*. And, consequently, all *Civil Government* is originally laid in *a natural Parental Authority*.[530]

## ORIGIN OF POLITICAL ORGANIZATION

The increased conflict between rising capitalism and declining feudalism was reflected in the social thought of the seventeenth century, particularly in relation to the rival theories as to the origin of society and political organization. The controversy reached its highest pitch in England, where a revolution was fought, and a king lost his head, as part of the dispute.

On the royalist side, Overall, Temple, and Filmer justified the status quo by means of the patriarchal theory, according to which the first father was the first king. Hobbes and Spinoza used the social contract theory in defense of royalty by maintaning that the people had voluntarily bound themselves to the king. The conquest theory was not much advocated any longer, though it is to be found in Pascal.

Among the antiroyalists, the social contract was still most popular and was a powerful weapon in the hands of Milton, Locke, and others.

### Overall

John Overall (1560–1619) used the patriarchal theory in support of the prerogative of James I.

To him that shall duly read the Scriptures, it will be plain and evident that the Son of God, having created our first parents, and purposing to multiply their seed into many generations, for the replenishing of the world with their posterity, did give to Adam for his time, and to the rest of the patriarchs and chief fathers successively before the flood, authority, power, and dominion over their children and offspring, to rule and govern them; ordaining by the law of nature, that their said children and offspring (begotten and brought up by them) should fear, reverence, honour, and obey them. Which power and authority before the flood, resting in the patriarchs, and in the chief fathers, because it had a very large extent, not only for the education of their said children and offspring, whilst they were young, but likewise for the ordering, ruling, and governing of them afterwards, when they came to men's estate. And for that also it had no superior authority, or power, over, or above it on earth.[531]

Noah lived, after the flood, three hundred and fifty years, and saw his children's children wonderfully multiplied; during which term of years he was the patriarch, or chief governor over them; ruling and ordering of them by virtue of that superiority, power, and authority which was given unto him by Almighty God, and was also warranted by the laws of nature and reason. . . . Also, the extent of this right and authority was so large, as that he lawfully distributed the whole world unto his said three sons, and their posterity. So that his said three sons, after him, were by the ordinance of God (the chief author of the said distribution) made three great princes; and also the sons of those three great princes (of whom about seventy are named) were the heads and governors of the families and nations that descended from them, according to their tongues, in their several countries.[532]

## Filmer

Robert Filmer (d. 1653) was another royalist who employed the patriarchal theory in the king's defense.

That the patriarchs . . . were endowed with kingly power, their deeds do testify; for as Adam was lord of his children, so his children under him had a command and power over their own children; but still with subordination to the first parent, who is lord-paramount over his children's children to all generations, as being the grandfather of his people.[533]

. . . erection of kingdoms came at first only by distinctions of families.[534]

It may seem absurd to maintain that kings now are the fathers of their people, since experience shows the contrary. It is true, all kings be not the natural parents of their subjects, yet they all either are, or are to be reputed, the next heirs to those first progenitors who were at first the natural parents of the whole people, and in their right succeeded to the exercise of supreme jurisdiction; and such heirs are not only lords of their own children, but also of their brethren, and all others that were subject to their fathers.[535]

## Hobbes

Thomas Hobbes (1588–1679) used the theory of social contract as weapon in favor of the British monarchy both before and after the Restoration.

. . . my Discourse of Civill and Ecclesiasticall Government, occasioned by the disorders of the present time, without partiality, without application, and without other designe, than to set before mens eyes the mutuall Relation between Protection and Obedience.[536]

Man is not a social animal.

The greatest part of those who have written aught concerning commonwealths, either suppose, or require us or beg of us to believe, that man is a creature born fit for society . . . Which axiom, though received by most, is yet certainly false; and an error proceeding from our too slight contemplation of human nature. For they who shall more narrowly look into the causes for which men come together, and delight in each other's company, shall easily find that this happens not because naturally it could happen no otherwise, but by accident. For if by nature one man should love another, that is, as man, there could no reason be returned why every man should not equally love every man, as being equally man; or why he should rather frequent those, whose society affords him honour or profit. We do not therefore by nature seek society for its own sake, but that we may receive some honour or profit from it; these we desire primarily, that secondarily.[537]

. . . to man by nature, or as man, that is, as soon as he is born, solitude is an enemy; for infants have need of others to help them live, and those of riper years to have them live well. Wherefore I deny not that men (even nature compelling) desire to come together. But civil societies are not mere meetings, but bonds, to the making whereof faith and compacts are necessary; the virtue whereof to children and fools, and the profit whereof to those who have not yet tasted the miseries which accompany its defects, is altogether unknown; whence it happens, that those, because they know not what society is, cannot enter into it; these, because ignorant of the benefit it brings, care not for it. Manifest therefore it is, that all men, because they are born in infancy, are born unapt for society. . . . Wherefore man is made fit for society not by nature, but by education.[538]

His basic thesis was that man is egocentric.

All society . . . is either for gain, or for glory; that is, not so much for love of our fellows, as for the love of ourselves.[539]

So that in the first place, I put for a generall inclination of all mankind, a perpetuall and restlesse desire of Power after power, that ceaseth onely in Death.[540]

As a result, in a state of nature there was a continual struggle for power.

. . . during the time men live without a common Power to keep them all in awe, they are in that condition which is called Warre; and such a warre, as is of every man, against every man.*[542]

From this condition, society developed by means of a social contract.

In such condition, there is not place for Industry; because the fruit thereof is uncertain: and consequently no Culture of the Earth; no Navigation, nor use of the commodities that may be imported by Sea; no commodious Building; no Instruments of moving, and removing such things as require much force; no Knowledge of the face of the Earth; no account of Time; no Arts; no Letters; no Society; and which is worst of all, continuall feare, and danger of violent death; And the life of man, solitary, poore, nasty, brutish, and short.[543]

It may peradventure be thought, there was never such a time, nor condition of warre as this; I believe it was never generally so, over all the world: but there are many places, where they live so now. For the savage people in many places of *America,* except the government of small Families, the concord whereof dependeth on naturall lust, have no government at all; and live at this day in that brutish manner, as I said before. Howsoever, it may be perceived what manner of life there would be, where there were no common Power to feare; by the manner of life, which man that have formerly lived under a peacefull government, use to degenerate into, in a civill Warre.[544]

Feare of oppression, disposeth a man to anticipate, or to seek ayd by society; for there is no other way by which a man can secure his life and liberty.[545]

The Passions that encline men to Peace, are Feare of Death; Desire of such things as are necessary to commodious living; and a Hope by their Industry to obtain them. And Reason suggesteth convenient Articles of Peace, upon which men may be drawn to agreement. These Articles, are they, which otherwise are called the Lawes of Nature.†[547]

A LAW OF NATURE, (*Lex Naturalis,*) is a Precept, or a generall Rule, found out by Reason, by which a man is forbidden to do, that, which is destructive of his life, or taketh away the means of preserving the same; and to omit that, by which he thinketh it may best be preserved.‡[549]

---

* " . . . amongst masterlesse men, there is perpetuall war, of every man against his neighbour."[541]

† "The finall Cause, End, or Designe of men, (who naturally love Liberty, and Dominion over others,) in the introduction of that restraint upon themselves, (in which wee see them live in Common-wealths), is the foresight of their own preservation, and of a more contented life thereby; that is to say, of getting themselves out from that miserable condition of Warre, which is necessarily consequent (as hath been shewn) to the naturall Passions of men, when there is no visible Power to keep them in awe, and tye them by feare of punishment to the performance of their Covenants, and observation of . . . Lawes of Nature."[546]

‡ " . . . the Lawes of Nature, which consist in Equity, Justice, Gratitude, and other morall Vertues on these depending, in the condition of meer Nature . . . are not properly Lawes, but qualities that dispose men to peace, and to obedience."[548]

*The laws of nature are immutable and eternal.*[550]

. . . a *commonwealth* . . . is made by the wills and agreement of men.[551]

The only way to erect such a Common Power, as may be able to defend them from the invasion of Forraigners, and the injuries of one another, and thereby to secure them in such sort, as that by their owne industrie, and by the fruites of the Earth, they may nourish themselves and live contentedly; is, to conferre all their power and strength upon one Man, or upon one Assembly of men, that may reduce all their Wills, by plurality of voices, into one Will: which is as much as to say, to appoint one Man, or Assembly of men, to beare their Person; and every one to owne, and acknowledge himselfe to be Author of whatsoever he that so beareth their Persons, shall Act, or cause to be Acted, in those things which concerne the Common Peace and Safetie; and therein to submit their Wills, every one to his Will, and their Judgements, to his Judgement. This is more than Consent, or Concord; it is a reall Unitie of them all, in one and the same Person, made by Covenant of every man with every man, in such manner, as if every man should say to every man, *I Authorise and give up my Right of Governing my selfe, to this Man, or to this Assembly of man, on this condition, that thou give up thy Right to him, and Authorise all his Actions in like manner.* This done, the Multitude so united in one Person, is called a COMMON-WEALTH, in latine CIVITAS. This is the Generation of that great LEVIATHAN, or rather (to speake more reverently) of that *Mortall God,* to which wee owe under the *Immortal God,* our peace and defence. For by this Authoritie, given him by every particular man in the Common-Wealth, he hath the use of so much Power and Strength conferred on him, that by terror thereof, he is inabled to forme the wills of them all, to Peace at home, and mutuall ayd against their enemies abroad. And in him consisteth the Essence of the Common-wealth; which (to define it,) is *One Person, of whose Acts a great Multitude, by mutuall Covenants one with another, have made themselves every one the Author, to the end he may use the strength and means of them all, as he shall think expedient, for their Peace and Common Defence.*

And he that carryeth this Person, is called SOVERAIGNE, and is said to have *Soveraigne Power;* and every one besides, his SUBJECT.[552]

A Multitude of men, are made *One* Person, when they are by one man, or one Person, Represented; so that it be done with the consent of every one of that Multitude in particular. For it is the *Unity* of the Representer, not the *Unity* of the Represented, that maketh the Person *One.* And it is the Representer that beareth the Person, and but one Person: And *Unity,* cannot otherwise be understood in Multitude.[553]

However, Hobbes later used a combination of the patriarchal and conquest theories in place of the social contract.

. . . the beginning of all dominion amongst men was in families. In which, first, the father of the family by the law of nature was absolute lord of his wife and children: secondly, made what laws amongst them he pleased: thirdly, was judge of all their controversies: fourthly, was not obliged by any law of man to follow any counsel but his own: fifthly, what land soever the lord sat down upon and made use of for his own and his family's benefit, was his propriety by the law of first possession, in case it was void of inhabitants before, or by the law of war, in case they conquered it. In this conquest what enemies they took and saved, were their servants. Also such men as wanting possessions of lands, but furnished with arts necessary for man's life, came to dwell in the family for protection, became their subjects, and submitted themselves to the laws of the family.[554]

He similarly had theories as to the evolution of other aspects of culture. For instance, he anticipated Bachofen's matrilineal hypothesis.

. . . in the state of nature it cannot be known who is the *father,* but by the testimony of the *mother;* the child therefore is his whose the mother will have it, and therefore her's. Wherefore the original dominion over *children* belongs to the *mother:* and among men no less than other creatures, the birth follows the belly.*[556]

Man was first a simple food-gatherer.

. . . from the beginning there were vines and ears of corn growing here and there in the fields; but no care was taken for the planting and sowing of them. Men lived therefore upon acorns; or if any were so bold as to venture upon the eating of those unknown and doubtful fruits, they did it with danger of their health.[557]

He has the following to say on the evolution of science and philosophy:

The faculty of Reasoning being consequent to the use of Speech, it was not possible, but that there would have been some generall Truths found out by Reasoning, as ancient almost as Language it selfe. The Savages of America, are not without some good Morall Sentences; also they have a little Arithmetick, to adde, and divide in Numbers not too great: but they are not therefore Philosophers. For as there were Plants of Corn and Wine in small quantity dispersed in the Fields and Woods, before men knew their vertue, or made use of them for their nourishment, or planted them apart in Fields, and Vineyards; in which time they fed on Akorns, and drank Water: so also there have been divers true, generall, and profitable Speculations from the beginning; as being the naturall plants of humane Reason: But they were at first but few in number; men lived upon grosse Experience; there was no Method; that is to say, no Sowing, nor Planting of Knowledge by it selfe, apart from the Weeds, and common Plants of Error and Conjecture: And the cause of it being the want of leasure from procuring the necessities of life, and defending themselves against their neighbours, it was impossible, till the erecting of great Common-wealths, it should be otherwise. *Leasure* is the mother of *Philosophy;* and *Commonwealth,* the mother of *Peace,* and *Leasure:* Where first were great and flourishing *Cities,* there was first the study of *Philosophy.*[558]

Now, the greatest commodities of mankind are the arts; namely, of measuring matter of motion; of moving ponderous bodies; of architecture; of navigation; of making instruments for all uses; of calculating the celestial motions, the aspects of the stars, and the parts of time; of geography, *&c.* By which sciences, how great benefits men receive is more easily understood than expressed. These benefits are enjoyed by almost all of the people of Europe, by most of those of Asia, and by some of Africa: but the Americans, and they that live near the Poles, do totally want them. But why? Have they sharper wits than these? Have not all men one kind of soul, and the same faculties of mind? What, then, makes this difference, except philosophy? Philosophy, therefore, is the cause of all these benefits . . . [for they] have learned the rules of civil life sufficiently. Now, the knowledge of these rules is moral philosophy.[559]

Religion evolved from fear of the unknown.

*Feare* of power invisible, feigned by the mind, or imagined from tales publiquely allowed, RELIGION; not allowed, SUPERSTITIION.[560]

---

* "If there by no Contract, the Dominion is in the Mother. For in the condition of meer Nature, where there are no Matrimoniall lawes, it cannot be known who is the Father, unlesse it be declared by the Mother: and therefore the right of Dominion over the Child dependeth on her will, and is consequently hers."[555]

Anxiety for the future time, disposeth men to enquire into the causes of things: because the knowledge of them, maketh men the better able to order the present to their best advantage.[561]

And they that make little, or no enquiry into the natural causes of things, yet from the feare that proceeds from the ignorance it selfe, of what it is that hath the power to do them much good or harm, are enclined to suppose, and feign unto themselves, severall kinds of Powers Invisible; and to stand in awe of their own imaginations; and in time of distresse to invoke them; as also in the time of an expected good successe, to give them thanks; making the creatures of their own fancy, their Gods. By which means it hath come to passe, that from the innumerable variety of Fancy, men have created in the world innumerable sorts of Gods. And this Feare of things invisible, is the naturall Seed of that, which every one in himself calleth Religion; and in them that worship, or feare that Power otherwise than they do, Superstition.

And this seed of Religion, having been observed by many; some of those that have observed it, have been enclined thereby to nourish, dresse, and forme it into Lawes; and to adde to it of their own invention, any opinion of the causes of future events, by which they thought they should best be able to govern others, and make unto themselves the greatest use of their Powers.[562]

Hobbes used the organic analogy in his analysis of society.

. . . by Art is created that great LEVIATHAN called a COMMON-WEALTH, or STATE, (in latine CIVITAS) which is but an Artificiall Man; though of greater stature and strength than the Naturall, for whose protection and defence it was intended; and in which, the *Soveraignty* is an Artificiall *Soul,* as giving life and motion to the whole body; The *Magistrates,* and other *Officers* of Judicature and Execution, artificiall *Joynts; Reward* and *Punishment* (by which fastned to the seate of the Soveraignty, every joynt and member is moved to performe his duty) are the *Nerves,* that do the same in the Body Naturall; The *Wealth* and *Riches* of all the particular members, are the *Strength; Salus Populi* (the *peoples safety*) its *Businesse; Counsellors,* by whom all things needfull for it to know, are suggested unto it, are the *Memory; Equity* and *Lawes,* an artificiall *Reason* and *Will; Concord, Health; Sedition, Sicknesse;* and *Civill war, Death.* Lastly, the *Pacts* and *Covenants,* by which the parts of this Body Politique were at first made, set together, and united, resemble that *Fiat,* or the *Let us make man,* pronounced by God in the Creation.[563]

Having spoken of the Generation, Forme, and Power of a Common-wealth, I am in order to speak next of the parts thereof. And first of Systemes, which resemble the similar parts, or Muscles of a Body naturall. By SYSTEMES; I understand any numbers of men joyned in one Interest, or one Businesse.[564]

. . . I shall speak of the parts Organicall, which are Publique Ministers.

A PUBLIQUE MINISTER, is he, that by the Soveraign, (whether a Monarch, or an Assembly,) is employed in any affaires, with Authority to represent in that employment, the Person of the Common-wealth.[565]

THE NUTRITION of a Common-wealth consisteth, in the *Plenty,* and *Distribution* of *Materials* conducing to Life: In *Concoction,* or *Preparation;* and (when concocted) in the *Conveyance* of it, by convenient conduits, to the Publique use.[566]

Mony [is] the Bloud of a Common-wealth.[567]

The Procreation, or Children of a Common-wealth, are those we call *Plantations,* or *Colonies;* which are numbers of men sent out from the Common-wealth, under a Conductor, or Governour, to inhabit a Forraign Country.[568]

Hitherto I have set forth the nature of Man, (whose Pride and other Passions have compelled him to submit himselfe to Government;) together with the great power of his Governour, whom I compared to *Leviathan,* taking that comparison out of the two last verses of the one and fortieth of *Job;* where God having set forth the great power of *Leviathan,* calleth him King of the Proud. . . . But because he is mortall, and subject to decay, as all other Earthly creatures are; and because there is that in heaven, (though not on earth) that he should stand in fear of, and whose Lawes he ought to obey; I shall in the next following Chapters speak of his Diseases, and the causes of his Mortality; and of what Lawes of Nature he is bound to obey.[569]

Amongst the *Infirmities* therefore of a Common-wealth, I will reckon in the first place, those that arise from an Imperfect Institution, and resemble the diseases of a naturall body, which proceed from a Defectuous Procreation.[570]

In the second place, I observe the *Diseases* of a Common-wealth, that proceed from the pyson of seditious doctrines.[571]

[A few others are also given.[572]]

Lastly, when in a warre (forraign, or intestine,) the enemies get a finall Victory; so as (the forces of the Common-wealth keeping the field no longer) there is no farther protection of Subjects in their loyalty; then is the Common-wealth DISSOLVED, and every man at liberty to protect himself by such courses as his own discretion shall suggest unto him. For the Sovereign, is the publique Soule, giving Life and Motion to the Common-wealth; which expiring, the Members are governed by it no more, than the Carcasse of a man, by his departed (though Immortall) Soule.[573]

By arguing against the freedom of the will, Hobbes made an important advance on Descarte's analysis of biological organisms as machines. Once man was shown to be completely subject to natural laws, a science of man could be developed.

Neither is the freedom of willing or not willing, greater in man, than in other living creatures. For where there is appetite, the entire cause of appetite hath preceded; and, consequently, the act of appetite could not choose but follow, that is, hath of necessity followed. . . . And therefore such a liberty as is free from necessity, is not to be found in the will either of men or beasts. But if by liberty we understand the faculty or power, not of willing, but of doing what they will, then certainly that liberty is to be allowed to both, and both may equally have it, whensoever it is to be had.[574]

For he is *free* to do a thing, that may do it if he have the will to do it, and may forbear, if he have the will to forbear. And yet if there be a *necessity* that he shall have the *will* to do it, the action is necessarily to follow: and if there be a *necessity* that he shall have the *will* to forbear, the forbearing also will be necessary. The question therefore is not, whether a man be a *free agent,* that is to say, whether he can write or forbear, speak or be silent, according to his *will;* but, whether the *will* to write, and the *will* to forbear, come upon him according to his *will,* or according to anything else in his own power. I acknowledge this *liberty,* that I *can* do if I *will;* but to say, I can *will* if I *will,* I take to be an absurd speech.[575]

. . . because man's will, that is every volition or act of the will and purpose of man had a *sufficient,* and therefore a *necessary* cause, and consequently every *voluntary* action was *necessitated.*[576]

I conceive that nothing taketh beginning from *itself,* but from the *action* of some other immediate *agent* without itself. And that therefore, when first a man hath an *appetite* or *will* to do something, to which immediately before he had no appetite nor will, the *cause* of his *will*, is not the *will* itself, but *something* else not in his own disposing. So that whereas it is out of controvery, that of *voluntary* actions the will is the *necessary* cause, and by this which is said, the will is also *caused* by other things whereof it disposeth not, it followeth, that *voluntary* actions have all of them *necessary* causes, and therefore are necessitated.[577]

His interest in social laws is shown in this statement:

The skill of making, and maintaining Common-wealths, consisteth in certain Rules, as does Arithmetique and Geometry; not (as Tennis-play) on Practise onely; which Rules, neither poor men have the leisure, nor men that have had the leisure, have hitherto had the curiosity, or the method to find out.[578]

As a final point, it should be mentioned that before La Peyrère and Spinoza, Hobbes analyzed the Old Testament from a historical point of view.[579]

## Spinoza

The standpoint from which Benedict de Spinoza (1632–77) investigated man is best expressed in his own words.

Philosophers conceive of the passions which harass us as vices into which men fall by their own fault, and, therefore, generally deride, bewail, or blame them, or execrate them, if they wish to seem unusually pious. And so they think they are doing something wonderful, and reaching the pinnacle of learning, when they are clever enough to bestow manifold praise on such human nature, as is nowhere to be found, and to make verbal attacks on that which, in fact, exists. For they conceive of men, not as they are, but as they themselves would like them to be. Whence it has come to pass that, instead of ethics, they have generally written satire, and that they have never conceived a theory of politics, which could be turned to use, but such as might be taken for a chimera, or might have been formed in Utopia, or in that golden age of the poets when, to be sure, there was least need of it. . . .

But statesmen, on the other hand, are suspected of plotting against mankind, rather than consulting their interests, and are esteemed more crafty than learned. No doubt nature has taught them, that vices will exist, while men do. And so, while they study to anticipate human wickedness, and that by arts, which experience and long practice have taught, and which men generally use under the guidance more of fear than of reason, they are thought to be enemies of religion, especially by divines, who believe that supreme authorities should handle public affairs in accordance with the same rules of piety, as bind a private individual. Yet there can be no doubt, that statesmen have written about politics far more happily than philosophers. For, as they had experience for their mistress, they taught nothing that was inconsistent with practice. . . .

Therefore, on applying my mind to politics, I have resolved to demonstrate by a certain and undoubted course of argument, or to deduce from the very condition of human nature, not what is new and unheard of, but only such things as agree best with practice. And that I might investigate the subject-matter of this science with the same freedom of spirit as we generally use in mathematics, I have laboured carefully, not to mock, lament, or execrate, but to understand human actions; and to this end I have looked upon passions, such as love, hatred, anger, envy, ambition, pity, and the other perturbations of the mind, not in the light of vices of human nature, but as properties, just as pertinent to it, as are heat, cold, storm, thunder, and the like to the nature of the atmosphere, which phenomena, though inconvenient, are yet necessary, and have fixed causes, by means of which we endeavour to understand their nature, and the mind has just as much pleasure in viewing them aright, as in knowing such things as flatter the senses.[580]

"Man thinks,"[581] and "some ideas or notions exist which are common to all men."[582]

. . . those notions which are called common . . . are the foundations of our reasoning.[583]

But in spite of his reason, man is not usually rational.

It is very seldom indeed that men live according to the guidance of reason.[584]

Inasmuch as men are led . . . more by passion than reason, it follows, that a multitude come together . . . not at the suggestion of reason, but of some common passion.[585]

There are three basic emotions: joy, sorrow, and desire.

. . . besides these three—joy, sorrow, and desire—I know of no other primary affect, the others springing from these.[586]

Following Descartes and Hobbes, Spinoza considered man to be under the control of natural laws.

It is impossible that a man should not be a part of nature, and that he should suffer no changes but those which can be understood through his own nature alone, and of which he is the adequate cause.[587]

The will cannot be called a free cause, but can only be called necessary.[588]

It is difficult to determine his theory of the origin of man because he deliberately shied away from it.

. . . it would be easy to explain on this basis [i.e., God's commandment to Adam not to eat the forbidden fruit] the whole history or allegory of the first man. But I prefer to pass over the subject in silence, because, in the first place, I cannot be absolutely certain that my explanation would be in accordance with the intention of the sacred writer; and, secondly, because many do not admit that this history is an allegory, maintaining it to be a simple narrative of facts.[589]

However, he undoubtedly did not take the Old Testament account too literally. Besides his remark in the preceding passage, as a result of his biblical criticism* he maintained that Genesis is merely Moses' view on creation.[593] In addition, he referred to Adam as "the first man to whom God was revealed."[594]

As to the purpose of his political works, Spinoza says:

I start from the natural rights of the individual, which are co-extensive with his desires and power, and from the fact that no one is bound to live as another pleases, but is the guardian of his own liberty. I show that these rights can only be transferred to those whom we depute to defend us, who acquire with the duties of defence the power of ordering our lives, and I thence infer that rulers possess rights only limited by their power, that they are the sole guardians of justice and liberty, and that their subjects should act in all things as they dictate.[595]

He believed in the social contract theory, and used it in much the same way as did Hobbes.

* "[Spinoza's analysis[590] is a classic of biblical criticism. His conclusion was] that all the books . . . are compilations, and that the events therein are recorded as having happened in old time."[591]

"The sacred books were not written by one man, nor for the people of a single period, but by many authors of different temperaments, at times extending from first to last over nearly two thousand years, and perhaps much longer.[592]

. . . men are not born fit for citizenship, but must be made so.[596]

For men are . . . by nature enemies.[597]

. . . every one . . . seeks his own interest.[598]

The natural right of the individual man is . . . determined, not by sound reason, but by desire and power.[599]

Whatsoever, therefore, an individual (considered as under the sway of nature) thinks useful for himself, whether led by sound reason or impelled by the passions, that he has a sovereign right to seek and to take for himself as he best can, whether by force, cunning, entreaty, or any other means; consequently he may regard as an enemy anyone who hinders the accomplishment of his purpose.[600]

. . . in the state of Nature . . . every man is his own judge, possessing the absolute right to lay down laws for himself, to interpret them as he pleases, or to abrogate them if he thinks it convenient.[601]

[However,] the mere state of nature, [is one] in which everyone lives after his own mind at the great risk of his life.[602]

It is very seldom indeed that men live according to the guidance of reason; on the contrary, it so happens that they are generally envious and injurious to one another. But, nevertheless, they are scarcely ever able to live a solitary life, so that to most men the definition of man that he is a social animal entirely commends itself, and indeed it is the case that far more advantages than disadvantages arise from the common society of man . . . by mutual help they can much more easily procure the things they need, and . . . it is only by their united strength that they can avoid the dangers which everywhere threaten them.[603]

. . . human management and watchfulness can greatly assist towards living in security and warding off the injuries of our fellow-men, and even of beasts.* Reason and experience show no more certain means of attaining this object than the formation of a society with fixed laws, the occupation of a strip of territory, and the concentration of all forces, as it were, into one body, that is the social body.[605]

The formation of society serves not only for defensive purposes, but is also very useful, and, indeed, absolutely necessary, as rendering possible the division of labour. If men did not render mutual assistance to each other, no one would have either the skill or the time to provide for his own sustenance and preservation: for all men are not equally apt for all work, and no one would be capable of preparing all that he individually stood in need of. Strength and time, I repeat, would fail, if every one had in person to plough, to sow, to reap, to grind corn, to cook, to weave, to stitch, and perform the other numerous functions required to keep life going; to say nothing of the arts and sciences which are also entirely necessary to the perfection and blessedness of human nature. We see that people in uncivilized barbarism lead a wretched and almost animal life, and even they would not be able to acquire their few rude necessaries without assisting one another to a certain extent.†[607]

* " . . . two dominions stand towards each other in the same relation as do two men in the state of nature, with this exception, that a commonwealth can provide against being oppressed by another; which a man in the state of nature cannot do, seeing that he is overcome daily by sleep, often by disease or mental infirmity, and in the end by old age, and is besides liable to other inconveniences, from which a commonwelath can secure itself."[604]

† "The strength of one man would scarcely suffice to obtain these things if men did not mutually assist one another."[606]

Inasmuch as men are led . . . more by passion than reason, it follows, that a multitude comes together, and wishes to be guided, as it were, by one mind, not at the suggestion of reason, but of some common passion—that is . . . , common hope, or fear, or the desire of avenging some common hurt. But since fear of solitude exists in all men, because no one in solitude is strong enough to defend himself, and procure the necessaries of life, it follows that men naturally aspire to the civil state; nor can it happen that men should ever utterly dissolve it.[608]

. . . many more advantages than disadvantages arise from their common union.[609]

. . . for the ends of every social organization and commonwealth are . . . security and comfort.[610]

Now if men were so constituted by nature that they desired nothing but what is designated by true reason, society would obviously have no need of laws: it would be sufficient to inclucate true moral doctrines; and men would freely, without hesitation, act in accordance with their true interests. But human nature is framed in a different fashion: every one, indeed, seeks his own interest, but does not do so in accordance with the dictates of sound reason, for most men's ideas of desirability and usefulness are guided by their fleshly instincts and emotions, which take no thought beyond the present and the immediate object. Therefore, no society can exist without government, and force, and laws to restrain and repress men's desires and immoderate impulses.[611]

Nevertheless, no one can doubt that it is much better for us to live according to the laws and assured dictates of reason, for, as we said, they have men's true good for their object. Moreover, every one wishes to live as far as possible securely beyond the reach of fear, and this would be quite impossible so long as everyone did everything he liked, and reason's claim was lowered to a par with those of hatred and anger; there is no one who is not ill at ease in the midst of enmity, hatred, anger, and deceit, and who does not seek to avoid them as much as he can. When we reflect that men without mutual help, or the aid of reason, must needs live most miserably, . . . we shall plainly see that men must necessarily come to an agreement* to live together as securely and well as possible if they are to enjoy as a whole the rights which naturally belong to them as individuals, and their life should be no more conditioned by the force and desire of individuals, but by the power and will of the whole body. This end they will be unable to attain if desire be their only guide (for by the laws of desire each man is drawn in a different direction); they must, therefore, most firmly decree and establish that they will be guided in everything by reason (which nobody will dare openly to repudiate lest he should be taken for a madman), and will restrain any desire which is injurious to a man's fellows, that they will do to all as they would be done by, and that they will defend their neighbour's rights as their own.

How such a compact as this should be entered into, how ratified and established, we will now inquire.†

. . . in general no one will abide by his promises, unless under the fear of a greater evil, or the hope of a greater good. . . . This consideration should have very great weight in forming a state. However, if all men could be easily led by reason alone, and could recognize what is best and most useful for a state, there would be no one who would not forswear deceit, for every one would keep most religiously to their compact in their desire for the chief good, namely, the preservation of the state, and would cherish

* " . . . the compact by which the right of free action was ceded."[612]

† " . . all men, whether barbarous or civilized, everywhere frame customs, and form some kind of civil state."[613]

good faith above all things as the shield and buckler of the commonwealth. However, it is far from being the case that all men can always be easily led by reason alone; everyone is drawn away by his pleasure, while avarice, ambition, envy, hatred, and the like so engross the mind that reason has no place therein. Hence, though men make promises with all the appearances of good faith, and agree that they will keep to their engagement, no one can absolutely rely on another man's promise unless there is something behind it. Everyone has by nature a right to act deceitfully, and to break his compacts, unless he be restrained by the hope of some greater good, or the fear of some greater evil.

However, as we have shown that the natural right of the individual is only limited by his power, it is clear that by transferring, either willingly or under compulsion, this power into the hands of another, he in so doing necessarily cedes also a part of his right; and further, that the sovereign right over all men belongs to him who has sovereign power, wherewith he can compel men by force, or restrain them by threats of the universally feared punishment of death; such sovereign right he will retain only so long as he can maintain his power of enforcing his will; otherwise he will totter on his throne, and no one who is stronger than he will be bound unwillingly to obey him.*[615]

In order that the true doctrines of reason, that is . . . the true Divine doctrines might obtain absolutely the force of law and right, it was necessary that each individual should cede his natural right, and transfer it either to society as a whole, or to a certain body of men, or to one man. Then, and not till then, does it first dawn upon us what is justice and what is injustice, what is equity and what is iniquity.†[617]

Spinoza treats of the evolution of property.

. . . nature offers nothing that can be called this man's rather than another's; but under nature everything belongs to all—that is, they have authority to claim it for themselves. But under dominion . . . it is by common law determined what belongs to this man, and what to that.[618]

Furthermore, in the state of nature, there is nothing which any man can less claim for himself, and make his own, than the soil, and whatever so adheres to the soil, that he cannot hide it anywhere, nor carry it whither he pleases. The soil, therefore, and whatever adheres to it in the way we have mentioned, must be quite common property of the commonwealth—that is, of all those who, by their united force, can vindicate their claim to it, or of him to whom all have given authority to vindicate his claim.[619]

. . . by the power of the commonwealth alone is anyone master of definite property.[620]

In addition, he considered the problem of the evolution of religion.

. . . the state of nature is, both in nature and in time, prior to religion. . . . The state of nature must by no means be confounded with a state of religion, but must be conceived as without either religion or law, and consequently without sin or wrong. . . .

We must, then, fully grant that the Divine law and right originated at the time when men by express covenant agreed to obey God in all things, and ceded, as it were, their natural freedom, transferring their rights to God.[621]

---

* "Now, we have seen that in forming a state the power of making laws must either be vested in the body of citizens, or in a portion of them, or in one man. For, although men's free judgements are very diverse, each one thinking that he alone knows everything, and although complete unanimity of feeling and speech is out of the question, it is impossible to preserve peace, unless individuals abdicate their right of acting entirely on their own judgement. Therefore, the individual justly cedes the right of free action, though not of free reason and judgement."[614]

† " . . . without such a compact, none but natural rights exist."[616]

Men would never be superstitious, if they could govern all their circumstances by set rules, or if they were always favoured by fortune: but being frequently driven into straits where rules are useless, and being often kept fluctuating pitiably between hope and fear by the uncertainty of fortune's greedily coveted favours, they are consequently, for the most part, very prone to credulity. The human mind is readily swayed this way or that in times of doubt, especially when hope and fear are struggling for mastery, though usually it is boastful, over-confident, and vain . . . . in adversity they know not where to turn, but and pray for counsel from every passer-by. No plan is then too futile, too absurd, or too fatuous for their adoption; the most frivolous causes will raise them to hope, or plunge them into despair—if anything heppens during their fright which reminds them of some past good or ill, they think it portends a happy or unhappy issue, and therefore (though it may have proved abortive a hundred times before) style it a lucky or unlucky omen. Anything which excites their astonishment they believe to be a portent signifying the anger of the gods or of the Supreme Being, and, mistaking superstition for religion, account it impious not to avert the evil with prayer and sacrifice. . . .

Superstition, then, is engendered, preserved, and fostered by fear.[622]

As men are accustomed to call Divine the knowledge which transcends human understanding, so also do they style Divine, or the work of God, anything of which the cause is not generally known.[623]

Similarly, if the Jews were at a loss to understand any phenomenon, or were ignorant of its cause, they referred it to God. Thus a storm was termed the chiding of God, thunder and lightning the arrows of God, for it was thought that God kept the winds confined in caves, His treasuries.[624]

He argued in favor of the psychic unity of mankind.

. . . all have one common nature.[625]

. . . in regard to intellect and true virtue, every nation is on a par with the rest.[626]

. . . men's natural passions are everywhere the same; and if wickedness more prevails, and more offences are committed in one commonwealth than in another, it is certain that the former has not enough pursued the end of unity, nor framed its laws with sufficient forethought; and that, therefore, it has failed in making quite good its right as a commonwealth. . . .

But as the vices and inordinate licence and contumacy of subjects must be imputed to the commonwealth, so, on the other hand, their virtue and constant obedience to the laws are to be ascribed in the main to the virtue and perfect right of the common wealth.[627]

But nature forms individuals, not peoples; the latter are only distinguishable by the differences of their language, their customs, and their laws,* while from the two last— i.e., customs and laws,—it may arise that they have a peculiar disposition, a peculiar manner of life, and peculiar prejudices. If, then, the Hebrews were harder of heart than other nations, the fault lay with their laws or customs.[629]

It may be concluded that these gifts [i.e., the characteristics of human nature] are not peculiar to any nation, but have always been shared by the whole human race, unless, indeed, we would indulge the dream that nature formerly created men of different kinds.[630]

---

* "Nations . . . are distinguished from one another in respect to the social organization and the laws under which they live and are governed."[628]

## Selden

Among the anti-royalists, John Selden (1584–1654) used the social contract theory against the king.

If our fathers have lost their libertye—whether may wee not labour to regaine it. Answer: wee must look to the contract; if that be rightly made wee must stand to it.[631]

A King is a thing men have made for their owne sakes for quietness sake.[632]

Every Law is a Contract betwixt the Prince & the people & therefore to bee kept.[633]

To know what obedience is due to the prince you must looke into the contract betwixt him & his people, as if you would know what Rent is due to the Landlord from the Tenant, You must looke into the Lease.[634]

He gave the usual description of the evolution of political organization.

Times . . . near the golden age . . . have left but few notes of expressly binding lawes, the main government consisting in the arbitrary disposition of those, in whom being chosen as princes for their eminency in justice, and consequently in all other virtues (as *Deioces* was of the *Medes*) it was rather an office than a title of dignity, to undergo the style of monarch.[635]

That supreme title of *king* or *emperor* . . . hath a two-fold original, to which all supreme kingdoms have relation; either from the power of the sword, or *conquest,* used by some ancestor of the present kings, who thence, as heirs, derive their sovereignty in the territories, and over the people of their kingdoms; or by some *choice* proceeding from the opinion of the virtue and nobleness of him that is chosen.[636]

Under what time the *beginning of kingdoms* or the *first king* should be placed, is most uncertain. For, although in the time before the flood, there be no express mention in the holy story of a king, and that the common opinion be, that in *Nimrod* or *Belus* (father to *Ninus*) the first monarchy began after the flood; yet there is reason enough to conjecture, that there were kings also long before both him and the flood.[637]

## Milton

John Milton (1608–74) was a powerful anti-royalist advocate of the social contract. The purpose of his political writings was "to assert the people's common rights against the unrighteous despotism of kings."[638]

No man who knows aught, can be so stupid to deny that all men naturally were borne free, being the image and resemblance of God himself, and were by privilege above all the creatures, born to command and not to obey: and that they liv'd so. Till from the root of *Adams* transgression, falling among themselves to doe wrong and violence,* and forseeing that such courses must needs tend to the destruction of them all†, they agreed by common league to bind each other from mutual injury, and joyntly to defend themselves against any that gave disturbance or opposition to such agreement.‡ Hence came

---

* "To live safe and free, without suffering violence and wrong, to this end it was that men first entered into a polity."[639]

† " . . . lest the stronger oppress the weaker, and thus those whom their mutual safety and protection had brought together to be disunited and divided by injury and violence, and reduced to a savage life again."[640]

‡ "For it was for this very reason that at first men entered into societies: not that any one might insult over all the rest, but that in case any should injure another, law might not be wanting, and a judge between man and man, whereby the injured might be protected or at least avenged."[641]

Citties, Townes and Common-wealths.* And because no faith in all was found sufficiently binding, they saw it needfull to ordaine som authoritie, that might restrain by force and punishment what was violated against peace and common rights. This authoritie and power of self-defence and preservation being originally and naturally in every one of them, and unitedly in them all, for ease, for order, and least each man should be his own partial Judge, they communicated and deriv'd either to one, whom for the eminence of his wisdom and integritie they chose above the rest, or to more than one whom they thought of equal deserving: the first was call'd a King; the other Magistrates. Not to be thir Lords and Maisters (though afterward those names in som places were giv'n voluntarily to such as had been Authors of inestimable good to the people) but, to be thir Deputies and Commissioners, to execute, by vertue of this intrusted power, that justice which else every man by the bond of nature and of Cov'nant must have executed for himself, and for one another. And to him that shall consider well why among free Persons, one man by civil right should beare authority and jurisdication over another, no other end or reason can be imaginable.[643]

Hence the king exists for the people, and consequently the people are above him and to be preferred to him; which being allowed, there can be no right of the king whereby he, the inferior, may oppress or enslave the people, the superior. Since the king has no right to do wrong, the right of the people remains by nature supreme; and therefore, by that right whereby, before kings were instituted, men first united their strength and counsels for their mutual defense, by that right whereby, for the preservation of all men's liberty, peace, and safety, they appointed one or more to govern the rest, by the same right they may punish or depose, for cowardice or folly or dishonour or treachery, those very persons whom for their valour or wisdom they had advanced to the government, or any others that rule disorderly; since nature hath regarded and doth regard the good not of one, or of a few, but of all in general, whatever become of one man's or of a few men's power.[644]

. . . then may the people as oft as they shall judge it for the best, either choose him or reject him, retaine him or depose him . . . meerly by the liberty and right of free born Men, to be govern'd as seems to them best.[645]

## Locke

Filmer's most important opponent was John Locke (1632–1704), who countered the former's patriarchal theory with that of social contract.

To understand political power aright, and derive it from its original, we must consider what estate all men are naturally in, and that is, a state of perfect freedom to order their actions, and dispose of their possessions and persons as they think fit, within the bounds of the Law of Nature, without asking leave or depending upon the will of any other man.[646]

God, having made man such a creature that, in His own judgement, it was not good for him to be alone, put him under strong obligations of necessity, convenience, and inclination, to drive him into society, as well as fitted him with understanding and language to continue and enjoy it. The first society was between man and wife, which gave beginning to that between parents and children, to which, in time, that between master and servant came to be added.[647]

---

* "Without magistrates and civil government there can be no commonwealth, no human society, no living in the world."[642]

[The relations between husband and wife,[648] and master and servant,[649] were also based upon a social contract.]

Men being, as has been said, by nature all free, equal, and independent, no one can be put out of this estate and subjected to the political power of another without his own consent, which is done by agreeing with other men, to join and unite into a community for their comfortable, safe, and peacable living, one amongst another, in a secure enjoyment of their own properties, and a greater security against any that are not of it. This any number of men may do, because it injures not the freedom of the rest; they are left, as they were, in the liberty of the state of Nature. When any number of men have so consented to make one community or government, they are thereby presently incorporated, and make one body politic, wherein the majority have a right to act and conclude the rest.[650]

Locke also refuted Herbert's doctrine of innate ideas by means of comparative ethnographic material,[651] which he used in the fashion customary among cosmopolitan skeptics.

Whether there be any such moral principles, wherein all men do agree, I appeal to any who have been but moderately conversant in the history of mankind, and looked abroad beyond the smoke of their own chimneys. Where is that practical truth which is universally received, without doubt or question, as it must be if innate? I easily grant that there are great numbers of opinions which, by men of different countries, education, and tempers, are received and embraced as first and unquestionable principles; many whereof, both for their absurdity as well as opposition to one another, it is impossible should be true. But yet all those propositions, how remote soever from reason, are so sacred somewhere or other, that men even of good understanding in other matters, will sooner part with their lives, and whatever is dearest to them, than suffer themselves to doubt, or others to question, the truth of them.[652]

. . . if we look abroad to take a view of men as they are, we shall find that they have remorse, in one place, for doing or omitting that which others, in another place, think they merit by.

He that will carefully peruse the history of mankind, and look abroad into the several tribes of men, and with indifferency survey their actions, will be able to satisfy himself, that their is scarce that principle of morality to be named, or rule of virtue to be thought on . . . which is not, somewhere or other, slighted or condemned by the general fashion of whole societies of men, governed by practical opinions and rules of living quite opposite to theirs.[653]

There is a psychic unity of mankind; group differences are culturally determined.

Had you or I been born at the Bay of Soldania, possibly our thoughts and notions had not exceeded those brutish ones of the Hottentots that inhabit there. And had the Virginia king Apochancana been educated in England, he had been perhaps as knowing a divine, and as good a mathematician as any in it; the difference between him and a more improved Englishman lying barely in this, that the exercise of his faculties was bounded within the ways, modes, and notions of his own country, and never directed to any other or further inquiries.[654]

One remark implies that he had in mind a unilinear conception of cultural evolution such as the Scotch evolutionists had in the eighteenth century and the English evolutionists in the nineteenth.

Thus, in the beginning, all the world was America, and more so than that is now.[655]

He was opposed to the geographic interpretation of cultural phenomena.

. . . several nations of the Americans . . . are rich in land and poor in all the comforts of life; whom Nature, having furnished as liberally as any other people with the materials of plenty—*i.e.,* a fruitful soil, apt to produce in abundance what might serve for food, raiment, and delight; yet, for want of improving it by labour, have not one hundredth part of the conveniences we enjoy, and a king of a large and fruitful territory there feeds, lodges, and is clad worse than a day labourer in England.[656]

## Sidney

Algernon Sidney (1622–83) was another of Filmer's opponents.

. . . how numerous soever families may be upon the increase of mankind, they are all free, till they agree to recede from their own right, and join together in or under one government, according to such laws as best please themselves.[657]

We have . . . seen . . . that the first Fathers of Mankind left all their Children independent on each other, and in an equal liberty of providing for themselves: that every man continu'd in this liberty, till the number so increas'd, that they became troublesom and dangerous to each other; and finding no other remedy to the disorders growing, or like to grow among them, join'd many Familys into one civil Body, that they might the better provide for the conveniency, safety, and defence of themselves and their Children.[658]

The Contracts made between Magistrats, and the Nations that created them, were real, solemn, and obligatory.[659]

Reason leads them to this: no one man or family is able to provide what is requisite for their convenience or security, whilst every one has an equal right to every thing, and none acknowledges a superior to determine the controversies, that upon such occasions must continually arise, and will probably be so many and great, that mankind cannot bear them. . . . The liberty of one is thwarted by that of another; and whilst they are all equal, none will yield to any, otherwise than by a general consent. This is the ground of all just governments; for violence or fraud can create no right; and the same consent gives the form to them all, how much soever they differ from each other.[660]

# IV

# THE EIGHTEENTH CENTURY

T HE EIGHTEENTH century was characterized by naturalism, which in anthropology meant that man was viewed as a natural phenomenon, part of the universe and subject to its laws.

To the scientist, nature appeared in the light of a gigantic mechanical contrivance, operated by a connected and coherent system of "springs and balances," whose purpose and function it was possible to discover by patient research. It was an easy step from this assumption about nature to the general position that man, hitherto an anomaly in the scheme of things, must also fall within the scope of the same laws: he was part of the natural world, and, as such, must be subject to its economy. And from this, again, it followed that all man's activities—intellectual, moral, religious, political, economic— ought to be susceptible to scientific treatment, and become intelligible on this basis, like the natural order. . . . The task of the eighteenth century was to apply the experimental and inductive method, by which Science was achieving its conquests, to ethics, politics, religion, and economics; in a word, to complete the subjugation of all cosmic phenomena to the mind of man.[1]

## PHYSICAL ANTHROPOLOGY

**Haller**

In the field of comparative anatomy, Albrecht von Haller (1708–77) made important contributions to the study of comparative neurology.[2]

**Daubenton**

Louis Jean Marie Daubenton (1716–99) pointed out the difference in position of the *foramen magnum* in various animals and its relation to their posture.[3]

**Bradley**

In the eighteenth century, the morphological relationship between man and the other animals was usually acknowledged.

An early systematist, Richard Bradley (1666–1732), was aware of the morphological similarity between man and other animals. However, he, as well as others, made a dichotomy on the basis of man's posession of a "soul" and "reason."

The *Apes* and *Monkeys* of several Kinds are naturally disposed to imitate the Actions of Men; but indeed the Figure and Disposition of their Parts agree much more with those in Mankind, than the Parts of any other Creature.[4]

[He concludes a chapter, "Of *Quadrupedes,* or such *Animals* of the Viviparous Race,

175

as have four Legs or Branches to their Bodies," with the following statement:] I suppose
it may be wonder'd at, that hitherto I have not mention'd Mankind, who is so remarkable
a Creature, and Lord of all the rest; I confess, was I to have placed him where the Parts
of his Body would most agree with those of the created Bodies mention'd in this Treatise,
I must have set him in the middle of this Chapter; but I suppose my Reader will excuse
me, if I shew him so much regard, that I rather speake of him in the summing up of my
Scale, than let him be encompass'd with wild Beasts.[5]

[When he does discuss man at length, he observes:] Man, altho' he is Lord of all, and
has a Power of Ordering and Governing all living Creatures, which relate to our *Globe,*
yet he has many Particulars in his Frame, which bear Analogy with the Parts of those
Creatures he is ordain'd to govern. The Harmony which Nature maintains in the Generation and Production of *Quadrupedes,* is not contradicted in HIM. The Functions of several
Parts in Brutes direct them to perform what the same Parts would do in Mankind, was he
not endow'd with Reason to guide . . . and overrule what is brutal in him.[6]

He gave a classification of human races.

I proceed to take notice of the several Kinds of Men, whose Difference is remarkable.
We find five Sorts of Men; the *White Men,* which are *Europeans,* that have *Beards;*
and a sort of *White Men* in *America* (as I am told) that only differ from us in having no
*Beards.* The third sort are the *Malatoes,* which have their *Skins* almost of a *Copper* Colour,
*small Eyes,* and *strait black Hair.* The fourth Kind are the *Blacks,* which have *strait black
Hair:* And the fifth are the *Blacks* of *Guiney,* whose *Hair* is *curl'd,* like the *Wool* of a *Sheep,*
which difference is enough to shew us their Distinctions; for, as to their Knowledge, I
suppose there would not be any great Difference, if it was possible they could be all born
of the same Parents, and have the same Education, they would vary no more in Understanding than Children of the same House.[7]

## Linnaeus

Carl von Linné (1707–78) had to take man into account in his taxonomic
system. As early as 1732 he wrote on the relation of man to other primates.

In the first edition (1735) of *Systema naturae*[8] man was classed under "Anthropomorpha" (see accompanying chart).

## I. QUADRUPEDIA
*Body* hairy   *Feet* four   Females viviparous, lactiferous

| ANTHROMORPHA Fore-teeth on both sides or none | HOMO | Know thyself | H | Europaeus albesc. Americanus rubesc. Asiaticus fuscus Africanus nigr. |
|---|---|---|---|---|
| | SIMIA | Anterior          Posterior Digits. 5 ............... 5 | | Simia cauda carens Papio   Satyrus Cercopithecus Cynocephalus |
| | BRADYPUS | Posterior the same as the anterior Digits. 3. or 2......... 3 | | Ai      *Ignavus* Tardigradus[9] |

But to decide concerning our own species. If we contemplate the characters of our teeth, hands, fingers, and toes, it is impossible not to perceive how very nearly we are related to Baboons and Monkeys, the wild men of the woods. In as much therefore as these are found to be carnivorous, the question is decided with respect to ourselves.[10] [He adds this "Paradoxon":] *Satyrus,* tailed, hairy, bearded, with a human body, much given to gesticulations, extremely lascivious, is a species of ape, if one has ever been seen. The *tailed men,* also, of whom modern travellers relate so much, is of the same genus.[11]

In the second edition (1740)[12] there are slight modifications.

CLASSIS  I

QUADRUPEDIA

*Ordo* 1.

ANTHROPOMORPHA. *Teeth* four fore-teeth, or none.
1.  *Homo. Know thyself.*
    *Homo* varieties:  Europaeus albus          Asiaticus fuscus
                       Americanus rubescens     Africanus niger
2.  *Simia . . .*
3.  *Bradypus . . .*
4.  *Myrmecophaga.*[13]

The Paradoxon of the first edition was repeated verbatim.[14]

The sixth edition (1748)[15] was somewhat similar.

QUADRUPEDIA

*Ordo* 1.

ANTHROPOMORPHA

*Teeth* incisors 4 upper & parallel. *Mammae* pectoral.
1.  HOMO. KNOW THYSELF.
    1.  Homo *varieties* Europaeus *albus*        Asiaticus *fuscus*
                        Americanus *rufescens*    Africanus *niger*
    2.  SIMIA . . .
    3.  BRADYPUS.[16]

The last revision, that of the tenth edition (1758–59),[17] gave more information, particularly on the differentia for the races of man.

MAMMALIA

I.  PRIMATES
Foreteeth, upper 4, parallel
Petoral mammae, 2
1.  *Homo* know thyself
    Sapiens    1.  H. Diurnus; varying by culture and place.
    *Ferus*        on all fours, mute, hairy.
    *Amercanus*  α.  reddish, choleric, erect.
                    *Hair* black, straight, thick; *Nostrils* wide; *Face* harsh, *Beard* scanty.
                    *Obstinate,* merry, free.
                    *Paints* himself with fine red lines.
                    *Regulated* by customs.

*Europaeus** β.  white, sanguine, muscular.
              *Hair* flowing, long. Eyes blue.
              *Gentle,* acute, inventive.
              *Covered* with close vestments.
              *Governed* by laws.

*Asiaticus*    γ.  sallow, melancholy, stiff.
              *Hair* black. *Eyes* dark.
              *Severe,* haughty, avaricious.
              *Covered* with loose garments.
              *Ruled* by opinions.

*Afer*         δ.  black, phlegmatic, relaxed.
              *Hair* black, frizzled. *Skin* silky. *Nose* flat. *Lips* tumid.
              *Women* without shame. *Mammae* lactate profusely.
              *Crafty,* indolent, negligent.
              *Anoints* himself with grease.
              *Governed* by caprice.

*Monstrosus* . . . .
Troglodytes   2.  H. nocturnus
              Homo sylvestris Orang Outang . . .
2.  *Simia* . . .
3.  *Lemur* . . .
4.  *Vespertilio.*[20]

While a young man, he puzzled over the problem of the causes of racial differences.

The people [at Enånger] seemed somewhat larger in stature than in other places, especially the men. I inquired whether the children are kept longer at the breast than is usual with us, and they answered in the affirmative. They are allowed that nourishment more than twice as long as in the other places. I have a notion that Adam and Eve were giants, and that mankind from one generation to another, owing to poverty and other causes, have diminished in size. Hence perhaps the diminutive stature of the Laplanders.[21]

There is a striking difference in stature between the inhabitants of Helsingland and those of Lapland, nor is the reason of this difference all obscure,

1.  If we give a young puppy plenty of food, he will grow large; if but little, he will turn out small.

2.  If kept warm, he will also grow to a much larger size than if he is always inured to cold.

The same remarks may be applied to the people in question.[22]

---

\* He classified man in Sweden as follows:

CLASSIS I
Quadrupedia
I.  *Anthropomorpha*
Homo

1.  THE MEN inhabiting Sweden are
"α.  *Goths,* of tall stature, hair white and straight, the iris of the eye ashen blue.
"β.  *Finns,* muscular body, hair long and yellow, the iris of the eye dark.
"γ.  *Lapps,* small thin body, hair black, straight, short, the iris of the eye blackish.
"δ.  *Variations* and mixtures of α. and β. and the others who have immigrated into Sweden, in the way that may be seen over all Europe."[18]
"The young women in Finland have much more swelling bosoms than those of Lapland."[19]

However, he was skeptical of the extent of innate physical differences.

. . . the question put by Dr. Rosen, "why are the Laplanders so swift-footed?"
To which I answer, that it arises not from any one cause, but from the cooperation of many.

1. The Laplanders, unlike us, wear no heels to their half boots . . . .
2. These people are accustomed to running from infancy . . . .
3. Freedom from hard labour is another cause . . . .
4. Habitual exercise of muscles . . . .
5. Animal food . . . .
6. The Laplander is satisfied with a small quantity of food at once . . . .
7. I examined their knees, ankles, and feet, but could not perceive the least difference in their shape from those of other countries, except perhaps that the sole of the foot seemed rather more concave, at the inner side, than usual. How far this may make any difference, a better mechanic than I am must determine.
8. All the Laplanders are of a small stature.[23]

In a similar manner he answered the question "Why are the Laplanders so healthy?"[24]

In 1746 he defended his classification of man as a quadruped.

No one has any right to be angry with me, if I think fit to enumerate man amongst the quadrupeds. Man is neither a stone nor a plant, but an animal, for such is his way of living and moving; nor is he a worm, for then he would have only one foot; nor an insect, for then he would have antennae; nor a fish, for he has no fins; nor a bird, for he has no wings. Therefore, he is a quadruped, has a mouth made like that of other quadrupeds, and finally four feet, on two of which he goes, and uses the other two for prehensive purposes; and indeed, to speak the truth, as a natural historian according to the principles of science, up to the present time I have not been able to discover any character by which man can be distinguished from the ape; for there are somewhere apes which are less hairy than man, erect in position, going just like him on two feet, and recalling the human species by the use they make of their hands and feet, to such an extent, that the less educated travellers have given them out as a kind of man. Speech, indeed, seems to distinguish man from other animals; but after all this is only a sort of power or result, and not a characteristic mark taken from number, figure, proportion, or position; so that it is a matter of the most arduous investigation to describe the exact specific difference of man. But there is something in us, which cannot be seen, whence our knowledge of ourselves depends—that is, *reason,* the most noble thing of all, in which man excels to a most surprising extent all other animals.*

No one, therefore, can very easily deny that man is an animal.[29]

In a letter to a colleague, written in 1747, he gave the reason for his deliberate ambiguity when discussing man.

You disapprove of my having located Man among the Anthropomorphi. But man

* "Nature teaches the brute creation to distinguish, without a preceptor, what is useful from what is hurtful, while man is left to his own inquiries."[25]

" . . . it is reason in which man is pre-eminent. In no other faculty does he so much excel other animals."[26]

"Man, my hearers, is distinguished from all other animals principally by *reason,* through which he surpasses them to such a degree and in so many ways, that we must confess that nature here has made its greatest leap."[27]

In another place he stated that man differs from other animals in the possession of a soul."[28]

knows himself. Now we may, perhaps, give up those words. It matters little to me what name we use; but I demand of you, and of the whole world, that you show me a generic character—one that is according to generally accepted principles of classification, by which to distinguish between Man and Ape. I myself most assuredly know of none. I wish someone would indicate one to me. But, if I had called man an ape, or vice versa, I should have fallen under the ban of all the ecclesiastics. It may be that as a naturalist I ought to have done so.[30]

In 1760 he painted a broad picture of man's relation to the rest of organic life.

. . . we must pursue the great chain of nature till we arrive at its origin; we should begin to contemplate her operations in the human frame, and from thence continue our researches through the various tribes of quadrupeds, birds, reptiles, fishes, insects, and worms, till we arrive at the vegetable creation . . . . the farther this natural chain is pursued from our species, the more simple we find it.[31]

Since he appreciated man's similarity to the other primates, it becomes interesting to know whether or not he believed in evolution. Inasmuch as he wrote both pro annd con and was cautious in the expression of heresies, the question cannot be answered. In some passages he argued for the fixity of species.

. . . no new species are produced at this time of day.[32]

Every genus is natural and was in the beginning of things created such.[33]

A single pair, one of each sex, of each species, of living creatures, was created in the beginning. . . .
We believe, on divine testimony, that God created a single human pair,—one male and one female.
The inspired writer, Moses, relates that they were placed in the garden of Eden; and that there Adam imposed names on all the animals which were brought before him by God.[34]

Men and all animals increase and multiply in such a manner, that however few at first, their numbers are continually and gradually increasing. If we trace them backwards, from a greater to a lesser number, we at length arrive at one original pair.[35]

Moreover, if we consider the *generation* of Animals, we find that each produces an offspring after its own kind, as well as Plants, *Taenias,* and Coral-lines; that all are propagated by their branches, by bud, or by seed; and that from each proceeds a germ of the same nature with its parent; so that all living things, plants, animals, and even mankind themselves, form one "chain of universal Being," from the beginning to the end of the world: in this sense truly may it be said, that there is nothing new under the sun.[36]

. . . of all the species originally formed by the Deity, not one is destroyed.[37]

However, at other times he advocated the doctrine of the modifiability of species.[38]

Species and genus are always the work of nature; varieties, often that of art, class and order, the result of nature and art united.[39]

. . . it seems probable, that many plants, which now appear different species of the same genus, may in the beginning have been but one plant, having arisen merely from hybrid generation.[40]

Here is a new employment for botanists, to attempt the production of new species of vegetables, by scattering the pollen of various plants over various widowed females. . . .

I am persuaded by many considerations, that those numerous and most valuable varieties of plants which are used for culinary purposes, have been produced in this manner, as the several kinds of cabbages, lettuces, &c.; and I apprehend this is the reason of their not being changed by a difference of soil. Hence I cannot give my assent to the opinion of those, who imagine all varieties to have been occasioned by change of soil; for, if this were the case, the plants would return to their original form, if removed again to their original situation.[41]

## Söderberg and Hoppe

Two dissertations written under Linné examined the relations between man and other animals. Ole Söderberg (fl. 1748) wrote:

... it is for us to inquire what man has beyond the other animals. Anatomy teaches us that man possesses heart, brain, entrails, nerves, bones, muscles; that he moves himself, touches, tastes, smells, hears, and sees, exactly like brute animals. It is, however, true that you will find two peculiarities in man, of which the other animals are destitute,— namely *admiration* and *speech*. So far as the external senses go, animals perceive the same things that we do, but being destitute of any distinct perception, they cannot apply reflection to any objects whatsoever, or that attention of looking at everything, which a man does when absorbed in admiration.[42]

Christian Emmanuel Hoppe (fl. 1760) expanded Linné's treatment of the Anthropomorpha other than *Homo sapiens*.

Amongst all the productions of the terraqueous globe, nothing so much resembles mankind as the genus of the *Simiae*. Their faces, hands, feet, arms, legs, breast, and intestines bear, in most respects, a strong resemblance to ours. Their habits, and ingenuity in practising tricks and jokes, besides their imitation of others (that is, their readiness in following the fashion of the age), make them so like ourselves, that it is difficult to draw any natural distinction between man and his imitator—the ape.[43]

I can discover scarcely any mark by which man can be distinguished from the apes, unless, perhaps, in the corner teeth alone,—a point still to be determined by experience, since neither in the face, nor in the feet, nor in the erect gait, nor in any other point of his external structure, does man differ from every one of the species of apes.[44]

I should run to great length if I were to describe here the customs and manners of apes; but I will only say a little about those I may call our relations,—that is, of those kinds of the ape who go upright like ourselves, and stand on two feet, and in their physiognomy and the palms of their hands are exactly like ourselves.[45]

... no kind of brutes approaches so near man as the apes, and especially the anthropomorpha, in which we not only see a stature exactly like our own, but very similar habits; for not only the females, but also the males cherish their young with more than paternal affection, carry them in their arms, nurse them in their bosoms, take care of and defend them.[46]

As for me, I am still uncertain, by what characteristic mark the troglodytes can be distinguished from man, according to the principles of natural history. For there are so many things so alike in these kinds of apes and man, such as the structure of the almost bare body, the face, the ears, mouth, teeth, hands, breasts; and also in the food, imitation and gesticulations in those species which walk upright and are properly called *anthropomorpha,* that it is very difficult to find marks sufficient to divide the genus.[47]

## Buffon

George Louis Leclerc, Count de Buffon (1707–88), did not make any substantial advance upon Linné in regard to man; in fact, his conservatism often prevented him from going as far.

He appreciated the similarity of structure in animals.

It is this envelope, or cover . . . which constitutes the distinction between different animals. The internal part, which is the basis of the animal oeconomy, is common to every animated being, with exception; and, as to its mode, it is nearly the same in man and in all animals which consist of flesh and blood. But the external cover is exceedingly diversified, and the greatest differences originate from the extremities of this cover.[48]

[Man] perceived that man, quadrupeds, cetaceous animals, birds, reptiles, insects, trees, and herbs, were nourished, expanded, and reproduced by the same law . . . . taking another animal, we always find the same fund of organization, the same senses, the same viscera, the same bones, the same flesh, the same motion of the fluids, the same play and action of the solids. In all of them he found a heart, veins, and arteries, and the same organs of circulation, respiration, digestion, nutrition, and secretion; in all of them he found a solid structure composed of the same pieces, and nearly situated in the same manner. This plan proceeds uniformly from man to the ape, from the ape to the quadrupeds, from quadrupeds to cetaceous animals, to birds, to fishes, and to reptiles: This plan, I say, when well apprehended by the human intellect, exhibits a faithful picture of animated Nature, and affords the most general as well as the most simple view under which she can be considered: And, when we want to extend it, and to pass from the animal to the vegetable, we perceive this plan, which had first varied only by shades, degenerating from reptiles to insects, from insects to worms, from worms to zoophytes, from zoophytes to plants; and, though changed in all its external parts, still preserving the same character, the principle features of which are nutrition, growth, and reproduction. These features are common to all organized substances. They are eternal and divine; and, instead of being effaced by time, it only renews and renders them more conspicuous.[49]

He even searches for species intermediate between man and other animals.

The four-handed animals fill the interval between man and the animals; and the two-handed species constitute a mean term in the distance betwen man and the cetaceous tribes.[50]

But, as Nature knows none of our definitions, as she has not classified her productions by bundles or genera, and as her progress is always gradual and marked by minute shades, some intermediate animal should be found between the ape and baboon. This intermediate species actually exists, and is the animal which we call *magot,* or the *Barbary ape.*[51]

His data forced him to acknowledge the resemblance between man and the apes.

What I call an *ape* is an animal without a tail, whose face is flat, whose teeth, hands, fingers, and nails resemble those of man, and who, like him, walks erect on two feet.[52]

This orang-outang or pongo is only a brute, but a brute of a kind so singular, that man cannot behold it without contemplating himself, and without being thoroughly convinced that his body is not the most essential part of his nature.[53]

[In the orang-outang] the . . . parts of the body, head, and members, both external and internal, so perfectly resemble those of man, that we cannot make the comparison without being astonished that such a similarity in structure and organization should not produce the same effects. The tongue, and all the organs of speech, for example, are the same as in man; and yet the orang-outang enjoys not the faculty of speaking; the brain has the same figure and proportions; and yet he possesses not the power of thinking. Can there be a more evident proof than is exhibited in the orang-outang, that matter alone, though perfectly organized, can produce neither language nor thought, unless it be animated by a superior principle?[54]

In fine, the orang-outang has a greater resemblance to man than even to the baboons or monkeys.[55]

Nevertheless, he refused to accept the affinity between man and the apes.

Man, it is true, resembles the other animals in the material part of his being; and, in the enumeration of natural existences, we are obliged to rank him in the class of animals . . .

When we compare man with the animal creation, we find in both a material organized body, senses, flesh and blood, motion, and many other striking resemblances. But all these analogies are external, and authorise us not to pronounce, that the nature of man is similar to that of the brute.[56]

We have often remarked, that Nature proceeds in her operations by imperceptible degrees. This truth, which otherwise admits of no exception, is here totally reversed. Between the faculties of man and those of the most minute animal, the distance is infinite. This is a clear proof, that the nature of man is different from that of the brute creation; that he himself constitutes a separate class from which there are numberless degrees of descent, before we arrive at the state of the mere animal; for, if man were of the same rank with the animals, there would be in nature a certain number of beings less perfect than man, and superior to any animal we are acquainted with; and those intermediate beings would descend imperceptibly from man to the monkey tribes. But no such beings exist. The passage is sudden and from a thinking being to a material one, from intellectual faculties to mechanical powers, from order and design to blind impulse, from reflection and choice to ungovernable appetite. . . . Man is a reasonable being; the animal is totally deprived of that noble faculty; And as there is no intermediate point between a positive and a negative, between a rational and an irrational animal, it is evident that man's nature is entirely different from that of the animal; that the latter only resembles the former in the external or material part.[57]

We should, therefore, conclude, that all animals are of the same nature, and that the nature of man is not only far superior, but likewise of a very different kind from that of the brute.[58]

The important difference lies in man's possession of a soul.

. . . the soul . . . . has been conferred on man alone, by which he is enabled to think and reflect, and, as the brutes are purely material, and neither think nor reflect, and yet act, and seem to be determined by motives, we cannot hesitate in pronouncing the principle of motion in them to be perfectly mechanical, and to depend absolutely on their organization.[59]

. . . man himself, though a distinct species, and infinitely removed from that of all other animals, being only of a middle size, has a greater number of neighbouring species than the very large kinds. In the history of the orang-outang . . . if figure alone be regarded, we might consider this animal as the first of apes, or the most imperfect of men;

because, except the intellect, the orang-outang wants nothing that we possess, and, in his body, differs less from man than from the other animals which receive the denomination of *apes*.

Hence mind, reflection, and language depend not on figure, or on the organization of the body. These are endowments peculiar to man.[60]

If our judgement were limited to figure alone, I acknowledge that the ape might be regarded as a variety of the human species. The Creator has not formed man's body on a model absolutely different from that of the mere animal. He has comprehended the figure of man, as well as that of all other animals, under one general plan. But, at the same time that he has given him a material form similar to that of the ape, he has penetrated this animal body with a divine spirit . . . .

Whatever resemblance, therefore, takes place between the Hottentot and the ape, the interval which separates them is immense; because the former is endowed with the faculties of thought and of speech.[61]

The relative degree of immaturity at birth is another important difference.

With regard to the ape, whose nature we are endeavouring to ascertain, however similar to man, he is so strongly marked with the features of brutality, that it is distinguishable from the moment of his birth. He is then proportionally stronger and better formed than the infant: He grows faster: The support of his mother is necessary for a few months only: His education is purely individual, and consequently as limited as that of the other animals.

Hence the ape, notwithstanding his resemblance to man, is a brute, and, instead of approaching our species, holds not the first rank among the animals; because he is by no means the most intelligent.[62]

Buffon also inquired into the difference between human and subhuman societies.

Having thus compared man with the brutes, when taken individually, I shall now compare man in society with the gregarious tribes, and endeavour to investigate the cause of that species of industry which is so remarkable in some animals, even of the lowest and most numerous orders.[63]

The nests of birds, . . . the cells of bees, the collections of foods laid up by the ant, the field-mouse, &c. suppose not any intelligence in those animals, nor proceed from particular laws established for each species, but depend, like every other animal operation, on number, figure, motion, organization, and feeling, which are general laws of Nature, and common to all animated beings.[64]

Whence proceeds this uniformity in all the operations of animals? Why does every species perform the same work in the very same manner? And why is the execution of different individuals neither better nor worse than that of every other? Can there be a stronger proof that their operations are only the results of pure mechanical impulse?[65]

He discussed the races of man in a consideration of

. . . the varieties that appear among men in different regions of the earth. These varieties may be reduced to three heads: 1. The colour; 2. The figure and stature; and, 3. The dispositions of different people.[66]

However, this section on "The varieties of the human species"[67] is based upon mere geographic distribution and is a mixture of physical anhropology and ethnography.

He believed in monogenesis and was an ardent defender of species fixity.

Every species having been originally created, the first individual served as a model to their descendants.[68]

... the existence of species is constant.[69]

He made the following remarks on the causes of race differences in order to uphold the biblical version of monogenesis.

Three causes . . . must be admitted, as concurring in the production of those varieties which we have remarked among the different nations of this earth: 1. The influence of climate; 2. Food, which has a great dependance on climate; and, 3. Manners, on which climate has, perhaps, a still greater influence.[70]

The climate may be regarded as the chief cause of the different colours of men. But food, though it has less influence upon colour, greatly affects the form of our bodies. Coarse, unwholesome, and ill prepared food, makes the human species degenerate. All those people who live miserably, are ugly and ill-made. . . . The air and the soil have great influence upon the figure of men, beasts, and plants. In the same province, the inhabitants of the elevated and hilly parts are more active, nimble, handsome, ingenious, and beautiful, than those who live in the plains, where the air is thick and less pure.[71]

Whenever man began to change his climate, and to migrate from one country to another, his nature was subject to various alterations. In temperate countries, which we suppose to be adjacent to the place where he was originally produced, these alterations have been slight; but they augmented in proportion as he receded from this station: And, after many ages had elapsed; after he had traversed whole continents, and inter-mixed with races already degenerated by the influence of different climates; after he was habituated to the scorching heats of the South, and the frozen regions of the North; the changes he underwent became so great and so conspicuous, as to give room for suspecting, that the Negro, the Laplander, and the White, were really different species, if, on the one hand, we were not certain, that one man only was originally created, and, on the other, that the White, the Laplander, and the Negro, are capable of uniting, and of propagating the great and undivided family of the human kind. Hence those marks which distinguish men who inhabit different regions of the earth, are not original, but purely superficial. It is the same identical being who is varnished with black under the Torrid Zone, and tawned and contracted by extreme cold under the Polar Circle. . . .

The earth is divided into two great continents. The antiquity of this division exceeds that of all human monuments; and yet man is more ancient, for he is the same in both worlds. The Asiatic, the European, and the Negro, produce equally with the American. Nothing can be a stronger proof that they belong to the same family, than the facility with which they unite to the common stock. The blood is different, but the germ is the same. The skin, the hair, the features, and the stature, have varied, without any change in internal structure.[72]

The impression of each species is a figure, the principal features of which are en-graven in characters which can never be effaced. But all the accessory shades and touches are greatly diversified; no individual has a perfect resemblance to another; no species exists without a number of varieties. In the human species, which bears the strongest marks of divinity the impression varies from white to black, from small to great, & c. The Laplander, the Patagonian, the Hottentot, the European, the American, and the Negro, though sprung from the same parents, have by no means the similarity of brothers.

All species, therefore, are subject to individual differences: But the constant varieties, perpetuated through successive generations, belong not equally to every species. The more dignified the species, its figure is the more fixed, and admits of fewer varieties.[73]

Upon the whole, every circumstance concurs in proving, that mankind are not composed of species essentially different from each other; that on the contrary, there was originally but one species, who, after multiplying and spreading over the whole surface of the earth, have undergone various changes by the influence of climate, food, mode of living, epidemic diseases, and the mixture of dissimilar individuals; that, at first, these changes were not so conspicuous, and produced only individual varieties; that these varieties became afterwards specific, because they were rendered more general, more strongly marked, and more permanent, by the continual action of the same causes; that they are transmitted from generation to generation, as deformities or diseases pass from parents to children; and that, lastly, as they were originally produced by a train of external and accidental causes, and have only been perpetuated by time and the constant operation of these causes, it is probable that they will gradually disappear, or, at least, that they will differ from what they are at present, if the causes which produced them should cease, or their operation be varied by other circumstances and combinations.[74]

He stated that man came to the New World from northeastern Asia.

With regard to their origin, I have no doubt, independent of theological considerations, that it is the same with ours. The resemblance of the North American savages to the oriental Tartars, renders it probable, that they originally sprung from the same stock. The late discovery by the Russians of several lands and islands beyond Kamtschatka, which extend nearly as far as the west part of the Continent of America, leave no room to question the possibility of communication, provided these discoveries were well attested, and the lands lay contiguous. But, even supposing considerable intervals of sea, is it not extremely probable that some people had crossed these intervals in quest of new countries, or that they were thrown upon the American coasts by tempests?[75]

## Hermann

Johann Hermann (1738–1800) was another systematist who included man in the primates.[76]

## Zimmerman

Eberhard August Wilhelm von Zimmerman (1743–1815) wrote on man in his *Speciman zoologiae geographicae*.[77]

## Pennant

Thomas Pennant (1726–98) wrote a *History of Quadrupeds* (1771)[78] which reflected the reactionary view in taxonomy.

I copy Mr. RAY, in his greater division of animals into hoofed, and digitated.[79]

He refused to accept the Linnean classification and gave as one of his reasons:

I reject his first division, which he calls *Primates,* or Chiefs of the Creation; because my vanity will not suffer me to rank mankind with *Apes, Monkies, Maucaucos,* and *Bats,* the companions LINNAEUS has allotted us even in his last System.[80]

Therefore, excluding man from consideration entirely, he classified the lower primates as follows:

DIV. II.   Digitated Quadrupeds.
SECT.   I. Anthropomorphos.[81]

To "Anthropomorphos" he appended this note:

*Animals approaching the human form:* A term to be taken in a limited sense; to be applied to all of this section, as far as relates to their feet, which serve the uses of hands in eating, climbing, or carrying any thing: to the flatness of the nails, in many species; and to some resemblance of their actions, resulting from the structure of their parts only, not from any superior sagacity to that of most others of the brute creation.[82]

## Blaumenbach

The last important systematist of the eighteenth century to be considered is Johann Friedrich Blumenbach (1752–1840). His disbelief in the concept of a chain of being was so great[83] that he classified man in a separate order from that of the other primates, let alone other mammals.

I.   Bimanus
    1.   *Homo*
II.   Quadrumana
    2.   *Simia*
    3.   *Papio*
    4.   *Cercopithecus*
    5.   *Lemur*
III.   Bradypoda [etc.][84]

[He then considers] the points, in which . . . man differs from other animals. . . .
First, I shall enumerate those things which affect the external conformation of the human body.
Secondly, those which affect the internal conformation.
Thirdly, the functions of the animal economy.
Fourthly, the endowments of the mind.
Fifthly, I mean to add a few words about the disorders peculiar to man.
And sixthly, I shall reckon up those points, in which man is commonly, but *wrongly*, thought to differ from the brutes.[85]

[I. Concerning the "external conformation of the human body."]
    A)  The erect position;
    B)  The broad, flat pelvis;
    C)  The two hands;
    D)  The regular and close set rows of teeth.[86]

[II. Concerning "the internal conformation."] It will be necessary to divide this discussion into two heads; first, by investigating those things which man alone, or only a few other animals with him, has not got; secondly, those things which are peculiar to him.[87]

[A.] *Internal parts which man is without.*
    [ 1.] . . . the subcutaneous muscle. . . .
    [ 2.] . . . the *rete mirabile arteriosum* . . . .
    [ 3.] . . . the *musculus oculi suspensorius s. bulbosus s. septimus* . . . .
    [ 4.] . . . the human foetus has no allantoid membrane . . . .
    [ 5.] The intermaxillary bone.[88]

[B.] *Differences between some internal parts of man and those of animals* . . . .

To begin with the head, besides some things of less moment, man has, it seems, the smallest crystalline lens (the cetacea excepted) in proportion, and it is less convex in the adult than in other animals; the large occipital foramen is placed more forward than in quadrupeds, and there are other things of the same kind. The mass of the brain is the largest of all, [etc.]*

The position of the heart is peculiar to man, [etc.][90]

[III. Concerning "the functions of the animal economy."] . . . man . . . has beyond all other mammals the most delicate and subtle cellular substance.

I am either very much mistaken, or the softness of that envelope is to be counted among the chief prerogatives by which man excels the rest of the animals. . . . I am thoroughly persuaded that to the flexible softness of this mucous membrane in man is owing his power of accustoming himself more than every other mammal to every climate, and being able to live in every region under the sun . . .[91]

To this aptitude for accommodation admirably answers that . . . physiological property of man, namely, *his slow growth, long infancys* and *late puberty.* . . .†

There are also some particulars to be mentioned about the sexual functions. Man has everywhere no particular time of the year, as the brutes, in which he desires to copulate. To men alone is conceded the prerogative of nocturnal pollutions. . . . The menstrual flux, on the other hand, is not less peculiar to women.[96]

[IV. Reason is] that prerogative of man which makes him lord and master of the rest of the animals. . . . the cause of this dominion does not reside in his bodily strength. It must therefore be referred exclusively to the gifts of the mind and their superiority. And these gifts in which man so far surpasses the rest of the animals, of whatever disposition and nature they may be, we will call *reason.*‡ Nature . . . has made man so as to be omniv-

---

* "As [to] the brain, the most noble entrail of the animal body. . . . The principal points in which its [i.e., that of a mandrill] base differs from the human organ are these. The two anterior lobes of the brain are almost entirely unified. The cerebellum is large in proportion to the brain. . . . The *pons varolii* is separated from the *medulla oblongata* by no apparent fissure, but is joined on, and down continuously with it. Not a vestige of the pyramidal or olivary bodies. . . . The *medulla oblongata* much thicker than in man. . . . The second pair of nerves which were united in one great mass, and then again divided at the very entrance of the orbits, was cut off before the separation. No *rete mirabile.*"[89]

† " . . . man . . . is born naked and weaponless, furnished with no instinct, entirely dependent on society and education. This excites the flame of reason by degrees, which at last shows itself capable of supplying, by itself, all the defects in which animals seem to have the advantage over man. Man brought up amongst the beasts, destitute of intercourse with man, comes out a beast. The contrary however never occurs to beasts which live with man. Neither the beavers, nor the seals, who live in company, nor the domestic animals which enjoy our familiar society, come out endowed with reason."[92]

"Of all animals he alone seems to be placed on the earth *altogether naked and defenceless.*"[93]

"Man is, in himself, a defenceless, helpless creature. No other animal continues so long in a state of infancy; no other is so long before it obtains its teeth; no other is so long before it can stand; no other arrives so late at puberty. Even his greatest advantages, Reason and Speech, are but germs, developed, not spontaneously, but by external assistance, cultivation, and education. This necessity of assistance, and his numerous urgent wants, prove the natural destination of man for *social connexion.*"[94]

"Man is a domestic animal."[95]

‡ "Instinct always remains the same, and is not advanced by cultivation, nor is it smaller or weaker in the young animal than in the adult. Reason, on the contrary, may be compared to a developing germ, which in the process of time, and by the accession of a social life, and other external circumstances, is as it were developed, formed, and cultivated. . . .

"Man then alone is destitute of what are called *instincts,* that is, certain congenital faculties for protecting himself from external injury, and for seeking nutritious foods, &c. All his instincts are artificial, and of the others there are only the smallest traces to be seen. Mankind therefore would be very wretched

orous and an inhabitant of the whole world. But this unlimited liberty of diet and locality, according to the almost infinite variety of climate, soil, and other circumstances,
brings with it also multifarious wants which cannot be met or remedied in one way alone.
His Creator has therefore fortified him with the power of reason and invention, in order
that he may accommodate himself to those conditions. . . . Thus, to compress a good deal
in a few words, man has made tools for himself, and so Franklin has acutely defined him
as *a tool-making animal;* thus he has prepared for himself arms and weapons; thus he has
found out ways of eliciting fire; and thus, in order that one man may use the advantages
and assistance of another, he has invented *language,* which again must be considered as one
of the things peculiar to man, since it is not like the sounds of animals, conventional,
but, as the arbitrary variety of language proves, has been invented and turned to use by
him.[101]*

Besides that other manifestation of the mind I have just spoken of, I mean language,
two others must be mentioned . . . I mean *laughter,* the companion of cheerfulness, and
*tears.*[103]†

[V and VI are less important.[104]]

Blumenbach then undertook an examination of the races of man. In the first
edition (1770) of *De generis humani varietate nativa* he classified man into four races.

. . . although there seems to be so great a difference between widely separate nations,
that you might easily take the inhabitants of the Cape of Good Hope, the Greenlanders,
and the Circassians for so many different species of man, yet when the matter is thoroughly considered, you see that all do so run into one another, and that one variety of mankind
does so sensibly pass into the other, that you cannot mark out the limits between them[105]

were it not preserved by the use of *reason,* of which other animals are plainly destitute. I am sure they
are only endowed with innate or comman and truly material sense (which is not wanting either to man)."[97]
   "Of the intellectual faculties, there are many possessed by man in common with most other animals,
such as Perception, Attention, and the two internal senses as they are called, Memory and Imagination.
   "Others are almost wholly confined to animals, so that but slight traces of them are found in man,
viz. the natural impulses or instincts: on the other hand, man is in exclusive possession of Reason."[98]

* "From what has been said, the direct difference between the voice and speech of animals is plain, since
we consider that man alone ought to be held to possess *speech,* or the voice of reason, and beasts only the
language of the affections. In process of time, the mind becomes developed, and finds out how to express
its ideas with the tongue. Young children give names to those they love, which is the case with no animal, although they can distinguish their master and those familiar to them well enough. Those stories
are utterly undeserving of attention which the old travellers related about the language of certain distant
nations, who they said were endowed with nothing but an inarticulate and, as it were, brutish voice.
It is indeed beyond all doubt that the fiercest nations, the Californians, the inhabitants of the Cape of
Good Hope, &c. have a peculiar sort of speech, and plenty of definite words, and that animals on the
contrary, whether they be like man in structure, as the famous orang-utan is, or approach man in intelligence, to use the words of Pliny about the elephant, are destitute of speech, and can only emit a few and
those equivocal sounds. That speech is the work of reason alone, appears from this, that other animals,
although they have nearly the same organs of voice as man, are entirely destitute of it."[99]

   "Man, besides the voice which is born with him, has also invented *speech.*"[100]
† "It has been disputed whether brutes have the same affections of the mind as man. This is a very difficult
question, if we examine the ways in which men express joy and sorrow, and especially laughter and
tears. That animals can cry is certain, since they have organs exactly like those in man for weeping; but
we must go deeper and enquire whether they do so in consequence of feeling sorrow. It is said to be
so with some animals . . . so that it is probable that weeping from sadness is common to animals and
man. About laughter as the effect of joy there seems more doubt. Some animals have peculiar ways of
expressing tranquillity or joy, but I do not think that a change in the muslces of the face, or the utterance
of cacchination, has been observed in any other animal but man."[102]

. . . The first and most important to us (which is also the primitive one) is that of Europe, Asia this side of the Ganges, and all the country situated to the north of the Amur, together with that part of North America, which is nearest both in position and character of the inhabitants. Though the men of these countries seem to differ very much amongst each other in form and colour, still when they are looked at as a whole they seem to agree in many thing with ourselves. The second includes that part of Asia beyond the Ganges, and below the river Amur, which looks towards the south, together with the islands, and the greater part of those countries which are called Australia. Men of dark colour, snub noses, with winking eyelids drawn outwards at the corners, scanty, and stiff hair. Africa makes up the third. There remains finally, for the fourth, the rest of America, except so much of the North as was included in the first variety.[106]

In the second edition (1781) he revised his classification by dividing man into five races, which he adhered to in all subsequent works.

Formerly in the first edition of this work I divided all mankind into four varieties; but after I had more accurately investigated the different nations of Eastern Asia and America, and, so to speak, looked at them more closely, I was compelled to give up that division, and to place in its stead the following five varieties, as more consonant to nature.

The first of these and the largest [the Caucasian,[107]] which is also the primeval one, embraces the whole of Europe, including the Lapps, whom I cannot in any way separate from the rest of the Europeans, when their appearance and their language bear such a testimony to their Finnish origin; and that western part of Asia . . .; also northern Africa, and lastly, in America, the Greenlanders and the Esquimaux; for I see in these people a wonderful difference from the other inhabitants of America; and, unless I am altogether deceived, I think they must be derived from the Finns. All these nations regarded as a whole are white in colour, and, if compared with the rest, beautiful in form.

The second variety [the Mongolian,[108]] comprises the rest of Asia. . . . The inhabitants of this country are distinguished by being of brownish colour, more or less verging to the olive, straight face, narrow eye-lids, and scanty hair . . .

The third variety [the Ethiopian,[109]] comprises what remains of Africa, besides that northern part which I have already mentioned. Black men, muscular, with prominent upper jaws, swelling lips, turned up nose, very black curly hair.

The fourth [the American,[110]] comprises the rest of America, whose inhabitants are distinguished by their copper colour, their thin habit of body, and scanty hair.

Finally, the new southern world makes up the fifth [the Malayan[111]] . . .; the men throughout being of a very deep brown colour, with broad nose, and thick hair.[112]

Each of these five principal races contains besides one or more nations which are distinguished by their more or less striking structure from the rest of those of the same division. Thus the Hindoos might be separated as particular subvarieties from the Caucasian; the Chinese and Japanese from the Mongolian; the Hottentots from the Ethiopian; so also the North American Indians from those in the southern half of the new world; and the black Papuans in New Holland, & c. from the brown Otaheitans and other islanders of the Pacific Ocean.[113]

The Caucasian must, on every physiological principle, be considered as the primary or intermediate of these five principal Races. The two extremes into which it has deviated, are on the one hand the Mongolian, on the other the Ethiopian. The other two Races from transitions between them; the American between the Caucasian and Mongolian; and the Malayan between the Caucasian and Ethiopian.[114]

[This investigation] brings us to that conclusion, which seems to flow spontaneously from physiological principles applied by the aid of critical zoology to the natural history of mankind; which is, *That no doubt can any longer remain but that we are with great probability right in referring all and singular as many varieties of man as are at present known to one and the same species.*[*116]

There is but one species of the genus Man; and all people of every time and every climate with which we are acquainted, may have originated from one common stock.[117]

This brings up the problem of the causes of racial differences.

. . . the genital liquid is only the shapeless material of organic bodies, composed of the innate matter of the organic kingdom, but differing in the force it shows, according to the phenomena; by which its first business is under certain circumstances of maturation, mixture, place, & to put on the form destined and determined by them.[118]

. . . it happens that the continuous action, carried on for several series of generations of some peculiar stimuli in organic bodies . . . has great influence in sensibly diverting the formative force from its accustomed path, which deflection is the most bountiful source of degeneration, and the mother of varieties properly so called. So now let us go to work and examine one by one the chief of these stimuli.[119]

[1.] Climate.[120]
[2.] Diet.[121]
[3.] Mode of life.[122]
[4.] Hybrid generation.[123]
[5.] Hereditary peculiarities of animals from diseased temperament.[124]
[6.] Problem proposed. Can mutilations and other artifices give a commencement to native varieties of animals?[125]

These factors are then used to explain the morphological differences to be found in the races of man.[126]

## Tyssot de Patot

Other scholars besides systematists dealt with problems in physical anthropology. Since the material is scattered and many writers dealt with a variety of topics, the data will be presented chronologically.

In his novel, *Voyages et avantures de Jaques Masse,*[127] Simon Tyssot de Patot (b. 1655) took up the usual questions of the creation of man, the relation between man and other animals, and the reasons for racial differences.

To speak the Truth, the first time that I gave it [i.e., the Bible] a Reading . . . I took it for an ill-concerted Romance, to which however I gave the Name of Sacred Stories. The Book of *Genesis* seem'd to me to be meer Fiction.[128]

. . . at the third Reading of the Bible I concluded, that the Creation of the World, and the Fall of Man, [etc.] . . . were only Types, Allegories, Emblems, Figures, and Shadows.[129]

[A physician in the story says:] Other Creatures having Organs like to ours, have no doubt the same Perceptions, and 'tis only the Degree of more or less, that can constitute the Difference. The Beasts therefore have Reason; and tho' they don't shew it, 'tis only

* " . . . it has been asserted that the negroes are specifically different in their bodily structure from other men, and must also be placed considerable in the rear, from the condition of their obtuse mental capacities. Personal observation, combined with the accounts of trustworthy and unprejudiced witnesses, has, however, long since convinced me of the want of foundation in both these assertions."[115]

for want, perhaps, of Speech to give Names, as we do, to things which affect them by being put in Motion; for, in other Matters, they are very capable of distinguishing—
Here our Physician was interrupted on a sudden.[130]

As soon as the Body [of a Negro] was put into our Hands, we dissected it, in form. All the Parts of it were disposed like those of the Body of a white Man, at least, we observ'd no Difference; but what surpris'd us was, to find immediately under the *Epidermis,* a very thin delicate Membrane. . . . We concluded that this must be the true Cause of the Blackness of this Race of Men, forasmuch as this Tunick stifles, and no doubt absorbs the Rays of Light. . . . This gave occasion to a strong Debate concerning the Origin of the *Ethiopians,* which, when we consider this remarkable Difference, seems not to be the same with other Men. Upon this Principle I was going to draw Consequences which would have tended to no less than the intire Subversion of the System of the Sacred Author in Debate [i.e., he was advocating polygenesis]. But I was silenc'd by being told, That there were many things, which it was the Will of Heaven we should admire, but are forbid to dive into.[131]

### Fabricius

Johann Albert Fabricius (1668–1736) still insisted upon the correctness of the Old Testament account of man's creation.

[His conclusion is that] from all these various facts, which up to this time have been collected together, nothing can be deduced, as I have shown, to invalidate the credit which is due to the inspired writer, Moses, who derives all mankind from the protoplast of one parent.[132]

For example, he explained the differences in color between the various races in the following manner:

These two things, I consider, have been discovered, and result from the investigation, —that aliment, water, and the air we inhale, have just as powerful an influence as the rays of the sun, or the scorching of cold, in altering the body and inducing a black colour . . .
Secondly. It may be the case that, in long successions of generations, nature may degenerate from the very purest white to the deepest black, until at last this becomes so confirmed in the body that it remains, and is propagated with the blood itself and is an efficient cause of carrying on the blackness to posterity.[133]

### Atkins

However, John Atkins (1685–1757) argued for polygenesis.

From the River *Senega* in *Africa,* 15°N. to almost its Southern Extremity in 34° they are all black and woolly, the natural Cause of which, must ever perplex Philosophers. I know *Malpighius,* and from him others, ascribe these different Colours in Men to a Tinge from that recticular or mucous Substance under the Cuticle, not considering the Question as strongly returns; How even that should become so oppositely coloured as it does, in this remarkable Division of Mankind into Blacks and Whites? The Gradations *Europeans* make toward a Mulatto Dye, seem well enough solved from the Fineness of their Skins, and Approaches to the Sun, whose Heat, more or less, easily eliminates the thin Parts of the Mucosity, and leaves the Remainder dark; as the clearest Liquors, they say, will have some Sediment; but how so entire and opposite a Change is made, as in Negroes, is not so soon answered. There are these Objections; *First,* that the Proximity of the Sun, has not the same Influence on other Animal in *Guiney,* nay, *their Sheep have*

*Hair* contrary to that closer Contexture of the Skin, which is supposed to contribute to the Production of Wool in the human Species. *Secondly,* no *European* totally changes by length of Cohabitation with them, neither in Generation begets a Black, but a Mulatto, not a wooly, but hairy Race, which ever remain so. *Thirdly,* the Palms and Soles of Negroes Feet, by Friction and constant Use, becomes whiter than other Parts; so does the Cuticle, supplied in other Places of the Body, after Scalds, or being otherwise peeled off; which could not well be, methinks, if the Colour of it were owing to the aforesaid Mucosity, unless Nature be allowed to take partial Methods in the tinging of it. *Fourthly, Americans,* or other Nations in the same, or Parallels of Latitude, where the Sun equally influences, are not black; And, *lastly,* even in this *Negroland,* there are a Race of a bright yellow Colour, as though painted . . .

From the Whole, I imagine that White and Black must have descended of different Protoplasts; and that there is no other Way of accounting for it.*[135]

## Pluche

Noel Antoine Pluche (1688–1761) was another who took the position that animals operate by instinct, man by reason.[136]

## Bougeant

Guillaume Hyacinthe Bougeant (1690–1743) wrote a clever book in defense of the existence of reason in, and the use of language by, animals, as an argument against the Cartesians.

Have Beasts any Understanding? If they have, they speak. But how do they speak? These shall be the three Heads of this Dissertation.[137]

[1.] It is certain that Beasts have an intelligent Faculty, be the Principle of it what it will.[138]

They must have a Knowledge and a Sentiment like ours; and from what passes within us, they must be jealous, choleric, perfidious, ungrateful, and self-interested like ourselves. They must be either gay or sad according to Events or their present Disposition. They must have Love and Hatred, and Desire for multiplying their Species, an Affection for their Young, and a Care to bring them up: In a Word, they must do all what they do, and which seems incomprehensible to us when a spiritual Soul is not granted them. However, it may be proper to observe, that . . . *God* has been minded to humble them with regard to their very Reason, by making them depend on Organs so very gross, that it is infinitely inferior to that of Men. Thence it happens, that we now and then judge that Beasts do some acts of Reason; but we have great Reason to believe, that they never make many coherent and reflected Judgements like ourselves, because their Organs will not allow of Motions so delicate.[139]

[2.] I very seriously am of the Opinion that Beasts do speak and understand each other every whit as well and sometimes better than we do.[140]

First, let us evidence the Possibility of it. In the common Use, what we call speaking is making one's self understood by a sequel of Words articulated, whereby Men have

* "The black Colour, and wooly Tegument of these *Guineans, is* what first obtrudes it self on our Observation, and distinguishes them from the rest of Mankind, who no where else, in the warmest Latitudes, are seen thus totally changed; nor removing, will they ever alter, without mixing in Generation. I have taken notice in my *Navy-Surgeon,* how difficultly the Colour is accounted for; and tho' it be a little Heterodox, I am persuaded the black and white Race have, *ab origine,* sprung from different-coloured first Parents."[134]

agreed to express such an Idea or Sentiment; and the total Collection of these Words is what we call a Language, which is different among different Nations. If Beasts speak, they certainly do it not by means of a Language of this Kind. But is it impossible, without this Assistance, to make one's self understood, and to speak in reality? Of this we cannot possibly doubt. . . . When we are pleased, every thing in us speaks. Do we not every Day speak by certain Looks, by a Motion of the Head, a Gesture, nay! The least Sign in the World? Imagine to yourself . . . a Nation of Dumb-People. Do you think they would not deliver their Minds to each other, and by Cries, Gestures, Looks, and Postures, supply the Want of our Words and Phrases? . . . They have no Tongues; but why should they not have Speech. The thing evidently is possible: Let us now examine whether it is necessary.[141]

. . . many Species of Beasts are made to live in Society at large, and the others either to live Male and Female in a kind of House-keeping, or in a kind of Family with their Young till they are brought up . . . . if you suppose that they have not a Language among themselves to understand each other, be it what you will, you can no longer conceive how their Society could subsist.[142]

In a Word, no more Communication, no more Society.[143]

Cannot Instinct, some will say, supply the Want of a Language? . . .

The Objection has something specious in it, but it must be examined to the Bottom. What is Instinct? It is a Sentiment void of Reflection, whose Principle is unknown; a blind Desire, an undeliberate Biass, a mechanick Motion of our Soul, which prompts us to do a Thing without knowing any Reason why. This Sentiment, if there is such a Thing, is commonly so intricate in Men, that it remains without Effect: Only it is thought to produce very singular Effects in some of them. It is wonderful in Beasts, they say, and by it their most Admirable Actions are explained. Nothing in reality is more convenient than this Instinct. But when will Men cease to mistake Words for Things? 1. What we call Instinct is something very obscure and unknown in itself. 2. What Proofs have we that Beasts have more of this Instinct than Men? . . . 3. But since we cannot refuse Beasts a knowing Faculty, why do we give them a needless Instinct? Why should we attribute to this unknown Instinct what may be the simple Effect of their Understanding; and since it is really in consequence of a Knowing Faculty that Man performs the same Operations, why should not the same Principle also rule in Beasts? . . . I am even apt to think that what we call Instinct is a meer *Ens Rationis,* a Name void of reality, a Remain of Peripatetic Philosophy.[144]

[3.] . . . their Language . . . is uniform, and with regard to each Species, at all Times and in all the Countries in the World, for ever the same: Whereas in the human Kind not only each Nation has its peculiar Language, but the Dialect of every People varies perpetually, and after a certain Time it is no longer what it was.[145]

But shall I conclude without giving you a particular Dictionary of the Language of Beasts? That must be: For you are sensible that the thing is impossible. There would be as many different Dictionaries as there are different Species of Beasts.[146]

. . . the Language of Beasts . . . is very limited, since it does not extend beyond the Necessaries of Life.[147]

The whole Language of Beasts amounts to expressing the Sentiment of their Passions, and all their Passions may be reduced to a very small Number, *viz*. Pleasure, Pain, Anger, Fear, Love, the Desire of eating, the Care of their Young. If then you intend to have the Dictionary of the Language of Beasts, observe them in the Circumstances of these different Passions, and as they commonly have but one Expression for each, you will soon compose your Dictionaries.[148]

I shall here make you a Confession, that will reduce the whole Languag to almost nothing. I mean that you must absolutely retrench from it whatever is called Phrase or grammatical Construction, not excepting the most Contracted. . . . For in good Truth, Beasts in a Manner cannot express any thing more th*u*n the Name of the Passions they feel.[149]

Observe . . . that this Simplicity or Sterility in the Language of Beasts, will appear . . . less defective to you, if you consider that its Imperfection is replaced by Miens, Gestures, and Motions, which are a kind of Language very intelligible, and a Supplement of the Vocal Expression. A Dog for Instance, has no vocal Expression to ask Pardon when he finds you are angry with him; but what does he do? Why he humbles himself before you; he cringes at your Feet in the Posture of a Supplicant.[150]

## Maillet

Benoît de Maillet (1656–1738) was one of the first to state that "all the species which now live in the globe might have been there naturally produced."[151] He developed a theory of biological evolution, the basic thesis of which was that "the races of terrestrial animals proceeded from those of the sea."[152]

He included man in this conception of evolution.

. . . the men who now inhabit the earth, are descended from other men, who lived originally in the sea.[153]

His evidence for this proposition consisted of accounts of mermen and mermaids.[154]

Because man is descended from different kinds of acquatic animals, "there are different species of men."[155]

## Hughes

Griffith Hughes (fl. 1750) was an advocate of the psychic unity of mankind, though he suspended judgment when considering the problem of the origin of the races of man.[156] In discussing the Negro slaves in Barbados, he attempted to show that group differences are the result of cultural and geographic factors.

The Capacities of their Minds in the common Affairs of Life are but little inferior, if at all, to those of the *Europeans*. If they fail in some Arts, it may be owing more to their Want of Education, and the Depression of their Spirits by Slavery, than to any Want of natural Abilities; for an higher Degree of improved Knowledge in any Occupation would not much alter their Condition for the better.

That Slavery not only depresses, but almost brutalizes human Nature, is evident from the low and abject State of the present *Grecians,* when compared with their learned and glorious ancestors.[157]

I must . . . beg leave to endeavour (a Thing hitherto unattempted) to ascertain some reasonable Cause of that general Observation, that the Inhabitants of hot Countries are of a more volatile and lively Disposition, and more irascible in general, than the Inhabitants of the Northern Part of the World. . . . Nor it is with me a Doubt, whether different Climates may not cause a constitutional Difference.

. . . it will not be difficult to explain, in some measure, the Reason of so visible a constitutional Difference in the Inhabitants of hot and cold Climates. . . . Influence on the Body must, in a great measure, depend upon the regular or irregular Motion of . . . the Blood; Now, when this is checked in its Circulation, either by a sudden Pressure of an heavy Atmosphere, or the . . . of the Winds from warm to cold; the Animal Spirits, which before were agreeably diffused through the whole Body [no longer are so] . . . .

Thus far have we briefly endeavoured to account, from the Nature of the Climate, and the Mechanism of the human body, for that volatile Disposition, so peculiar to the Inhabitants of hot Climates: That Irascibility of Temper, likewise, which is ascribed to them, is, in a great measure, the natural Consequence of the above-mentioned Disposition; for, as Water that is already hot, will, with a little additional Heat, boil over, so when the Animal Spirits are in a high Flow, and the Will, by the Propensity of long-rooted Habits, unhappily assists, and is bent to gratify some favourite Passion, the Transition from a Degree of Sprightliness to Irascibility is natural and easy.[158]

## Kames

Henry Home, Lord Kames (1696–1782), made the usual dichotomy between man and other animals on the basis of reason versus instinct.

. . . neither experience nor argument is required to prove, that a horse is not an ass, or that a monkey is not a man.[159]

The actions of brute creatures are generally directed by instinct, meaning blind impulse or desire, without any view to consequences. Man is framed to be governed by reason: he commonly acts with deliberation, in order to bring about some desirable end. . . . At the same time, there are human actions that are not governed by reason, nor are done with any view to consequences. Infants, like brutes, are mostly governed by instinct, without the least view to any end, good or ill. And even adult persons act sometimes instinctively.[160]

He also made the usual distinction on the basis of speech.[161]

Kames was an advocate of polygenesis.

. . . there are different races or kinds of men, and . . . these races or kinds are naturally fitted for different climates: whence we have reason to conclude, that originally each kind was placed in its proper climate, whatever change may have happened in later times by war or commerce.[162]

America has not been peopled from any part of the old world. The external appearance of the inhabitants, makes this conjecture approach a certainty; as they are widely different in appearance from any other known people.[163]

If we can rely on the conjectures of an eminent writer [i.e., Buffon], America emerged from the sea later than any other part of the known world: and supposing the human race to have been planted in America by the hand of God later than the days of Moses, Adam and Eve might have been the first parents of mankind, *i.e.,* of all who at that time existed, without being the first parents of the Americans.[164]

No race is innately inferior to any other, though temperamental differences exist.

The colour of the Negroes . . . affords a strong presumption of their being a different species from the Whites; and I once thought, that the presumption was supported by inferiority of understanding in the former. But it appears to me doubtful, upon second thoughts, whether that inferiority may not be occasioned by their condition. A man never ripens in judgment nor in prudence but by exericising these powers. At home, the negroes have little occasion to exercise either: they live upon fruits and roots, which grow without culture: they need little clothing: and they erect houses without trouble or art. Abroad, they are miserable slaves, having no encouragement either to think or to act. Who can say how far they might improve in a state of freedom, were they obliged, like Europeans, to procure bread with the sweat of their brows? Some nations in Negroland, particularly that of Whidah, have made great improvements in government, in police, and in manners. The negroes on the Gold coast are naturally gay: they apprehend readily what is said to them, have a good judgment, are equitable in their dealings, and accommodate themselves readily to the manners of strangers. And yet, after all, there seems to be some original difference between the Negroes and Hindows. In no country are food and raiment procured with less labour than in the southern parts of Hindostan, where the heat is great: and yet no people are more industrious than the Hindows.[165]

Different tribes are distinguishable no less by internal disposition than by external figure.[166]

## Wesley

John Wesley (1703–91) believed that all animals, including man, were supernaturally created.

God, in creating the first individual of each species, animal or vegetable, not only gave a form to the dust of the earth, but a principle of life.[167]
God made the body of man.[168]

He accepted the concept of the chain of being.

The whole progress of nature is so gradual, that the entire chasm from a plant to man, is filled up with divers kinds of creatures, rising one above the other, by so gentle an ascent, that the transitions from one species to another, are almost insensible.[169]

Next to man in the visible creation are Beasts. And certainly, with regard to the structure of the body, the difference is not extremely great between man and other arnimals, only in this, that the stature of man is erect, and his form more elegant; that no beast has the feet of a man, much less a hand so admirable fitted for every purpose: and lastly, that no other animal has a brain so large in proportion to its bulk as man.[170]

We cannot . . . deny, that there is something in brutes which perceives the impressions made by outward objects; and that they perform a thousand actions which can never be explained by mere mechanism. . . .
It is true, some things in brutes as well as in men may be mechanically accounted for, but others cannot; so that we are constrained to own there is in them also some superior principle, of whatever kind it be, which is endued with sense, perception, and various appetites . . . this principle is immaterial[171]

## Camper

Petrus Camper (1722–89) delivered a course of lectures entitled, "Two discourses on the analogy which exists between the structure of human bodies and those of quadrupeds, birds, and fish."[172]

[However,] man is the most perfect of all animals. . . . The grand corporeal advantage enjoyed by man is, that he can walk, and even sit, in an erect attitude.[173]

The striking resemblance between the race of Monkies and of Blacks, particularly upon a superficial view, has induced some philosophers to conjecture that the race of blacks originated from the commerce of the whites with ourangs and pongos; or that these monsters, by gradual improvements, finally became men.

This is not the place to attempt a full confutation of so extravagant a notion. . . . I shall simply observe at present, that the whole generation of apes, from the largest to the smallest, are quadrupeds, not formed to walk erect;* and that from the very construction of their larynx, they are incapable of speech.† Further: They have a great similarity with the canine species, particularly respecting the organs of generation. The diversities observable in these parts, seem to mark the boundaries which the Creator has placed between the various classes of animals.[176]

He was convinced of supernatural monogenesis.

No man who contemplated the whole human race as it is now spread over the face of the earth, without a predilection for hypothesis, can doubt of its having descended from a single pair, that were formed by the immediate hand of God, long after the world itself had been created and had passed through numberless changes. From this pair all the habitable parts of the earth were gradually propagated.[177]

Since we are totally ignorant at what period after the formation of the globe man was created, and the human race began to spread over the earth, we shall confine ourselves to the differences in the human species that now exist.[178]

People are distinguished according to the grand divisions of the continents, into Europeans, Africans, Asiatics, and Americans.[179]

Having contemplated the inhabitants of various nations with great attention, I conceived that a striking difference was occasioned . . . by the position of the inferior maxilla, . . . the breadth of the face, and the quadrangular form of this maxilla.[180]

The first observation led him to the discovery of the facial angle. For comparative purposes in its investigation, he developed the plane which served him as a standard for the measurement of skulls.[181]

[Camper's plane:] An horizontal line has been drawn through the lower part of the nose . . . and the orifice of the ear . . .; and the . . . skulls were arranged with care on the line . . .; attention being also paid to the direction of the *jugale,* or cheekbone.[182]

[Summary on the facial angle:] The two extremities . . . of the facial lines are from 70 to 100 degrees, from the negro to the Grecian antique; make it under 70, and you describe an ourang or an ape; lessen it still more, and you have the head of a dog.[183]

On the breadth of the face, he offered the following comparative ratios:

|          | Vertex-Gnathion: Eurion-Eurion | Eurion-Eurion: Zygion-Zygion[184] |
|----------|:------------------------------:|:---------------------------------:|
| Orang    | $19\frac{1}{2}$:14             | 14:14                             |
| Negro    | 27:20                          | 20:18                             |
| Calmuck  | 32:20                          | 20:24                             |
| European | 29:23                          | 23:20                             |

As to the causes of racial differences, Camper followed Buffon.

. . . the climate, under which we include the influence of air, of food, and customs,

---

* Camper made a classic study of the anatomy of the orang.[174]

† "Having dissected the whole organ of voice in the Orang, in apes, and several monkies, I have a right to conclude, that Orangs and apes are not made to modulate the voice like men: for the air passing by the *rima glottidis* is immediately lost in the ventricles or ventricle of the neck, as in apes and monkies, and must consequently return from thence without any force and melody within the throat and mouth of these creatures: and this seems to me the most evident proof of the incapacity of Orangs, apes, and monkies, to utter any modulated voice, as ineded they never have been observed to do."[175]

is of itself sufficient to give some particular and appropriated form to the bones; and consequently to the softer parts. When we add the different diseases peculiar to some countries, which cooperate with the above causes, we shall not be suprised that a similar diversity should be found in the human species dispersed over different parts of the globe; as may be observed in plants, fowls, quadrupeds, &c.[185]

Finally, he was interested in the morphological development of man from birth to old age.[186]

## Formey

Jean Henri Samuel Formey (1711–97) described the chain of being in order to draw the usual theological moral.

*Nature distinguishes its Works by Differences of very narrow Limits.* Such is the Nature of its Works, that their Perfections rise almost in an imperceptible Gradation. We shall begin at the lowest Stage; and these unquestionably are inanimate Things, as the Earth and the Stones. This Class admits of a Division into an Infinity of Species; and the successive Order, in which they follow each other, is such, that the Differences betwixt the two Species in Contact are so minute, as frequently to perplex Observation; but the Perfection of these Beings rises through a Progression of innumerable Degrees, till, at length, inanimate Creatures attain very near to the Perfection of the coarsest organized Bodies. If we consider the regular Texture and Arrangement of Salts and Gems which form the principal Species of inanimate Things; and we compare them with the lowest Plants; how small the Difference! In the Former the Structure is surprising, but without internal Motion or Life; whereas in the Latter we observe some Slight Trace of Motion, and the Limits, separating the Mineral Kingdom from the Vegetable, cannot admit of a closer Contraction.

In examining the latter the like Order appears: The least Plants seem to rise very little above the most perfect Gems, and this Perfection augments through several thousand Gradations, one Species differing very little from that immediately following or preceding it, so that, at length, the Perfection of Plants is carried to such a Pitch as to appear equal to the least of Animals. The Difference of Plants and Animals is this: The former are without Sensation and local Motion, whereas Animals are endued with both these Attributes. Such then are the Limits placed betwixt Plants and Animals, but how near are they! for some Plants have an Appearance of Sensation, and some Animals seem inanimate. There are Animals which, by all preceding Ages, were taken for Plants, or even for Stones.

In Animals, Perfection rises through an infinite Series up to Man, whom Reason and Speech distinguish from Brutes. But are not these Limits likewise contiguous? On one Side we see Men with scarce a Glimmering of Reason; and, on the other, Animals with all the Appearances of it. Thus every Genus grows up to Perfection so insensibly, that what distinguishes the immediately more Perfect from the less Perfect, is scarce perceivable. It is even to be presumed that these Limits, however intricate they appear to us, again decrease likewise infinitely through innumerable Creatures of several Thousands of other Worlds. Thus it is that Nature points out to us Infinitude, as the distinctive Character of its adorable Author.[187]

## Ferguson

Adam Ferguson (1723–1816) made a few observations on physical anthropology.

The human form is erect, furnished with articulations and muscles fitted to retain this posture, and to move it with ease and safety.

The hand and the arm of man is an instrument and a weapon, not a prop or support to his body.

His form and posture are well fitted to observation, to the use of reason, and to the practice of arts.[188]

Speech is universal to mankind, and peculiar to the human species.[189]

Mankind may be referred to six different races.

The *European,* the *Samoeide,* the *Tartar,* the *Hindoo,* the *Negro,* and the *American.*[190]

## Gregory

John Gregory (1724–73) analyzed the differences between man and other animals.

Man has been usually considered as a Being that has no analogy to the rest of the Animal Creation. . . . But this conduct is very weak and foolish. Nature is a whole, made up of parts which tho' distinct, are yet intimately connected with one another. This connection is so close, that one species often runs into another so imperceptibly, that it is difficult to say where one begins and the other ends. This is particularly the case with the lowest of one species, and the highest of that immediately below it. On this account no one link of the great chain can be perfectly understood, without the knowledge, at least, of the links that are nearest it.

In comparing the different species of Animals, we find each of them possessed of powers and faculties peculiar to themselves, and admirably adapted to the particular sphere of action which Providence has allotted them. But, amidst that infinite variety which distinguishes each species, we find many qualities in which they are all similar, and some which they have in common.

Man is evidently at the head of the Animal Creation. . . . If he is not the only Animal possest of reason, he has it in a degree so greatly superior, as admits of no comparison. . . .

One Animal governs another only by superior force or cunning. . . . There is no sense of superiority or subordination among them.

Their want of language seems owing to their having no regular train or order in their ideas, and not to any deficiency in their organs of speech. . . .

There is a remarkable uniformity in the works of Animals. . . . On the contrary, among Mankind, every individual thinks and acts in a way almost peculiar to himself. . . .

All Animals express pain and pleasure by cries and various motions of the body; but laughter and shedding of tears are peculiar to Mankind. . . . But above all, they are distinguished by the Moral Sense, and the happiness flowing from religion, and from the various intercourses of social life.[191]

The advantages, which Mankind possess above the rest of the Animal Creation, are principally derived from Reason, from the Social Principle, from Taste, and from religion.[192]

[1.] . . . other Animals . . . are governed solely by the unerring principle of Instinct, whereas Men are directed by other principles of action along with this, particularly by the feeble and fluctuating principle of Reason.[193]

Instinct is a principle common to us and the whole Animal world. . . .

Reason indeed is but a weak principle in Man, in respect of Instinct, and is generally a more unsafe guide.—The proper province of Reason is to investigate the causes of things, to shew us what consequences will follow from our acting in any particular way, to point out the best means of attaining an end, and, in consequence of this, to be a check upon our Instincts, our tempers, our passions, and our tastes: But these must still be the immediately impelling principles of action. In truth, life, without them, would not only be joyless and insipid, but quickly stagnate and be at an end.[194]

[2.] The next distinguishing principle of Mankind, which was mentioned, is that which unites them into societies, and attaches them to one another by sympathy and affection. This principle is the source of the most heart-felt pleasure which we ever taste.[195]

Nature has made no individual, nor any class of people, independent of the rest of their Species, or sufficient for their own happiness.[196]

[3.] The advantages derived to Mankind from Taste, by which we understand the improved use of the powers of the Imagination, are confined to a very small number.[197]

[4.] We proceed now to consider that principle of Human Nature which seems in a peculiar manner the characteristic of the species, the Sense of Religion.[198]

## Goldsmith

Oliver Goldsmith (1728–74) was a follower of Buffon.

In taking a cursory view of the form of quadrupeds, we may easily perceive, that of all the ranks of animated nature, they bear the nearest resemblance to man. This similitude will be found more striking when, erecting themselves on their hinder feet, they are taught to walk forward in an upright posture. We shall then see that all their extremities in a manner correspond with ours, and present us with a rude imitation of our own. In some of the ape kind the resemblance is so striking, that anatomists are puzzled to find in what part of the human body man's superiority consists; and scarcely any but the metaphysician can draw the line that divides them.[199]

In the Ape kind we see the whole external machine strongly impressed with the human likeness and capable of the same exertions: these walk upright, want a tail, have fleshy posteriors, and calves to their legs, and feet nearly like ours.[200]

. . . of all the races of animated nature, man is least affected by the soil where he resides, and least influenced by the variations of vegetable sustenance: equally unaffected by the luxuriance of the warm climates, or the sterility of the poles, he has spread his habitations over the whole earth . . . man may be called the animal of every climate, and suffers but very gradual alterations from the nature of any situation.[201]

He classified man into six races.

If we look round the world, there seem to be not above six* distinct varieties in the human species, each of which is strongly marked, and speaks the kind seldom to have mixed with any other. But there is nothing in the shape, nothing in the faculties, that shows their coming from different originals;† and the varieties of climate, of nourishment, and custom, are sufficient to produce every change.[204]

The first distinct race of men is found round the polar regions. The Laplanders, the Esquimaux Indians, the Samoeid Tartars, the inhabitants of Nova Zembla, the Borandians,

* "I have taken four of these varieties from Linnaeus; those of the Laplanders and Tartars from Mr. Buffon."[202]

† "That we have all sprung from one common parent, we are taught both by reason and religion to believe; and we have good reason to think that the Europeans resemble him more than any of the rest of his children."[203]

the Greenlanders, and the natives of Kamtschatka, may be considered as one peculiar race of people. . . .

The second great variety in the human species seems to be that of the Tartar race. . . .

To this race of men, also, we must refer the Chinese and the Japanese. . . .

Another, which makes the third variety in the human species, is that of the southern Asiatics . . . The nations that inhabit the peninsula of India seem to be the principal stock. . . .

The fourth striking variety in the human species, is to be found among the negroes of Africa. . . .

The inhabitants of America make a fifth race. . . .

The sixth and last variety of the human species, is that of the Europeans and the nations bordering on them.[205]

. . . hair . . . colour differs in different tribes and races of people. The Americans, and the Asiatics, have their hair black, thick, straight, and shining. The inhabitants of the torrid climates of Africa have it black, short, and woolly. The people of Scandinavia have it red, long, and curled; and those of our own and the neighbouring countries, are found with hair of various colours.[206]

The under jaw in a Chinese face falls greatly more backward than with us.[207]

## Robertson

William Robertson (1721–93) believed in monogenesis.

We know, with infallible certainty, that all the human race spring from the same source, and that the descendants of one man, under the protection as well as in obedience to the command of Heaven, multiplied and replenished the earth.[208]

He therefore had the task of explaining the existence of man in the New World. He first established criteria for differentiating between diffusion and independent invention.

Nothing can be more frivolous or uncertain than the attempts to discover the original of the Americans merely by tracing the resemblance between their manners and those of any particular people in the ancient continent. If we suppose two tribes, though placed in the most remote regions of the globe, to live in a climate nearly of the same temperature, to be in the same state of society, and to resemble each other in the degree of their improvement, they must feel the same wants and exert the same endeavours to supply them. The same objects will allure, the same passions will animate them, and the same ideas and sentiments will arise in their minds. . . . Had Lafitau, Garcia, and many other authors attended to this, they would not have perplexed a subject, which they pretend to illustrate, by their fruitless endeavours to establish an affinity between various races of people, in the old and new continents, upon no other evidence than such a resemblance in their manners as necessarily arises from the similarity of their condition. There are, it is true, among every people, some customs which, as they do not flow from any natural want or desire peculiar to their situation, may be denominated usages of arbitrary institution. If between two nations settled in remote parts of the earth, a perfect agreement with respect to any of these should be discovered, one might be led to suspect that they were connected by some affinity. If, for example, a nation were found in America that consecrated the seventh day to religious worship and rest, we might justly suppose that it had derived its knowledge of this usage, which is of arbitrary institution, from the Jews. But, if it were discovered that another nation celebrated the first appearance of every now moon with extraordings demonstrations of joy we should not be entitled to conclude that the observation of this monthly festival was borrowed from the Jews, but ought to consider it merely as the expression of that joy which is natural to man on the return of the planet which guides and cheers him in the night. The instances of customs, merely arbitrary, common to the inhabitants of both hemispheres, are, indeed, so few and so equivocal, that no theory concerning the population of the New World ought to be founded upon them.*[210]

He then attempted to show that man migrated to the New World from northwestern Asia.

We may lay it down as a certain principle in this inquiry, that America was not peopled by any nation of the ancient continent which had made considerable progress in civilization. The inhabitants of the New World were in a state of society so extremely rude as to be unacquainted with those arts which are the first essays of human ingenuity in its advance towards improvement. Even the most cultivated nations of America were strangers to many of those simple inventions which were almost coeval with society in other parts of the world, and were known in the earliest periods of civil life with which we have any acquaintance. From this it is manifest, that the tribes which originally migrated to America, came off from nations which must have been no less barbarous than their posterity, at the time when they were first discovered by the Europeans. For, although the elegant or refined arts may decline or perish, amidst the violent shocks of those revolutions and disasters to which nations are exposed, the necessary arts of life, when once they have been introduced among any people, are never lost. . . . We may conclude, then, that the Americans sprung from some people, who were themselves in such an early and unimproved stage of society, as to be unacquainted with all those necessary arts, which continue to be unknown among their posterity when first visited by the Spaniards.[211]

From considering the animals with which America is stored, we may conclude that the nearest point of contact between the old and new continents is towards the northern extremity of both, and that there the communication was opened, and the intercourse carried on between them. All the extensive countries in America which lie within the tropics, or approach near to them, are filled with indigenous animals of various kinds, entirely different from those in the corresponding regions of the ancient continent. But the northern provinces of the New World abound with many of the wild animals which are common in such parts of our hemisphere as lie in a similar situation. The bear, the wolf, the fox, the hare, the deer, the roebuck, the elk, and several other species, frequent the forests of North America, no less than those in the north of Europe and Asia. It seems to be evident, then, that the two continents approach each other in this quarter, and are either united, or so nearly adjacent that these animals might pass from the one to the other.[212]

The actual vicinity of the two continents is so clearly established by modern discoveries, that the chief difficulty with respect to the peopling of America is removed.[213]

Thus the possibility of communication between the continents in this quarter rests no longer upon mere conjecture, but is established by undoubted evidence. Some tribe,

* "At the time when Robert Bruce began his reign in Scotland, the same form of government was established in all the kingdoms of Europe. This surprising similarity in their constitution and laws demonstrates that the nations which overturned the Roman empire, and erected these kingdoms, though divided into different tribes and distinguished by different names, were either derived originally from the same source, or had been placed in similar situations."[209]

or some families of wandering Tartars, from the restless spirit peculiar to their race, might migrate to the nearest islands, and, rude as their knowledge of navigation was, might, by passing from one to the other, reach at length the coast of America, and give a beginning to population in that continent.[214]

## Hunter

John Hunter (1728–93) was skeptical of the biblical version of the creation of the world,[215] and shocked some of his contemporaries[216] by stating that there are fossils "many thousand centuries" old.[217] In regard to man, after quoting an "Account of a Hill in which Human Bones are found, near Rome,"* by James Hall (1761–1832), he comments as follows:

This hill must have been formed before the Romans took possession of this place, and, probably, by the formation of the hill, the Tiber made its way in this direction, for it cuts the hill across. This is probably the only instance met with of human bones being in such a state. But in future ages, when the present rivers may take a new turn, through localities in which are deposited human bones, many may be found; for, in sinking the caissons for Blackfriars Bridge, a human skull was found twelve feet under the bed of the river; and there is in the British Museum a human skull taken out of the Tiber thickly incrusted with a brownish substance. Or when the sea shall leave its now situation, human bones may be found, as also everything of art, in a Fossil state.[219]

Though ambiguous, one passage seems to hint at biological evolution.

### On the Origin of Species

Does not the natural gradation of animals, from one to another, lead to the original species? And does not that mode of investigation gradually lead us to the knowledge of that species? Are we not led on to the wolf by the gradual affinity of the different varieties in the dog? Could we not trace out the gradation in the cat, horse, cow, sheep, fowl, & c., in a like manner.[220]

The human . . . seems to have most of original forms, or fewer forms in common [with those of other animals].†[222]

The monkey in general may be said to be half beast and half man; it may be said to be the middle stage.[223]

Unlike most of his contemporaries, Hunter did not make the customary dichotomy between instinct and reason, attributing the former to lower animals and the latter to man.

Whatever impulse of action we have which does not arise from the knowledge of the

* "The hill is about 100 feet high above the level of the plain along which it passes. . . .

"1st. the upper part, on which the vegetable earth rests, is a bed (A) sixty or eighty feet thick, of a kind of tufa . . .

"2nd. A stratum of rolled pebbled (B) . . . This stratum is about three feet thick in one place, and tapers from right to left to the thickness of a few inches, on an extent of thirty or forty yards.

"3rd. Another stratum of tufa (C) . . . This stratum is eight or ten feet thick.

"4th. A second stratum of gravel (D) . . . This stratum reaches down about twelve feet . . .

"We found the bones . . . in the first stratum of gravel (B), between the two beds of tufa. . . . There is the greatest reason to suppose that the place where they were found has never been moved since the tufa came there; that is, that the bones and the stones of the stratum were placed there by the same cause, and previous to the formation of the upper bed of tufa (A)."[218]

† "When I compared the human with the quadruped . . . it always put me in mind of two machines of the same kind, one made by an artist, the other only an imitation of it made by a novice."[221]

event, or from a motive, is 'instinct'; and whatever action arises from an intention, is 'reason.'[224]

Than that animals have reason, nothing can be more clear; for all animals can go mad; by which they lose all instinctive and acquired properties of the mind.[225]

All animals . . . are . . . ruled by natural and instinctive principles. But the Human . . . [is] an animal of art. . . .

Nothing shows more the superiority of the Human over the brute, than the variety of ways in which he shall perform any natural and instinctive action.[226]

Man is a more perfect or complicated animal than any other, . . . is able to live in a much greater variety of circumstances than any other animal, and has more opportunities of exercising the faculties of his mind.[227]

Men, at first . . . were guided by instinctive principles, and a kind of habit arising out of practice; for civilization, cultivation, and improvement took place at first by slow and almost imperceptible degrees. Men, then, hardly considering what they did know, perhaps they knew but little in proportion to what they saw, the transition from one improvement to another was gradual; whereby they almost lost sight of the past by its having become familiar to them; and they had not the means nor the disposition to record it farther than by narration, which is called 'Tradition.'[228]

Hunter was an adherent of the theory of innate sociality.

### Of the Sociability of Man and of Animals

The mixing the different tribes of men is much more difficult than that of other animals. Men's minds are linked together by a much greater variety of circumstances than other animals are: men become attached to systems, to peculiarities; and in proportion to the attachment to their own, they despise those of others. Animals confine their connexions to acquaintance only.

The instinctive principle in animals to associate with each other may be classified under the following heads, each head having its degree of power; viz. acquaintance simple, tribe, genus, species, sex, and last of all, family. However, I believe the instinctive principle of family to associate beyond the first, or acquaintance, is only in those cases where the family is large, more especially where each is to assist in the economy of the family; this will include the human kind, common bee, humble bee, hornet, wasp, &c. . . .

This instinctive principle to associate is natural to all animals, but is much stronger in some than in others; and, when increased by acquaintance, it becomes stronger; and, indeed, so much so, as to appear at first view rather an acquired principle: for, the natural bent of strangers, even of the same species, is to quarrel and fight; but then they associate afterwards. However, I believe that it is not so much the natural disposition in every species, except excited by some circumstances, viz. towards a stranger. . . .

The same principle exists in the Human race; Men have their degrees of attraction towards each other according as they are circumstanced in life. In close connexions he is sociable, excepting interests clash (in which case no animal is sociable). In the crowd he forms his likings, dislikings, and indifferences. But, take him to Siberia, and let him meet the man he most disliked in his own country; he will immediately become sociable with that man. He is, in such a situation, deprived of the acquired cause of sociability, viz. acquaintance; and he feels the want of such: so that the moment the object of acquaintance presents himself, he associates with him; for the dislike arose from having had great choice.[229]

Another characteristic of man is imitation.

Imitation is so much a principle in Man that it distinguishes families, towns, and nations.[230]

## Monboddo

To his contemporaries, James Burnett, Lord Monboddo (1714–99), was chiefly known as the atheist or, at best, the eccentric, who believed that the orangoutang was human.

He saw the chain of being in terms of the scholastic powers of the soul.

. . . it seems to be a law of nature, that no species of thing is formed at once, but by steps and progression from one stage to another.[231]

*That mind,* which pervades and animates the whole universe, is the principle of that motion which is essential to all physical bodies, is the foundation . . . of all kinds of life, the *vegetable,* the *animal,* and the *rational.* In like manner, the *vegetable* is the foundation of the *animal,* and the *animal* again of the *rational.* So that there is no void in this part of nature, any more than in the corporeal; but every kind of life is inseparably connected with another, all hanging together in one indissoluble chain, and each supporting, or supported by the other.[232]

And here it may be observed, how full and compleat, according to my system, the scale of nature is in this matter of *mind* and how it arises, by just degrees, one step above another. First, there is that *mind* which simply moves *body* in a certain determined direction. This is the lowest kind of *mind,* of least variety and excellence, and below what the antients called $\Psi\Upsilon XN$ or *life;* yet it is essential, according to Aristotle, to a *physical body.* Next to that is the *mind* which *moves* the vegetable with much greater variety, producing, by its various motions, the nutrition, growth, and propagation of the plant: This is what is known by the name of *the vegetable life.* Next to it is the *animal life,* producing still greater variety of motion; for it has sensation superadded to the vegetable life, by which the animal *perceives,* and has communication with objects external. And, last of all, comes *intellect,* which is essentially distinguished from the other three, by *consciousness;* for none of the other three knows what it does, whereas intellect recognises itself, as well as other natures.[233]

He made the usual distinction between man and other animals on the basis of the former's possession of reason.

. . . that prime faculty, which makes the chief distinction betwixt our nature and that of the brute . . . [is] intellect.[234]

What . . . according to my system chiefly distinguishes Human Nature from that of the brute is not the actual possession of higher faculties, but the greater capacity of acquiring them.[235]

. . . it may not be improper, first, to take a general view of the *powers* of *human nature,* beginning with those that are from *nature immediately,* and next considering such as are *acquired.* The first operate without any previous use, exercise, or instruction: The other are the fruit of our own industry; and, before they can be exercised, the habit must be first formed, by art, experience, or custom. Of the first kind, most certainly, are those with which we are born; and with them therefore we shall begin.

They are but few in number: one of the most remarkable of them is the power of *motion,* and that natural impulse . . . well known by the name of *instinct,* which directs an infant to apply that power of motion to the drawing its nourishment from the breast of the mother by the action of sucking. Besides this, we have that habit of body which makes us susceptible of nourishment, of growth, and all the vital functions. Whether we have distinct perceptions of sense, such as of seeing and hearing, I think may justly be doubted; . . . we have them not in any the least degree of perfection, till in process of time the organs have acquired a certain degree of firmness, and we by experience have learned the proper use of them.[236]

These seem to be all the *faculties* which we are *actually* in possession of when we first come into the world. The rest of our nature at that time is made up of *capacities merely,* or, to use the fashionable world, which I think not improper, of *capabilities:* for it is with us, as with other animals, at the time of our birth, almost all the powers of our nature lie concealed, and, as it were, folded up, till time and opportunity display them, and bring them into exertion: And indeed in that state, I cannot discover, that, with respect to actual powers, either of mind or body, there is any difference betwixt us and those other animals; or, if there be any, the advantage is on the side of the brute; for his body then is commonly more vigorous, and his instincts stronger and more active.

But with respect to latent *powers* and *capabilities,* there appears to be a wonderful difference, insomuch that it is difficult to say, even at this day, after so much observation and experience, what the capabilities of a nature so various and so excellent as ours are. . . .

The next thing to be considered is, what natural powers we are possessed of, when we have attained to perfect age. And these I think may be reduced to the following heads: 1*st,* The perfect use of all the five senses; 2*dly,* Greater strength of body, and power of bodily motion; 3*dly,* The faculty of propagating the kind; and, *lastly,* with respect to the mind, *instinct,* at that time of life, is more perfect, and less liable to error, directing us not only to the preservation of the individual, but to the continuation of the species. This last instinct still remains; and also another, which makes us abhor destruction, and fly from danger and pain: but I am persuaded, that, before we were so much under the guidance of reason, or rather that bastard kind of reason commonly called *opinion,* we had many more instincts, directing us to the means of preserving and providing for both the individual and the offspring . . . But, after we had formed opinions concerning what was good or ill, profitable or otherwise, in human life, and forsaking the guidance of nature and instinct, had resigned ourselves to the government of these opinions, and become the artificial creatures we now are, we lost those instincts by degrees, and nature yielded to artificial habit.

These are the *natural* powers belonging to our species at present; and we are next to speak of the *acquired* or adventitious powers, which we have added to our natures by our own industry and sagacity. Of this kind are all the sciences, all the arts liberal and mechanic, all the commodities and pleasures of life, even civil society itself, and almost every thing belonging to it: And, if we rightly consider the matter, we shall find, that our nature is chiefly constituted of acquired habits, and that we are much more creatures of custom and art than of nature. It is a common saying, that habit (meaning custom) is a second nature. I add, that it is more powerful than the first, and in a great measure destroys and absorbs the original nature: For it is the capital and distinguishing characteristic[237] of our species, that we can *make* ourselves, as it were, over again, so that the *original* nature in us can hardly be seen; and it is with the greatest difficulty that we can distinguish it from the *acquired.**

What chiefly makes this difficulty, is the facility with which we perform the operations

* " . . . man, in his natural state, is the WORK OF GOD; but, as we now see him, he may be said, properly enough, to be *the work of man.*"[238]

" . . . man is so much a creature of art, that it is a matter of nice discernment to separate what is artificial in him from what is purely natural."[239]

" . . . human nature . . . is almost wholly composed of artificial habits."[240]

that proceed from those acquired habits, and which makes us think them natural. Then many of them are acquired by such insensible degrees, and in our earliest years, that we do not perceive the progress that has been from *capacity* to *habit;* and, finding ourselves possessed of them, without knowing how, we rashly conclude them to be the gift of nature.[241]

His most startling proposition was that the orangoutang is human.

. . . the Orang Outangs . . . are of our species, and though they have made some progress in the arts of life, they have not advanced so far as to invent a language.[242]

In some of his private letters he qualified this statement.

. . . there can be no sort of reason why we should doubt that this wild man, or *Ouran Outang*, is a real man, or at least a being most nearly allied to us in his rational faculty.[243]

. . . the Orang-Outang belong[s] . . . to us . . . [because of] his use of a stick.* From which, and many other circumstances, it appears to me evident that he is much above the Simian race, to which I think you very rightly disclaim the relation of brother, though I think that race is of kin to us, though not so nearly related.

For the large monkeys, or baboons, appear to me to stand in the same relation to us, that the ass does to the horse, or our gold-finch to the canary-bird.[245]

Monboddo believed in innate psychological differences between the races.

. . . the habits and disposition of mind, and by consequence, the aptitude to learn anything, are qualities which go to the race, as well as the shape and other bodily qualities.[246]

. . . there appear to be whole nations, who have not at all, in any degree worth observing, this creative power of *genius* [in the "fine arts"]. Of this kind, is the great nation of the Chinese. . . .

On the other hand, the Greek nation appears to have been the nation of the greatest genius that ever existed. . . .

It appears, therefore, that in our species, as in other species of animals, the excellency of it is confined to certain races of the animals, in certain countries of the earth, not diffused over the whole species.[247]

## Long

Edward Long (1734–1813) attempted to show that the Negro race did not belong to the same species as the other races of man, probably in order to rationalize the slavery in Jamaica which he was describing.

The particulars wherein they differ most essentially from the Whites are, first, in respect to their bodies, viz. . . . the dark membrane which communicates that black colour to their skins,† which does not alter by transportation into other climates . . . the Blacks

---

* "And if there were nothing else to convince me that the Orang Outang belongs to our species, his using sticks as a weapon would alone be sufficient."[244]

† He wrote against Buffon's theory of geographical causes for racial differences: "to admit the force of this reasoning, we must suppose the world to be much older than has been generally believed. The Aethiopian is probably not at all blacker now than he was in the days of Solomon. The nations of Nicaragua and Guatimila, on the American continent, have not acquired this black tincture, although many more generations have passed since they were first discovered by the Europeans that Mr. Buffon thinks sufficient for changing a Negroe from black to white. . . . Further, as this change is supposed by Mr. Buffon to be gradual, some proof of it would doubtless appear in the course of one or two centuries. But we do not find, that the posterity of those Europeans, who first settled in the hottest parts of the West Indies,

born here, to the third and fourth generation, are not at all different in colour from those Negroes who are brought directly from Africa; whence it may be concluded very properly, that Negroes, or their posterity, do not change colour, though they continue ever so long in a cold climate.

Secondly, A covering of wool, like the bestial fleece, instead of hair.

Thirdly, The roundness of their eyes, the figure of their ears, tumid nostrils, invariable thick lips, and general large size of the female nipples, as if adapted by nature to the particular conformation of their childrens mouths.

Fourthly, The black colour of the lice which infest their bodies. . . . It is known, that there is a very great variety of these insects; and some say, that almost all animals have their peculiar sort.

Fifthly, Their bestial or fetid smell.[249]

It is not a variety of climate that produces various complexions.[250]

[But the environment does produce some other effects.] The effect of climate is not only remarkable in the structure of their [i.e., the native whites of Jamaica] eyes, but likewise in the extraordinary freedom and suppleness of their joints, which enable them to move with ease, and give them a surprising agility, as well as gracefulness in dancing. Although descended from British ancestors, they are stamped with these characteristic deviations. Climate, perhaps, has had some share in producing the variety of feature which we behold among the different societies of mankind, scattered over the globe: so that, were an Englishman and woman to remove to China, and there abide, it may be questioned, whether their descendants, in the course of a few generations, constantly residing there, would not acquire something of the Chinese cast of countenance and person? I do not indeed suppose, that, by living in Guiney, they would exchange their hair for wool, or a white cuticle for a black: change of complexion must be referred to some other cause. I have spoken only of those Creoles who never have quitted the island; for they, who leave it in their infancy, and pass into Britain for education, where they remain until their growth is pretty well compleated, are not so remarkably distinguished either in their features or limbs.[251]

I shall next consider their disparity, in regard to the faculties of their mind. . . .

In general, they are void of genius, and seem almost incapable of making any progress in civility or science. They have no plan or system of morality among them . . . it being a common known proverb, that all people on the globe have some good as well as ill qualities, except the Africans.[252]

The examples which have been given of Negroes born and trained up in other climates, detract not from that general idea of narrow, humble intellect, which we affix to the inhabitants of Guiney. We have seen *learned horses, learned* and even *talking dogs* in England; who, by dint of much pains and tuition, were brought to exhibit the signs of a capacity

are tending towards this black complexion, or are more tawny than an Englishman might become by residing five or six years in Spain, and exposing himself to the sun and air during his residence. It would likewise happen, that the progeny of Negroes brought from Guiney two hundred years ago, and transplanted into a colder climate, would be comparatively less black than the natives of that part of Africa, from whence their progenitors were removed; but no such effect has been observed. And lastly, the whole fabric of Mr. Buffon's hypothesis is subverted at once, by the race of *Albinoes,* in the very heart of Guiney; who, although subject to the same intense heat of climate, which, he says, has caused the black colour of Negroes, are unaccountably exempted from the influence of this cause, though equally exposed to it. Without puzzling our wits, to discover the occult causes of this diversity of colour among mankind, let us be content with acknowledging, that it was just as easy for Omnipotence to creat black-skinned, as white-skinned men; or to create five millions of human beings, as to create one such being."[248]

far exceeding what is ordinarily allowed to be possessed by those animals.[253]

When we reflect on the nature of these men, and their dissimilarity to the rest of man-kind, must we not conclude, that they are a different species of the same *genus*? Of other animals, it is well known, there are many kinds, each kind having its proper species subordinate thereto: and why shall we insist, that man alone, of all other animals, is undiversified in the same manner?[254]

Having proved to his satisfaction that the Negro is not to be classified as *Homo sapiens,* he modified Monboddo's scheme and placed the Negro and orang as intermediate between man and the lower primates.

[Do] we [not] find so many irresistible proofs which denote his [i.e., man's] conformity to the general system of the world? In this system we perceive a regular order and grada-tion, from inanimate to animate matter; and certain links, which connect the several *genera* one with another; and, under these *genera,* we find another gradation of species, comprehending a vast variety, and, in some classes, widely differing from each other in certain qualities. We ascend from mere inert matter into the animal and vegetable king-doms, by an almost imperceptible deviation; and these two are again nearly connected by a very palpable similitude; so that, where the one ends, the other seems to begin.[255]

If, amidst the immense variety of all animal beings which people the universe, some animal, for example, the body of a man, be selected to serve as a criterion, with which all the other organized beings are to be compared; it will be found, that, although all these beings exist abstractedly, and all vary by differences infinitely graduated, yet, at the same time, there appears a primitive and general design, or model, that may be very plainly traced.[256]

When we come to examine . . . the monkey-kind, or *anthropomorphits,* so called by naturalists, because they partake more or less of the human shape and disposition; we here observe the palpable link which unites the human race with the quadruped, not in exterior form alone, but in the intellectual quality.[257]

[After quoting Buffon on the morphological[258] and psychological similarities between the orang and man, he concludes:][259] we allow to these orang-outangs a degree of intel-lect not restricted wholly to instinct, but approaching, like the frame of their organs, to an affinity with humans.[260]

His imitation and mimickry of human gestures and movements, which come so near in semblance to the result of thought, set him at a great distance from brute animals, and in a close affinity to man. If the essence of his nature consists entirely in the form and organization of the body, he comes nearer to man than any other creature, and may be placed in the second class of animal beings.

If he is a creature *sui generis,* he fills up the space between mankind and the ape, as this and the monkey tribe supply the interval that is between the oran-outang and the quad-rupeds.[261]

That the oran-outang and some races of black men are very nearly allied, is, I think, more than probable.[262]

. . . the natives of the whole tract, comprised under the name of Negro-land, are all black, and have wool instead of hair. . . . As we recede from Negro-land, this blackness gradually decreases, and the wool as gradually changes to lank hair, which is at first of a short staple, but is found longer, the further we advance. We observe the like gradations of the intellectual faculty, from the first rudiments perceived in the monkey kind, to the more advanced stages of it in apes, in the *oran-outang,* that type of man, and the Guiney

Negroes; and ascending from the varieties of this class to the lighter casts, until we mark its utmost limit of perfection in the pure White.[263] . . . The measure of the several orders and varieties of these Blacks may be as compleat as that of any other race of mortals; filling up that space, or degree, beyond which they are not destined to pass; and discriminating them from the rest of men, not in *kind,* but in *species.*[264]

## Hunter

John Hunter (d. 1809) attempted to provide explanations for the various differences which exist between races, for he was a monogenesist.

. . . each and every species of animals has been circumscribed within fixed boundaries from the beginning by Divine Wisdom.[265]

. . . my opinion is that men must be held to be of the same species. And as in the vegetable kingdom, the same species sometimes comprehends many varieties, which all depend upon the climate, the soil, and cultivation, so to use the language of botanists, the diversities of men are to be considered as varieties of the same species, and, in the same way, to be deduced from natural causes.

No one can be ignorant how much influence events have in affecting and changing men. On these depend almost all disorders, and the numerous changes in the human body.[266]

In order that I may conduct my work on some plan, I have thought it best to divide it into four parts; in the first of which I shall treat of the colour of men; in the second, of stature and form; in the third, of the excess or defect of parts, or other differences; and in the fourth, of the mental faculties.[267]

[1.] The varieties of colour are wonderful.[268]

What is the cause of such different colours? To this the answer is difficult.[269]

[He finally decides that the most probable factors are] the heat of the sun, and the effects of the air, where any one is exposed to it.[270]

[2.] The differences of human stature are far from being small.[271]

. . . we must now find out what are the . . . causes which . . . explain the varieties of human stature.

Of these the principal are climate, food, exercise, and labour.[272]

I must now speak of the varieties of form. . . . I confess that I cannot understand how the forms of men and the lineaments of the face come to be so diverse from each other as they are.[273]

[3.] The "defect or excess of parts of the human body" are the result of geographic and cultural factors.[274]

[4.] The mental varieties seem equal to and sometimes greater than the bodily varieties of man.[275]

. . . men's minds do not seem to me to differ so much by the fortune of birth as by the use and exercise of reason, and the faculties of the mind come out smaller or greater by use, almost in the same way as those of the body. And as there are several reasons for this exercise, I will consider them under three heads; position, education, and the affections of the mind.

As to the first; If one be in a place where insuperable impediments, or none at all, are placed in the way of action, in the first place he gives himself up to despair, in the other to idleness, and equally in either case does nothing. And, in fact, the Samoeides and the negroes seem placed in similar circumstances. If, on the contrary, all the necessities of life are uncertain to anyone on account of the climate, the soil, or some other reason, what does he do? Instantly he struggles to make them more secure by art and industry. . . . Since then the force of circumstances is so powerful to excite and amplify the reason, so also the affections of the mind, and especially the desires, are of great influence towards the same end.

What has not been done for science and knowledge, especially in the government and administration of public affairs, through benevolence, or emulation, or envy, ambition, and glory?

No one doubts the important part that education and discipline play in forming and stimulating the mind. . . .

Has conformation any thing to do with the increase or diminution of the mental faculties? . . . something must be attributed to congenital conformation and stamina but more to exertion, so far as calls are made for it by position, mental affections, and education, in the matter of reason and prudence.

Travellers have exaggerated the mental varieties far beyond the truth, who have denied good qualities to the inhabitants of other countries, because their mode of life, manners, and customs have been excessively different from their own. For they have never considered, that when the Tartar tames his horse, and the Indian erects his wig-wam, he exhibits the same ingenuity which an European general does in manoeuvering his army, or Inigo Jones in building a palace.[276]

There is nothing in which men differ so much as in their customs. They are of innumerable origins. Climate, soil, diet, occupations, laws, religion, individual men, government, the institution of monarchy, or a republic, with a thousand other things, create and alter their customs in a marvellous way.[277]

However various the causes may be, which create and alter the customs of men, there is but one which can make them lasting, stable and, as it were, eternal. This is imitation, the most powerful principle in man. By this we acquire customs, manners, and almost every thing. Sometimes indeed its power is such that against our will we are compelled to imitate others. From this source depends the resemblance of customs in the family, the city, or the nation. . . .

There are truly few, who judge for themselves, what customs are right or wrong, and they are still fewer who, whilst they think for themselves, and differ from the mob, go on to accomodate and alter their customs according to their own opinions.[278]

## Herder

Johann Gottfried von Herder (1744–1803) was another who saw man in relation to the rest of organic life.

The mass of active powers and elements, from which the Earth was formed, contained, probably, as a chaos, all that was to be, and could be, on it. At stated periods, air, fire, water, the earth, arose from these spiritual and material *stamina*. Various combinations of water, air, and light, must have taken place, before the seeds of the first vegetable organization, of moss perhaps, could have appeared. Many plants must have sprung up and died, before organized animals were produced; and among these, insects and birds, acquatic and nocturnal animals, must have preceded the more perfect animals of the land and the day; till finally, to crown the organization of our Earth, Man, the *Microcosm*, arose. He, the son of all elements and being, their choicest summary and the flower of creation, could not but be the last darling child of Nature; whose formation and reception various evolutions and changes must have preceded.[279]

Now it is incontestable, that amid all the differences of earthly creatures a certain uniformity of structure, and as it were a *standard form,* appear to prevail, convertible into the most abundant variety. The similitude of the bony frame of land animals is obvious: head, body, hands, and feet, are the chief parts in all; and even in their principal limbs are fashioned after one prototyde, but infinitely diversified. The internal structure of beasts renders the proposition still more evident; and many rude external figures strongly resemble man in the principal internal parts. Amphibia deviate more from this standard: birds, fishes, insects, and acquatic animals, the last of which are lost in the vegetable or fossil world, still more. Farther our eyes cannot penetrate: but these transitions render it not improbable, that in marine productions, plants, and even inanimate things as they are called, one and the same groundwork of organization may prevail, though infinitely more rude and confused.[280]

The higher we ascend . . . the more complicated are the parts.[281]

[Nature] seemed to pursue one great end. This great end is evidently to approach that organic form, in which the greatest combination of clear ideas, and the most diversified and free use of various senses and limbs, could take place: and this it is, that constitutes the greater or less humanity of beasts. It is no sport of the will: but a result of the diverse forms, that could be no otherwise combined to that end, to which nature would combine them; namely, to an employment of thoughts, senses, powers, and desires, in this proportion, to such an end, and no other.[282]

[He takes up the] structure of plants and animals compared with regard to the organization of man.[283]

The upright posture of man is natural to him alone: nay, it is the organism of the whole destination of the species, and its most distinguishing character.[284]

[The upright posture of man produces the following effects:

[1. Reason.[285]. For example, the bee's] mind is included in its organizations, and intimately interwoven with it. Thus it operates conformably to it; finely, and with art, but in a very narrow and confined circle.[286]

The teachable creature [man,] must learn, as he receives from nature less knowledge: he must exercise his powers, because he receives less power from nature.[287]

[2. Development of the "higher senses," i.e., sight and hearing, rather than smell and taste.[288]]

[3. The arts.[289]]

[4. Language.[290]] The beast [on the other hand,] that has a voice recurs to its aid, when it feels any propensity, and is desirous to express its feelings, whether of joy or sorrow. It gesticulates little, and those only speak by signs, which are comparatively denied an animated voice. The tongue of some animals is so formed, as even to be capable of producing human words, the signification of which they do not understand: the external organization, particularly when tutored by man, runs before the internal capacity.[291]]

[5. Physical delicacy, but with adaptability.[292]]

. . . what raised man above the brute, and prevented him, even in his rudest state, from being degraded to the rank of a beast? It will be said, reason and speech.[293]

We have seen, that the reason and humanity of man depend on education, language, and tradition: and that in this respect he differs totally from the brute, which brings its infallible instinct into the world with it.[294]

Hitherto we have considered the Earth as an abode of the human species in general;

and endeavoured to mark the rank, that man holds among the living creatures, by which it is inhabited. Having thus formed an idea of his general nature, let us proceed, to contemplate the various appearances he assumes on this globular stage.[295]

[He gives a geographic and cultural interpretation of racial differences based upon the inheritance of acquired characteristics.[296]]

Notwithstanding the varieties of the human form, there is but one and the same species of man throughout the whole of our earth.[297]

. . . everywhere he still continues man: for, even in what appear to be the features of the greatest inhumanity among these people [i.e., the Eskimo] is humanity visible, when they are closely examined.[298]

Mankind, destined to humanity, were to be from their origin a brotherly race, of one blood, and formed by one guiding tradition; and thus the whole arose, as each individual family now arises, branches from one stem, plants from one primitive nursery.[299]

. . . the human species originated in Asia.[300]

Herder gave a discussion on facial angles, following Camper.[301]

### Smith

Samuel Stanhope Smith (1750–1819) defended monogenesis for religious reasons. He said of his work:

. . . as its object is to establish the unity of the human species, by tracing its varieties to their natural causes, it has an obvious and intimate relation with religion, by bringing in science to confirm the verity of the Mosaic history.[302]

. . . all the varieties of men may have sprung from the same original stock.[303]

Of the chief causes of the varieties of the human species I shall treat under the heads *Of Climate,—Of the State of Society,—*and, *Of the Manner of Living.*[304]

Climate, modes of living, national customs and ideas, and the degree of civilization to which a people have arrived, all have an influence on the figure of the bony substratum of the head, as well as on the features of the countenance.[305]

I am inclined . . . to ascribe the apparent dullness of the negro principally to the wretched state of his existence first in his original country, where he is at once a poor and abject savage, and subjected to an atrocious despotism; and afterwards in those regions to which he is transported to finish his days in slavery, and toil. Genius, in order to its cultivation, and the advantageous display of its power, requires freedom: it requires reward, the reward at least of praise, to call it forth; competition to awaken its ardor; and examples both to direct its operations, and to prompt its emulation.[306]

He was opposed to the theory of cultural evolution.

. . . man, originally formed by a wise and beneficent Creator, was instructed by him in the duties, and the most necessary arts of life. Thus were laid, in the very commencement of the race, the foundation of domestic, social, and civil order.[307]

### Goethe

Johann Wolfgang von Goethe (1749–1832) applied the principle of continuity to organic life.

Nature can compass her purpose only *in sequence.* She makes no jumps. She could not, for example, produce a horse, had not all the other animals *preceded* on which, as a ladder, she ascends to the structure of the horse.[308]

This also applies to man.

Man is most closely akin to the animals.[309]

. . . how much of the animal is still left in man.[310]

However, he too made a dichotomy between man and the rest of the animals on the basis of reason.

If anything like reason shows itself in the brute creation, it is long before we can recover from our amazement; for, although the animals stand so near to us, they yet seem to be divided from us by an infinite gulf, and to be entirely subject to the rule of necessity.[311]

On the other hand, he was so convinced of the principle of continuity that he was not satisfied with the proposition of contemporary anatomists to the effect that man differed from other animals in his lack of the intermaxillary bone and did not rest until in 1784 he was able to announce jubilantly to his friend Herder, "I have found—neither gold nor silver, but what gives me inexpressible delight—the *os intermaxillare* in man.[312]

He applied the principle of continuity in another way through his concept of the archetype.

. . . my vision . . . is a discernment of the essential form with which nature continually plays, as it were, and in playing brings forth the manifold forms of life.[313]

This was first applied to plants in *Die Metamorphose der Pflanzen* (1790),[314] and later extended to all organic life.

This . . . we have no hesitation in maintaining: that all the more perfect organisms, among them fishes, amphibians, birds, mammals, and at the head of these last man, are all formed after one archetype that simply varies more or less and is continually developing and transforming itself through propagation.[315]

An illustration of the application of this doctrine will be given from plant life.

. . . all forms of plants may, perhaps, be developed from a single form.[316]

The changeableness of plant forms which I had long been observing awoke in me the idea that the forms about us were not originally fixed and determined, but that there had been given to them, along with a singular tenacity of generic and specific character, a fortunate mobility and flexibility by which they were able to accommodate themselves to such varied terrestrial conditions, and to form and transform themselves accordingly.[317]

[Much earlier he has discussed] the influence which the altitude of the mountain region evidently had on plants.[318]

## Kant

Immanuel Kant (1724–1804) also discussed the similarity of structure in organisms.

. . . if the naturalist would not waste his labour he must in judging of things, the concept of any of which is indubitably established as a natural purpose (organised beings), always lay down as basis an original organisation, which uses that very mechanism in order to produce fresh organised forms or to develop the existing ones into new shapes (which, however, always result from that purpose and conformably to it).

It is praiseworthy by the aid of comparative anatomy to go through the great creation organised natures, in order to see whether there may not be in it something similar to a system and also in accordance with the principle of production. For otherwise we should have to be content with the mere principle of judgement (which gives no insight into their production) and, discouraged, to give up all claim to *natural insight* in this field. The agreement of so many genera of animals in a certain common schema, which appears to be fundamental not only in the structure of their bones, but also in the disposition of their remaining parts,—so that with an admirable simplicity of original outline, a great variety of species has been produced by the shortening of one member and the lengthening of another, the involution of this part and the evolution of that,—allows a ray of hope, however faint, to penetrate into our minds, that here something may be accomplished by the aid of the principle of the mechanism of nature (without which there can be no natural science in general.) This analogy of forms, which with all their differences seem to have been produced according to a common original type, strengthens our suspicions of an actual relationship between them in their production from a common parent, through the gradual approximation of one animal-genus to another—from those in which the principle of purposes seems to be best authenticated, *i.e.,* from man, down to the polype, and again from this down to mosses and lichens, and finally to the lowest stage of nature noticeable by us, viz. to crude matte. And so the whole Technic of nature, which is so incomprehensible to us in organised beings that we believe ourselves compelled to think on different principle for it, seems to be derived from matter and its powers according to mechanical laws (like those by which it works in the formation of crystals).

Here it is permissible for the *archaeologist* of nature to derive from the surviving traces of its oldest revolutions, according to all its mechanism known or supposed by him, that great family of creatures (for so we must represent them if the said thoroughgoing relationship is to have any ground). He can suppose the bosom of mother earth, as she passed out of her chaotic state (like a great animal), to have given birth in the beginning to creatures of less purposive form, that these again gave birth to others which formed themselves with greater adaptation to their place of birth and their relations to each other; until this womb becoming torpid and ossified, limited its births to definite species not further modifiable, and the manifoldness remained as it was at the end of the operation of that fruitful formative power.[319]

## Beattie

James Beattie (1735–1803) was interested in the differences between human and subhuman forms of communication.

Man is the only animal that can speak. For speech implies the arrangement and separation of our thoughts; and this is the work of reason and reflection. Articulate sounds resembling speech may be uttered by parrots, by ravens, and even by machines; but this is not speech, because it implies neither reflection, nor reason, nor any separation of successive thoughts; because, in a word, the machine or parrot does not, and cannot, understand the meaning of what it is thus made to utter.

The *natural* voices of brute animals are not, however, without meaning. But they differ from speech in these three respects. First, man speaks by art and imitation; whereas brutes utter their voices without being taught, that is, by the instinct of their nature. Secondly, the voices of brutes are not separable into simple elementary sounds, as the speech of man is; nor do they admit of that amazing variety whereof our articulate voices are susceptible. And, thirdly, they seem to express, not separate thoughts or ideas, but such feelings, pleasant and painful, as it may be necessary, for the food of those animals, or for the benefit of man, that they should have the power of uttering.[320]

## Darwin

Erasmus Darwin (1731–1802) had an evolutionary view of man.

> Imperious man, who rules the bestial crowd,
> Of language, reason, and reflection proud,
> With brow erect who scorns this earthy sod,
> And styles himself the image of his God;
> Arose from rudiments of form and sense,
> And embryon point, or microscopic ens![321]

In *The Temple of Nature* he gave the biblical version of the creation of man[322] but added the following note:

The mosaic history of Paradise and of Adam and Eve has been thought by some to be a sacred allegory, designed to teach obedience to divine commands, and to account for the origin of evil . . . and . . . that this account originated with the magi or philosophers of Egypt, with whom Moses was educated, and that this part of the history, where Eve is said to have been made from a rib of Adam might have been an hieroglyphic design of the Egyptian philosophers, showing their opinion that Mankind was originally of both sexes united, and was afterwards divided into males and females: an opinion in later times held by Plato, and I believe by Aristotle.[323]

He believed in the modifiability of species.

. . . the great globe itself, and all that it inhabit, appear to be in a perpetual state of mutation and improvement.[324]

. . . animals seem to have undergone great changes, as well as the inanimate parts of the earth, and are probably still in a state of gradual improvement.[325]

[There is] some change which these animals have undergone in the gradual progression of the formation of the earth, and of all that it inhabit.[326]

This change takes place as a result of the "desires" of the organism.

. . . the three great objects of desire, which have changed the forms of many animals by their exertions to gratify them, are those of lust, hunger, and security.*[328]

He had an elaborate theory of man's evolution.

The earth was originally covered with water, as appears from some of its highest mountains, consisting of shells cemented together by a solution of part of them, as in the limestone rocks of the Alps; Ferber's Travels. It must be therefore concluded, that animal life began beneath the sea. Nor is this unanalogous to what still occurs, as all quadrupeds and mankind in their embryon state are acquatic animals; and thus may be said to resemble gnats and frogs. The fetus in the uterus has an organ called the placenta, the fine extremities of the vessels of which permeate the arteries of the uterus, and the blood of the fetus becomes thus oxygentated from the passing stream of the maternal arterial blood; exactly as is done by the gills of fish from the stream of water, which they occasion to pass through them.[329]

From thus meditating on the great similarity of the structure of the warm-blooded animals, and at the same time of the great changes they undergo both before and after their nativity; and by considering in how minute a portion of time many of the changes

---

* "Many . . . parts of animals . . . have arisen from their three great desires of lust, hunger, and security."[327]

of animals above described have been produced; would it be too bold to imagine, that in the great length of time, since the earth began to exist, perhaps millions of ages before the commencement of the history of mankind, would it be too bold to imagine, that all warm-blooded animals have arisen from one living filament, which THE GREAT FIRST CAUSE endued with animality, with the power of acquiring new parts, attended with new propensities, directed by irritations, sensations, volitions, and associations; and thus possessing the faculty of continuing to improve by its own inherent activity, and of delivering down those improvements by generation to its posterity, world without end?[330]

Shall we then say that the vegtable living filament was originally different from that of each tribe of animals . . .? And that the productive living filament of each of those tribes was different originally from the other? or, as the earth and ocean were probably peopled with vegetable productions long before the existence of animals, and many families of these animals long before other families of them, shall we conjecture that one and the same kind of living filaments is and has been the cause of all organic life?[331]

This idea of the gradual formation and improvement of the animals' world accords with the observations of some modern philosophers . . . [and] seems not to have been unknown to the ancient philosophers.[332]

The arguments which have been adduced to show, that mankind and quadrupeds were formerly in an hermaphrodite state, are first deduced from the present existence of breasts and nipples in all the males; which latter swell on titillation like those of the females, and which are said to contain a milky fluid at their birth. . . .[333]

Secondly, from the apparent progress of many animals to greater perfection. . . .

It has been supposed by some, that mankind were formerly quadrupeds as well as hermaphrodites; and that some parts of the body are not yet so convenient to an erect attitude as to a horizontal one; as the fundus of the bladder in an erect posture is not exactly over the insertion of the urethra; whence it is seldom completely evacuated, and thus renders mankind more subject to the stone, than if he had preserved his horizontality: these philosophers, with Buffon and Helvetius, seem to imagine, that mankind arose from one family of monkeys on the banks of the Mediterranean; who accidentally had learned to use the adductor pollicis, or that strong muscle which constitutes the ball of the thumb, and draws the point of it to meet the points of the fingers; which common monkeys do not; and that this muscle gradually increased in size, strength, and activity, in successive generations; and by this improved use of the sense of touch, that monkeys acquired clear ideas, and gradually became men.[334]

. . . the progress of mankind in arts and sciences, which continues slowly to extend, and to increase, seems to evince the youth of human society; whilst the unchanging state of the societies of some insects, as of the bee, wasp, and ant, which is usually ascribed to instinct, seems to evince the longer existence, and greater maturity of those societies.[335]

He believed in polygenesis.

The nations, which possess Europe and a part of Asia and Africa, appear to have descended from one family, and to have had their origin near the banks of the Mediterranean, as probably in Syria, the site of Paradise, according to the Mosaic history. This seems highly probable from the similarity of the structure of the languages of these nations, and from their early possession of similar religions, customs, and arts, as well as from the most ancient histories extant.* . . .

Other families of mankind, nevertheless, appear to have arisen in other parts of the

* "The Eleusinian mysteries were invented in Egypt, and afterwards transferred into Greece along with most of the other early arts and religions of Egypt."[336]

habitable earth, as the language of the Chinese is said not to resemble those of this part of the world in any respect. And the inhabitants of the islands of the South-Sea had neither the use of iron tools, nor of the bow, nor of wheels, nor of spinning, nor had learned to coagulate milk, or to boil water, though the domestication of fire seems to have been the first great discovery that distinguished mankind from the bestial inhabitants of the forest.[337]

However, for all his evolutionism, Darwin still differentiated between man and other animals.

> Proud Man alone in wailing weakness born,*
> No horns protect him, and no plumes adorn;
> No finer powers of nostril, ear or eye,
> Teach the young Reasoner to pursue or fly.—
> Nerved with fine touch above the bestial throngs,
> The hand, first gift of Heaven! to man belongs;
> Untipt with claws the circling fingers close,
> With rival points the bending thumbs oppose,
> Trace the nice lines of Form with sense refined,
> And clear ideas charm the thinking mind.[339]

The human species in some of their sensations are much inferior to animals, yet the accuracy of the sense of touch, which they possess in so eminent a degree, gives them a great superiority of understanding; as is well observed by the ingenious Mr. Buffon.†[341]

It was before observed, how much the superior accuracy of our sense of touch contributes to increase our knowledge; but it is the greater energy and activity of the power of volition, that marks mankind, and has given them the empire of the world.[342]

The facility of the use of the voluntary power, which is owing to the possession of the clear ideas acquired by our superior sense of touch, and afterwards of vision, distinguishes man from brutes, and has given him the empire of the world, with the power of improving nature by the exertions of art.[343]

## White

Charles White (1728–1813) based his analysis of man on the conception of the chain of being.

Nature descends by gradual and imperceptible steps from man down to the least organized beings.[344]

Everyone who has made Natural History an object of study, must have been led occasionally to contemplate the beautiful gradation that subsists amongst created being, from the highest to the lowest. From man down to the smallest reptile, who existence can be discovered only by the microscope, Nature exhibits to our view an immense chain of beings, endued with various degrees of intelligence and active powers, suited to their stations in the general system.[345]

---

* " . . . not only the growth of those peculiar parts of animals, which are first wanted to secure their subsistence, are in general furthest advanced before their nativity: but some animals come into the world more completely formed throughout their whole system than others; and are thence much forwarder in all their habits of motion."[338]

† "There is . . . at this time an old monkey shewn in Exeter Change, London, who having lost his teeth, when nuts are given him, takes a stone into his hand, and cracks them with it one by one; thus using tools to effect his purpose like mankind."[340]

. . . there is a general gradation from man through the animal race; from animals to vegetables, and through the whole vegetable system. By gradation, I mean the various degrees in the powers, faculties, and organization. The gradation from man to animals is not by one way; the person and actions descend to the orang-outang, but the voice to birds.*[347]

[There is] a *gradation,* as well of the human race, as of the animal and vegetable kingdoms in general.[348]

. . . there exist material differences in the organization and constitution of various tribes of the human species; and not only so, but . . . these differences, generally, mark a regular gradation, from the white European down through the human species to the brute creation. From which it appears, that in those particulars where in mankind excel brutes, the European excels the African.[349]

From the numerous facts which have been adduced, it must appear evident, that various differences exist in the human race; some of which are generally known,—but others, it is presumed, have never been before pointed out. In the bony system, it has been shewn that the head,† the arms,‡ and the feet, differ materially; characteristic differences have also been pointed out in the hair, the colour of the skin, the complexion, the being adapted to a particular climate, and the being subject to different diseases in the same situation.

There are but two ways of accounting for this great diversity in the human frame and constitution. 1. To suppose that the diversity, great as it is, might be produced from one pair, by the slow operation of natural causes. 2. or to suppose that different species were originally created with those distinctive marks which they still retain.[353]

On the . . . [latter] hypothesis we can easily account for . . . diversities in the human race; or rather indeed, the hypothesis itself presumes upon such diversities. Besides, we find that, in those animals which most nearly resemble man in their bodily conformation, there are a great number of species differing but in small degrees one from another. The same observation, indeed, may be extended to the animal kingdom in general. Why then should we seek to infringe this apparent law of nature in regard to man, unless to serve an hypothesis?[354]

Different species of men being once admitted, it will become a proper object of physiological enquiry to determine their number and [character?], with the merits, excellencies, and defects of each. In pursuing this enquiry there is no doubt but gradation will afford the proper clue to direct us. What the number of species may be, is not perhaps easy to determine. . . . The Negro, the American, some of the Asiatic tribes, and the European, seem evidently to be different species.

Ascending the line of gradation, we come at last to the white European; who being most removed from the brute creation, may, on that account, be considered as the most

---

* "The orang-outang has the person, the manner, and the action of man; the parrot, the bullfinch, &c. have such vocal organization as to command the powers of speech, of singing, and whistling; while the elephant enjoys the faculty of reason in an eminent degree."[346]

† Among other data, he gives illustrations of the comparative profiles of various animals and races of man.[350]

‡ "I measured the arms of about fifty negroes;—men, women, and children, born in very different climates; and found the lower arm longer than in Europeans, in proportion to the upper arm and to the height of the body."[351]

His data is put into some of the earliest anthropometric tables which give comparative material from Negroes, whites, Tyson's "pigmy," and a "monkey."[352]

beautiful of the human race.* No one will doubt his superiority in intellectual powers; and I believe it will be found that his capacity is naturally superior also to that of every other man.†[357]

## ARCHEOLOGY

The eighteenth century interest in the local antiquities of western Europe is exemplified in the work of John Carter (1748–1817)[358]. Besides the continuation of the Académie des Inscriptions et Belles Lettres, the eighteenth century also saw the formation of the Society of Antiquaries of London, whose *Archaeologia*[359] contained much archeological material, particularly on the remains of Roman Britain.

Classical archeology received a great impetus from the excavations at Herculaneum begun in 1738[360] and at Pompeii in 1748. Roman ruins were magnificently pictured by Giovanni Battista Piranesi (1720–78),[361] while a noteworthy contribution to Greek archeology was made by Richard Chandler (1738–1810) and others in the *Ionian Antiquities*,[362] a work which even influenced the fashions of the day.

As to paleolithic and neolithic artefacts, the informed consensus was that they were the man-made remains of societies in which the use of metals was unknown. This was the position, for example, of George André Helwig (1666–1748) in his *Lithographia angerburgica*[363] and of Nicolas Mahudel (1673–1747).[364]

### Montfaucon

Bernard de Montfaucon (1655–1741) gave the following discussion of such artefacts.

In the Year 1685, M. *de Cocherel,* a Gentleman of *Normandy,* in the Diocess of *Evreux,* seeing two Stones on a Hill near the Place of *Cocherel,* fancied that this distinguished something concealed in the Earth: He caused the two Stones to be removed, and to dig underneath. The Workmen in digging the Earth, met with a Sepulchre composed of five rough Stones of enormous Greatness. There were two Skulls found therein, and underneath each of them a hard Stone cut in the Form of an Ax; one, which is of the Stone called *Pyrites,* is six or seven Inches long, and one and a half broad; the Extremity that was the Edge and Cut was very sharp, and terminated in sharp Corners. The other, which is of fine oriental Giade, greenish, and spotted with Silver, is also shaped like an Ax, is perforated at one of its Extremities, and is three Inches long and two Broad. . . .

Under these two Carkasses there was a great Stone, which they took away, and there was found underneath the Bones of two other Bodies, who had also their Hatchets of Stone under their Heads: Their Figure was the same as the former; but the Stones were of another Colour, and of a different kind: In the same place there were three Urns filled with Coals.

By enlarging the Ditch, the Workmen met with from sixteen to eighteen other Bodies stretched out side by side on the same Line; their Heads were turned towards the South, and their Arms extended aside of their Bodies, each of them had a Stone under their Head,

---

* The following is one piece of evidence in his proof of this proposition: "Where, except on the bosom of the European woman, [are] two such plump and snowy white hemispheres, tipt with vermillion?"[355]

† However, he generously grants souls to Negroes.[356]

and a Hatchet, as the former. The Bodies were of the common Stature . . . and their Skulls much harder and thicker than ordinary. . . . The Stone-hatchets were all of the same Shape, but of different Colour, reddish, blackish, and other Colours.

There were found three Bones pointed like the Head of a Halbert, which formerly had been fixed to long Staffs, for to make Lances and Pikes of them. One of these was the Bone of a Horse's Leg. There were also Points found, some of Ivory, and other of Stone which had served for Heads of Arrows. From whence it appears that these Barbarians had not any Use either of Iron, or Copper, or of any other Metal. A little Piece of a Hart's Horn, that was found in the same place, had served for to fasten one of these Axes in: This Horn had a Hole in one of its Extremities, for to fix an Helve therein.

Aside of these Bodies, where the Ground was eight Inches higher, was found a great Quantity of Bones half burnt; and amongst these Bones an heap of Stones, upon which was an earthern Urn broken and full of Coals: Above the Bones was a Lay of Ashes, a Foot and a half high. Among the Bones there was found, which is remarkable, two pieces of a Skull of ordinary Thickness, and at the left Corner of this Space a great Stone almost round, upon which were three other less Stones. . . .

This is the Relation that M. *Cocherel* gave me of his Discovery, under whose Direction and View every thing was dug up. . . .

There is not the least doubt but that this was the Sepulchre of the two Nations, and of the highest Antiquity. Those whole Bodies laid on the same Line were of some barbarrous Nation, that knew not yet the Use either of Iron, or of any Metal. The two which were in the Sepulchre built of great Stones, were 'tis likely Chiefs or Princes of that Nation, which was the Reason that one of them had an Ax made of precious Stone. The burnt Bodies were *Gauls,* who burnt the Bodies of their Dead, as we have just said. Or perhaps these Barbarians had been taken in War, and were afterwards sacrificed to the *Manes* of the deceased *Gauls,* which is what is most probable to be believed.[365]

## Anonymous, in Gordon

In 1726, speaking of a Scotch site, an anonymous writer wrote:

. . . in the . . *Cairn,* there was found an Instrument of Stone, of the flinty Kind, resembling a Wedge; such are very common in *Scotland,* and we meet with them frequently in the Hitories and Descriptions of the Northern Parts of *Europe;* they have been considered as a Sort of Arms, which the Ancients made us of, before the Use of Brass and Iron.[366]

Like Montfaucon, the same person noticed differences in stratification and burial customs and drew the proper inferences.

I had the Honour of being with my Lord *Pembroke* . . . when his Lordship caused above twenty of the *Tumuli* to be opened, that lie about Stonehenge. . . . That several Sorts of People, in a Succession of Time, had been bury'd there, was evident from the different Manners of Interrments, that disclosed themselves: Some of the Skeletons had been deposited upon the Surface of the Ground, at the Bottom of the Barrow, properly called Χωμα, being a Heap of Earth plainly poured upon the Bodies. Others had their Bones elevated from the Level of the Soil, and laid within 20 Inches of the Top of the Barrow; but probably at their first Interrment lay under a thicker Covering, since the Rains must necessarily, in so long a Tract of Years, have wash'd down a great deal of the incumbent Earth. . . . Near these Barrows, or *Tumuli,* we observed another Manner of Interrment, which I never saw any where else; This was, several Inclosures, exactly Circular, consisting of a small Trench and Bank within it, all of them had a little Rising in the

Center, scarcely so big as a Mole-hill, and others none at all perceptible. Two of these we opened, precisely in the Middle, and at about two Foot from the Surface, came to the *Stratum* of Chalk that runs under the whole Heath, in which we found a circular Cavity, cut about two Foot diameter, and filled with human Bones and Ashes.[367]

## Buffon

George Louis Leclerc, Count de Buffon (1707–88), was another who properly interpreted these artefacts.

The first men . . . began with sharpening into the figures of axes those hard flints, those *thunder-stones,* which their descendents imagined to have been produced by thunder, and to have fallen from the clouds, but which, in reality, are the first monuments of human art.[368]

## Lyttelton

Charles Lyttelton (1714–68), in a paper read to the Oonden Society of Antiquaries in 1766(?),[369] also argued for the antiquity of stone artefacts.

The stone I have now the honour of laying before you for your inspection, was found some years ago on ploughing some new inclosed pasture ground, near Spurnston, in the parish of St. Cuthbert, Carlisle, in a little hillock, or raised piece of ground, about four yards one way, and three the other, a little above a foot in height, consisting entirely of earth.

It is undoubtedly what Gesner, Aldrovand, and other early writers on Natural Philosophy, very absurdly name *Ceraunia,* or *Thunder-bolts,* affirming that they fall from the clouds in storms of thunder. . . .

There is not the least doubt of these stone instruments having been fabricated in the earliest times, and by barbarous people, before the use of iron or other metals was known; and from the same cause spears and arrows were headed with flint and other hard stones; abundance of which, especially of the latter, are found in Scotland, where they are, by the vulgar, called *Elfs arrows (lamiarum sagittae),* and some few here in England. . . .

This which now lies before you being found in a *tumulus,* inclines me to pronounce it a military weapon, answering to the steel or iron battle-ax in later times, for warlike instruments only, or, at least, for the most part, were interred with the bodies or ashes of men in the early ages of the world . . . these were British instruments of war, and used by them before they had the art of making arms of brass or iron; but I go farther, and am persuaded that when they fabricated these stone weapons, they had no knowledge at all of these metals; and that must have been at a very early period indeed, as in Julius Caesar's time they had abundance of *scythed* chariots, which probably were introduced here by the Phoenicians some ages before; since the Gauls, who together with the Britons had one common origin, had no use of these chariots. . . .

On the whole, I am of opinion that these stone axes are by far the most ancient remains existing at this day of our British ancestors, and probably coeval with the first inhabitants of this island.[370]

## Douglas

James Douglas (1753–1819) was of the same opinion.

From the known fact, that similar arrow-heads as are found in our antient sepulchres are used at this day by the barbarous natives of the globe, it is a natural and reasonable inference that they were used by a barbarous people who were, at a certain period, the inhabitants of this island.[371]

They are evidences of a people not in the use of malleable metal; and it therefore implies, that, wherever these arms are found in barrows, they are incontestible the relics of a primitive barbarous people, and preceding the aera of those barrows in which brass or iron arms are found.[372]

## Esper

Johann Friedrich Esper (1732–81) found human artefacts and skeletal material in association with extinct animals in Franconian caves.[373]

## Frere

John Frere (1740–1807) discovered flint artefacts associated with extinct animals, and in undisturbed strata of some depth.

I take the liberty to . . . lay before the Society some flints found in the parish of Hoxne, in the county of Suffolk, which, if not particularly objects of curiosity in themselves, must, I think, be considered in that light, from the situation in which they were found. See Pl. XIV, XV [in the original].

They are, I think, evidently weapons of war, fabricated and used by a people who had not the use of metals. They lay in great numbers at the depth of about twelve feet, in a stratified soil, which was dug into for the purpose of raising clay for bricks.

The strata are as follows:
1. Vegetable earth 1½ feet.
2. Argill 7½ feet.
3. Sand mixed with shells and other marine substances 1 foot.
4. A gravelly soil, in which the flints are found, generally at the rate of five or six in a square yard, 2 feet.

In the same stratum are frequently found small fragments of wood, very perfect when first dug up, but which soon decompose on being exposed to the air; and in the stratum of sand, (No. 3,) were found some extraordinary bones, particularly a jaw-bone of enormous size, of some unknown animal, with the teeth remaining in it. . . .

The situation in which these weapons were found may tempt us to refer them to a very remote period indeed; even beyond that of the present world; but whatever our conjectures on that head may be, it will be difficult to account for the stratum in which they lie being covered with another stratum, which, on that supposition, may be conjectured to have been once the bottom, or at least the shore, of the sea. The manner in which they lie would lead to the persuasion that it was a place of their manufacture and not of their accidental deposit; and the numbers of them were so great that the man who carried on the brick-work told me that, before he was aware of their being objects of curiousity, he had emptied baskets full of them into the ruts of the adjoining road.[374]

## Stukeley

William Stukeley (1687–1765) made studies of megalithic remains in England.[375]

## Barton

Benjamin Smith Barton (1766–1815) wrote the first book on North American archeology; his *Observations on Some Parts of Natural History*[376] is, in the words of ts subtitle, "An account of several remarkable vestiges of an ancient date, which have been discovered in different parts of North America."

He was particularly impressed by mounds, and after giving a review of the literature and descriptions of a few sites which he presumably had observed himself, he concludes:

These are the principal facts I have been able to collect from different sources, both public and private, concerning AMERICAN ANTIQUITIES; and, I flatter myself, they are sufficiently numerous to convince even obstinacy and incredulity, that various parts of the NORTHERN CONTINENT of the NEW WORLD, have formerly been inhabited by a people, who had made considerable advances towards those arts which are almost inseperable from the dawn of CIVIL SOCIETY.[377]

On the origin of the American Indian, he had the following theory:

I am induced to think, that the DANES have contributed to the peopling of AMERICA; and that the TOLTECAS, or whatever nation it may have been, that contructed the eminences and fortifications in that continent [of Middle America], were their descendents.[378]

## ETHNOGRAPHY AND ETHNOLOGY

A great deal of valuable ethnographic information on exotic cultures is contained in the accounts of eighteenth century explorers.[379] Carl von Linné's (1707–78) *Iter lapponicum* (1732) is an especially good work, particularly for the technology of the Lapps.

Meanwhile, classical scholars extended the knowledge of Greek and Roman cultures.[380]

As a result of the beginnings of the romantic movement, much interest was centered upon the folklore of European countries. In England, Thomas Percy's (1729–1811) *Reliques of Ancient English Poetry* (1765)[381] is a classic in the field: another important English collector was Joseph Ritson (1752–1803).[382]

### Goethe

Johann Wolfgang von Goethe (1749–1832) was a respectable ethnographer. His descriptions of the Roman carnival[383] and the festival of St. Roch at Bingen[384] might well excite the envy of professional ethnographers. He tells how he decided to write the former account.

It was the second time I had seen the Carnival, and very soon it struck me that this popular festival, like any other recurring part of the web of life, must have its determined history.

This thought reconciled me to the hubbub. It now assumed in my eyes the character of an important natural production and national event. From this point of view the spectacle interested me. I observed minutely the course of the follies, and how withal everything went off in a certain prescribed form and appropriateness. Thereupon I noted down the particular events in their order, a preparation which, later on, I used for the essay appended. At the same time I requested my housemate, Georg Schütz, to make a hasty drawing and colouring of the particular masks.[385]

Goethe was also a keen folklorist.

[He once wrote to Herder:] I have, in fact, brought with me from Alsace twelve ballads, which I have secured in my wanderings, from the mouths of the most aged women.[*] A piece of good luck! for their grandchildren all sing, "I only love Ismene" . . . they are the old tunes as God created them.[387]

While at Bingen he made a collection of weather proverbs[388] and variants of the legend of St. Roch.

In accordance with a wish that had been expressed, the company now related the graceful legend and moreover did so as if in competition, children and parents helping one another, as the case might be.

From this we could perceive the real nature of a legend, when flitting from mouth to mouth, and from ear to ear. Of contradictions there were none, but an endless variety of forms, which resulted from different persons taking a different interest in the several incidents; thus at one time one circumstance was set aside, and at another brought prominently forward.[389]

## Others

Antiquaries continued their local observations and were increasingly impressed by survivals, a phenomenon which played so important a role in the thinking of the English evolutionists of the nineteenth century. For example, John Brand (1744–1806) remarked:

Tradition has in no instance so clearly evinced her faithfulness as in the transmittal of vulgar rites and popular opinions. . . .

It must be confessed that many of these are mutilated, and, as in the remains of ancient statuary, the parts of some have been awkwardly transposed: they preserve, however, the principal traits that distinguish them in their origin.

Things that are composed of such flimsy materials as the fancies of a multitude do not seem calculated for a long duration; yet have these survived shocks by which even empires have been overthrown, and preserved at least some form and colour of identity, during a repetition of changes both in the religious opinions and civil polity of states.[390]

An important antiquary at the beginning of the century was Edward Lhuyd (1660–1709).[391]

Interest became so great that a number of organizations and periodicals were devoted to local and foreign customs. The Academie des Inscriptions et Belles-Lettres added the *Mémoirs de littérature et beaux-arts*[392] to its previously established *Histoire et mémoires*.[393] In England, the *Gentleman's Magazine*[394] devoted much space to local ethnography.[395] In 1770 the Society of Antiquaries of London began its *Archaeologia,*[396] and a privately published *Antiquarian Repertory*[397] had a brief existence. The movement spread, and in 1788 the Asiatic Society of Bengal proudly issued the first number of *Asiatick Researches.*[398]

A kind of social survey is Daniel Defoe's (1661–1731) *A Tour thro' the Whole Island of Great Britain* (1724–27),[399] but in the last quarter of the eighteenth century there began to appear from the pens of social reformers specialized monographs based upon intensive empirical investigations. Thus. while engaged in his study of prisons,[400] he gives a picture of John Howard (1726–90), who

"carries his weighing-scales in his pocket": when your jailor answers, "The prisoner's

* "[Goethe] was the first German who actually went among the 'folk' to collect their songs. Herder was getting his from books."[386]

allowance of food is so and so: and we observe it sacredly; here, for example, is a ration."
—"Hey! a ration this?" and solid John suddenly produces his weighing-scales; weighs it, marks down in his tablets what the actual quantity of it is. That is the art and manner of the man.[401]

Howard himself described his work in the following words:

The distress of prisoners, of which there are few who have not some imperfect idea, came more immediately under my notice when I was sheriff of the county of *Bedford* [in 1773]; and the circumstances which excited me to activity in their behalf was, the seeing, some—who by the verdict of juries were declared *not guilty;* some—on whom the grand jury did not find such an appearance of guilt as subjected them to trial; and some—whose prosecutors did not appear against them;—after having been confined for months, dragged back to gaol, and locked up again till they should pay *sundry fees* to the gaoler, the clerk of assize, *&c.*

In order to redress this hardship, I applied to the justices of the county for a salary to the *gaoler* in lieu of *his* fees. The bench were properly affected with the grievance, and willing to grant the relief desired: but they wanted a precedent for charging the county with the expence. I therefore rode into several neighbouring counties in search of one; but I soon learned that the same injustice was practiced in them; and looking into the prisons, I beheld scenes of calamity, which I grew daily more and more anxious to alleviate. In order therefore to gain a more perfect knowledge of the particulars and extent of it, by various and accurate observations, I visited most of the *county gaols* in England.

Seeing in two or three of them some poor creatures, whose aspect was singularly deplorable, and asking the cause of it, the answer was, "they were lately brought from the *bridewells."* This started a fresh subject of inquiry. I resolved to inspect the bridewells: and for that purpose travelled again into the counties where I had been; and, indeed, into all the rest; examining *houses of correction, city* and town *gaols.*[402]

I made it my business to collect materials, the authenticity of which could not be disputed.[403]

Another important work was *The State of the Poor,*[404] by Frederick Morton Eden (1766–1809).

The difficulties, which the labouring classes experienced, from the high price of grain, and of provisions in general, as well as of cloathing and fuel, during the years 1794 and 1795, induced me, from motives both of benevolence and personal curiosity, to investigate their condition in various parts of the kingdom. As I advanced in my enquiries, the subject became so interesting, that I persuaded myself the result would be acceptable to the Public, if I should be able to lay before them accurate details respecting the present state of the Labouring part of the community, as well as the actual Poor.*[406]

Private opinion, and private passions, will, in spite of us all, too often interfere, and bias and influence the most honest and intelligent minds, in their judgements respecting even matters of fact.[407]

It frequently requires a large experience, aided by much sagacity, to trace, amid a multitude of causes, those particular ones which contribute most to produce a numerous Poor.[408]

The following are some of his conclusions:

Paupers, comparatively speaking, are but rarely found among those employed in agriculture.[409]

* His data were gathered on the basis of a questionnaire which is reprinted in his monograph.[405]

. . . manufacturers more commonly become Paupers than labourers in husbandry.[41]

In the eighteenth century the question of the migration of peoples interested many scholars, and though because of a lack of adequate anthropological information they did not always come out with the right answer, still their analysis of the problem resulted in an enumeration of the criteria for diffusion and independent invention which is still valid.

### La Créquinière

— de La Créquinière (fl. 1704) maintained that the East Indies had been populated by the Israelites.

I have made it my Business to inquire only after that which the *Indians* have in common with other *Ancient People,* but more particularly with the *Jews,* without entring upon that great Question, *viz.* Whether those who in the Days of *Pekah* the Son of *Remaliah* the King of *Israel,* were carry'd into *Assyria* by *Tiglethpileser,* or those whom *Shalmaneser* transported thither under the Reign of *Hoseah,* did not so far penetrate into the *Indies* that they communicated to the People there, those things wherein we observe them now to resemble the *Jews?* Or, whether *God* in giving a *Law* to his People, did not prescribe to them many things which other Nations observ'd before, as being good in themselves?[41]

### Newton

Isaac Newton's (1642–1727) *The Chronology of Ancient Kingdoms Amended*[41] is based upon the idea of Egypt as the center of diffusion. His examples include oracles,[413] images with their legs crossed,[414] idolatry,[415] adoration of dead kings and queens,[416] and the alphabet.[417] The following is a sample of his reasoning

*Lycaon* [of Arcadia] sacrificed children, and therefore his father might come with his people from the Shepherds in *Egypt,* and perhaps from the regions of *Heliopolis,* where they sacrificed men, 'till *Amos* abolished that custom.[418]

### Pluche

Noel Antoine Pluche (1688–1761) followed Warburton in his analysis of the "Origine of Idolatry."

We sometimes are amazed at the conformity found in many respects between the practices of the people of God [i.e., the Israelites], and those of the nations given over to the grossest idolatry. . . .

Neither did the Hebrews receive from the Heathens, nor these from the former, such usages as are common to both: but they all resemble each other in some particular points because they have preserved several innocent customs borrowed from the remotest antiquity, even from Noah's family, from which they all took their original.[419]

### Linnaeus

Carl von Linné (1707–78) tried his hand at historical reconstruction, too.

. . . the Lapps . . . plainly show from their manners, diet, clothing, and language, that they are descended from the same nation as the Samoyeds.[420]

### Parsons

James Parsons (1705–70) maintained that "*America* was peopled from the *Eastern* parts of *Tartary.*"[421]

The agreement of the manners and customs of people, though never so remote from each other; the religious practices of the inhabitants of any two places being exactly the same; and the superstitious observations of certain things to be avoided, or put in execution, according to their notions of good or bad luck attending; but especially the essential, or chief point of their *theology* being the same, will surely put it beyond all doubt, that the people are from the same origin; notwithstanding the distance of time and place, from their first separation.[422]

The chief difficulty that seemed to occur to the curious inquirers, who formerly considered this matter, was the vast distance which they supposed to have been, between the most *Eastern* land of *Asia,* and the most *Western* of the *American* continent; and certainly, such considerations would have great weight against every proof arising from the manners, customs, religion and other circumstances of the people in both places; upon account of the supposed long navigation, which could hardly be thought in the power of the people of *East Tartary* to perform: and yet, I must confess, that a sameness in the most weighty customs of any two people, though at never so great a distance, would influence me to think them sprung from the same source, in former ages, notwithstanding any argumentative supposition that might be brought against me; because I really think it impossible, that an exact agreement can be in any distant places, between the manners, &c. of the people, by chance; especially too, when such a similarity is visible in the majority of their customs. However, the case is far otherwise than was suspected, with regard to the distance, by sea, from *Asia* to *America.*[423]

. . . we have now very sufficient proofs, that both continents are so near each other, as to remove all manner of doubt concerning the first inhabitants of *America,* on that side of the world.[424]

## Monboddo

James Burnett Lord Monboddo (1714–99) was another precursor of Elliot Smith who considered Egypt to be the center of universal diffusion.

Egypt is the native country of all Arts, Sciences, and Philosophy, and . . . from thence they have been derived to all the Nations.[425]

## Herder

To Johann Gottfried von Herder (1744–1803), Asia was the center of universal diffusion.

Here everything struck a deep root; religion, filial reverence, despotism! The nearer we are to Asia, the more are these, as ancient, eternal habits, at home.[426]

He used the age-area hypothesis to prove that man originated in Asia,[427] arguing on the basis of language,[428] writing,[429] domestication of animals,[430] agricutlure,[431] science and technology,[432] political organization,[433] and folklore.[434]

[For example, on political organization:] where do we find the most ancient and extensive monarchies? where have the empires of the world found their firmest establishment? China has maintained its ancient constitution for some thousands of years; and though this unwarlike country has been more than once overrun by Tartar hordes, the vanquished have always civilized their vanquishers, and inured them to the chains of their old constitution. What form of government in Europe can make a similar boast? The most ancient hierarchy upon earth reigns on the mountains of Tibet: and the castes of Hindus indicate their primeval establishment, from the deep rooted power, which has been for ages a second nature to the gentlest of people. Warlike or peacable established monarchies, on the Tigris and Euphrates, on the banks of the Nile and the mountains of Media, interfere in the history of the western nations in the remotest times; and even on the heights of Tartary the unrestricted liberty of the hordes was interwoven with a despotism of the khans, whence the principles of many European forms of government have been derived. From every corner of the world, the nearer we approach Asia, the nigher we come to firmly established kingdoms, in which the unlimited power of the monarch has been for thousands of years so deeply impressed on the minds of the people, that the king of Siam laughed at a nation without a king, as an abortive birth destitute of a head. The most established despotisms in Africa are seated nearest to Asia: the more distant they are from it, the ruder the state of tyranny, till at length it is lost among the Kaffirs in the patriarchal condition of the shepherd. In the southern ocean, the nearer we come to Asia, the deeper we find arts, manufactures, pomp, and the spouse of pomp, monarchical despotism, rooted; the farther we are from it, as in the remote islands, in America, and on the barren verge of the southern world, the more simple constitutions of society occur in a ruder state, the freedom of voices and independence of families; so that some historians have deduced even the two American monarchies of Mexico and Peru from the neighborhood of despotic governments in Asia.[435]

## Jones

William Jones (1746–94) was particularly interested in historical reconstruction.[436] He paid attention to the methodology involved and developed criteria to distinguish between diffusion and independent invention.

We cannot justly conclude, by arguments preceding the proof of facts, that one idolatrous people must have borrowed their deities, rites, and tenets from one another; since Gods of all shapes and dimensions may be framed by the boundless powers of imagination, or by the frauds and follies of men, in countries never connected; but, when features of resemblance, too strong to have been accidental, are observable in different systems of polytheism, without fancy or prejudice to colour them, and improve the likeness, we can scarce help believing, that some connection has immemorially subsisted between the several nations, who have adopted them.[437]

He used the evolutionary principle of development from the simple to the complex.

. . . the fundamental [chronological] rule [is,], that *natural, and most human, operations, proceed from the simple to the compound.*[438]

He attempted to develop a critical method that would enable him to utilize folklore; a problem that was reattacked with no greater success in the nineteenth century.

There seem to have been four principal sources of all mythology. I. Historical, or natural, truth has been perverted into fable by ignorance, imagination, flattery, or stupidity. . . . II. The next source of them appears to have been a wild admiration of the heavenly bodies, and, after a time, the systems and calculations of Astronomers. . . . III. Numberless divinities have been created solely by the magick of poetry; whose essential business it is, to personify the most abstract notions, and to place a nymph or a genius in every grove and almost in every flower. . . . IV. The metaphors and allegories of moralists and metaphysicians have been also very fertile in Deities.[439]

The numerous *Puranas* and *Itihasas,* or poems mythological and heroick, are completely in our power; and from them we may recover some disfigured, but valuable, pictures of ancient manners and governments; while the popular *tales* of the Hindus, in prose and in verse, contain fragments of history; and even in their *dramas* we may find as many real characters and events, as a future age might find in our own plays, if all histories of *England* were, like those of *India,* to be irrecoverably lost.[440]

He divided the history of man into four periods.

. . . the true History of the World seems obviously divisible into *four* ages or periods; which may be called, first, the *Diluvian,* or purest age; namely, the times preceding the deluge, and those succeeding it till the mad introduction of idolatry at Babel; next, the *Patriarchal,* or pure, age; in which, indeed, there were mighty hunters of beasts and of men, from the rise of patriarchs in the family of SEM to the simultaneous establishment of great Empires by the descendants of his brother HAM; thirdly, the *Mosaick,* or less pure, age; from the legation of MOSES, and during the time, when his ordinances were comparatively well-observed and uncorrupted; lastly, the *Prophetical,* or *impure,* age, beginning with the vehement warnings given by the Prophets to apostate Kings and degenerate nations, but still subsisting and to subsist, until all genuine prophecies shall be fully accomplished.[441]

The following is a summary of his conclusions in the field of historical reconstruction.

Let us begin with a short review of the propositions, to which we have gradually been led, and separate such as are morally certain, from such as are only probable: that the first race of *Persians* and *Indians,* to whom we may add the *Romans* and *Greeks,* the *Goths,* and the old *Egyptians* or *Ethiops,* originally spoke the same language and professed the same popular faith, is capable, in my humble opinion, of incontestable proof; that the *Jews* and *Arabs,* the *Assyrians,* or second *Persian* race, the people who spoke the *Syriack,* and a numerous tribe of *Abyssinians,* used one primitive dialect wholly distinct from the idiom just mentioned, is, I believe, undisputed, and, I am sure, indisputable; but that the settlers in *China* and *Japan* had a common origin with the *Hindus,* is no more than highly probable; and, that all the *Tartars,* as they are inaccurately called, were primarily of a third separate branch, totally different from the two others in language, manners, and features, may indeed be plaudably conjectured, but cannot . . . be perspicuously shown, and for the present therefore must be merely assumed. Could these facts be verified by the best attainable evidence, it would not, I presume, be doubted, that the whole earth was peopled by a variety of shoots from the *Indian, Arabian,* and *Tartarian* branches, or by such intermixtures of them, as, in a course of ages, might naturally have happened.

Now I admit without hesitation the aphorism of LINNAEUS, that "in the beginning GOD created one pair only of every living species, which has a diversity of sex". . . . If the human race then be, as we may confidently assume, of one nature species, they must all have proceeded from one pair; . . . they must people in time the region where they first were established, and their numerous descendants must necessarily seek new countries, as inclination might prompt, or accident lead, them; they would of course migrate in separate families and clans, which, forgetting by degrees the language of their common progenitor, would form new dialects to convey new ideas, both simple and complex; natural affection would unite them at first, and a sense of reciprocal utility, the great and only cement of social union in the absence of publick honour and justice, for which in evil times it is a general substitute, would combine them at length in communities more or less regular; laws would be proposed by a part of each community, but enacted by the whole; and governments would be variously arranged for the happiness or misery of the governed, according to their own virtue and wisdom, or depravity and folly; so that, in less than three thousand years, the world would exhibit the same appearances, which we may actually observe on it in the age of the great *Arabian* impostor [Mohammed].

On that part of it, to which our united researches are generally confined, we see *five* races of men peculiarly distinguished, in the time of MUHAMMED, for their multitude and extent of dominion, but we have reduced them to *three,* because we can discover no more, that essentially differ in language, religion, manners, and other known characteristicks: now those three races, how variously soever they may at present be dispersed and inter-mixed, must (if the preceding conclusions be justly drawn) have migrated originally from a central country, to find which is the problem proposed for solution. . . .

Thus then have we proved, that the inhabitants of *Asia,* and consequently, as it might be proved, of the whole earth, sprang from three branches of one stem: and that those branches have shot into their present state of luxuriance in a period comparatively short, is apparant from a fact universally acknowledged, that we find no certain monument, or even probable tradition, of nations planted, empires and states raised, laws enacted, cities built, navigation improved, commerce encouraged, arts invented, or letters con-trived, above twelve or at most fifteen or sixteen centuries before the birth of CHRIST, and from another fact, which cannot be controverted, that seven hundred or a thousand years would have been fully adequate to the supposed propagation, diffusion and establish-ment of the human race. . . . [He then uses the Old Testament as evidence for these state-ments[442] and concludes:] If MOSES then was endued with supernatural knowledge, it is not longer probable only, but absolutely certain, that the whole race of man proceeded from *Iran,* as from a centre, whence they migrated at first in three great colonies; and that those three branches grew from a common stock, which had been miraculously pre-served in a general convulsion and inundation of this globe. . . .

From the testimonies adduced in the six last annual discourses, and from the additional proofs laid before you, or rather opened, on the present occasion, it seems to follow, that the only human family after the flood established themselves in the northern parts of *Iran;* that, as they multiplied, they were divided into three distinct branches, each retaining little at first, and losing the whole by degrees, of their common primary language, but agreeing severally on new expressions for new ideas; that the branch of YAFET was *enlarged* in many scattered shoots over the north of *Europe* and *Asia,* diffusing themselves as far as the western and eastern seas, and, at length in the infancy of navigation, beyond them both: that they cultivated no liberal arts, and had no use of letters, but formed a variety of dialects, as their tribes were variously ramified; that, secondly, the children of HAM, who founded in *Iran* itself the monarchy of the first *Chaldeans,* invented letters, observed and named the luminaries of the firmament, calculated the known *Indian* period of *four hundred and thirty-two thousand years,* or an *hundred and twenty* repetitions of the *saros,* and contrived the old system of Mythology, partly allegorical, and partly grounded on idolatrous veneration for their sages and lawgivers; that they were dispersed at various intervals and in various colonies over land and ocean; that the tribes of MISR, CUSH, and RAMA settled in *Africk* and *India;* while some of them having improved the art of sailing, passed from *Egypt, Phenice,* and *Phrygia,* into *Italy* and *Greece,* which they found thinly peopled by former emigrants, of whom they supplanted some tribes, and united them-selves with others, whilst a swarm from the same hive moved by a northerly course into *Scandinavia,* and another, by the head of the *Oxus,* and through the passes of *Imaus,* into *Cashghar* and *Eighur, Khata* and *Khoten,* as far as the territories of *Chin* and *Tancut,* where letters have been used and arts immemorially cultivated; nor is it unreasonable to believe, that some of them found their way from the eastern isles into *Mexico* and *Peru,* where traces were discovered of rude literature and Mythology analogous to those of *Egypt* and *India;* that, thirdly, the old *Chaldean* empire being overthrown by the *Assyrians* under CAYUMERS, other migrations took place, especially into *India,* while the rest of SHEM'S progeny, some of whom had before settled on the Red Sea, peopled the whole *Arabian* peninsula, pressing close on the nations of *Syria* and *Phenice;* that, lastly, from all the three families were detached many bold adventurers of an ardent spirit and a roving disposition, who disdained subordination and wandered in separate clans, till they settled in distant isles or in deserts and mountainous regions; that, on the whole, some colonies might have migrated before the death of their venerable progenitor, but that states and empires could scarce have assumed a regular form, till fifteen or sixteen hundred years before the *Christian* epoch, and that, for the first thousand years of that period, we have no history unmixed with fable, except that of the turbulent and variable, but eminently distinguished, nation descended from ABRAHAM.[443]

Jones also wrote on ethnography,[444] linguistics,[445] comparative literature,[446] and comparative law,[447] while his "Remarks on the island of Hinzuan or Johanna"[448] is an acculturation study of a region which

exhibits a curious instance of the slow approaches toward civilization, which are made by a small community, with many natural advantages, but with few means of improving them.[449]

His travels gave him a cosmopolitan outlook.

Men will always differ in their ideas of civilization, each measuring it by the habits and prejudices of his own country.[450]

He sought for social laws.

The practical use of history, in affording particular *examples* of civil and military wisdom, has been greatly exaggerated; but *principles* of action may certainly be collected from it.[451]

## LINGUISTICS

### Leibniz

Gottfried Wilhelm von Leibniz (1646–1716) was interested in linguistics.

First, he sought for an inherent meaning in phonemes and roots.

I know it has been customary to say in the schools and almost everywhere else that the *meanings* of words are arbitrary (*ex instituto*) and it is true that they are not determined by a natural necessity, but they are nevertheless determined by reasons sometimes natural, in which chance has some share, sometimes moral, where choice enters.[452]

. . . root words . . . [are] formed . . . by chance but upon natural grounds. Those which signify the sounds of animals or have come from them furnish examples. Such, for example, is the Latin *coaxare* attributed to the frogs, which has some relation to *couaquen* or *quaken* in German. Nor it seems that the noise of these animals is the primordial root of other words of the German language. [Examples are given.]. . . . And there are many others in which the same thing appears. For it seems that the ancient Germans, Kelts, and other peoples allied to them have employed by a natural instinct the letter R to signify a violent movement and a noise like that of this letter. It appear in $\dot{\rho}\dot{\epsilon}\omega$, *fluo, rinnen, rüren (fluere), rutir (fluxion),* the *Rhine, Rhone, Roer (Rhenus, Rhodanus, Eradinus, Rura), rauben (rapere, ravir), Radt (rota), radere (raser), raschen,* a word difficult to translate into French; it signifies a noise like that which the wind or a passing animal stirs up in the leaves or the trees, or is made by a trailing dress; *rekken* (to stretch with violence), whence it comes that *reichen* is to reach; that *der Rick* signifies a long stick or perch useful for suspending anything, in this kind of Plat-tütsch or Low Saxon which is (spoken) near Brunswick; that *Rige, Reihe, regula, regere,* refer to length of a straight course; and that *Reck* has signified a thing or person very extended and long, and in particular a giant, and then a powerful and rich man, as it appears in the *reich* of the Germans and in the *riche* or *ricco* of Semi-Latins. In Spanish *ricos hombres* means the nobles or chief men; and this makes it plain at the same time how metaphor, synecdoche, and metonymy have caused words to pass from one signification to another without our being able always to trace them. This noise and violent movement is noticed also in *Riss* (rupture) with which the Latin *rumpo,* the Greek ῥῆγνυμι, the French *arracher,* the Italian *straccio* are connected. Now as the letter R signifies naturally a violent movement, the letter L designates a gentler one. [Examples of the same type are then given.][453]

Second, he was interested in comparative philology.

Now the language or the dialect of these ancient Goths is different from the modern German, although it has the same linguistic basis. The ancient Gallic is still more different, to judge by the language most nearly approaching the true Gallic, which is that of the country of Wales, Cornwall, and Basse-Bretagne; but the Irish differs therefrom still more and shows us traces of a Britannic, Gallic, and German language, still more ancient. But all these languages come from one source, and may be taken as modifications of one and the same language, which may be called the *Keltic*. Thus the ancients called both the Germans and Gauls *Kelts;* and in going back farther in order to understand the origin both of the Keltic and the Latin and Greek, which have many roots in common with the Germanic or Keltic tongues, we may conjecture that this fact arises from the common origin of all these peoples descended from the *Scythians,* who, having come from the Black Sea, passed the Danube and the Vistula, and of whom one part may have gone into Greece, the other have filled Germany and the Gauls; a consequence of the hypothesis which makes the Europeans come from Asia. [He then discusses the Finno-Ugric and other Asiatic languages and continues:]. . . . Now all these languages of Scythia have many roots common among themselves and with ours, and it is found that even the Arabic (under which the Hebrew, the ancient Punic, the Chaldee, the Syriac, the Ethiopic of the Abyssinians are to be comprised) has so great a number of them and an agreement so manifest with ours that it cannot be attributed to chance alone, nor even to commerce alone, but rather to favor the view of the common origin of all nations, and of a primitive root language. If the Hebrew or the Arabic approaches the nearest to it, it must be at least much changed, and the German seems to have preserved more completely the natural.[454]

And I mention in passing that the names of rivers, having ordinarily come from the farthest known antiquity, show best the old language and the ancient inhabitants; hence they deserve particular investigation. And languages in general being the most ancient monuments of peoples, before writing and the arts, show best the origin and cognations and migrations. Hence etymologies much extended would be curious and significant; but it is necessary to unite the languages of many peoples, and not to make too many leaps from one nation to another far distant without having good verifications, in which process it is especially useful to have intervening peoples as guarantees. And in general credence must be given to etymologies only when there is a quantity of concurrent evidence.[455]

In time all the languages of the world will be recorded and placed in the dictionaries and grammars, and compared together; this will be of very great use both for the knowledge of things, since names often correspond to their properties (as is seen by the names of plants among different peoples), and for the knowledge of our mind* and the wonderful variety of its operations. Not to speak of the origin of nations, which is known by means of solid etymologies which the comparison of languages will best furnish.[457]

It is certain at least that the Teutonic language and antiquities enter into the majority of the researches into European origins, customs, and antiquities. And I wish that learned men would make as much of them in the languages of the Wallachians, Biscayans, Slavonians, Finns, Turks, Persians, Armenians, Georgians, and others, the better to discover the harmony which would particularly be of service, as I have just said, in clearing up the origin of nations.[458]

## Parsons

Some eighteenth century scholars still imagined Hebrew to be the parent of all languages, a corollary of the Old Testament narrative, and a contemporary poet laughed at

> those learned philologists, who chase
> A panting syllable through time and space,
> Start it at home, and hunt it in the dark
> To Gaul, to Greece, and into Noah's ark.[459]

A modification of this theory was given by James Parsons (1705–1770), whose thesis was that Celtic is the remnant of the "Japhetan" parent of European languages.

. . . the more I enquired, the more nearly related the *Irish* and *Welsh* languages appeared . . . and . . . an appearance of the highest antiquity was very striking in *these two* languages; and this opinion grew into a conclusion, of their being the originals of Europe.[460]

I have endeavoured to trace the languages of *Europe* to their source; and I think I have discovered that which was previous to the *Greek* tongue, all over *Asia Minor, Scythia* and *Greece*. And this was the *Japhetan,* called afterwards the *Pelasgian,* and then *Gomerian* and *Magogian,* or *Scythian* language; which is now to be found only in *Ireland,* the *Highlands* of *Scotland,* and *Wales.*[461]

Now, it is hard to say when the *Japhetan* language began; there is a suspicion of its being related to the *Hebrew,* among some ingenious gentlemen, either as a mutilated dialect of it, or as a sister-dialect with that, of some more ancient antediluvian tongue. . . . However this may be, since we cannot think that *Japhet*'s people, or those of *Shem,* were at all concerned in the affair of *Babel,* we must suppose them both to have been languages of the antediluvian world, and both in the house of *Noah:* even as many families in every nation, at this time, speak two languages . . . for it cannot be supposed that *Japhet,* who was near one hundred years old when he went into the ark, could have learned a new language, when there were no people but the few of his own family upon the face of the earth.[462]

Such conclusions no more than mildly arouse one's curiosity at present, but what is interesting is that, in attempting to prove his thesis, he based one of his arguments upon phonetic shifts between related languages, thus anticipating Grimm.

---

* "I truly think that languages are the best mirrors of the human mind, and that an exact analysis of the signification of words would show us better than anaything else the workings of the understanding."[456]

If we enter into a little reflection upon our own language, we shall find, that the same word is pronounced differently in different places, and, accordingly, such persons as are not versed in classical learning, will be apt to write as they pronounce; and so lose the original root of the word. This is one cause of the degeneracy of a language, and often of the alienation of the true sense of the expression.

Another cause of the introduction of new words into a language is, that, in the original migration of a people, they meet a great number of things, which were unknown in the places from whence they departed; for the productions of nature, and other incidental matters, are not the same in all places; and hence an invention of new words must ensue.

Again, in a long tract of time, when the subdivisions of the same people have been settled in remote places, and their language, which, before their separation, was the same, has undergone, in each division, in habitations very remote from one another, several such changes as I have mentioned; they have appeared very strange and different to their former relations, in their future incursions and depredations . . . . these changes consist in a deviation of the sense, or a different syllabication, and, consequently, pronunciation, of the same word; still retaining the same signification.[463]

Let us, however, by way of examplification, first attend to the present state of some languages of *Europe,* which have a considerable share of the *Latin* in them; and these are the *French, Italian* and *Spanish.*[464]

[He then gives comparative word lists to show the similarities.[465]]

Again, the same kind of differences are also manifest between the *Greek,* and the *Latin* derived from it.[466]

[A comparative word list is given.[467]]

And, in a word, the same kind of mutilation in the *Greek* and *Latin* words, derived from the ancient *Pelasgian.*[468]

[He gives word lists for some of the Celtic languages, which are compared with Greek and Latin.[469]]

Now, although some mention is made already of the causes of the changes of words, which are adopted in the different languages; yet, for the better elucidation of this matter, it will be necessary to be a little more particular in enumerating the specific manner in which the changes are made; by which the reader will be able to discern more clearly the identity of the words, notwithstanding the apparent differences, and the many alterations that will occur in the list of them, nd to make the necessary allowances for them.

And first, there will appear a deviation of sense, or ideal difference, in the same word, or in its different syllabications; but still retaining an affinity of meaning, and manifesting the same origin. . . .

Another alteration consists of the transposition of letters, or syllables. . . .

Other alterations arise in words, which have the same root, or meaning, from the addition of initial letters, whether consonants or vowels; or of middle vowels, or gutterals, to words in one language, which have them not in the original. . . .

The additions, and omissions of labial letters, palatials, vowels, mutes, liquids, variations of initial syllables, changes of termination, changes of vowels, changes of labial and of palatial letters, as well as of linguals, although they make such differences as would seem sufficient to cause a total alienation of the relation and sense of words, in both these original languages; yet their affinity to each other, and their being the parents of others, in various tongues, still are manifest to every impartial and judicious reader, in the midst of such seeming difficulties. . . .

A few examples, in this place, will make all these assertions very manifest; let us take some words, each of which had the same signification in every one of the *European* tongues, and we shall see, at one view, the alterations they have gone through; and also, that, notwithstanding such changes, or deviations, they must be owned to have been originally the same word. . . .

| | | |
|---|---|---|
| | | All these are derived from the *Magogian nathair,* changing only |
| *Mag.* | Nathair. | the initial. . . . This is mutilated by the *Germans,* and other *Northern* |
| *Gomer.* | Taad. | nations, in chusing another initial letter, and varying it otherwise |
| *Greek* | πατηρ. | also: and we have adopted their mode in our *English* tongue. Some |
| *Latin* | Pater. | of those countries say, *fader, faeder, phadaer;* some, *fater, fatter,* |
| *French* | Pere. | *bader, bater;* others, *feer, veer, vayer, vader;* others, *haita, heite;* and |
| *Italian* | Padre. | we, in *England,* have had it from the *Saxons* four different ways in |
| *Hisp.* | Padre. | a course of years, thus: *fadiir, fadir, fader,* and now *father.* |
| *Port.* | Pae. / Pay. | These are the variations in the *West* and *North-west* of *Europe;* and it is very remarkable, that, of all the Eastern nations, not one but |
| *Manx* | Ayr. | the *Persian* has a word agreeing with this. The *Persians* have *Pader* |
| *Gothic* | Atta. | and *Peder.* . . . Most others of the people of *Asia* seem to follow the |

*Hebrews,* in the title for a father: these and the *Samaritans* say *ab;* the *Rabins, av; Chaldeans, abba; Syrians, aboh; Arabians, aba* and *abu* . . . the *Aethiopians* say, *abi.*[470]

In a later section, entitled, "Observations upon the causes of some differences in the names of the *numberals* of the *European nations,*" he continues the subject. He first gives a table of the words for numerals; the following sample is for "4."

| | |
|---|---|
| Magogian, Irish | Cathair |
| Gomerian, Welsh | Pedwar |
| Greek | Tessares |
| Latin | Quatuor |
| Italian | Quatro |
| Spanish | Quatro |
| French | Quatre |
| German | Vier |
| Dutch | Vier |
| Swedish | Fyra |
| Danish | Fire |
| Saxon | Feower |
| English | Four |
| Polish | Czterzi |
| Russian | Shatiry |
| Hungarian | Negy[471] |

The sound shifts involved for each instance of every numeral is then analyzed; e.g.:

. . . the number *four* has two alterations in the *Welsh;* the *k,* which is always put for *ch,* in the *Gomerian* language, being changed, in the *Welsh,* into *p,* and the *th* of *Irish* into *w.* This difference plainly indicates, that the *Irish ceathoir* was the original, in the very *Gomerian;* for, if we compare the *Welsh pedwar* with the *Greek tessares,* we shall easily see that both these are a deviation from the original *ceathoir* . . . the *Latin* . . . *quatuor* and *ceathoir* are the same word, the *q* and *ch* being both palatial characters . . . the *Greek* . . .

*tessares* derived only from *ceathoir* . . . by changing the initial *ch* into *t,* and the middle *th* into a double *s* . . .

The *Germans* made another change in the name of this number; for instead of the *ch,* or *q,* they make the initial letter a *v, vier,* which would sound, with the former, *chier,* or *quier.* Now, although in the *Magogian,* the root of this name, is *chathoir,* yet the *Irish* pronounce it as if it was a monosyllable, *chair,* and sometimes express the aspirate without the *t,* but in so soft a manner, as to make it seem but one syllable. . . . The *Dutch* have followed the *Germans,* in adopting the same word; and the *Saxons* have made it still rougher and stronger, by changing the *v* into an *f,* and pronounce it *feower,* from whom the *English* say *four.* The *Poles* appear to to have followed the same mode . . . *cz* being put in place of the original *chea,* or *qua* . . . but the *Poles* and *Hungarians* have deviated from the original much.[472]

This is followed by "Remarks on the names of the numerals of the *Asiatic* nations," preceded by another list of numerals; again those for "4" are given here.

| | |
|---|---|
| Bengalian | Charr |
| Persian | Char |
| Turkish | Dewet |
| Hebrew | Arbaa |
| Mallays | Ampat |
| Chinese | Suze[473] |

My reasons for introducing the name of the number of any of the *Asiatic* regions, when I am expressly pursuing the origin of the *European* languages only, are two; first, to shew that two of them are actually derived from the old *Scythian,* or *Magogian* names, which are the *Bengalian* and *Persian:* and, secondly, that the other four, the *Turkish, Hebrew, Malays* and *Chinese,* have not the least affinity to those original, nor to one another.[474]

[In the word for "4"] the *ch* . . . in the *Magogian,* is always pronounced like the . . . *English k;* whereas, the *Persians* and *Indians* pronounce them as we do in *chain.*[475]

Satisfied that he had proved his thesis, Parsons posed a problem that many of the nineteenth century philologists were to try to solve.

The reader might thus be led to know the origin of most nations, by tracing words to different places, and thereby find out the source of their languages also, which would be a very desirable and useful research for the learned.[476]

## Marsden

William Marsden (1754–1836) was another linguist who interested himself in sound shifts, this time in connection with Malayo-Polynesian languages.

[After giving comparative word lists, he continues:] For tracing the connexion of the words of the accompanying specimens, it is ncessary to remark, that there are several letters or simple sounds, which, though to our organs they seem distinct, are often confounded and transposed in rude languages. These are probably such as are produced by conformations of the mouth nearly similar, and a difference in such sounds, on a comparison of words, is not to be esteemed essential, though it may occasion a considerable alteration, if two or more happen to concur in the same. The change is still greater when a second corruption of the same letter takes place, on a word's passing into a third language; though to a person tolerably versed in them there is not a doubt of the derivation and analogy. For example, *Eedong,* in Malays, became *Eerong* in Javanese and *Oorong* in the Madagascar language: and *Duo* in Malays, is in Otaheitian R*ooa,* in Savuan R*ooe* and in Mongeraye *Loolaye.* The letters usually confounded are L and R, P and F, D and T, D and R, B and V, Oo and R; besides many others in which the articulation is less marked.[477]

## Monboddo

As a consequence of his theory of Egypt as the center of universal diffusion, James Burnett, Lord Monboddo (1714–99), was led to the belief that the language of the Old World, at least, belonged to a single linguistic stock.

I think it probable, that all the languages spoken in Europe, all Asia, if you will, and some part of Africa, are dialects on one parent-language, which probably was invented in Egypt.[478]

. . . there are three marks of affinity betwixt languages. The *first* is, The similarity of the sound of words signifying the same thing in both languages; *2dly,* The similarity of termination in particular; and, *lastly,* Similarity of flection, in forming cases, genders, numbers, and tenses. If the words have only the first kind of resemblance, the connection betwixt the two languages is remote. . . . But, if besides this first mark, the two languages have likewise the second, the connection becomes much greater. . . . But if the third mark of resemblance likewise concurs, if the flection be the same, or nearly the same, then we pronounce, without hesitation, that they are either the same language, or dialects of the same language very akin to one another.[479]

. . . the Greek, Latin, Teutonic or Gothic, Hebrew or Phoenician, were originally the same language.[480]

As to the Oriental languages, it is certain that the Hebrew, Phoenician, Syriac, Chaldaic, and Arabic, have all such an affinity, that either one of them must be the parent language of the rest, or they must be all children of some common parent.[481]

Now it appears to me evident, that . . . the Teutonic, the Persian, the Greek, and its most ancient dialect the Latin[482] . . . must have come off from the parent-stock at times so different.[483]

. . . we can trace arts from Egypt into India; and from India, according to our Arabian travellers, the Chinese got their religion and laws, and we may presume likewise their language.[484]

It was on this a priori basis, rather than as a result of empirical investigation, that he anticipated Jones's discovery of the affinity between Sanskrit and the other Indo-European languages. In 1774 he stated:

[There is a] probability . . . of a resemblance . . . betwixt the Bramin and Greek languages, which I think the more likely that I am persuaded both Indians and Greeks got their language, and all their other arts, from the same parent-country, viz. Egypt.[485]

In 1787, but before he had heard of Jones's conclusions, he gave some evidence for his thesis.

. . . from what we hear of the Indian Sanscrit language . . . we are sure that, in some respects, it resembles very much the Greek, particularly in the verbs, of which the Sanscrit has a class that are conjugated in the same manner as the verbs in -$\mu\iota$ in Greek.[486]

[To this statement he gives the following note:] This curious fact is averred by a gentleman from India, whom I know, Mr Brassey.[487]

After reading a reprint of Jones's paper, which the author had sent him, he replied:

... the most curious thing concerning this language [i.e., Sanskrit] ... is its affinity with the Greek, and the most ancient dialect of Greek, the Latin. This affinity is so great that either the Greek is a dialect of the Sanscrit, or they are both dialects of the same parent language. ... Now the question is this: where, or whence, did the Greeks learn this language? They certainly did not go to India to learn it, nor did the Indians come to them. And if so, I can find no other place where they could have learned it except Egypt, where we know they learned all their arts and sciences, and—as it appears—language among other arts. So that here we have discovered that the ancient language of Egypt was Sanscrit.[488]

## Jones

In 1786, William Jones (1746–94) showed that Sankrit belonged to the Indo-European linguistic stock, along with Greek, Latin, Germanic, Celtic, and Persian.

The *Sanscrit* language, whatever be its antiquity, is of a wonderful structure; more perfect than the *Greek,* more copious than the *Latin,* and more exquisitely refined than either, yet bearing to both of them a stronger affinity, both in the roots of verbs and in the forms of grammar, than could possibly have been produced by accident; so strong, indeed, that no philologer could examine them all three, without believing them to have sprung from some common source, which, perhaps, no longer exists: there is a similar reason, though not quite so forcible, for supposing that both the *Gothick* and the *Celtick,* though blended with a very different idiom, had the same origin with the *Sanscrit;* and the old *Persian* might be added to the same family.[489]

He was also interested in the Semitic-Hamitic stock.

That the written *Abyssinian* language, which we call *Ethiopick,* is a dialect of old *Chaeldean,* and a sister of *Arabick* and *Hebrew,* we know with certainty, not only from the great multitude of identical words, but (which is a far stronger proof) from the similar grammatical arrangement of the several idoms.[490]

## Gibbon

Edward Gibbon (1737–94) believed in the great antiquity of Gaelic.

Irish Language—It is believed that Irish was the ancient language of the Scythians. ... One must agree that Irish differs greatly from Gallic, from Bas Breton, and from Basque; but it is not less certain that here is found a number of words, which, if they are not taken from Latin, come from the same source, that is to say, from Celtic. I have come across in Irish many terms of the language of the people of Pays de Vaud; words which I have not found in the dictionaries of the three other dialects nor in Germanic. One proof of the antiquity of Irish is that its letters are purely Greek letters; and as there were only seventeen of them, it was necessary that they had been received before the Trojan war, since it was only during that famous siege that Palamedes added to the Greek alphabet the four letters which have been attributed to them; and of these four the Irish alphabet has none, no more than of the four of which Simonides was the inventor. It follows that it is the alphabet of Cadmus which the inhabitants of Ireland received, and not the Ionian alphabet adopted by all of Greece. The Irish have added to this the "f" only, and as they write it in the Latin and not as "ρ", it is probable that they did not adopt it until after the emperor Claudian had it added to the Latin alphabet. A language which can only be that of Cadmus is assuredly of the greatest antiquity and is preserved more completely than any other which is known. In regard to its abundance, the author of the Dictionary in fact states in its preface that of all the dead or living languages none is richer in words nor more elegant in expression than Irish.[491]

## Doig

David Doig (1719–1800) wrote a treatise on the languages of the world.

If we call all the different dialects of the various nations that now inhabit the known earth, languages, the number is truly great; and vain would be his ambition who should attempt to learn them, though but imperfectly. We will begin with naming the principal of them: There are four, which may be called original or mother-languages, and which seem to have given birth to all that are now spoken in Europe. These are the *Latin, Celtic, Gothic,* and *Sclavonian.* It will not, however, be imagined, from the term *original* given to these languages, that we believe them to have come down to us, without any alteration, from the confusion of tongues at the building of the tower of Babel. We have repeatedly declared our opinion, that there is but one truly original language, from which all others are derivatives variously modified.* The four languages just mentioned are original only as being the immediate parents of those which are now spoken in Europe.

I.   From the *Latin* came,
1. The Portuguese.
2. Spanish.
3. French.
4. Italian.
    From the *Celtic,*
5. The Erse . . .
6. The Welsh.
7. The Irish.
8. Basse-Bretagne.
    From the *Gothic,*
9. The German.
10. The Low Saxon or Low German.
11. The Dutch.
12. The English . . .
13. The Danish.
14. The Norwegian.
15. Swedish.
16. Icelandic.
    From the *Sclavonian,*
17. The Polonese.
18. The Lithuanian.
19. Bohemian.
20. Transylvanian.
21. Moravian.
22. The modern Vandalian . . .
23. The Croatian.
24. The language of the Calmucs and Cossacs.

* "Hebrew and Chaldean were originally spoken by the same family, and of course were the same between themselves, and were actually the first language upon earth."[492]

25. Thirty-two different dialects of nations who inhabit the north-eastern parts of Europe and Asia, and who are descended from the Tartars and Huno-Scythians.[493]

The languages of the other continents are merely listed; no attempt is made to establish relationships.[494] However, in an earlier part of the work Doig has pointed out some relationships.

. . . the Arabian language . . . is evidently one of the sister dialects of the Hebrew. Both, we imagine, were originally the same.[495]

[In discussing] the Chaldean, Phoenician, Ethiopian or Abyssinian, and Egyptian Languages . . . [he remarks:] there is a very strict connection and dialectical analogy among these languages.[496]

He saw the relationship between these latter languages and Hebrew and Arabic. However, he also believed in "the Egyptian origin of the Shanscrit."[497] Persian, too, provided difficulties:

. . . the oldest languages of Persia were Chaldaic and Shanscrit: and . . . when they had ceased to be vernacular, the Pahlavi and Send were deduced from them respectively, and the Parsi either from the Zend, or immediately from the dialect of the Brahmins: but all had perhaps a mixture of Tartarian.[498]

Chinese was the greatest puzzle of all.

The language of the Chinese is totally different from those of all other nations, and bears very strong signatures of an original tongue.[499]

## Tooke

According to John Horne Tooke (1736–1812) language has two functions.

The first aim of Language was to *communicate* our thoughts: the second, to do it with *despatch*.[500]

Language was not rationally invented.

Language, it is true, is an Art. . . . But an art springing from necessity, and originally invented by artless men; who did not sit down like philosophers to invent.[501]

. . . there are only *two* sorts of words which are *necessary* for the communication of our thoughts. . . .
1. Noun, and
2. Verb.[502]

All other parts of speech are corruptions derived from these two.

As far as relates to . . . prepositions and conjunctions, I hope it is by this time pretty evident that, instead of *invention,* the *classes* of them spring from *corruption;* and that, in this respect, the Savage languages are upon an equal footing with the languages (as they are called) of *art,* except that the former are less corrupted: and that Savages have not only as *separate and distinct ideas* of those relations as we have, but that they have this advantage over us (an advantage in point of intelligibility, though it is a disadvantage in point of brevity), that they also *express* them separately and distinctly.[503]

He emphasized the importance of Gothic and Anglo-Saxon in English etymology.

I am persuaded that all future etymologists (and perhaps some philosophers) will acknowledge their obligation to me. . . .

They shall no more expose themselves by unnatural forced conceits to derive the

English and all other languages from the Greek or the Hebrew, or some imaginary primeval tongue. The Conjunctions of *every* language shall teach them whither to direct and where to stop their inquiries: for wherever the evident meaning and origin of the conjunctions of any language can be found, there is the certain source of the whole.[504]

[He attempted to] lead the way to their better acquaintance with the parent language, which ought long ago to have made a part of the education of our youth. And I flatter myself that one of the consequences of my present inquiry will be, to facilitate and abridge the tedious and mistaken method of instruction which had too long continued in our seminaries: the time which is at present allotted to Latin and Greek, being amply sufficient for the acquirement also of French, Italian, Anglo-Saxon, Dutch, German, Danish and Swedish. Which will not seem at all extraordinary, when it is considered that the five last mentioned (together with English) are little more than different dialects of one and the same language.[505]

However, he exaggerated the importance of earlier Germanic languages.

But it is a great mistake, into which both the Italian and Latin etymologists have fallen, to suppose that all the Italian must be found in the Latin, and all the Latin in the Greek: for the fact is otherwise. The bulk and foundation of the Latin language is Greek: but great part of the Latin is the language of our Northern ancestors, grafted upon the Greek. And to our Northern language the etymologist must go, for that part of the Latin which the Greek will not furnish: and there, without any twisting or turning or ridiculous forcing and torturing of words, he will easily and clearly find it. We want therefore the testimony of no historians to conclude that the founders of the Roman state and of the Latin tongue came not from Asia, but from the North of Europe. For the language cannot lye. And from the language of every nation we may with certainty collect its origin. In the same manner . . . all the Italian, which cannot be easily shewn to be Latin, can be easily shewn to be our Northern language.[506]

## Beattie

James Beattie (1735–1803) made a passing remark on some of the Indo-European languages.

Greek and Latin resemble one another not a little: whence it is probable, that both were derived from some primitive tongue more ancient than either. The modern languages of France, Spain, Italy, and Portugal, resemble one another very much; and we know they are in a great measure derived from the ancient Latin.[507]

## Others

Edward Lhuyd (1660–1709) studied the Celtic languages,[508] and Johan Ihre (1707–80) the Germanic.[509] William Drake (1723–1801), as a result of a comparison of English and Gothic, came to the conclusion that "the English language is purely Teutonick, radically derived from the Gothick and Saxon, the universal parents of most of the Northern European tongues."[510]

Peter Simon Pallas' (1741–1811) *Sravnitelniye slovari*[511] is a compilation of word lists from various European and Asiatic languages; the second edition,[512] edited by T. J. von Mirijevo, also includes languages from Africa and the Americas.

# V

# EIGHTEENTH CENTURY SOCIAL ANTHROPOLOGY:
## MAN'S NATURE

## MAN'S NATURE

IN THE EIGHTEENTH century much consideration was given to the analysis of human nature, an interest which was reflected in the novels of Richardson and Austen. Most students emphasized man's sociality, and some gave it the status of an instinct.

A point of great interest at this time was the analysis of conscience. There were three major schools of thought. The first, led by Shaftesbury, considered conscience to be a primitive faculty. The other two reduced it to simpler elements; Gay and his followers, to association; Hume, Smith, and others, to sympathy.

### Toland

John Toland (1670–1722) made much of the constraint of culture.

You greatly complain, MADAM, that you are still a Captive to several Prejudices; and I wonder more how you came to get rid of so many.[1]

. . . every one with whom he [i.e., the infant] has afterwards to do, endeavours to deprave his Reason from the very beginning; so that not remembering when, or where, or how he came by many of his Notion, he's tempted to believe that they proceed from Nature it self, and is astonish'd to find that any shou'd call the Truth of 'em in question.[2]

When we come abroad into the World, we find all those Errors to be in so high a Credit, that every one is gaz'd on as a Monster, who is out of this universal Mode: or if by some lucky chance we shou'd happen to be undeceiv'd, yet the prevailing Power of Interest will make us hypocritically (of, if you please, prudently) to pretend the contrary, for fear of losing our Fortunes, Quiet, Reputation, or Lives. This confirms others in their Prejudices by our example, as much as if we were deceiv'd our selves; for knowing nothing of our Minds but by our outward Actions, which appear so like their own, they judg us to be of the same Persuasion.[3]

But no sort of Prejudices stick closer to us, or are harder to be eradicated, than those of the Society wherein we live and had our Education. This holds equally true of their civil Customs and religious Rites, of their Notions and Practices.[4]

Thus the Body of the People in all Places of the World do greedily imbibe whatever they are taught to imitate or to respect from their Infancy, and without further Evidence are ready to die for the Truth of it in old Age.[5]

. . . our Prejudices govern us.[6]

He derived religion from worship of the dead.

It seems evident from the remotest Monuments of Learning, that all Superstition originally related to the Worship of the Dead, being principally deriv'd from Funeral Rites.[7]

The People begun it [i.e., the idea of immortality], from them their Children learnt it, at last it became a part of all mens Education (as it happens to Opinions generally reciv'd) and so the Learned themselves believ'd it before they had a reason for it. 'Tis true, the Vulgar, who are not us'd to Reflections, embrac'd to ever afterwards (as they do still) upon Trust or from Authority: but not so with the Philosophers, who offer'd many probable Arguments for the Soul's separate Existence and eternal Duration.[8]

It will not . . . appear unlikely that Men very early learnt to have the same Conceptions of God himself, which they had before of their earthly Princes: and after thus fancying him mutable, jealous, revengeful, and arbitrary, they next endeavour'd to procure his Favor much after the same manner that they made their court to those who pretended to be his Representatives or Lieutenants, nay to be Gods themselves, or to be descended of heavenly Parentage, as the antient Monarchs us'd to do.[9]

## Shaftesbury

Anthony Ashley Cooper, Earl of Shaftesbury (1671–1713), made a shrewd defense of man's sociality against Hobbes.

For to understand the manners and constitutions of men in common, 'tis necessary to study man in particular, and know the creature as he is in himself, before we consider him in company, as he is interested in the State, or joined to any city or community.[10]

That which is of original and pure nature, nothing beside contrary habit and custom (a second nature) is able to displace.[11]

The young of most other kinds . . . are instantly helpful to themselves, sensible, vigorous, know to shun danger and seek their good. A human infant is of all the most helpless, weak, infirm. And wherefore should it not have been thus ordered? Where is the loss in such a species? Or what is man the worse for this defect, amidst such large supplies? Does not this defect engage him more strongly to society, and force him to own that he is purposely, not by accident, made rational and sociable; and can no otherwise increase or subsist than in that social intercourse and community which is his natural state? Is not both conjugal affection and natural affection to parents, duty to magistrates, love of a common city, community, or country, with the other duties and social parts of life, deduced from hence and founded in these very wants?[12]

. . . we may with justice surely place it as a principle, "That if anything be natural, in any creature or any kind, 'tis that which is preservative of the kind itself, and conducing to its welfare and support." If in original and pure nature it be wrong to break a promise, or be treacherous, 'tis as truly wrong to be in any respect inhuman, or any way wanting in our natural part towards human kind. If eating and drinking be nautral, herding is so too. If any appetite or sense be natural, the sense of fellowship is the same. If there be anything of nature in that affection which is between the sexes, the affection is certainly as natural towards the consequent offspring; and so again between the offspring themselves, as kindred and companions, bred under the same discipline and economy. And thus a clan or tribe is gradually formed; a public is recognised; and besides the pleasure found in social entertainment, language, and discourse, there is so apparent a necessity for continuing this good correspondency and union, that to have no sense or feeling of this kind, no love of country, community, or any thing in common, would be the same as to be insensible even of the plainest means of self-preservation, and most necessary condition of self-enjoyment.

How the wit of man should so puzzle this cause as to make civil government and society appear a kind of invention and creature of art, I know not. For my own part, methinks, this herding principle, and associating inclination, is seen so natural and strong in most men, that we might readily affirm 'twas even from the violence of this passion that so much disorder arose in the general society of mankind.[13]

'Tis ridiculous to say there is any obligation on man to act sociably or honestly in a formed government, and not in that which is commonly called the state of nature. For, to speak in the fashionable language of our modern philosophy: "Society being founded on a compact, the surrender made of every man's private unlimited right, into the hands of the majority, or such as the majority should appoint, was of free choice, and by a promise." Now the promise itself was made in the state of nature: and that which could make a promise obligatory in the state of nature, must make all other acts of humanity as much our real duty and natural part. Thus faith, justice, honesty, and virtue, must have been as early as the state of nature, or they could never have been at all. The civil union, or confederacy, could never make right or wrong, if they subsisted not before. He who was free to any villiany before his contract, will and ought to make as free with his con- tract when he sees fit. The natural knave has the same reason to be a civil one, and may dispence with his politic capacity as oft as he sees occasion. 'Tis only his word stands in his way. . . . A man is obliged to keep his word. Why? Because he has given his word to keep it. . . . Is not this a notable account of the original of moral justice, and the rise of civil government and allegiance.[14]

First, he supported the gregarious theory of society;[15] he spoke of "how natural an affection there is towards government and order among mankind."[16]

All men have naturally their share of this combining principle.[17]

A public spirit can come only from a social feeling or sense of partnership with human kind.[18]

Second, he believed in the existence of a "social or natural affection."[19]

And for real society, there could be none between such as had no other sense than that of private good.[20]

You have heard it, my friend, as a common saying, that interest governs the world. But, I believe, whoever looks narrowly into the affairs of it will find that passion, humour, caprice, zeal, faction, and a thousand other springs, which are counter to self-interest, have as considerable a part in the movements of this machine. There are more wheels and counterpoises in this engine than are easily imagined.[21]

[Man's sociality is fundamental] since often through this affection, and for the sake of the person beloved, the greatest hardships in the world have been submitted to, and even death itself voluntarily embraced without any expected compensation. For where should the ground of such an expectation lie? Not here in this world, surely; for death puts an end to all. Not yet hereafter, in any other; for who has ever thought of providing a heaven of future recompense for the suffering virtue of lovers?[22]

Philosophers indeed there have been that denied man to have any such instinct as that which led to the good of society or his fellows, and consequently dissuaded him from the public service and from obeying such unnatural motions as these, if he found any such in himself. And this for certain is most true, that if man be not by nature sociable, he is the foolishest creature on earth to make society or the public the least part of his real care or concern. But if when he tries to shake off this principle, he has either no success or makes things worse with him than before, it is a shrewd presumption of what he is *born to*.[23]

. . . a life without natural affection, friendship, or sociableness would be found a wretched one were it to be tried.[24]

It has already been shown, that in the passions and affections of particular creatures there is a constant relation to the interests of a species or common nature. This has been demonstrated in the case of natural affection, parental kindness, zeal for posterity, concern for the propagation and nurture of the young, love of fellowship and company, compassion, mutual succour, and the rest of this kind. Nor will any one deny that this affection of a creature towards the good of the species or common nature is as proper and natural to him as it is to any organ, part, or member of an animal body, or mere vegetable, to work in its known course and regular way of growth. 'Tis not more natural for the stomach to digest, the lungs to breathe, the glands to separate juices, or other entrails to perform their several offices, however they may by particular impediments be sometimes disordered or obstructed in their operation.[25]

His third argument for man's sociality was "his natural moral sense,"[26] i.e., his instinctive conscience.[27]

[Man has a] natural sense of right and wrong.[28]

Sense of right and wrong therefore being as natural to us as natural affection itself, and being a first principle in our constitution and make, there is no speculative opinion, persuasion, or belief, which is capable immediately or directly to exclude or destroy it.[29]

## Hutcheson

Francis Hutcheson (1694–1746) was a follower of Shaftesbury. He proposed two theses in "An inquiry concerning the original of our ideas of virtue or moral good":[30]

'I. That some Actions have to Men an *immediate Goodness;*' or, 'that by a *superior Sense,* which I call a *Moral one,* we perceive Pleasure in the Contemplation of such Actions in others, and are determin'd to love the Agent, (and much more do we perceive Pleasure in being conscious of having done such Actions our selves) without any View of further *natural Advantage* from them.'

II. It may perhaps also appear, 'That what excites us to these Actions which we call *Virtuous,* is not an Intention to obtain even this *sensible Pleasure;* much less the *future Rewards* from Sanctions of Laws, or any other *natural Good,* which may be the Consequence of the *virtuous* Action; but an entirely different Principle of Action from Interest or Self-Love.'[31]

[I. The existence of a "moral sense."] *Virtue* is not pursu'd from the *Interest* or *Self-love* of the *Pursuer,* or any Motives of his own Advantage.[32]

We must then certainly have other Perceptions of *moral Actions* than those of *Advantage:* And that power of receiving these Perceptions may be call'd a MORAL SENSE, since the Definition agrees to it, *viz. a Determination of the Mind, to receive any Idea from the Presence of an Object which occurs to us, independently of our Will.*[33]

But *Virtue* it self, or *good Dispositions* of Mind, are not directly taught, or produc'd by *Instruction;* but are the *Effect* of the *great* AUTHOR of all things, who forms our *Nature* for them.[34]

It remains then, 'That . . . the AUTHOR of *Nature* . . . has given us a MORAL SENSE, to direct our Actions, and to give us still *nobler Pleasures;* so that while we are only intending the *Good* of others, we undesignedly promote our own greatest *private Good*.'[35]

Our *Sense* of *Virtue* generally leads us exactly enough according to our Opinions; and therefore the absurd Practices which prevail in the World, are much better Arguments that Men have no *Reason*, than that they have no *moral Sense* of Beauty in *Actions*.[36]

[II. The existence of "benevolence":] let us next establish the *true one* [i.e., "Spring of virtuous Actions"], *viz. some Determination of our Nature to study the Good of others; or some Instinct, antecedent to all Reason from Interest, which influences us to the Love of others;* even as the *moral Sense* above suppos'd, determines us to *approve* the Actions which flow from *this Love* in our selves or others.[37]

. . . there is a *universal Determination* to *Benevolence* in *Mankind,* even toward the most distant parts of the Species.[38]

*This Love* makes them *Parts* of our selves.[39]

. . . there is something in Actions which is apprehended *absolutely good;* and this is *Benevolence,* or a Tendency to the *publick natural Happiness* of *rational Agents*.[40]

[Therefore] Men have, by NATURE, a *moral Sense of Goodness* in Actions, and . . . they are capable of *disinterested Love*.[41]

## Butler

Joseph Butler (1692–1752), the greatest member of the Shaftesbury school, particularly directed his attack against Hobbes and Mandeville.

. . . it may not be amiss to give the reader the whole argument here in one view.

Mankind has various instincts and principles of action, as brute creatures have; some leading most directly and immediately to the good of the community, and some most directly to private good.

Man has several which brutes have not; particularly reflection or conscience, an approbation of some principles or actions, and disapprobation of others.

Brutes obey their instincts or principles of action, according to certain rules; suppose the constitution of their body, and the objects around them.

The generality of mankind also obey their instincts and principles, all of them; those propensions we call good, as well as the bad, according to the same rules; namely, the constitution of their body, and the external circumstances which they are in. (Therefore it is not a true representation of mankind to affirm, that they are wholly governed by self-love, the love of power and sensual appetites: since, as on the one hand they are often actuated by these, without any regard to right or wrong; so on the other it is manifest fact, that the same persons, the generality, are frequently influenced by friendship, compassion, gratitude; and even a general abhorrence of what is base, and liking of what is fair and just, takes its turn amongst the other motives of action] . . .

But that is not a complete account of man's nature. Somewhat further must be brought in to give us an adequate notion of it; namely, that one of those principles of action, conscience or reflection, compared with the rest as they all stand together in the nature of man, plainly bears upon it marks of authority over all the rest, and claims the absolute direction of them all, to allow or forbid gratification: a disapprobation of reflection being in itself a principle manifestly superior to a mere propension.[42]

. . . the comparison will be between the nature of man as respecting self, and tending to private good, his own preservation and happiness; and the nature of man as having respect to society, and tending to promote public good, the happiness of that society. These ends do indeed perfectly coincide; and to aim at public and private good are so far from being inconsistent, that they mutually promote each other.*[45]

From this review and comparison of the nature of man as respecting self, and as respecting society, it will plainly appear, that there are as real and the same kind of indications in human nature, that we were made for society and to do good to our fellow-creatures; as that we were intended to take care of our own life and health and private good: and that the same objections lie against one of these assertions, as against the others. For,

First, There is a natural principle of *benevolence* in man,[46] which is in some degree to *society*, what *self-love* is to the *individual*. And if there be in mankind any disposition to friendship; if there be any such thing as compassion, for compassion is momentary love; if there be any such things as the paternal or filial affections; if there be any affection in human nature, the object and end of which is the good of another; this is itself benevolence, or the love of another. Be it ever so short, be it in ever so low a degree, or ever so unhappily confined; it proves the assertion, and points out what we were designed for, as really as though it were in a higher degree and more extensive. I must however remind you that though benevolence and self-love are different; though the former tends most directly to public good, and the latter to private: yet they are so perfectly coincident, that the greatest satisfactions to ourselves depend upon our having benevolence in a due degree; and that self-love is one chief security of our right behaviour towards society. It may be added, that their mutual coinciding, so that we can scarce promote one without the other, is equally a proof that we were made for both.

Secondly, This will further appear, from observing that the *several passions and affections,* which are distinct both from benevolence and self-love, do in general contribute and lead us to *public* good as really as to *private*. . . . It is enough to the present argument, that desire of esteem from others, contempt and esteem of them, love of society as distinct from affection to the good of it; indignation against successful vice, that these are public affections or passions; have an immediate respect to others, naturally lead us to regulate our behaviour in such a manner as will be of service to our fellow-creatures. If any of these may be considered likewise as private affections, as tending to private good; this does not hinder them from being public affections too, or destroy the good influence of them upon society, and their tendency to public good. . . . Thus sum is, men have various appetites, passions, and particular affections, quite distinct both from self-love and from benevolence: all of these have a tendency to promote both public and private good, and may be considered as respecting others and ourselves equally and in common: but some of them seem most immediately to respect others, or tend to public good; others of them most immediately to respect self, or tend to private good: as the former are not benevolence, so the latter are not self-love: neither sort are instances of our love either to ourselves or others; but only instances of our Maker's care and love both of the individual and the species, and proofs that He intended we should be instruments of good to each other, as well as that we should be so to ourselves.

Thirdly, There is a principle of reflection in men, by which they distinguish between,

---

* "Every man is to be considered in two capacities, the private and public; as designed to pursue his own interest, and likewise to contribute to the good of others. Whoever will consider, may see, that in general there is no contrariety between these; but that from the original constitution of man, and the circumstances he is placed in, they perfectly coincide, and mutually carry on each other. But, amongst the great variety of affections or principles of action in our nature, some in their primary attention and design seem to belong to the single or private, others to the public or social capacity."[43]

"That there are some particular pursuits or actions concerning which we cannot determine how far they are owing to one, and how far to the other, proceeds from this, that the two principles are frequently mixed together, and run up into each other."[44]

approve and disapprove their own actions. We are plainly constituted such sort of creatures as to reflect upon our own nature. The mind can take a view of what passes within
itself, its propensions, aversions, passions, affections, as respecting such objects, and in
such degrees; and of the several actions consequent thereupon. In this survey it approves
of one, disapproves of another, and towards a third is affected in neither of these ways,
but is quite indifferent. This principle in man, by which he approves or disapproves his
heart, temper, and actions, is conscience. . . . And that this faculty tends to restrain men
from doing mischief to each other, and leads them to do good, is too manifest to need
being insisted upon. . . . There is therefore this principle of reflection or conscience in
mankind. It is needless to compare the respect it has to private good, with the respect
it has to public; since it plainly tends as much to the latter as to the former, and is commonly thought to tend chiefly to the latter. . . .

From this comparison of benevolence and self-love, of our public and private affections, of the courses of life they lead to, and of the principle of reflection or conscience
as respecting each of them it is as manifest, that we were made for society, and to promote
the happiness of it; as that we were intended to take care of our own life, and health,
and private good.

And from this whole review must be given a different draught of human nature from
what we are often presented with. Mankind are by nature so closely united, there is such
a correspondence between the inward sensations of one man and those of another, that
disgrace is as much avoided as bodily pain, and to be the object of esteem and love as
much desired as any external goods: and in many particular cases, persons are carried on
to do good to others, as the end their affection tends to and rests in; and manifest that they
find real satisfaction and enjoyment in this course of behaviour. There is such a natural
principle of attraction in man towards man, that having trod the same tract of land, having
breathed in the same climate, barely having been born in the same artificial district or
division, becomes the occasion of contracting acquaintances and familiarities many years
after: for anything may serve the purpose. Thus relations merely nominal are sought and
invented, not by governors, but by the lowest of the people; which are found sufficient
to hold mankind together in little fraternities and copartnerships: weak ties indeed, and
what may afford fund enough for ridicule, if they are absurdly considered as the real
principles of that union: but they are in truth merely the occasions, as anything may be
of anything, upon which our nature carries us on according to its own previous bent
and bias; which occasions therefore would be nothing at all, were there not this prior
disposition and bias of nature. Men are so much one body, that in a peculiar manner they
feel for each other, sudden danger, resentment, honour, prosperity, distress; one or
another, or all of these, from the social nature in general, from benevolence, upon the
occasion of natural relation, acquaintance, protection, dependence; each of these being
distinct cements of society. And therefore to have no restraint from, no regard to others
in our behaviour, is the speculative absurdity of considering ourselves as single and independent, as having nothing in our nature which has respect to our fellow-creatures,
reduced to action and practice. And this is the same absurdity, as to suppose a hand, or
any part to have no natural respect to any other, or to the whole body.[47]

The sum of the whole is plainly this. The nature of man considered in his single capacity, and with respect only to the present world, is adapted and leads him to attain the
greatest happiness he can for himself in the present world. The nature of man considered
in his public or social capacity leads him to a right behaviour in society, to that course of
life which we call virtue. Men follow or obey their nature in both these capacities and
respects to a certain degree, but not entirely: their actions do not come up to the whole

of what their nature leads them to in either of these capacities or respects: and they often violate their nature in both. *I.e.* as they neglect the duties they owe to their fellow-creatures, to which their nature leads them; and are injurious, to which their nature is abhorrent: so there is a manifest negligence in men of their real happiness or interest in the present world, when that interest is inconsistent with a present gratification; for the sake of which they negligently, nay, even knowingly, are the authors and instruments of their own misery and ruin. Thus they are as often unjust to themselves as to others, and for the most part are equally so to both by the same actions.[48]

## Gay

To John Gay (1699–1745) the "moral sense" and "benevolence" were not instinctive, but arose through the association of ideas.

... though it be necessary in order to solve the principal actions of human life to suppose a moral sense (or what is signified by that name) and also publick affections; yet I deny that this moral sense, or these public affections, are innate or implanted in us. They are acquired either from our own observation or the imitation of others.[49]

There is one thing more to be observed . . . and that is, that we do not always (and perhaps not for the most part) make this association ourselves, but learn it from others: i.e. we annex pleasure or pain to certain things or actions because we see others do it, and acquire principles of action by imitating those whom we admire, or whose esteem we would procure: Hence the son too often inherits both the vices and party of his father, as well as his estate: Hence national virtues and vices, dispositions and opinions: And from hence we may observe how easy it is to account for what its generally call'd the prejudice of education; how soon we catch the temper and affections of those whom we daily converse with; how almost insensibly we are taught to love, admire or hate; to be grateful, generous, compassionate or cruel, &c.[50]

We first perceive or imagine some real good, i.e. fitness to promote our natural happiness, in those things which we love and approve of. Hence . . . we annex pleasure to those things. Hence those things and pleasure are so tied together and associated in our minds, that one cannot present itself, but the other will occur. And the association remains even after that which at first gave them the connection is quite forgot, or perhaps does not exist, but the contrary.[51]

Ambition is a desire of being esteemed. Hence a desire of being thought an object of esteem; hence of being an object of esteem; hence of doing laudable, i.e. useful actions . . . The title to the esteem of others, which ariseth from any meritorious action, is called honour. The pleasure arising from honour being paid to us, i.e. from others acknowledging that we are entitled to their esteem, is without a name. Modesty is the fear of losing esteem. The uneasiness or passion which ariseth from a sense that we have lost it, is called shame. So that ambition, and all those other passions and affections belonging to it, together with shame, arise from the esteem of others: which is the reason why this tribe of affections operate more strongly on us than any other, viz. because we perceive that as our happiness is chiefly dependent on the behaviour of others, so we perceive also that this behaviour is dependent on the esteem which others have conceived of us; and consequently that our acquiring or losing esteem, is in effect acquiring or losing happiness, and in the highest degree.[52]

## Inquiry

John Gay's analysis of conscience was followed by the anonymous author of

*An Inquiry into the Origin of Human Appetites and Affections, Shewing How Each Arises from Association* (1747).[53]

All the writers who have hitherto obliged the world, either with set treatises, or occasional essays, upon ethics, have, to a man, taken for granted, that the passions, or to speak more properly, the affections and dispositions of the mind, consequent upon, and taking their rise from the passions, or *original sensations* of the soul, were implanted there by the great Author of our beings.[54]

The same arguments, which the great Mr. Locke made use of, in order to prove there were no innate ideas, will, methinks, hold full as strong, and conclude with equal force against all *implanted* appetites whatever.[55]

To prevent all mistakes about the signification of the term instinct, it is proper to observe, once for all, as a matter of fact generally acknowledged, that every one of the human species is born with an implanted sense, instinct, or determination of nature (if this be more expressive than the other) leading it to seek and pursue such things as are necessary to its preservation, and to refuse and avoid such as are destructive to it*. . . . A child, for instance, is furnished with a sharp, impulsive instinct that will not suffer its nurse to forget its wants, which, in all cases, it proclaims by tears; a language, as it is rightly adapted to, so it is constantly used, in the tender years of infancy. Such instincts therefore I am so far from denying man to be possessed of at the time of his birth, that on the contrary they are both affirmed and maintained to be of such absolute necessity, that without them he could not survive many minutes in the world after his first entrance into it. It is the innateness of moral principles, or the natural determinations of will only, that, it is presumed, ought not to be admitted, or, that the mind should be pleased with some certain forms or kinds of acting, and displeased with others, antecedent to all instruction and information about them, and separate from all reflection on their necessary or probable tendencies to our happiness or misery, when upon enquiry into their rise and formation, or the particular time when, and the manner in which, they first began to operate, it is apprehended they will appear to be no other than certain associations of ideas, which we either make ourselves, or learn of others.[57]

. . . the whole tribe of human appetites and affections . . . seem to be no other than certain associations, which we form ourselves or learn from others, according to the particular course of life in which we are engaged, and in conformity to the situation we have been in.[58]

If moral principles, or determination of will, either to, or from action, were natural and therefore necessary, whence could arise such a difference and contrareity amongst them in different nations, or in the same nation at different junctures or periods of time?[59]

. . . by careful enquiry into the nature of the mind's furniture, and the various steps she takes in acquiring it, we find, that children are absolutely indifferent as to any moral form or species of action, till such times as they become acquainted with the different tendencies which different actions beat to human happiness or misery; and are taught to love and approve one sort of conduct, and to disapprove and dislike the contrary. This is plainly discernable by one who attends to that progress the human mind (if rightly

---

* ". . . approbation and disapproabation . . . is originally founded on a sense of private, personal happiness, though we afterwards approve and disapprove *characters,* love and hate *moral representations, virtuous* and *vicious forms,* and *certain species of public good or ill,* without any respect had to or connecting them with our happiness, which is in no ways concerned in exciting one or the other. . . . Whence we gather, that though no affection of any kind can originally arise from any other source than that of self-love, yet may we have the *desire of the happiness of others, without conceiving such happiness as the means of ours.*"[56]

taken care of) is continually making from its infancy, through the several intermediate stages of childhood and youth, up to mature life. Their young and tender minds can take in any sort of impressions, in whatever manner offered and communicated to them, whether from external objects, or by rational agents, and may be fashioned for virtue and vice just as their instructors please. . . . And in consequence of this pliableness of children's minds with regard to what is proposed to them, do we find such different and contrary approbations of moral characters in the world, and that mankind are so variously affected with the contemplation of them.[60]

From this difference in our approbation and disapprobation of moral characters, it is but a reasonable conclusion that we would draw, viz. that those actions which we stile virtuous, or vicious, are liked and disliked, not by nature and constitution, but from association* and habit.[62]

. . . active habits, as they may be properly called, are formed by long use and custom, and follow, as an effect, from that particular course of life men have been trained up in. It seems, the more we use ourselves to any way of business, the more it influences our practice, becomes woven in by degrees into our frame, or what makes a part of it, and generally constitutes our character in life.[63]

Many of our associations are voluntary and from ourselves. . . .

Other associations (and those the most considerable as to number and importance) grow out of the circumstances we are placed in, and are the necessary effect of that particular course of life we are brought up to. Some also we learn from imitation, or by taking the acts of others as the rule and measure of our own, or are taught by those we are brought up amongst, and have had converse with. We walk, we ride, we lie down; we eat, dress, visit, &c. as the mode in fashion is; we hope, fear; we love, hate; we approve and disapprove, according as our education and training-up have been, and in obedience to the prevailing custom of the age.[64]

We are now also able to account for that *internal* obligation, we are by some supposed to live under to the constant practice of those virtues, independently on all consideration of their being accessory to our happiness, which, I will venture to affirm, is only the effect of an association made in favour of virtue in general, or some particular derivation from it. The fact is, we are so constituted, as to have it in our power to acquire certain associations, or rather those associations grow upon us as we advance in years, which laying a bias upon the mind, we cannot so far withdraw ourselves from it but that in going against it, or in not conforming to it, we condemn ourselves for so doing, or are uneasy upon it. And from this, and no other source, results the obligation they talk of.[65]

## Mandeville

The Shaftesbury school was opposed by Bernard Mandeville (1670?–1733), who examined human nature in the tradition of Machiavelli and Hobbes. He insisted upon an empirical rather than a moralistic approach.

[An] unbiass'd Method of searching after Truth and enquiring into the Nature of Man and Society, [is here] made use of.[66]

If we would know the World, we must look into it.[67]

. . . more useful Knowledge may be acquired from unwearied Observation, judicious

* "*By association I mean that power or faculty by which the joint appearance of two or more ideas frequently in the mind, is for the most part changing into a lasting and sometimes into an inseparable union.*"[61]

Experience, and arguingfrom Facts *a posteriori,* than from the haughty Attempts of entring into first Causes, and reasoning *a priori.*[68]

He saw the important role of emotions and the unconscious[69] in determining man's actions.

One of the greatest Reasons why so few People understand themselves, is, that most Writers are always teaching Men what they should be, and hardly ever trouble their Heads with telling them what they really are. As for my Part, without any Compliment to the Courteous Reader, or my self, I believe Man (besides Skin, Flesh, Bones, *&c.* that are obvious to the Eye) to be a compound of various Passions, that all of them, as they are provoked and come uppermost, govern him by turns, whether he will or no.*[71]

*Cleomenes.* . . . when a Man has . . . lived up to the strictest Rules of good Breeding for many Years, and has gain'd the Esteem of all that know him, when his noble and polite Manner is become habitual to him, it is possible, he may in time forget the Principle he set out with, and become ignorant, or at least insensible of the hidden Spring, that gives Life and Motion to all his Actions.

*Horatio.* . . . I am not satisfied . . . how a Man of so much Sense, Knowledge and Penetration, one that understands himself so entirely well, should be ignorant of his own Heart, and the Motives he acts from. What is it that induces you to believe this, besides the Possibility of his Forgetfulness?

*Cleo.* I have two Reasons for it, which I desire may be seriously consider'd. The first is, that in what relates to ourselves, especially our own Worth and Excellency, Pride blinds the Understanding in Men of Sense and great Parts as well as in others, and the greater Value we may reasonably set upon ourselves, the fitter we are to swallow the grossest Flatteries in spight of all our Knowledge and Abilities in other Matters: Witness *Alexander the Great,* whose vast Genius could not hinder him from doubting seriously, whether he was a God or not. My second Reason will prove to us; that, if the Person in question was capable of examining himself, it is yet highly improbable, that he would ever set about it: For it must be granted, that in order to search into ourselves, it is required, we should be willing as well as able; and we have all the Reason in the World to think, that there is nothing, which a very proud Man of such high Qualifications would avoid more carefully, than such an Enquiry: Because for all other Acts of Self-denial he is repaid in his darling Passion [i.e., pride]; but this alone is really mortifying, and the only Sacrifice of his Quiet, for which he can have no Equivalent† . . . Therefore enquiring within, and boldly searching into ones own Bosom, must be the most shocking Employment, that a Man can give his Mind to, whose greatest Pleasure consists in secretly admiring himself.[73]

All Human Creatures are sway'd and wholly govern'd by their Passions, whatever fine Notions we may flatter our Selves with; even those who act suitably to their Knowledge, and strictly follow the Dictates of their Reason, are not less compell'd so to do by some Passion or other, that sets them to Work, that others, who bide Defiance and act contrary to Both, and whom we call Slaves to their Passions.[74]

Christians . . . are not bad for want of Faith, or wishing to be Good; but because they are not able to overcome their Appetites and curb their Passions.[75]

For we are ever pushing our Reason which way soever we feel Passion to draw it, and

---

* "He was opposed to freedom of will in men because each of them was prompted to do what he did, and over rul'd by a predominant Passion."[70]

† After an analysis of motivation by Cleomenes, Horatio says: "I can't endure to see so much of my own Nakedness."[72]

Self-love pleads to all human Creatures for their different Views, still furnishing every individual with Arguments to justify their Inclinations.[76]

He argued against the existence of instinctive gregariousness[77] and benevolence.[78] To Mandeville, it was "self-love" which was fundamental.

What belongs to our Nature, all Men may justly be said to have actually or virtually in them at their Birth.[79]

It is not easy to determine what Instincts, Properties, or Capacities other Creatures are either possess'd or destitute of, when those Qualifications fall not under our Senses.[80]

I believe . . . that . . . ["Passions"] are born with us, and belong to our Nature, that some of them are in us, or at least the Seeds of them, before we perceive them.[81]

All Passions and Instincts in general were given to all Animals for some wise End, tending to the Preservation and Happiness either of themselves or their Species.[82]

. . . the Seeds of every Passion are innate to us and no body comes into the World without them.[83]

. . . and all Passions center in Self-Love.[84]

. . . whether it has been given to other Animals besides ourselves or not, it is certain, that in our own Species every individual Person likes himself better than he does any other.[85]

. . . it is plain to me, that it flows from Man's nature, always to mind to Flatter, Love, and take Delight in himself. . . The Care of Self-Preservation we are born with.[86]

There is nothing so universally sincere upon Earth, as the Love which all Creatures, that are capable of any, bear to themselves; and as there is no Love but what implies a Care to preserve the thing beloved, so there is nothing more sincere in any Creature than his Will, Wishes, and Endeavours to preserve himself. This is the Law of Nature, by which no Creature is endued with any Appetite or Passion but what either directly or indirectly tends to the Preservation either of himself or his Species.[87]

Let us examine a Man's whole Life, from his Infancy to his Grave, and see, which of the two seems to be most natural to him; a Desire of Superiority, and grasping every thing to himself; or a Tendency to act according to the reasonable Notions of Right and Wrong; and we shall find, that in his early Youth the first is very conspicuous; that nothing appears of the second before he has receive'd some Instructions, and that this latter will always have less Influence upon his Actions, the more uncivilis'd he remains: From whence I infer, that the Notions of Right and Wrong are acquired; for if they were as natural, or if they affected us, as early as the Opinion, or rather the Instinct we are born with, of taking every thing to be our own, no Child would ever cry for his eldest Brother's Playthings.[88]

. . . we meet with Thousands [of phenomena] every Day to convince us, that Man centers every thing in himself, and neither loves nor hates, but for his own Sake. Every Individual is a little World by itself, and all Creatures, as far as their Understanding and Abilities will let them, endeavour to make that Self happy: This in all of them is the continual Labour, and seems to be the whole Design of Life. Hence it follows, that in the Choice of Things Men must be determin'd by the Perception they have of Happiness; and no Person can commit or set about an Action, which at that then Present time seems not to be the best to him.[89]

All untaught Animals are only solicitous of pleasing themselves, and naturally follow the bent of their own Inclinations, without considering the good or harm that from their being pleased will accrue to others.[90]

What we do for our Friends and Kindred, we do partly for our selves.[91]

Our Love to what never was within the reach of our Senses is but poor and inconsiderable, and therefore Women have no Natural Love to what they bear; their Affection begins after Birth: what they feel before is the result of Reason, Education, and the Thoughts of Duty. Even when Children first are Born the Mother's Love is but weak, and increases with the Sensibility of the Child, and grows up to a prodigious height, when by signs it begins to express his Sorrows and Joys, makes his Wants known, and discovers his Love to novelty and the multiplicity of his Desires.[92]

Besides "self-love" there is a "self-liking" which produces "pride," "shame," and "ambition," through which man develops the social sentiments.

*Cleomenes.* That Self-love was given to all Animals, at least, the most perfect, for Self-Preservation, is not disputed; but as no Creature can love what it dislikes, it is necessary, moreover, that every one should have a real liking to its own Being, superior to what they have to any other. . . .

*Horatio.* What Reason have you to suppose this Liking, which Creatures have for themselves, to be distinct from Self-love; since the one plainly comprehends the other?

*Cleo.* . . . I fancy, that, to encrease the Care in Creatures to preserve themselves, Nature has given them an Instinct, by which every Individual values itself above its real Worth; this in us, I mean, in man, seems to be accompany'd with a Diffidence, arising from a Consciousness, or at least an Apprehension, that we do over-value ourselves: It is this that makes us so fond of the Approbation, Liking and Assent of others; because they strengthen and confirm us in the good Opinion we have of ourselves. . . . Self-liking, give me Leave to call it.[93]

*Hor.* Self-love I can plainly see induces him to labour for his Maintenance and Safety, and makes him fond of every thing which he imagines to tend to his Preservation: But what good does the Self-liking do him? . . .

*Cleo.* . . . it seems to be that, which continually furnishes us with that Relish we have for Life, even when it is not worth having. . . . It doubles our Happiness in Prosperity, and buoys us up against the Frowns of adverse Fortune. It is the Mother of Hopes, and the End as well as the Foundation of our best Wishes.[94]

*Hor.* But what you call Self-liking is evidently Pride.

*Cleo.* I believe it is, or at least the Cause of it.[95]

Pride is that Natural Faculty by which every Mortal that has any Understanding over-values, and imagines better Things of himself than any impartial Judge, thoroughly acquainted with all his Qualities and Circumstances, could allow him.[96]

There is no Man that has any Pride, but he has some Value for his Reputation.[97]

The true Object of Pride or Vain-glory is the Opinion of others; and the most superlative Wish, which a Man possess'd, and entirely fill'd with it can make, is, that he may be well thought of, applauded, and admired by the whole World, not only in the present, but all future Ages.[98]

[Pride is] the Passion, that is so conspicuously the Occasion of all this, the palpable and only Cause of the Uneasiness we feel at the Thoughts of being despis'd.[99]

We are possess'd of no other Quality so beneficial to Society, and so necessary to render it wealthy and flourishing.[100]

. . . to define the Passion of Shame, I think it may be call'd *a sorrowful Reflexion on our wn Unworthiness, proceeding from an Apprehension that others either do, or might, if they knew ll, deservedly despise us.*[101]

. . . tho' Shame is a real Passion, the Evil to be fear'd from it is altogether imaginary, nd has no Existence but in our own Reflection on the Opinion of others.[102]

Ambition . . . is deeply riveted in human Nature.[103]

These social sentiments can overcome the instinctive form of self-love.

The Greediness we have after the Esteem of others, and the Raptures we enjoy in the Thoughts of being liked, and perhaps admired, are Equivalents that overpay the Conquest of the strongest Passions, and consequently keep us at a great Distance from all uch Words or Actions that can bring Shame upon us.[104]

. . . it is incredible, how many strange and widely different Miracles are and may be perform'd by the force of it [i.e., "Pride"]; as Persons differ in Circumstances and Inclinations. In the first place, there is no Danger so great, but by the help of his Pride a Man may slight and confront it; nor any manner of Death so terrible, but with the same Assistance, he may court, and if he has a firm Constitution, undergo it with Alacrity. In he second, there are no good Offices or Duties, either to others or ourselves . . . but Man of good Sense and Knowledge may learn to practise them from no better Principle han Vain-glory, if it be strong enough to subdue and keep under all other Passions, that may thwart and interfere with his Design.[105]

Self-love may make a Man destroy himself.[106]

Man's sociality came under Mandeville's analysis.

*Horatio.* But was not Man, by Nature, designed for Society?* . . .

*Cleomenes.* . . . Nature had design'd Man for Society, as she has made Grapes for Wine.

*Hor.* To make Wine is an Invention of Man. . . .

*Cleo.* And so it is to form a Society of independent Multitudes; and there is nothing hat requires greater Skill.[108]

From what we observe in the Behaviour of Brutes, we have Reason to think, that among the more perfect Animals, those of the same Species have a Capacity on many Occasions, to make their Wants known to one another; and we are sure of several, not only that they understand one another, but likewise that they may be made to understand us. In comparing our Species with that of other Animals, when we consider the Make of Man, and the Qualifications that are obvious in him, his superior Capacity in the Faculties of thinking and reflecting, beyond other Creatures, his being capable of learning to speak, and the Usefulness of his Hands and Fingers, there is no room to doubt, that he is more fit for Society than any other Animal we know.[109]

The undoubted Basis of all Societies is Government: This Truth, well examin'd into, will furnish us with all the Reasons of Man's Excellency, as to Sociableness. It is evident from it, that Creatures, to be rais'd into a Community, must, in the first Place, be governable: This is a Qualification that requires Fear, and some Degree of Understanding. . . . But to be governable, implies an Endeavour to please, and a Willingness to exert ourselves in behalf of the Person that governs: But Love beginning every where at Home, no Creature can labour for others, and be easy long, whilst Self is wholly out of the Question:

---

* ". . . by Society I understand a Body Politick, in which Man either subdued by Superior Force, or by Persuasion drawn from his Savage State, is become a Disciplin'd Creature, that can find his own Ends in Labouring for others, and where under one Head or other Form of Government each Member is render'd Subservient to the Whole, and all of them by cunning Management are made to Act as one."[107]

Therefore a Creature is then truly governable, when, reconcil'd to Submission, it has learn'd to construe his Servitude to his own Advantage; and rests satisfy'd with the Account it finds for itself, in the Labour it performs for others. Several kinds of Animals are, or may, with little Trouble, be made thus governable; but there is not one Creature so tame, that it can be made to serve its own Species, but Man; yet without this he could never have been made sociable.[110]

Societies . . . cannot exist without the Concurrence of human Wisdom: All of them must have a Dependence, either on mutual Compact, or the Force of the Strong, exerting itself upon the Patience of the Weak.[111]

*Hor.* If I have not misunderstood you, you would insinuate two Things: First, that the Fitness of Man for Society, beyond other Animals, is something real; but that it is hardly perceptible in Individuals, before great Numbers of them are joyn'd together, and artfully manag'd. Secondly, that this real Something, this Sociableness, is a Compound, that consists in a Concurrence of several Things, and not in any one palpable Quality, that Man is endued with, and Brutes are destitute of. . . . you must shew me, that in Society there is . . . something that individual Persons are not actually possess'd of, whilst they remain single, and which, likewise, is palpably adventitious to Multitudes, when joyn'd together . . . and . . . necessary and essential to the compleating of Society . . . .

*Cleo.* Such . . . is demonstrable in mutual Commerce: for if we examine every Faculty and Qualification, from and for which we judge and pronounce Man to be a sociable Creature beyond other Animals, we shall find, that a very considerable, if not the greatest Part of the Attribute is acquired, and comes upon Multitudes, from their conversing with one another. *Fabricando fabri fimus.* Men become sociable, by living together in Society.*[113]

We have so few Examples of human Creatures, that never convers'd with their own Species, that it is hard to guess, what Man would be, entirely untaught; but we have good Reason to believe, that the Faculty of Thinking would be very imperfect in such a one, if we consider; that the greatest Docility can be of no use to a Creature, whilst it has nothing to imitate, nor any body to teach it.[114]

Man is a rational Creature, but he is not endued with Reason when he comes into the World; nor can he afterwards put it on when he pleases, at once, as he may a Garment. Speech likewise is a Characteristick of our Species, but no Man is born with it.[115]

. . . a dozen Generations proceeding from two Savages would not produce any tolerable Language; nor have we reason to believe, that a Man could be taught to speak after Five and Twenty, if he had never heard others before that time.[116]

*Hor.* So that in the Compliment we make to our Species, of its being endued with Speech and Sociableness, there is no other Reality; than that by Care and Industry Men may be taught to speak, and be made sociable, if the Discipline begins when they are very young.

*Cleo.* Not otherwise. A thousand of our Species all grown up, that is above Five and Twenty, could never be made sociable, if they had been brought up wild, and were all Strangers to one another.

*Hor.* I believe they could not be civilis'd, if their Education began so late.

*Cleo.* But I mean barely sociable, as it is the Epithet peculiar to man; that is, it would be impossible by Art to govern them, any more than so many wild Horses, unless you

* "Civil Society, where Men are become taught Animals."[112]

had two or three times that Number to watch and keep them in awe. Therefore it is highly probable, that most Societies, and Beginnings of Nations, were form'd in the Manner Sir *William Temple* supposes it; but nothing near so fast: and I wonder how a Man of his unquestionable good Sense could form an Idea of Justice, Prudence, and Wisdom, in an untaught Creature; or think of a civilis'd Man, before there was any Civil Society, and even before Men had commenc'd to associate.[117]

*Hor.* How came Society into the World?

*Cleo.* As I told you, from private Families; but not without great Difficulty, and the Concurrence of many favourable Accidents; and many Generations may pass, before there is any Likelihood of their being form'd into a Society. . . . Self-preservation bids all Creatures gratify their Appetites, and that of propagating his Kind never fails to affect a Man in Health, many Years before he comes to his full Growth. If a wild Man and a wild Woman should meet very young, and live together for fifty Years undistrub'd, in a mild wholesome Climate, where there is plenty of Provisions, they might see a prodigious Number of Descendants: For in the wild State of Nature, Man multiplies his Kind much faster, than can be allow'd of in any regular Society. . . From . . . the Right, Men naturally claim to everything they can get, it must follow, that Man will look upon his Children as his Property, and make such use of them as is most consistent with his interest. . . . Natural Affection would prompt a wild Man to love, and cherish his Child; it would make him provide Food and other Necessaries for his Son, till he was ten or twelve Years old, or perhaps longer.* But this Affection is not the only Passion, he has to gratify; if his Son provokes him by Stubborness, or doing otherwise than he would have him, the Love is suspended; and if his Displeasure be strong enough to raise his Anger, which is as natural to him as any other Passion, it is ten to one, but he'll knock him down: If he hurts him very much, and the Condition, he has put his Son in, moves his Pity,† his Anger will cease; and, natural Affection returning, he'll fondle him again, and be sorry for what he has done. Now, if we consider, that all Creatures hate and endeavour to avoid Pain, and that Benefits beget Love in all that receive them, we shall find, that the Consequence of this Management would be; that the Savage Child would learn to love and fear his Father: These two Passions, together with the Esteem, which we naturally have for every thing that far excels us, will seldom fail of producing that Compound, which we call Reverence.[120]

It is our Parents, that first cure us of our natural wildness, and break in us the Spirit of Independency, we are all born with: It is to them we owe the first Rudiments of our Submission; and to the Honour and Deference, which Children pay to Parents, all Societies are oblig'd for the Principle of human Obedience. The Instinct of Sovereignty in our Nature, and the Waywardness of Infants, which is the Consequence of it, discover themselves with the least glimmering of our Understanding, and before: Children that have been most neglected, and the least taught, are always the most stubborn and obstinate; and none are more unruly, and fonder of following their own Will, than those that are least capable of governing themselves.[121]

Children, who convers'd with their own Species, though they were brought up by Savages, would be governable; and consequently . . . all such, when come to Maturity,

"The Savage's Wife, as well as himself, would be highly pleas'd to see their Daughters impregnated, and bring forth; and they would both take great Delight in their Grand-Children . . . Our Savage Pair would have a double Title to their Grand-Children, from their undoubted Property in each Parent of them; and all the Progeny being sprung from their own Sons and Daughters, without Intermixture of foreign Blood, they would look upon the whole Race to be their natural Vassals."[118]

". . . without a considerable mixture of it [i.e., pity] the Society could hardly subsist."[119]

would be fit for Society, how ignorant and unskillful soever their Parents might have been.

*Hor.* I thank you for it; for it has shewn me, that the very first Generation of the most brutish Savages, was sufficient to produce sociable Creatures.[122]

Mandeville believed in the psychic unity of mankind and was a cosmopolitan skeptic.

Human Nature is always the same.[123]

. . . there is no Difference between the original Nature of a Savage, and that of civiliz'd Man.[124]

Human Nature is every where the same: Genius, Wit and Natural Parts are always sharpened by Application, and may be as much improv'd in the Practice of the meanest Villany, as they can in the Exercise of Industry or the most Heroic Virtue.[125]

I affirm, that if we consult History both Ancient and Modern, and take a view of what has past in the World, we shall find that Human Nature since the Fall of *Adam* has always been the same, and that the Strength and Frailties of it have ever been conspicuous in one Part of the Globe or other, without any Regard to Ages, Climate, or Religion. . . . As Human Nature still continues the same, as it has always been for so many thousand Years, we have no great Reason to suspect a future Change in it, while the World endures.[126]

The same Motives may produce very different Actions, as Men differ in Temper and Circumstances.[127]

In the first place, Men differ in Temperament: Some are naturally of an active, stirring, others of an indolent, quiet Disposition; some of a bold, others of a meek Spirit. In the second, it is to be consider'd, that this Temperament in Men come to Maturity is more or less conspicuous, according as it has been either check'd or encourag'd by Education. Thirdly, that on these two depend the different Perception Men have of Happiness, according to which the Love of Glory determines them different ways. Some think it the greatest Felicity to govern and rule over others: Some take the Praise of Bravery and Undauntedness in Dangers to be the most valuable: Others, Erudition, and to be a celebrated Author: So that, tho' they all love Glory, they set out differently to acquire it.[128]

Remember what I have said of Education, and the Power of it; you may add Inclinations, Knowledge, and Circumstances; for as Men differ in all these, so they are differently influenced and wrought upon by all the Passions. There is nothing that some Men may not be taught to be ashamed of. The same Passion, that makes the well-bred Man and prudent Officer value and secretly admire themselves for the Honour and Fidelity they display, may make the Rake and Scoundrel brag of their Vices and boast of their Impudence.[129]

. . . the . . . way of gratifying one's Pride . . . depends upon Modes and Custom.[130]

He emphasized "this Tyranny which Custom usurps over us."[131]

. . . our Liking or Disliking of things Chiefly depends on Mode and Custom, and the Precept and Example of our Betters and such whom in one way or other we think to be Superior to us.[132]

In the choice of things we are more often directed by the Caprice of Fashions, and the Custom of the Age, than we are by solid Reason, or our own Understanding.[133]

In a tolerable Education we are so industriously and so assiduously instructed, from our most early Infancy, in the Cermonies of bowing, and pulling off Hats, and other Rules of Behaviour; that even before we are Men we hardly look upon a mannerly Deportment as a Thing acquired, or think Conversation to be a Science. Thousand things are call'd easy and natural in Postures and Motions, as well as Speaking and Writing, that have caus'd infinite Pains to others as well as ourselves, and which we know to be the Product of Art. What aukward Lumps have I known, which the Dancing-master has put Limbs to![134]

The child learns the customs of its group through "Man being born the most necessitous and most helpless Animal."[135]

. . . it is highly probable that the principal and most necessary Parts of the Machine are less elaborate in Animals, that attain to all the Perfection they are capable of, in three, four, five, or six Years at furthest, than they are in a Creature that hardly comes to Maturity, its full Growth and Strength, in five and twenty.[136]

. . . tho' some Animals perhaps live longer than we do, there is no Species that remains young so long as ours; and besides what we owe to the superior Aptitude to learn, which we have from the great Accuracy of our Frame and inward Structure, we are not a little indebted for our Docility, to the Slowness and long Gradation of our Encrease, before we are full grown: the Organs in other Creatures grow stiff, before ours are come to half their Perfection.[137]

The child adopts customs through its "fondness of Imitation."[138]

Children and even Infants are the Apes of others.[139]

It is Precept and the Examples of Parents, and those they Eat, Drink and Converse with, that have an Influence upon the Minds of Children.[140]

We are fond of imitating our Superiors from our Cradle, and whilst this Honour and Reverence to Parents continue to be paid by their Children, when they are grown Men and Women, and act for themselves, the Example is of singular use to all Minors, in teaching them their Duty, and not to refuse what they see others, that are older and wiser, comply with by Choice: For by this means, as their Understanding encreases, this Duty by degrees becomes a Fashion, which at last their Pride will not suffer them to neglect.[141]

[This was even true in the "first family."] He would make his Children, as soon as they were able, assist him in getting Food, and teach them, how and where to procure it. Savage Children, as they got Strength, would endeavour to imitate every Action they saw their Parents do, and every Sound they heard them make.[142]

Shame plays an important role in this process.

It is incredible how necessary an Ingredient Shame is to make us sociable.[143]

The Lessons of it, like those of *Grammar*, are taught us long before we have occasion for, or understand the Usefulness of them; for this Reason Children often are ashamed, and blush out of Modesty, before the Impulse of Nature I hint at [i.e., "Lust"] makes any Impression upon them. A Girl who is modestly educated, may, before she is two Years old, begin to observe how careful the Women, she converses with, are of covering themselves before Men; and the same Caution being inclucated to her by Precept, as well as Example, it is very probable that at Six she'll be ashamed of shewing her Leg, without knowing any Reason why such an Act is blameable, or what the Tendency of it is.[144]

I must put you in mind of what happens in early Education, by the first Rudiments of which Infants are taught, in the Choice of Actions to prefer the Precepts of others, to the Dictates of their own Inclinations; which in short is no more than doing as they are bid. To gain this Point, Punishments and Rewards are not neglected, and many different Methods are made use of; but it is certain, that nothing proves more often effectual for this Purpose, or has a greater Influence upon Children, than the Handle that is made of Shame; which, tho' a natural Passion, they would not be sensible of so soon, if we did not artfully rouze and stir it up in them, before they can speak or go: By which means, their Judgements being then weak, we may teach them to be asham'd of what we please, as soon as we can perceive them to be any ways affected with the Passion itself.[145]

In considering cultural evolution, Mandeville emphasized the social nature of inventions.

. . . there are very few [customs], that are the Work of one Man, or of one Generation; the greatest part of them are the Product, the joynt Labour of several Ages.[146]

I think of all Inventions of this sort . . . that they are the joint Labour of Many. Human Wisdom is the Child of Time. It was not the Contrivance of one Man, nor could it have been the Business of a few Years.[147]

What depth of Thought and Ingenuity, what Toil and Labour, and what length of Time must it have cost, before Man could learn from a Seed to raise and prepare so useful a Product as Linen . . . The Arts of Brewing, and making Bread, have by slow degrees been brought to the Perfection they now are in.[148]

*Cleomenes*. . . you shall find, that the Disturbance and Uneasiness, that must be caused by Self-liking, whatever Strugglings and unsuccessful Tryals to remedy them might precede, must necessarily produce at long run, what we call good Manners and Politeness.

*Horatio*. I understand you, I believe. Everybody, in this undisciplin'd State, being affected with the high Value he has for himself, and displaying the most natural symptoms, which you have describ'd, they would all be offended at the barefac'd Pride of their Neighbours: and it is impossible, that this should continue long among rational Creatures, but the repeated Experience of the Uneasiness they received from such Behaviour, would make some of them reflect on the Cause of it; which, in tract of time, would make them find out, that their own barefaced Pride must be as offensive to others, as that of others is to themselves.

*Cleo*. What you say is certainly the Philosophical Reason of the Alterations, that are made in the Behaviour of Men, by their being civiliz'd: but all this is done without reflection, and Men by degrees, and great Length of Time, fall as it were into these Things spontaneously.

*Hor*. How is that possible, when it must cost them Trouble, and there is a palpable Self-denial to be seen in the Restraint they put upon themselves?

*Cleo*. In the Pursuit of Self-preservation, Men discover a restless Endeavour to make themselves easy, which insensibly teaches them to avoid Mischief on all Emergencies: and when human Creatures once submit to Government, and are used to live under the Restraint of Laws, it is incredible, how many useful Cautions, Shifts, and Stratagems, they will learn to practise by Experience and Imitation, from conversing together; without being aware of the natural Causes, that oblige them to act as they do, *viz*. The Passions within, that, unknown to themselves, govern their Will and direct their Behaviour.[149]

The restless Industry of Man to supply his Wants, and his constant Endeavours to meliorate his Condition upon Earth, have produced and brought to Perfection many useful Arts and Sciences, of which the beginnings are of uncertain Aera's, and to which we can assign no other Causes, than Human Sagacity in general, and the joynt Labour of many Ages, in which Men have always employ'd themselves in studying and contriving Ways and Means to sooth their various Appetites, and make the best of their Infirmities. Whence had we the first Rudiments of Architecture; how came Sculpture and Painting to be what they have been these many hundred Years; and who taught every Nation the respective Languages they speak now? When I have a Mind to dive into the Origin of any Maxim or political Invention, for the Use of Society in general, I don't trouble my Head with enquiring after the Time or Country, in which it was first heard of, nor what others have wrote or said about it; but I go directly to the Fountain Head, human Nature itself, and look for the Frailty or Defect in Man, that is remedy'd or supply'd by that Invention: When Things are very Obscure, I sometimes make Use of Conjectures to find my Way.

*Hor.* Do you argue, or pretend to prove any thing from those Conjectures?

*Cleo.* No; I never reason but from the plain Observations which every body may make on Man, the *Phaenomena* that appear in the lesser World.[150]

## Society originated because of man's needs.

. . . the Sociableness of Man arises only from these Two things, *viz.* The multiplicity of his Desires, and the continual Opposition he meets with in his Endeavours to gratify them.[151]

The reciprocal Services which all Men pay to one another, are the Foundation of the Society.[152]

*Cleomenes.* . . . the Order, Oeconomy, and the very Existence of the Civil Society . . . is entirely built upon the Variety of our Wants, so the whole Superstructure is made up of the reciprocal Services, which Men do to each other. . . .

There are great Blessings that arise from Necessity; and that every Body is obliged to eat and drink, is the Cement of civil Society.[153]

The first thing that could make Man associate, would be common Danger, which unites the greatest Enemies: This Danger they would certainly be in, from wild Beasts, considering, that no uninhabited Country is without them, and the defenceless Condition, in which Men come into the World.[154]

It is not possible to know any thing, with Certainty, of Beginnings, where Men were destitute of Letters; but I think, that the Nature of the thing makes it highly probable, that it must have been their common Danger from Beasts of Prey.[155]

. . . when I reflect on the Passions, all Men are born with, and their Incapacity, whilst they are untaught; I can find no Cause or Motive, which is so likely to unite them together, and make them espouse the same Interest, as that common Danger they must always be in from wild Beasts, in uncultivated Countries; whilst they live in small Families, that all shift for themselves, without Government or Dependance upon one another: This first Step to Society, I believe to be an Effect, which that same Cause, the common Danger so often mentioned, will never fail to produce upon our Species in such Circumstances.[156]

. . . great Numbers of them have by mutual compact framed themselves into a Body Politick.*[159]

Now, pray Sir, is not the great End of Men's forming themselves into such Societies,

* In other places he speaks of " Regulations and Contracts, that had been agreed upon before,"[157] and " the Contract between the King and People."[158]

mutual Happiness; I mean, do not all individual Persons, from being thus combined, propose to themselves a more comfortable Condition of Life, than human Creatures, if they were to live like other wild Animals, without Tie or Dependance, could enjoy in a free and savage State?

*Horatio.* This certainly is not only the End, but the End which is every where attain'd to by Government and Society, in some Degree or other.[160]

*Cleo.* The second Step to Society, is the Danger Men are in from one another: for which we are beholden to that stanch Principle of Pride and Ambition, that all Men are born with. Different Families may endeavour to live together, and be ready to join in common Danger; but they are all of little use to one another, when there is no common Enemy to oppose. If we consider, that Strength, Agility, and Courage would in such a State be the most valuable qualifications, and that many Families could not live long together, but some, actuated by the Principle I named, would strive for Superiority: this must breed Quarrels, in which the most weak and fearful will, for their own Safety, always join with him, of whom they have the best Opinion.

*Hor.* This would naturally divide Multitudes into Bands and Companies, that would all have their different Leaders, of which the strongest and most valiant would always swallow up the weakest and most fearful.

*Cleo.* What you say agrees exactly with the Accounts we have of the unciviliz'd Nations, that are still subsisting in the World; and thus Men may live miserably many Ages.

*Hor.* The very first Generation, that was brought up under the Tuition of Parents, would be governable: and would not every succeeding Generation grow wiser than the foregoing?

*Cleo.* Without doubt they would encrease in Knowledge and Cunning: Time and Experience would have the same effect upon them as it has upon others; and in the particular things, to which they apply'd themselves, they would become as expert and ingenious as the most civiliz'd Nations: But their unruly Passions, and the Discords occasioned by them, would never suffer them to be happy; their mutual Contentions would be continually spoiling their Improvements, destroying their Inventions, and frustrating their Designs.[161]

It is probable that in the Wild State of Nature Parents would keep a Superiority over their Children, at least While they were in Strength, and that even afterwards the Remembrance of what the others had experienc'd might produce in them something between Love and Fear, which we call Reverence: It is probable likewise that the second Generation following the Example of the first, a Man with a little Cunning would always be able, as long as he lived and had his Senses, to maintain a Superior Sway over all his own Offspring and descendants, how numerous soever they might grow. But the old Stock once dead, the Sons would quarrel, and there could be no Peace long, before there had been War. Eldership in Brothers is of no great Force, and the Preeminence that is given to it only invented as a shift to live in Peace. Man as he is a fearful Animal, naturally not rapacious, loves Peace and Quiet, and he would never Fight, if no body offended him, and he could have what he fights for without it. To this fearful Disposition and the Aversion he has to his being disturb'd, are owing all the various Projects and Forms of Government. Monarchy without doubt was the first. Aristocracy and Democracy were two different Methods of mending the Inconveniencies of the first, and a mixture of these three an Improvement on all the rest.[162]

*Hor.* But don't you think, that the same Ambition, that made a Man aspire to be a

Leader, would make him likewise desirous of being obey'd in civil Matters, by the Numbers he led?

*Cleo.* I do; and moreover that, notwithstanding this unsettled and precarious way Communities would live in, after three or four Generations human Nature would be look'd into, and begin to be understood: Leaders would find out, that the more Strife and Discord there was amongst the People they headed, the less use they could make of them: this would put them upon various ways of curbing Mankind; they would forbid killing and striking one another; the taking away by force the Wives, or Children of others in the same Community: they would invent Penalties, and very early find out, that no body ought to be a Judge in his own Cause; and that old Men, generally speaking, knew more than young.*[164]

*Hor.* When once they have Prohibitions and Penalties, I should think all the Difficulty surmounted; and I wonder why you said, that thus they might live miserably for many Ages.

*Cleo.* There is one thing of great moment, which has not been named yet; and 'till that comes to pass, no considerable Numbers can ever be made happy: What signify the strongest Contracts, when we have nothing to shew for them; and what Dependance can we have upon oral Tradition, in Matters that require Exactness; especially whilst the Language that is spoken is yet very imperfect? Verbal Reports are liable to a thousand Cavils and Disputes, that are prevented by Records, which every body knows to be unerring Witnesses; and from the many Attempts that are made to wrest and distort the Sense of even written Laws, we may judge, how impracticable the Administration of Justice must be among all Societies that are destitute of them. Therefore the third and last Step to Society is the Invention of Letters. No Multitudes can live peacably without Government; no Government can subsist without Laws; and no Laws can be effectual long, unless they are wrote down: The Consideration of this is alone sufficient to give us a great Insight into the Nature of Man.[165]

Whence once Men come to be govern'd by written Laws, all the rest comes on a-pace. Now Property, and the Safety of Life and Limb, may be secured: This naturally will forward the Love of Peace, and make it spread. No number of Men, when once they enjoy Quiet, and no Man needs to fear his Neighbour, will be long without learning to divide and subdivide their Labour.[166]

*Hor.* What Time, how many Ages, do you think, it would require to have a well-civiliz'd Nation from such a Savage Pair as yours?

*Cleo.* That's very uncertain; and I believe it impossible, to determine any thing about it. From what has been said, it is manifest, that the Family descending from such a Stock would be crumbled into pieces, re-united, and dispers'd again several times, before the whole or any part of it could be advanced to any degree of Politeness. The best Forms of Government are subject to Revolutions, and a great many things must concur, to keep a Society of Men together, till they become a civiliz'd Nation.

*Hor.* Is not a vast deal owing, in the raising of a Nation, to the difference there is in the Spirit and Genius of People?

---

* He later qualified this: "*Cleo.* I would shew, that, on the one Hand, you can make no Multitudes believe contrary to what they feel, or what contradicts a Passion inherent in their Nature, and that, on the other, if you humour that Passion, and allow it to be just, you may regulate it as you please. . . .

"*Hor.* It is not in the Power then, you think, of Politicians to contradict the Passions, or deny the Existence of them, but that, when once they have allow'd them to be just and natural, they may guide Men in the Indulgence of them, as they please.

"*Cleo.* I do so."[163]

*Cleo.* Nothing, but what depends upon Climates, which is soon over-ballanc'd by skil-ful Government. Courage and Cowardice, in all Bodies of Men, depend entirely upon Exercise and Discipline. Arts and Sciences seldom come before Riches, and both flow in faster or slower, according to the Capacity of the Governours, the Situation of the People, and the Opportunities they have of Improvements; but the first is the Chief. . . .

*Hor.* But what is it at last, that raises opulent Cities and powerful Nations from the smallest Beginnings? . . .

*Cleo.* All the Ground Work, that is required to aggrandise Nations, you have seen in *the Fable of the Bees.*[167]

[In that first volume he] demonstrates in the first place, that the National Happiness which the Generality wish and pray for, is Wealth and Power, Glory and Worldly Greatness; to live in Ease, in Affluence and Splendour at Home, and to be fear'd, courted and esteem'd Abroad: In the second, that such a Felicity is not to be attain'd to without Avarice, Profuseness, Pride, Envy, Ambition and other Vices.[168]

It is this which leads him to his famous paradoxes:

Private Vices, Publick Benefits.[169]

Parties directly opposite,
Assist each other, as 'twere for Spight.[170]

Mandeville also considered the evolution of other aspects of culture.

In the first Ages, Man, without doubt, fed on the Fruits of the Earth, without any previous Preparation, and reposed himself naked like other Animals on the Lap of their common Parent.[171]

He spoke of the "Caves, Huts, Hovels, Tents and Barracks, with which Mankind took up at first,"[172] and also mentioned the evolution of weapons.[173]

Following is his discussion on the development of religion.

*Horatio.* I ask'd you, how Religion came into the World . . . what is it, that disposes him [man] to it?

*Cleomenes.* Fear. . . . Every Mischief and every Disaster that happens to him, of which the Cause is not very plain and obvious; excessive Heat and Cold; Wet and Drought, that are offensive; Thunder and Lightning, even when they do no visible Hurt; Noises in the dark, Obscurity itself, and every thing that is frightful and unknown, are all ad-ministring and contributing to the Establishment of this Fear. The wildest Man, that can be conceiv'd, by the time that he came to Maturity, would be wise enough to know, that Fruits and other Eatables are not to be had, either always, or every where: This would naturally put him upon hoarding, when he had good Store: His Provision might be spoil'd by the Rain; he would see that Trees were blasted, and yielded not always the same Plenty: He might not always be in Health, or his young ones might grow sick, and die, without any Wounds or external Force to be seen. Some of these Accidents might at first escape his Attention, or only alarm his weak Understanding, without oc-casioning much Reflection for some Time; but as they came often, he would certainly begin to suspect some invisible Cause; and, as his Experience encreased, be confirm'd in his Suspicion. It is likewise highly probable, that a Variety of different Sufferings, would make him apprehend several such Causes; and at last induce him to believe, that there was a great Number of them, which he had to fear. What would very much contribute to this credulous Disposition, and naturally lead him into such a Belief, is a false Notion, we imbibe very early, and which we may observe in Infants, as soon as by their Looks, their Gestures, and the Signs they make, they begin to be intelligible to us.

*Hor.* What is that, pray?

*Cleo.* All young Children seem to imagine, that every thing thinks and feels in the same Manner as they do themselves: And, that they generally have this wrong Opinion of Things inanimate, is evident, from a common Practice among them; whenever they labour under any Misfortune, which their own Wildness, and want of Care have drawn upon them. In all such Cases, you see them angry at and strike, a Table, a Chair, the Floor, or any thing else, that can seem to have been accessary to their hurting themselves, or the Production of any other Blunder, they have committed. . . . It is not to be imagin'd, that this natural Folly should be so easily cured in a Child, that is destitute of all Instruction and Commerce with his own Species, as it is in those, that are brought up in Society, and hourly improv'd by conversing with others, that are wiser than themselves; and I am persuaded, that a wild Man would never get entirely rid of it, whilst he lived.[174]

In the evolution of language, he derived speech from gesture in the same manner as Wundt did later.

*Horatio.* Pray what Language did your wild Couple speak, when first they met?

*Cleomenes.* From what I have said already it is evident, that they could have had none at all; at least, that is my Opinion. . . . I am persuaded, that Nature has made all Animals of the same kind, in their mutual Commerce, intelligible to one another, as far as is requisite for the Preservation of themselves and their Species: And as to my wild Couple, as you call them, I believe there would be a very good Understanding, before many Sounds past between them. It is not without some difficulty, that a Man born in Society can form an Idea of such Savages, and their Condition; and unless he has used himself to abstract thinking, he can hardly represent to himself such a State of Simplicity, in which Man can have so few Desires, and no Appetites roving beyond the immediate Call of untaught Nature: To me it seems very plain, that such a Couple would not only be destitute of Language, but likewise never find out or imagine, that they stood in need of any; or that the want of it was any real Inconvenience to them.

*Hor.* Why do you think so?

*Cleo.* Because it is impossible, that any Creature should know the Want of what it can have no Idea of: I believe, moreover, that if Savages, after they are grown Men and Women, should hear others speak, being made acquainted with the Usefulness of Speech, and consequently become sensible of the want of it in themselves, their Inclination to learn it would be as inconsiderable as their Capacity; and if they should attempt it, they would find it an immense labour, a thing not to be surmounted; because the Suppleness and Flexibility in the Organs of Speech, that Children are endued with, and which I have often hinted at, would be lost in them; and they might learn to play masterly upon the Violin, or any other the most difficult musical Instrument, before they could make any tolerable Proficiency in speaking. . . . When a Man's Knowledge is confin'd within a narrow Compass, and he has nothing to obey, but the simple Dictates of Nature, the Want of Speech is easily supply'd by dumb Signs; and it is more natural to untaught Men to express themselves by Gestures, than by Sounds; but we are all born with a Capacity of making ourselves understood, beyond other Animals, without Speech: To express Grief, Joy, Love, Wonder and Fear, there are certain Tokens, that are common to the whole Species. . . .

*Hor.* But if the old Stock would never either be able or willing to acquire Speech, it is impossible they could teach it their Children: Then which way could any Language ever come into the World from two Savages?

*Cleo.* By slow degrees, as all other Arts and Sciences have done, and length of time; Agriculture, Physick, Astronomy, Architecture, Painting, &c. From what we see in Children that are backward with their Tongues, we have reason to think, that a wild Pair would make themselves intelligible to each other by Signs and Gestures, before they would attempt it by Sounds: But when they lived together for many Years, it is very probable, that for the Things they were most conversant with they would find out Sounds, to stir up in each other the Idea's of such Things, when they were out of sight; these Sounds they would communicate to their young ones; and the longer they lived together the greater Variety of Sounds they would invent, as well for Actions as the Things themselves: They would find that the Volubility of Tongue, and Flexibility of Voice, were much greater in their young ones, than they could remember it ever to have been in themselves: It is impossible, but some of these young ones would, either by Accident or Design, make use of this superior Aptitude of the Organs at one time or other; which every Generation would still improve upon; and this must have been the Origin of all Languages, and Speech it self, that were not taught by Inspiration. I believe, moreover, that after Language (I mean such as is of human Invention) was come to a great degree of Perfection, and even when People had distinct Words for every Action in Life, as well as every Thing they meddled or convers'd with, Signs and Gestures still continued to be made for a great while, to accompany Speech; because both are intended for the same Purpose. . . . Because Signs confirm Words, as much as Words do Signs.

*Hor.* From what you have said, it should seem that Action is not only more natural, but likewise more ancient than Speech it self, which before I should have thought a Paradox.

*Cleo.* Yet it is true.[175]

Lastly, Mandeville discussed the factors influencing population size.

I believe that Wars of all sorts, as well as Diseases, are natural Means to hinder Mankind from encreasing too fast.[176]

## Burnet

Thomas Burnet (d. 1750) was an advocate of the sociality of man.

Mankind . . . being naturally sociable Creatures, are naturally capable of entring into Societies of themselves.[177]

In fact, one of his postulates was

That the End for which God made the World, was to do Good, or in other Words, that every Thing might be Happy according to its Nature, and by Consequence as Mankind are of a sociable Nature, and cannot be truly Happy without Society, it must have been one End of that Wisdom, that made us for our Happiness, that we should be united in Society.[178]

However, political organization developed only after the commission of the original sin.

### The Original of Government

And as to this it is certain, that whether 'twas deriv'd from God, or Men, the Original Reason, and Occasion of it was, the Corruption, or Imperfection of human Nature.

For tho' these would have been something in a State of Purity and Innocence, (had Mankind continued in that State) as there would have been a Difference of Degrees, of Superiority and Inferiority, as of Parents, and Children, and tho' they would probably have had some Rules of Order, as these are suppos'd to be amongst the Angels of Heaven, yet these would be nothing like (what we call) Government now in this State of Corruption we are in; that is, these would have been nothing like a Government of Coercion.[179]

## Pluche

Noel Antoine Pluche (1688–1761) was another who mantained that man is a social animal.

... the Intention of the Creator was to make this Earth an Habitation of Fellow-citizens, not an Hermitage for Anchorets. ...

This universal Passion for Society in Man is as much a Gift of the Creator as his very Arms are. ... the Love of Society is previous to all manner of Utility. It is the Intention of God: It is so far our natural Condition, that when our own Utility ceases, we do not however go out of Society, nor are we ever free from the Ties that bind us to it, as they were made by the divine Hand.[180]

## Amory

Thomas Amory's (1691?–1788) eccentric novel, *The Life and Opinions of John Buncle* (1756)[181] covers such a wide range of topics that there are some statements even of interest to the anthropologist.

Although apologetically so, he was a proponent of the psychological equality of the sexes.

... the faculties and imagination of women's minds, properly cultivated, may equal those of the greatest men.[182]

He believed in man's sociality.

I saw ... that in respect of mankind, our natural sense of right and wrong, points out to us the duties to be performed towards others, and the kind affections implanted by nature, excites us to the discharge of them: that by the law of our constitution and nature, justice and benevolence are prescribed; and aids and an intercourse of mutual offices required, not only to secure our pleasure and happiness, but to preserve ourselves in safety and in life; that the law of nature, or natural right, forbids every instance of injustice, a violation of life, liberty, health, property; and the exercise of our honourable, kind powers, are not only a spring of vigorous efforts to do good to others, and thereby secure the common happiness; but they really procure us a joy and peace, an inward applause and external advantages; while injustice and malice, anger, hatred, envy, and revenge, are often matter of shame and remorse, and contain nothing joyful, nothing glorious: in the greatest affluence, the savage men are miserable.[183]

The case however is, that the generality of mankind are too corrupt to be governed by the great universal law of social nature, and to gratify ambition, avarice, and the like, employ a cunning or power, to seize the natural rights and properties of others: and therefore, to natural virtue, grounded on the reason and fitness of things, in themselves, the first and principal mean of securing the peace and happiness of society, it was necessary to add two other grand principles, civil government and religion, and so have three conducible means to social happiness.[184]

Amory was bound by the orthodox literal interpretation of the Bible, and therefore his account of the development of religion[185] is of little interest. More curious is his analysis of the first language.

I am now convinced, not only that Hebrew was not the language of Paradise, or that Adam did not speak the tongue the old world used immediately before the confusion at Babel; but likewise, that the division there, was a division and confusion of the one language then spoken.[186]

Economy is the basic aspect of culture.

. . . industry and property . . . may be called the generative principle of empire.[187]

## Bolingbroke

Henry St. John, Viscount Bolingbroke (1678–1751), insisted upon the existence of laws of nature.

I say that the law of nature is the law of God.[188]

The laws of nature are general; and . . . the particular application of them, and the means of securing their effect, are left to human prudence.*[191]

Nature and truth are the same every where, and reason shews them every where alike.† But the accidental and other causes, which give rise and growth to opinions, both in speculation and practice, are of infinite variety; and where ever these opinions are once confirmed by custom and propagated by education, various, inconsistent, contradictory as they are, they all pretend (and all their pretences are backed by pride, by passion, and by interest) to have reason, or revelation, or both, on their side; tho neither reason nor revelation can be possibly on the side of more than one, and may be possibly on the side of none.‡[194]

The rough draughts, that have been thrown upon these papers, may help to shew that there is such a thing as the law of nature, antecedent to all other laws, and to the establishment of civil society; that this law is the law of reason collected " a posteriori " from the actual consitution of things, by experience and observation; that as instinct, affections, passions, and self-love that universal spring of the animal kind, were given to put us into action, so this law is given to guide and govern the human conduct.[195]

From the laws of nature, he proceeded to man's sociality.

Thus far the law of nature is plain: and this is sufficient to shew, how we are led by the hand of God, that is, by the circumstances in which he has ordained that we should be born; by the necessary dependence of children, by the instinct of parents, by information,§ by habit, and finally by reason; how we are led, I say, to civil thro natural society,

---

* " . . . marriages, within certain degrees of consanguinity and affinity, are forbid by political institutions and for political reasons; but are left indifferent by the law of nature, which determines nothing expressly about them."[189]

" . . the love of our country is a lesson of reason, not an institution of nature.   Education and habit, obligation and interest, attach us to it, not instinct."[190]

† "There are certain general principles, and rules of life and conduct, which always must be true, because they are conformable to the invariable nature of things. He who studies history as he would study philosophy, will soon distinguish and collect them, and by doing so will soon form to himself a general system of ethics and politics on the surest foundations, on the trial of these principles and rules in all ages, and on the confirmation of them by universal experience."[192]

‡ "The laws of nature are truly what my lord BACON stiles in aphorisms, the laws of laws. Civil laws are always imperfect, and often false deductions from them, or applications of them; nay they stand, in many instances, in direct opposition to them. It follows from hence, not that there is no natural law, but that civil laws have been made without a sufficient and constant regard to it."[193]

§ " . . how great soever a genius may be, and how much soever he may acquire new light and heat, as he proceeds in his rapid course, certain it is that he will never shine with the full lustre, nor shed the full influence he is capable of, unless to his own experience he adds the experience of other men and other ages."[196]

and are fitted to be members of one, by having been members of the other. This is the case of every one in particular, and has been that of mankind collectively considered.[197]

Men were never out of society; for if they were divided into families before they were assembled into nations, they were in society still from their original.[198]

There is a sort of geneology of law, in which nature begets natural law, natural law sociability, sociability union of societies by consent, and this union by consent the obligation of civil laws. When I make sociability the daughter of natural law, and the granddaughter of nature, I mean plainly this. Self-love, the original spring of human actions,* directs us necessarily to sociability. The same determination of nature appears in other animals. They all herd with those of their own species, with whom they sympathise more; whose language, perhaps, whether it consists in signs or sounds, they understand better, and from whom if individuals do not receive much good, they may have less evil to apprehend. This instinct operates, at least, as strongly in man.[202]

[As to] general sociability. To account for that, we have no need to recur to occult qualities. Instinct leads us to it, by a sense of pleasure: and reason, that recalling the past, foresees the future, confirms us in it, by a sense of happiness. Instinct is an inferior principle, and sufficient for the inferior ends to which other animals are directed. The necessities, the conveniences of life, and every agreeable sensation, are the objects of both. But happiness is a continued enjoyment of these, and that is an object proportioned to reason alone. Neither is obtained out of society; and sociability therefore is the foundation of human happiness.† Society cannot be maintained without benevolence, justice, and the other moral virtues. These virtues, therefore, are the foundations of society: and thus men are led, by a chain of necessary consequences, from the instinctive to the rational law of nature, if I may speak so. Self-love operates in all these stages. We love ourselves, we love our families, we love the particular societies, to which we belong, and our benevolence extends at last to the whole race of mankind. Like so many different vortices, the center of them all is self-love, and that which is the most distant from it is the weakest.[204]

On the basis of the laws of nature and man's sociality, he refuted Hobbes.

If any man should advance, that we ought to proceed on the known principles of mathematics, not because there are such in nature, but because mathematicians have made an agreement or compact to proceed upon them as if there were such, I suspect that he would be esteemed mad. What then was *Hobbes*, his predecessors, and his successors, who affirmed that all distinction between moral good and evil, just and unjust, is established solely by civil institution; and that our moral obligations are derived from the laws of society, not from the law of nature? . . . It seems then to me, that civil societies could not have been formed, nor the distinction of just and unjust, nor the honestum and decorum of life have been established, if there had not been, antecedently, such a law of nature as *Hobbes* denies, and directly opposite to that which he supposes.[205]

However you suppose the human race to have begun, societies, little indeed, but societies still, must have been co-eval with it. If there was a first man and a first woman, they and their children (for these could not nurse and educate themselves) must have

---

* "Self-love [is not only] the great spring of human actions[199] [but also the] universal spring of the animal kind."[200]

"The love of history seems inseparable from human nature, because it seems inseparable from self-love."[201]

† ". . . private good depends on the public, and the happiness of every individual on the happiness of society."[203]

constituted a first society. If numbers of men and women sprung out of the earth at once, there might be some contests among the men about these primitive ladies, and some violence might be employed, and some confusion might arise, in the immediate hurry of copulation. But after that, the same instinct, which had caused variance, would have formed societies. Families would have been soon raised, and the authority, subordination, order, and union, necessary to their well being, must have followed naturally, as we may observe that they do among the most savage people. Men never were, because they could never subsist, in a state of absolute individuality. Self-love, directed by instinct to mutual pleasure, made the union of man and woman. Self-love made that of parents and children. Self-love begat sociability; and reason, a principle of human nature, as well as instinct, improved it. Reason improved it, extended it to relations more remote, and united several families into one community, as instinct had united several individuals into one family. Reason performed this by the help of experience: and what is the effect of experience? It is not to make any thing new in nature, it is to discover what was in nature, tho unobserved before. We might say as truly that COLUMBUS discovered a new world, in the absolute as well as relative sense of the word, as to say with HOBBES, that when men distinguished between just and unjust, and made laws and institutions on that distinction, they made that to be just or unjust which was indifferent before. The natural obligation to exercise benevolence, to administer justice, and to keep compacts, is as evident to human reason, as the desire of happiness is agreeable to human instinct. We desire by instinct, we acquire by instinct. The natural desire leads us necessarily to the natural obligation: and we proceed, in this case, from intuitive to demonstrative knowledge, by the same sure steps, by which we proceed from the knowledge of our own, to that of God's existence. The law of nature, or of right reason, is the real original of all positive laws.[206]

On the whole, as fast as families united in larger societies, and the same plain and simple rules, the first rudiments of natural law, that had been sufficient under paternal government, were so no longer, but required greater extension and a greater variety of application. Philosophers and legislators arose, constituted governments, and made laws wisely and unwisely, agreeably and disagreeably to the nature of things, according to the general imperfection of human productions: but there would have been no societies to whom laws might be given, no pretence to give them, no disposition to receive them, if there had not been a primaeval law, a law by which the families of men were governed in that state which we commonly call a state of nature, and which laid the principles of future government in another state, to which they were advancing gradually. This primaeval law is that code wherein all the laws, to which God has subjected his human creatures, are contained. Civil laws are the glosses which sometimes explain and sometimes perplex it, which men make, and men may alter at their will; whilst the other remains immutable like that of God.[207]

In the next place, this [Hobbesian] hypothesis considers each man as an individual, no more a member of the great commonwealth of mankind than of any particular commonwealth, it supposes him to have a right to every thing, and to be a rival and enemy on that account to every other man; whereas it is not more evident that we are born to walk with our legs, and to handle things with our hands, than it is that we are born to assist, and to be assisted by one another. It is not more plain that each man cannot enjoy every thing, than it is that each man has not an unlimited right to enjoy every thing, or that the right of each man, where things are common, is limited by his real wants. It did not require more sagacity to discover these truths in a state of nature, than it did to reason and to act as unnaturally as mankind must have done in a perpetual ound of jealousy, precaution, and design, such as HOBBES had imagined it.[208]

He countered Hobbes's hypothesis as to the origin of society and political organization, with his own, based upon the previous arguments.

We are too apt to carry systems of philosophy beyond all our ideas, and systems of history beyond all our memorials.[209]

We have . . . neither in profane nor in sacred authors such authentic, clear, distinct, and full accounts of the originals of ancient nations, and of the great events of those ages that are commonly called the first ages, as deserve to go by the name of history, or as afford sufficient materials for chronology and history.[210]

It is impossible we should know, by history or tradition, how the first civil governments were established. . . . But we may guess with great probability, by analogy from what we know.[211]

On the whole, it cannot be doubted, I think, that the first societies of men were those of families formed by nature and governed by natural law, nor that kingdoms and states were the second.[212]

Many hypotheses have been made to account for the beginning of civil society, for the nature of it, and for the motives to it. All of them have some degree of probability, and might have some share in framing those political congregations and unions, by which mankind has been divided into distinct nations, and the great commonwealth, as the stoicians called it not improperly, into distinct states. But no one of these must pass for universal, nor be supposed to have done the work alone. In general we may say, that the foundations of civil or political societies were laid by nature, tho they are the creatures of art. Societies were begun by instinct, and improved by experience. They were disturbed early, perhaps as soon as they were formed, both from within and from without, by the passions of men: and they have been maintained ever since, in opposition to them, very imperfectly, and under great vicissitudes, by human reason, which is exercised in particular systems of law for particular states, in leagues and covenants between state and state, and in tacit agreements that constitute what is commonly called the law of nations.[213]

Antient traditions, sacred and prophane, how imperfect and uncertain soever they are, give us sufficient reason, by their concurrence in this general account, to believe that mankind was at first dispersed in families, which formed so many distinct societies under paternal government.[214]

If we are persuaded then, that this world, and the inhabitants of it had a beginning in time, we must of necessity assume that the first men and the first women, or that one man and one woman at least, were produced in full strength and vigor of body and mind, prompted by instinct to an act of which they might not foresee the consequence, and prompted by self-love, when they saw it, to love themselves in their children, and to nurse and educate their off-spring.

Thus natural societies and paternal governments began.[215]

. . . civil societies arose out of natural, as natural societies arose out of one another. When any of these grew too numerous to inhabit the same country, or dissension arose among them, as it happened in the case of ABRAHAM and LOT, and of ESAU and JACOB afterwards, they separated . . . but we may conclude, from reason and analogy both, that if families sometimes separated, they sometimes united too, for mutual conveniency; and that in this manner several little dynasties were formed, which had more settled establishments than the vagabond families.[216]

Neighbourhood, an intercourse of good offices, and, in a word, mutual conveniency, might give a beginning, by the union of independent families under compacts and covenants, to civil societies. But the principal cause of such artificial or political unions was of a very different kind. We cannot suppose, that all the members of every family lived in a state of uninterrupted concord. There was a quarrel, and one brother assassinated another, even in the family of the first man.[217]

The state of mankind altered extremely when families had been long separated, whatever the cause of separation was; and when the natural bands were not only loosened, but lost and forgot in the course of generations; when there was no longer any regard to one common ancestor; when there was no authority to interpose between different people, and to influence and direct their conduct, as paternal authority had done, where different members of the same family were alone concerned.[218]

As fast as the distribution of mankind into families, and as paternal government ceased, men went out of a natural into a political state.[219]

Thus it became necessary to establish a power superior to that of the fathers of families, and, as fast as men went out of the state of nature, to substitute artificial to natural government. This was not done all at once, I suppose, nor every where in the same nanner. But it seems most probable, that these governments were in general monarchical. I know that some writers have thought otherwise; but they have no more right to affirm than I have, who am far from affirming. We must all guess, and probabilities must be weighed.[220]

The first kings were limited monarchs. They earned the sovereignty by great and good actions, held it from their people, and were accountable to their people for the exercise of it. Such I mean as came to their crowns by consent, and in countries where common utility united families in civil society, and neither conquest nor the fear of it.[221]

I have said thus much, in order to shew that political societies grew out of natural, and that civil governments were formed not by the concurrence of individuals, but by the association of families.[222]

Though he stated that "nations, like men, have their infancy,"[223] Bolingbroke had a cyclical rather than a progressive theory of history.

Our physical and moral systems are carried round in one perpetual revolution, from generation to corruption, and from corruption to generation; from ignorance to knowledge, and from knowledge to ignorance; from barbarity to civility, and from civility to barbarity. Arts and sciences grow up, florish, decay, die, and return again under the same, or other forms, after periods which seems long to us, however short they may be, compared with the immense duration of the systems of created being.[224]

But since the ages of prophecy, as well as miracles, are past, we must content ourselves to guess at what will be, by what has been.[225]

The history of a culture is divided into epochs, each with its own characteristics.

A new situation, different from the former, begets new interests in the same proportion of difference; not in this or that particular state alone, but in all those that are concerned by vicinity or other relations . . . in one general system of policy. New interests beget new maxims of government, and new methods of conduct. These, in their turns, beget new manners, new habits, new customs. The longer this new constitution of affairs continues, the more will this difference increase: and altho some analogy may remain long between what preceded and what succeeds such a period, yet will this analogy soon become an object of mere curiosity, not of profitable enquiry. Such a period therefore is, in the true sense of the words, an epocha or aera, a point of time at which you stop, or from which you reckon forward.[226]

Bolingbroke had a Chesterfieldian conception of the functions of history.

The true and proper object of this application is a constant improvement in private and in public virtue . . . the study of history seems to me, of all other, the most proper to train us up to private and public virtue[227]

[1.] I think, that history is philosophy teaching by examples*. . . . Such is the imperfection of human understanding, such is the frail temper of our minds, that abstract or general propositions, tho ever so true, appear obscure or doubtful to us very often, till they are explained by examples; and that the wisest lessons in favor of virtue go but a little way to convince the judgement, and determine the will, unless they are enforced by the same means; and we are obliged to apply to ourselves what we see happen to other men. . . . But this is not the only advantage of instruction by example; for example appeals not to our understanding alone, but to our passions likewise. Example assuages these, or animates them; sets passion on the side of judgement, and makes the whole man of a piece; which is more than the strongest reasoning and clearest demonstration can do: and thus forming habits by repetition, example secures the observance of those precepts which examples insinuated.[230]

[2.; . . . history serves to purge the mind of those national partialities and prejudices that we are apt to contract in our education, and that experience for the most part rather confirms than removes: because it is for the most part confined, like our education.[231]

There is scarce any folly or vice more epidemical among the sons of men, than that ridiculous and hurtful vanity, by which the people of each country are apt to prefer themselves to those of every other; and to make their own customs, and manners, and opinions the standards of right and wrong, of true and false. The Chinese mandarins were strangely surprised, and almost incredulous, when the Jesuits shewed them how small a figure their empire made in the general map of the world. The Samojeds Wondered much at the Czar of Muscovy for not living among them: and the Hottentot, Who returned from Europe, stripped himself naked as soon as he came home, put on his bracelets of guts and garbage, and grew stinking and lousy as fast as he could. Now nothing can contribute more to prevent us from being tainted with this vanity, than to accustom ourselves early to contemplate the different nations of the earth, in that vast map which history spreads before us, in their rise and their fall, in their barbarous and civilized states, in the likeness and unlikeness of them all to one another, and of each to itself. By frequently renewing this prospect to the mind, the Mexican with his cap and coat of feathers, sacrificing a human victim to his god, will not appear more savage to our eyes, than the Spaniard with an hat on his head, and a gonilla round his neck, sacrificing whole nations to his ambition, his avarice, and even the wantonness of his cruelty.†[234]

[3.] . . . there is this further advantage in the study of history, that the improvement

"We ought always to keep in mind, that history is philosophy teaching by examples how to conduct ourselves in all the situations of private and public life."[228]

"The school of example, my lord, is the world: and the masters of this school are history and experience."[229]

". . . custom, that result of the passions and prejudices of many, and of the designs of a few: that ape of reason, who usurps her seat, exercises her power, and is obeyed by mankind in her stead. Men find it easy, and government makes it profitable, to concur in established systems of speculation and practice: and the whole turn of education prepares them to live upon credit all their lives.[232]

". . . every one thinks the system, as he speaks the language, of his country; at least there are few that think, and none that act, in any country, according to the dictates of pure unbiassed reason."[233]

we make by it extends to more objects, and is made at the expense of other men: whereas
that improvement, which is the effect of our own experience, is confined to fewer objects, and is made at our own expense.[235]

We are cast back, as it were, into former ages: we live with the men who lived before
us, and we inhabit countries that we never saw. Place is enlarged, and time prolonged,
in this manner; so that the man who applies himself early to the study of history, may acquire in a few years, and before he sets foot abroad in the world, not only a more extended knowledge of mankind, but the experience of more centuries than any of the
partriarchs saw.[236]

In the study of these [i.e., ideal histories] we shall find many a complete series of
events, preceded by a deduction of their immediate and remote causes, related in their
full extent, and accompanied with such a detail of circumstances, and characters, as may
transport the attentive reader back to the very time, make him a party to the councils,
and an actor in the whole scene of affairs. . . . Thus history becomes what she ought
to be.[237]

## Pope

Alexander Pope (1688–1744) was a follower of Bolingbroke. To him, man was
related to the other animals, but differed from them in the possession of reason.

> Far as Creation's ample range extends,
> The scale of sensual, mental pow'rs ascends:
> Mark how it mounts, to Man's imperial race,
> From the green myriads in the peopled grass:
> What modes of sight betwixt each wide extreme,
> The mole's dim curtain, and the lynx's beam:
> Of smell, the headlong lioness between,
> And hound sagacious on the tainted green:
> Of hearing, from the life that fills the Flood,
> To that which warbles thro' the vernal wood:
> The spider's touch, how exquisitely fine!
> Feels at each thread, and lives along the line:
> In the nice bee, what sense so subtly true
> From pois'nous herbs extract the healing dew?
> How Instinct varies in the grov'lling swine,
> Compar'd, half-reas'ning elephant, with thine!
> 'Twixt that, and Reason, what a nice barrier,
> For ever sep'rate, yet for ever near!
> Remembrance and Reflection how ally'd;
> What thin partitions Sense from Thought divide:
> And Middle natures, how they long to join,
> Yet never pass th' insuperable line!
> Without this just gradation, could they be
> Subjected, these to those, or all to thee?
> The pow'rs of all subdu'd by thee alone,
> Is not thy Reason all these pow'rs in one?[238]

This was a corollary of the chain of being.

> Vast chain of Being! which from God began,
> Natures ethereal, human, angel, man,

Beast, bird, fish, insect, what no eye can see,
No glass can reach; from Infinite to thee,
From thee to Nothing.—On superior pow'rs
Were we to press, inferior might on ours:
Or in the full creation leave a void,
Where, one step broken, the great scale's destroy'd:
From Nature's chain whatever link you strike,
Tenth or ten thousandth, breaks the chain alike.[239]

Reason and self-love are basic in man's nature.

Two Principles in human nature reign;
Self-love, to urge,* and Reason, to restrain.[241]

Self-love and Reason to one end aspire,
Pain their aversion, Pleasure their desire.[242]

However, man is a social animal.

Look round our World; behold the chain of Love
Combining all below and all above.
See plastic Nature working to this end,
The single atoms each to other tend,
Attract, attracted to, the next in place
Form'd and impell'd its neighbour to embrace.
See Matter next, with various life endu'd,
Press to one centre still, the gen'ral Good.
See dying vegetables life sustain,
See life dissolving vegetate again:
All forms that perish other forms supply,
(By turns we catch the vital breath, and die,)
Like bubbles on the sea of Matter born,
They rise, they break, and to that sea return.
Nothing is foreign: Parts relate to whole;
One all-extending, all-preserving Soul
Connects each being, greatest with the least;
Made Beast in aid of Man, and Man of Beast;
All serv'd, all serving, nothing stands alone;
The chain holds on, and where it ends, unknown.[243]

God in the nature of each being founds
Its proper bliss, and sets its proper bounds:
But as he fram'd a Whole, the Whole to bless,
On mutual Wants built mutual Happiness:
So from the first, eternal ORDER ran,
And creature link'd to creature, man to man.[244]

Heav'n forming each on other to depend,
A master, or a servant, or a friend,
Bids each on other for assistance call,
Till one Man's weakness grows the strength of all.
Wants, frailties, passions, closer still ally
The common int'rest, or endear the tie.[245]

* "For, Vice or Virtue, Self directs it still."[240]

There's not a blessing Individuals find,
But some way leans and hearkens to the kind:
No Bandit fierce, no Tyrant mad with pride,
No cavern'd Hermit, rests self-satisfy'd:
Who most to shun or hate Mankind pretend,
Seek an admirer, or would fix a friend:
Abstract what others feel, what others think,
All pleasures sicken, and all glories sink.[246]

Altruism develops from self-love.

Each loves itself, but not itself alone,
Each sex desires alike, 'till two are one.
Nor ends the pleasure with the fierce embrace;
They love themselves, a third time, in their race.
Thus beast and bird their common charge attend,
The mothers nurse it, and the sires defend;
The young dismiss'd to wander earth or air,
There stops the Instinct, and there ends the care;
The link dissolved, each seeks a fresh ambrace,
Another love succeeds, another race.
A longer care Man's helpless kind demands;
That longer care contracts more lasting bands:
Reflection, Reason, still the ties improve,
At once extend the int'rest, and the love;
With choice we fix, with sympathy we burn;
Each Virtue in each Passion takes its turn;
And still new needs, new helps, new habits rise,
That graft benevolence on charities.
Still as one brood, and as another rose,
These nat'ral love maintained, habitual those:
The last, scarce ripen'd into perfect Man,
Saw helpless him from whom their life began:
Mem'ry and fore-cast just returns engage,
That pointed back to youth, this one to age;
While pleasure, gratitude, and hope, combin'd,
Still spread the int'rest, and preserv'd the kind.
Nor think, in NATURE'S STATE they blindly trod;
The state of Nature was the reign of God:
Self-love and Social at her birth began,
Union the bond of all things, and of Man.[247]

Pope then portrays the evolution of culture.

Cities were built, Societies were made:
Here rose one little state; another near
Grew by like means, and join'd, thro' love or fear.
Did here the trees with ruddier burdens bend,
And there the streams in purer rills descend?
What War could ravish, Commerce could bestow,
And he return'd a friend, who came a foe.
Converse and Love mankind might strongly draw.

When Love was Liberty, and Nature Law.
Thus States were form'd; the name of King unknown,
'Till common int'rest plac'd the sway in one.
'Twas VIRTUE ONLY (or in arts or arms,
Diffusing blessings, or averting harms)
The same which in a Sire the Sons obey'd,
A Prince the Father of a People made.
   'Till then, by Nature crown'd, each Patriarch sate,
King, priest, and parent of his growing state;
On him, their second Providence, they hung,
Their law his eye, their oracle his tongue.
He from the wond'ring furrow call'd the food,
Taught to command the fire, control the flood,
Draw forth the monsters of th' abyss profound,
Or fetch th' aerial eagle to the ground.
'Till drooping, sick'ning, dying they began
Whom they rever'd as God to mourn as Man:
Then, looking up from sire to sire, explor'd
One great first father, and that first ador'd.
Or plain tradition that this All begun,
Convey'd unbroken faith from sire to son;
The worker from the work distinct was known,
And simple Reason never sought but one:
Ere Wit oblique had broke that steady light,
Man, like his Maker, saw that all was right;
To Virtue, in the paths of Pleasure, trod,
And own'd a Father when he own'd a God.
LOVE all the faith, and all th' allegiance then;
For Nature knew no right divine in Men,
No ill could fear in God, and understood
A sov'reign being but a sov'reign good.
True faith, true policy, united ran,
This was but love of God, and this of Man.
   Who first taught souls enslav'd, and realms undone,
Th' enormous faith of many made for one;
That proud exception to all Nature's laws,
T' invert the world, and counter-work its Cause?
Force first made Conquest, and that conquest, Law;
'Till Superstition taught the tyrant awe,
Then shar'd the Tyranny, then lent it aid,
And Gods of Conqu'rors, Slaves of Subjects made:
She 'midst the lightning's blaze, and thunder's sound,
When rock'd the mountains, and when groan'd the ground,
She taught the weak to bend, the proud to pray,
To Pow'r unseen, and mightier far than they:
She, from the rending earth and bursting skies,
Saw Gods descend, and fiends infernal rise:
Here fix'd the dreadful, there the blest abodes;
Fear made her Devils, and weak Hope her Gods;

Gods partial, changeful, passionate, unjust,
Whose attributes were Rage, Revenge, or Lust;
Such as the souls of cowards might conceive,
And, form'd like tyrants, tyrants would believe.
Zeal then, not charity, became the guide;
And hell was built on spite, and heav'n on pride,
Then sacred seem'd th' ethereal vault no more;
Altars grew marble then, and reek'd with gore:
Then first the Flamen tasted living food;
Next his grim idol smear'd with human blood;
With Heav'n's own thunders shook the world below,
And play'd the God an engine on his foe.
    So drives Self-love, thro' just and thro' unjust,
To one Man's pow'r, ambition, lucre, lust:
The same Self-love, in all, becomes the cause
Of what restrains him, Government and Laws.
For, what one likes if others like as well,
What serves one will, when many wills rebel?
How shall he keep, what, sleeping or awake,
A weaker may surprise, a stronger take?
His safety must his liberty restrain:
All join to guard what each desires to gain.
Forc'd into virtue thus by Self-defence,
Ev'n Kings learn'd justice and benevolence:
Self-love forsook the path it first pursu'd,
And found the private in the public good.
    'Twas then, the studious head or gen'rous mind,
Follow'r of God or friend of human kind,
Poet or Patriot, rose but to restore
The Faith and Moral Nature gave before;
Re-lum'd her ancient light, not kindled new;
If not God's image, yet his shadow drew:
Taught Pow'r's due use to People and to Kings,
Taught nor to slack, nor strain its tender strings,
The less, or greater, set so justly true,
That touching one must strike the other too;
'Till jarring int'rests, of themselves create
Th' according music of a well-mix'd State.[248]

    Man, like the gen'rous vine, supported lives;
The strength he gains is from th' embrace he gives.
On their own Axis as the Planets run,
Yet make at once their circle round the Sun;
So two consistent motions act the Soul;
And one regards Itself, and one the Whole.
    Thus God and Nature link'd the gen'ral frame,
And base Self-love and Social be the same.[249]

## Linné

Carl von Linné (1707–78) made a few scattered observations that are of interest to social anthropologists. One was on the nature of man.

. . . you, the miracle of nature's audacity, the chief of animals, for whose sake nature has produced every thing, are an animal, weeping, laughing, singing, speaking, docile, judging, wondering, very wise, but delicate, naked, defenceless by nature, exposed to all the contempt of fortune, dependent upon the assistance of others, of anxious mind, and desirous of protection, of wavering spirit, obstinate in hope, querulous in life, very slow in gaining wisdom.[250]

He spoke of the constraint of custom.

. . . you hold that to be right which is really wrong made public, which clothes you in the shroud of custom as soon as you are born, nourishes, educates, brings you up, rules you, according to which you are held to be honest, strong, wise, of good morals; thus governed you live according to custom, but not according to reason.[251]

He showed some interest in cultural evolution.

. . . the early times, when men had scarcely left off eating acorns.[252]

Ovid's description of the silver age is still applicable to the native inhabitants of Lapland. Their soil is not wounded by the plough, nor is the iron din of arms to be heard; neither have mankind found their way to the bowels of the earth, nor do they engage in wars to define boundaries. They perpetually change their abodes, live in tents, and follow a pastoral life, just like the patriarchs of old.[253]

Their discourse . . . ran on that useful sort of witchcract by which a thief is put to his wit's end and detected. The origin of these fables may partly be traced in history, and the rest is to be attributed to invention.[254]

## Buffon

George Louis Leclerc, Count de Buffon (1707–88) stressed the importance of the social factors in human development.

We are . . . ill qualified to distinguish the genuine gifts of Nature from what is acquired by education, art, and imitation.*[258]

Man becomes socialized through being reared in a primary group because of his helplessness at birth.

Nothing exhibits such a striking picture of weakness, of pain, and of misery, as the condition of an infant immediately after birth. Incapable of employing its organs or its senses, the infant requires every kind of succour and assistance: It is more helpless than the young of any other animal.[259]

Now, there are two kinds of education, which ought to be carefully distinguished, because their effects are extremely different; the education of the individual, which is common to man and the other animals; and the education of the species, which appertains to man alone. A young animal, both from natural incitements and from example, learns, in a few weeks, to do every thing its parents can perform. To an infant, several years are necessary before it acquires this degree of perfection; because, when brought forth, it is incomparably less advanced, weaker, and more imperfectly formed, than the

* " . . . we have no just idea of a man in a pure state of nature."[255]

" . . . the distance between man in a pure state of nature and a Hottentot, is greater than between a Hottentot and us."[256]

"An absolute savage, such as the boy brought up by the bear, [etc.] . . . would be a curious object to a philosopher, by the contemplation of which he might estimate the force of natural appetites."[257]

smaller animals. In early infancy, the mind is nothing, when compared to the powers it will afterwards acquire. In receiving individual education, therefore, the infant is much slower than the brute; but, for this very reason, it becomes susceptible of that of the species. The multiplicity of succours, the continual cares, which the state of imbecility for a long time requires, cherish and augment the attachment of the parents. In training the body, they cultivate the mind. The time employed in strengthening the former gives an advantage to the latter. The bodily powers of most animals are more advanced in two months than those of the infant in two years. Hence the time employed in bestowing on the infant its education, is as twelve to one, without estimating the fruits of what follows after this period, without considering that animals separate from their parents as soon as they can provide for themselves, and that, not long after this separation, they know each other no more. All education ceases the moment that the aid of the parents becomes unnecessary.[260]

. . . if abandoned before the age of three years, it would infallibly perish. Now, this necessary, and so long continued intercourse between mother and child, is sufficient to communicate to it all that she possesses: And though we should falsely suppose, that a mother, in a state of nature, possesses nothing, not even the faculty of speech, would not this long intercourse with her infant produce a language? Hence a state of pure nature, in which man is supposed neither to think nor speak, is imaginary, and never had an existence. This necessity of a long intercourse between parents and children produces society in the midst of a desert. The family understand each other by signs and sounds; and this first ray of intelligence, when cherished, cultivated, and communicated, unfolds, in process of time, all the germs of cogitation. As this habitual intercourse could not subsist long, without producing mutual signs and sounds, these signs and sounds, always repeated and gradually engraven on the memory of the child, would become permanent expressions. The catalogue of words, though short, forms a language which will soon extend as the family augments, and will always follow, in its improvement, the progress of society. As soon as society begins to be formed, the education of the infant is no longer individual, since the parents communicate to it not only what they derive from Nature, but likewise what they have received from their progenitors, and from the society to which they belong. It is no longer a communication between detached individuals, which, as in the animals, would be limited to the transmission of simple faculties, but an institution of which the whole species participate, and whose produce constitutes the basis and bond of society.[261]

We have seen, that all the actions which ought to be denominated *human*, are relative to society; that they depend, at first, on the mind, and afterwards on education, the physical principle of which is the long intercourse between the parents and children.[262]

Man derives all his power from society, which matures his reason, exercises his genius, and unites his force. Before the formation of society, man was perhaps the most savage and the least formidable of all animals.[263]

He gave a panorama of cultural evolution.

The first men. . . . Naked in mind as well as in body, exposed to the injuries of every element, victims to the rapacity of ferocious animals, which they were unable to combat, penetrated with the common sentiment of terror, and pressed by necessity, they must have quickly associated, at first to protect themselves by their numbers, and then to afford mutual aid to each other in forming habitations and weapons of defence. They began with sharpening into the figures of axes those hard flints, those *thunder-stones*, which their descendants imagined to have been produced by thunder, and to have fallen from the clouds, but which, in reality, are the first monuments of human art. They would soon extract fire from these flints by striking them against each other.

To destroy the brushwood and the forests, they would employ the flames derived from volcano's, or from their burning lavas; for, with the assistance of this powerful element, they cleared and purified the grounds which they chose to inhabit. With the axes of stone, they cut trees, and fabricated those weapons and utensils of which necessity first suggested the use; and, after being provided with clubs and other heavy armour, would not these first men discover the means of making lighter weapons to annoy at a distance? The tendon of an animal, the fibres of aloes, or the pliant bark of some ligneous plant, would serve them for a cord to unite the extremities of an elastic branch; with which they made their bow: To arm their arrows, they employed small sharp flints. In a short time they would have thread, rafts, and canoes; and in this state they would remain till little nations were formed. These nations were composed of a few families, or rather of the descendants of the same family, which is still the condition of those savages who live independent in such open and spacious territories as afford them game, fishes, and fruits. But, in territories which are narrowed by waters, or confined by high mountains, these small nations, after a great increase of population, were obliged to divide the land among themselves; and, from this moment, the earth became the inheritance of man. He took possession of it by his labour and cultivation; and the attachment to a native soil followed rapidly the first acts of property. As individual interest constitutes a part of national order, government and laws must have succeeded, and society must have assumed strength and consistence.

Nevertheless, these men, deeply affected with the miseries of their original state, and having still before their eyes the ravages of inundations, the conflagrations of volcano's, and gulfs opened by the succussions of the earth . . . gave rise to the fable of the Titans, and of their assaults against the Gods; the notion of the real existence of a malevolent being, with the terror and superstition which it unavoidably produced; all these sentiments, founded upon fear, took an unconquerable possession of the human mind.[264]

He continued with a discussion of the later history of man, based upon a degradation theory.[265] As to the center of the diffusion of culture, "the source of human knowledge must have arisen in the northern countries of Asia."[266]

Buffon made some remarks on the characteristics of "savage" man.

. . . savage man, having no idea of society.[267]

As they have but few ideas, their expressions are limited to the most common objects.[268]

He gave a geographic interpretation of culture.

[The] early civilization [of the Japanese and Chinese] may be ascribed to the fertility of the soil, the mildness of the climate, and the vicinity of the sea; while the Tartars, removed from the sea, and separated from the southern nations by high mountains, have continued to wander in their vast deserts, and under a climate, the rigour of which, especially in the northern parts of Tartary, could only be supported by a robust and uncultivated people.[269]

He minimized the importance of the role of the individual in affecting historical development.

Previous to the reign of Czar Peter I. the Russians, we are told, were almost entirely barbarous. [Then follows a description of their "unrefined" and "refined" customs of earlier times.] . . . Is it not apparent, from these circumstances, that the barbarity of the Russians had already begun to decay, and that their sovereign had not such amazing difficulties in polishing them, as some authors are desirous of insinuating? They are now a civilized and commercial people; they are fond of the arts and sciences, of public spectacles, of ingenious novelties. Such important changes cannot be produced by a great man; but a great man may be born in a fortunate moment.[270]

Buffon interested himself in the factors which determine the size of population.

Population depends more on society than Nature. Men would not be comparatively so numerous as the savage animals, if they were not united, and derived not mutual aid and succour from society. . . . But, though population be a result of society, it is the increased number of men which necessarily produces their unity.[271]

. . . the ordinary course of animated Nature, which, in general, is always the same: Its movements are performed on two steady pivots, unlimited fecundity, and those innumerable causes of destruction which reduce the product of this fecundity to a determined measure, and preserve, at all periods, nearly an equal number of individuals in each species.[272]

## Gray

In his *Elegy Written in a Country Church-Yard* (1751)[273] Thomas Gray (1716–71) based one of his most romantic ideas on the importance of social factors in personality development.

> Perhaps in this neglected spot is laid
>   Some heart once pregnant with celestial fire;
> Hands, that the road of empire might have sway'd,
>   Or wak'd to extasy the living lyre.
>
> But Knowledge to their eyes her ample page
>   Rich with the spoils of time did ne'er unroll;
> Chill Penury repress'd their noble rage,
>   And froze the genial current of the soul.
>
> Full many a gem of purest ray serene,
>   The dark unfathom'd caves of ocean bear:
> Full many a flower is born to blush unseen,
>   And waste its sweetness on the desert air.
>
> Some village-Hampden, that with dauntless breast
>   The little Tyrant of his fields withstood,
> Some mute inglorious Milton here may rest,
>   Some Cromwell guiltless of his country's blood.
>
> Th' applause of list'ning senates to command,
>   The threats of pain and ruin to despise,
> To scatter plenty o'er a smiling land,
>   And read their hist'ry in a nation's eyes,
>
> Their lot forbad: nor circumscrib'd alone
>   Their growing virtues, but their crimes confin'd;
> Forbad to wade through slaughter to a throne,
>   And shut the gates of mercy on mankind,
>
> The struggling pangs of conscious truth to hide,
>   To quench the blushes of ingenuous shame,

Or heap the shrine of Luxury and Pride
　　With incense kindled at the Muse's flame.

Far from the madding crowd's ignoble strife,
　　Their sober wishes never learn'd to stray:
Along the cool sequester'd vale of life
　　They kept the noiseless tenor of their way.

## Cowper

William Cowper (1731–1800) showed man's need for society in "Verses, supposed to be written by Alexander Selkirk, during his solitary abode in the Island of Juan Fernandez" (1782).

I am monarch of all I survey,
　　My right there is none to dispute,
From the centre all round to the sea,
　　I am lord of the fowl and the brute.
O solitude! where are the charms
　　That sages have seen in thy face?
Better dwell in the midst of alarms,
　　Than reign in this horrible place.

I am out of humanity's reach,
　　I must finish my journey alone,
Never hear the sweet music of speech.—
　　I start at the sound of my own.

The beasts that roam over the plain
　　My form with indifference see,
They are so unacquainted with man,
　　Their tameness is shocking to me.

Society, friendship, and love,
　　Divinely bestowed upon man,
Oh had I the wings of a dove,
　　How soon would I taste you again!

## Herder

Johann Gottfried von Herder (1744–1803) began his *Ideen zur Philosophie der Geschichte der Menschheit* with a consideration of man as a part of the cosmos and as subject to its laws.

. . . everything in nature is connected.[274]

. . . man is but a small part of the whole; and his history, like that of the grub, is intimately interwoven with that of the web he inhabits.[275]

. . . man is also a part of the creation, and in his wildest extravagances and passions must obey laws, not less beautiful and excellent than those, by which all the celestial bodies move.[276]

Wherever or whatever I may be, I shall be, as I now am, a power in the universal system of powers, a being in the inconceivable harmony of some *world of God*.[277]

. . . for we, with this our Earth, and everything upon it, evidently form but a small fragment of the great whole.[278]

. . . the whole Earth is made for him [i.e., man]; he for the whole Earth.[279]

His approach was empirical.

. . . throughout the whole creation we know nothing, except by what it is, and what it effects.[280]

The metaphysician . . . sets out with establishing a certain idea of the mind, and from this deduces everything, that can be deduced, wherever, or under whatever circumstances, it may be found. The philosopher of history can proceed on no abstract notion, but on history alone; and he is in danger of forming erroneous conclusions, if he does not generalize at least in some degree the numerous facts before him. I shall attempt to explore the way, however: yet, instead of launching out into the ocean, I shall rather coast along the shore; or, to speak in plain terms, confine myself to undoubted facts, and such as are generally considered so, distinguishing them from my own conjectures, and leaving it to those who are more fortunate, to arrange and employ them in a better manner.[281]

In natural philosophy we never reckon upon miracles: we observe laws, which we perceive everywhere equally effectual, undeviating, and regular. And shall man, with his powers, changes, and passions, burst these chains of nature?[282]

This philosophy will first and most eminently guard us from attributing the facts, that appear in history, to the particular hidden purposes of a scheme of things unknown to us, or the magical influence of invisible powers, which we would not venture to name in connexion with natural phenomena. Fate reveals its purposes through the events that occur, and as they occur: accordingly, the investigator of history develops these purposes merely from what is before him, and what displays itself in its whole extent. Why did the enlightened Greeks appear in the world? Because Greeks existed; and existed under such circumstances, that they could not be otherwise than enlightened. Why did Alexander invade India? Because he was Alexander, the son of Philip; and from the dispositions his father had made, the deeds of his nation, his age and character, his reading of Homer, &c., knew nothing better, that he could undertake. But if we attribute his bold resolution to the secret purposes of some superior power, and his heroic achievements to his peculiar fortune; we run the hazard, on the one hand, of exalting his most senseless and atrocious actions into designs of the deity; and, on the other, of detracting from his personal courage and military skill; while we deprive the whole occurrence of its natural form. He who takes with him into natural history the fairy belief, that invisible sylphs tinge the rose, or hang its cup with pearly dew-drops, and that little spirits of light encase themselves in the body of the glow-worm, or wanton in the peacock's tail, may be an ingenious poet, but will never shine as a naturalist or historian. History is the science of what is, not of what possibly may be according to the hidden designs of fate.[283]

How, therefore, came Europe by its cultivation, and the rank it obtained by it above other countries? Time, place, necessity, the state of affairs, the stream of events, impelled it to this: but, above all, its *peculiar industry in the arts, the result of many common exertions,* procured it this rank.[284]

Natural history has reaped no advantage from the philosophy of final causes, the sectaries of which have been inclined, to satisfy themselves with probable conjecture, instead of patient inquiry: how much less the history of mankind, with its endlessly complicated machinery of causes mutually acting upon each other![285]

Let us, therefore, contemplate this, like any other natural phenomenon, the causes and effects of which we would investigate freely, without any preconceived hypothesis.[286]

Thus contemplated, every thing arbitrary and irrational vanishes from history. In t, as in every production of nature, all, or nothing, is fortuitous: all, or nothing, is arbitrary. Every phenomenon in history is a natural production.[287]

He was a cosmopolitan, and this determined his use of the comparative method.

The mind nobly expands, when it is able to emerge from the narrow circle, which climate and education have drawn round it, and learns from other nations at least what may be dispensed with by man. How much, that we have been accustomed to consider as absolutely necessary, do we find others live without, and consequently perceive to be by no means indispensable! Numberless ideas, which we have often admitted as the most general principles of the human understanding, disappear, in this place and that, with the climate, as the land vanishes like a mist from the eye of the navigator. What one nation holds indispensable to the circle of its thoughts, has never entered into the mind of a second, and by a third has been deemed injurious.[288]

Is there any species of barbarity, to which some man, some nation, nay frequently a number of nations, have not accustomed themselves; so that many, perhaps most, have even fed on the flesh of their fellow-creatures? Is there a wild conception the mind can frame, which has not been actually rendered sacred by hereditary tradition, in one place or another? . . . I am persuaded, no form of human manners is possible, which some nation, or some individual, has not adopted.[289]

If, then, we would philosophise on the history of our species, let us reject, as far as possible, all narrow modes of thinking, taken from the constitution of one region of the Earth, the doctrines of a single school. Let us consider as the purpose of Nature, not what man is with us, or what, according to the notions of some dreamer, he ought to be; but what he is on the Earth in general, and at the same time in every region in particular; or to what the copious variety of circumstances in the hand of Nature can any where fashion him.[290]

After the biological analysis of man given above in the section on physical anthropology, Herder continued:

. . . having gone over the figure and natural powers of man, I come to his mind, and attempt to investigate its variable faculties, as they exist throughout the wide World, from indirect, defective, and partly questionable accounts.[291]

The basic factors are racial and geographic.

The appetites of the human spirit vary with their form and climate.*[296]

However, he did not neglect the influence of culture.

The human fancy is everywhere organic and climatic, but it is everywhere led by tradition.[297]

* "It is true, we are ductile clay in the hand of Climate;[292] but her fingers mould so variously, and the laws, that counteract them, are so numerous, that perhaps the genius of mankind alone is capable of combining the relations of all these powers in one whole."[293]

"The gentic power is the mother of all the forms upon earth, climate acting merely as an auxiliary or antagonist."[294]

" . . . on the opposition between genesis and climate. . . . Nature has drawn determinate lines round her species. . . . But, that the rose can admit of variation, that the dog can acquire something wolfish, is conformable to experience: yet here the variation is producible only by slow or speedy violence done to the resisting organic powers. Thus both the contending principles act with great force, yet each in its own way. Climate is a chaos of causes, very dissimilar to each other, and in consequence acting slowly and in various ways, till at length they penetrate to the internal parts, and change them by habit, and by the genetic power itself: this resists long, forcibly, uniformly, and like itself; but as it is not independent of external affections, it also must accommodate itself to them in length of time."[295]

The practical understanding of the human species has every where grown up under the wants of life; but every where it is a blossom of the genius of the people, a son of tradition and custom.[298]

The feelings and inclination of men are everywhere conformable to their organization, and the circumstances in which they live, but they are every where swayed by custom and opinion.[299]

The happiness of man . . . is every where climatic and organic, the offspring of practice, tradition, and custom.[300]

. . . the inequality of men is not so great by nature, as it is rendered by education; as the qualities of the very same people under different forms of government show.[301]

In fact, Herder believed in the inheritance of socially acquired characteristics.

It has long been questioned, whether there be innate ideas: and in the common acceptation of the words the answer must certainly be in the negative. But if we understand them to signify a predisposition to receive, connect, and expand certain ideas and images, nothing appears to make against the affirmative, and every thing for it. If a child can inherit six fingers, if the family of the *porcupine-man* in England could derive from their parent his unnatural excrescences, if the external form of the head and face be often transmitted, as it evidently is, from father to son; would it not be strange, that the form of the brain, perhaps even in its finest organic divisions, should not be hereditary likewise?[302]

. . . man . . . sought fame in perils; and to surmount them was the most precious jewel of his life. This disposition descended from father to son: the rudiments of education promoted it, and in a few generations the tendency became hereditary. No other man is affected by the sound of the horn, and the voice of the hound, like him who is born a hunter: to this the impressions he received in his childhood contribute. Nay, frequently the countenance of the hunter, and the structure of his brain, are transmitted to his posterity. It is the same with all the other ways of life of free, active nations.[303]

He stressed man's sociality.

. . . considering man among his brethren, let us ask: is he by nature a beast of prey towards his fellows, is he an unsocial being? By his make he is not the former; and by his birth the latter still less. Conceived in the bosom of Love, and nourished at the breast of Affection, he is educated by men, and receives from them a thousand unearned benefits. Thus he is actually formed in and for society, without which he could neither have received his being, nor have become a man.[304]

As all the tender affections, except imparting and receiving love, are satisfied with *participation;* Nature has formed man most of all living creatures for *participating* in the fate of others, having framed him as it were out of all the rest, and organized him similarly to every part of the creation in such a degree, that he can feel with each. The structure of his fibres is so fine, delicate, and elastic, his nerves are so diffused over every part of his vibrating frame, that, like an image of the all sentient deity, he can put himself almost in the place of every creature, and can share its feelings in the degree necessary to the creature, and which his own frame will bear without being disordered; nay even at the hazard of disordering it.[305]

. . . there is a human nature, that is, a cooperation of individuals, which alone makes us men.[306]

The first society arose in the paternal habitation, being cemented by the ties of blood,

f confidence, and love. . . . Here lies the ground of a necessary *human society*, without
which no man could grow up, and the species could not multiply. Man is therefore *born
for society*: this the affection of his parents tells him; this, the years of his protracted
infancy.[307]

The natural state of man is society; for in this he is born and brought up; to this
he is led by the awakening propensities of his youth; and the most pleasing appelations
of father, son, brother, sister, lover, friends, are ties of the law of Nature, that exist in
very primitive society of men.[308]

The human infant is plastic and helpless at birth.

. . . our specific character lies in this, that, born almost without instinct, we are formed
to manhood only by the practice of a whole life.[309]

For no one of us became man of himself: the whole structure of his humanity is connected by a spiritual birth, education, with his parents, teachers, friends; with all the
circumstances of his life, and consequently with his countrymen and their forefathers;
and lastly with the whole chain of the human species, some link or other of which is
continually acting on his mental faculties.[310]

. . . throughout his whole life, he is not only a child in reason, but a pupil of the
reason of others. Into whatever hands he falls, by them he is formed.[311]

. . . living beings like ourselves contribute to instruct us, fashion us, and form our
habits.[312]

. . . every one becomes a man only by means of education.[313]

As man at his natural birth springs not from himself, equally remote is he from being
selfborn in the use of his mental faculties. Not only is the germ of our internal disposition genetic, as well as our bodily frame, but every development of this germ depends
on fate, which planted us in this place or in that, and supplied us with the means by which
we were formed, according to time and circumstances. Even the eye must learn to see,
the ear to hear; and no one can be ignorant with what art language, the principal instrument of thought, is acquired. Nature has evidently calculated our whole mechanism,
with the condition and duration of each period of our lives, for this foreign aid. The
brain of infants is soft, and suspended from the skull: its strata are slowly formed; it
grows firmer with increasing years, and gradually hardens, till at length it will receive
no more new impressions. It is the same with the organs and with the faculties of a
child: those are tender, and formed for imitation; these imbibe what they see and hear
with wonderfully active attention, and internal vital power. Thus man is an artificial
machine; endued with a genetic disposition, it is true, and plenitude of life; but the
machine does not work itself, and the ablest of mankind must learn how to work it.
Reason is the aggregate of the experiences and observations of the mind, the sum of
the education of man, which the pupil ultimately finishes in himself, as an extraneous
artist, after certain extraneous models.[314]

The child learns by imitation, uncritically accepting the customs of its group.

All education must spring from imitation and exercise, by means of which the model
passes into the copy.[315]

The ignorant child listens with curiosity to the tales, which flow into his mind like
his mother's milk, like choice wine of his father, and form its nutriment. They seem to
him to explain what he has seen: to the youth they account for the way of life of his tribe,
and stampt the renown of his ancestors: the man they introduce to the employment

suited to his nation and climate, and thus they become inseparable from his whole life. The Greenlander and Tungus see in reality all their lives only what they heard of in their infancy, and thus they believe it to be evidently true.[316]

Herder pointed out that man adapts himself to new environmental conditions culturally, rather than morphologically—an observation later repeated by Wallace in the nineteenth century.

The habitable land of our Earth is accumulated in regions, where most living beings act in the mode best adapted to them.[317]

Of all these changeable, modifiable, adaptable creatures, man is the most adaptable.[318]

Thus man was led to clothe himself; and no sooner had he acquired this and a few other arts, but he was capable of enduring any climate, and taking possession of every part of the Earth. Few animals, scarcely any indeed except the dog, have been able to follow him into every region; and then how greatly has the form of these been changed! how much has their native constitution been altered! Man alone has but little varied, and this in no essential part. It is astonishing how uniformly he has retained his nature, when we contemplate the variations, that have taken place in other migrating animals.[319]

He showed the importance of language in the development of man.

Speech alone has rendered man human, by setting bounds to the vast flood of his passions, and giving them rational memorials by means of words.[320]

Language is the special means of improving man.[321]

By speech alone we all attain to reason*; and by tradition, by belief in the words of our fathers, to speech.[323]

In man, nay even in the ape, there is a peculiar disposition to imitation, which appears to be by no means the consequence of rational conviction, but the immediate offspring of organic sympathy. As one string resounds to another, and the vibrating capacity of all bodies increases with their more equable density and homogeneity; the human organization, being the most exquisite of all, is of necessity more peculiarly formed, to repeat the tones of all other beings, and sympathetic with them.[324]

But man did not attain the artificial characteristic of his species, reason, by all this mimicry: he arrived at it by speech alone.[325]

By it men welcomed one another into society, and knit the bonds of love. It framed laws and united families: it alone renders a history of mankind, in transmitted modifications of the heart and mind, possible.[326]

All the arts and sciences of mankind have been invented through imitation, reason, and language.[327]

Thus he got into the road to every art, through nothing but the internal generation of a distinct mark, and the retention of it in a fact, or some other note; in short, through language. Through it, and it alone, were observation, recognition, remembrance, possession, and a chain of thought, possible; and thus in time were born the arts and sciences, daughters of designating reason, and imitation for some purpose.[328]

Writing is a necessary factor in the development of civilization.

If language has been the means of improving men as *men*, writing is the means of improving them in *erudition*. All nations, who have been destitute of this artificial tradition, have remained, according to our ideas, uncultivated; while they, who have enjoyed

---

* " . . . without speech he could not attain to reason."[322]

t but imperfectly, have immortalized their understanding and laws by embalming them
n letters.[329]

Language is related to the rest of culture.

A nation has no idea, for which its language has no word.[330]

*A philosophical comparison of languages* would form the best essay on the history and
diversified character of the human heart and understanding: for every language bears
the stamp of the mind and character of a people. Not only do the organs of speech vary
with climates, not only are there certain sounds and letters peculiar to almost every
nation, but the giving of names, even in denoting audible things, nay in the immediate
xpressions of the passions, in interjections, varies over all the Earth. With respect to
visible things, and subjects of cool reflextion, this variation is still greater, and in al-
egorical expressions, in figures of speech, in the structure of a language lastly, in the
elation, arrangement, and connexion of its parts, it is almost infinite: though still the
genius of a people is no where more displayed than in the physiognomy of their language. For instance, whether a nation have many names, or much action; how it expresses time and person; to what order of ideas it is attached; is often extremely character-
stic in nice features. Many nations have a particular language for either sex: in others
even condition is discriminated in the simple word *I*. The verbs of active nations have
n abundance of moods: refined nations have a number of modifications of things, which
they have exalted to abstract notions. Finally, the most singular part of human languages
s the delineation of men's feelings, the expressions of love and esteem, of reproof and
dulation, in which the weaknesses of a people are often laughably displayed.[331]

Culture itself has a history and is subject to natural laws.

. . . reason, the essence of man, and its organ, tradition, have been inherited through
series of successive generations.[332]

The whole history of mankind is a pure natural history of human powers, actions, and
propensities, modified by time and place.[333]

[However,] It had never entered into my mind, by employing a few figurative expressions, the *childhood, infancy, manhood,* and *old age* of our species, the chain of which was
pplied, as it was applicable, only to a few nations, to point out a highway, on which
the *history of culture,* to say nothing of the *philosophy of history at large,* could be traced
with certainty.[334]

Our philosophy of history shall not wander in this path of the Averroean system,
ccording to which the whole human species possesses but one mind; and that indeed
of a very low order, distributed to individuals only piecemeal. On the other hand, were
to confine every thing to the individual, and deny the existence of the chain, that
connects each to others and to the whole, I should run equally counter to the nature of
man, and his evident history.[335]

Hence the principles of this philosophy becomes as evident, simple, and indubitable,
s the natural history of man itself is: they are called *tradition and organic powers.* All educa-
ion must spring from imitation and exercise, by means of which the model passes into
the copy; how can this be more aptly expressed than by the term tradition? But the
mitator must have powers to receive what is communicated or communicable, and
onvert it into his own nature, as the food by means of which he lives. Accordingly,
what and how much he received, whence he derives it, and how he uses, applies it, and
makes it his own, must depend on his own, the receptive powers. So that the education
of our species is in a double sense genetic and organic: genetic, inasmuch as it is com-

municated; organic, as what is communicated is received and applied. Whether we nam
this second genesis of man *culture* from the culture of the ground, or *enlightening* fro
the action of light, is of little import; the chain of light and culture reaches to the en
of the Earth. Even the inhabitant of California or Tierra del Fuego learns to make an
use the bow and arrow: he has language and ideas, practices and arts, which he learned
as we learn them: so far, therefore, he is actually cultured and enlightened, though i
the lowest order. Thus the difference between enlightened and unenlightened, culture
and uncultured nations, is not specific; it is only in degree.[336]

He was not satisfied with simplified explanations of historical events; fo
example, in discussing the decline of Rome he warned, "let the reader extend hi
views, and not confine them to a single cause of the ruin of that state."[337]

Indeed, no occurrence in human affairs stands alone: arising from anterior causes, th
spirit of the times, and the dispositions of nations, it is to be considered only as the dia
the hand of which is moved by internal springs.[338]

He was an advocate of the theory of social progress; "he would doubt as littl
of their [i.e., men's] progress, as of the most indisputable physical truth."[3?]

Nothing in nature stands still: every thing exerts itself, and pushes on. Could w
contemplate the first periods of creation, and see how one kingdom of nature was erecte
on another; what a series of powers urging onward would be displayed progressivel
unfolding themselves![340]

If our species be destined to approach, in the eternal path of an asymptote, a poir
of perfection, which it does not know, and which, with all the labour of a Tantalus, :
can never touch.[341]

Therefore he spoke of "the chain of improvement,"[342] and "the varied progressiv
improvement of the human mind."[343]

From the laws of their internal nature, reason and justice must gain more footin
among men in the course of time, and promote a more durable humanity.*[345]

[First.] Times connect themselves together, in virtue of their nature; and with ther
the child of time, the race of mankind, with all its operations and productions.[346]

. . . a certain progress of the human species is inseparable from the progress of time
as far as man is included in the family of time and earth.[347]

Secondly. The habitations of mankind render the progress of the human specie
still more evident.[348]

To him the earth is given; and he will not desist, till it is wholly his own, at least a
regards knowledge and use. Are we not already ashamed, that one hemisphere of ou
planet remained for so long a time as unknown to us, as if it had been the other sid
of the moon?[349]

Third. In consequence of the internal nature of the human minds, its activity ha
hitherto been employed solely on means of grounding more deeply the humanity an
cultivation of our species, and extending them farther.[350]

. . . every good employment of the human understanding necessarily must and wil
at some time or other, promote humanity.[351]

Every addition to the useful arts secures men's property, diminishes their labou

* "[The goal of this progress is] humanity, that is, reason and equity in all conditions, and in all occupa
tions of men."[344]

extends their sphere of activity, and necessarily lays therewith the foundations of farther cultivation and humanity.[352]

Reason . . . and the effective joint activity of mankind, keep on their unwearied course.[353]

## Goethe

Johann Wolfgang von Goethe (1749–1832) made a profound investigation of the dynamic and social factors in personality development.

First, he considered personality as a dynamic thing, the product of the individual's successive interactions with his environment.

The life of a man, *that* is his character.[354]

. . . everything that happens to us leaves some trace behind it, everything contributes imperceptibly to form us.[355]

Altogether, the most important part of an individual's life is that of development, and mine is concluded in the detailed volumes of " Dichtung und Wahrheit."[356]

[In *Dichtung und Wahrheit*] I had to represent the development of a child grown to be considerable, how in given circumstances the bent of my genius had asserted itself.[357]

[The end or purpose of his autobiography is:] Does it give an idea of the gradual development of a personality?[358]

How else does character finally prove itself, if it is not formed by the activity of the day, by reflective agencies which counteract each other? Who would venture to determine the value of contingencies, impulses, after-effects? Who dare estimate the influence of elective affinities? At all events, he who would presume to estimate what man is, must take into consideration what he was, and how he became so.[359]

Second, he emphasized the importance of the fact that the infant is born into a social group with a culture.

Not only what is born with him, but also what he acquires, makes the man.[360]

It is very strange how certain modes of thought become general, and can, for some length of time, be maintained, and for long actually regarded as something existing in human nature.[361]

. . . we are born in an artificial state, and it is far easier to make it more artificial still, than to return to what is simple.[362]

People are always talking about originality; but what do they mean? As soon as we are born, the world begins to work upon us, and this goes on to the end.[363]

For what then is man, in and through himself? When he opens his eyes and ears, he cannot avoid objectivity, example, tradition; he educates himself by these.[364]

In fact, when endeavouring to estimate the value of any unusual degree of talent, it is but a poor expedient rashly to speculate where the man may have derived all his advantages. A child growing up to manhood does not find Nature presented to him in all its simplicity and nakedness; for the divine power of his ancestors has created for him a second world in the already existing world. Enforced habits, usages, popular customs, venerable traditions, precious monuments, useful laws, and the many glorious productions of art, enthral and influence him to such a degree, that he is never quite able to distinguish between what is original in him and what hereditary.[365]

Third, the individual is born with certain potentialities; the culture of the group determines which are to be developed, and which inhibited.

Much within us that is peculiarly our own, we are not allowed to develop in outward acts; much that we need from without for the perfection of our character is withheld; while, on the other hand, much is forced upon us which is as alien to us as it is burdensome.[366]

We are indeed born with faculties; but we owe our development to a thousand influences of the great world, from which we appropriate to ourselves what we can, and what is suitable to us.[367]

Any talent, the development of which is not favored by time and circumstances, and must on that account work its way through a thousand obstacles, and get rid of a thousand errors, must always be at a disadvantage, when compared with a contemporary one that has the opportunity to cultivate itself with facility and act to the extent of its capacity without opposition.[368]

It may therefore always be maintained that native talent is indeed indispensable to production, but equally indispensable is a commensurate development in the provinces of nature and art.[369]

The author no more than the man of action can fashion the conditions under which he is born and under which he acts. Each one, even the greatest genius, suffers in some respects from the social and political conditions of his age, just as in other respects he benefits by them.*[371]

... the main function of biography seems to be, to exhibit the man in relation to his times, and to show to what extent this environment was inimical or propitious to him; how he evolved from it a philosophy of the world and of men, and in what way he, in his turn, if an artist, poet, or author, reproduced this philosophy in concrete form.[372]

Fourth, the means by which the individual adjusts to his environment, both social and natural, are themselves social products.

But, in fact, we are all collective beings, let us place ourselves as we may. For how little *have* we, and *are* we, that we can strictly call our own property? We must all receive and learn both from those who were before us, and from those who are with us. Even the greatest genius would not go far if he tried to owe everything to his own internal self.[373]

If I could give an account of all that I owe to great predecessors and contemporaries, there would be a small balance in my favour.[374]

[The works of Raphael] demanded the culture of a series of centuries to achieve.[375]

There is through all art a filiation. If you see a great master, you will always find that he used what was good in his predecessors, and that it was this which made him great. Men like Raphael do not spring out of the ground.[376]

What are the conditions that produce a classical national author? He must, in the first place, be born in a great commonwealth, which after a series of great and historic events has become a happy and unified nation. He must find in his countrymen loftiness of disposition, depth of feeling, and vigor and consistency of action. He must be thoroughly pervaded with the national spirit, and through his innate genius feel capable of sympathizing with the past as well as the present. He must find his nation in a high state of civilization, so that he will have no difficulty in obtaining for himself a high degree of culture.

* He later qualified this: "A mediocre talent is, indeed, always biassed by its age, and must be fed by the elements of the age . . . [but] great geniuses . . . have a foundation in themselves, and keep free from the mode of thinking which belongs to their time."[370]

He must find much material already collected and ready for his use, and a large number of more or less perfect attempts made by his predecessors. And finally, there must be such a happy conjuncture of outer and inner circumstances that he will not have to pay dearly for his mistakes, but that in the prime of his life he may be able to see the possibilities of a great theme and to develop it according to some uniform plan into a well-arranged and well-constructed literary work.[377]

Goethe insisted that everything, including man, is subject to natural law.

Even what is most unnatural is Nature.[378]

Man obeys her laws even in opposing them: he works with her even when he wants to work against her.[379]

... whatever is produced by a great mind is also nature.[380]

Everything repeats itself in the grand course of the world's history; a careful observer will notice this everywhere.[381]

The characteristics of a culture depend upon the genius of the people.

Every nation has peculiarities by which it is distinguished from the others, and it is by these distinguishing traits that nations are also attracted to and repelled from one another. The external expressions of these inner idiosyncracies appear to the others in most cases strikingly disagreeable, or, if endurable, merely amusing. This is why, too, we always respect a nation less than it deserves. The inner traits, on the other hand, are not known or recognized, by foreigners or even by the nation itself; for the inner nature of a whole nation, as well as the individual man, works all unconsciously. At the end we wonder, we are astounded, at what appears.[382]

However, geography plays a part.

... not only the inborn peculiarities of race, but soil and climate, aliment and occupation, combine to form the character of a people. It is also to be borne in mind, that the primitive races mostly took possession of a soil that pleased them; and, consequently, where the country was already in harmony with their own inborn character.[383]

... nowhere, perhaps, in the history of art does the national character, the climatic influence, play so beautiful a part as in the Rhine countries.[384]

Its stage of development also affects a culture.*

All eras in a state of decline and dissolution are subjective; on the other hand, all progressive eras have an objective tendency.[387]

The more genius a century possesses the more are individual things furthered.[388]

Nevertheless, he sometimes gave a quasi-social interpretation of cultural events.

As the military and physical strength of a nation develops from its internal unity and cohesion, so must its aesthetic and ethical strength grow gradually from a similar unanimity of feeling and ideas.[389]

Literature decays only as men become more and more corrupt.[390]

Goethe vacillated when considering the role of the individual in history.

... man may often be considered as an instrument in a higher government of the world,—as a vessel found worthy for the reception of a divine influence. I say this, whilst I consider how often a single thought has given a different form to whole centuries,

---

* "It is impossible to understand the present without a knowledge of the past."[385]
" ... only through comprehension of the past is the present intelligible."[386]

and how individual men have, by their expressions, imprinted a stamp upon their age, which has remained uneffaced, and has operated beneficially upon succeeding generation.[391]

[He said of Napoleon:] What a compendium of the world![392]

. . . personal influence . . . often produced great effects without being much heard of. This showed how little history can be relied upon; as, in fact, no one can tell why or wherefore one thing or another is done.[393]

The individual limited to his own part is heedless of the great whole.[394]

I am opposed to the view that any single man can cause the decline of an art. Much, which it is not so easy to set forth, must co-operate to this end. The decline of the tragic art of the Greeks could no more have been caused by Euripides, than could that of sculpture by any great sculptor who lived in the time of Phidias, but was inferior to him. For when an epoch is great, it proceeds in the path of improvement, and an inferior production is without results. But what a great epoch was the time of Euripides! It was the time, not of a retrograde, but of a progressive taste. Sculpture had not yet reached its highest point, and painting was still in its infancy.[395]

. . . as centuries pass from the severe to pleasing, they form man's taste at the same time—indeed, create him after the same law.[396]

## Darwin

To Erasmus Darwin (1731–1802) man's love and sympathy are the basis of society.

> Love and Sympathy with potent charm
> Warm the cold heart, the lifted hand disarm;
> Allure with pleasures, and alarm with pains,
> And bind Society in golden chains.[397]

> hail the DEITIES OF SEXUAL LOVE!
> All forms of Life shall this fond Pair delight,
> And sex to sex the willing world unite;
> Shed their sweet smiles in Earth's unsocial bowers,
> . . .
> And give SOCIETY his golden chain.*[400]

> Parturient Sires caress their infant train,
> And heaven-born STORGE† weaves the social chain;
> Successive births her tender cares combine,
> And soft affections live along the line.[401]

He contrasted social man with the unsocial animals.

> In these lone births no tender mothers blend
> Their genial powers to nourish or defend;
> No nutrient streams from Beauty's orbs improve
> These orphan babes of solitary love;
> Birth after birth the line unchanging runs,
> And fathers live transmitted in their sons;
> Each passing year beholds the unvarying kinds,

---

* "[Love] binds SOCIETY in silken chains."[398]
† "The Greek word Storgè is used for the affection of parents to children."[399]

The same their manners, and the same their minds.[402]

Man is imitative and sympathetic.

> Last, as observant Imitation stands,
> Turns her quick glance, and brandishes her hands,
> With mimic acts associate thoughts excites,
> And storms the soul with sorrows or delights;
> Life's shadowy scenes are brighten'd and refin'd,
> And soft emotions mark the feeling mind.
>
> The Seraph, SYMPATHY, from Heaven descends,
> And bright o'er earth his beamy forehead bends;
> On Man's cold heart celestial ardor flings,
> And showers affection from his sparkling wings;
> Rolls o'er the world his mild benignant eye
> . . .
> And charms the world with universal love.
>
> O'er the thrill'd frame his words assuasive steal,
> And teach the selfish heart what other feel;
> With sacred truth each erring thought control.
> Bind sex to sex, and mingle soul with soul;
> From heaven, He cried, descends the moral plan,
> And gives Society to savage man.[403]

Like Tarde in the nineteenth century, Darwin thought of imitation as the fundamental mechanism in social interaction.[404]

> And IMITATION marks the mind of Man.[405]
> Hence when the inquiring hands with contact fine
> Trace on hard forms the circumscribing line;
> Which then the language of the rolling eyes
> From distant scenes of earth and heaven supplies;
> Those clear ideas of the touch and sight
> Rouse the quick sense to anguish or delight;
> Whence the fine power of IMITATION springs,
> And apes the outlines of external things;
> With ceaseless action to the world imparts
> All moral virtues, languages, and arts.
> First the charm'd Mind mechanic powers collects,
> Means for some end, and causes of effects;
> Then learns from other Minds their joys and fears,
> Contagious smiles and sympathetic tears.[406]

To which may be added, that this propensity to imitation not only appears in the actions of children, but in all the customs and fashions of the world; many thousands tread in the beaten paths of others, who precede or accompany them, for one who traverses regions of his own discovery.*[408]

. . . the immediate cause of our propensity to imitation above that of other animals

---

* "Not only the greatest part of mankind learn all the common arts of life by imitating others, but brute animals seem capable of acquiring knowledge with greater facility by imitating each other, than by any methods by which we can teach them."[407]

arises from the greater facility, with which by the sense of touch we acquire the ideas of the outlines of objects, and afterwards in consequence by the sense of sight.[409]

The origin of this propensity to imitation has not been deduced from any known principle; when any action presents itself to the view of a child, as of whetting a knife, or threading a needle; the parts of this action in respect of time, motion, figure, are imitated by parts of the retina of his eye; to perform this action therefore with his hands is easier to him than to invent any new action; because it consists in repeating with another set of fibres, viz. with the moving muscles, what he had just performed by some parts of the retina; just as in dancing we transform the times of the motions from the actions of the auditory nerves to the muscles of the limbs. Imitation therefore consists of repetition, which is the easiest kind of animal actions; as the ideas or motions become presently associated together; which adds to the facility of their production; as shown in *Zoonomia*, Vol. I. sect. XXII. 2.[410]

Imitations resolve themselves into four kinds, voluntary, sensitive, irritative, and associative. The voluntary imitations are, when we imitate deliberately the actions of others, either by mimicry, as in acting a play, or in delineating a flower; or in the common actions of our lives, as in our dress, cookery, language, manners, and even in our habits of thinking. . . .

The sensitive imitations are the immediate consequences of pleasure or pain, and these are often produced even contrary to the effects of the will. Thus many young men on seeing cruel surgical operations become sick, and some even feel pain in the parts of their own bodies, which they see tortured or wounded in others. . . .

. . . irritative imitations are daily observable in common life; thus one yawning person shall set a whole company a yawning; and some have acquired winking of the eyes or impediments of speech by imitating their companions without being conscious of it.

Besides the three species of imitations above described there may be some associative motions, which may imitate each other in the kind as well as in the quantity of their action; but it is difficult to distinguish them from the associations of motion.[411]

From our aptitude to imitation arises what is generally understood by the word sympathy, so well explained by Dr. Smith of Glasgow. Thus the appearance of a cheerful countenance gives us pleasure, and of a melancholy one makes us sorrowful. . . .

The effect of this powerful agent in the moral world, is the foundation of all our intellectual sympathies with the pains and pleasures of others, and is in consequence the source of all our virtues. For in what consists our sympathy with the miseries or with the joys of our fellow creatures, but in an involuntary excitation of ideas in some measure similar or imitative of those which we believe to exist in the minds of the persons whom we commiserate or congratualte![412]

There are two ways by which we become acquainted with the passions of others: first, by having observed the effects of them, as of fear or anger, on our own bodies, we know at sight when others are under the influence of these affections. So children long before they can speak, or understand the language of their parents, may be frightened by an angry countenance, or soothed by smiles and blandishments.

Secondly, when we put ourselves into the attitude that any passion naturally occasions, we soon in some degree acquire that passion; hence when those that scold indulge themselves in loud oaths and violent actions of the arms, they increase their anger by the mode of expressing themselves; and, on the contrary, the counterfeited smile of pleasure in disagreeable company soon brings along with it a portion of the reality, as is well illustrated by Mr. Burke. *(Essay on the Sublime and Beautiful.)*

These are natural signs by which we understand each other, and on this slender basis is built all human language. For without some natural signs no artificial ones could have been invented or understood, as is very ingeniously observed by Dr. Reid. ((*Inquiry into the Human Mind.*)[413]

Darwin believed in the evolution of culture.

The story of Hercules seems of great antiquity, as appears from the simplicity of his dress and armour, a lion's skin and a club; and from the nature of many of his exploits, the destruction of wild beasts and robbers. This part of the history of Hercules seems to have related to times before the invention of the bow and arrow, or of spinning flax.[414]

The discovery of fire was of primary importance; the following is part of his invocation to the nymphs of primeval fire:

> Nymphs! your soft smiles uncultur'd man subdued,
> And charm'd the Savage from his native wood;
> You, while amazed his hurrying Hords retire
> From the fell havoc of devouring FIRE,
> Taught, the first Art! with piny rods to raise
> By quick attrition the domestic blaze,
> Fan with soft breath, with kindling leaves provide,
> And list the dread Destroyer on his side.[415]

He accepted the Euhemeristic theory of the origin of religion.

The Deities of Egypt, and afterwards of Greece, and Rome, were derived from men famous in those early times, as in the ages of hunting, pasturage, and agriculture.[416]

Language evolved from gestures.

It must have already appeared to the reader, that all other animals, as well as man, are possessed of this natural language of the passions, expressed in signs or tones; and we shall endeavour to evince, that those animals, which have preserved themselves from being enslaved by mankind, and are associated in flocks, are also possessed of some traditional knowledge.[417]

[He gives examples among turkeys, rabbits, dogs, and nightingales.*[419]]

The origin of this universal language is a subject of highest curiousity. [Then follows an analysis of the biological basis of gesture similar to that found in Charles Darwin's *Expression of the Emotions.*][420]

> When strong desires or soft sensations move
> The astonish'd Intellect to rage or love;
> Associate tribes of fibroud motions rise,
> Flush the red cheek, or light the laughing eyes.
> Whence ever-active Imitation finds
> The ideal trains, that pass in kindred minds;
> Her mimic arts associate thoughts excite
> And the first LANGUAGE enters at the sight.

---

* "A curious circumstance is mentioned by Kircherus de Musurgia, in his "Chapter de Lusciniis." 'That the young nightingales, that are hatched under other birds, never sing till they are instructed by the company of other nightingales.' And Johnston affirms, that the nightingales that visit Scotland, have not the same harmony as those of Italy, (Pennant's *Zoology*, octavo, p. 255), which would lead us to suspect, that the singing of birds, like human music, is an artificial language rather than a natural expression of passion."[416]

Thus the jealous quails or village-cocks inspect
Each other's necks with stiffened plumes erect;
Smit with the wordless eloquence, they know
The rival passion of the threatening foe.
So when the famish'd wolves at midnight howl,
Fell serpents hiss, or fierce hyenas growl;
Indignant Lions rear their bristling mail,
And lash their sides with undulating tail.
Or when the Savage-Man with clenched fist
Parades, the scowling champion of the list;
With brandish'd arms, and eyes that roll to know
Where first to fix the meditated blow;
Association's mystic power combines
Internal passions with external signs.

From these dumb gestures first the exchange began
Of viewless thought in bird, and beast, and man;
And still the stage by mimic art displays
Historic pantomime in modern days;
And hence the enthusiast orator affords
Force to the feebler eloquence of words.

Thus the first LANGUAGE, when we frown'd or smiled,
Rose from the cradle, Imitation's child;
Next to each thought associate sound accords,*
And forms the dulcet symphony of words;[422]
The tongue, the lips articulate; the throat
With soft vibration modulates the note;[423]
Love, pity, war, the shout, the song, the prayer
Form quick concussions of elastic air.

Hence the first accents bear in airy rings
The vocal symbol of ideal things,
Name each nice change appulsive powers supply
To the quick sense of touch, or ear or eye.
Or in fine traits abstracted form suggest
Of Beauty, Wisdom, Number, Motion, Rest;
Or, as within reflex ideas move,
Trace the light steps of Reason, Rage, or Love.
The next new sounds adjunctive thought recite,
As hard, odorous, tuneful, sweet, or white.
The next the fleeting images select
Of action, suffering, causes and effect.[424]

With language came the development of reason.

As the soft lips and pliant tongue are taught
With other minds to interchange the thought;
And sound, the symbol of the sense, explains
In parted links the long ideal trains;

---

* "Words were originally the signs or names of individual ideas; but in all known languages many of them by changing their terminations express more than one idea, as in the cases of nouns, and the moods and tenses of verbs."[421]

From clear conceptions of external things
The facile power of Recollection springs.

Whence REASON's empire o'er the world presides,
And man from brute, and man from man divides.[425]

Ages remote by thee, VOLITION, taught
Chain'd down in characters the winged thought;
With silent language mark'd the letter'd ground,
And gave to sight the evanescent sound.*
Now, happier lot! enlightened realms possess
The learned labours of the immortal Press;
Nursed on whose lap the births of science thrive,
And rising Arts the wrecks of Time survive.[427]

As our ideas consist of successive trains of the motions, or changes of figure, of the extremities of the nerves of one or more of our senses, as of the optic or auditory nerves; these successive trains of motion, or configuration, are in common life divided into many links, to each of which a word or name is given, and is called an idea. This chain of ideas may be broken into more or fewer links, or divided in different parts of it, by the customs of different people. Whence the meanings of the words of one language cannot always be exactly expressed by those of another; and hence the acquirement of different languages in their infancy may affect the modes of thinking and reasoning of whole nations, or of different classes of society; as the words of them do not accurately suggest the same ideas, or parts of ideal trains; a circumstance which has not been sufficiently analysed.[428]

He thought the whole world was progressing toward perfection.

From having observed the gradual evolution of the young animal or plant from its egg or seed; and afterwards its successive advances to its more perfect state, or maturity; philosophers of all ages seem to have imagined, that the great world itself had likewise its infancy and its gradual progress to maturity.[429]

Perhaps all the productions of nature are in their progress to greater perfection! an idea countenanced by modern discoveries and deductions concerning the progressive formation of the solid parts of the terraqueous globe, and consonant to the dignity of the Creator of all things.[430]

The size of population is limited by a number of factors.

human progenies, if unrestrain'd,
By climate friended, and by food sustain'd,
O'er seas and soils, prolific hordes! would spread
Erelong, and deluge their terraqueous bed;
But war, and pestilence, disease, and dearth,
Sweep the superfluous myriads from the earth.[431]

## Godwin

William Godwin (1756–1836) saw the human infant as born without instincts and merely a bundle of potentialities, to be formed by its social milieu.

* "The application of mankind, in the early ages of society, to the imitative arts of painting, carving, statuary, and the casting of figures in metals, seems to have preceded the discovery of letters; and to have been used as a written language to convey intelligence to their distant friends, or to transmit to posterity the history of themselves, or of their discoveries."[426]

We bring into the world with us no innate principles: consequently we are neither virtuous nor vicious as we first come into existence.[432]

Our virtues and vices may be traced to the incidents which make the history of our lives.[433]

Mind is in its infancy nearly . . . the creature of contingencies. But the farther it advances, the more it individualises. Each man has habits and prejudices that are properly his own.[434]

Thus there are three principal causes by which the human mind is advanced towards a state of perfection; literature, or the diffusion of knowledge through the medium of discussion, whether written or oral; education, or a scheme for the early impression of right principles upon the hitherto unprejudiced mind; and political justice, or the adoption of any principle of morality and truth in the practice of a community.[435]

Man is subject to natural law, and therefore there is no freedom of the will.

. . . mind as well as matter exhibits a constant conjunction of events and affords a reasonable presumption as to the necessary connection of those events.[436]

. . . man considered as an individual . . . is operated upon by exterior causes immediately, producing certain effects upon him independently of the exercise of reason; and he is operated upon by exterior causes mediately, their impressions furnishing him with materials for reflection and assuming the form of motives to act or to refrain from acting. But the latter of these, at least so far as related to man in a civilised state, may stand for the whole. He that would change the character of the individual would miserably misapply his efforts if he principally sought to effect this purpose by the operations of heat and cold, dryness and moisture upon the animal frame. The true instruments of moral influence are desire and aversion, punishment and rewards, the exhibition of general truth, and the development of those punishments and rewards which wisdom and error by the very nature of the thing constantly bring along with them. . . .

As is the character of the individual, so may we expect to find it with nations and great bodies of men. The operations of law and political institution will be important and interesting, the operations of climate trifling and unworthy of notice. Thus there are particular professions, such as that of the priesthood, which must always operate to the production of a particular character.[437]

Following Paine, he distinguished between society and political organization.

. . . it is . . . necessary . . . carefully to distinguish between society and government. Men associated at first for the sake of mutual assistance.* They did not foresee that any restraint would be necessary to regulate the conduct of individual members of the society towards each other or towards the whole. The necessity of restraint grew out of the errors and perverseness of a few.[439]

He speculated on the evolution of language.

Its beginning was probably from those involuntary cries, which infants for example are found to utter in the earliest stages of their existence, and which, previously to the idea of exciting pity or procuring assistance, spontaneously arise from the operation of pain upon our animal frame. These cries, when actually uttered, become a subject of perception to him by whom they are uttered; and, being observed to be constantly associated with certain preliminary impressions and to excite the idea of those impressions

---

* "Men would never have associated if they had not imagined that in consequence of that association they would mutually conduce to the advantage and happiness of each other."[438]

in the hearer, may afterward be repeated from reflection and the desire of relief. Eager desire to communicate any information to another, will also prompt us to utter some simple sound for the purpose of exciting attention: this sound will probably frequently recur to organs unpractised to variety, and will at length stand as it were by convention for the information intended to be conveyed. But the distance is extreme from these simple modes of communication, which we possess in common with some of the inferior animals, to all the analysis and abstraction which languages require . . .

But, though it be by no means impossible, to trace the causes that concurred to the production of language, and to prove them adequate to their effect, it does not the less appear like an endless labyrinth. The distance is immeasurable between the three or four vague and inarticulate sounds uttered by animals, and the copiousness of lexicography or the regularity of grammar.[440]

He appreciated the fact of the interdependence of the aspects of culture.

[There is an] intimate connection of the different parts of the social system . . . as it relates to the intercourse of individuals or to the maxims and institutes of states and nations.[441]

As did Brown, he objected to the theory of the natural decay of a culture.

[He opposes] the proposition which affirms that nations like individuals are subject to the phenomena of youth and old age, and that when a people by luxury and depravation of manners have sunk into decreptitude, it is not in the power of legislation to restore them to vigour and innocence.[442]

[He gave the following refutation:]

[1.] The condition of nations is more fluctuating, and will be found less obstinate in its resistance to a consistent endeavour for their improvement, than that of individuals.[443]

[2.] Add to this that generations of men are perpetually going off the stage, while other generations succeed.[444]

[3.] Lastly, the power of social institutions changing the character of nations is very different from and infinitely greater than any power which can ordinarily be brought to bear upon a solitary individual.[445]

In fact, he opposed to this notion that of a general and continuing social progress.

Is it possible for us to contemplate what he [i.e., man] has already done without being impressed with a strong presentiment of the improvements he has yet to accomplish? There is no science that is not capable of additions; there is no art that may not be carried to a still higher perfection. If this be true of all other sciences, why not of morals? If this be true of all other arts, why not of social institution? The very conception of this as possible is in the highest degree encouraging. If we can still farther demonstrate it to be a part of the natural and regular progress of mind, our confidence and our hopes will then be complete.[446]

## Rush

Benjamin Rush (1745–1813) made "An inquiry into the influence of physical causes upon the moral faculty" (1786).[447]

It is immaterial, whether the physical causes that are to be enumerated act upon the moral faculty through the medium oft he senses, the passions, the memory, or the imagination. Their influence is equally certain, whether they act as remote, predisposing, or occasional causes.

1. The effects of CLIMATE upon the moral faculty claim our first attention. Not only individuals, but nations, derive a considerable part of their moral, as well as intellectual character, from the different portions they enjoy of the rays of the sun. Irascibility, levity, timidity, and indolence, tempered with occasional emotions of benevolence, are the moral qualities of the inhabitants of warm climates, while selfishness, tempered with sincerity and integrity, form the moral character of the inhabitants of cold countries. The state of the weather, and the seasons of the year also, have a visible effect upon moral sensibility. The month of November, in Great Britain, rendered gloomy by constant fogs and rains, has been thought to favour the perpetration of the worst species of murder, while the vernal sun, in middle latitudes, has been as generally remarked for producing gentleness and benevolence.

2. The effects of DIET upon the moral faculty are more certain, though less attended to, than the effects of climate. "Fulness of bread," we are told, was one of the predisposing causes of the vices of the cities of the plain. The fasts so often inculcated among the Jews were intended to lessen the incentives to vice; for pride, cruelty, and sensuality, are as much the natural consequences of luxury, as apoplexies and palsies. But the *quality* as well as the quantity of aliment has an influence upon morals; hence we find the moral diseases that have been mentioned are most frequently the offspring of animal food. . . .

3. The effects of CERTAIN DRINKS upon the moral faculty are not less observable than upon the intellectual powers of the mind. Fermented liquors, of a good quality, and taken in a moderate quantity, are favourable to the virtues of candour, benevolence and generosity; but when they are taken in excess, or when they are of a bad quality, and taken even in a moderate quantity, they seldom fail of rousing every latent spark of vice into action. . . . Water is the universal sedative of turbulent passions; it not only promotes a general equanimity of temper, but it composes anger. . . .

4. EXTREME HUNGER produces the most unfriendly effects upon moral sensibility.

5. I hinted formerly . . . [that] the moral faculty . . . was frequently impaired by madness. I beg leave to add further upon this head, that not only madness, but the hysteria and hypochondriasis, as well as all those other states of the body, whether idiopathic or symptomatic, which are accompanied with preternatural irritibility, sensibility, torpor, stupor, or mobility of the nervous system, dispose to vice, either of the body or of the mind. . . .

6. INDLENESS is the parent of every vice. . . .

7. The effects of EXCESSIVE SLEEP are intimately connected with the effects of idleness upon the moral faculty. . . .

8. The effects of bodily pain upon the morals are not less remarkable than upon the intellectual powers of the mind. . . . The effects of bodily pain . . . [operate] in rousing and directing the moral faculties. . . .

9. Too much cannot be said in favour of CLEANLINESS, as a physical means of promoting virtue. . . .

10. I hope that I shall be excused in placing SOLITUDE among the physical causes which influence the moral faculty, when I add, that I confine its effects to persons who are irreclaimable by rational or moral remedies. . . .

11. Connected with solitude, as a mechanical means of promoting virtue, SILENCE deserves to be mentioned. . . .

12. The effects of MUSIC upon the moral faculty have been felt and recorded in every country. . . .

13. The ELOQUENCE of the PULPIT is nearly allied to music in its effects upon the moral faculty. . . .

14. ODOURS of various kinds have been observed to act in the most sensible manner upon the moral faculty. Brydone tells us, upon the authority of a celebrated philosopher in Italy, that the peculiar wickedness of the people who live in the neighbourhood of Aetna and Vesuvius is occasioned chiefly by the smell of the sulpher, and of the hot exhalations which are constantly discharged from these volcanoes. Agreeable odours seldom fail to inspire serenity, and to compose the angry spirits. . . .

15. It will be sufficient only to mention LIGHT and DARKNESS, to suggest facts in favour of the influence of each of them upon the moral sensibility. . . . [He adds the following footnote:] The temperature of the air has a considerable influence upon moral feeling. Henry the Third of France was always ill humoured, and sometimes cruel, in cold weather. There is a damp air which comes from the sea in Northumberland county in England which is known by the same of the *Seafret;* from its inducing fretfulness in the temper.

16. It is to be lamented, that no experiments have as yet been made to determine the effects of all the different species of AIRS, which chemistry has lately discovered; upon the moral faculty. I have authority, from actual experiments, only to declare, that dephlogisticated air, when taken into the lungs, produces cheerfulness, gentleness, and serenity of mind.

17. What shall we say of the effects of MEDICINES upon the moral faculty? . . . Clouds and darkness still hang upon this part of my subject. . . .

Thus I have enumerated the principal causes which act mechanically upon morals.[448]

## COSMOPOLITANISM

In the eighteenth century cosmopolitanism was no longer confined to a few independent men but spread among the educated classes generally.

### The Religion of Nature Consider'd

The anonymous author of *The Religion of Nature Consider'd*[449] realized that "what Education, Example or Custom recommend, may in time become so habitual, as to be reputed natural."[450]

By reading *Ross's View of all Religions, Purchas's Pilgrim,* or any other Account of Religions, Countries or Customs of People throughout the World, we become capable of judging of them both jointly and severally, and knowing in what respects they agree with, or are better or worse than our own. *Reason* then becomes useful to us, in considering, comparing and collating one with another, and distinguishing, as near as we are able, Truth from Error, Barbarous from Civil, Right from Wrong: but if we have never heard nor read, of any Religion or Country beside our own, if we have not had so much as an Intimation that there are such and such Places and Persuasions in the World, besides *England* and the *Church established; Reason,* I imagine, wou'd think nothing about it, but content itself with that stock of Knowledge it has already attain'd to, without attempting to make discoveries of things that the Mind has not the least Notion or Idea of.[451]

### Goldsmith

Oliver Goldsmith's (1728–74) *The Citizen of the World* (1762)[452] was based upon an anti-ethnocentric theme.

When I had just quitted my native country, and crossed the Chinese wall, I fancied every deviation from the customs and manners of China was a departing from nature; I smiled at the blue lips and red foreheads of the Tonguese; and could hardly contain when I saw the Daures dress their heads with horns. The Ostiacs powdered with red earth; and the Calmuck beauties, tricked out in all the finery or sheep-skin, appeared highly ridiculous; but I soon perceived that the ridicule lay not in them, but in me; that I falsely condemned others for absurdity, because they happened to differ from a standard originally founded in prejudice or partiality.[453]

Similarly, one might recall the contemporary popularity of Montesquieu's *Lettres persanes* (1721)[454] and Voltaire's *Zadig* (1747).[455]

## Franklin

An interesting example of cosmopolitanism is "The savages of North America" (1784)[456] by Benjamin Franklin (1706–90), which contains a number of examples of the superiority of the American Indians over the western Europeans.

Savages, we call them, because their manners differ from ours, which we think the perfection of civility; they think the same of theirs.

Perhaps, if we could examine the manners of different nations with impartiality, we should find no people so rude as to be without rules of politeness; nor any so polite as not to have some remains of rudeness.[457]

In another work he brought up the subject of physical beauty and then hastened to qualify his remark .

But perhaps I am partial to the complexion of my country, for such kind of partiality is natural to mankind.[458]

## Steuart Denham

To James Steuart Denham (1712–80) cosmopolitanism was a prerequisite for every social scientist.

The speculative person who, removed from the practice, extracts the principles of this science from *observation* and *reflection,* should divest himself, as far as possible, of every prejudice in favour of established opinions, however reasonable, when examined relatively to particular nations: he must do his utmost to become a citizen of the world, comparing customs, examining minutely institutions which appear alike, when in different countries they are found to produce different effects: he should examine the cause of such differences with the utmost diligence and attention. It is from such inquiries that the true principles are discovered.[459]

Man is a social animal.

Man we find acting uniformly in all ages, in all countries, and in all climates, from the principles of self-interest, expediency, duty, or passion.* In this he is alike, in nothing else.

These motives of human actions produce such a variety of circumstances, that if we consider the several species of animals in the creation, we shall find the individuals of no class so unlike to one another, as man to man. No wonder then if people differ in opinion with regard to every thing almost which relates to our species.

* " . . . how seldom does man follow what prudence directs ! "[460]

As this noble animal is a sociable creature, both from necessity* and inclination, we find also, in all ages, climates, and countries, a certain modification of government and subordination established among them. Here again we are presented with as great a variety, as there are different societies; all however agreeing in this, that the end of a *voluntary* subordination to authority is with a view to promote the general good.[463]

Every society has a particular "spirit."

The spirit of a people is formed upon a set of received opinions relative to three objects; morals, government, and manners: these once generally adopted by any society, confirmed by long and constant habits, and never called in question, form the basis of all laws, regulate the form of every government, and determine what is commonly called the customs of a country.[464]

If one considers the variety which is found in different countries, in the distribution of property, subordination, genius of people, proceeding from the variety of forms of government, laws, climate, and manners, one may conclude, that the political oeconomy in each must necessarily be different.[465]

Anticipating Tolstoy and the twentieth century social anthropologists, he stated that for new customs to be accepted, they must be in harmony with the culture.

Freedom itself, *imposed* upon a people groaning under the greatest slavery, will not make them happy, unless it is made to undergo certain modifications, relative to their established customs.[466]

This is so true, that many examples may be found, of a people's rejecting the most beneficial institutions, and even the greatest favours, merely because some circumstance had shocked their established customs.[467]

He developed a theory of generations to explain cultural change, similar to that of some later German historians.

The spirit of a people changes no doubt of itself, but by slow degrees. The same generation commonly adheres to the same principles, and retains the same spirit. In every country we find two generations upon the stage at a time; that is to say, we may distribute into two classes the spirit which prevails; the one amongst men between twenty and thirty, whose opinions are forming; the other of those who are past fifty, when opinions and habits are formed and confirmed. A person of judgement and observations may foresee many things relative to government, from an exact attention to the rise and progress of new customs and opinions.[468]

Like Pascal, Steuart Denham was impressed by the role of the trivial in history.

Let us consult the revolutions of all countries, and we shall find, that the most trivial circumstances have had a greater influence on such events, than the more weighty reasons, which are always set forth as the real motives.[469]

The kingdom of Spain was lost for a violence committed upon chastity; the city of Genoa for a blow.[470]

---

* "Of all animals, man appears to be born with least instinct for his preservation, either against danger, or to procure sustenance."[461]

" . . . no truth is intuitive before it be learned; even the shutting of the eye upon the approach of hurt to that delicate organ: The most involuntary action, the most instinctive, instantaneous, and truly irresistible of any one, is learned by infants and other animals; they have it not the moment they come into the world. On the other hand, many very abstruse demonstrations in geometry may be called intuitive truths, when once they are fully understood."[462]

The evolution of religion is based upon the existence of an instinct of curiosity in man.

. . . man . . . has . . . an instinct which . . . appears to be peculiar to him; it is that of enquiring into the cause of all he perceives, and . . . he begins to be afraid whenever he does not discover it. . . . From this habit of enquiring into the causes of every thing, and of feeling anxiety whenever we do not discover them, undoubtedly arises the idea of an invisible being, which we figure to ourselves as the hidden cause of them. Such is, in my opinion, the true origin of a Supreme Being, impressed in man *by the instinct of his nature.* . . .

The first men, and those who are in the grossest ignorance, make to themselves Gods of thunder, of hurricanes, of the sun, of the moon, of great men after their death, &c.; that is, they ascribe to those kinds of things, the effects which they cannot ascribe to any other cause.[471]

Like so many others of his time, he gave some attention to population.

I am . . . to examine the natural and rational causes of multiplication. . . .

The fundamental principle of the multiplication of all animals, and consequently of man, is generation; the next is food: generation gives existence, food preserves it. . . . Now in all countries found inhabited, as in those which have been found desolate, if the state of animals be inquired into, the number of them will be found in proportion to the quantity of food produced by the earth, *regularly throughout the year,* for their subsistence.[472]

From what has been said, we may conclude, that the numbers of mankind must depend upon the quantity of food produced by the earth for their nourishment; from which, as a corollary, may be drawn,

That mankind have been, as to numbers, and must ever be, in proportion to the food produced; and that the food produced will be in the compound proportion of the fertility of the climate, and the industry of the inhabitants.

From this last proposition it appears plain, that there can be no general rule for determining the number of inhabitants necessary for agriculture, not even in the same country.[473]

## HISTORIANS OF CHRISTIANITY

The seventh-century historical analysis of the Bible was extended in the eighteenth century to an empirical-historical view of Christianity itself. Thus the naturalistic world view was finally applied to the sacred religion of western Europe.

### Middleton

Conyers Middleton (1685–1750) applied the methods of secular historical criticism to Christianity and thus brought the religion of western Europe under the same type of analysis as other aspects of its culture.

He began with an anti-Catholic thesis that had been used since the Reformation by Erasmus* and others.

---

* "There be which honour certain saints with certain ceremonies . . . which honouring of saints truly, except it be referred from the respect of corporal commodities or incommodities unto Christ, is not for a christian man, insomuch that it is not far from the superstitiousness of them which in time past vowed the tenth part of their goods to Hercules, to the intent they might wax rich, or a cock to Esculapius that they might be recovered of their diseases: or which sacrificed a bull to Neptunus that they might have good passage by sea and prosperous sailing. The names be changed, but verily they have both one end and intent."[474]

... that System of Ceremonies and doctrines, which is peculiar to the *Romish Church* ... the source of which I have undertaken to lay open, and by an historical deduction of facts, to trace it's origin in a direct line, from *Pagan* down to *Popish Rome*.[475]

I ... undertook to prove; an *exact Conformity,* or *Uniformity* rather, of *Worship,* between *Popery* and *Paganism;* for since, as I have shewn ... we see the *present people of Rome* worshipping in the *same Temples;* at the *same Altars;* sometimes the same Images; and always with the *same Ceremonies,* as the *old Romans;* they must have more charity, as well as *skill in distinguishing,* that I pretend to have, who can absolve them from the *same superstition* and *idolatry,* of which we condemn their *Pagan Ancestors.*[476]

Second, he made the Bible an object of historical criticism. The following were his fundamental propositions:

[1.] *That the* Jews *borrowed some of their Ceremonies and Customs from* Aegypt.[477]

All that I pretend to intimate, is, from the near Resemblance of many Customs, that the *Jews* might probably have borrowed them from *Aegypt.*[478]

[2.] *That the Scriptures are not of absolute and universal Inspiration.*[479]

[He argued that it was] a *wrong principle* ... [to maintain] that *every single passage of the Scriptures, we call Canonical, must needs be received, as the very word and as the voice of God himself.*[480]

But the Pentateuch states that it was written by Moses under supernatural inspiration. How does Middleton answer this?

*Moses was ... a wise and excellent Man, just such an one as Minos and the other Lawgivers of Greece; these imputed their Laws to the Gods, as Moses had done before them.*[481]

He attacked the literal interpretation of the Bible, himself preferring an allegorical interpretation, which often was merely a thin disguise for skepticism.

*God in the beginning created the World and all Things in it,* ... But whether this was brought about *exactly and literally,* according to every circumstance of the *Mosaic account;* with all the *Form and Machinery,* of *six days labour;* a *Paradise,* &c. as it is not, in my judgement, material to inquire, so I shall not take upon me to determine.[482]

An interesting passage is his substitution of a naturalistic explanation for the origin of the diversity of languages in opposition to the story of the Tower of Babel.

I have proved* ... that the *dispersion of Mankind* and *peopling of the World,* must of course be the certain and necessary effect of an *encreasing Multitude,* flowing from the Reason and Nature of Things, exclusive of any *Miracle or the extraordinary Interposition of God;* so what I pretend to shew now, is, that the *Variety of Languages* may with *some colour of Reason and Probability* be accounted for too in the same way, as the natural and necessary Consequence of such Dispersion.

Let's consider Mankind in its infant State, as yet but one Family, tho' daily growing and encreasing so fast, as to be forced in Proportion to that Encrease to break off and separate from each other into several Parties or Colonies in quest of fresh Quarters and Provisions. ...

Now as this Dispersion must have happened, whilst Mankind was yet rude and barbarous, unacquainted with Arts and Sciences, and even the common Inventions and

---

* " ... a multitude daily growing cannot *hang together in clusters;* must of necessity *disperse,* in proportion to the encrease of their numbers; *want of room* will force them to seek *new quarters.*"[483]

Conveniencies of Life; so the Production of such Arts, the Improvement of Knowledge and Science, and the new Demands of Life daily arising must necessarily produce a *new Language* in each single Nation or separate People, unknown in a great measure to the rest of their Fellow Creatures. For as Names are generally but arbitrary Signs, not drawn from the Nature or Qualities of the Things themselves, but formed by Fancy or Accident and confirmed by Use; so every thing new must necessarily create not onely a new Name, but a different one too from what the same thing, when invented, would obtain in a different People.

And thus a Difference of Languages being once established, the Mixture and Composition of several of them together, which follows of course from Conquests and the familiar Intercourse of different Nations, is another inexhaustible Source and Cause of multiplying that same Variety.[484]

In his next series of works Middleton proceeded to attack the Catholic doctrine of miracles.

I propose to observe the following method. . . .

II. To throw together all, which . . . [the early Christian church] Fathers . . . have delivered, concerning the conditions of the persons who are said to be indued with . . . [miraculous] gifts, and to have wrought the miracles, to which they appeal.

III. To illustrate the particular characters and opinions of the Fathers, who attest those miracles; so as to enable us to determine with more exactness, what degree of credit may be due to their testimony.

IV. To review all the several kinds of miracles, which are pretended to have been wrought, and to observe, from the nature of each, how far the credibility of them may reasonably be suspected.[485]

II. . . . strolling wonder-workers, by a dexterity of juggling, which art, not Heaven had taught them, imposed upon the credulity of the pious Fathers, whose strong prejudices and ardent zeal for the interest of Chrisitianity, would dispose them to embrace, without examination, whatever seemed to promote so good a cause.[486]

III. The authority of a writer, who affirms any quaestionable fact, must depend on the character of his veracity and of his judgement.[487]

[After a consideration of the early fathers, particularly Justin Martyr and Irenaeus,[488] he concludes:]

Now, from what I have above collected, it is certain, that if a gross absurdity of opinions, and the belief of things impossible, be the proof of a weak mind; if exposition of the Scriptures, void of reason and common sense, betray a great want of judgement, then we may justly charge those defects upon these ancient fathers. . . .

As to the quaestion of their veracity, it may admit perhaps some debate, and it will probably be thought harsh in the opinion of many, to suspect men of such piety and sanctity of life, either of the invention, or the propagation of known forgeries. Yet there are many things so peremptorily affirmed, without any ground of truth or probability by the two Fathers, whose characters I have been considering, as to give us too much cause for such a suspicion.[489]

[However, he later considers the social milieu, rather than deliberate fraud, to have produced their stories of the miraculous;] opinions, wholly absurd and contrary to nature, may gain credit and establishment through ages and nations, which, by the force of education, custom, and example, have once contracted a superstitious and credulous turn.[490]

For a mind, so totally possessed by superstitious fancies, and disturbed by vain terrors, could not have either the judgement to discern, or the inclination to examine, or the courage even to suspect the pretensions of those vagrant Jugglers, who, in those primitive ages, were so numerous, and so industriously employed in the affair of deluding their fellow creatures. Every man will perceive, how easy it must have been to men of that class, whether Heathens, Jews, or Christians, (for they are all allowed to have had such impostors among them) to impose the tricks of their art, as the effects of a supernatural power, on a multitude already persuaded, that they lived on magic ground, exposed at every step to snares and charms contrived by malicious Spirits, perpetually haunting them, and watching every unguarded moment, to get possession both of their souls and bodies.[491]

IV. [He argues that the miracles either never occurred or were the result of natural causes.[492]]

[His conclusion is that] the forged miracles of the fourth century give us just reason to suspect the pretensions of every other age both before and after it. . . . [for] the earlier miracles rest on no better foundation, nor are supported by any better evidence, than the later.[493]

Finally, there are a couple of remarks on methodology.

. . . human nature has always been the same, agitated by the same appetites and passion, and liable to the same excuses and abuses of them, in all ages and countries of the world; so that our experience of what passes in the present age, will be the best comment on what is delivered to us concerning the past.[494]

To conclude, the chief purpose of these inquiries, is, to shew, that Christianity cannot be defended to the satisfaction of speculative and thinking men, but by reducing it to it's original simplicity, and stripping it of the false glosses, and sytem, with which it has been incumbered, through the prejudices of the pious, as well as the art of the crafty and interested. One of the principal of the incumbrances, as far as I am able to judge, is the notion, which is generally inculcated by our Divines, concerning *the perpetual inspiration and infallibility of the Apostles and Evangelists:* a notion, which has imparted such difficulties and perplexities into the system of Christian religion, as all the wit of man has not been able to explane: which yet will all be easily solved, and vanish at once, by admitting onely the contrary notion, *that the Apostles were fallible:* which is a sort of proof that generally passes with men of sense for demonstrative; being of the same kind, by which *Sir Isaac Newton* has convinced the world, of the truth of his philosophical principles. . . .

The case is the same in Theological, as in natural inquiries: it is experience alone, and the observation of facts, which can illustrate the truth of principles.[495] Facts are stubborn things, deriving their existence from nature, and tho' frequently misrepresented and disguised by art and false colors, yet cannot be totally changed, or made pliable to the Systems, which happen to be in fashion; but, sooner or later, will always reduce the opinions of men, to a compliance and uniformity with themselves.

Wherefore, as we learn from dayly experience that prejudice, passion, want of memory, knowledge or judgement naturally produce obscurity, inaccuracy and mistakes in all modern writings whatsoever; so when we see the same effects in antient writings, how sacred soever they may be deemed, we must necessarily impute them to the same causes. This is what sense and reason prescribe.[496]

## Gibbon

Edward Gibbon (1737–94) was familiar with many cultures; as a boy "I swallowed with voracious appetite the descriptions of India and China, of Mexico and Peru";[497] "the Dynasties of Assyria and Egypt were my top and cricket ball."[498]

Consequently his cosmopolitanism is no surprise.

Without a philosophical knowledge of antiquity, we should be induced to do too much honour to humankind. The influence of custom would be little known. We should every moment be apt to confound the incredible and the absurd.[499]

But what is too absurd for mankind?[500]

The laws of honour are different in different ages; and a behaviour which in Augustus was decent, would have covered Aeneas with infamy.[501]

He was interested in ethnographic and comparative material.

What a retrospect is it to a genius truly philosophical, to see the most absurd opinions received among the most enlightened people; to see barbarians, on the other hand, arrive at the knowledge of the most sublime truths; to find true consequences falsely deduced from the most erroneous principles; admirable principles, bordering on the verge of truth, without ever conducting thither; languages formed on ideas, and yet those ideas corrected by such languages; the springs of morality universally the same; the opinions of contentious metaphysics universally varied, and generally extravagant, accurate only while superficial, but subtile, obscure and uncertain whenever they were profound. A philosophical work written by an Iroquouis, tho' full of absurdities, would be to us an inestimable performance. It would present us with a singular instance of the nature of the human mind, placed in circumstances we have never experienced, and influenced by customs and religious opinions totally different from ours. Sometimes it would surprize and instruct us, by the contrariety of ideas, that would thence necessarily arise; we should be led to enquire into the reasons, and trace the mind from errour to errour: Sometimes, again, we should see our own principles, but deduced by different means, and almost always peculiarly modified and altered. We should hence learn, not only to acknowledge, but to feel the force of prejudice; we should learn never to be surprized at apparent absurdity, and often to suspect the truth of what might appear to want no confirmation.[502]

I read *Mr. Mallet's Introduction to the History of Denmark*, with *a Translation of the Edda*, the sacred book of the ancient Celts. We have now a half a dozen of bibles, if we include our own. A valuable work might be written, giving a philosophical picture of the religions, their genius, reasonings and influence on the manners, government, philosophy, and poetry of their respective votaries.[503]

He applied Middleton's method to the history of Christianity and thus was one of the first to see western Europe's sacred religion as a social phenomenon subject to natural laws—a procedure which scandalized many of his contemporaries[504].

Our curiosity is naturally prompted to inquire by what means the Christian faith obtained so remarkable a victory over the established religion of the earth. To this inquiry, an obvious but satisfactory answer may be returned; that it was owing to the convincing evidence of the doctrine itself, and to the ruling providence of its great Author. But, as truth and reason seldom find so favourable a reception in the world, and as the wisdom of Providence frequently condescends to use the passions of the human heart, and the general circumstances of mankind, as instruments to execute its purpose; we may still be permitted, though with becoming submission, to ask not indeed what were the first, but what were the secondary causes of the rapid growth of the Christian church.* It will, perhaps, appear that it was most effectually favoured and assisted by the five following causes: I. The inflexible, and, if we may use the expression, intolerant zeal of the Christians, derived, it is true, from the Jewish religion, but purified from the narrow and unsocial spirit which, instead of inviting, had deterred the Gentiles from embracing the law of Moses. II. The doctrine of a future life, improved by every additional circumstance which could give weight and efficacy to that important truth. III. The miraculous powers ascribed† to the primitive church. IV. The pure and austere morals of the Christians. V. The union and discipline of the Christian republic, which gradually formed an independent and increasing state in the heart of the Roman empire.[508]

Gibbon was an empiricist; for example, in a criticism of Blackstone he stated:

I have entirely omitted a metaphysical inquiry upon the nature of laws in general, eternal and positive laws, and a number of sublime terms, which I admire as much as I can without understanding them. Instead of following this high priori road, would it not be better humbly to investigate the desires, fears, passions, and opinions of the human being; and to discover from thence what means an able legislator can employ to connect the private happiness of each individual with the observance of those laws which secure the well-being of the whole.[509]

Gibbon's most complete expression of a philosophy of history is to be found in his youthful *Essai sur l'étude de la littérature.*

. . . in war, in politics, in religion, the most important effects have proceeded from the most simple causes.‡[511]

History is, to a philosophical genius, what play was to the Marquis Dangeau. He saw a system, regularity and connection, where others only perceived the wanton caprices of chance. The knowledge of history is to the philosopher that of causes and effects.§[513]

Among a multitude of historical facts, there are some, and those by much the majority, which prove nothing more than that they are facts. There are others which may be useful in drawing a partial conclusion, whereby the philosopher may be enabled to judge of the motives of an action, or some peculiar features in a character: these relate only to single links of the chain. Those whose influence extends throughout the whole system, and which are so intimately connected as to have given motion to the springs of action, are very rare; and what is still more rarely to be met with is, a genius who knows how to distinguish them, amidst the vast chaos of events wherein they are jumbled, and deduce them, pure and unmixt, from the rest.

It will appear unnecessary to observe to those, whose judgement is superior to their erudition, that causes ought always to be proportioned to their effects; that it is wrong to trace the character of an age, from the conduct of an individual; or to estimate from a single effort, often forced and destructive, the strength and riches of a state.[514]

Design has been often observed to govern the actions of a great man; a ruling principle has been perceived in his character; hence theoretical minds have conceived the notion,

---

* " . . it is my intention to remark only such human causes as were permitted to second the influence of revelation."[505]

"I had . . . flattered myself that an age of light and liberty would receive, without scandal, an enquiry into the *human* causes of the progress and establishment of Christianity."[506]

† He delicately hinted at his own skepticism in regard to miracles.[507]

‡ " . . . all those trifling but decisive causes which so often influence the fate of empires and the councils of the wisest monarchs."[510]

§ "History . . . undertakes to record the transactions of the past, for the instruction of future, ages."[512]

that mankind in general are as systematical in practice as in speculation. They have pretended to discover art in our passions, policy in our foibles, dissimulation in our caprices; in a word, by their endeavours to enhance the merit of the understanding, they have done little honour to the art.

Justly disgusted at such excessive refinement, and displeased to see those pretensions extended to mankind in general which should be confined to a Philip or a Caesar, others of a more natural turn have run into the other extreme. These have entirely banished art from the moral world, in order to substitute accident in its room. According to them, weak mortals act altogether from caprice: the phrenzy of a madman raises up the pillars of an empire, and the weakness of a woman throws them down.

The study of general and determinate causes should be agreeable to both parties; as in this the one would, with pleasure, see the pride of man humbled; the motives of his action unknown to himself; a puppet moved by foreign wires; and from particular liberty would see the origin of general necessity. The other also, would find in the study of general causes, that connection they so much admire, and ample room for indulging these speculations for which their genius is turned.

What a wide field opens itself to my reflection! The theory of general causes would, in the hands of a Montesquieu, become a philosophical history of man. He would display these causes operating in the rise and fall of empires; successively assuming the appearance of accident, or prudence, of courage, and of cowardice; acting without the concurrence of particular causes, and sometimes directly against them. Superior to a fondness for his own system, that meanest passion in a philosopher, he would discover that, notwithstanding the extensive influence of those causes, its effect must necessarily be confined, and that it would principally display itself in general events; in such whose slow, but certain, operation works imperceptibly a change on the face of things, particularly on religion, on manners, and indeed every thing that depends on opinion. Such would in part be the lesson such a philosopher would give on the subject.[515]

In those great events, wherein, from the diversity of actors, whose views, situation, and character, are different, there arises an unity of action, or rather of effect; it is perhaps only into general causes we must look for the springs of those.

In more particular events, the process of nature is very different from that of the philosophers. In nature there are few effects so simple as to owe themselves to one sole cause; whereas our philosophers are generally attached to one cause, sole and universal. Let us avoid this precipice: on the contrary, if an action appears ever so little complicated, let us admit of general causes, not excluding either hazard or design.[516]

Some years later he remarked:

There are few observers who possess a clear and comprehensive view of the revolutions of society; and who are capable of discovering the nice and secret springs of action which impel, in the same uniform direction, the blind and capricious passions of a multitude of individuals.[517]

He applied his philosophy of history in *The History of the Decline and Fall of the Roman Empire;* at different places in the book he attempted to analyze the factors which produced the decline of Rome. Most often he used a cultural interpretation, but one factor which he took into consideration was a biological "principle of decay." Perhaps the best approach is to give his analyses chronologically.

It was scarcely possible that the eyes of contemporaries should discover in the public felicity the latent causes of decay and corruption. This long peace, and the uniform government of the Romans, introduced a slow and secret poison into the vitals of the empire. The minds of men were gradually reduced to the same level, the fire of genius was extinguished, and even the military spirit evaporated.[518]

Since Romulus, with a small band of shepherds and outlaws, fortified himself on the hills near the Tiber, ten centuries had already elapsed. During the first four ages, the Romans, in the laborious school of poverty, had acquired the virtues of war and government: by the vigorous exertion of those virtues, and by the assistance of fortune, they had obtained, in the course of the three succeeding centuries, an absolute empire over many countries of Europe, Asia, and Africa. The last three hundred years had been consumed in apparent prosperity and internal decline. The nation of soldiers, magistrates, and legislators, who composed the thirty-five tribes of the Roman people, was dissolved into the common mass of mankind, and confounded with the millions of servile provincials, who had received the name, without adopting the spirit, of Romans. A mercenary army, levied among the subjects and barbarians of the frontier, was the only order of men who preserved and abused their independence. . . .

The limits of the Roman empire still extended from the Western Ocean to the Tigris, and from Mount Atlas to the Rhine and the Danube. To the undiscerning eye of the vulgar, Philip appeared a monarch no less powerful than Hadrian or Augustus had formerly been. The form was still the same, but the animating health and vigour was fled. The industry of the people was discouraged and exhausted by a long series of oppressions. The discipline of the legions, which alone, after the extinction of every other virtue, had propped the greatness of the state, was corrupted by the ambition, or relaxed by the weakness, of the emperors. The strength of the frontiers, which had always consisted in arms rather than in fortifications, was insensibly undermined; and the fairest provinces were left exposed to the rapaciousness or ambition of the barbarians, who soon discovered the decline of the Roman empire.[519]

A long period of calamity or decay must have checked the industry, and diminished the wealth, of the people; and their profuse luxury must have been the result of that indolent despair which enjoys the present hour and declines the thoughts of futurity. The uncertain condition of their property discouraged the subjects of Theodosius from engaging in those useful and laborious undertakings which require an immediate expense and promise a slow and distant advantage. The frequent examples of ruin and desolation tempted them not to spare the remains of a patrimony which might, every hour, become the prey of the rapacious Goth.* And the mad prodigality which prevails in the confusion of a shipwreck or a siege may serve to explain the progress of luxury amidst the misfortunes and terrors of a sinking nation.

The effeminate luxury which infected the manners of the courts and cities had instilled a secret and destructive poison into the camps of the legions.[521]

But its fall was announced by a clearer omen than the flight of vultures: the Roman government appeared every day less formidable to its enemies, more odious and oppressive to its subjects. The taxes were multiplied with the public distress; economy was neglected in proportion as it became necessary; and the injustice of the rich shifted the unequal burden from themselves to the people, whom they defrauded of the *indulgencies* that might sometimes have alleviated their misery. The severe inquisition, which confiscated their goods and tortured their persons, compelled the subjects of Valentinian to prefer the more simple tyranny of the Barbarians, to fly to the woods and mountains, or to em-

* "Cold, poverty, and a life of danger and fatigue, fortify the strength and courage of Barbarians."[520]

brace the vile and abject condition of mercenary servants. They abjured and abhorred the name of Roman citizens, which had formerly excited the ambition of mankind. The Armorican provinces of Gaul, and the greatest part of Spain, were thrown into a state of disorderly independence, by the confederations of the Bagaudae; and the Imperial ministers pursued with proscriptive laws, and ineffectual arms, the rebels whom they had made. If all the Barbarian conquerors had been annihilated in the same hour, their total destruction would not have restored the empire of the West; and, if Rome still survived, she survived the loss of freedom, of virtue, and of honour.[522]

. . . the decline of Rome was the natural and inevitable effect of immoderate greatness. Prosperity ripened the principle of decay; the causes of destruction multiplied with the extent of conquest; and, as soon as time or accident had removed the artificial supports, the stupendous fabric yielded to the pressure of its own weight. The story of its ruin is simple and obvious; and, instead of inquiring why the Roman empire was destroyed, we should rather be surprised that it had subsisted so long. The victorious legions, who, in distant wars, acquired the vices of strangers and mercenaries, first oppressed the freedom of the republic, and afterwards violated the majesty of the purple. The emperors, anxious for their personal safety and the public peace, were reduced to the base expedient of corrupting the discipline which rendered them alike formidable to their sovereign and to the enemy; the vigour of the military government was relaxed, and finally dissolved, by the partial institutions of Constantine; and the Roman world was overwhelmed by a deluge of Barbarians.[523]

As the happiness of a *future* life is the great object of religion, we may hear, without surprise or scandal, that the introduction, or at least the abuse, of Christianity had some influence on the decline and fall of the Roman empire.*[525]

In all the pursuits of active and speculative life, the emulation of states and individuals is the most powerful spring of the efforts and improvements of mankind. . . . The Byzantine subjects were degraded to an abject and languid temper, the natural effect of their solitary and insulated state.[526]

They held in their lifeless hands the riches of their fathers, without inheriting the spirit which had created and improved that sacred patrimony: they read, they praised, they compiled, but their languid souls seemed alike incapable of thought and action . . . a succession of patient disciples became in their turn the dogmatic teachers of the next servile generation.[527]

Gibbon believed in the evolution of culture.

The origin and changes of our religion and government, of our arts and manners, afford an entertaining and often an instructive subject of speculation. . . . We contemplate the gradual progress of society from the lowest ebb of primitive barbarism, to the full tide of modern civilization.[528]

M. de Buffon speaks of complete vessels being found in the heart of mountains at a very great distance from the sea. A fact, indeed, of a very extraordinary nature, which shews us a lively glimpse of a former world, and of arts cultivated by men who inhabited some country now overwhelmed by the sea, in ages when the modern Alps were buried under the waters.[529]

Like the nineteenth-century English evolutionists, he equated children with "savages."

* "I believed, and . . . I still believe, that the propagation of the gospel and triumph of the Church are inseparably connected with the decline of the Roman Monarchy."[524]

. . . it is in rude ages and to youthful minds that the marvellous is most attractive.[530]

Society originated through social contract.

When the injustice of some, and the weakness of others, showed the necessity for civil society, individuals were obliged to renounce their beloved, but pernicious, independence. All particular wills were melted down into the general will of the public; by which, under the sanction of definite punishments, men became bound to regulate their conduct.[531]

He used the age-area hypothesis in the reconstruction of linguistic development.

In the origin of human speech, a method must have been wanted, and sought, and found, of discriminating the several individuals of the same tribe, who were mingled in the daily offices, even of savage life. In every language the invention of proper and personal names must be at least as ancient as the use of appellative words. The truth of this remark is attested by the ancient continent from India to Spain, from the lakes of Canada to the hills of Chili, the same distinctions were familiar to the inhabitants of the New World; and our navigators who have recently explored the islands of the South Sea, and their testimony to the general practice of mankind.[532]

Gibbon gave the usual eighteenth-century account of the evolution of religion as a result of fear,[533] but he also flirted with the euhemeristic theory; thus, he spoke of "the scythe, the invention or emblem of Saturn,"[534] and of the "arrival of Saturn (or his religious worship) in a ship."[535]

Like so many others of his time, he was an advocate of social progress.

The discoveries of ancient and modern navigators, and the domestic history, or tradition, of the most enlightened nations, represent the *human savage,* naked both in mind and body, and destitute of laws, of arts, of ideas, and almost of language.* From this abject condition, perhaps the primitive and universal state of man, he has gradually arisen to command the animals, to fertilise the earth, to traverse the ocean, and to measure the heavens. His progress in the improvement and exercise of his mental and corporeal faculties has been irregular and various, infinitely slow in the beginning, and increasing by degrees with redoubled velocity; ages of laborious ascent have been followed by a moment of rapid downfall; and the several climates of the globe have felt the vicissitudes of light and darkness. Yet the experience of four thousand years should enlarge our hopes, and diminish our apprehensions; we cannot determine to what height the human species may aspire in their advances towards perfection; but it may safely be presumed that no people, unless the face of nature is changed, will relapse into their original barbarism. The improvements of society may be viewed under a threefold aspect. 1. The poet or philosopher illustrates his age and country by the efforts of a *single* mind; but these superior powers or reason or fancy are rare and spontaneous productions, and the genius of Homer, or Cicero, or Newton, would excite less admiration, if they could be created by the will of a prince or the lessons of a preceptor. 2. The benefits of law and policy, of trade and manufactures, of arts and sciences, are more solid and permanent; and *many* individuals may be qualified, by education and discipline, to promote, in their respective stations, the interest of the community. But this general order is the effect of skill and labour; and the complex machinery may be decayed by time or injured by violence. 3. Fortunately for mankind, the more useful, or, at least, more necessary arts can be performed without superior talents or national subordination; without the powers of *one* or

* "Fancy or perhaps reason may still suppose an extreme and absolute state of nature far below the level of these savages [of New Holland], who had acquired some arts and instruments."[536]

the union of *many*. Each village, each family, each individual, must always possess both ability and inclination to perpetuate the use of fire and of metals; the propagation and service of domestic animals; the methods of hunting and fishing; the rudiments of navigation; the imperfect cultivation of corn or other nutritive grain; and the simple practice of the mechanic trades. Private genius and public industry may be extirpated; but these hardy plants survive the tempest, and strike an everlasting root into the most unfavourable soil. The splendid days of Augustus and Trajan were eclipsed by a cloud of ignorance; and the Barbarians subverted the laws and palaces of Rome. But the scythe, the invention or emblem of Saturn, still continued annually to mow the harvests of Italy; and the human feasts of the Laestrygons have never been renewed on the coast of Campania.

Since the first discovery of the arts, war, commerce, and religious zeal have diffused, among the savages of the Old and New World, those inestimable gifts: they have been successively propagated; they can never be lost. We may therefore acquiesce in the pleasing conclusion that every age of the world has increased, and still increases, the real wealth, the happiness, the knowledge, and perhaps the virtue, of the human race.[537]

### Evanson

Edward Evanson (1731–1805) was another who applied the principles of historical criticism to the New Testament. In a book on the four gospels, he wrote:

. . . these Evangelical histories contain such gross, irreconcilable contradictions, that no close reasoning, unprejudiced minds can admit the truth and authenticity of them all.

It is an obvious maxim, that, in the investigation of the doctrines of Christianity, the first necessary step is to enquire into the truth and authenticity of those original writings in which they are contained: but the misfortune is, that nobody takes this important, necessary step of the inquiry, in any firm and satisfactory manner.[538]

## LAW OF NATURE

With the increasing secularization of society, more and more educated people began to lose interest in the minutiae which divided the innumerable Christian sects and sought for a rational rather than an authoritarian set of general principles which would satisfy their religious needs. This was the role of natural religion in the eighteenth century.

### Tindal

Matthew Tindal (1653–1733) was one of the foremost expositors of natural religion based upon the law of nature.

I shall attempt to shew you, That Men, if they sincerely endeavour to discover the will of God, will perceive, that there's a *Law of Nature,* or *Reason;* which is so call'd, as being a Law, which is common, or natural, to all rational Creatures; and that this Law, like its Author, is absolutely perfect, eternal, and unchangeable; and that the design of the Gospel was not to add to, or take from this Law; but to free Men from that load of Superstition, which had been mix'd with it: So that TRUE CHRISTIANITY is not a Religion of yesterday, but what God, at the beginning, dictated, & still continues to dictate to Christians, as well as others.[539]

If so, it follows, That the *Christian* Religion has existed from the beginning; and that

God, both *then,* and *ever since,* has continu'd to give all Mankind sufficient means to know it; and that 'tis their duty to know, believe, profess, and practise it: so that *Christianity,* tho' the name is of a later date, must be as old, and as extensive, as humane-nature; and as the Law of our creation, must have been then implanted in us by God himself.[540]

By *Natural Religion,* I understand the belief of the existence of a God, and the sense and practice of those duties, which result from the knowledge we, by our Reason, have of him, and his perfections; and of ourselves, and our own imperfections; and of the relation we stand in to him, and to our fellow-creatures; so that the *Religion of Nature* takes in every thing that is founded on the reason & nature of things.[541]

. . . there's a Religion of Nature & Reason written in the hearts of every one of us from the first Creation, by which all Mankind must judge of the truth of any instituted Religion whatever.[542]

*Natural* Religion . . . as I take it, differs not from *Reveal'd,* but in the manner of its being communicated: The one being the internal, as the other the external revelation of the same unchangeable will of a Being, who is alike at all times infinitely wise and good.[543]

. . . the Religion of Nature is an absolutely perfect Religion; and . . . external Revelation can neither add to, nor take from its perfection: and . . . true Religion, whether internally or externally reveal'd, must be the same.[544]

Tindal was not impressed by the current theory of social progress.

What impartial Man, who has compar'd the former, & present condition of Mankind, can think the World much mended since the times of *Tiberius?* or tho' ever so well vers'd in Church-History, can, from the conduct of Christians, find, that they are arriv'd to any higher state of perfection, than the rest of Mankind, who are suppos'd to continue in their degeneracy, & corruption?[545]

## Blackstone

William Blackstone (1723–80) was the last great jurist to employ the law of nature as the basis of law. He made the following analysis of that law of nature:

The will of his [i.e., man's] Maker is called the law of Nature. For as God, when he created matter, and endued it with a principle of mobility, established certain rules for the perpetual direction of that motion, so, when he created man, and endued him with freewill to conduct himself in all parts of life, he laid down certain immutable laws of human nature, whereby that freewill is in some degree regulated and restrained, and gave him also the faculty of reason to discover the purport of those laws.*[547]

He accepted man's sociality.

If man were to live in a state of nature, unconnected with other individuals, there would be no occasion for any other laws than the law of nature and the law of God. Neither could any other law possibly exist: for a law always supposes some superior who is to make it; and, in a state of nature, we are all equal, without any other superior but Him who is the author of our being. But man was formed for society; and, as is demonstrated by the writers on this subject, is neither capable of living alone, nor indeed has the courage to do it.[548]

He upheld the gregarious theory of society.

The only true and natural foundations of society, are the wants and fears of individuals. Not that we can believe, with some theoretical writers, that there ever was a time when

* "This law of nature, being coeval with mankind, and dictated by God himself."[546]

there was no such thing as society either natural or civil; and that, from the impulse of reason, and through a sense of their wants and weaknesses, individuals met together in a large plain, entered into an original contract, and chose the tallest man to be their govern or. This notion of an actually existing unconnected state of nature, is too wild to be seriously admitted: and besides it is plainly contradictory to the revealed accounts of the primitive origin of mankind, and their preservation two thousand years afterwards; both which were effected by the means of single families. These formed the first natural society among themselves; which, every day extending its limits, laid the first though imperfect rudiments of civil or political society: and when it grew too large to subsist with con venience in that pastoral state, wherein the patriarchs appear to have lived, it necessarily subdivided itself by various migrations into more. Afterwards, as agriculture increased which employs and can maintain a much greater number of hands, migrations became less frequent: and various tribes, which had formerly separated, reunited again; sometimes by compulsion and conquest, sometimes by accident and sometimes perhaps by compact But though society had not its formal beginning from any convention of individuals, actuated by their wants and their fears; yet it is the *sense* of their weakness and imperfection that *keeps* mankind together; that demonstrates the necessity of this union; and that therefore is the solid and natural foundation, as well as the cement of civil society. And this is what we mean by the original contract of society; which, though perhaps in no instance it has ever been formally expressed at the first institution of a state, yet in nature and reason must always be understood and implied, in the very act of associating together: namely, that the whole should protect all its parts, and that every part should pay obedi ence to the will of the whole, or, in other words, that the community should guard the rights of each individual member, and that (in return for this protection) each individual should submit to the laws of the community; without which submission of all it was im possible that protection could be certainly extended to any.

For when civil society is once formed, government at the same time results of course, as necessary to preserve and to keep that society in order. Unless some superior be con stituted, whose commands and decisions all the members are bound to obey, they would still remain as in a state of nature, without any judge upon earth to define their several rights, and redress their several wrongs.[549]

Blackstone also discussed the evolution of property.[550]

## SOCIAL CONTRACT

As has been seen, the social contract theory was the ideological weapon of rising capitalism against dying feudalism, and in the eighteenth century that theory was used for the last time. In France, the feudal aristocracy kept its power until the last decade of the century, and Rousseau used the contract theory in favor of a democratic regime. In the New World there was a struggle for colonial independence on the part of the North American colonies against Great Britain; Paine was the revolutionary voice of this movement.

### Rousseau

Jean Jacques Rousseau (1712–78) was interested in the development of social science for purposes of reform.

Of all human sciences the most useful and most imperfect appears to be that of mankind: and I will venture to say, the single inscription on the Temple of Delphi contained a precept more difficult and more important than is to be found in all the huge volumes that moralists have ever written.[551]

. . . everything takes place according to the natural order.[552]

General laws should always be distinguished from individual causes that may modify their effects.[553]

There is often a great deal of difference between the will of all and the general will; the latter considers only the common interest, while the former takes private interest into account, and is no more than a sum of particular wills: but take away from these same wills the pluses and minuses that cancel one another, and the general will remains as the sum of the differences.[554]

Every political society is composed of other smaller societies of different kinds, each of which has its interests and its rules of conduct: but those societies which everybody perceives, because they have an external and authorized form, are not the only ones that actually exist in the State; all individuals who are united by a common interest compose as many others, either transient or permanent, whose influence is none the less real because it is less apparent, and the proper observation of whose various relations is the true knowledge of public morals and manners. The influence of all these tacit or formal associations causes, by the influence of their will, as many different modifications of the public will.[555]

The following are a few examples of social laws.

The daily ebb and flow of the tides are not more regularly influenced by the moon, than the morals of a people by the progress of the arts and sciences. As their light has risen above our horizon, virtue has taken flight, and the same phenomenon has been constantly observed in all times and places.[556]

It appears that the feeling of humanity evaporates and grows feeble in embracing all mankind, and that we cannot be affected by the calamities of Tartary or Japan, in the same manner as we are by those of European nations.[557]

He distinguished between primary and secondary aspects of culture.

The mind, as well as the body, has its needs: those of the body are the basis of society, those of the mind its ornaments.[558]

But, as has been stated, his greatest interest was in the evolution of culture.

. . . we must look for the origin of those differences which now distinguish men, who, it is allowed, are as equal among themselves as were the animals of every kind, before physical causes had introduced those varieties which are now observable among some of them.[559]

I conceive that there are two kinds of inequality among the human species; one, which I call natural or physical, because it is established by nature, and consists in a difference of age, health, bodily strength, and the qualities of the mind or of the soul: and another, which may be called moral or political inequality, because it depends on a kind of convention, and is established, or at least authorised by the consent of men. This latter consists of the different privileges, which some men enjoy to the prejudice of others; such as that of being more rich, more honoured, more powerful or even in a position to exact obedience.[560]

The philosophers, who have inquired into the foundations of society, have all felt the necessity of going back to a state of nature; but not one of them has got there.[561]

For it is by no means a light undertaking to distinguish properly between what is original and what is artificial in the actual nature of man, or to form a true idea of a state which no longer exists, perhaps never did exist, and probably never will exist*; and of which, it is, nevertheless, necessary to have true ideas, in order to form a proper judgment of our present state. It requires, indeed, more philosophy than can be imagined to enable any one to determine exactly what precautions he ought to take, in order to make solid observations on this subject; and it appears to me that a good solution of the following problem would be not unworthy of the Aristotles and Plinys of the present age. *What experiments would have to be made, to discover the natural man? And how are those experiments to be made in a state of society?*[563]

Let us begin then by laying facts aside, as they do not affect the question. The investigations we may enter into, in treating this subject, must not be considered as historical truths, but only as mere conditional and hypothetical reasonings, rather calculated to explain the nature of things, than to ascertain their actual origin; just like the hypotheses which our physicists daily form respecting the formation of the world. Religion commands us to believe that, God Himself having taken men out of a state of nature immediately after the creation, they are unequal only because it is His will they should be so: but it does not forbid us to form conjectures based solely on the nature of man, and the beings around him, concerning what might have become of the human race, if it had been left to itself.[564]

So that, without having recourse to the supernatural information given us on this head, or paying any regard to the changes which must have taken place in the internal as well as the external, conformation of man, as he applied his limbs to new uses, and fed himself on new kinds of food, I shall suppose his conformation to have been at all times what it appears to us at this day; that he always walked on two legs, made use of his hands as we do, directed his looks over all nature, and measured with his eyes the vast expanse of Heaven.

If we strip this being, thus constituted, of all the supernatural gifts he may have received, and all the artificial faculties he can have acquired only by a long process; if we consider him, in a word, just as he must have come from the hands of nature, we behold in him an animal weaker than some, and less agile than others; but, taking him all round, the most advantageously organised of any. I see him satisfying his hunger at the first oak, and slaking his thirst at the first brook; finding his bed at the foot of the tree which afforded him a repast; and, with that, all his wants supplied.

While the earth was left to its natural fertility and covered with immense forests, whose trees were never mutilated by the axe, it would present on every side both sustenance and shelter for every species of animal. Men, dispersed up and down among the rest, would observe and imitate their industry, and thus attain even to the instincts of the beasts, with the advantage that, whereas every species of brutes was confined to one particular instinct, man, who perhaps has not any one peculiar to himself, would appropriate them all, and live upon most of those different foods, which other animals shared among themselves and thus would find his subsistence much more easily than any of the rest.

Accustomed from their infancy to the inclemencies of the weather and the rigour of the seasons, inured to fatigue, and forced, naked and unarmed, to defend themselves and their prey from other ferocious animals, or to escape them by flight, men would acquire a robust and almost unalterable constitution.[565]

* ". . . this supposed primitive state."[562]

Solitary, indolent, and perpetually accompanied by danger, the savage cannot but be fond of sleep; his sleep too must be light, like that of the animals, which think but little and may be said to slumber all the time they do not think. Self-preservation being his chief and almost sole concern, he must exercise most those faculties which are most concerned with attack or defence, either for evercoming his prey, or for preventing him from becoming the prey of other animals. On the other hand, those organs which are perfected only by softness and sensuality will remain in a gross and imperfect state, incompatible with any sort of delicacy; so that, his senses being divided on this head, his touch and taste will be extremely coarse, his sight, hearing and smell exceedingly fine and subtle. Such in general is the animal condition, and such, according to the narratives of travellers, is that of most savage nations. . . .

Hitherto I have considered merely the physical man; let us now take a view of him on his metaphysical and moral side.

I see nothing in any animal but an ingenious machine, to which nature hath given senses to wind itself up, and to guard itself, to a certain degree, against anything that might tend to disorder or destroy it. I perceive exactly the same things in the human machine, with this difference, that in the operations of the brute, nature is the sole agent, whereas man has some share in his own operations, in his character as a free agent. The one chooses and refuses by instinct, the other from an act of free-will*: hence the brute cannot deviate from the rule prescribed to it, even when it would be advantageous for it to do so; and, on the contrary, man frequently deviates from such rules to his own prejudice. . . .

Every animal has ideas, since it has senses; it even combines those ideas in a certain degree; and it is only in degree that man differs, in this respect, from the brute. Some philosophers have even maintained that there is a greater difference between one man and another than between some men and some beasts. It is not, therefore, so much the understanding that constitutes the specific difference between the man and the brute, as the human quality of free agency. Nature lays her commands on every animal, and the brute obeys her voice. Man receives the same impulsion, but at the same time knows himself at liberty to acquiesce or resist: and it is particularly in his consciousness of this liberty that the spirituality of his soul is displayed. For physics may explain, in some measure, the mechanism of the senses and the formation of ideas; but in the power of

* " . . . the brutes . . . are mere slaves of instinct."[566]

"Plants are fashioned by cultivation, man by education."[567]

"When our life begins our needs begin too."[568]

" . . man's education begins at birth; before he can speak or understand he is learning."[569]

"As man's first state is one of want and weakness, his first sounds are cries and tears. The child feels his needs and cannot satisfy them, he begs for help by his cries. Is he hungry or thirsty? there are tears; is he too cold or too hot? more tears; he needs movement and is kept quiet, more tears; he wants to sleep and is disturbed, he weeps. The less comfortable he is, the more he demands change. He has only one language because he has, so to say, only one kind of discomfort. In the imperfect state of his sense organs he does not distinguish their several impressions; all ills produce one feeling of sorrow.

"These tears, which you think so little worthy of your attention, give rise to the first relation between man and his environment; here is forged the first link in the long chain of social order.

"When the child cries he is uneasy, he feels some need which he cannot satisfy; you watch him, see this need, find it, and satisfy it."[570]

"Children learn the meaning of signs by their effects; they have no other meaning for them."[571]

"As their strength increases, children have also less need for tears. They can do more for themselves, they need the help of others less frequently. With strength comes the sense to use it. It is with this second phase that the child becomes conscious of himself. During every moment of his life memory calls up the feeling of sense; he becomes really one person, always the same, and therefore capable of joy or sorrow. Hence we must begin to consider him as a moral being."[572]

willing or rather of choosing, and in the feeling of this power, nothing is to be found but acts which are purely spiritual and wholly inexplicable by the laws of mechanism.

However, even if the difficulties attending all these questions should still leave room for differences in this respect between men and brutes, there is another very specific quality which distinguishes them, and which will admit of no dispute. This is the faculty of self-improvement, which, by the help of circumstances, gradually develops all the rest of our faculties, and is inherent in the species as in the individual: whereas a brute is, at the end of a few months, all he will ever be during his whole life, and his species, at the end of a thousand years, exactly what it was the first year of that thousand. . . .

Savage man, left by nature solely to the direction of instinct, or rather indemnified for what he may lack by faculties capable at first of supplying its place, and afterwards of raising himself much above it, must accordingly begin with purely animal functions: thus seeing and feeling must be his first condition, which would be common to him and all other animals. To will, and not to will, to desire and to fear, must be the first, and almost the only operations of his soul, till new circumstances occasion new developments of his faculties.

Whatever moralists may hold, the human understanding is greatly indebted to the passions, which, it is universally allowed, are also much indebted to the understanding. It is by the activity of the passions that our reason is improved; for we desire knowledge only because we wish to enjoy; and it is impossible to conceive any reason why a person who has neither fears nor desires should give himself the trouble of reasoning. The passions, again, originate in our wants, and their progress depends on that of our knowledge; for we cannot desire or fear anything, except from the idea we have of it, or from the simple impulse of nature. Now savage man, being destitute of every species of intelligence, can have no passions save those of the latter kind: his desires never go beyond his physical wants. The only good he recognises in the universe are food, a female, and sleep: the only evils he fears are pain and hunger. I say pain, and not death: for no animal can know what it is to die; the knowledge of death and its terrors being one of the first acquisitions made by man in departing from an animal state.[573]

. . . men in a state of nature . . . [had] no moral relations or determinate obligations one with another.[574]

[Thus, he spoke of] the little care which nature has taken to unite mankind by mutual wants, and to facilitate the use of speech, . . . she has contributed little to make them sociable, and has put little of her own into all they have done to create such bonds of union. It is in fact impossible to conceive why, in a state of nature, one man should stand more in need of the assistance of another, than a monkey or a wolf of the assistance of another of its kind: or, granting that he did, what motive could induce that other to assist him; or, even then, by what means they could agree about the conditions.[575]

[However, he was opposed to Hobbes's conception of the state of nature as a state of war.[576]]

. . . contemplating the first and most simple operations of the human soul, I think I can perceive in it two principles prior to reason, one of them deeply interesting us in our own welfare and preservation, and the other exciting a natural repugnance at seeing any other sensible being, and particularly any of our own species, suffer pain or death. It is from the agreement and combination which the understanding is in a position to establish between these two principles, without its being necessary to introduce that of sociability, that all the rules of natural right appear to me to be derived.[577]

[1.] Egoism must not be confused with self-respect: for they differ both in themselves and in their effects. Self-respect is a natural feeling which leads every animal to look to its own preservation, and which, guided in man by reason and modified by compassion, creates humanity and virtue. Egoism is a purely relative and factitious feeling, which arises in a state of society, leads each individual to make more of himself than of any other, causes all the mutual damage men inflict one on another, and is the real source of the " sense of honour." This being understood, I maintain that, in our primitive condition, in the true state of nature, egoism did not exist; for as each man regarded himself as the only observer of his actions, the only being in the universe who took any interest in him, and the sole judge of his deserts, no feeling arising from comparisons he could not be led to make could take root in his soul; and for the same reason, he could know neither hatred nor the desire for revenge, since these passions can spring only from a sense of injury: and as it is the contempt or the intention to hurt, and not the harm done, which constitutes the injury, men who neither valued nor compared themselves could do one another much violence, when it suited them without feeling any sense of injury. In a word, each man, regarding his fellows almost as he regarded animals of different species, might seize the prey of a weaker or yield up his own to a stronger, and yet consider these acts of violence as mere natural occurrences, without the slightest emotion of insolence or despite, or any other feeling than the joy or grief of success or failure.[578]

[2.] Mandeville well knew that, in spite of all their morality, men would have never been better than monsters, had not nature bestowed on them a sense of compassion, to aid their reason: but he did not see that from this quality alone flow all those social virtues, of which he denied man the possession. But what is generosity, clemency or humanity but compassion applied to the weak, to the guilty, or to mankind in general? Even benevolence and friendship are, if we judge rightly, only the effects of compassion, constantly set upon a particular object: for how is it different to wish that another person may not suffer pain and uneasiness and to wish him happy? Were it even true that pity is no more than a feeling, which puts us in the place of the sufferer, a feeling, obscure yet lively in a savage, developed yet feeble in civilised man; this truth would have no other consequence than to confirm my argument. Compassion must, in fact, be the stronger, the more the animal beholding any kind of distress identifies himself with the animal that suffers.* Now, it is plain that such identification must have been much more perfect in a state of nature than it is in a state of reason. It is reason that engenders self-respect, and reflection that confirms it: it is reason which turns man's mind back upon itself, and divides him from everything that could disturb or afflict him. . . .

It is then certain that compassion is a natural feeling, which, by moderating the violence of love of self in each individual, contributes to the preservation of the whole species. It is this compassion that hurries us without reflection to the relief of those who are in distress: it is this which in a state of nature supplies the place of laws, morals and virtues, with the advantage that none are tempted to disobey its gentle voice. . . .[580]

With passions so little active, and so good a curb, men, being rather wild than wicked, and more intent to guard themselves against the mischief that might be done them, than to do mischief to others, were by no means subject to very perilous dissensions.[581]

. . . in this primitive state, men had neither houses, nor huts, nor any kind of property

* "Indeed, how can we let ourselves be stirred by pity unless we go beyond ourselves, and identify ourselves with the suffering animal, by leaving, so to speak, our own nature and taking his. We only suffer so far as we suppose he suffers; this suffering is not ours but his. So no one becomes sensitive till his imagination is aroused and begins to carry him outside himself.[579]

whatever; every one lived where he could, seldom for more than a single night; the sexes united without design, as accident, opportunity or inclination brought them together, nor had they any great need of words to communicate their designs to each other; and they parted with the same indifference. The mother gave suck to her children at first for her own sake; and afterwards, when habit had made them dear, for theirs: but as soon as they were strong enough to go in search of their own food, they forsook her of their own accord; and, as they had hardly any other method of not losing one another than that of remaining continually within sight, they soon became quite incapable of recognising one another when they happened to meet again.[582]

Let us conclude then that man in a state of nature, wandering up and down the forests, without industry, without speech, and without home, an equal stranger to war and to all ties, neither standing in need of his fellow-creatures nor having any desire to hurt them, and perhaps even not distinguishing them one from another; let us conclude that, being self-sufficient and subject to so few passions, he could have no feelings or knowledge but such as befitted his situation; that he felt only his actual necessities, and disregarded everything he did not think himself immediately concerned to notice, and that his understanding made no greater progress than his vanity. If by accident he made any discovery, he was the less able to communicate it to others, as he did not know even his own children. Every art would necessarily perish with its inventor, where there was no kind of education among men, and generations succeeded generations without the least advance; when, all setting out from the same point, centuries must have elapsed in the barbarism of the first ages; when the race was already old, and man remained a child.[583]

Having proved that the inequality of mankind is hardly felt, and that its influence is next to nothing in a state of nature, I must next show its origin and trace its progress in the successive developments of the human mind. Having shown that human *perfectibility,* the social virtues, and the other faculties which natural man potentially possessed, could never develop of themselves, but must require the fortuitous concurrence of many foreign causes that might never arise, and without which he would have remained for ever in his primitive condition, I must now collect and consider the different accidents which may have improved the human understanding while depraving the species, and made man wicked while making him sociable; so as to bring him and the world from that distant period to the point at which we now behold him.

I confess that, as the events I am going to describe might have happened in various ways, I have nothing to determine my choice but conjectures: but such conjectures become reasons, when they are the most probable that can be drawn from the nature of things, and the only means of discovering the truth. The consequences, however, which I mean to deduce will not be barely conjectural; as, on the principles just laid down, it would be impossible to form any other theory that would not furnish the same results, and from which I could not draw the same conclusions.[584]

The first man who, having enclosed a piece of ground, bethought himself of saying *This is mine,* and found people simple enough to believe him, was the real founder of civil society. . . . But there is a great probability that things had then already come to such a pitch, that they could no longer continue as they were; for the idea of property depends on many prior ideas, which could only be acquired successively, and cannot have been formed all at once in the human mind. Mankind must have made very considerable progress, and acquired considerable knowledge and industry which they must also have transmitted and increased from age to age, before they arrived at this last point of the state of nature. Let us then go farther back, and endeavour to unify under a single point of view that slow succession of events and discoveries in the most natural order.

Man's first feeling was that of his own existence, and his first care that of self-preservation. The produce of the earth furnished him with all he needed, and instinct told him how to use it. Hunger and other appetites made him at various times experience various modes of existence; and among these was one which urged him to propagate his species— a blind propensity that, having nothing to do with the heart, produced a merely animal act. The want once gratified, the two sexes knew each other no more; and even the offspring was nothing to its mother, as soon as it could do without her.

Such was the condition of infant man; the life of an animal limited at first to mere sensations, and hardly profiting by the gifts nature bestowed on him, much less capable of entertaining a thought of forcing anything from her. But difficulties soon presented themselves, and it became necessary to learn how to surmount them: the height of the trees, which prevented him from gathering their fruits, the competition of other animals desirous of the same fruits, and the ferocity of those who needed them for their own preservation, all obliged him to apply himself to bodily exercises. He had to be active, swift of foot, and vigorous in fight. Natural weapons, stones and sticks, were easily found: he learnt to surmount the obstacles of nature, to contend in case of necessity with other animals, and to dispute for the means of subsistence even with other men, or to indemnify himself for what he was forced to give up to a stronger.

In proportion as the human race grew more numerous, men's cares increased. The difference of soils, climates and seasons, must have introduced some differences into their manner of living. Barren years, long and sharp winters, scorching summers which parched the fruits of the earth, must have demanded a new industry. On the seashore and the banks of rivers, they invented the hook and line, and became fishermen and eaters of fish. In the forests they made bows and arrows, and became huntsmen and warriors. In cold countries they clothed themselves with the skins of the beasts they had slain. The lightning, a volcano, or some lucky chance acquainted them with fire, a new resource against the rigours of winter; they next learned how to preserve this element, then how to reproduce it, and finally how to prepare with it the flesh of animals which before they had eaten raw.

This repeated relevance of various beings to himself, and one to another, would naturally give rise in the human mind to the perceptions of certain relations between them. Thus the relations which we denote by the terms, great, small, strong, weak, swift, slow, fearful, bold, and the like, almost insensibly compared at need, must have at length produced in him a kind of reflection, or rather a mechanical prudence, which would indicate to him the precautions most necessary to his security.

The new intelligence which resulted from this development increased his superiority over other animals, by making him sensible of it. He would now endeavour, therefore, to ensnare them, would play them a thousand tricks, and though many of them might surpass him in swiftness or in strength, would in time become the master of some and the scourge of others. Thus, the first time he looked into himself, he felt the first emotion of pride; and, at a time when he scarce knew how to distinguish the different orders of beings, by looking upon his species as of the highest order, he prepared the way for assuming pre-eminence as an individual.

Other men, it is true, were not then to him what they now are to us, and he had no greater intercourse with them than with other animals; yet they were not neglected in his observations. The conformities, which he would in time discover between them, and between himself and his female, led him to judge of others which were not then per-

ceptible; and finding that they all behaved as he himself would have done in like circumstances, he naturally inferred that their manner of thinking and acting was altogether
in conformity with his own. This important truth, once deeply impressed on his mind,
must have induced him, from an intuitive feeling more certain and more rapid than any
kind of reasoning, to pursue the rules of conduct, which he had best observe towards
them, for his own security and advantage.

Taught by experience that the love of well-being is the sole motive of human actions,
he found himself in a position to distinguish the few cases, in which mutual interest might
justify him in relying upon the assistance of his fellows; and also the still fewer cases in
which a conflict of interests might give cause to suspect them. In the former case, he
joined in the same herd with them, or at most in some kind of loose association, that
laid no restraint on its members, and lasted no longer than the transitory occasion that
formed it. In the latter case, every one sought his own private advantage, either by
open force, if he thought himself strong enough, or by address and cunning, if he felt
himself the weaker.

In this manner, men may have insensibly acquired some gross ideas of mutual undertakings, and of the advantages of fulfilling them: that is, just so far as their present and
apparent interest was concerned: for they were perfect strangers to foresight, and were
so far from troubling themselves about the distant future, that they hardly thought of
the morrow. If a deer was to be taken, every one saw that, in order to succeed, he must
abide faithfully by his post: but if a hare happened to come within the reach of any one
of them, it is not to be doubted that he pursued it without scruple, and, having seized
his prey, cared very little, if by so doing he caused his companions to miss theirs.

It is easy to understand that such intercourse would not require a language much
more refined than that of rooks or monkeys, who associate together for much the same
purpose. Inarticulate cries, plenty of gestures, and some imitative sounds, must have been
for a long time the universal language; and by the addition, in every country, of some
conventional articulate sounds (of which, as I have already intimated, the first institution
is not too easy to explain) particular languages were produced*; but these were rude

* "The first language of mankind, the most universal and vivid, in a word the only language man needed,
before he had occasion to exert his eloquence to persuade assembled multitudes, was the simple cry of
nature.   But as this was excited only by a sort of instinct on urgent occasions, to implore assistance in
case of danger, or relief in case of suffering, it could be of little use in the ordinary course of life, in which
more moderate feelings prevail. When the ideas of men began to expand and multiply, and closer communication took place among them, they strove to invent more numerous signs and a more copious
language. They multiplied the inflections of the voice, and added gestures, which are in their own nature
more expressive, and depend less for their meaning on a prior determination. Visible and movable objects
were therefore expressed by gestures, and audible ones by imitative sounds: but, as hardly anything can
be indicated by gestures, except objects actually present or easily described, and visible actions; as they are
not universally useful—for darkness or the interposition of a material object destroys their efficacy—and
as besides they rather request than secure our attention; men at length bethought themselves of substituting for them the articulate sounds of the voice, which, without bearing the same relation to any
particular ideas, are better calculated to express them all, as conventional signs. Such an institution could
only be made by common consent, and must have been effected in a manner not very easy for men whose
gross organs had not been accustomed to any such exercise. It is also in itself still more difficult to conceive, since such a common agreement must have had motives, and speech seems to have been highly
necessary to establish the use of it.

"It is reasonable to suppose that the first words made use of by mankind had a much more extensive
signification than those used in languages already formed, and that ignorant as they were of the division
of discourse into its constituent parts, they at first gave every single word the sense of a whole proposition.
When they began to distinguish subject and attribute, and noun and verb, which was itself no common
effort of genius, substantives were at first only so many proper names; the present infinitive was the only
tense of verbs; and the very idea of adjectives must have been developed with great difficulty; for every

and imperfect, and nearly such as are now to be found among some savage nations.

Hurried on by the rapidity of time, by the abundance of things I have to say, and by the almost insensible progress of things in their beginnings, I pass over in an instant a multitude of ages; for the slower the events were in their succession, the more rapidly may they be described.

These first advances enabled men to make others with greater rapidity. In proportion as they grew enlightened, they grew industrious. They ceased to fall asleep under the first tree, or in the first cave that afforded them shelter; they invented several kinds of implements of hard and sharp stones, which they used to dig up the earth, and to cut wood; they then made huts out of branches, and afterwards learnt to plaster them over with mud and clay. This was the epoch of the first revolution, which established and distinguished families, and introduced a kind of property, in itself the source of a thousand quarrels and conflicts. As, however, the strongest were probably the first to build themselves huts which they felt themselves able to defend, it may be concluded that the weak found it much easier and safer to imitate, than to attempt to dislodge them: and of those who were once provided with huts, none could have any inducement to appropriate that of his neighbour; not indeed so much because it did not belong to him, as because it could be of no use, and he could not make himself master of it without exposing himself to a desperate battle with the family which occupied it.

The first expansions of the human heart were the effects of a novel situation, which united husbands and wives, fathers and children, under one roof. The habit of living together soon gave rise to the finest feelings known to humanity, conjugal love and paternal affection. Every family became a little society, the more united because liberty and reciprocal attachment were the only bonds of its union.* The sexes, whose manner of life had been hitherto the same, began now to adopt different ways of living. The women became more sedentary, and accustomed themselves to mind the hut and their children, while the men went abroad in search of their common subsistence. From living a softer life, both sexes also began to lose something of their strength and ferocity: but, if individuals became to some extent less able to encounter wild beasts separately, they found it, on the other hand, easier to assmble and resist in common.

The simplicity and solitude of man's life in this new condition, the paucity of his wants, and the implements he had invented to satisfy them, left him a great deal of leisure, which

adjective is an abstract idea, and abstractions are painful and unnatural operations.

"Every object at first received a particular name without regard to genus or species, which these primitive originators were not in a position to distinguish; every individual presented itself to their minds in isolation, as they are in the picture of nature. If one oak was called A, another was called B; for the primitive idea of two things is that they are not the same, and it often takes a long time for what they have in common to be seen: so that, the narrower the limits of their knowledge of things, the more copious their dictionary must have been."[585]

"[In turn, language affected reason:] Let it be considered how many ideas we owe to the use of speech; how far grammar exercises the understanding and facilitates its operation."[586]

" . . . languages, as they change the symbols, also modify the ideas which the symbols express. Minds are formed by language, thoughts take their colour from its ideas."[587]

* "The most ancient of all societies, and the only one that is natural, is the family: and even so the children remain attached to the father only so long as they need him for their preservation. As soon as this need ceases, the natural bond is dissolved. The children, released from the obedience they owed to the father, and the father, released from the care he owed to his children, return equally to independence. If they remain united, they continue so no longer naturally, but voluntarily; and the family itself is then maintained only by convention. . . .

"The family then may be called the first model of political societies: the ruler corresponds to the father, and the people to the children; and all, being born free and equal, alienate their liberty only for their own advantage."[588]

he employed to furnish himself with many conveniences unknown to his fathers. . . .

We can here see a little better how the use of speech became established, and insensibly improved in each family, and we may form a conjecture also concerning the manner in which various causes may have extended and accelerated the progress of language, by making it more and more necessary. Floods or earthquakes surrounded inhabited districts with precipices or waters: revolutions of the globe tore off portions from the continent, and made them islands. It is readily seen that among men thus collected and compelled to live together, a common idiom must have arisen much more easily than among those who still wandered through the forests of the continent. Thus it is very possible that after their first essays in navigation the islanders brought over the use of speech to the continent: and it is at least very probable that communities and languages were first established in islands, and even came to perfection there before they were known on the mainland.

Everything now begins to change its aspect. Men, who have up to now been roving in the woods, by taking to a more settled manner of life, come gradually together, form separate bodies, and at length in every country arises a distinct nation, united in character and manners, not by regulations or laws, but by uniformity of life and food, and the common influence of climate. Permanent neighbourhood could not fail to produce, in time, some connection between different families. Among young people of opposite sexes, living in neighbouring huts, the transient commerce required by nature soon led, through mutual intercourse, to another kind not less agreeable, and more permanent. Men began now to take the difference between objects into account, and to make comparisons; they acquired imperceptibly the ideas of beauty and merit, which soon gave rise to feelings of preference. In consequence of seeing each other often, they could not do without seeing each other constantly. A tender and pleasant feeling insinuated itself into their souls, and the least opposition turned it into an impetuous fury: with love arose jealousy; discord triumphed, and human blood was sacrificed to the gentlest of all passions.

As ideas and feelings succeeded one another, and heart and head were brought into play, men continued to lay aside their original wildness; their private connections became every day more intimate as their limits extended. They accustomed themselves to assemble before their huts round a large tree; singing and dancing, the true offspring of love and leisure, became the amusement, or rather the occupation, of men and women thus assembled together with nothing else to do. Each one began to consider the rest, and to wish to be considered in turn; and thus a value came to be attached to public esteem. Whoever sang or danced best, whoever was the handsomest, the strongest, the most dexterous, or the most eloquent, came to be of most consideration; and this was the first step towards inequality, and at the same time towards vice. From these first distinctions arose on the one side vanity and contempt and on the other shame and envy: and the fermentation caused by these new leavens ended by producing combinations fatal to innocence and happiness.

As soon as men began to value one another, and the idea of consideration had got a footing in the mind, every one put in his claim to it, and it became impossible to refuse it to any with impunity. Hence arose the first obligations of civility even among savages; and every intended injury became an affront; because, besides the hurt which might result from it, the party injured was certain to find in it a contempt for his person, which was often more insupportable than the hurt itself.

Thus, as every man punished the contempt shown him by others, in proportion to his opinion of himself, revenge became terrible, and men bloody and cruel. This is precisely the state reached by most of the savage nations known to us. . . .

But it must be remarked that the society thus formed, and the relations thus established among men, required of them qualities different from those which they possessed from their primitive constitution. Morality began to appear in human actions, and every one, before the institution of law, was the only judge and avenger of the injuries done him, so that the goodness which was suitable in the pure state of nature was no longer proper in the new-born state of society. Punishments had to be made more severe, as opportunities of offending became more frequent, and the dread of vengeance had to take the place of the rigiour of the law. Thus, though men had become less patient, and their natural compassion had already suffered some diminution, this period of expansion of the human faculties, keeping a just mean between the indolence of the primitive state and the petulant activity of our egoism, must have been the happiest and most stable of epochs. . . . [Most] savages . . . have been found in this state. . . .

So long as men remained content with their rustic huts, so long as they were satisfied with clothes made of the skins of animals and sewn together with thorns and fishbones, adorned themselves only with feathers and shells, and continued to paint their bodies different colours, to improve and beautify their bows and arrows and to make with sharp-edged stones fishing boats or clumsy musical instruments; in a word, so long as they undertook only what a single person could accomplish, and confined themselves to such arts as did not require the joint labour of several hands, they lived free, healthy, honest and happy lives, so long as their nature allowed, and as they continued to enjoy the pleasures of mutual and independent intercourse. But from the moment one man began to stand in need of the help of another; from the moment it appeared advantageous to any one man to have enough provisions for two, equality disappeared, property was introduced, work became indispensable, and vast forests became smiling fields, which man had to water with the sweat of his brow, and where slavery and misery were soon seen to germinate and grow up with the crops.

Metallurgy and agriculture were the two arts which produced this great revolution. The poets tell us it was gold and silver, but, for the philosophers, it was iron and corn, which first civilised men, and ruined humanity. Thus both were unknown to the savages of America, who for that reason are still savage: the other nations also seem to have continued in a state of barbarism while they practised only one of these arts. One of the best reasons, perhaps, why Europe has been, if not longer, at least more constantly and highly civilised than the rest of the world, is that it is at once the most abundant in iron and the most fertile in corn.

It is difficult to conjecture how men first came to know and use iron. . . .

With regard to agriculture, the principles of it were known long before they were put in practice; and it is indeed hardly possible that men, constantly employed in drawing their subsistence from plants and trees, should not readily acquire a knowledge of the means made use of by nature for the propagation of vegetables. It was in all probability very long, however, before their industry took that turn, either because trees, which together with hunting and fishing afforded them food, did not require their attention; or because they were ignorant of the use of corn, or without instruments to cultivate it; or because they lacked foresight to future needs; or lastly, because they were without means of preventing others from robbing them of the fruit of their labour.

When they grew more industrious, it is natural to believe that they began, with the help of sharp stones and pointed sticks, to cultivate a few vegetables or roots around their huts; though it was long before they knew how to prepare corn, or were provided with the implements necessary for raising it in any large quantity; not to mention how essential it is, for husbandry, to consent to immediate loss, in order to reap a future gain—a precaution very foreign to the turn of a savage's mind; for, as I have said, he hardly foresees in the morning what he will need at night.

The invention of the other arts must therefore have been necessary to compel mankind to apply themselves to agriculture. No sooner were artificers wanted to smelt and forge iron, than others were required to maintain them; the more hands that were employed in manufactures, the fewer were left to provide for the common subsistence, though the number of mouths to be furnished with food remained the same: and as some required commodities in exchange for their iron, the rest at length discovered the method of making iron serve for the multiplication of commodities. By this means the arts of husbandry and agriculture were established on the one hand, and the art of working metals and multiplying their uses on the other.

The cultivation of the earth necessarily brought about its distribution; and property, once recognised, gave rise to the first rules of justice; for, to secure each man his own, it had to be possible for each to have something. Besides, as men began to look forward to the future, and all had something to lose, every one had reason to apprehend that reprisals would follow any injury he might do to another. This origin is so much the more natural, as it is impossible to conceive how property can come from anything but manual labour: for what else can a man add to things which he does not originally create, so as to make them his own property? Is it the husbandman's labour alone that, giving him a title to the produce of the ground he has tilled, gives him a claim also to the land itself, at least till harvest; and so, from year to year, a constant possession which is easily transformed into property. . . .

In this state of affairs, equality might have been sustained, had the talents of individuals been equal, and had, for example, the use of iron and the consumption of commodities always exactly balanced each other; but, as there was nothing to preserve this balance, it was soon disturbed; the strongest did most work; the most skilful turned his labour to best account; the most ingenius devised methods of diminishing his labour: the husbandman wanted more iron, or the smith more corn, and, while both laboured equally, the one gained a great deal by his work, while the other could hardly support himself. Thus natural inequality unfolds itself insensibly with that of combination, and the difference between men, developed by their different circumstances, becomes more sensible and permanent in its effects, and begins to have an influence, in the same proportion, over the lot of individuals.

Matters once at this pitch, it is easy to imagine the rest. I shall not detain the reader with a description of the successive invention of other arts, the development of language, the trial and utilisation of talents, the inequality of fortunes, the use and abuse of riches, and all the details connected with them which the reader can easily supply for himself.*

---

* In another work he gives the evolution of religion. "What makes the deaf suspicious and the lower classes superstitious? Ignorance of the things about us, and of what is taking place around us."[589]

"The perception of our action upon other bodies must have first induced us to suppose that their action upon us was effected in like manner. Thus man began by thinking that all things whose action affected him were alive. He did not recognise the limits of their powers, and he therefore supposed that they were boundless; as soon as he supplied them with bodies they became his gods. In the earliest times men went in terror of everything and everything in nature seemed alive. The idea of matter was developed as slowly as that of spirit, for the former is itself an abstraction. Thus the universe was peopled with gods like themselves. The stars, the winds, and the mountains, rivers, trees, and towns, their very dwellings, each had its soul, its god, its life. The teraphim of Laban, the manitos of savages, the fetishes of negroes, every work of nature and of man, were the first gods of mortals; polytheism was their first religion and idolatry their earliest form of worship. The idea of one God was beyond their grasp, till little by little they formed general ideas, and they rose to the idea of a first cause and gave meaning to the word 'substance,' which is at bottom the greatest of abstractions."[590]

I shall confine myself to a glance at mankind in this new situation.

Behold then all human faculties developed, memory and imagination in full play, egoism interested, reason active, and the mind almost at the highest point of its perfection. Behold all the natural qualities in action, the rank and condition of every man assigned him; not merely his share of property and his power to serve or injure others, but also his wit, beauty, strength or skill, merit or talents: and these being the only qualities capable of commanding respect, it soon became necessary to possess or affect them. . . . In a word, there arose rivalry and competition on the one hand, and conflicting interests on the other, together with a secret desire on both of profiting at the expense of others. All these evils were the first effects of property, and the inseparable attendants of growing inequality.

Before the invention of signs to represent riches, wealth could hardly consist in anything but lands and cattle, the only real possessions men can have. But, when inheritances so increased in number and extent as to occupy the whole of the land, and to border on one another, one man could aggrandise himself only at the expense of another; at the same time the supernumeraries, who had been too weak or too indolent to make such acquisitions, and had grown poor without sustaining any loss, because, while they saw everything change around them, they remained still the same, were obliged to receive their subsistence, or steal it, from the rich; and this soon bred, according to their different characters, dominion and slavery, or violence and rapine. The wealthy, on their part, had no sooner begun to taste the pleasure of command, than they disdained all others, and, using their old slaves to acquire new, thought of nothing but subduing and enslaving their neighbours. . . .

Thus, as the most powerful or the most miserable considered their might or misery as a kind of right to the possession of others, equivalent, in their opinion, to that of property, the destruction of equality was attended by the most terrible disorders. Usurpations by the rich, robbery by the poor, and the unbridled passions of both, suppressed the cries of natural compassion and the still feeble voice of justice, and filled men with avarice, ambition and vice. Between the title of the strongest and that of the first occupier, there arose perpetual conflicts, which never ended but in battles and bloodshed. The newborn state of society thus gave rise to a horrible state of war; men thus harassed and depraved were no longer capable of retracing their steps or renouncing the fatal acquisitions they had made, but, labouring by the abuse of the faculties which do them honour, merely to their own confusion, brought themselves to the brink of ruin. . . .

It is impossible that men should not at length have reflected on so wretched a situation, and on the calamities that overwhelmed them. The rich, in particular, must have felt how much they suffered by a constant state of war, of which they bore all the expense; and in which, though all risked their lives, they alone risked their property. Besides, however speciously they might disguise their usurpations, they knew that they were founded on precarious and false titles. . . . Destitute of valid reasons to justify and sufficient strength to defend himself, able to crush individuals with ease, but easily crushed himself by a troop of bandits, one against all, and incapable, on account of mutual jealousy, of joining with his equals against numerous enemies united by the common hope of plunder, the rich man, thus urged by necessity, conceived at length the profoundest plan that ever entered the mind of man: this was to employ in his favour the forces of those who attacked him, to make allies of his adversaries, to inspire them with different maximes, and to give them other institutions as favourable to himself as the law of nature was unfavourable.

With this view, after having represented to his neighbours the horror of a situation which armed every man against the rest, and made their possessions as burdensome to them as their wants, and in which no safety could be expected either in riches or in poverty, he readily devised plausible arguments to make them close with his design. "Let us join," said he," to guard the weak from oppression, to restrain the ambitious, and to secure to every man the possession of what belongs to him: let us institute rules of justice and peace, to which all without exception may be obliged to conform; rules that may in some measure make amends for the caprices of fortune, by subjecting equally the powerful and the weak to the observance of reciprocal obligations. Let us, in a word, instead of turning our forces against ourselves, collect them in a supreme power which may govern us by wise laws, protect and defend all the members of the association, repulse their common enemies, and maintain eternal harmony among us."

Far fewer words to this purpose would have been enough to impose on men so barbarous and easily seduced; especially as they had too many disputes among themselves to do without arbitrators, and too much ambition and avarice to go long without master. . . .

Such was, or may well have been, the origin of society and law,* which bound new fetters on the poor, and gave new powers to the rich; which irretrievably destroyed natural liberty, eternally fixed the law of property and inequality, converted clever usurpation into unalterable right, and, for the advantage of a few ambitious individuals, subjected all mankind to perpetual labour, slavery, and wretchedness. It is easy to see how the establishment of one community made that of all the rest necessary, and how, in order to make head against united forces, the rest of mankind had to unite in turn. Societies soon multiplied and spread over the face of the earth, till hardly a corner of the world was left in which a man could escape the yoke, and withdraw his head from beneath the sword which he saw perpetually hanging over him by a thread. Civil rights having thus become the common rule among the members of each community, the law of nature maintained its place only between different communities, where, under the name of the right of nations, it was qualified by certain tacit conventions, in order to make commerce practicable, and serve as a substitute for natural compassion, which lost, when applied to societies, almost all the influence it had over individuals, and survived no longer except in some great cosmopolitan spirits, who, breaking down the imaginary barriers that separate different peoples, follow the example of our Sovereign Creator, and include the whole human race in their benevolence.

But bodies politic, remaining thus in a state of nature among themselves, presently experienced the inconveniences which had obliged individuals to forsake it; for this state became still more fatal to these great bodies than it had been to the individuals of whom they were composed. Hence arose national wars, battles, murders, and reprisals, which shock nature and outrage reason; together with all those horrible prejudices which class among the virtues the honour of shedding human blood. . . . Such were the first effects which we can see to have followed the division of mankind into different communities. But let us return to their institutions. . . .

Government had, in its infancy, no regular and constant form. The want of experience and philosophy prevented men from seeing any but present inconveniences, and they thought of providing themselves against others only as they presented themselves. In spite of the endeavours of the wisest legislators, the political state remained imperfect, because it was little more than the work of chance; and, as it has begun ill, though time

* "Look into the motives which have induced men, once united by their common needs in a general society, to unite themselves still more intimately by means of civil society: you will find no other motive than that of assuring the property, life and liberty of each member by the protection of all."[591]

revealed its defects and suggested remedies, the original faults were never repaired. It was continually being patched up. . . . Society consisted at first merely of a few general conventions, which every member bound himself to observe; and for the performance of covenants the whole body went security to each individual. Experience only could show the weakness of such a constitution, and how easily it might be infringed with impunity, from the difficulty of convicting men of faults, where the public alone was to be witness and judge: the laws could not but be eluded in many ways; disorders and inconveniences could not but multiply continually, till it became necessary to commit the dangerous trust of public authority to private persons, and the care of enforcing obedience to the deliberations of the people to the magistrate. For to say that chiefs were chosen before the confederacy was formed, and that the administrators of the laws were there before the laws themselves, is too absurd a supposition to consider seriously.[592]

Without entering at present upon the investigations which still remain to be made into the nature of the fundamental compact underlying all government, I content myself with adopting the common opinion concerning it, and regard the establishment of the political body as a real contract between the people and the chiefs chosen by them: a contract by which both parties bind themselves to observe the laws therein expressed, which form the ties of their union.* The people having in respect of their social relations concentrated all their wills in one, the several articles, concerning which this will is explained, become so many fundamental laws, obligatory on all the members of the State without exception, and one of these articles regulated the choice and power of the magistrates appointed to watch over the execution of the rest. This power extends to everything which may maintain the constitution, without going so far as to alter it. It is accompanied by honours, in order to bring the laws and their administrators into respect. The ministers are also distinguished by personal prerogatives, in order to recompense them for the cares and labour which good administration involves. The magistrate, on his side, binds himself to use the power he is entrusted with only in conformity with the intention of his constituents, to maintain them all in the peaceable possession of what belongs to them, and to prefer on every occasion the public interest to his own.[594]

By the social compact we have given the body politic existence and life; we have now by legislation to give it movement and will. For the original act by which the body is formed and united still in no respect determines what it ought to do for its preservation.

What is well and in conformity with order is so by the nature of things and independently of human conventions. All justice comes from God, who is its sole source; but if we knew how to receive so high an inspiration, we should need neither government nor laws. Doubtless, there is a universal justice emanating from reason alone, but this

"I suppose men to have reached the point at which the obstacles in the way of their preservation in the state of nature show their power of resistance to be greater than the resources at the disposal of each individual for his maintenance in that state. That primitive condition can then subsist no longer; and the human race would perish unless it changed its manner of existence.

"But, as men cannot engender new forces, but only unite and direct existing ones, they have no other means of preserving themselves than the formation, by aggregation, of a sum of forces great enough to overcome the resistance. These they have to bring into play by means of a single motive power, and cause to act in concert. . . .

"If then we discard from the social compact what is not of its essence, we shall find that it reduces itself to the following terms—

" ' *Each of us puts his person and all his power in common under the supreme direction of the general will, and, in our corporate capacity, we receive each member as an indivisible part of the whole.*' "[593]

justice, to be admitted among us, must be mutual. . . . Conventions and laws are therefore needed to join rights to duties and refer justice to its object. In the state of nature, where everything is common, I owe nothing to him whom I have promised nothing; I recognize as belonging to others only what is of no use to me. In the state of society all rights are fixed by law, and the case becomes different.

But what, after all, is a law? . . . laws . . . are acts of the general will.[595]

The passage from the state of nature to the civil state produces a very remarkable change in man, by substituting justice for instinct in his conduct, and giving his actions the morality they had formerly lacked. Then only, when the voice of duty takes the place of physical impulses and right of appetite, does man, who so far had considered only himself, find that he is forced to act on different principles, and to consult his reason before listening to his inclinations. Although, in this state, he deprives himself of some advantages which he got from nature, he gains in return others so great, his faculties are so stimulated and developed, his ideas so extended, his feelings so ennobled, and his whole soul so uplifted, that, did not the abuses of this new condition often degrade him below that which he left, he would be bound to bless continually the happy moment which took him from it for ever, and, instead of a stupid and unimaginative animal, made him an intelligent being and a man.[596]

I have endeavoured to trace the origin and progress of inequality, and the institution and abuse of political societies, so far as these are capable of being deduced from the nature of man merely by the light of reason, and independently of those sacred dogmas which give the sanction of divine right to sovereign authority.[597]

## Rousseau used the organic analogy.

I shall take the liberty of making use of a very common, and in some respects inaccurate, comparison. . . .

The body politic, taken individually, may be considered as an organised, living body, resembling that of man. The sovereign power represents the head; the laws and customs are the brain, the source of the nerves and seat of understanding, will and senses, of which the Judges and Magistrates are the organs: commerce, industry, and agriculture are the mouth and stomach which prepare the common subsistence; the public income is the blood, which a prudent *economy,* in performing the functions of the heart, causes to distribute through the whole body nutriment and life: the citizens are the body and members, which make the machine live, move and work; and no part of this machine can be damaged without the painful impression being at once conveyed to the brain, if the animal is in a state of health.

The life of both bodies is the self common to the whole, the reciprocal sensibility and internal correspondence of all the parts. Where this communication ceases, where the formal unity disappears, and the contiguous parts belong to one another only by juxtaposition, the man is dead, or the State is dissolved.[598]

## There is for nations, as for men, a period of youth.[599]

The body politic, as well as the human body, begins to die as soon as it is born, and carries in itself the causes of its destruction.[600]

As nature has set bounds to the stature of a well-made man, and outside those limits, makes nothing but giants or dwarfs, similarly, for the constitution of a State to be at its best, it is possible to fix limits that will make it neither too large for good government, nor too small for self-maintenance. In every body politic there is a *maximum* strength which it cannot exceed and which it only loses by increasing in size. Every extension of the social tie means its relaxation; and, generally speaking, a small State is stronger in proportion than a great one.[601]

As the particular will acts constantly in opposition to the general will, the government continually exerts itself against the Sovereignty. The greater this exertion becomes, the more the constitution changes; and, as there is in this case no other corporate will to cretate an equilibrium by resisting the will of the prince, sooner or later the prince must inevitably suppress the Sovereign and break the social treaty. This is the unavoidable and inherent defect which, from the very birth of the body politic, tends ceaselessly to destroy it, as age and death end by destroying the human body.

There are two general courses by which government degenerates: *i.e.* when it undergoes contraction, or when the State is dissolved.

Government undergoes contraction when it passes from the many to the few, that is, from democracy to aristocracy, and from aristocracy to royalty. To do so is its natural propensity. . . .

The dissolution of the State may come about in either of two ways.

First, when the prince ceases to administer the State in accordance with the laws, and usurps the Soverign power. A remarkable change then occurs: not the government, but the State, undergoes contraction; I mean that the great State is dissolved, and another is formed within it, composed solely of the members of the government, which becomes for the rest of the pople merely master and tyrant. So that the moment the government usurps Sovereignty, the social compact is broken, and all private citizens recover by right their natural liberty, and are forced, but not bound, to obey.

The same thing happens when the members of the government severally usurp the power they should exercise only as a body; this is as great an infraction of the laws, and results in even greater disorders. There are then, so to speak, as many princes as there are magistrates, and the State, no less divided than the government, either perishes or changes its form.[602]

The life-principle of the body politic lies in the sovereign authority. The legislative power is the heart of the State; the executive power is its brain, which causes the movement of all the parts. The brain may become paralysed and the individual still live. A man may remain an imbecile and live; but as soon as the heart ceases to perform its functions, the animal is dead.[603]

He sought for objective criteria of excellence of governments and decided upon size of population.

For my part, I am continually astonished that a mark so simple is not recognised, or that men are of so bad faith as not to admit it. What is the end of political association? The preservation and prosperity of its members. And what is the surest mark of their preservation and prosperity? Their numbers and population. Seek then nowhere else this mark that is in dispute. The rest being equal, the government under which, without external aids, without naturalisation or colonies, the citizens increase and multiply most, is beyond question the best. The government under which a people wanes and diminishes is the worst. Calculators, it is left for you to count, to measure, to compare.[604]

Students of population took up the challenge, as will be seen.

To Rousseau, personality was influenced by both social milieu and natural surroundings.

It is in fact easy to see that many of the differences which distinguish men are merely the effect of habit and the different methods of life men adopt in society. Thus a robust or delicate constitution, and the strength or weakness attaching to it, are more frequently the effects of a hardy or effeminate method of education than of the original endowment of the body. It is the same with the powers of the mind; for education not only makes a difference between such as are cultured and such as are not, but even increases the differences which exist among the former, in proportion to their respective degrees of culture: as the distance between a giant and a dwarf on the same road increases with every step they take. If we compare the prodigious diversity, which obtains in the education and manner of life of the various orders of men in the state of society, with the uniformity and simplicity of animal and savage life, in which every one lives on the same kind of food and in exactly the same manner, and does exactly the same things, it is easy to conceive how much less the difference between man and man must be in a state of nature than in a state of society, and how greatly the natural inequality of mankind must be increased by the inequalities of social institutions.

But even if nature really affected, in the distribution of her gifts, that partiality which is imputed to her, what advantage would the greatest of her favourites derive from it, to the detriment of others, in a state that admits of hardly any kind of relation between them? Where there is no love, of what advantage is beauty? Of what use is wit to those who do not converse, or cunning to those who have no business with others?[605]

. . . a hot climate . . . seems always to inflame the passions.[606]

Liberty, not being a fruit of all climates, is not within the reach of all peoples. The more this principle, laid down by Montesquieu, is considered, the more its truth is felt; the more it is combated, the more chance is given to confirm it by new proofs.[607]

## Paine

Thomas Paine (1737–1809) premised the rights of man and his sociality.

. . . all men are born equal, and with equal natural rights.[608]

Natural rights are those which appertain to man in right of his existence.[609]

As Nature created him for social life, she fitted him for the station she intended. In all cases she made his natural wants greater than his individual powers.

No one man is capable, without the aid of society, of supplying his own wants; and those wants acting upon every individual, impel the whole of them into society, as naturally as gravitation acts to a center.

But she has gone further. She has not only forced man into society, by a diversity of wants, which the reciprocal aid of each other can supply, but she has implanted in him a system of social affections, which, though not necessary to his existence, are essential to his happiness. There is no period in life when this love for society ceases to act. It begins and ends with our being.[610]

In short, man is so naturally a creature of society, that it is almost impossible to put him out of it[611]

He distinguished between society and political organization, which had previously been confused, making the former the result of sociality according to the gregarious theory, and the latter the result of social contract.

Great part of that order which reigns among mankind is not the effect of government. It had its origin in the principles of society and the natural constitution of man. It existed prior to government, and would exist if the formality of government was abolished. The mutual dependence and reciprocal interest which man has upon man, and all parts of a civilized community upon each other, create that great chain of connection which holds it together.[612]

Some writers have so confounded society with government, as to leave little or no distinction between them; whereas they are not only different, but have different origins. Society is produced by our wants, and government by our wickedness; the former promotes our happiness *positively*, by uniting our affections; the latter negatively, by restraining our vices. The one encourages intercourse, the other creates distinctions. The first is a patron, the last a punisher.

Society in every state is a blessing, but government, even in its best state, is but a necessary evil; in its worst state, an intolerable one; for when we suffer, or are exposed to the same miseries *by a government*, which we might expect in a country *without government*, our calamity is heightened by reflecting that we furnish the means by which we suffer.

Government, like dress, is the badge of lost innocence: the palaces of kings are built on the ruins of bowers of paradise. For, were the impulses of conscience clear, uniform, and irresistibly obeyed, man would need no other lawgiver; but that not being the case, he finds it necessary to surrender up a part of his property to furnish the means for the protection of the rest; and this he is induced to do by the same prudence which in every other case, advises him out of two evils to choose the least. *Wherefore,* security being the true design and end of government, it unanswerably follows, that whatever *form* thereof appears most likely to ensure it to us with the least expense and greatest benefit, is preferable to all others.

In order to give a clear and just idea of the design and end of government, let us suppose a small number of persons settled in some sequestered part of the earth, unconnected with the rest; they will then represent the first peopling of any country, or of the world. In this state of natural liberty, society will be their first thought. A thousand motives will excite them thereto; the strength of one man is so unequal to his wants, and his mind so unfitted for perpetual solitude, that he is soon obliged to seek assistance and relief of another, who in his turn requires the same. Four or five united would be able to raise a tolerable dwelling in the midst of a wilderness; but *one* man might labour out the common period of life without accomplishing anything: when he had felled his timber he could not remove it, nor erect it after it was removed; hunger in the meantime would urge him from his work, and every different want call him a different way. Disease, nay even misfortune, would be death; for though neither might be mortal, yet either would disable him from living, and reduce him to a state in which he might rather be said to perish than to die.

Thus necessity, like a gravitating power, would soon form our newly-arrived emigrants into society, the reciprocal blessings of which would supersede and render the obligations of law and government unnecessary while they remained perfectly just to each other: but as nothing but Heaven is impregnable to vice, it will unavoidably happen, that in proportion as they surmount the first difficulties of emigration, which bound them together in a common cause, they will begin to relax in their duty and attachment to each other; and this remissness will point out the necessity of establishing some form of government to supply the defect of moral virtue.*

---

* " . . . as man must have existed before governments existed, there necessarily was a time when governments did not exist . . . The fact therefore must be, that the *individuals themselves,* each in his own personal and sovereign right, *entered* into a compact with each other to produce a government."[613]

"[But even the social contract is possible only because of man's instinctive sociality;] *government is nothing more than a national association acting on the principles of society.*"[614]

"The social compact would dissolve, and justice be extirpated from the earth, or have only a casual existence were we callous to the touches of affection."[615]

Some convenient tree will afford them a State House, under the branches of which the whole colony may assemble to deliberate on public matters. It is more than probable that their first-laws will have the title only of regulations, and be enforced by no other penalty than public disesteem, In this first parliament every man, by natural right, will have a seat.

But as the colony increases, the public concerns will increase likewise, and the distance at which the members may be separated, will render it too inconvenient for all of them to meet on every occasion as at first, when their number was small, their habitations near, the public concerns few and trifling. This will point out the convenience of their consenting to leave the legislative part to be managed by a select number chosen from the whole body, who are supposed to have the same concerns at stake which those have who appointed them, and who will act in the same manner as the whole body would were they present. If the colony continue increasing, it will become necessary to augment the number of representatives, and that the interest of every part of the colony may be attended to, it will be found best to divide the whole into convenient parts, each part sending its proper number; and that the *elected* might never form to themselves an interest separate from the *electors,* prudence will point out the propriety of having elections often; because as the *elected* might by that means return and mix again with the general body of the *electors* in a few months, their fidelity to the public will be secured by the prudent reflection of not making a rod for themselves. And as this frequent interchange will establish a common interest with every part of the community, they will mutually and naturally support each other, and on this (not on the unmeaning name of king) depends the *strength of government and the happiness of the governed.*

Here, then, is the origin and rise of government; namely, a mode rendered necessary by the inability of moral virtue to govern the world; here, too, is the design and end of government, viz. freedom and security. And however our eyes may be dazzled with show, or our ears deceived by sound; however prejudice may warp our wills, or interest darken our understanding; the simple voice of nature and reason will say, 'tis right.[616]

Mankind being originally equals in the order of creation, the equality could only be destroyed by some subsequent circumstances; the distinctions of rich and poor may in a great measure be accounted for, and that without having recourse to the harsh, ill-sounding names of oppression and avarice. Oppression is often the *consequence,* but seldom or never the *means* of riches; and though avarice will preserve a man trom being necessitously poor, it generally makes him too timorous to become wealthy.

But there is another and greater distinction, for which no truly natural or religious reason can be assigned, and that is, the distinction of men into KINGS and SUBJECTS. Male and female are the distinctions of nature, good and bad the distinctions of heaven; but how a race of men came into the world so exalted above the rest, and distinguished like some new species, is worth inquiring into, and whether they are the means of happiness and misery to mankind.

In the early days of the world, according to the scripture chronology, there were no kings; the consequence of which was, there were no wars; it is the pride of kings which throws mankind into confusion. Holland without a king hath enjoyed more peace for this last century than any of the monarchical governments in Europe. Antiquity favors the same remark; for the quiet and rural lives of the first patriarchs hath a happy something in them, which vanishes away when we come to the history of Jewish royalty.

Government by kings was first introduced into the world by the heathens, from whom the children of Israel copied the custom.[617]

To the evil of monarchy we have added that of hereditary succession; and as the first is a degrading and lessening of ourselves, so the second, claimed as a matter of right, is an insult and imposition on posterity. For all men being originally equals, no one by birth could have a right to set up his family in perpetual preference to all others forever, and though himself might deserve *some* decent degree of honors of his con-contemporaries, yet his descendants might be far too unworthy to inherit them. . . .

This is supposing the present race of kings in the world to have had an honorable origin: whereas it is more than probable, that, could we take off the dark covering of antiquity and trace them to their first rise, we should find the first of them nothing better than the principle ruffian of some restless gang, whose savage manners or preeminence in subtility obtained him the title of chief among plunderers: and who by increasing in power, and extending his depredations, overawed the quiet and defenseless to purchase their safety by frequent contributions. . . . Perhaps the disorders which threatened, or seemed to threaten, on the decease of a leader, and the choice of a new one (for elections among ruffians could not be very orderly) induced many at first to favor hereditary pretensions; by which means it happened, as it hath happened since, that what at first was submitted to as a convenience, was afterwards claimed as a right.*[619]

Paine realized that the development of personality depended upon the social milieu in which the individual finds himself.

It appears to general observation, that revolutions create genius and talents; but those events do no more than bring them forward. There is existing in man, a mass of sense lying in a dormant state, and which, unless something excites it to action, will descend with him, in that condition, to the grave.[620]

## POLITICAL PRAGMATISTS

### Justi

In the eighteenth century the German cameralists were the most important group of political pragmatists, and the best of them was Johann Heinrich Gottlob von Justi (1720–71.)

People have always been obliged to observe appropriate rules in exploiting their estates, and rulers of republics have found themselves constrained to adopt expedient measures both for organizing the state and for thrift and order in the same. This is the essential in the economic and cameral sciences.[621]

The economic and cameral sciences are those which teach economy on a large scale with the means of the state, or which put us in possession of the measures by which the general means of a commonwealth may be preserved, increased, and reasonably applied to its ultimate purpose of happiness.[622]

. . . the economic and cameral sciences . . . give us precisely that insight which we most need for the purposes of civic and social life. The government of republics cannot endure without them, and there is no social institution or class or mode of life which could do without them entirely.[623]

Societies are not rational.

People are governed by the help of prejudices. The passions are the first sources

* "It could have been no difficult thing in the early and solitary ages of the world, while the chief employment of men was that of attending flocks, for a banditti of ruffians to overrun a country, and lay it under contributions. Their power being thus established, the chief of the band contrived to lose the name of robber, in that of monarch; and hence the origin of monarchy and kings."[618]

and the springs of all human actions. . . . The strength and weakness of a state therefore depends on the character of the prejudices with which the citizens are filled.[624]

Justi was aware of the interdependence of the parts of culture; he spoke of "the correlation of this great system and the influence which all circumstances of the entire system have on each other."[625]

. . . the internal security of a state consists in such a well ordered disposition of the same, that all parts of the body of the state are held in their appropriate connection and in the consequent rest.[626]

He had the usual theory of the evolution of society and political organization.

The constitution and properties of republics are opposed to the state of natural freedom. Before men lived in republics, they lived in a state of natural freedom. Consequently, if we want to discuss the origin of republics, we must first go back to the state of natural freedom.[627]

[1. Original state of wildness.] According to the information of the oldest secular writers, they lived in forests, cliffs, and caves.[628]

In this very first state of natural freedom, or rather first wildness, which must even still precede the state of natural freedom, the human organisms did not have the idea of forcing each other to live according to their own will.[629]

They were not subject to laws other than those that originated from their own volition, or the ones which they imposed upon themselves. If they recognised the laws of nature above themselves, they did so because these were only laws which originated from their own nature, through their immediate and narrowest consequence; for all supposed laws of the right of nature, which are derived from far-fetched propositions, and which cannot be recognized without acquiring profound knowledge, and without much science, are chimeras of scholars, of which one never thought in the state of natural freedom. If children were subjected to their parents, these were laws which followed from their natural condition, from their need and consequently by definition. If someone changed his work, he was first to do that with the special quality of his condition, or of his needs, and these were laws which he imposed upon himself. In all other cases he could not be subjected to external laws unless he was forced to do so. Men at that time were in the condition in which free princes and states now are, that is, to force continually or to be forced.[630]

Men in their first state of their natural freedom could only have had very few concepts, and they were probably not very different from cattle.[631]

[2. State of natural freedom.] The state of natural freedom did not begin until men had acquired such a degree of knowledge and concepts that their reasoning began. . . . In this first state of natural freedom all people were probably composed of hunters and fishers. . . . If men in the first state of natural freedom were hunters and fishers, everyone lived according to his own laws; however, they had few occasions to force each other, because their needs were still so slight. However, this first state produced social life, the origin of which we must deal with more thoroughly.[632]

Those who derive the origin of the social life of men from inclination and drive, which is by nature rooted in all creatures equally, make a great mistake, I feel. In the present state of affairs we are hardly able to judge correctly whether or not we have a natural drive for society. The natural drive, which so many people believe thy have, may be based upon the habit, which has been changed into nature, of associating with men, and it may rest mainly on the emptiness of their minds, as a result of which they are unable to occupy themselves with themselves, and that is why they feel the desire to pass the time away. A conclusion concerning man cannot be drawn from the social life of animals. If we would draw the proper conclusion from this, we should imagine man to have only an animal nature, and then we should recognize him as a real ferocious animal, as he still is, the most ferocious animal on the whole surface of our planet, from whose tricks and teeth only a very few creatures are safe; and who, not like other ferocious animals, robs in order to satisfy his hunger, but who strangles creatures in order to satisfy his whims, lust, vanity, and enjoyment of overabundance. However, animals do not live in societies. Their nature is opposed to social life. They will only hinder each other in robbing. At least they would disagree every time over the distribution of the loot, as the experience of all ferocious animals shows us. Every ferocious animal hunts for himself, and isolates himself from others for this purpose; and likewise men, if they were without all recognition and concepts, and only in the state of animals, would certainly behave likewise. The drive to seek a spouse, which all ferocious animals have, is not a societal drive. Many, after the act of procreation has occurred, or at least after the young are grown, do not care much about their spouse.[633]

It is much more probable that reason alone is the true cause of the social life of man. As soon as men have increased their knowledge and concepts, as soon as they have left the merely animal life and opened their eyes to the great many conveniences which they did not know before, they must also see the great advantage which they can have from the mutual assistance of other men, and this must move them to social life. . . . However, to see these advantages presupposes reason, and to distribute equally and justly the things that were gotten through common endeavor presupposes concepts of justice, which is not a fruit of a nature drive, but reason which has been budding through acquired knowledge.[634]

[3. Civil society.] It is usually stated that republics have been derived from fear of incursions. It is more probable that they grew out of the governing skill of families; that is, the patriarch must necessarily have had a certain prestige and power over his children and servants, which descended at his death to his eldest son, until in the course of time it amounted to a real rulership. We have many evidences that this was the fact, but of course they do not account for great empires, which have always been formed by force of arms.[635]

He also dealt with the evolution of subsistence.

The history as well as the nature of the matter, and the growth of human reasoning, teaches us that all peoples have gone through the stages of hunters and fishers to pastoralists, from pastoralists to agriculturalists, and finally from agriculturalists to scholars, artists, and merchants.[636]

## Sonnenfels

Joseph von Sonnenfels (1733–1817) was another cameralist of some interest. He disagreed with Justi, advocating man's sociality and the gregarious theory of society.

The isolated man is not man in a *state of nature*; his condition would be a state of constant *helplessness:* but he feels his lack, he feels that he can remedy his lack, that he is able to improve his condition: reason, which differentiates him from animals, permits him to see the means by which he can reach a better condition: their means is *socialization with his own kind*. The *state of nature* of man is therefore *society:* the *domestic,* the *conjugal,* the *paternal* society, are so many stages through which he comes nearer to the *greater* society which includes all others.[637]

The concept of an isolated man is perhaps only a literary abstraction. Man is always in society.[638]

The *isolated man* was at the mercy of every attack of unequal power: his *security* was no greater than the *force* with which he could defend against *attack*. *Two* men, whose physical force excelled his own, were already dangerous to his security. Therefore he sought to *increase* his force through *combination* with *more*. The *isolated* man felt *needs* for the sustenance of his life, which could be attained neither by his bodily force, nor his spiritual force, nor even by his time; he sought to satisfy *these* needs through this, that with his diligence he came to help the needs of *other* men, and to receive from them in return those things which he lacked. The *isolated man* lacked a thousand *comforts,* the lack of which he felt, the possession of which would make his external situation pleasanter and his *existence* happier: he sought to achieve the *comforts* through *socialization* with others. The larger the society now was, into which he placed himself, the greater was the *amount* of opposition which he could exert in every circumstance, and through that could make his security certain. The more *numerous* the society was, the more frequent its *needs,* the easier he found ways to get what he wanted from some one to whom he supplied what was lacking. The more numerous the society, the *more various* were the products of her diligence, the easier was it for him to satisfy each of his needs and *comforts*. The goal of civil society, the *security and comfort of life,* was therefore achieved through the *enlargement* of the society, and *according to its size*. This goal always remains the same at later periods: the same *means* will also remain effective.[639]

The great society is the *state*. The transition into which has given the members a new *name,* has put them in new *relationships,* the men have become citizens; beings who through the nature of their self-chosen condition, now have as *parts* their relationship to a *whole,* are united as members of a *moral body*. The effect of this unification is *unity of purpose, unity of will, unity of force*.[640]

He dealt with the problem of population size.

This *population* has its *limits,* or its so-called *maximum;* and these limits are drawn from the *nature of the states,* from the *political* and *physical* situation, and the circumstances. Genoa will not reach the populousness of France: the bare rocks of Malta will not support as many inhabitants as fertile Sicily; the sandy Mark Brandenburg not as many as Bohemia.[641]

## Priestley

Joseph Priestley (1733–1804) numbered among his other accomplishments a preoccupation with political science. He based his approach upon the psychic unity of mankind, i.e., "the principle that human nature was the same thing then that it is now."[642]

Jews are *men,* and men are beings, whose affections and actions are subject to as strict rules as those of the animate or inanimate parts of nature. Their conduct, therefore, must be accounted for on such principles as always have influenced the conduct of men, and such as we observe still to influence men.[643]

Man's sociality was also premised.

[Men are] beings who, from the commencement to the close of this mortal life, can hardly subsist but as members of some particular community, and are, moreover, capable of the most extensive social connexions.[644]

In his *Lectures on History and General Policy* (1788),[645] Priestley gave his views on social science.

That the observations I have collected . . . may be the most intelligible and useful, I shall dispose of them in the following method: considering,

I. The general uses of history.

II. The sources of history.

III. What is necessary or useful to be known previous to the study of history.

IV. Directions for the more easy acquiring and retaining a knowledge of history.

V. Proper objects of attention to an historian. And under this head I shall consider the several subjects of *general policy,* or the circumstances that chiefly contribute to render civil societies secure, numerous, and happy, as being the most important of all objects of attention to readers of history.[646]

[I.] . . . the general *uses* of history. These may be exhibited under three heads: 1. History serves to amuse the imagination and interest the passions in general. 2. It improves the understanding. And, 3, It tends to strengthen the sentiments of virtue.[647]

But the capital advantage we derive from history under this head [i.e., 2] is, that from this source only can be derived all future improvements in the science of *government.*[648]

This grand science is still in its infancy. Men of the greatest reflection and experience could not pretend to pronounce, with any degree of certainty, what, for instance, would be the consequence of any considerable change in our own constitution and government, or that of other nations. And do we not frequently see that our ablest ministers of state, who give the closest attention to the internal policy of the kingdom, are obliged to change their measures, in consequence of being disappointed in their expectations from them?[649]

So important is this science of government, that nothing can be more worthy of the study of those who have sufficient abilities, and who are friends of mankind; and the only foundation on which men who think, and who are not carried away by their own imaginations, will build any conclusions, is *historical facts.* Hypotheses built upon arguments *a priori,* are least of all tolerable. Here observation and experience are the only safe guides.[650]

Human nature, with the various interests and connexions of men in a state of society, is so complex a subject, that nothing can be safely concluded *a priori* with respect to it. Every thing that we can depend upon must be derived from *facts.*[651]

For want of acquaintance with history, we are apt to pronounce, *a priori,* many things to be impossible, which in fact really exist, and are very safe.[652]

. . . all acting is at random without regard to some theory. Indeed, it is impossible to act at all without some *view,* and that view directed by some *hypothesis,* to which the event is expected to conform. Is it not then better to form to ourselves the best hypothesis about human actions that we can collect from reading and observation, than to act absolutely at random; and is it not better and safer to follow a more perfect theory, than a more imperfect one?[653]

. . . in politics, as in every other branch of study, all just reasoning on the connexion of cause and effect is capable of being reduced to practice.[654]

It is only the observation of historical facts that can authorize us to advance any thing with certainty upon this subject.[655]

[[II.] Under this second head, *Of the Sources of History,* I propose to enumerate all, or at least the principal, methods that have been made use of for transmitting to posterity the knowledge of past events.[656]

[Of particular interest to the anthropologist are:]
[1. "Oral tradition."] It must be confessed, and it is obvious to conveive, that this method of conveying historical knowledge must have been very imperfect, and inadequate for several important uses of history.[657]

[2. Diffusion.] . . . customs . . . are easily transferred with the people that migrate, wherever they go; and . . . they are . . . useful to an historian, as they assist him in tracing the origin of colonies, which would naturally retain the customs of their mother country.*[661]

[3. Interdependence between aspects of culture.] For so extensive is the connexion of things with one another, that every thing written or done, in any period of time, is necessarily related, in a thousand ways, to many other things that were transacted at the same time; and therefore cannot help bearing some marks and traces of those related particulars.[662]

Language takes a tincture from the civil policy, the manners, customs, employment, and taste of the nation that uses it.[663]

The laws and customs of a country shew clearly what was the manner of living and the occupation of the original inhabitants of it. . . . The changes of manners and way of living may be traced in the changes of the laws.[664]

[4. Survivals.] Many things in the present state of any law are unintelligible without the knowledge of the history and progress of it.[665]

[For example, dueling] is a remarkable instance of the continuance of an *effect* after the *cause* hath ceased to operate. Nobody at this day imagines that single combat is a proper *appeal to God,* or that he who is in the right has any advantage in the combat over him that is in the wrong; yet a man thinking himself innocent and injured, and perhaps having a wife and family, will voluntarily expose his life to an equal risk with that of a man whom he despises as a nuisance to society, because he has been insulted by him.[666]

[III.] . . . if a person have further and scientific views in the study of history, he will find several branches of knowledge, and some articles of previous information, extremely useful, and in a manner necessary.[667]

[These are:]

---

* For example, *The History of the Corruptions of Christianity* is based upon the phenomenon of acculturation: "The causes of the corruptions were almost wholly contained in the established opinions of the heathen world, and especially the philosophical part of it; so that when those Heathens embraced Christianity, they mixed their former tenets and prejudices with it."[658]

" . . . my proper and ultimate object [of the book is] that every thing which I deem to be a *corruption of Christianity* has been a departure from the original scheme, or an innovation. It will also be seen, that I have generally been able to trace every such corruption to its proper source, and to shew what circumstances in the state of things, and especially of other prevailing opinions and prejudices, made the alteration, in doctrine or practice, sufficiently natural, and the introduction and establishment of it easy. And if I have succeeded in this investigation, this *historical method* will be found to be one of the most satisfactory modes of argumentation, in order to prove that what I object to is really a corruption of genuine Christianity, and no part of the original scheme."[659]

" . . . the corruption of Christianity, in every article of faith or practice, was the natural consequence of the circumstances in which it was promulgated."[660]

[1.] . . . the knowledge of *human nature*. . . .

[2.] *Philosophical knowledge*. . . .

[3.] *Astronomy*. . . .

[4 & 5.] But those sciences which are of the most constant and general use to an historian, so as to have deserved to be called the *two eyes of history*, are *geography* and chronology.[668]

[6.] . . . how to make a just estimate of the riches and power of ancient and remote nations, and to compare them with those of our own age and nation, by means of the expressions which historians have used to denote the riches and power of states, and particularly by the sums of money which are occasionally mentioned in their writings.[669]

[IV. This section consists of critical remarks on historians, compendia, tables, etc.[670]]

[V. Government[671] and law[672] are essential to a nation. He then considers the conditions which make a nation rich, happy, populous, and secure.[673]]

Priestley believed in the evolution of culture and gave a picture of primitive man on the basis of

the most credible accounts we have of the state of mankind in the earliest ages, in almost all parts of the world; when they lived in caves, or huts made of the branches of trees and earth, when they had no clothing but leaves, or the raw hides of animals, and no food but the fruit and roots which the earth produced of itself; or sometimes the flesh of animals which they might happen to surprise, eaten raw, or with very little preparation.[674]

He gave a brief exposition of his theory of the evolution of language.

It is natural to suppose that the first words which mankind, in the most early stages of the world, would invent and apply, would be names for sensible objects; as of animals, vegetables, the parts of the human body, the sun, moon, &c.[675]

. . . gestures being equally significant with words, we often have recourse to them to express a passion, or a simple intention, with more force.[676]

Amazing as is the power and advantage of *speech* for the communication of ideas, it is, in several respects, infinitely inferior to the art of *writing;* since by the one the power of communication is confined both in point of view of time and place, and in the other it is absolutely unconfined with respect to both. By words we can converse only with those are present with us, but by means of writing we become acquainted with who the sentiments and transactions of men in all ages and all nations of the world. It connects, as it were, the living, the dead, and the unborn; for, by writing, the present age can not only receive information from the greatest and wisest of mankind before them, but are themselves able to convey wisdom and instruction to the latest posterity.[677]

## Volney

Constantin François Chasseboef, Conte de Volney (1757–1820) was a humanitarian interested in social science for reform purposes.

The *third* kind of utility which History affords. . . . consists in collecting and meditating on all the facts which relate to the formation of societies and the mechanism of governments, with the view of obtaining general or particular results, calculated to serve as terms of comparison in analogous or similar cases. In this light, History, considered universally, is a vast collection of moral and social experiments which mankind make involuntarily and very expressively on themselves, and in which every people, by exhibiting varied combination of events, passions, causes and effects, unfolds to the attentive observer all the springs and mechanisms of human nature.[678]

. . . man vainly ascribes his misfortunes to obscure and imaginary agents; in vain he seeks as the source of his evils mysterious and remote causes. In the general order of the universe his condition is, doubtless, subject to inconveniences, and his existence governed by superior powers; but those powers are neither the decrees of a blind fatality, nor the caprices of whimsical and fantastic beings. Like the world of which he forms a part, man is governed by natural laws, regular in their course, uniform in their effects, immutable in their essence; and those laws,—the common source of good and evil,— are not written among the distant stars, nor hidden in codes of mystery; inherent in the nature of terrestrial beings, interwoven with their existence, at all times and in all places, they are present to man: they act upon his senses, they warn his understanding, and give to every action its reward or punishment. Let man then know these laws! let him comprehend the nature of the elements which surround him, and also his own nature, and he will know the regulators of his destiny; he will know the causes of his evils and the remedies he should apply.[679]

Self-love is the basis of man's nature.

. . . self-love, the desire of happiness, aversion to pain, become the essential and primary laws imposed on man by nature herself—the laws which the directing power, whatever it be, has established for his government—and which laws, like those of motion in the physical world, are the simple and fruitful principle of whatever happens in the moral world.[680]

*Q.* Explain the principles of the law of nature with relation to man.

*A.* They are simple; all of them are comprised in one fundamental and single precept.

*Q.* What is that precept?

*A.* It is self-preservation. . . .

*Q.* How does nature order man to preserve himself?

*A.* By two powerful and involuntary sensations, which it has attached, as two guides, two guardian Geniuses to all his actions: the one a sensation of pain, by which it admonishes him of, and deters him from everything that tends to destroy him; the other, a sensation of pleasure, by which it attracts and carries him towards everything that tends to his preservation and the development of his existence.[681]

However, man is also a social animal.

*Q.* But can man individually acquire this knowledge necessary to his existence, and to the development of his faculties?

*A.* No; not without the assistance of his fellow men, and by living in society.

*Q.* But is not society to man a state against nature?

*A.* No: it is on the contrary a necessity, a law that nature imposed on him by the very act of his organization; for, first, nature has so constituted man, that he cannot see his species of another sex without feeling emotions and an attraction, which induce him to live in a family, which is already a state of society; secondly, by endowing him with sensibility, she organized him so that the sensations of others reflect within him, and excite reciprocal sentiments of pleasure and of grief, which are attractions, and indissoluble ties of society; thirdly, and finally, the state of society, founded on the wants of man, is only a further means of fulfilling the law of preservation: and to pretend that this state is out of nature, because it is more perfect, is the same as to say, that a bitter and wild fruit of the forest, is no longer the production of nature, when rendered sweet and delicious by cultivation in our gardens. . . .

*Q.* What is man in the savage state?

*A.* A brutal, ignorant animal, a wicked and ferocious beast.

*Q.* Is he happy in that state?

*A.* No; for he only feels momentary sensations, which are habitually of violent wants which he cannot satisfy, since he is ignorant by nature, and weak by being isolated from his race.

*Q.* Is he free?

*A.* No; he is the most abject slave that exists; for his life depends on everything that surrounds him: he is not free to eat when hungry, or rest when tired, to warm himself when cold; he is every instant in danger of perishing; wherefore nature offers but fortuitous examples of such beings; and we see that all the efforts of the human species, since its origin, sorely tends to emerge from that violent state by the pressing necessity of self-preservation.

*Q.* But does not this necessity of preservation engender in individuals egotism, that is to say self-love? and is not egotism contrary to the social state?

*A.* No; for if by egotism you mean a propensity to hurt our neighbor, it is no longer self-love, but the hatred of others. Self-love, taken in its true sense, not only is not contrary to society, but is its firmest support, by the necessity we lie under of not injuring others, lest in return they should injure us.

Thus man's preservation, and the unfolding of his faculties, directed towards this end, teach the true law of nature in the production of the human being; and it is from this essential principle that are derived, are referred, and in its scale are weighed, all ideas of good and evil, of vice and virtue, of just and injust, of truth or error, of lawful or forbidden, on which is founded the morality of individual, or of social man.[682]

*Q.* What is society?

*A.* It is every reunion of men living together under the clauses of an expressed or tacit contract, which has for its end their common preservation.[683]

He was aware of the constraint of culture.

[In religion] you confessed yourselves . . . to be only the echoes of your fathers.[684]

Imposed by authority, inculcated by education, and maintained by example, they pass from age to age, and strengthen their empire from habit and inattention.[685]

. . . to religious quarrels there is no end, since the prejudices of infancy and education almost unavoidably exclude impartial reasoning.[686]

Man is a product of the social conditions in which he is reared.

We may kill men; but we cannot kill things, nor the circumstances which produce them.[687]

Like modern psychiatrists, Volney emphasized the importance of childhood in personality.

. . . the early habits and impressions of childhood, the force of which is such, that, *after much consideration,* I am now *clearly of the opinion,* that the moral system of man has assumed, at the age of five years, a shape and tendency which it will retain through life. New or late events may unfold it, but the character contains nothing new; all proceeds from the seed sown in childhood.[688]

*Les ruines* is an attempt to answer this question:

. . . *by what secret causes do empires rise and fall; from what sources spring the prosperity and misfortunes of nations; on what principles can the peace of society, and the happiness of man be established?*[689]

He used the usual description of the evolution of culture[690] to prove the following thesis:

The cupidity of man and his ignorance,—these are the evil genii which have wasted the earth! These are the decrees of fate which have overthrown empires![691]

Thus agitated by their own passions, men, whether collectively or individually taken, always greedy and improvident, passing from slavery to tyranny, from pride to baseness, from presumption to despondency, have made themselves the perpetual instruments of their own misfortunes.

These, then, are the principles, simple and natural, which regulated the destiny of ancient states. By this regular and connected series of causes and effects, they rose or fell, in proportion as the physical laws of the human heart were respected or violated; and in the course of their successive changes, a hundred different nations, a hundred different empires, by turns humbled, elevated, conquered, overthrown, have repeated for the earth their instructive lessons.[692]

He was an enthusiastic believer in social progress.

Are men still in their forests, destitute of everything, ignorant, stupid and ferocious? Are all the nations still in that age when nothing was seen upon the globe but brutal robbers and brutal slaves? If at any time, in any place, individuals have ameliorated, why shall not the whole mass ameliorate? If partial societies have made improvements, what shall hinder the improvement of society in general? And if the first obstacles are overcome, why should the others be insurmountable?[693]

This amelioration is a necessary effect of the laws of nature; for, by the law of sensibility, man as invincibly tends to render himself happy as the flame to mount, the stone to descend, or the water to find its level.[694]

Volney was interested in cultural evolution; his theory of the evolution of religion has already been mentioned; and he was opposed to the biblical account of the origin and development of man and his culture.[695] He based his methodology on unilinear evolution.

. . . the more we study the manners of savage nations, the greater light is thrown upon the nature of man, and the history and origin of society, and especially on the situation of the nations of antiquity. I have often been struck with the analogy subsisting between the Indians of North America, and the nations so much extolled of ancient Greece and Italy.[696]

He also wrestled with the problem of independent invention versus diffusion.

[After pointing out some similarities between the theologies of the Old and the New World, he continues:] I mean not to insinuate that the Indians have borrowed their doctrines from Scythia or Greece. Shamanism, or the system of Buddtha, may possibly have spread itself throughout the old world, where it is found even at the extremities of Spain, Scotland, and Denmark; but it is quite as possible that it is a native product of the human mind, since it every where bears an intimate relation to the habits and condition of the people who profess it.[697]

Finally, he developed a sort of statistical "Notes and Queries," according to the following topics:

I.   Physical state of the country

1.  Geographic situation
2.  Climate
3.  State of the soil
4.  Natural products
II.  Political state
1.  Population
2.  Agriculture
3.  Industry
4.  Commerce
5.  Government and administration[698]

# POPULATION

Scattered statements on population have been given throughout this work, but in the eighteenth century a group of students made a concentrated attack upon the problem of population growth as a natural phenomenon.

### Cantillon

Richard Cantillon (d. 1734) has a section on population in his *Essai sur la nature du commerce en general* (1755),[699] the gist of which is:

Experience shews that Trees, Plants, and other Vegetables can be increased to any Quantity which the Extent of Ground laid out for them can support.

The same Experience shews that all kinds of Animal Creation are to be multiplied to any Quantity which the Land allotted to them can support. . . . People . . . are necessarily proportioned to their Means of Living and do not exceed the number the Country can support according to their standard of life.[700]

### Chalmers

George Chalmers (1742–1825) wrote:

The Lord Chief Justice Hale formerly, and Sir James Stuart, and the Count de Buffon, lately considered men, as urged, like other animals, by natural instincts; as directed, like them, by the same motives of propagation; and as subsisted afterwards, or destroyed, by similar means.

It is instinct, then, which, according to those illustrious authors, is the cause of procreation; but it is food, that keeps population full, and accumulates numbers. The force of the first principle, we behold in the multitudes, whether of the fish of the sea, the fowls of the air, or the beasts of the field, which are yearly produced: we perceive, however, the essential consequence of the last, from the vast numbers, that annually perish for want.

Experience indeed evinces, to what an immense extent domestic animals may be multiplied, by providing abundance of food. In the same manner, mankind have been found to exist, and increase, in every condition, and in every age, according to the standard of their subsistence, and to the measure of their comforts.[701]

### Franklin

Benjamin Franklin (1706–90) showed that the rate of population growth depends upon the type of community.

1. Tables of the proportion of marriages to births, of deaths to births, of marriages to the number of inhabitants, &c., formed on observations made upon the bills of mortality, christenings, &c. of populous cities, will not suit countries; nor will tables formed on observations made on full-settled old countries as Europe, suit new countries as America.

2. For people increase in proportion to the number of marriages, and that is greater in proportion to the ease and convenience of supporting a family. When families can be easily supported, more persons marry, and earlier in life.

3. In cities, where all trades, occupations, and offices are full, many delay marrying till they can see how to bear the charges of a family; which charges are greater in cities, as luxury is more common; may live single during life and continue servants to families, journeymen to trades, &c.; hence cities do not, by natural generation, supply themselves with inhabitants; the deaths are more than the births.

4. In countries full settled the case must be nearly the same; all lands being occupied and improved to the height, those who cannot get land must labor for others that have it; when laborers are plenty their wages will be low; by low wages a family is supported with difficulty; this difficulty deters many from marriage, who therefore long continue servants and single. Only as the cities take supplies of people from the country, and thereby make a little more room in the country, marriage is a little more encouraged there, and the births exceed the deaths.

5. Europe is generally full settled with husbandmen, manufacturers, &c., and therefore cannot know increase in people. . . .

6. Land being . . . plenty in America, and so cheap that a laboring man that understands husbandry can in a short time save money enough to purchase a piece of new land sufficient for a plantation, whereon he may subsist a family, such are not afraid to marry. . . .

7. Hence, marriages in America are more general, and more generally early than in Europe.[702]

. . . till it [i.e., North America] is fully settled, labor will never be cheap here, where no man continues long a laborer for others, but gets a plantation of his own; no man continues long a journeyman to a trade, but goes among those new settlers and sets up for himself, &c.[703]

There is, in short, no bound to the prolific nature of plants or animals, but what is made by their crowding and interfering with each other's means of subsistence.[704]

## Wallace

Robert Wallace (1697–1771) made one of the most influential studies of population in the eighteenth century.

. . . through various causes, there has never been such a number of inhabitants on the earth at any one point of time, as might have been easily raised by the prolific virtue of mankind.

The causes of this paucity of inhabitants, and of this irregularity of increase, are manifold. Some of them may be called physical, as they depend entirely on the course of nature, and are independent of mankind. Others are moral, and depend on the affections, the passions, and the institutions of men. Among the physical causes, some are more constant: such as the temperature of the air; the extreme heat or cold of some climates; the barrenness of some regions of the earth; and the unfavourableness of the climate or natural product of some soils to generations. Other causes of this kind are more variable: such as, the inclemency of particular seasons; plagues; famines; earthquakes; and inundations of the sea; which sweep off great numbers of men, as well as of other animals, and prevent the quicker replenishing of the earth.

That these natural causes have had a baneful influence, cannot be doubted. Yet it is probable, that this might be prevented in some degree, perhaps in even a great measure, by the skill and the industry of men, and by wholesome laws and institutions; at least, that all these natural causes taken together, excepting perhaps the incurable barrenness or unwholesomeness of some particular regions, have not so bad an effect as those which have moral causes, which arise from the passions and the vices of men, and which have a more constant and more powerful influence on the world.

To this last article we may refer the many destructive wars which men have waged against one another; great poverty; corrupt institutions either of a civil or of a religious kind; intemperance; debauchery; irregular amours; idleness; luxury; and whatever either prevents marriage, or weakens the generating faculties of men, or renders them either negligent or incapable of educating their children, and of cultivating the earth to advantage. It is chiefly to such destructive causes we must ascribe the small number of men.[705]

A rude and barbarous people, living by hunting, by fishing, or by pasturage, or on the spontaneous product of the earth, without agriculture, can never be so numerous as a people inhabiting the same tract of land, who are well skilled in agriculture, as uncultivated can never maintain so many inhabitants as cultivated lands. In every country, there shall always be found a greater number of inhabitants, *caeteris paribus,* in proportion to the plenty of provisions it affords, as plenty will always encourage the generality of the people to marry.

Hence it is evident, that the world could not be best peopled in rude and ignorant ages, while men lived chiefly on the spontaneous fruits of the earth, and were not instructed in agriculture; and that in whatever age we find a country grossly ignorant of agriculture, we may be assured that country must have been but thinly inhabited.[706]

He took into consideration the influence of the standard of living upon marriage and the birth rate.

Food and clothes, houses, and a little furniture, are necessary for all. And, if a nation be laborious and industrious, these necessaries will be in such abundance, that almost every one will have them at an easy rate. Hence, while a people preserve their simple taste, and continue to be industrious, they will multiply prodigiously. But when this simplicity of taste is lost, which must always happen in proportion as operose manufactures increase; though they continue to be industrious, yet more of the people will apply themselves to the less necessary manufactures, and fewer to provide what is more substantial; and as the proportion of those who apply to elegant manufactures increases, and fewer hands are employed in providing foods, necessaries will become more scarce; toys will abound, and trifles will become more necessary for the bulk of the people. This will still keep them dear, though they be in plenty. Hence living even in the most simple manner will become more expensive; consequently, mankind be less able to support families, and be less encouraged to marry.[707]

## Malthus

Thomas Robert Malthus (1766–1834) gave the classic exposition of the principles of population growth.

[First, he notices] the constant tendency in all animated life to increase beyond the nourishment prepared for it.[708]

The germs of existence contained in this earth, if they could freely develop themselves, would fill millions of worlds in the course of a few thousand years. Necessity, that imperious, all-pervading law of nature, restrains them within the prescribed bounds. The race of plants and the race of animals shrink under this great restrictive law; and man cannot by any efforts of reason escape from it.[709]

But as, by that law of our nature which makes food necessary to the life of man, population can never actually increase beyond the lowest nourishment capable of supporting it, a strong check on population, from the difficulty of acquiring food, must be constantly in operation.[710]

Agriculture is not only, as Hume states, that species of industry, which is chiefly requisite to the subsistence of multitudes, but it is in fact the *sole* species by which multitudes can exist; and all the numerous arts and manufactures of the modern world, by which such numbers appear to be supported, have no tendency whatever to increase population, except so far as they tend to increase the quantity and to facilitate the distribution of the products of agriculture.[711]

It may safely be pronounced . . . that population, when unchecked, goes on doubling itself every twenty-five years, or increases in a geometrical ratio. . . .

It may be fairly pronounced . . . that, considering the present average state of the earth, the means of subsistence, under circumstances the most favourable to human industry, could not possibly be made to increase faster than in an arithmetical ratio.[712]

. . . the following propositions are intended to be proved:—

1. Population is necessarily limited by the means of subsistence.

2. Population invariably increases where the means of subsistence increase, unless prevented by some very powerful and obvious checks.

3. These checks, and the checks which repress the superior power of population, and keep its effects on a level with the means of subsistence, are all resolvable into moral restraint, vice and misery.[713]

The ultimate check to population appears then to be a want of food, arising necessarily from the different ratios according to which population and food increases. But this ultimate check is never the immediate check, except in cases of actual famine.

The immediate check may be stated to consist in all those customs, and all those diseases, which seem to be generated by a scarcity of the means of subsistence; and all those causes, independent of this scarcity, whether of a moral or physical nature, which tend prematurely to weaken and destroy the human frame.

These checks to population, which are constantly operating with more or less force in every society, and keep down the number to the level of the means of subsistence, may be classed under two general heads—the preventive, and the positive checks.

The preventive check, as far as it is voluntary, is peculiar to man, and arises from that distinctive superiority in his reasoning faculties, which enables him to calculate distant consequences. The checks to the indefinite increase of plants and irrational animals are all either positive, or, if preventive, involuntary. . . .

The positive checks to population are extremely various, and include every cause, whether arising from vice or misery, which in any degree contributes to shorten the natural duration of human life. Under this head, therefore, may be enumerated all unwholesome occupations, severe labour and exposure to the seasons, extreme poverty, bad nursing of children, great towns, excesses of all kinds, and the whole train of common diseases and epidemics, wars, plague, and famine.[714]

... in Modern Europe the positive checks to population prevail less, and the preventive checks more than in past times and in the more uncivilized parts of the world.[715]

He stressed the fact that man is subject to natural law.

In New Jersey the proportion of births to deaths, on an average of 7 years, ending with 1743, was 300 to 100. In France and England the average proportion cannot be reckoned at more than 120 to 100. Great and astonishing as this difference is, we ought not to be so wonder-struck at it, as to attribute it to the miraculous interposition of Heaven. The causes of it are not remote, latent and mysterious, but near us, round about us, and open to the investigation of every inquiring mind. It accords with the most liberal spirit of philosophy to believe that no stone can fall, or plant rise, without the immediate agency of divine power. But we know from experience, that these operations of what we call nature have been conducted almost invariably according to fixed laws. And since the world began, the causes of population and depopulation have been probably as constant as any of the laws of nature with which we are acquainted.

The passion between the sexes has appeared in every age to be so nearly the same, that it may always be considered, in algebraic language, as a given quantity. The great law of necessity, which prevents population from increasing in any country beyond the food which it can either produce or acquire, is a law so open to our view, so obvious and evident to our understandings, that we cannot for a moment doubt it. The different modes which nature takes to repress a redundant population, do not indeed appear to us so certain and regular; but though we cannot always predict the mode, we may with certainty predict the fact. If the propotion of the births to the deaths for a few years indicates and increase of numbers much beyond the proportional increased or acquired food of the country, we may be perfectly certain that, unless an emigration take place, the deaths will shortly exceed the births, and that the increase which had been observed for a few years cannot be the real average increase of the population of the country. If there were no other depopulating causes, and if the preventive check did not operate very strongly, every country would without doubt be subject to periodical plagues and famines.[716]

In regard to social progress, he spoke of "the probable improvement of society."[717]

## THEOLOGICAL STATISTICIANS

The statistical regularity discovered by Graunt in the preceding century was in the eighteenth century used by theologians as arguments for the existence of a god.

### Derham

William Derham (1657–1735) seems to have been the first to give a statistical proof of the existence of a god.

It appears from our best account of these matters, that in our *European* parts, and I believe the same is throughout the world; that, I say, there is a certain rate and proportion in the propagation of mankind: such a number marry, so many are born, such a number die; in proportion to the number of persons in every nation, country, or parish. And as to births, two things are very considerable: one is the proportion of males and females, not in a wide proportion, not an uncertain, accidental number at all adventures; but nearly equal. Another thing is, that a few more are born than appear to die, in any certain place; which is an admirable provision for the extraordinary emergencies and occasions of the world; to supply unhealthful places, where death out-runs life; to make up the ravages of great plagues and diseases, and the depredations of war and the seas; and to afford a sufficient number for colonies in the unpeopled parts of the earth. . . .

And now upon the whole matter, What is all this but admirable and plain management? What can the maintaining, throughout all ages and places, these proportions of mankind, and all other creatures; this harmony in the generations of men be, but the work of One that ruleth the world?[718]

## Süssmilch

Derham was followed by Johann Peter Süssmilch (1707–67).

That a constant, general, great, perfect, and beautiful order reigns in birth, increase, and spread; in life, death, and in the causes of deaths; this is the thing which will be shown in this work.[719]

# VI

# EIGHTEENTH-CENTURY SOCIAL ANTHROPOLOGY: DEGRADATION VERSUS PROGRESS

## DEGRADATION VERSUS PROGRESS

I N THE EIGHTEENTH century the theory of social progress triumphed over that of social degradation. However, a few men still advocated the latter doctrine.

### Swift

Jonathan Swift (1667–1745) supported his patron Temple, and spoke of "our degenerate days."[1]

### Doig

David Doig (1719–1800) was one of Kames' orthodox opponents.

. . . if mankind were *originally savages,* the *Mosaic history* must unquestionably be false; and therefore the author was flattered with the hope, that his letters, of which the tendency is to overturn that hypothesis, might be of some use to the cause of revelation.[2]

[He believed] mankind . . . to have been originally civilized.[3]

. . . there did exist, time immemorial, somewhere in the eastern parts of the world, a society of people who were never in the savage state.[4]

. . . all the learning, religion, laws, arts, and sciences, and other improvements that have enlightened Europe, a great part of Asia, and the northern coast of Africa, were so many rays diverging from two points, on the banks of the Euphrates and the Nile. In proportion as nations receded from these two sources of humanity and civilization, in the same proportion were they more immersed in ignorance and barbarism.[5]

An interesting use of the age-area hypothesis!

He argued against cultural evolution by denying the principle of social progress.

. . . the tendency towards progressive improvement, implanted in the human soul, is not altogether so vigorous as modern philosophers generally represent it.*[7]

In fact, he countered this with the principle of degeneration.

There seems to be in human nature, an innate propensity towards degeneracy, even in

---

* "None of the nations which were savages or barbarians, at the period of their first appearance in history, have ever been known to move one step forward towards a civilized state, 'till impelled by some external circumstance; a phoenomenon which does not seem to favour the progressive motion of the human species towards a state of civilization."[6]

a state of the highest improvement.[8]

He explained the existence of simpler societies by means of this latter principle.

. . . man once civilized, in a certain degree, may relapse into the savage, or, at least, into the barbarous state.[9]

In another work he gave one of the common theories on the origin of theology and mythology.[10]

### Farquhar

On the other side of the question was George Farquhar (1677?–1707).

I must beg you, Sir, to lay aside your Superstitious Veneration for Antiquity, and the usual Expressions on that Score; that the present Age is illiterate, or their taste is vitiated; that we live in the decay of Time, and the Dotage of the World is fall'n to our Share— 'Tis a mistake, Sir, the World was never more active or youthful.[11]

### Dennis

John Dennis (1657–1734) wrote:

'Tis ridiculous and pedantick to imagine, that the natural Powers of the Soul were stronger or more excellent in the Ancients than they are in the Moderns. And as to Experience we have vastly the Advantage of them. When we consider Experience, as my Lord *Bacon* observes, we are properly the Ancients, who live in the elder Ages of the World, and have the Advantage of the Knowledge of Three thousand Years over the first Writers. Not but that at the same time that I assert the Equality of Faculties in the Moderns, and the Advantage of their Experience, I freely acknowledge the actual Preheminence that several of the Ancients have over the Moderns; but I have sufficiently shewn in the *Advancement of Modern Poetry*,[12] that that actual Preheminence proceeded from accidental [cultural] Causes, and not from any Superiority of Faculties in those ancient Authors.[13]

### Turgot

Anne Robert Jacques Turgot (1727–81) was the great eighteenth century exponent of the theory of social progress.

The phenomena of nature, subject as they are to unvarying laws, are enclosed within a circle whose revolutions are ever the same; everything is born and born again, everything perishes; and in the successive generations that reproduce the vegetal and the animal forms, times does but restore at every moment the image of what it has already made to disappear.

The succession of men, on the contrary, offers from century to century, an ever varied spectacle. Reason, passions, liberty, give rise unceasingly to new events: All the ages of mankind are enchained, one with another, by a sequence of causes and effects that binds the present to the whole preceding past. The arbitrary signs of speech and writing, by giving men the means wherewith to make sure of the possession of their ideas and to communicate them to others, have formed from individual stores of knowledge a common treasure, that one generation transmits to another, like unto a heritage continually augmented by the discoveries of each century; and the human race, considered from its origin, appears to the eyes of a philosopher to be an immense whole, having like every individual its own childhood and its own stages of growth.*

* "[In this he anticipated Comte's law of three stages.] Men, when they began to reason in regard to the phenomena which were offered to their observation, sought the cause of these phenomena before they

Societies are established and nations formed. They become dominant one after another and yield to other nations. Empires rise and fall. Laws and forms of government succeed one another. Arts, and sciences are discovered and perfected one after another; and one after another, as they are hastened or delayed in their progress, they pass from climate to climate. Interest, ambition, and vainglory at every instant change the face of the world and inundate the earth with blood. In the midst of their ravages, manners grow refined, the mind of man becomes enlightened, nations leave their isolation to draw nearer one another; commerce and politics unite at last all the parts of the globe; and the total mass of human kind, through alternations of calm and agitation, of evil days and good, ever advances, though with dragging pace, towards a higher degree of perfection.*

We cannot, within the limits here prescribed for us, display before your eyes a picture so vast: we shall try only to point out the thread that runs through the advances of the human mind; and some reflections on the birth of sciences and arts, their accretions, their fluctuating fortunes, drawn from the sequence of historical facts, will form the simple plan of this discourse.

The Sacred Books after having enlightened us as to the creation of the Universe, the origin of men, and the birth of the first arts, show us soon thereafter the human race concentrated anew in a single family by a universal flood. Scarcely had it begun to make good its losses than the miraculous confusion of tongues forced men to disperse. The necessity of busying themselves with pressing demands for food in sterile deserts that put only wild beasts at their disposal obliged them to wander away from one another in every direction and hastened their diffusion throughout the Universe. Soon the first traditions were forgotten; the nations, separated by vast spaces and still more by the diversity of languages, unknown one to another, were almost all plunged into the same barbarism in which we still see the Americans.

But the resources of nature and the prolific seeds of science are found wherever there are men. The loftiest heights of knowledge are and can be nothing but developments of combinations of the first ideas given us by the senses, just as the edifice whose height most astonishes our eyes rests of necessity upon the same earth we press beneath our feet. And the same senses, the same organs, the spectacle of the same Universe have everywhere

had any real knowledge of the phenomena themselves; and, as the true causes could only be discovered with the lapse of time, they imagined false causes for them."[14]

"[1. 'Theological stage.'] Before the relation between physical facts was known, there was nothing more natural than to suppose that they were produced by intelligent beings, invisible and like ourselves; for what else would they have resembled? Everything that happened without man's having had a part in it had its god, to the worship of whom fear or hope soon gave rise; and this worship was later developed in the light of the regard paid to powerful men; for gods were only men more powerful or less perfect; according as they were the work of an age more or less enlightened as to the true perfections of mankind.

"[2. 'Metaphysical stage.'] When philosophers had recognized the absurdity of these fables, without having, however, acquired true light upon natural history, they imagined they could explain the causes of phenomena by means of abstract expressions, such as *essences* or *faculties,* expressions which yet explained nothing, and in regard to which men reasoned as if they had been *beings,* new divinities substituted for the old. These analogies were followed out, and faculties were multiplied to account for each effect.

"[3. 'Positive stage.'] It was only later, when the mechanical action of bodies upon one another was observed, that from this mechanical relation were drawn other hypotheses that mathematicians could develop and experience verify. That is why physics ceased to degenerate into a bad metaphysics only after a long progress in the arts and in chemistry had multiplied combinations of bodies after more intimate communication between societies had made geographical knowledge more extensive, after facts had become more certain, and the very practice of the arts had been put under the eyes of philosophers. Printing, literary and scientific journals, and the memoirs of academies have augmented certitude to the point that only the details are today in doubt."[15]

* "Different series of events take place in the different countries of the world, and all, as by as many separate routes, at last concur in the same purpose, the upbuilding of the ruins of the human mind."[16]

given men the same ideas, just as the same needs and the same propensities have every-where taught them the same arts.

At long intervals a feeble light begins to pierce the night overspreading the nations and becomes more and more diffused. The inhabitants of Chaldea, nearer the source of the first traditions, the Egyptians, the Chinese, appear to outstrip the remaining peoples. Others follow them afar; one step in advance leads to another; the inequality of nations grows greater; the arts are just coming to birth; there, they advance with great strides towards perfection; further off, they halt in mediocrity; elsewhere, the primeval darkness is not yet dissipated; and, in its infinitely varied inequalities, the present state of the Universe, presenting to our eyes at a single moment all the delicate shadings of barbarism and culture existent throughout the earth, shows us, so to speak, at a single glance the monuments, the vestiges of every advance of the mind of man, the image of all the states through which he has passed, and the history of all the ages.

Is not nature then everywhere the same? And if she guides all men to the same truths, if their very errors are alike, why do they not all advance with equal step on the road traced out for them? No doubt the mind of man everywhere contains within itself the seeds of the same achievements; but nature, not impartial in the bestowal of her gifts, has given to certain minds a fulness of talent that she has refused to others; circumstances develop these talents or leave them buried in obscurity; and from the infinite variety of such cir-cumstances springs the inequality that marks the progress of nations.

Barbarism makes all men equal; and in the earliest times, all those who are born with genius find almost the same obstacles and the same resources. Time passes, and societies are formed and grow\*: The hates of nations, and ambition—or rather avarice, the sole ambition of barbaric peoples—multiply wars and devastation. Conquests and revolutions commingle in a thousand ways, peoples, tongues, and manners. Mountain chains, great rivers, and seas, by putting limits to the movement of peoples and so to their intermingling, brought about the formation of languages of a more general nature, each of which became a bond for several nations. In this way these natural features parcelled out, as one might say, all the tongues of the Universe into a certain number of groups. The tillage of fields made habitations more permanent. It nourished more men than it kept busy, and thenceforth imposed on those it left unoccupied the necessity of becoming useful or redoubtable to those who worked the soil. Hence cities, commerce, the arts of use and those of elegance, diversity of occupations, differences of education, greater inequality of conditions; hence, the leisure that allows genius, freed from the burden of elemental needs, to leave the narrow sphere in which they hold it and direct all its forces to the culture of the arts; hence, the stricter carriage and more rapid pace of the human mind, drawing with it all parts of society, and receiving from their perfection a livelier activity. Passions and genius developed together; ambition gained strength; politics opened to it ever wider vistas; victories once gained had more lasting consequences than before and gave rise to empires whose laws, manners, and government, diversely modifying the genius of men, become a kind of general education for the nations, establishing between people and people the same difference that education sets between man and man.

Re-united, rent asunder, each erected on the ruins of another, the empires came in rapid succession. The rounds of change through which they passed brought into being one by one all possible political conditions, united and disjoined all the elements of polit-ical bodies. There was, as one might say, an ebb and flow of power from one nation to another, and in the same nation from the princes to the multitude and from the multitude to the princes. Amidst these fluctuations, everything tends gradually towards equilibrium,

* "The recurrence of needs that are ever forcing men back into society and bending them to its laws."[17]

and assumes at length a calmer and more stable position. Ambition, by creating great States from the crumbled remains of a host of little ones, itself puts limits to its own ravages. War now brings desolation but to the frontiers of empires; city and country begin to breathe in the midst of peace; the bonds of society hold in unity a greater number of men; the spread of enlightenment becomes more rapid and more widely extended; and arts, sciences, and manners progress at a more rapid pace. As the tempests that have convulsed the deeps of the sea, so the evils that are inseparable from social upheavels disappear; the good remains, and humanity moves onward to perfection. In the midst of this varied combination of events, sometimes favorable, sometimes adverse, whose conflicting influences must at last be self-destructive, there is an unceasing action of the genius which nature, though bestowing it on certain individuals, has yet spread throughout the mass at almost equal intervals; and its effects become sensible with time.

Its progress, slow at first, unnoticed, buried in the general oblivion into which time precipitates all human things, rises with them from darkness by the invention of *writing*. Precious invention! which seemed to give the peoples that first possessed it wings to outstrip the other nations! Inestimable invention! which snatches from the power of death the memory of great men and examples of valor and integrity, unites times and places, fixes the fugitive thought, and assures it lasting existence, whereby the products, the opinions, the experiences, the discoveries accumulated through all the ages serve as groundwork and as stairs on which posterity may rise ever higher![18]

Turgot's *Réflexions sur la formation et le distribution des richesse* (1769–70)[19] contains an extensive exposition of the evolution of economy, part of which follows.

The first Cultivator has taken the seed he has sown from plants which the earth had of itself produced; while waiting for the harvest he has lived by hunting and fishing, and upon wild fruits: his tools have been branches of trees, torn down in the forests, shaped with stones sharpened against other stones; he has himself captured in the chase animals wandering in the woods or caught them in his traps; he has brought them into subjection and trained them; he has made use of them first for food and afterwards to help him in his labour.[20]

In a time when there was still a large quantity of uncultivated lands which belonged to no one, one might possess cattle without being a Proprietor of lands. It is even probable that mankind has almost everywhere begun to collect flocks and live on their produce before it gave itself up to the more toilsome labour of agriculture. It would seem that the Nations which cultivated the earth in the most ancient times are those which have found in their Country kinds of animals more susceptible of being tamed, and that have been led in this way from the wandering and restless life of the Peoples who live by the chase and fishing to the more tranquil life of Pastoral Peoples. Pastoral life necessitates dwelling for a longer time in the same place; it affords more leisure; more opportunities to study the difference of soils, to observe the march of nature in the production of those plants which serve for the support of cattle. Perhaps it is for this reason that the Asiatic Nations have been the first to cultivate the earth, and that the Peoples of America have remained so long in the state of Savages.[21]

. . . the lands have been cultivated before they have been divided; that very cultivation having been the sole motive for division and for the law which assures to each his property. Now the first who have cultivated have probably cultivated as much ground as their forces permitted, and consequently more than was necessary for their support.

Even if this state could have existed, it could not possbily have been durable; each man, as he got from his field nothing but his subsistence, and had nothing wherewith to pay the labour of the others, could only supply his other wants in the way of shelter, clothing, etc., by his own labour; and this would be almost impossible; *every piece of land by no means produces everything.*

He whose land was only fit for grain and would produce neither cotton nor hemp would be without cloth wherewith to clothe himself. Another would have a piece of land fit for cotton which would not produce grain. A third would be without wood wherewith to warm himself, while a fourth would be without grain wherewith to feed himself. Experience would soon teach each what was the kind of product for which his land would be best adapted, and he would limit himself to the cultivation of that particular crop, in order to procure for himself the things he was devoid of by means of exchange with his neighbours; and these, having in turn made the same reflections, would have cultivated the crop best suited to their field and abandoned the cultivation of all the others.[22]

The crops which the land produces to satisfy the different wants of man cannot serve that purpose, for the most part, in the state which nature gives them; they must undergo various changes and be prepared by art. Wheat must be converted into flour and then into bread; hides must be tanned or dressed.[23]

The same motive which has established the exchange of crop for crop between the Cultivators of different kinds of soil must, then, have necessarily brought about the exchange of crop for labour between the Cultivators and another part of the society, which shall have preferred the occupation of preparing and working up the produce of the land to that of growing it. Everyone profited by this arrangement, for each by devoting himself to a single kind of work succeeded much better in it. The Husbandman obtained from his field the greatest amount of produce possible, and procured for himself much more easily all the other things he needed by the exchange of his surplus than he would have done by his own labour. The Shoemaker, by making shoes for the Husbandman, obtained for himself a part of the latter's harvest. Each workman laboured to satisfy the wants of the workmen of all the other kinds, who, on their side, all laboured for him.[24]

Up to this point we have not yet distinguished the Husbandman from the Proprietor of the lands; and in fact they were not originally distinct. It is by the labour of those who have been first to till the field, and who have enclosed them, in order to secure to themselves the harvest, that all the lands have ceased to be common to all, and that landed properties have been established. Until the societies have been consolidated, and the public force, or law, now becomes superior to individual force, has been able to guarantee to each man the tranquil possession of his property against all invasion from without, a man could retain the ownership of a field only in the way he had acquired it and by continuing to cultivate it. It would not have been safe to get his field cultivated by somebody else, who, having taken all the trouble, would have had difficulty in understanding that the whole havest did not belong to him. Moreover, in this early time, as every industrious man would find as much land as he wished, he could not be tempted to till the soil for others. It was necessary that every proprietor should cultivate his field himself, or give it up altogether.[25]

In the times bordering on the beginning of the societies, it was almost impossible to find men who were ready to cultivate the soil which belonged to others; since, as all the grounds were not yet occupied, those who wished to labour preferred to clear new lands and cultivate them on their own account. This is pretty much the position in which people find themselves in all the new colonies.

Violent men have therefore conceived the idea of obligating other men by force to labour for them; and they have had slaves.[26]

But the land filled up, and was more and more cleared. The best lands at length came o be all occupied. There remained for the last comers only the sterile soils rejected by the first. But in the end all land found its master, and those who could not have properties had at first no other resource than that of exchanging the labour of their arms, in the employments of the stipendiary class, for the superflous portion of the crops of the cultivating Proprietor.[27]

He also discussed the evolution of religion, giving additional material to that found in his treatment of the three stages of social evolution.

Men oblivious of the first traditions, struck by the phenomena made known by the senses, assumed that all effects, not due to their own action, had been produced by beings like themselves, but invisible and more powerful, whom they put in the place of the divinity. . . . All the objects of nature had their gods, who, having been formed in the likeness of men, had men's attributes and vices. Superstition through- out the Universe gave its consecration to the caprices of imagination; and the only true God, alone worthy of adoration, was known but in a corner of the earth, by the people whom he had expressly chosen.[28]

## Condorcet

Marie Jean Antoine Nicolas Caritat, Marquis de Condorcet (1743–94), elaborated on Turgot's theory.

Man is born with the faculty of receiving sensations. . . .

Sensations are accompanied with pleasure or pain, and man has the further faculty of converting these momentary impressions into durable sentiments of a corresponding nature, and of experiencing these sentiments either at the sight or recollection of the pleasure or pain of beings sensitive like himself. And from this faculty, united with that of forming and combining ideas, arise between him and his fellow-creatures, the ties of interest and duty, to which nature has affixed the most exquisite portion of our felicity, and the most poignant of our sufferings.

Were we to confine our observations to an enquiry into the general facts and unvarying laws which the developement of these faculties presents to us, in what is common to the different individuals of the human species, our enquiry would bear the name of metaphysics.

But if we consider this development in its results, relative to the mass of individuals co-existing at the same time on a given space, and follow it from generation to generation, it then exhibits a picture of the progress of the human intellect. This progress is subject to the same general laws, observable in the individual development of our faculties*; being the result of that very development considered at once in a great number of individuals united in society. But the result which every instant presents, depends upon that of the preceding instants, and has an influence on the instants which follow.

The picture, therefore, is historical; since subjected as it will be to perpetual variations, it is formed by the successive observation of human societies at the different eras through which they have passed. It will accordingly exhibit the order in which the changes have taken place, explain the influence of every past period upon that which follows it, and thus show, by the modifications which the human species have experienced, in its incessant renovation through the immensity of ages, the course which it has pursued, and the steps

* "The only ground for belief in the truth of natural sciences, is that universal laws, known or unknown, which regulate the phenomena of the universe are necessary and constant; and why is the principle any the less true for the development of the intellectual and moral faculties of man than for other operations of nature?"[29]

which it has advanced towards knowledge and happiness. From these observations on what man has heretofore been, and what he is at present, we shall be led to the means of securing and of accelerating the still further progress, of which, from his nature, we may indulge the hope*. . . . The course of this progress may doubtless be more or less rapid, but it can never be retrograde.[33]

I shall divide the space through which I mean to run, into nine grand epochs; and shall presume in a tenth, to advance some conjectures upon the future destiny of mankind.[34]

## FIRST EPOCH

### Men united into hordes

We have no direct information by which to ascertain what has preceded the state of which we are now to speak; and it is only by examining the intellectual or moral faculties, and the physical constitution of man, that we are enabled to conjecture by what means he arrived at this first degree of civilization. . . .

A society consisting of a family appears to be natural to man. Formed at first by the want which children have of their parents, and by the affection of the mother, as well as that of the father, though less general and less lively, time was allowed, by the long continuance of this want, for the birth and growth of a sentiment which must have excited the desire of perpetuating the union. The continuance of the want was also sufficient for the advantages of the union to be felt. A family placed upon a soil that afforded easy subsistence, might afterwards have multiplied and become a horde.

Hordes that may have owed their origin to the union of several distinct families, must have been formed more slowly and more rarely, the union depending on motives less urgent and the concurrence of a greater number of circumstances.

The art of fabricating arms, of preparing aliments, of procuring the utensils requisite for this preparation, of preserving these aliments as a provision against the seasons in which it was impossible to procure a fresh supply of them—these arts, confined to the most simple wants, were the first fruits of a continued union, and the first features that distinguished human society from the society observable in many species of beasts.

In some of these hordes, the women cultivate round the huts, plants which serve for food and supercede the necessity of hunting and fishing. In others, formed in places where the earth spontaneously offers vegetable nutriment, a part of the time of the savage is occupied by the care of seeking and gathering it. In hordes of the last description, where the advantage of remaining united is less felt, civilization has been observed very little to exceed that of a society consisting of a single family. Meanwhile there has been found in all the use of an articulate language.

More frequent and more durable connections with the same individuals, a similarity of interests, the succour mutually given, whether in their common hunting or against an enemy must have equally produced both the sentiment of justice and a reciprocal affection between the members of the society. In a short time this affection would transform itself into an attachment to the society.

The necessary consequence was a violent enmity, and a desire of vengeance not to be extinguished, against the enemies of the horde.

The want of a chief, in order to act in common, and thereby defend themselves the better, and procure with greater ease a more certain and more abundant subsistence, intro-

* " . . . the unlimited perfectibility of mankind . . . is a universal law of nature."[30]

In another work he speaks of "the ever-increasing progress of enlightenment"[31] and "the necessary progress of the human race."[32]

duced the first idea of public authority into these societies. In circumstances in which the whole horde was interested, respecting which a common resolution must be taken, all those concerned in executing the resolution were to be consulted. The weakness of the females, which exempted them from the distant chace and from war, the usual subjects of debate, excluded them alike from these consultations. As the resolutions demanded experience, none were admitted but such as were supposed to possess it. The quarrels that arose in a society disturbed its harmony, and were calculated to destroy it: it was natural to agree that the decision of them should be referred to those whose age and personal qualities inspired the greatest confidence. Such was the origin of the first poltical institutions.

The formation of a language must have preceded these institutions. The idea of expressing objects by conventional signs appears to be above the degree of intelligence attained in this stage of civilization; and it is probable they were only brought into use by length of time, by degrees, and in a manner in some sort imperceptible. . . .

Regular movements adjusted to each other in due proportions, are capable of being executed with a less degree of fatigue; and they who see, or hear them, perceive their order and relation with greater facility. For both these reasons they form a source of pleasure. Thus, the origin of the dance, of music and of poetry, may be traced to the infant state of society. . . .

The only science known to savage hordes, are a slight and crude idea of astronomy, and the knowledge of certain medicinal plants employed in the cure of wounds and diseases; and even these are already corrupted by a mixture of superstition.

. . . We can here perceive the beginning . . . of the formation of a class of men the depositaries of the elements of the sciences or processes of the arts, of the mysteries or ceremonies of religion, of the practices of superstition, and frequently even of the secrets of legislation and polity.[35]

## SECOND EPOCH

### PASTORAL STATE OF MANKIND
*Transition from that to the Agricultural State*

The idea of preserving certain animals taken in hunting, must readily have occurred, when their docility rendered the preservation of them a task of no difficulty, when the soil round the habitations of the hunters afforded these animals an ample subsistence, when the family possessed a greater quantity of them than it could for the present consume, and at the same time might have reason to apprehend the being exposed to want, from the ill success of the next chace, or the intemperance of the seasons.

From keeping these animals as a simple supply against a time of need, it was observed that they might be made to multiply, and thus furnish a more durable provision. Their milk afforded a farther resource: and those fruits of a flock, which, at first, were regarded only as a supplement to the produce of the chace, became the most certain, most abundant and least painful means of subsistence. Accordingly the chace ceased to be considered as the principal of these resources, and soon as any resource at all; it was pursued only as a pleasure, or as a necessary precaution for keeping beasts of prey from the flocks, which, become more numerous, could no longer find round the habitations of their keepers a sufficient nourishment.

A more sedentary and less fatiguing life afforded leisure favorable to the developement of the mind. Secure of subsistence, no longer anxious respecting their first and indispensable wants, men sought, in the means of providing for those wants, new sensations.

The arts made some progress. . . .

Wool was used for apparel, and cloth substituted in the place of skins.

Family societies became more urbane, without being less intimate. As the flocks of each could not multiply in the same proportion, a difference of wealth was established. Then was suggested the idea of one man sharing the produce of his flocks who had no flocks, and who was to devote his time and strength to the care they require. Then it was found that the labor of a young and able individual was of more value than the expence of his bare subsistence; and the custom was introduced of retaining prisoners of war as slaves, instead of putting them to death.

Hospitality, which is practised also among savages, assumes in the pastoral state a more decided and important character. . . .

Manners of course must have softened. . . .

A great variety of articles employed in satisfying the different wants, and great number of instruments to prepare these wants, and a greater inequality in their distribution, gave energy to exchange, and converted it into actual commerce: it was impossible it should extend without the necessity of a common measure and a species of money being felt.

Hordes became more numerous. . . .

Each nation had its chief for the conduct of war; but being divided into tribes, from the necessity of securing pasturage, each tribe had also its chief. This superiority was attached almost universally to certain families.

The consuls of the chiefs of the family or tribe decided, from ideas of natural justice or of established usage, the numerous and intricate disputes that already prevailed. The tradition of these decisions, by confirming and perpetuating the usage, soon formed a kind of jurisprudence more regular and coherent than the progress of society had rendered in other respects necessary. The idea of property and its rights had acquired a greater extent and precision. The division of inheritances becoming more important, there was a necessity of subjecting it to fixed regulations. The agreements that were entered into being more frequent, were no longer confined to such simple objects; they were to be subjected to forms; and the manner of verifying them, to secure their execution, had also its laws.

[There was] . . . a slight degree of improvement in astronomy.

. . . More regular forms of worship begin to be established, and systems of faith less coarsely combined. . . .

Languages were enriched without becoming less figurative or less bold . . . Songs, poetry, and instruments of music were improved during a leisure that produced an audience more peaceable, and at the same time more difficult to please, and allowed the artist to reflect on his own sentiments, examine his first ideas, and form a selection from them.

It could not have escaped observation that some plants yielded the flocks a better and more abundant subsistence than others. The advantage was accordingly felt of favoring the production of these, of separating them from plants less nutritive, unwholesome, and even dangerous; and the means of effecting this were discovered.

In like manner, where plants, grain, the spontaneous fruits of the earth, contributed with the produce of the flocks to the subsistence of man, it must equally have been observed how these vegetables multiplied; and the care must have followed of collecting them nearer to the habitations; of separating them from useless vegetables, that they might occupy a soil to themselves; of securing them from untamed beasts, from the flocks, and even from the rapacity of other men.

These ideas must have equally occurred, and even sooner, in more fertile countries, where the spontaneous productions of the earth almost sufficed of themselves for the support of men; who now began to devote themselves to agriculture.

In such a society, and under a happy climate, the same space to ground produces, in corn, roots, and fruit, wherewith to maintain a greater number of men than if employed as pasturage. Accordingly. . . agriculture became the most plentiful source of subsistence, the first occupation of men; and the human race arrived at the third epoch of its progress.

There are people who have remained, from time immemorial, in one of the two states we have described. They have not only not risen of themselves to any higher degree of improvement, but the connection and commercial intercourse they have had with nations more civilized have failed to produce this effect. Such connections and intercourse have communicated to them some knowledge, some industry, and a great many vices, but have never been able to draw them from their state of mental stagnation.

The principle causes of this phenomenon are to be found in climate; in habit; in the sweets annexed to this state of almost complete independence, an independence not to be equalled but in a society more perfect even than our own; in the natural attachment of man to opinions received from his infancy, and to the customs of his country; in the aversion that ignorance feels to every sort of novelty; in bodily and more especially mental indolence, which suppress the feeble and as yet scarcely existing spark of curiosity; and lastly, in the empire which superstition already exercises over these infant societies.[36]

## THIRD EPOCH

*Progress of mankind from the agricultural state to the invention of
alphabetical writing*

. . . Agriculture attaches man to the soil which he cultivates. . . .

Each parcel of land has a master, to whom alone the fruits of it belong. . .

In the two former states of society, every individual, or every family at least, practised nearly all the necessary arts.

But when there were men, who, without labor, lived upon the produce of their land, and others who received wages; when occupations were multiplied, and the processes of the arts became more extensive and complicate, common interest soon enforced a separation of them. It was perceived, that the industry of an individual, when confined to fewer objects, was more complete; that the hand executed with greater readiness and precision a smaller number of operations that long habit had rendered more familiar; that a less degree of understanding was required to perform a work well, when that work had been more frequently repeated. . . .

Thus to the three classes of men before distinguishable in pastoral life, that of proprietors, that of the domestics of their family, and lastly, that of slaves, we must now add, that of the different kinds of artisans, and that of merchants. . . .

Some nations remained dispersed over the country. Others united themselves in towns, which became the residence of the common chief, called by a name answering to the word KING.[37]

## FOURTH EPOCH

*Progress of the human mind in Greece, till the division of sciences
about the age of Alexander.*[38]

## FIFTH EPOCH

*Progress of the sciences, from their division to their decline*[39]

## SIXTH EPOCH

*Decline of learning, to its restoration about the*
*period of the Crusades*[40]

## SEVENTH EPOCH

*From the first progress of the sciences about the period of their revival in the*
*west, to the invention of the art of printing*[41]

## EIGHTH EPOCH

*From the invention of printing to the period when the sciences and*
*philosophy threw off the yoke of authority*[42]

## NINTH EPOCH

*From the time of Descartes, to the formation of the French republic*[43]

## TENTH EPOCH

*Future progress of mankind*[44]


## CULTURAL EVOLUTION

In this section a group of writers will be considered whose main contributions were in the field of cultural evolution.

### Warburton

William Warburton (1698–1779) gave a Hobbesian account of the state of nature and the origin of society.

The general appetite of self-preservation being most indispensable to every animal, nature hath made it the strongest of all.[45]

. . . man, in a state of nature, soon ran into very violent excesses; and never thought he had sufficiently provided for his own being, till he had deprived his fellows of the free enjoyment of theirs. Hence, all those evils of mutual violence, rapine, and slaughter, which, in a state of nature, where all are equal, must needs be abundant. . . .

Thus was *Society* invented for a remedy against injustice; and a *Magistrate,* by mutual consent, appointed, to give it a sanction. . . Where it is to be observed, that though society provides for all those conveniencies and accomodations of a more elegant life, which man must have been content to have lived without, in a state of nature; yet it is more than probable that these were never thought of when Society was first established; but that they were the mutual violences and injustices, at length become intolerable, which set men upon contriving this generous remedy.[46]

Warburton's influence lay in his hypotheses on the evolution of language and writing.

LANGUAGE, as appears from the nature of the thing, from the records of history, and from the remains of the most ancient languages yet remaining, was at first extremely rude, narrow, and equivocal: so that men would be perpetually at a loss, on any new conception or uncommon accident, to explain themselves to another; the art of inlarging language by a scientific analogy being a late invention: this would necessarily set them upon supplying the deficiencies of speech by apt and significant SIGNS. Accordingly, in the first ages of the world, mutual converse was upheld by a mixed discourse of words and ACTIONS.[47]

Men soon found out two ways of communicating their thoughts to one another; the first by SOUNDS, and the second by FIGURES: for there being frequent occasion to have their compositions either perpetuated, or communicated at a distance, the way of figures or characters was next thought upon, after sounds (which were momentary and confined), to make their conceptions lasting and extensive.

The first and most natural way of communicating our thoughts by marks or figures, is by tracing out the images of things. So the early people, to express the idea of a man or horse, delineated the form of those animals. Thus the first essay towards writing was a mere picture.[48]

But the incoveniences attending the too great bulk of the volume in writings of this kind, would soon set the more ingenious and better civilized people upon contriving methods to abridge their characters: and of all the improvements of this kind, that which was invented by the EGYPTIANS, and called HIEROGLYPHICS, was by far the most celebrated.[49]

But the obscurity which attended the scantiness of heiroglyphic characters, joined to the enormous bulk of picture volumes, set men upon contriving a third change in this kind of writing: of which the CHINESE have given us a famous example. . . The CHINESE writing. . . threw out the images, and retained only the marks; which they increased to a prodigious number.[50]

On the whole, therefore, we see, that before the institution of letters to express SOUNDS, all characters denoted only THINGS; 1. By *representation*. 2. By *analogy* or *symbols*. 3. By *arbitrary* institution.[51]

Thus we have brought down the general history of Writing, by a gradual and easy descent, from a PICTUE to a LETTER; for Chinese marks. . . are on the very border of letters; an ALPHABET invented to express *sounds* instead of *thing* being only a compendium of that large volume of arbitrary marks.[52]

## Condillac

Étienne Bonnot de Condillac (1714–80) was particularly interested in the evolution of language.

We must . . . observe languages; nay, if we wish to know what they were in their origin, we must observe the language of action, by which they have been made. It is here we shall begin.

The elements of the language of action were born with man, and these elements are the organs which the Author of nature gave us.* Thus there is an innate language, though there are no innate ideas. Indeed, it was necessary that the elements of a language . . . should precede our ideas, because, without signs of any species, it would be impossible for us to analyse our thoughts, in order to account to ourselves for what we think, that is, to see it distinctly.

Therefore our exterior conformation is so adapted to our state of existence, as to be capable of representing all that occurs in the soul; and this is the expression of our

* " . . . the wants and faculties are properly what we call the nature of each animal, and thereby we only mean to say that an animal was born with certain wants and faculties. But since the wants and faculties depend on the organization, and vary with it; it follows that by nature we understand the conformation of the organs, and in fact, such it is in its principle."[53]

feelings and judgements; so that when it speaks, nothing can be hidden.

The peculiar quality of action does not consist in mere analysing; for the action only represents the feelings, because it is their effect; it represents at once all those feelings which we experience in the same instant, and the simultaneous ideas in the mind are naturally simultaneous in the language or action by which we express them . . .

Men begin to speak the language of action as soon as they feel, and they then speak it without designing to communicate their thoughts; they will only make the effort to speak, in order to make themselves understood, when they shall have remarked that they have been understood; but in the beginning they predetermine nothing, because they have not yet observed any thing.

Therefore, all is in a confused state to them, as to their language, and they discern in it nothing, as long as they shall not have learned to analyse their thoughts.

But though all is confused in their language, yet it includes all they feel; it includes all they can discern in it, when they come to know how to analyse their thoughts; that is, *desires, fears, judgments, reasonings,* in one word, all the operations of which the soul is capable. For if all these modifications of sensation were not in it, analysis could not find them there. Let us then see how men learn from nature to analyse all these things.

They want to assist each other; therefore each of them is desirous to make himself understood, and consequently to understand himself.

At first they obey nature; and without design, as we have just remarked, they say at once all they feel, because it is natural for their action to do so. However, he who listens with the eyes will not understand, if he does not decompose this action, in order to observe its movements one after another. But it is natural for him to decompose it; and therefore he decomposes it before he has formed any design to do so. For if he sees at once all its movements at first sight, he looks only at those which strike him the most forcibly; at the second view, he looks at others; and at the third, at others still. He observes them, therefore, successively ; and thus, without knowing it in form, they are analysed in fact.

Each of these men will therefore remark, sooner or later, that he never understands others better, than after having decomposed their action, and by consequence he will be able to remark, that in order to make himself understood, he must decompose his action. Then he will by degrees contract a habit of repeating, one after another, the movements which nature causes him to make at once, and the language of action will naturally become for him an analytical method. I say a method, because the succession of movements will not be done arbitrarily, and without rules: for the action being the effect of wants and circumstances, it is natural that it should be decomposed in the order of those very wants and circumstances; and though this order may vary, and does vary, it can never be arbitrary. Thus, in a picture, the place of each personage, his action and character are determined, when the subject is given, with all its circumstances.

By decomposing his action, a man decomposes his thoughts for himself, as well as for others; he analyses it, and he makes himself understood, because he understands himself.

As the whole actions form the picture of the whole thought, the partial actions are as many pictures of the ideas which make each a part of this compounded whole. Therefore, if he seeks to decompose these partial actions, he will likewise decompose the several ideas of which they are the signs, and he will continually form new and distinct ideas.

These means, the only means by which he is able to analyse his thought, will be sufficient to unfold it in all its most minute shades; for the first signs of a language being given, we only resort to consult analogy, and it will furnish all others.

There are, therefore, no ideas which the language of action cannot express; and it will express them with so much the more clearness and precision, as analogy will shew more sensibly in the series of signs which shall have been chosen.

Absolutely arbitrary signs would not be understood, because not being analogous, the acceptation of a known sign would not lead to the acceptation of an unknown sign. And truly it is analogy which constitutes the whole artifice of languages. They are easy, clear, precise, in proportion as analogy is more sensible or visble in them.[54]

Because of the relevance of this analysis to the modern conception of the role and effects of communication, Condillac's earlier and less abstract treatment of the subject is also given here.

The habit of intellectual operations in our first parents was not the effect of experience; for immediately after their creation they were rendered capable, by the extraordinary assistance of the Deity, of reflecting and of communicating their thoughts to each other. But suppose that some time after the deluge two children, one male, and the other female, wandered about in the deserts, before they understood the use of any sign.[55]

So long as the abovementioned children lived asunder, the operations of their minds were confined to perception and consciousness . . . to attention . . . to reminiscence . . . and to a very limited exercise of the imagination.[56]

When they came to live together, they had occasion to enlarge and improve these first operations; because their mutual converse made them connect with the cries of each passion, the perceptions which they naturally signified. They generally accompanied them with some motion, gesture or action, whose expression was yet of a more sensible nature. For example, he who suffered, by being deprived of an object which his wants had rendered necessary to him, did not confine himself to cries or sounds only; he used some endeavors to obtain it, he moved his head, his arms, and every part of his body. The other, struck with this sight, fixed his eye on the same object, and perceiving some inward emotions which he was not yet able to account for, he suffered in seeing his companion suffer. From that very instant he felt himself inclined to relieve him, and he followed this impression to the utmost of his power. Thus by instinct alone they asked and gave each other assistance. I say *by instinct alone:* for as yet there was no room for reflexion. One of them did not say to himself. *I must make such particular motions to render him sensible of my want, and to induce him to relieve me:* nor the other, *I see by his motions that he wants such a thing, and I will let him have it:* but they both acted in consequence of the want which pressed them most.

And yet the same circumstance could not be frequently repeated, but they must have accustomed themselves at length to connect with the cries of the passions and with the different motions of the body, those perceptions which were expressed in so sensible a manner. The more they grew familiar with those signs, the more they were in a capacity of reviving them at pleasure. Their memory began to acquire some sort of habit, they were able to command their imagination as they pleased, and insensibly they learned to do by reflexion what they had hitherto done merely by instinct. At first both of them acquired the habit of discerning by those signs the sensations which each other felt at that moment,and afterwards they make use of them in order to let each other know their past sensations. For example, he who saw a place in which he had been frightened, mimicked those cries and movements which were the signs of fear, in order to warn the other not to expose himself to the same danger.

The use of those signs insensibly enlarged and improved the operations of the mind, and on the other hand these having acquired some improvement, perfected the signs, and rendered the use of them more familiar. Experience shews that these two things assist each other. . . .

By these particulars we see in what manner the cries of the passions contributed to enlarge the operations of the mind, by giving occasion naturally to the mode of speaking by action; a language which in its infancy, probably consisted only in contorsions and violent agitations, being thus proportioned to the slender capacity of this young couple.

And yet when once they had acquired the habit of connecting some ideas with arbitrary signs, the natural cries served them for a pattern, to frame a new language. They articulated new sounds, and by repeating them several times, and accompanying them with some gesture which pointed out such objects as they wanted to be taken notice of, they accustomed themselves to give names to things. The first progress of this language was nevertheless very slow. The organ of speech was so inflexible, that it could not easily articulate any other than a few simple sounds. The obstacles which hindered them from pronouncing others, prevented them even from suspecting that the voice was susceptible of any further variation, beyond the small number of words which they had already devised.

Let us suppose this young couple to have had a child, who being pressed by wants which he could not without some difficulty make known, put every part of his body into motion. His tongue, being extremely pliant, made an extraordinary motion, and pronounced a new expression. As those wants continued to press the child, this occasionaed a repetition of the same efforts; again he moved his tongue in the same manner as at first, and articulated the same sound. The parents surprized, having at length guessed his meaning, gave him what he wanted, but tried as they gave it him, to repeat the same word. The difficulty they had to pronounce it, shewed that they were not of themselves capable of inventing it.

For the same reason this new language was not much improved. The child's organ for want of exercise quickly lost all its flexibility. His parents taught him to communicate his thoughts by action; the sensible images of this mode of speaking, being much easier to him than articulate sounds. Chance alone could give rise to some new words; and doubtless it must have been a long time, before their number could be considerably increased by so slow a method. The mode of speaking by action, at that time so natural, was a great obstacle to surmount. How could they leave it for another, whose advantages were not yet foreseen, and whose difficulties were so obvious?

In proportion as the language of articulate sounds became more copious, there was more need of seizing early opportunities of improving the organ of speech, and for preserving its first flexibility. Then it appeared as convenient as the mode of speaking by action: they were both indiscriminately used; till at length articulate sounds became so easy, that they absolutely prevailed.

There was therefore a time when conversation was supported by a language intermixed with words and gestures.[57]

Throughout the foregoing discussions, Condillac mentioned the interdependence of signs and ideas; he treated this problem at great length.

Lower animals adjust by the association of ideas; man, by signs.

. . . brutes . . . represent to themselves an absent object, only because the image of it in their brain is closely connected with the object present. It is not their memory which directs them to a place, where the day before they met with nourishment; but it is because the sensation of hunger is so strongly connected with the ideas of that place and of the road leading to it, that these ideas are revived, as soon as they feel the sensation.[58]

By following the explications here given, we may frame a clear idea of what is comnonly called *instinct*. It is the imagination, which at the presence of the object, revives the perceptions immediately connected with it, and thereby directs every species of animals without the assistance of reflexion.[59]

. . . the use of signs is the real cause of the progress of imagination, contemplation and memory.[60]

It is even by their connection alone with these signs that the imagination is capable of reviving them at will.[61]

. . . the facility of connecting our ideas produces the imagination, contemplation, and memory.[62]

Signs are of three types.

I distinguish three sorts of signs: 1. Accidental signs, or the objects which particular circumstances have connected with some of our ideas, so as to render the one proper to revive the other. 2. Natural signs, or the cries which nature has established to express the passions of joy, of fear, or of grief, &c. 3. Instituted signs, or those which we have chosen ourselves, and bear only an arbitrary relation to our ideas.[63]

An analysis is given "Of the operation by which we give signs to our ideas."[64]

This operation is the result of the imagination, which presents signs to the mind with which, it had been as yet unacquainted; and of the attention which connects them with our ideas. It is one of the most esential operations in the study of truth; and yet it is one of those which are least known. I have already shewn the use and necessity of signs in acquiring a habit of the operations of the mind. I shall now demonstrate the same thing, considering them in regard to the different species of ideas.*[67]

Arithmetic furnishes us with a very sensible example of the necessity of signs. If after having given name to a unit, we did not successively imagine others for the several ideas which we form by the multiplication of this first one, it would be impossible for us to make any progress in the knowledge of numbers. We discern different combinations, only because we have cyphers which are themselves very distinct. Take away these cyphers, take away all the signs in use, and we shall find it impossible to preserve any idea of those combinations. Can we form to ourselves a notion even of the smallest number, without considering several objects, each of which is in some measure the sign to which we affix the unit? For my part, I perceive the numbers *two* or *three*, only as I represent to myself two or three different objects. If I proceed to the number *four*, I am obliged for greater ease, to imagine two objects on one side and two on the other; coming to the number *six*, I cannot help distributing them by two and two, or three and three; and if I have a mind to go further, I shall soon be under a necessity of considering several units as a single one, and to reunite them for this purpose in a single object.[68]

Hence it is beyond all manner of doubt, that if a person wanted only to calculate for himself, he would be equally obliged to invent signs, as if he wanted to communicate his calculations. But why should that which is true in arithmetic, not be the same in other sciences? Should we be capable ever to reflect on metaphysics and morals, if we had not invented signs to fix our ideas, in proportion as we formed new combinations?

* "Let us conclude that in order to have ideas on which we may be capable of reflecting, we have need of imagining signs that may serve as chains to the different combinations of simple ideas; and that our notions are exact, no farther than as we have invented regular signs to fix them."[65]

"As the [analytical] statue cannot yet use signs it cannot classify ideas, and consequently it cannot have ideas as general as ours."[66]

Should not words be the same in regard to our ideas in the several sciences, as cyphers are to our ideas in arithmetic? In all probability the ignorance of this truth is one of the causes of the confusion which prevails in works of metaphysics and morality.[69]

The mind is so limited that we cannot revive a great number of ideas to render them all at the same time the subject of our reflexion. And yet it is oftentimes necessary that we should consider several of them together. This we do with assistance of signs, which, by being combined, makes us consider them as if they were only one idea.[70]

From this truth it likewise appears, how simple and how admirable are the springs of human knowledge. The soul has felt various sensations and operations: how then shall it dispose of these materials? By gestures, by signs, by sounds, by cyphers, by letters; by instruments so foreign as these from our ideas, we set them to work, in order to raise ourselves even to the sublimest knowledge. The materials are the same in all men; but the art of making use of signs varies; and from thence the inequality which is to be observed among mankind.

Take away from a superior genius the use of characters; and you debar him of a deal of knowledge to which a person of middling abilities may easily attain. Take away from him likewise the use of speech; and the fate of mutes will shew you to what narrow limits you confine him. In fine, deprive him of the use of all sorts of signs, so as he shall not be able to make the least gesture with propriety, in order to express the most ordinary thought; and he will be no more to you than a driveler.[71]

In *La logique*, Condillac argued that language itself is an analytical method. In fact, the entire discussion so far is a remarkable anticipation of logical positivism and its offshoots in their linguistic aspects.

We shall easily conceive how languages are analytical methods, if we have conceived how the language of action is itself such a metod; and if we have comprehended the truth, that were it not for this latter language, it would not have been in the power of men to analyse their thoughts; we shall at once perceive that, if they ceased speaking the language of action, they could not analyse their thoughts, if they had not substituted for the language of action a language of articulate sounds. Analysis is performed, and can be performed only by the aid of signs.

Nay, we must remark that, if it had not been at first performed by the help of signs, symbols, or representatives of the language of action, it would never have been executed with the articulate sounds of our languages. Indeed, how should a word have become the sign of an idea, if that idea could not have been shewn in the language of action? And how could this language have expressed it, if it had not caused it to be observed separately from every other. . . .

Men only thought of making analyses, after having observed that they had already, and without premeditation, made some: they only thought of speaking the language of action, to make themselves understood, after having observed that they had been by that means understood. They will likewise only have thought of speaking with articulate sounds, after having observed that they had spoken with such sounds; and languages have begun before men formed any project of making a language.

It is thus they have been orators and poets, before they thought of being either In one word, whatever they have become, such they were at first by the operation of nature alone; and they only studied to be again so, when they had observed what nature had caused them to do, without previous study. . . .

As men analysed without knowing it, they did not remark that if they had exact ideas, they owed them solely to analysis. They therefore did not know all the importance of this method, and they analysed less in proportion as the want of analysing was less felt.[72]

Condillac also dealt with the evolution of other aspects of culture, including science and technology,[73] art (literature,[74] music,[75] dance,[76] and pantomime[77]), religion,[78] writing,[79] and political organization and law.[80]

Like many others before and since, he was puzzled by the differential development of culture in various societies.

> . . . we should resolve two questions, which have been often discussed, and never, I think, rightly decided. It is to know the reason why the arts and sciences do not flourish alike in all ages and countries; and why men of eminence in every kind are generally cotemporaneous.[81]

> The causes which contribute to the display of abilities are as follows. 1. The climate is an essential condition.* 2. It is requisite that the form of government be settled, so as to fix the character of a nation.† 3. It is this that gives a character to the language by multiplying such phrases as express the prevailing taste of a people.‡ 4. This is brought about very slowly in languages formed upon the ruin of others: but when once these obstacles are surmounted, then the rules of analogy are established, the language makes some improvements, and there is an opportunity to display one's abilities.§ We see therefore the reason why great writers do not indifferently flourish in all ages, and why they make their appearance sooner in some, and later in other countries. It remains now for us to inquire how it happens that great men of every kind are generally contemporaries.

> As soon as a man of genius discovers the character of a language, he expresses it strongly in his writings. With this assistance other ingenious persons, who would not perhaps have been able to find it out of themselves, see it very plain, and express it after his example, each in his own way. The language is insensibly enriched with a multitude of new turns of expressions, which from the relation they bear to its character, enlarge it more and more; and analogy becomes as it were a lamp, whose light continually increases, to direct a greater number of writers. Then the public eye is naturally fixed on those who distinguish themselves from the crowd: the taste of these become the prevailing taste of the nation: each person in the several subjects to which he applies himself, uses that discernment which he learnt of those ingenious persons: abilities begin to ferment: the several arts assume their proper character; and men of superior merit in every branch of learning make their appearance.[86]

* "The climate is not . . . the cause of the progress of the arts and sciences; it is required only as an essential condition."[82]

† "To form the character of a people two things contribute, climate and government. From the climate arises a greater degree of vivacity or of phlegm; and of course a disposition to one form of government preferably to another. But these dispositions are changed by a thousand circumstances. The sterility, fruitfulness, or situation of a country; the respective interests of the inhabitants compared to those of their neighbours; the restless spirits who disturb it, while the government is not yet settled on a solid basis; the extraordinary men whose superior abilities eclipse those of their fellow citizens; these and several other causes contribute to alter, and sometimes intirely to destroy the first propensities which a nation derives from its climate. The character therefore of a people undergoes very near the same changes as their government, nor does it fix, till the latter has received a settled form."[83]

‡ "As government influences the character of a people, so the character of a people influences that of language. . . . Upon the whole . . . it appears that every language expresses the character of the people that speak it."[84]

§ "The circumstances favourable to the displaying of talents, are always to be found in a nation, when the language begins to have fixed principles and a settled standard: such a period is therefore the epocha of great men."[85]

## Blacklock

Monboddo wrote that Thomas Blacklock (1721–91)

conjectures, that the first language among men was *music,* and that, before our ideas were expressed by articulate sounds, they were communicated by tones, varied according to different degrees of gravity or acuteness: For he considers language to be of so difficult invention, that it could not have been attained to at once, without trying every more obvious variation of the voice, such as that of musical tones, which we first learned by imitation of the birds; and, having in that way become musicians, it was natural enough to think of applying the variation of tones to a purpose of utility as well as pleasure, namely, the communication of ideas. And he adds, that, when it was found necessary to enlarge the expression of language by the addition of articulation, the tones were still preserved.[87]

## ETHOLOGICAL INTERPRETATIONS

No one of the stature of Barclay appeared in the eighteenth century to explain culture in terms of the ethos or "genius" of the society.

## Harris

James Harris (1709–80) spoke of the effect of the ethos of a society upon its language.

. . . we shall be led to observe, how Nations, like single Men, have their *peculiar* Ideas; how these *peculiar* Ideas become THE GENIUS OF THEIR LANGUAGE, since the *Symbol* must of course correspond to its *Archetype;* how the *wisest* Nations, have the *most* and *best Ideas,* will consequently have the *best* and *most copious Languages;* how others, whose Languages are motley and compounded, and who have borrowed from different countries different Arts and Practices, discover by WORDS, to whom they are indebted for THINGS.[88]

He argued for man's sociality on the basis of the nature of language.

If Men by nature had been framed for Solitude, they had never felt an Impulse to converse one with another.[89]

. . . a WORD may be defined *a Voice articulate, and significant by Compact.*[90]

## Chastellux

François Jean Chastellux (1734–88) was another writer to whom every society had a "genius."

[He speaks] of that original character, of that spirit which presides at the formation of people, and at the establishment of nations.[91]

. . . the character, the genius of a people, is not solely produced by the government they have adopted, but by the circumstances under which they were originally formed.[92]

Thus, states, like individuals, are born with a particular complexion, the bad effects of which may be corrected by regimen and habits, but can never be entirely changed. Thus, legislators, like physicians, ought never to flatter themselves that they can bestow, at pleasure, a particular temperament on bodies politic, but strive to discover what they already have, and thence study to remedy the incoveniences, and multiply the advantages resulting from it.[93]

[For example, the] Virginians differ essentially from the inhabitants to the north and eastward of the Bay, (of Chesapeak) not only in the nature of their climate, that of their soil, and the objects of cultivation peculiar to it, but in that indelible character which is imprinted on every nation at the moment of its origin, and which by perpetuating itself from generation to generation, justifies the following great principle, that *every thing which is, partakes of that which has been*.[94]

Now, to discover the natural tendency of a nation, not only must we examine its actual legislation, but the opposition which may exist between the government and prejudices, between the laws and habits; the re-action, in short, which these different moving powers may produce, one upon the other.[95]

. . . *every thing that is, partakes of what has been;* and to attain a thorough knowledge of any people, it is not less necessary to study their history than their legislation.[96]

There are also racial differences.

[In reporting his experiences in the southern part of the United States, he speaks of the negroes, whose situation would be still more lamentable, did not their natural insensibility extenuate, in some degree, the sufferings annexed to slavery.[97]

. . . the more we regard the negroes, the more must we be persuaded that the difference between them and us, consists in something more than complexion.[98]

He was aware of man's sociality.

It is . . . difficult to define what human nature hath fixed, relative to the state of society; but it is, at once, frivolous and useless to propose these questions: "Are men in a state of mutual and perpetual war?" "are they born the friends or the enemies of each other?" . . they are friends, whilst lending to each other a reciprocal support, they can the more easily satisfy their mutual wants: they are enemies, whilst circumstances establishing a competition amongst themselves, several strive to obtain that which one only can enjoy.[99]

If we regard as natural, all which is within the order of nature; all which is accomplished in consequence of its powers and its laws, then is there a state of nature as peculiar to the city, as to the country; to the tradesman, as to the husbandman; to the man that launches out into society, as to him that buries himself in solitude.[100]

He distinguished between society and political organization, which were so often confused.

One great, and common error, amidst a multitude of other errors, is the confounding the people with the government.[101]

He was a cosmopolitan.

There is nothing so fantastical and extraordinary but an instance of it may be found amongst mankind.[102]

What ridiculous opinions have not prevailed in the world, from the time of the Grecian sophists to the theologians of our days?[103]

However, there are some traits inherent in man, though modified by culture.

. . . morality, which can never differ from the real interest of society, appears sometimes to be local and modified by times and circumstances.[104]

. . . legislation, morals, and customs maintain such an empire over the passions, that they may give rise to infinite differences in the social state.[105]

He thought that the characteristic of a language was related to the degree of simplicity of the culture of which it was a part.

. . . the more ignorant and unpolished a nation is, the more its language abounds with metaphors and comparisons. They are the artful expedients of the mind, to elude that exact definition, which so frequently baffles all her powers.[106]

The development of the arts also depends on social conditions.

The arts, let us not doubt it, can never flourish, but where there is a great number of men. They must have large cities, they must have capitals.[107]

Finally, *De la félicité publique* was written to prove the reality of social progress; "in the moral sciences, one may always observe a slow, but continual progress,"[108] as well as "the general progress of our intellectual faculties."[109]

[The] sole end of all government, [is] the acquisition of the greatest welfare of the greatest number of individuals.[110]

Let us now seek out for some distinguishing mark, some particular symptoms which may serve as the standards of this Public Happiness. The two proofs which will naturally present themselves, are agriculture, and population. I name agriculture before population, because that whenever a large quantity of land, within a nation not composed of an extensive number of individuals, is industriously, and carefully cultivated, the consequence must be, that this nation will consume a great deal, and add to the necessary aliments of life, those comforts, and conveniencies, which form the happiness of life. If, on the contrary, the increase of the people be in proportion to the increase of agriculture, what can be concluded from hence, but that this multiplication of the human species, like the multiplication of every other species, arises solely from their well-being? Agriculture is, therefore, not only a distinguishing mark of the felicity of the people, but anterior, and preferable to the symptoms of population.[111]

. . . we are always mistaken in establishing too general principles, or rather in the consequences which we draw from these principles.

*Subsistence is the standard of population.* Were the quantity of subsistence to decrease, *the number of individuals must decrease in the same proportion.* It must decrease, without doubt: in the same proportion? that is another affair; or, at least, it can only be at the close of a very long period that this proportion will be found exact.[112] [This qualification exists because of differences in the standard of living.][113]

## IDEALISTIC INTERPRETATIONS

From the eighteenth century on, few scholars used the crude theological interpretation of history. In its stead there developed an idealistic school, of which Hegel was to be the greatest exponent, to whom the history of a culture was the unfolding and development of an idea. This conception was indebted to the theological group for its teleological viewpoint and to the ethological school for the belief that every society has an idea or ethos.

### Lessing

To Gotthold Ephraim Lessing (1729–81) cultural change was fundamentally the history of the growth of the race's spiritual nature through revelation.

That which Education is to the Individual, Revelation is to the Race.

Education is Revelation coming to the Individual Man; and Revelation is Education

which has come, and is yet coming, to the Human Race.
... Revelation [is to] be conceived of as the Educator of Humanity.[114]

Education has its *goal*, in the Race, no less than in the Indivudual. That which is ducated is educated for something.

The flattering prospects which are opened to the pupil, the Honour and Well-being which are painted to him, what are they more than means of educating him to become a man, who, when these prospects of Honour and Well-being have vanished, shall be able to do his Duty?

This is the aim of human education, and should not the Divine education extend as ar? Is that which is successful in the way of Art with the individual, not to be successful n the way of Nature with the whole? Blasphemy! Blasphemy![115]

## Kant

Immanuel Kant (1724–1804) followed Hobbes in considering that the state of nature was a state of war.

A state of Peace among men who live side by side with each other, is not the natural state. The state of nature is rather a state of War; for although it may not always present the outbreak of hostilities, it is nevertheless continually threatened with them. The state of Peace must, therefore, be established; for the mere cessation of hostilities furnished no security against their recurrence, and where there is no guarantee of peace between neighbouring States—which can only be furnished under conditions that are regulated by Law—the one may treat the other, when proclamation is made to that effect, as an enemy.[116]

However, the social contract by which political organization is explained is merely an intellectual construct.

We have before us the idea of an "Original Contract" as the only condition upon which a civil and, therefore, wholly rightful constitution can be founded among men, and as the only basis upon which a State can be established. But this fundamental condition— whether called an "original contract" or a "social compact"—may be viewed as the coalition of all the private and particular wills of a people into one common and public Will, having a purely juridical legislation as its end. But it is not necessary to presuppose this contract or compact, to have been actually a fact: nor indeed is it possible as a fact. We have not to deal with it as if it had first to be proved from history that a people into whose rights and obligations we have entered as their descendants, did actually on a certain occasion execute such a contract, and that a certain evidence or instrument regarding it of an oral or written kind, must have been transmitted so as to constitute an obligation that shall be binding in any existing civil constitution. In short, this idea is merely an idea of Reason; but it has undoubtedly a practical reality. For it ought to bind every legislator by the condition that he shall enact such laws as might have arisen from the united will of a whole people; and it will likewise be binding upon every subject, in so far as he will be a citizen, so that he shall regard the Law as if he had consented to it of his own will. This is the test of the rightfulness of every public law. If the law be of such a nature that it is impossible that the whole people could give their consent to it, it is not a just law ... But if it be merely possible that a people could consent to a law, it is a duty to regard it as just, even supposing that the people were at the moment in such a position or mood, that if it were referred to them, their consent to it would probably be refused.[117]

Kant viewed man and society as subject to natural law.

Whatever metaphysical theory may be formed regarding the *Freedom of the Will*, i holds equally true that the *manifestations of the Will* in human actions, are determined lik all other external events, by universal natural laws. Now History is occupied with the nar ration of these manifestations as facts, however deeply their causes may lie concealed Hence in view of this natural principle of regulation, it may be hoped that when th play of the freedom of the human Will is examined on the great scale of universal history a regular march will be discovered in its movements; and that, in this way, what appear to be tangled and unregulated in the case of individuals, will be recognised in the histor of the whole species as a continually advancing, though slow, development of its origina capacities and endowment. Thus marriages, births and deaths appear to be incapable o being reduced to any rule by which their numbers might be calculated beforehand, or account of the great influence which the free will of man exercises upon them; and yet th annual Statistics of great countries prove that these events take place according to constan natural laws. In this respect they may be compared with the very inconstant changes o the weather which cannot be determined beforehand in detail, but which yet, on the whole do not fail to maintain the growth of plants, the flow of rivers, and other natural process es, in a uniform and uninterrupted course. Individual men, and even whole nations little think, while they are pursuing their own purposes—each in his own way and ofter one in direct opposition to another—that they are advancing unconsciously under th guidance of a Purpose of Nature which is unknown to them, and that they are toiling for the realisation of an End which, even if it were known to them, might be regarded as o little importance.[118]

He then attempted to discover the trend of society in accordance with these natural laws;

to try whether he [i.e., the philosopher] cannot discover a *universal purpose of Nature* ir this paradoxical movement of human things, and whether in view of this purpose, a history of creatures who proceed without a plan of their own, may nevertheless b possible according to a determinate plan of Nature.[119]

All the capacities implanted in a Creature by nature, are destined to unfold themselves completely and conformably to their End, in the course of time.[120]

In Man, as the only rational creature on earth, those natural capacities which are directed towards the use of his Reason, could be completely developed only in the species and not in the individual.[121]

Nature has willed that Man shall produce wholly out of himself all that goes beyond the mechanical structure and arrangement of his animal existence, and that he shall participate in no other happiness or perfection but what he has procured for himself, apart from Instinct, by his own Reason.[122]

The means which Nature employs to bring about the development of all the capacities implanted in men, is their mutual Antagonism in society, but only so far as this antagonism becomes at length the cause of an Order among them that is regulated by Law.[123]

The greatest practical Problem for the human race, to the solution of which it is compelled by Nature, is the establishment of a Civil Society, universally administering Right according to Law.[124]

This Problem is likewise the most difficult of its kind, and it is the latest to be solved by the Human Race.[125]

The problem of the establishment of a perfect Civil Constitution is dependent on the problem of the regulation of the external relations between the States conformably to

Law; and without the solution of this latter problem it cannot be solved.[126]

The history of the human race, viewed as a whole, may be regarded as the realization of a hidden plan of Nature to bring about a political Constitution, internally, and for this purpose, also externally perfect, as the only state in which all the capacities implanted by her in Mankind can be fully developed.[127]

A philosophical attempt to work out the Universal History of the world according to the plan of Nature in its aiming at a perfect Civil Union, must be regarded as possible, and as even capable of helping forward the purpose of Nature.[128]

This idea of a Universal History is no doubt to a certain extent of an *a priori* character, but it would be a misunderstanding of my object were it imagined that I have any wish to supplant the empirical cultivation of History, or the narration of the actual facts of experience. It is only a thought of what a philosophical mind—which, as such, must be thoroughly versed in History—might be induced to attempt from another standpoint.[129]

He expressed his belief in social progress.

. . . as the human race is continually advancing in civilisation and culture as its natural purpose, so it is continually making progress for the better in relation to the moral end of its existence, and . . . this progress although it may be sometimes interrupted, will never be entirely broken off or stopped.[130]

## IDEOLOGICAL INTERPRETATIONS

In the ideological interpretation of history, a dichotomy is made of culture into the ideas of a people and their customs, with the former aspect the one which determines the characteristics of the culture.

### Voltaire

To Voltaire the controlling force [of history] is intellectual; and the conditions prevailing at any time are the outcome of ideas operating through individuals, classes, and institutions, which are themselves the expression of these ideas. . . . He visualized history as the clash of ideas and the progressive expansion of the human mind through the triumph of reason.[131]

François Marie Arouet de Voltaire (1694–1778) was the formost representative of the ideological school. He said of his *Essai sur les mœurs et l'esprit des nations* (1745–56):[132]

The object was the history of the human spirit, and not the detail of the facts almost always described; it is not a question of looking, for example, for the family which was lord of Puiset, or which the lord of Montlhéry, who made war on the kings of France, but rather to see by what degrees one comes from the barbarous rusticity of those times to the civility of ours. . . .*

* "My principle object is to know, as far as I can, the customs of peoples, and to study the human spirit; I will regard the order of succession of kings and chronology as my guides, but not as the object of my work."[133]

"You are at length resolved, then, to surmount the disgust you conceived from reading the "Modern History" since the decay of the Roman Empire, and to receive a general idea of the nations which inhabit and ravage the face of the earth. All that you seek to learn in this immensity of matter, is only that which deserves to be known; the genius, the manners and customs of the principal nations, supported by facts, of which no intelligent person should be ignorant. The aim of such an inquiry is not to know the precise

It is then the history of opinion which it is necessary to write, and by that the chaos of events, of factions, of revolutions and of crimes, becomes worthy of being presented for the regard of the wise.[137]

One sees in history so conceived, errors and prejudices succeeding one another and expelling truth and reason. One sees the clever and the fortunate enslave the foolish and crush the unfortunate; and again, these clever and these fortunate ones themselves are the playthings of fortune, as much as the slaves whom they govern. Finally, men understand themselves a little as a result of this tableau of their misfortunes and their foolishness. Societies come with time to rectify their ideas; men learn to think.[138]

My principal aim had been to follow the revolutions of the human spirit in those of governments.*[140]

Opinion has . . . changed a great part of the earth. Not only empires have disappeared without leaving a trace, but religions have been engulfed in these vast ruins.[141]

However, other aspects of culture reciprocally influence men and ideas.

As there are opinions which have absolutely changed the conduct of men, there are arts which have also changed everything in the world: such is that of gunpowder.[142]

Three things unceasingly influence the mind of man: climate,† government, and religion; this is the only way to explain the enigma of this world.[144]

Besides his interest in cultural history, Voltaire displayed his cosmopolitanism in not limiting his *Essai* to Greek, Roman, and western European history, but also including China and India:

. . . what places the Chinese above all the other nations of the world is that neither their laws, nor manners, nor the language exclusively spoken by their men of learning, have experienced any change in the course of about four thousand years. Yet this nation and that of India, the most ancient of all that are now subsisting, those which possess the largest and most fertile tracts of territory, those which had invented nearly all the arts almost before we were in possession of any of them, have been always omitted, down to our time, in our pretended universal histories.[145]

He also believed in the psychic unity of mankind.

. . . whatever concerns human nature is the same from one end of the universe to the other, and . . . what is dependent upon custom differs, or, if there is any resemblance, it is the effect of chance. The dominion of custom is much more extensive than that of nature, and influences all manners and all usages. It diffuses variety over the face of the universe. Nature establishes unity, and everywhere settles a few invariable principles; the soil is still the same, but culture produces various fruits.[146]

It is true that varying customs make us attach the idea of justice to different things. What is a crime in Europe will be a virtue in Asia, just as German dishes do not please French palates: but God has so made Germans and French that they both like good living. All societies, then, will not have the same laws, but no society will be without laws.[147]

year in which the brutal sovereign of a barbarous people was succeeded by a prince unworthy of historical notice."[134]

And of the *Siècle de Louis XIV* (1751)[135]: "It is not only the life of Louis XIV that we propose to write; we have a greater object in view. We mean to set before posterity not only the portrait of one man's actions but that of the spirit of mankind in general, in the most enlightened of all ages."[136]

* "Opinion has made laws."[139]

† However, he later wrote against geographic determinism.[143]

In fact, all men are subject to natural law.

There is evidently a grand mathematical principle **directing** all nature, and affecting every thing produced.[148]

In the multitude of revolutions which we have seen from one end of the universe to the other, there seems to have been a fated chain of causes by which mankind have been carried away, as the waves and sands are driven by the wind.[149]

[Like Hobbes, he opposed the freedom of the will.] In what then consists your liberty, if not in the power that your body has acquired of performing that which from absolute necessity your will requires? . . . you necessarily will the ideas only which are presented to you. . . . Your will is not free, but your actions are. You are free to act when you have the power of acting.[150]

The entire cosmos consists of a series of interrelated causes and effects.

We come now to one of the most striking examples of those turns of fortune, which are in fact no other than the necessary concatenation of all events in the world.[151]

However, in any given phenomenon only a limited number of previous events are influential in its production.

Present events . . . are not the offspring of all past events, they have their direct lines, but with a thousand small collateral lines they have nothing to do.[152]

The cause of every event is contained in some precedent event; this no philosopher has ever called in question. If Caesar's mother had never gone through the Caesarian operation, Caesar had never subverted the commonwealth; he could never have adopted Octavius, and Octavius could never have chosen Tiberius for his successor in the empire. The marriage of Maximilian with the heiress of Burgundy and the Low Countries, gave rise to a war which lasted two hundred years. But Caesar's spitting on the right or left side, or the Duchess of Burgundy's dressing her head in this manner or in that, could have halted nothing in the general plan of providence.

It follows, therefore, that there are some events which have consequences and others which has none. Their chain resembles a geneological tree, same branches of which disappear at the first generation, whilst the race is continued by others. There are many events which pass away without ever generating others.[153]

The likelihood of subverting these natural laws is diminished by the irrationality of social phenomena.

. . . laws have proceeded, in almost every state, from the interest of the legislator, from the urgency of the moment, from ignorance, and from superstition, and have accordingly been made at random, and irregularly, just in the same manner in which cities have been built.[154]

He follows Bolingbroke's conception of the function of history.

What would constitute useful history? That which should teach us our duties and our rights, without appearing to teach them.[155]

Charles XII, King of Sweden . . . and his rival, Peter Alexiowitz, by far the greater man of the two, are universally admitted to be the most illustrious persons who have appeared for upwards of twenty centuries. The trifling pleasure, however, of relating extraordinary events was not our only motive for engaging in this work; we flattered ourselves that it might be of some little use to princes, should it ever happen to fall into their hands. No king, surely, can be so incorrigible as, when he reads the "History of Charles XII.," not to be cured of the vain ambition of making conquests.[156]

The history of a prince, in our opinion, is not to relate every thing he did, but only what he did worthy of being transmitted to posterity.[157]

He was skeptical of historical reconstructions of the culture of early man.

All the origins of nations are evidently fables. The reason is that men must have lived long in society, and have learned to make bread and clothing (which would be matters of some difficulty) before they acquired the art of transmitting all their thoughts to posterity (a matter of greater difficulty still). . . .

The history, therefore, of preceding periods, could be transmitted by memory alone; and we well know how the memory of past events changes from one generation to another. The first histories were written only from the imagination. Not only did every people invent its own origin, but it invented also the origin of the whole world.[158]

Thus reason is insulted in our universal histories, and the little knowledge we might have of antiquity stifled under a heap of overstrained conjectures.[159]

Nevertheless, he tried his hand at reconstructions. He was opposed to the idea that the earliest man lived in isolation and without a family,[160] and he indulged in conjectures about the social organization[161] and language[162] of early man. As to religion, it originated in fear of the unknown.

Astonishing effects of nature were beheld—harvest and barrenness, fair weather and storms, benefits and scourges; and the hand of a master was felt.[163]

Last, Voltaire had a dynamic conception of culture.

Nature everywhere presents evidence of these remarkable revolutions; and if stars have been lost in the immensity of space, if the seventh of the Pleiades has long since disappeared, if others have vanished from sight into the milky way, should we be surprised that this little globe of ours also undergoes perpetual changes?[164]

We say of a man, that he was brave at such a time; in like manner we should say in speaking of a nation, they were of this or that character in such a year, and under such a government.[165]

## Schiller

Johann Christoph Friedrich von Schiller (1759–1805) was a cultural evolutionist.

The discoveries that have been made by European navigators upon distant oceans and along distant coasts, afford us a spectacle as instructive as it is entertaining. They show us tribes occupying the most varied degrees of culture, as children of various ages are grouped around a full-grown man, and remind him by their example of what he has been and from what point he has started on his course. A wise hand seems to have reserved these rude tribes for a period when we would have become sufficiently advanced in civilization to make a useful application of this discovery to ourselves, and to restore the lost beginnings of our race by the reflections of this mirror. How humiliating and gloomy is the image which these tribes present to us of our infancy! and yet it is not the first degree where we see them. At the beginning, man was a much lower creature. These tribes already constitute political bodies, peoples; it is only by extraordinary exertions that man was enabled to form a political society. . . .

This is what we were. Eighteen hundred years ago Caesar and Tacitus found us not much better.[166]

[The function of history is] showing the workings of the delicate mechanism by which the quiet hand of Nature has developed man's powers from the commencement of the world, according to an immutable design, and . . . indicating the progressive evolutions of this great design in every age.[167]

All the preceding ages have unconsciously and unintentionally endeavoured to prepare the advent of our humane century.[168]

These mechanisms operate universally, according to the principle of the uniformity of nature.

. . . the uniformity and immutable oneness of the laws of nature and of the human mind, in consequence of which oneness the events of the remotest antiquity recur in our age, if similar circumstances act as determining causes.[169]

The goal of society is a moral state, which is achieved by means of the arts.

. . . three different moments or stages of development can be distinguished, which the individual man, as well as the whole race, must of necessity traverse in a determinate order if they are to fulfil the circle of their determination. No doubt, the separate periods can be lengthened or shortened, through accidental causes which are inherent either in the influence of external things or under the free caprice of men; but neither of them can be overstepped, and the order of their sequence cannot be inverted either by nature or by the will. Man, in his *physical* condition, suffers only the power of nature; he gets rid of this power in the *aesthetical* condition, and he rules them in the *moral* state.*[172]

The dynamic [or physical] state can only make society simply possible by subduing nature through nature; the moral (ethical) state can only make it morally necessary by submitting the will of the individual to the general will. The aesthetic state alone can make it real, because it carries out the will of all through the nature of the individual. If necessity alone forces man to enter into society, and if his reason engraves on his soul social principles, it is beauty only that can give him a social *character;* taste alone brings harmony into society, because it creates harmony in the individual. All other forms of perception divide the man, because they are based exclusively either in the sensuous or in the spiritual part of his being. It is only the perception of beauty that makes of him an entirety, because it demands the co-operation of his two natures. All other forms of communication divide society, because they apply exclusively either to the receptivity or to the private activity of its members, and therefore to what distinguishes men one from the other. The aesthetic communication alone unites society, because it applies to what is common to all its members.[173]

## PHYSICAL INTERPRETATIONS

The eighteenth century saw the beginning of a tendency to employ physical

* "But perhaps there is a vicious circle in our previous reasoning? Theoretical culture must it seems bring along with it practical culture, and yet the latter must be the condition of the former. All improvement in the political sphere must proceed from the ennobling of the character. But, subject to the influence of a social constitution still barbarous, how can character become ennobled? It would then be necessary to seek for this end an instrument that the state does not furnish, and to open sources that would have preserved themselves pure in the midst of political corruption.

"I have now reached the point to which all the considerations tended that have engaged me up to the present time. This instrument is the art of the beautiful; these sources are open to us in its immortal models."[170]

"[For example:] Convinced by my preceding letters, you agree with me on this point, that man can depart from his destination by two opposite roads, that our epoch is actually moving on these two false roads, and that it has become the prey, in one case, of coarseness, and elsewhere of exhaustion and depravity. It is the beautiful that must bring it back from this twofold departure."[171]

and mathematical approaches toward social phenomena. Students of the young social sciences could not help contrasting their puny results with the elaborate body of generalizations that constituted the latter sciences and sometimes came to the conclusion that the best way to hasten the development of their own fields was to take over wholesale the methods and techniques of those more advanced. Berkeley and Boscovich were the eighteenth century forerunners of the mathematical economists, the mathematical sociologists, and historians like Henry Adams.

## Berkeley

George Berkeley (1685–1753) developed a mechanical theory of society.

If we consider the whole scope of the creation that lies within our view, the moral and intellectual, as well as the natural and corporeal, we shall perceive throughout a certain correspondence of the parts, a similitude of operation and unity of design, which plainly demonstrate the universe to be the work of one infinitely good and wise Being; and that the system of thinking beings is actuated by laws derived from the same divine power which ordained those by which the corporeal system is upheld.

From the contemplation of the order, motion, and cohesion of natural bodies, philosophers are now agreed that there is a mutual attraction between the most distant parts at least of this solar system. All these bodies that revolve round the sun are drawn towards each other, and towards the sun, by some secret, uniform and never-ceasing principle. Hence it is that the earth (as well as the other planets) without flying off in a tangent line, constantly rolls about the sun, and the moon about the earth, without deserting her companion in so many thousand years. And as the larger systems of the universe are held together by this cause, so likewise the particular globes derive their cohesion and consistence from it.

Now, if we carry our thoughts from the corporeal to the moral world, we may observe in the Spirits or Minds of men a like principle of attraction, whereby they are drawn together in communities, clubs, families, friendships, and all the various species of society. As in bodies, where the quantity is the same, the attraction is strongest between those which are placed nearest to each other, so it is likewise in the minds of men, *caeteris paribus*, between those which are most nearly related. Bodies that are placed at the distance of many million of miles may nevertheless attract and constantly operate on each other, although this action do not shew itself by an union or approach of those distant bodies, so long as they are withheld by the contrary forces of other bodies, which, at the same time, attract them different ways, but would, on the supposed removal of all other bodies, mutually approach and unite with each other. The like holds with regard to the human soul, whose affection towards the individuals of the same species who are distantly related to it is rendered inconspicuous by its more powerful attraction towards those who have a nearer relation to it. But as those are removed the tendency which before lay concealed doth gradually disclose itself.

A man who has no family is more strongly attracted towards his friends and neighbours; and, if absent from these, he naturally falls into an acquaintance with those of his own city or country who chance to be in the same place. Two Englishmen meeting at Rome or Constantinople soon run into a familiarity. And in China or Japan Europeans would think their being so a good reason for their uniting in particular converse. Farther, in case we supposed ourself translated into Jupiter or Saturn, and there to meet a Chinese or other more distant native of our own planet, we should look on him as a near relaon, and readily commence a friendship with him. These are natural reflexions, and such as may convince us that we are linked by an imperceptible chain to every individual of the human race.

The several great bodies which compose the solar system are kept from joining together at the common centre of gravity by the rectilinear motions the Author of nature has impressed on each of them; which, concurring with the attractive principle, form their respective orbits round the sun: upon the ceasing of which motions, the general law of gravitation that is now thwarted would shew itself by drawing them all into one mass. After the same manner, in the parallel case of society, private passions and motions of the soul do often obstruct the operation of that benevolent uniting instinct implanted in human nature; which, notwithstanding, doth still exert, and will not fail to shew itself when those obstructions are taken away.

The mutual gravitation of bodies cannot be explained any other way than by resolving it into the immediate operation of God, who never ceases to dispose and actuate his creatures in a manner suitable to their respective beings. So neither can that reciprocal attraction in the minds of men be accounted for by any other cause. It is not the result of education, law, or fashion; but is a principle originally ingrafted in the very first formation of the soul by the Author of our nature.

And as the attractive power in bodies is the most universal principle which produceth innumerable effects, and is a key to explain the various phenomena of nature; so the corresponding social appetite in human souls is the great spring and source of moral actions. This it is that inclines each individual to an intercourse with his species, and models every one to that behaviour which best suits with the common well-being. Hence that sympathy in our nature whereby we feel the pains and joys of our fellow creatures. Hence that prevalent love in parents towards their children, which is neither founded on the merit of the object, nor yet on self-interest. It is this that makes us inquisitive concerning the affairs of distant nations which can have no influence on our own. It is this that extends our care to future generations, and excites us to acts of beneficence towards those who are not yet in being, and consequently from whom we can expect no recompense. In a word, hence rises that diffusive sense of Humanity so unaccountable to the selfish man who is untouched with it, and is, indeed, a sort of monster or anomalous production.[174]

He repeatedly insisted upon the sociality of animals, including man.

Do you not . . . observe a natural union and consent between animals of the same kind; and that even different kinds of animals have certain qualities and instincts whereby they contribute to the exercise, nourishment, and delight of each other?[175]

Should it not therefore seem to follow, that reasonable creatures were, as the philosophical Emperor [i.e., Marcus Aurelius] observes, made for one another?[176]

That men have certain instinctive sensations or passions from nature, which makes them amiable and useful to each other, I am clearly convinced. Such are a fellow-feeling with the distressed, a tenderness for our offspring, an affection towards our friends, our neighbours, and our country, an indignation against things base, cruel, or unjust. These passions are implanted in the human soul, with several other fears and appetites, aversions and desires, some of which are strongest and uppermost in one mind, others in another.[177]

However, unlike many of his contemporaries, he did not believe in the existence of an instinctive "moral sense."

May not this be sufficiently accounted for by conscience, affection, passion, education, reason, custom, religion; which principles and habits, for aught I know, may be what you metaphorically call a moral sense?[178]

Berkeley was an advocate of social progress.

I have long observed that there is a gradual progress in human affairs. The first care of mankind is to supply the cravings of nature; in the next place they study the conveniences and comforts of life. But the subduing prejudices, and acquiring knowledge that Herculean labour, is the last; being what demands the most perfect abilities, and to which all other advantages are preparative.[179]

## Beccaria

Cesare Bonesana, Marchesi de Beccaria (1735?–94), argued that laws of nature applied to man result only in a statistical regularity.

In political arithmetic the calculations of probabilites must be substituted for mathematical exactness.[180]

It is impossible to reduce the turbulent activity of men to a geometric harmony without any irregularity or confusion. As the constant and most simple laws of nature do not prevent aberrations in the movements of the planets, so, in the infinite and contradictory attractions of pleasure and pain, disturbances and disorder cannot be prevented by human laws.[181]

Cultural disorganization is a result of social disintegration.

The larger society grows, the smaller fraction of the whole does each member of it become, and the more is the feeling of the commonwealth diminished, unless care be taken by the laws to reinforce it. Societies, like human bodies, have their circumscribed limits, extension beyond which involves inevitably a disturbance of their economy.[182]

It is impossible to prevent all the disorders that may arise in the universal conflict of human passions. Their increase depends on that of population and on the crossing of private interests, which cannot be directed with geometrical exactness to the public welfare. In political arithmetic the calculation of probabilities must be substituted for mathematical exactness. Glance at the history of the world, and you will see disorder increase with the increase of the bounds of empire; thus national feeling being to the same extent diminished, the general inducement to crime increases with the greater interest of each individual in such disorders, and on this account the necessity for aggravating penalties ever continues to increase.[183]

Beccaria made a few observations on the evolution of culture.

The multiplication of the human race, slight in the abstract, but far in excess of the means afforded by nature, barren and deserted as it originally was, for the satisfaction of men's ever increasing wants, caused the first savages to associate together. The first unions necesarily led to others to oppose them, and so the state of war passed from individuals to nations.

Laws are the conditions under which men, leading independent and isolated lives, joined together in society, when tired of living in a perpetual state of war, and enjoying a liberty which the uncertainty of its tenure rendered useless. Of this liberty they voluntarily sacrificed a part, in order to enjoy the remainder in security and quiet.[184]

We shall see, if we open histories, that laws . . . have generally been nothing but the instrument of the passions of some few men, or the result of some accidental and temporary necessity.[185]

. . . in proportion as men's minds become softened in the social state, their sensibility increases.[186]

. . . moral sentiments, [are] the product only of many ages and of much bloodshed, the slowest and most difficult attainment of the human mind.[187]

## CULTURAL INTERPRETATIONS

### Moyle

Walter Moyle (1672–1721) gave a cultural explanaton of the rise and fall of Rome.

[Part 1.] I have attempted to take a short Survey of the Civil and Ecclesiastical Constitution of the *Roman* Commonwealth, together with the various Changes and Revolutions of their Government, deduc'd from their true and natural Causes, down to the last great Reformation of their Government, and the Foundation of a more equal Commonwealth.[188]

. . . the Rise and Progress of the *Roman* Greatness were wholly owing to the mighty Confluence of People from all Parts of the World.[189]

These Periods and Revolutions of Empires are the natural Transmigrations of Dominion, from one Form of Government to another; and make the common Circle in the Generation and Corruption of all States. The Succession of these Changes POLYBIUS knew from Experience, but not from their true natural Causes: for he plainly derives these Alterations from moral Reasons; such as Vices and Corruptions, the Oppression and Tyranny of their Governors, which made the People impatient of the Yoke, and fond of new Forms; and not from the Change of the only true Ground and Foundation of Power, *Property.* To confute this great Man, I only appeal to the Examples of the famous Monarchies of *Rome* (under the Emperors) and of *Turkey;* which being founded on the Ballance of Land, after so many Successions of effeminate and tyrannical Princes, stood firm; and the People, provok'd often by their Oppressions, rebell'g against the Monarch, but never against the Monarchy: for while the Root of Power continues, the Government will last, tho the Branches are lopp'd off. But the first *Roman* Empire not being founded on the steddy Ballance, the People, who were in possession of it, wanted nothing but Oppression to make them exert their Power, and nothing but a Tyrant to set them free.

Thus it appears that Land is the true Center of Power, and that the Ballance of Dominion changes with the Balance of Property*; as the Needle in the Compass shifts its Point just as the great Magnet in the Earth changes its Place. This is an eternal Truth and confirm'd by the Experience of all Ages and Governments; and so fully demonstrated by the Great HARRINGTON in his *OCEANA,* that 'tis as difficult to find out new Arguments for it, as to resist the Cogency of the old.[191]

[Part 2.] The Subject of this following Part is the Declension and Decay of the *Roman* Government.[192]

The Reasons of the Corruption and Ruin of the *Roman* Commonwealth, may be reduc'd to these general Heads.

The negligent Execution of the Laws and Orders on which the Popular Government was founded.†

---

* " . . . that eternal Principle, that *Equality of Possession, makes Equality of Power.*"[190]

† "The ill Execution of the Laws and Orders on which the Popular Government was founded, proceeded from these two causes.

"Z. That the Government was not often enough reduced to its first Principles.

Some original Defects in the first Constitution of the Government.*

And lastly, to some succeeding Laws and Institutions in favour of an Aristocratical Government, or of an absolute Monarchy.[195]

## Melon

Jean François Melon (1675–1738) had a cultural interpretation of social evolution and progress.

Societies are removed from the Condition of Savages, only in Proportion to the Greater, and the more general Conveniencies they procure to themselves.[196]

According to the Progress of Arts, Men, at first, tilled the Ground by the Strength of their Arms alone, and afterwards, by the Help of Instruments, which, in the Beginning, afforded small Assistance; but Experience rendered them, by Degrees, much more useful. This Progress of Industry, hath no Bounds.[197]

He believed in the psychic unity of mankind.

We have all of us, the Seeds of the same Passions, in us; Education alone varieth their Effects.[198]

He appreciated the interdependence of the parts of culture.

There is such an intimate Connexion between the Parts of Society, that one of them cannot be hurt, without offending the others.[199]

Melon was one of the first to speak of the professional criminal.

The Trade of a Beggar, a School of Thievery, to which there is only wanting Letters of Licence, encreaseth, and is perpetuated by Father to Son, almost by Hereditary Right; For the Son, really succeededth the Father, in Stations, remarkable for a plentiful Harvest of Alms.[200]

## Law

John Law (1671–1729) gave the usual description of the evolution of money.[201] More interesting is his cultural interpretation of social phenomena.

If want of Honesty and Laziness were Natural, they would be so to Mankind; or if peculiar to a People, this would be so to the *Dutch* rather than to us: The Air of *Holland* is grosser which inclines to Laziness; and the Country not producing wherewith to maintain the Inhabitants, would force them to Rob or Cheat their Neighbours, or one another. But it is more Reasonable to think Laziness and want of Honesty are Vices, the consequences of Poverty; and Poverty the consequence of a faulty Administration.[202]

---

"2. From the alteration of their way of living. Cicero, and from him Macchiavel, and other modern Writers of Politicks, lay down for a certain Maxim, That Commonwealths cannot subsist, unless they are frequently renew'd by their Magistrates, either by reviving the Reverence and Terror of the Laws, or by restoring the antient Virtue and Discipline, or by a thorow reformation of those Corruptions and Disorders, which length of Time, a loose Administration, and the depravity of human Nature will introduce into the soundest and firmest Constitutions of Government."[193]

* " . . as all natural Bodies are born with Seeds of Dissolution in their own Frame, so these great artificial Bodies, Commonwealths, are founded with . . such original Flaws in their first Constitution, as, in some Periods of time, corrupt and dissolve them . . . the most considerable of which were [in Rome], The making the Monarchy elective; allowing such a Share of Property to the Commons; increasing the number of People by naturalizing all Foreigners, and trusting Arms in their hands."[194]

## Harris

Joseph Harris (1702–64) stated that social differentiation is a factor in increasing social integration.

Men are endued with various talents and propensities, which naturally dispose and fit them for different occupations; and are . . . under a necessity of betaking themselves to particular arts and employments, from their inability of otherwise acquiring all the necessaries they want, with ease and comfort: This creates a dependance of one men upon another, and naturally unites men into societies.[203]

He also gave a social explanation of cultural phenomena.

Idleness is the bane of society; the great source of vice and confusion; the fore-runner of public distress and calamity. Industry produces the contrary effects.[204]

Harris had the current conception of the evolution of money.[205]

# VII

# EIGHTEENTH-CENTURY SOCIAL ANTHROPOLOGY:
## THE INSTITUTIONALISTS AND
## THE SCOTCH SCHOOL

### INSTITUTIONALISTS

O N THE BASIS of the interrelations which exist between the various aspects of culture, the institutionslists analyzed the relationships between them.

### Montesquieu

Charles Louis de Secondat, Baron de la Brede et de Montesquieu (1689–1755), was one of the greatest figures in the social science of the eighteenth century. His interest was empirical rather than normative, and he used the comparative method for the discovery of social laws. In the words of Rousseau:

Montesquieu . . . was not concerned with the principles of political law; he was content to deal with the positive laws of settled governments; and nothing could be more different than these two branches of study.[1]

First, he affirmed the existence of social laws.

. . . as men have been sensible of the same passions in all ages, the occasions which give rise to great revolutions, are various, but the causes are for ever the same.[2]

Fortune never interposes in the government of this world . . . There are a set of general causes, either moral or physical, which operate in every monarchy, and either raise and maintain it, or else involve it in ruin. All accidental conjunctures are subordinate to these causes; and if the hazard of a battle, which in other words is no more than a particular cause, has been destructive to a state, some general cause presided and made a single battle be the inevitable ruin of that state. In a word, the tendency of the main principle draws after it all the particular incidents.[3]

I have first considered mankind; and the result of my thoughts has been, that amidst such an infinite diversity of laws and manners, they were not solely conducted by the caprice of fancy.

I have laid down the first principles, and have found that the particular cases follow naturally from them; that the histories of all nations are only consequences of them; and that every particular law is connected with another law, or depends on some other of a more general extent.[4]

De l'esprit des lois is primarily an institutional analysis of law. It begins with an analysis of the nature of law.

Laws, in their most general signification, are the necessary relations arising from the nature of things. In this sense all beings have their laws: the Deity his laws, the material world its laws, and intelligences superior to man their laws, the beasts their laws, man his laws.

They who assert, that *a blind fatality produced the various effects we behold in this world,* talk very absurdly; for, can any thing be more unreasonable than to pretend that a blind fatality could be productive of intelligent beings?

There is, then, a primitive reason; and laws are the relations subsisting between it and different beings, and the relations of these to one another.

God is related to the universe, as Creator and Preserver; the laws by which he created all things, are those by which he preserves them. He acts according to these rules, because he knows them; he knows them, because he made them; and he made them, because they are relative to his wisdom and power.

Since we observe that the world, though formed by the motion of matter, and void of understanding, subsists through so long a succession of ages, its motions must certainly be directed by invariable laws; and could we imagine another world, it must also have constant rules, or it would inevitably perish.

These rules are a fixed and invariable relation. In bodies moved, the motion is received, increased, diminishes, lost, according to the relations of the quantity of matter and velocity; each diversity is *uniformity,* each change is *constancy.*

Particular intelligent beings may have laws of their own making, but they have some likewise which they never made. Before there were intelligent beings, they were possible; they had therefore possible relations, and consequently possible laws. Before laws were made, there were relations of possible justice. To say that there is nothing just or unjust but what is commanded or forbidden by positive laws, is the same as saying, that before the describing of a circle, all the radii were not equal.

We must therefore acknowledge relations of justice antecedent to the positive law by which they are established; as for instance, that if human societies existed, it would be right to conform to their laws; if there were intelligent beings that had received a benefit of another being, they ought to show their gratitude; if one intelligent being had created another intelligent being, the latter ought to continue in its original state of dependence; if one intelligent being injures another, it deserves a retaliation; and so on.

## Montesquieu proceeds to explain his approach.

Law in general is human reason, inasmuch as it governs all the inhabitants of the earth; the political and civil laws of each nation ought to be only the particular cases in which human reason is applied.

They should be adapted in such a manner to the people for whom they are framed, that it is a great chance if those of one nation suit another.

They should be relative to the nature and principle of each government; whether they form it, as may be said of politic laws; or whether they support it, as in the case of civil institutions.

They should be relative to the climate of each country, to the quality of its soil, to its situation and extent, to the principal occupation of the natives, whether husbandmen, huntsmen, or shepherds: they should have a relation to the degree of liberty which the constitution will bear; to the religion of the inhabitants, to their inclinations, riches, numbers, commerce, manners, and customs. In fine, they have relations to each other, as also to their origin, to the intent of the legislator, and to the order of things on which they are established; in all which different lights they ought to be considered.

This is what I have undertaken to perform in the following work. These relations I shall examine, since all these together constitute what I call the *Spirit of Laws.*

I have not separated the political from the civil institutions: for as I do not pretend to treat of laws, but of their spirit; and as this spirit consists in the various relations which the laws may have to different objects, it is not so much my business to follow the natural order of laws, as that of these relations and objects.[8]

Then follows his institutional investigation.

[1. The relations between law and government[9]]

[2a.] Of Laws in the Relation they bear to a Defensive Force.[10]

[2b.] Of Laws in the Relation they bear to Offensive Force.[11]

[3a.] Of the Laws which establish Political Liberty, with regard to the Constitution.[12]

[3b.] Of the Laws that form Political Liberty, as Relative to the Subject.[13]

But the intelligent world is far from being so well governed as the physical. For though the former has also its laws, which of their own nature are invariable, it does not conform to them so exactly as the physical world. This is, because, on the one hand, particular intelligent beings are of a finite nature, and consequently liable to error; and on the other, their nature requires them to be free agents. Hence they do not steadily conform to their primitive laws; and even those of their own instituting they frequently infringe.

Whether brutes be governed by the general laws of motion, or by a particular movement, we can not determine. Be that as it may, they have not a more intimate relation to God than the rest of the material world; and sensation is of no other use to them, than in the relation they have either to other particular beings or to themselves.

By the allurement of pleasure they preserve the individual, and by the same allurement they preserve their species. They have natural laws, because they are united by sensation; positive laws they have none, because they are not connected by knowledge. And yet they do not invariably conform to their natural laws; these are better observed by vegetables, that have neither understanding nor sense. . . .

Man, as a physical being, is like other bodies, governed by invariable laws. As an intelligent being, he incessantly transgresses the laws established by God, and changes those of his own instituting. He is left to his private direction, though a limited being, and subject, like all finite intelligencies, to ignorance and error: even his imperfect knowledge he loses; and as a sensible creature, he is hurried away by a thousand impetuous passions. Such a being might every instant forget his Creator; God has therefore reminded him of his duty by the laws of religion. Such a being is liable every moment to forget himself; philosophy has provided against this by the laws of morality. Formed to live in society, he might forget his fellow-creatures; legislators have therefore by political and civil laws confined him to his duty.[5]

Antecedent to the above-mentioned laws are those of nature, so called, because they derive their force entirely from our frame and existence. In order to have a perfect knowledge of these laws, we must consider man before the establishment of society: the laws received in such a state would be those of nature.

The law which impressing on our minds the idea of a Creator inclines us towards him, is the first in importance, though not in order, of natural laws. Man in a state of nature would have the faculty of knowing, before he had acquired any knowledge. Plain it is that his first ideas would not be of a speculative nature; he would think of the preservation of his being, before he would investigate its original. Such a man would feel nothing in himself at first but impotency and weakness; his fears and apprehensions would be excessive; as appears from instances (were there any necessity of proving it) of savages found in forests, trembling at the motion of a leaf, and flying from every shadow.

In this state every man, instead of being sensible of his equality, would fancy himself inferior. There would therefore be no danger of their attacking one another; peace would be the first law of nature. . . .

Next to a sense of his weakness man would soon find that of his wants. Hence another law of nature would prompt him to seek for nourishment.

Fear, I have observed, would induce men to shun one another; but the marks of this fear being reciprocal, would soon engage them to associate. Besides, this association would quickly follow from the very pleasure one animal feels at the approach of another of the same species. Again, the attraction arising from the difference of sexes would enhance this pleasure; and the natural inclination they have for each other, would form a third law.

Besides the sense or instinct which man possesses in common with brutes, he has the advantage of acquiring knowledge; and thence arises a second tie, which brutes have not. Mankind have therefore a new motive of uniting; and a fourth law of nature results from the desire of living in society.[6]

As soon as mankind enter into a state of society they lose their sense of their weakness; equality ceases, and then commences the state of war.

Each particular society begins to feel its strength, whence arises a state of war betwixt different nations. The individuals likewise of each society become sensible of their force; hence the principal advantages of this society they endeavour to convert to their own emolument, which constitutes a state of war betwixt individuals.

These two different kinds of states give rise to human laws. Considered as inhabitants of so great a planet, which necessarily contains a variety of nations, they have laws relative to their mutual intercourse, which is what we call the *law of nations*. As members of a society that must be properly supported, they have laws relative to the governors and the governed, and this we distinguish by the name of *politic law*. They have also another sort of laws, as they stand in relation to each other; by which is understood the *civil law*.[7]

After this analysis of the origin and nature of law,

[4.] Of the Relation which the Levying of Taxes and the greatness of the Public Revenues have to Liberty.[14]

[5.] Of Laws as Relative to the Nature of the Climate.[15]

A cold air constringes the extremities of the external fibres of the body; this increases their elasticity, and favours the return of the blood from the extreme parts to the heart. It contracts those very fibres; consequently it increases also their force. On the contrary a warm air relaxes and lengthens the extremes of the fibres; of course it diminishes their force and elasticity.

People are therefore more vigorous in cold climates. Here the action of the heart and the reaction of the extremities of the fibres are better performed, the temperature of the humours is greater, the blood moves freer towards the heart, and reciprocally the heart has more power. This superiority of strength must produce various effects; for instance, a greater boldness, that is, more courage; a greater sense of superiority, that is, less desire of revenge; a greater opinion of security, that is, more frankness, less suspicion, policy and cunning. In short, this must be productive of very different tempers. . . . The inhabitants of warm countries are, like old men, timorous; the people in cold countries are, like young men, brave. . . .

In cold countries, they have very little sensibility for pleasure; in temperate countries, they have more; in warm countries, their sensibility is exquisite. As climates are distinguished by degrees of latitude, we might distinguish them also in some measure, by those of sensibility. . . .

It is the same with regard to pain; which is excited by the laceration of some fibre of the body. The author of nature has made it an established rule that this pain should be more acute in proportion as the laceration is greater: now it is evident that the large bodies and coarse fibres of the people of the north, are less capable of laceration than the delicate fibres of the inhabitants of warm countries; consequently the soul is there less sensible of pain. You must flay a Muscovite alive to make him feel.

From this delicacy of organs peculiar to warm climates, it follows, that the soul is most sensibly moved by whatever relates to the union of the two sexes: here every thing leads to this object.

In nothern climates scarce has the animal part of love a power of making itself felt. In temperate climates, love attended by a thousand appendages, endeavours to please by things that have at first the appearance, though not the reality of this passion. In warmer climates it is liked for its own sake; it is the only cause of happiness; it is life itself.

In southern countries a machine of delicate frame, but strong sensibility, resigns itself either to a love which rises and is incessantly laid in a seraglio, or to a passion which leaves women in a greater independence, and is consequently exposed to a thousand inquietudes. In northern regions a machine robust and heavy, finds a pleasure in whatever is apt to throw the spirits into motion, such as hunting, travelling, war, and wine. If we travel towards the north, we meet with people who have few vices, many virtues, and a great share of frankness and sincerity. If we draw near the south, we fancy ourselves entirely removed from the verge of morality; here the strongest passions are productive of all manner of crimes, each man endeavouring, let the means be what they will, to indulge his inordinate desires. In temperate climates we find the inhabitants inconstant in their manners, as well as in their vices and virtues: the climate has not a quality determinate enough to fix them.

The heat of the climate may be so excessive as to deprive the body of all vigour and strength. Then the faintness is communicated to the mind; there is no curiosity, no enterprize, no generosity of sentiment; the inclinations are all passive; indolence constitutes the utmost happiness; scarcely any punishment is so severe as mental employment; and slavery is more supportable than the force and vigour of mind necessary for human conduct.[16]

It is the variety of wants in different climates, that first occasions a difference in the manner of living, and this gave rise to a variety of laws. Where people are very communicative, there must be particular laws; and others where there is but little communication.[17]

[6.] Of Laws in the Relation they bear to the Nature of the Soil.[18]

The goodness of the land, in any country, naturally establishes subjection and dependence. The husbandmen, who compose the principle part of the people, are not very jealous of their liberty; they are too busy and too intent on their own private affairs. A country which overflows with wealth is afraid of pillage, afraid of any army. . . .

Thus, monarchy is more frequently found in fruitful countries, and a republican government in those which are not so.[19]

The barrenness of the earth renders men industrious, sober, inured to hardship, courageous, and fit for war; they are obliged to procure by labour what the earth refuses to bestow spontaneously. The fertility of a country gives ease, effeminacy, and a certain fondness for the preservation of life.[20]

[6a. Relations between law and the means of subsistence.]

The laws have a very great relation to the manner in which the several nations procure their subsistence. There should be a code of laws of a much larger extent for a nation attached to trade and navigation, than for a people who are content with cultivating the earth. There should be a much greater for the latter, than for those who subsist by their flocks and herds. There must be a still greater for these, than for such as live by hunting.[21]

Let us see in what proportion countries are peopled, where the inhabitants do not cultivate the earth. As the produce of uncultivated land, is to that of land improved by culture; so the number of savages in one country, is to that of husbandmen in another: and when the people who cultivate the land, cultivate also the arts, this is also in such proportion as would require a minute detail.

They can scarcely form a great nation. If they are herdsmen and shepherds, they have need of an extensive country to furnish subsistence for a small number; if they live by hunting, their number must be still less, and in order to find the means of life, they must constitute a very small nation.

Their country commonly abounds with forests; which, as the inhabitants have not the art of draining off the waters, are filled with bogs; here each troop canton themselves, and form a petty nation.[22]

There is this difference between savage and barbarous nations: the former are dispersed clans, which, for some particular reason, cannot be joined in a body; and the latter are commonly small nations, capable of being united. The savages are generally hunters; the barbarians are herdsmen and shepherds.[23]

[7.] Of Laws in Relation to the Principles which form the general Spirit, the Morals and Customs of a Nation.[24]

Mankind are influenced by various causes, by the climate, by the religion, by the laws, by the maxims of government, by precedents, morals, and customs*; from whence is formed a general spirit of nations.

In proportion as, in every country, any one of these causes acts with more force, the others in the same degree are weakened. Nature and the climate rule almost alone over the savages; customs govern the Chinese; the laws tyrannize in Japan; morals had formerly all their influence at Sparta; maxims of government, and the ancient simplicity of manners, once prevailed at Rome.[26]

. . . in all countries and governments morality is requisite.[27]

Nations are in general very tenacious of their customs.[28]

In the infancy of societies, the leading men in the republic form the constitution; afterwards, the constitution forms the leading men in the republic.[29]

Man, that flexible being, conforming in society to the thoughts and impressions of others.[30]

Self-love, and a fondness for our preservation, changes itself into so many shapes, and acts by so many contrary principles, that it leads us to sacrifice our existence for the very sake of existence; and such is the estimate we make of ourselves, that we consent to die by a natural and obscure sort of instinct, which makes us love ourselves even more than our lives.[31]

[8.] Of Laws in Relation to Commerce.[32]

Commerce is a cure for the most destructive prejudices; for it is almost a general rule,

* "I do not deny that the climate may have produced great part of the laws, manners, and customs of this nation: but I maintain that its manners and customs have a close connexion with its laws."[25]

that wherever we find agreeable manners, there commerce flourishes: and that whereve
there is commerce, there we meet with agreeable manners.

. . . Commerce has every where diffused a knowledge of the manners of all nations
these are compared one with another, and from this comparison arise the greatest ad
vantages.

Commercial laws, it may be said, improve manners for the same reason as they destro
them. They corrupt the purest morals; this was the subject of Plato's complaints; and w
every day see, that they polish and refine the most barbarous.[33]

[9.] Of Laws in Relation to the Use of Money.[34]

. . . it is impossible but wealth must give power.[35]

[10.] Of Laws in the Relation they bear to the Number of Inhabitants.[36]

[11.] Of Laws as Relative to Religion.[37]

Like many of his contemporaries, Montesquieu was fascinated by the problem
of the rise and fall of Rome. He attributed this to a number of factors, of which
the following are of particular interest to anthropologists.

. . . the circumstance which chiefly raised the Romans to the sovereignty of the world
was, their laying aside their own customs as soon as they met with better among the
people they conquered; and it is well known that they fought successively against al
nations.[38]

If the unbounded extent of the Roman empire proved the ruin of the republic, th
vast compass of the city was no less fatal to it.[39]

Authors enlarge very copiously on the divisions which proved the destruction o
Rome; but their readers seldom discover those divisions to have been always necessar
and inevitable. The grandeur of the republic was the only source of that calamity, an
exasperated popular tumults into civil wars.[40]

When virtue is banished, ambition invades the minds of those who are disposed t
receive it, and avarice possesses the whole community. The objects of their desire
are changed; what they were fond of before, is become indifferent; they were free, whil
under the restraint of laws, but they would fain now be free to act against law; and as eac
citizen is like a slave who has run away from his master, what was a maxim of equity
he calls rigour; what was a rule of action, he styles constraint; and to precaution, h
gives the name of fear. Frugality, and not the thirst of gain, now passes for avarice
Formerly the wealth of individuals constituted the public treasure; but now this i
become the patrimony of private persons. The members of the commonwealth ric
on the public spoils, and its strength is only the power of a few, and the licentiousnes
of many.[41]

### Falconer

William Falconer (1744–1824) was a follower of Montesquieu.

Vegetable productions, separately considered, appear to be limited by nature to
certain climate and situation. . . . The same is true, though with greater latitude, o
the animal kingdom, in which the same general rule prevails as in the vegetable. . .

Man, however, appears to be an exception to this rule, and to be enabled to subsis
in almost every climate and situation. . . .

Nor is man less capable of subsisting on a great variety of aliments. . . . But notwith
standing this assistance afforded by nature, it may be justly doubted if this universalit
of the human species be not owing more to his rational faculties, which enable hir

to supply the defects, and correct the exhuberances of particular climates and situations, than merely his animal formation. . . .

But although man is enabled to subsist, by means of these succours from his rational faculties, he is still liable to be considerably affected, both in body and mind, by external circumstances, such as climate, situation, &c. To enumerate some of these, with their general effects, which relate to or influence the disposition and temper, the manners, intellects, laws and customs, form of government, and religion of mankind, is the purpose of the following pages.[42]

I must beg leave to take notice of a general mistake, which appears to me to have pervaded the works of every writer upon this subject; which is, the making their position too universal.

The Effects of Climate, &c. are all of them general, and not particular; and if a considerable majority of the nations, as well as the individuals, that live under a certain climate, are affected in a certain manner, we may pronounce decisively on its influence, even though there may be some exceptions. It must likewise be taken into consideration, that the influence of one of the above causes often correct the other. Thus a hot climate naturally renders men timid and slothful; but the necessity induced by a barren country, number of inhabitants, animal diet, and a savage way of life, may, any of them, correct this tendency of the climate, and dispose the manners to a different turn.

. . . But the effect of climate, in these instances, is not surpressed, but overpowered; it still exists, but its effect is not discernable: remove the impediment to its action, and it immediately exerts itself . . . The effects of each of the causes here described, when combined together, overpower, temper, and modify one another in many instances; but have each of them a separate existence and action, however they may concur with one another in the general effect.[43]

Less than half of the work is taken up with geographic and related factors, which are considered under the following headings:

Book I. On the Effect of Climate
Book II. On the Influence of Situation and Extent of a Country
Book III. On the Influence of the Nature of the Country itself
Book IV. On the Influence of Population
Book V. On the Influence of the Nature of Food and Diet

Book VI, "On the Influence of Way of Life," constitutes more than half of the book, and is in effect an institutional analysis according to these subheadings:

Chap. I. On the influence of a savage state.
Chap. II. Influence of a barbarous state or way of life upon mankind.
Chap. III. On the effects of agriculture upon mankind.
Chap. IV. On the effects of a commercial life upon mankind.
Chap. V. On the effects of literature and science.
Chap. VI. On the effects of luxury and refinement.

It is thus seen that Falconer's interpretation of culture is what in the nineteenth century would have been termed "materialistic," except for the last two chapters of Book VI.

His description of the stages in cultural evolution may be of some interest.

The progress of civilisation may be divided into several stages; each of which, however, separately, comprehends divers degrees of improvement.[44]

[1.] The first and lowest stage of civilisation, of which I shall speak, is that generally called savage, where the people subsist by hunting or fishing, and on the spontaneous produce of the earth; and are ignorant, at least in general, of the nature of private property, particularly money. Some latitude must, however, be allowed this description, as there is scarce any people to whom it is strictly applicable.[45]

[2.] I now come to the second stage of civilisation, [barbarism]. . . .

This may be supposed to comprehend the period from the invention of property and money, to the general use of agriculture and cultivation of lands. This division, as well as the former, admits of several intermediate stages or degrees. . . . [It is] a state wherein the feeding of cattle is the means of subsistence; and hunting or fishing are not practised with that intention, in a national view at least.[46]

[3.] We must now advance a step farther, and consider the . . . next stage, when men betake themselves to agriculture as a way of life, and general mode of existence.[47]

[4.] The next stage . . . is that of commerce.[48]

## Brown

John Brown (1715–66) made an institutional analysis of the turmoils of the times in order to find remedies for these troubles.

. . . the Writer thought it not amiss to offer his Sentiments on the present State and Situation of his country, at a *Crisis* so important and alarming.[49]

Superficial, though zealous, Observers, think that they see the Source of all our public Miscarriages in the particular and accidental Misconduct of Individuals. This is not much to be wondered at, because it is so easy a Solution. . . .

But a candid and mature Consideration will probably convince us, that the Malady lies deeper than what is commonly suspected: and, on impartial Enquiry, it will probably be found springing, not from varying and incidental, but from permanent and established Causes.[50]

Among all these various Causes, none perhaps so much contributes to raise or sink a Nation, as the Manners and Principles of its People.[51]

[He then analyzes the effect of the English economy upon the other aspects of culture and concludes:] it seems evident, that our present effeminate Manners and Defect of Principle have arisen from our exorbitant Trade and Wealth, left without Check, to their natural Operations and uncontrouled Influence. And that these Manners, and this Defect of Principle, by weakening or destroying the national Capacity, Spirit of Defence, and Union, have produced such a general Debility as naturally leads to Destruction.[52]

Brown opposed the common idea of the natural death of societies and cultures.

The World has been long amused with a trite and hacknied Comparison between the Life of Man, and that of States; in which it is pretended that they both proceed in the same irrevocable Manner; from Infancy to Maturity, from Maturity to Death: A Comparison, perhaps as groundless as it is common. The human Body contains, in its very Texture, the Seeds of certain Dissolution. . . . But in Societies, of whatever Kind, there seems no such necessary or essential Tendency to Dissolution, The human Body is *naturally* mortal; the political, only so by *Accident*. . . . But there appears nothing in the internal Construction of any State, that tends inevitably to Dissolution, analogous to those Causes in the human Frame, which lead to certain Death.[53]

There are two Causes, essentially distinct, though often interwoven, by which a free state may perish. These are, *external* and *internal* Violence: *Invasions* from Abroad, or *Dissentions* at Home: The Rage of foreign *War*, or domestic *Faction*.[54]

... in all *polished States* these [i.e., the fine] Arts have a natural Tendency towards *Corruption,* unless checked and chastised by wholesome Institutions. This Tendency ariseth not from the Nature of the Arts themselves; but from that *Period of Manners,* which tends to pervert them from their *proper Ends.* ...

More particularly, in a great and powerful Kingdom, where additional Degrees of Wealth should flow in with every Tide; these, especially in a Time of Peace, must inevitably be followed by new Degrees of inventive Luxury, and an unwearied Passion for Dissipation and Amusement.[55]

On the basis of the psychic unity of mankind, he showed that personality differences are the reuslt of varying social milieus.

... all Orders of Men being born with an equal Tendency to Virtue or Vice; their adopting the One, or falling into the Other, depends chiefly on the Temptations to which their *Rank* exposes them.[56]

[He then] points out the Circumstances which naturally tend, upon the Whole, to form the several Ranks into ... distinct Characters.[57]

... in the Period of savage Manners, the Power of *abstract Reasoning* is always weak, and is often found to have *no Place.*[58]

Towards the end of his life Brown became interested in the evolution of culture. He published his book on poetry and music and contemplated a "Principles of Christian Legislation," which was to contain "An analysis of the various Religions, Manners, and Polities of Mankind, in their several Gradations."[59]

*A Dissertation on the Rise, Union, and Power, the Progressions, Separations, and Corruptions, of Poetry and Music,* to give it its full title, is an interesting example of the degree of development of the evolutionary approach in the eighteenth century.

The Purpose of the following Dissertation ... is to trace the *Rise, Union,* and *Progression* of *Poetry* and *Music,* as they are found to exist in their several Kinds and Gradations among Mankind; thence to consider the Causes which have produced that *Separation* under which they now lie, and and have often lain, among the more polished Nations; and in Conclusion, to point out the *Circumstances* in which, and the *Means* by which, they may possibly be *again united.*[60]

[The work] is prosecuted ... by deducing things from their state in savage life, through the several stages of civilized society.[61]

Whatever is founded in such *Passions* and *Principles* of Action, as are *common* to the whole *Race* of *Man,* will be most effectually investigated, as to its *Origin* and *Progress,* by viewing Man in his *savage* or *uncultivated* State. Here, before Education and Art have cast their Veil over the human Mind, its various Powers throw themselves out, and all its Workings present themselves instantly, and without Disguise.

It may be affirmed with Truth, that, for Want of beginning our Inquiries at this early and neglected Period, and by viewing Man under his State of *Civilization* only, many curious and interesting Questions have been left involved in Darkness, which might have been clearly unfolded by a free and full Research into the Passions, Propensities, and Qualities of savage Man ... he intends to treat the present Subject in the Way now proposed, by deducing his Argument from the first great and original Fountain of *savage Life* and *Manners.*[62]

By examining savage Life, where untaught Nature rules, we find that the *agreeable*

*Passions* of Love, Pity, Hope, Joy, and Exultation, no less than their *Contraries* of Hate, Revenge, Fear, Sorrow, and Despair, oppressing the human Heart by their mighty Force, are thrown out by the three Powers of *Action, Voice,* and *articulate Sounds.* The *Brute* Creatures express their Passions by the two first of These; some by *Action,* some by *Voice,* and some by *both* united: Beyond these, *Man* has the added Power of *articulate Speech:* The same Force of *Association* and *Fancy* which gives him *higher Degrees* and a *wider Variety* of Passion, gives rise to this *additional Power* of expressing those passions which he feels.

Among the *Savages* who are in the *lowest Scale* of the human Kind, these several Modes of expressing their Passions are found altogether suited to their wretched State. Their *Gestures* are *uncouth* and *horrid:* Their *Voice* is thrown out in *Howls* and *Roarings:* Their *Language* is like the *Gabbling of Geese.*

But if we ascend a Step or two higher in the Scale of savage Life, we shall find this *Chaos* of *Gesture, Voice,* and *Speech,* rising into an agreeable *Order* and *Proportion.* The natural Love of a *measured Melody,* which Time and Experience produce, throws the *Voice* into *Song,* the *Gesture* into *Dance,* the *Speech* into *Verse* or *Numbers.* The Addition of musical *Instruments* comes of Course: They are but *Imitations* of the human Voice, or of other natural Sounds, produced gradually by frequent Trial and Experiment.[63]

While these free and warlike Savages continue in their present *unlettered* State of Ignorance and Simplicity, no material Improvements in their *Song-Feasts* can arise. But let us suppose that the Use of *Letters* should come among them, and, as a Cause or Consequence of *Civilization,* be cultivated with that Spirit which is natural to a free and active People; and many notable Consequences would appear. Let us consider the most probable and striking among these natural Effects.

1. Their Idea of *Music* in its most *inlarged* Sense, would probably comprehend the three united Circumstances of *Melody, Dance,* and *Poem.* . . .

2. In the early Periods of such a Commonwealth, the *Chiefs* or *Legislators* would often be the *principal Bards, Poets,* or *Musicians.* . . .

3. Hence, their most ancient *Gods* would naturally be styled *Singers* and *Dancers.* . . .

4. Measured Periods, or in other Words, *Rythm, Numbers,* and *Verse,* would naturally arise. . . .

5. Their earliest *Histories* would be written in Verse. . . .

6. Their most ancient *Maxims, Exhortations, Proverbs,* or *Laws,* would probably be written in Verse. . . .

7. Their *religious Rites* would naturally be performed or accompany'd by *Dance* and *poetic Song.* . . .

8. Their *earliest Oracles* would probably be delivered in *Verse,* and *sung* by the Priest or Priestess of the supposed God. . . .

9. Their poetic *Songs* would be of a *legislative* Cast; and being drawn chiefly from the Fables or History of their own Country, would contain the most essential Parts of their *religious, moral,* and *political* Systems. . . .

10. MUSIC, in the extended Sense of the Word (that is, including *Melody, Dance,* and *poetic Song*) would make an essential and principal Part in the *Education* of their Children. . . .

11. *Melody, Dance,* and *poetic Song,* therefore, thus *united,* must gain a *great* and *universal* Power over the Minds and Actions of such a People. . . .

12. If their warlike Character continued, the *Dance* would naturally *separate* from the *poetic Song;* and would itself become a *distinct Exercise* or *Art,* for the Sake of increasing their Strength and Agility of Body, as the Means of rendering them invincible in War. . . .

13. After a certain Period of Civilization, the complex Character of *Legislator* and *Bard* would *separate,* or be seldom united. . . .

14. In the Course of Time, and Progress of Polity and Arts, a *Separation* of the several *Kinds* of *poetic Song* would arise. . . .

15. *Hymns* or *Odes* would be composed, and *Sung* by their Composers at their festal Solemnities. . . .

16. The *Epic Poem* would naturally arise, and be sung by its Composers at their public Solemnities. . . .

17. From an *Union* of these two, a certain rude Outline of *Tragedy* would naturally arise. . . .

18. In Process of Time, this barbarous Scene would improve into a more perfect Form: Instead of *relating,* they would probably represent, by Action and Song united, those great or terrible Atchievements which their Heroes had performed. . . .

19. If the *Choir* should be *established* by general Use, and should animate the Solemnity by *Dance* as well as *Song;* the *Melody, Dance,* and *Song* would of Course *regulate* each other, and the *Ode* or *Song* would fall into *Stanzas* of some *particular Kind.* . . .

20. Another Consequence of an *established Choir* would be an unvaried Adherence to the *Unities* of *Place* and *Time.* . . .

21. Not only the Part of the tragic *Choir,* but the *Episode* or *interlocutory* Part would be also *sung.* . . .

22. While the Nation held its *fierce* and *warlike* Character, the *tragic* Representations would chiefly turn on Subjects *distressful* or *terrible.* . . .

23. Their Tragedy being intended as a *visible Representation* of their ancient Gods and Heroes, it would be natural for them to invent some Means of *strengthening* the *Voice,* and *aggrandising* the *Visage* and *Person,* as the Means of compleating the Resemblance. . . .

24. As their Tragic *Poets* would be *Singers,* so they would be *Actors,* and perform some capital Part in their own Pieces for the State. . . .

25. *Musical Contests* would be admitted as *public Exercises* in such a State. . . .

26. The Profession of *Bard* would be held as very honourable, and of high Esteem. . . .

27. *Odes,* or *Hymns,* would naturally make a Part of their *domestic Entertainments:* and the *Chiefs* would be proud to signalize themselves by their Skill in *Melody* and *Poetic Song.* . . .

28. When *Music,* that is, *Melody* and *Poem,* thus *united,* had attained to this State of relative Perfection, it would be regarded as a *necessary Accomplishment.* . . .

29. The Genius of their *Poem* and *Melody,* would *vary* along with their *Manners.* . . .

30. As a Change of *Manners* must influence their *Poem* and *Melody,* so, by a reciprocal Action, a Change in *These* must influence *Manners:* For we have seen, that They were the *established Vehicle* of all the great Principles of Education.

31. A Provident Community, of Principles uncommonly severe, would probably fix both the *Subjects* and *Movements* of *poetic Song* and *Dance,* by *Law.* . . .

32. In a Society of more libertine and relaxed Principles, the Corruption of their *Poem* and *Melody* would naturally arise, along with the Corruption of Manners . . . and the Bards, Poets, or Musicians, would be the immediate Instruments of this Corruption. . . .

32. In Consequence of this Corruption, a gradual and total *Separation* of the *Bard's* complex Character would ensue. For the *Chief* would now no longer pride himself on the Character of *Poet* or Performer; nor the *Man* of *Genius* and *Worth* descend to the Profession of *Lyrist, Singer,* or *Actor.*[64]

The following is Brown's picture of the origin of comedy.

1. "Their casual Strokes of Raillery would improve into written Invectives, which would occasionally be sung by their sarcastic Choirs." . . .

2. "Narrative or Epic Poems of the *invective* or *comic* Kind would likewise arise, and be occasionally sung at their public Festivals." . . .

3. "From these two Species (the *choral* and *narrative* united) the first rude Outline of *Comedy* would arise." . . .

4. " While the salutary Principles of Legislation should prevail, Comedy thus formed, would be little encouraged by the Leaders of the State." . . .

5. "A provident Community, of Principles uncommonly severe, might even banish this Species of Poem, as destructive to their State." . . .

6. "If in a State of more relaxed Principles, where such Comedy had been tolerated, a general Corruption of Manners should take Place among the People; and if by any means, such a corrupt People should overpower the Magistrates, and assume to themselves the Reins of Government; then, this Species of Comedy would rise into Credit, and be publicly established." . . .

7. "The Ridicule and Invective of their Comedy, thus established, would be pointed chiefly against those Magistrates, or private Men, whose Qualities would be hateful to the debauched Populace." . . .

8. "If a *Tyranny* should suddenly erect itself on the Ruins of such a People, it would by its Authority *silence* this Species of Comedy." . . .

9. "The Poets would probably find a Subterfuge, for the Gratification of the People; and continue to represent *real Characters* under *feigned Names*." . . .

10. "If a great Conqueror should arise, and, by subduing a Variety of Nations, should open a Communication between such a State and others of more luxurious and refined Manners, this *second* Species of Comedy would naturally receive a *Polish*; and, instead of the indirect personal Invective, would assume the more delicate Form of general Raillery, and become a Picture of human Life."[65]

In a section "Of the Rise and Progress of the *pastoral* Species", he has the following to say:

. . . the Manners of Savages depend more on the *Barrenness* or *Fertility* of their *Soil*, than on the mere Influences of *Climate, Heat,* or *Cold*. The *Wants* that arise from a barren Soil, and the Methods of *Violence* necessary to relieve them, naturally produce the *ferocious* Character. The spontaneous Productions of a fertile Soil bring an *unsought* Relief to the Wants of it's Inhabitants: hence their Character is naturally *indolent* and *peaceful*.

From the *first* of these *Causes* we have found the natural Origin of the *grand* and *terrible* Kinds of Poetry, among the *mountainous* Districts and *warlike* Tribes of GREECE. From the *second*, we may naturally expect to find the Origin of the *mild* and *peaceful* Pastoral, in the fertile Vales of *Sicily*.[66]

To Brown, "this natural Progression"[67] of the arts is the result of natural laws operating on human beings whose psychological characteristics were everywhere alike; "the Principles of savage Nature (making Allowance for the Difference of Soil and Climate) are every where the same."[68]

Their earliest Histories were written in Verse.[69]

The *Universality* of the Fact is allowed by All. Such an universal Coincidence, therefore, must spring from some . . . Cause, such as ariseth unalterably from Nature, and takes Place among the savage Tribes in an universal and unvaried Manner.[70]

. . . the Birth and Progress of the *tragic* Species . . . was indeed the *natural Progress* of Passion expressed by *Melody, Dance,* and *Song*. We have seen, that an Union of Narration and concurrent Shouts of Praise takes Place even in the rude Festivals of the savage

Tribes: 'Tis altogether repugnant, therefore, to the Nature of Things to suppose, when *Letters* had given Accents to the Rapture of the surrounding Audience, and moulded the Ode into Form, that this natural Union should not be upheld. Though, therefore, the first Rise and Progress of the tragic Species in GREECE were hid in Darkness, through a Want of recording History, yet, from a Similarity of Causes and Effects which we find among the barbarous Nations of AMERICA, we might fairly conclude, that it had not a *casual*, but a *certain Rise* from *Nature;* according to the Principles here given.[71]

## Winckelmann

Johann Joachim Winckelmann (1717–68) put the study of classical art upon a scientific basis.

*The History of Art* is intended to show the origin, progress, change, and downfall of art, together with the different styles of nations, periods, and artists, and to prove the whole, as far as it is possible, from the ancient monuments now in existence.[22]

The following is, in a few words, the design of this treatise on the History of Art. In the first place, I shall speak, generally, of the shape with which art commenced; next, of the different materials upon which it is worked; and lastly, of the influence of climate upon it.[73]

As to the first point, he developed a theory of the evolution of art.

The arts which are dependent on drawing have, like all inventions, commenced with the necessary; the next object of research was beauty; and, finally, the superfluous followed: these are the three principal stages in art.[74]

... the earliest essays, especially in the drawing of figures, have represented, not the manner in which a man appears to us, but what he is; not a view of his body, but the outline of his shadow. From this simplicity of shape the artist next proceeded to examine proportions; this inquiry taught exactness; the exactness hereby acquired gave confidence, and afterwards success, to his endeavours after grandeur, and at last gradually raised art among the Greeks to the highest beauty. After all the parts constituting grandeur and beauty were united, the artist, in seeking to embellish them, fell into the error of profuseness; art consequently lost its grandeur; and the loss was finally followed by its utter downfall.[75]

Art commenced with the simplest shape, and by working in clay,—consequently, with a sort of statuary; for even a child can give a certain form to a soft mass, though unable to draw anything on a surface, because merely an idea of an object is sufficient for the former, whereas for the latter much other knowledge is requisite; but painting was afterwards employed to embellish sculpture.

Art appears to have originated in a similar way among all the nations by which it has been cultivated; and there is no sufficient reason for assigning any particular country as the land of its birth, for every nation has found within itself the first seed of those things which are indispensable. ... But as the earliest essays appear to have been made on figures of the divinities, the era in which art was invented consequently differs according to the age of each nation, and the earlier or later introduction of religious worship.[76]

In dealing with the third topic, he goes beyond geographic determinism and considers the influence of other aspects of culture upon art.

The superiority which art acquired among the Greeks is to be ascribed partly to the influence of climate, partly to their constitution and government, and the habits of thinking which originated therefrom, and, in an equal degree, to the respect for the artist, and the use and application of art.[77]

## Pauw

Cornelius de Pauw (1739–99) gave the following explanation of his approach:

When the art of studying the customs, manners, and characters of nations began to be reduced to fixed rules, the expediency was perceived of acquiring, in the first place, exact ideas relative to the state of population, the extent, as well as cultivation of country, and the nature of climate. Researches were afterwards to be made on the mode of living, and the expedients devised by each political society to satisfy the wants of the first and second necessity. The propriety is obvious of introducing what belongs to rural oeconomy, previous to any discussions on the arts, which are the offspring of agriculture. When all these objects are attained with some degree of precision, the more difficult task may be undertaken of examining religion and government.[78]

But before we proceed with any discussions relative to the peculiarities of the inhabitants, it will be necessary to describe the qualities of their native soil; for by these their genius and manners must have been affected, on a thousand different occasions.[79]

Nevertheless, there are also innate racial differences.

. . . those nations condemned to eternal mediocrity . . . the Chinese and Egyptians.[80]

## Raynal

Guillaume Thomas François Raynal (1713–96) was an institutionalist who achieved great popularity in his day by writing on the effects of commerce upon the rest of culture.

No event has been so interesting to mankind in general, and to the inhabitants of Europe in particular, as the discovery of the new world, and the passage to India by the Cape of Good Hope. It gave rise to a revolution in the commerce, and in the powers of nations; and in the manners, industry, and government of the world. At this period, new connections were formed by the inhabitants of the most distant regions, for the supply of wants they had never before experienced. The productions of climates situated under the equator, were consumed in countries bordering on the pole; the industry of the north was transplanted to the south; and the inhabitants of the west were cloathed with the manufactures of the east: a general intercourse of opinions, laws and customs, diseases and remedies, virtues and vices, was established among men. . . . How has the condition of these several people been affected by these discoveries?[81]

. . . viewing those beautiful regions, in which the arts and sciences flourish, and which have been for so long obscured by ignorance and barbarism, I have said to myself: Who is it that hath digged these canals? Who is it that hath dried up these plains? Who is it that has founded these cities? Who is it that hath collected, clothed, and civilized these people? Then I have heard the voice of all the enlightened men amonn them, who have answered: This is the effect of commerce.[82]

The connections of commerce are very close. One of its branches cannot experience any opposition, without the others being sensible of it. Commerce connects peoples and fortunes together, and establishes the intercourse of exchanges. It is one entire whole, the several parts of which, attract, support, and balance each other. It resembles the human body, all the parts of which are affected, when one of them does not fulfill the functions that were destined to it.[83]

[He sums up his procedure as follows:] We have first described the state of Europe before the discovery of the East and West Indies.

After this we have pursued the uncertain, tyrannical, and sanguinary progress of the settlements formed in these distant regions.

It now remains to unfold the influence which the intercourse established with the New World has had upon the opinions, government, industry, arts, manners, and happiness of the Old.[84]

He was an advocate of the gregarious theory of society.

Society naturally results from population, and government is a part of the social state.[85]

. . . man are by nature formed for society.[86]

He briefly mentioned the role of social factors in personality development.

The people are formed and fashioned by the arts they profess. If there be some occupations which soften and degrade the human race, there are others by which it is hardened and repaired.[87]

## Heeren

Arnold Hermann Ludwig Heeren (1760–1842) used the comparative method as a result of his cosmopolitanism.

It is . . . one of the worst errors, into which we but too frequently fall, to consider ourselves as the standard of what is or can be done by other nations, in other countries, and under other circumstances.[88]

The ethos of a society determines the character of its customs.

Whoever undertakes to write the history of any particular states-system . . . ought, above all things, to possess a right conception of its general character. . . . In every society of moral beings, and consequently, therefore, in every society or union of states, certain general ideas, from which the leading motives of conduct originate, will of necessity prevail, without there being any occasion to assume the fact of a generally adopted system of action. These ideas, however, agreeably to their nature, cannot possibly remain unaltered, for the very reason that the leading minds do not. . . . To have a correct apprehension, therefore, of the ruling ideas of each age, and to exhibit the particular maxims arising from them, will be the first requisite of the historian. . . . These remarks will serve to vindicate the plan adopted by the author. It was his intention not merely to furnish a sketch of the various revolutions brought about in the political relations of modern Europe, together with the several events springing out of them, though this would certainly form the most important part of his undertaking; but also to exhibit, at the same time, their foundation in the prevailing ideas of each age, and as well with regard to the particular leading states, considered as prominent actors in the system, to illustrate the formation of their respective characters and consequent modes of action.[89]

There are few subjects in history which have been so little illustrated, especially with reference to their consequences, as the characters of nations and their branches. And yet it is these peculiarities, which, in a certain degree, form the guiding thread in the web of the history of nations. From whatever they may proceed, whether from original descent, or the earliest institutions, or from both, experience teaches that they are almost indelible. The difference between the Doric and Ionic tribes, runs through the whole of Grecian history.[90]

The different character of the Grecian states necessarily exercised an influence on the character of the statesmen, who appeared in them. Where the law exercised unlimited power, as it did in Sparta, there was no room for demagogues like those of Athens. But difference of time was as influential as the difference of constitutions. How then could it be otherwise expected, than that with the increasing culture of the nation, there should be a change in the influence and conduct of those who were at its head.[91]

He tried to discover the aspect of culture that was basic in determining these "general ideas," a problem that interested Marx in the succeeding century.

It is not easy to decide, whether the culture of a nation proceeds originally from their sacred or their civil institutions. The character of the domestic relations, the proper application of the means provided for the easier and more regular support of life, agriculture, and husbandry, constitute the first foundation of national culture; but even these can make but little progress without the assistance of religion. Without the fear of the gods, marriage loses its sanctity, and property its security.[92]

Some of Heeren's institutional remarks follow.[93]

As the priests never formed a distinct order, and still less a caste, in Greece, the religion never became a religion of state to such a degree as in other countries.[94]

[In a discussion of the political organization of Greece:] The reciprocal influence between national economy and that of the state, is so great and so natural, that it was necessary to premise a few observations respecting the former.[95]

The relation which exists between science and political institutions, is of a twofold nature. It may be asked, What has the state done for the promotion of the sciences? And also, What influence in return have the sciences, or any particular branch of them, exerted on the state?[96]

Whether in our inquiries on the political institutions of Greece, their poetry and arts must be considered,—will hardly be made a question by any of my readers. Almost every one of the preceding chapters has served to show how closely they were connected with the state. Yet our remarks must be limited to the question: What was the nature, and what were the consequences of this connexion?[97]

Religious notions, it is true, do not seem to have a very near connexion with political, but even if the union of the state with its acknowledged forms of worship were less strict, these could seldom be overthrown without entailing the fall of more than can be originally forseen.[98]

In the case of a conquering nation, the institutions of war are so intimately mixed up with its constitution that, even in a work principally devoted to the arts of peace, the former cannot be entirely passed over.[99]

[The reason for the difficulty of reform in Asiatic monarchies:] the inseparable connexion . . . between religion and legislation, must greatly embarrass, if not altogether obstruct, the development of a constitution. A new system of laws would have been equivalent to a change of religion; and even a partial modification of the former would have been looked upon as an innovation on the latter. The difficulties attending such innovations are obvious, but they must have been considerably increased when (as was often the case) not only the ceremonies of religion but those of the court were in the custody of a separate caste, whose interest it was to discourage any attempt to change.[100]

No doubt . . . can exist respecting the close connection between trade and religion.[101]

Heeren was interested in tracing the growth of culture and, on the basis of a unilinear conception of evolution, used contemporary "primitive" groups as representative of earlier stages of development.

. . . our observations on such tribes as are still in their political infancy supply us with data respecting the progress of ancient nations, which we shall in vain expect from the history of the latter.[102]

The great question respecting the rise and first formation of states, which hitherto has been little more than an object of speculation, seems here [i.e., in central Africa] likely to be historically answered. Religion, legislation, national law, all appear here in their infancy.[103]

[In a description of Africa, he states:] We have already seen all the various gradation, from the complete savage, as described by Hanno, whose rank might have been disputed by the ourang-outang, to the hunting and fishing tribes; and again, from the latter to the nomad herdsman.[104]

This is his treatment of cultural evolution:

The first bond of community existing among men was, beyond all question, the natural one of *domestic* ties. It is greatly to be doubted whether any people ever existed, among whom the law of marriage, or the domestic alliance of the two sexes, did not prevail; and even if an instance or two could be cited, it may safely be pronounced that such a state of society would resolve itself into barbarism.[105]

This bond, however, of consanguinity, is much more extensive and powerful among savage tribes than among civilized nations. The different members of the family do not, as with us, devote themselves, as soon as they have attained a certain age, to various occupations in the world without, and thus separate from the parent-stock, All pursue the same occupation, whether it be hunting or the tending of cattle. Consequently the families remain united: they gradually form Tribes, and the Tribes—Nations.[106]

We do not consider the formation of such societies to be the result of a formal, social *compact*—the very idea of which is a variance with the condition of a people still in their infancy:—nor do we think that anything like the *discovery* of a constitution took place at a definite period; but we believe it to have grown insensibly out of the exigencies and the passions of mankind. All this was so far from being the result of theory, that it is probable the notion of a theory never entered the heads of the first founders of states, whatever may have been thought of subsequently; and in consequence of this want of system at their commencement, the different forms of government assumed a variety of character, which the theorist finds it hard to reduce to the classifications of modern systems.*[111]

The judical institutions of a nation proceed from very simple beginnings. Where they are left to be developed by circumstances and the necessities of the times, they cannot but become more and more intricate; since with the progress of culture, new relations arise, both at home and with foreign countries. In the heroic age [of Greece], Kings sat on the tribunals of justice, though even then arbitrators were not unusual. There existed

* " . . . the origin of political constitutions was, at the first, exceedingly simple, and as far as possible from being the effect of deliberate intention or established principles : and being much more the result of circumstances and necessity."[107]

"To require that the human race should advance without interruption to its more perfect state, by the path which reason points out, is to mistake our nature, and to forget that we are not creatures of pure reason, but of reason mixed and alloyed with passion. It is difficult for individual man to tread that path, but for the crowd, which only approaches its objects by circuitous ways, it is impossible."[108]

"The judicial institutions of the Greeks were the creation of time and circumstances. The form, therefore, which they eventually assumed, could not well correspond to the requisitions of a theory."[109]

"The constitutions of their cities, like those of the moderns, were framed by necessity, and developed by circumstances."[110]

at that time no written laws; questions were decided by prescrpition, and good common sense, directed by a love of justice.

When nations begin to emerge from the rude condition of savages, the first necessity which is felt, is that of personal security, and next, the security of property. National legislation has always commenced with the criminal code and the police laws; the rights of citizens were defined more slowly, and at a later period; because it was not sooner necessary.[112]

In analyzing the factors that produce civilization, Heeren hesitated when considering a biological interpretation.

From whence proceeds this superiority, this universal sovereignty of so small a region as Europe? . . .

Here attention is drawn to one important circumstance, of which the cautious inquirer almost fears to estimate the value. Whilst we see the surface of the other continents covered with natives of different, and almost always of dark colour, (and, in so far as this determines the race, of different races,) the inhabitants of Europe belong only to one race. It has not, and it never had, any other native inhabitants than white nations. Is the white man distinguished by greater natural talents? Has he by means of them precedence over his coloured brethren? This is a question which physiology cannot answer at all, and which history must answer with timidity. Who will absolutely deny that the differences of organization, which attend on the difference in colour, can have an influence on the more rapid or more difficult unfolding of the mind? But, on the other hand, who can demonstrate this influence, without first raising that secret veil, which conceals from us the reciprocal connexion between body and mind? And yet we must esteem it probable; and how much does this probability increase in strength, if we make inquiries of history? The great superiority which the white nations in all ages and parts of the world have possessed, is a matter of fact, which cannot be done away with by denials. It may be said, that this was the consequence of external circumstances, which favoured them more. But has this always been so? And why has it been so? And, further, why did those darker nations, which rose above the savage state, attain only to a degree of culture of their own; a degree which was passed neither by the Egyptian nor by the Mongolian, neither by the Chinese nor the Hindoo? And among the coloured races, why did the black remain behind the brown and the yellow? If these observations cannot but make us inclined to attribute differences of capacity to the several branches of our race, they do not on that account prove an absolute want of capacity in our darker fellow-men, nor must they be urged as containing the whole explanation of European superiority. This, only, is intended; experience thus far seems to prove, that a greater facility in developing the powers of mind belongs to the nations of a clear colour; but we will welcome the age which shall contradict this experience, and exhibit cultivated nations of negroes.[113]

In his estimation, geography has an important influence on the production of civilization.[114]

But however high or low this natural [biological] precedency of the Europeans may be estimated, no one can fail to observe, that the physical qualities of this continent offer peculiar advantages, which may serve not a little to explain the above-mentioned phenomenon.

Europe belongs almost entirely to the northern temperate zone. . . . Thus our continent has in no part the luxuriant fruitfulness of tropic regions; but also no such ungrateful climates, as to make the care for the mere preservation of life exhaust the whole strength of its inhabitants. Europe, except where local causes put obstacles in the way, is throughout susceptible of agriculture. To this it invites, or rather compels; for it is as little adapted to the life of hunters as of herdsmen. . . . No European nation ever lived in tents; the well-wooded plains offered in abundance the materials for constructing those huts which the inclement skies required. Its soil and climate were peculiarly fitted to accustom men to that regular industry, which is the source of all prosperity.[115]

[In another place he speaks of] the great influence which the natural circumstances of country and climate have upon the destiny of the human race.[116]

[After a description of the geography of central Asia, he continues:] This natural condition of the soil, added to another peculiarity, the almost total absence of woods or forests, has had great influence in determining the manner of life of the inhabitants of those regions. . . . these vast and level plains are accordingly studded, instead of with cities and houses, with tents and encampments, the ordinary abodes of these migratory tribes, often surrounded for leagues by their innumerable flocks and herds of sheep and cattle, of horses and camels, which constitute their riches, and supply all, or nearly all, their limited wants. . . .

Their social relations have, as might be expected, been greatly influenced by these peculiarities of their situation. It is impossible that they should adopt those civil constitutions to which we have been accustomed from our youth, and which are the consequences of settled habitations, domestic tranquility, and established possessions. The place of these was supplied by the natural bond of consanguinity; which became proportionably stronger than among Europeans, inasmuch as it embraced not only individual families, but whole tribes and nations.[117]

Also, acculturation is necessary for a civilization to develop.

One of the most interesting spectacles which history affords us, is the spread of nations by peaceable colonization . . . in a great measure, the civilization of the whole human race, depend very much upon these peaceful means of advancement. The continual intercourse with their colonies enlivens and extends the knowledge of the mother states; and besides this, it infallibly promotes the development of political ideas, and what is founded upon it, the perfecting of civil government. The portion of the people separated from the parent country undergo some change in every new settlement, as the difference in the nature of the country, and favourable or unfavourable circumstances necessarily give a new direction to the mind. In such cases, where society in a manner sets out anew, many improvements are easily and necessarily made, which could scarcely be adopted where everything is become fixed and settled. . . . And thus, amid the rise and fall of empires, the advances of man in civilization, in all its multitudinous forms, is perpetuated and secured.[118]

Civilization being generally the result of commerce.[119]

. . . the whole course of history tends to prove, that the countries which became the staples or the depots of this commerce, uniformly attained a high degree of opulence and refinement; which, however, gradually changed their habits and corrupted the manners of their inhabitants; at the same time that these were softened, sowing among them the seeds of luxury, and consequently of decline and ruin. The result of this . . . has been, the mutual intercourse and civilization of nations; which, if they had continued unconnected, would have remained still in their infancy, as must be the case with all isolated nations, even if by some strong instinctive effort they succeed in emerging from their original barbarism.[120]

The geographical situation of this town [i.e., Geneval] undoubtedly contributed to produce a collision of ideas, such as could not easily take place elsewhere. Placed upon the borders of France, Italy, and Switzerland, it enjoyed a degree of intellectual prosperity to which each of the neighbouring states contributed its share.[121]

Thus the great conclusion, so interesting and important for human nature and its history, becomes in a manner forced upon us: THE FIRST SEATS OF COMMERCE WERE ALSO THE FIRST SEATS OF CIVILIZATION. Exchange of merchandise led to exchange of ideas, and by this mutual friction was first kindled the sacred flame of moral and intellectual culture.[122]

## SCOTCH SCHOOL

The outstanding characteristic of the Scotch school was its approach to the problem of cultural evolution; its method and conclusions, if not its data, were equal to those of the English evolutionary school of the nineteenth century. The former, like the latter, built a unilinear theory of evolution upon the premise of the psychic unity of mankind. In the field of man's nature, the Scotch group advocated man's social nature and a gregarious theory of society.

### Smith

To Adam Smith (1723–90), self-love was fundamental in human nature.

Every man, as the Stoics used to say, is first and principally recommended to his own care; and every man is certainly, in every respect, fitter and abler to take care of himself than of any other person. Every man feels his own pleasures and his own pains more sensibly than those of other people. The former are the original sensations—the latter the reflected or sympathetic images of those sensations. The former may be said to be the substance—the latter the shadow.[123]

. . . man has almost constant occasion for the help of his brethren, and it is in vain for him to expect it from benevolence only. He will be more likely to prevail if he can interest their self-love in his favour, and shew them that it is for their own advantage to do for him what he requires of them. . . . It is not from the benevolence of the butcher, the brewer, or the baker, that we expect our dinner, but from their regard to their own interest. We address ourselves, not to their humanity but to their self-love, and never talk to them of our necessities but of their advantages. Nobody but a beggar chuses to depend chiefly upon the benevolence of his fellow-citizens. Even a beggar does not depend upon it entirely.[124]

He therefore used an argument similar to Mandeville's "Private vices, public benefits" in defense of *laissez faire.*

The natural effort of every individual to better his own condition, when suffered to exert itself with freedom and security, is so powerful a principle, that it is alone, and without any assistance, not only capable of carrying on the society to wealth and prosperity, but of surmounting a hundred impertinent obstructions with which the folly of human laws too often incumbers its operations.[125]

This self-love is not limited to the individual alone; it extends to others as well, because of the social relations that exist between men.

After himself, the members of his own family, those who usually live in the same house with him, his parents, his children, his brothers and sisters, are naturally the objects of his warmest affections. They are naturally and usually the persons upon whose happiness or misery his conduct must have the greatest influence. He is more habituated to sympathize with them: he knows better how every thing is likely to affect them, and his sympathy with them is more precise and determinate than it can be with the greater part of other people. It approaches nearer, in short, to what he feels for himself.[126]

The children of brothers and sisters are naturally connected by the friendship which, after separating into different families, continues to take place between their parents. Their good agreement improves the enjoyment of that friendship—their discord would disturb it. As they seldom live in the same family, however, though of more importance to one another than to the greater part of other people, they are of much less than brothers and sisters. As their mutual sympathy is less necessary, so it is less habitual, and, therefore, proportionably weaker.

The children of cousins, being still less connected, are of still less importance to one another; and the affection gradually diminishes as the relation grows more and more remote.

What is called affection is in reality nothing but habitual sympathy. Our concern in the happiness or misery of those who are the objects of what we call our affections; our desire to promote the one and to prevent the other, are either the actual feeling of that habitual sympathy, or the necessary consequences of that feeling. Relations being usually placed in situations which naturally create this habitual sympathy, it is expected that a suitable degree of affection should take place among them. We generally find that it actually does take place;—we therefore naturally expect that it should; and we are, upon that account, more shocked when upon any occasion we find that it does not.[127]

I consider what is called natural affection as more the effect of the moral than of the supposed physical connection between the parent and the child.[128]

A father is apt to be less attached to a child who, by some accident, has been separated from him in its infancy, and who does not return to him till it is grown up to manhood. The father is apt to feel less paternal tenderness for the child; the child less filial reverence for the father.[129]

The same principles that direct the order in which individuals are recommended to our beneficence, direct that likewise in which societies are recommended to it.[130]

Though our effectual good offices can very seldom be extended to any wider society than that of our own country, our good will is circumscribed by no boundary, but may embrace the immensity of the universe.[131]

Besides, it should not be forgotten that man has need of others.

In civilized society he stands at all time in need of the co-operation and assistance of great multitudes. . . . man has almost constant occasion for the help of his brethren.[132]

In every species of animals the connexion between the sexes is just as much as is necessary for the propagation and support of the species. Quadrupeds, whenever the female impregnates, have no farther desire for each other; the support of the young is no burden to the female, and there is no occasion for the assistance of the male. Among birds some such thing as marriage seems to take place, they continue the objects of desire to each other, their connexion remains for a considerable time, and they jointly support the young; but whenever the young can shift for themselves all further inclination ceases. In the human species women by their milk are not capable of providing long for their children. The assistance of the husband is therefore necessary for their sustenance, and this ought to make marriage perpetual. . . . We may observe an utility in this constitution of our nature that children have so long a dependence upon their parents, to bring down their passions to theirs, and thus be trained up at length to become useful members of society. Every child gets this piece of education, even under the most worthless parent.[133]

Therefore, man is a social animal.

It is thus that man, who can subsist only in society, was fitted by nature to that situation for which he was made. All the members of human society stand in need of each other's assistance, and are likewise exposed to mutual injuries. Where the necessary assistance is reciprocally afforded from love, from gratitude, from friendship, and esteem, the society flourishes and is happy. All the different members of it are bound together by the agreeable bands of love and affection, and are, as it were, drawn to one common centre of mutual good offices.

But though the necessary assistance should not be afforded from such generous and disinterested motives, though among the different members of the society there should be no mutual love and affection, the society, though less happy and agreeable, will not necessarily be dissolved. Society may subsist among different men, as among different merchants, from a sense of its utility, without any mutual love or affection; and though no man in it should owe any obligation, or be bound in gratitude to any other, it may still be upheld by a mercenary exchange of good offices according to an agreed valuation.[134]

Nature, when she formed man for society, endowed him with an original desire to please, and an original aversion to offend his brethren. She taught him to feel pleasure in their favourable, and pain in their unfavourable regard. She rendered their approbation most flattering and most agreeable to him for its own sake; and their disapprobation most mortifying and most offensive.

But this desire of approbation, and this aversion to the disapprobation of his brethren, would not alone have rendered him fit for that society for which he was made. Nature, accordingly, has endowed him, not only with a desire of being approved of, but with a desire of being what ought to be approved of; or of being what he himself approves of in other men. The first desire could only have made him wish to appear to be fit for society. The second was necessary in order to render him anxious to be really fit. The first could only have prompted him to the affectation of virtue, and to the concealment of vice. The second was necessary in order to inspire him with the real love of virtue, and with the real abhorrence of vice.[135]

. . . the chief part of human happiness arises from the consciousness of being beloved.[136]

It is this desire for approbation which produces ambition and its effects.[137]

Sympathy is another phenomenon of importance in man's nature.

How selfish soever man may be supposed, there are evidently some principles in his nature, which interest him in the fortune of others, and render their happiness necessary to him, though he derives nothing from it, except the pleasure of seeing it. Of this kind is pity or compassion, the emotion which we feel for the misery of others, when we either see it, or are made to conceive it in a very lively manner. That we often derive sorrow from the sorrow of others, is a matter of fact too obvious to require any instances to prove it; for this sentiment, like all the other original passions of human nature, is by no means confined to the virtuous and humane, though they perhaps may feel it with the most exquisite sensibility. The greatest ruffian, the most hardened violator of the laws of society, is not altogether without it.

As we have no immediate experience of what other men feel, we can form no idea of the manner in which they are affected, but by conceiving what we ourselves should feel in the like situation. Though our brother is upon the rack, as long as we ourselves are at our ease, our senses will never inform us of what he suffers. They never did, and never can, carry us beyond our own person, and it is by the imagination only that we can form any conception of what are his sensations. Neither can that faculty help us to this any other way, than by representing to us what would be our own, if we were in his case. It is the impressions of our own senses only, not those of his, which our imaginations copy. By the imagination we place ourselves in his situation, we conceive ourselves enduring all the same torments, we enter as it were into his body, and become in some measure the same person with him, and thence form some idea of his sensations, and even feel something which, though weaker in degree, is not altogether unlike them. His agonies, when they are thus brought home to ourselves, when we have thus adopted and made them our own, begin at last to affect us, and we then tremble and shudder at the thought of what he feels. For as to be in pain or distress of any kind excites the most excessive sorrow, so to conceive or to imagine that we are in it, excites some degree of the same emotion, in proportion to the vivacity or dulness of the conception.

That this is the source of our fellow-feeling for the misery of others, that it is by changing places in fancy with the sufferer, that we come either to conceive or to be affected by what he feels, may be demonstrated by many obvious observations, if it should not be thought sufficiently evident of itself. When we see a stroke aimed, and just ready to fall upon the leg or arm of another person, we naturally shrink and draw back our own leg or our own arm; and when it does fall, we feel it in some measure, and are hurt by it as well as the sufferer. . . .

Neither is it those circumstances only, which create pain or sorrow, that call forth our fellow-feeling. Whatever is the passion which arises from any object in the person principally concerned, an analogous emotion springs up, at the thought of his situation, in the breast of every attentive spectator. Our joy for the deliverance of those heroes of tragedy or romance who interest us, is as sincere as our grief for their distress, and our fellow-feeling with their misery is not more real than that with their happiness. We enter into their gratitude towards those faithful friends who did not desert them in their difficulties; and we heartily go along with their resentment against those perfidious traitors who injured, abandoned, or deceived them. In every passion of which the mind of man is susceptible, the emotions of the bystander always correspond to what, by bringing the case home to himself, he imagines should be the sentiments of the sufferer.

Pity and compassion are words appropriated to signify our fellow-feeling with the sorrow of others. Sympathy, though its meaning was, perhaps, originally the same, may now, however, without much impropriety, be made use of to denote our fellow-feeling with any passion whatever.[138]

Sympathy . . . does not arise so much from the view of the passion, as from that of the situation which excites it. We sometimes feel for another, a passion of which he himself seems to be altogether incapable; because, when we put ourselves in his case, that passion arises in our breast from the imagination, though it does not in his from the reality. We blush for the impudence and rudeness of another, though he himself appears to have no sense of the impropriety of his own behaviour; because we cannot help feeling with what confusion we ourselves should be covered, had we behaved in so absurd a manner.[139]

The next point of interest is Smith's treatment of mores and conscience.

In treating of the principles of morals there are two questions to be considered. First, wherein does virtue consist—or what is the tone of temper, and tenor of conduct, which constitutes the excellent and praiseworthy character, the character which is the natural object of esteem, honour, and approbation? And, secondly, by what power or faculty in the mind is it that this character, whatever it be, is recommended to us? or, in other words, how and by what means does it come to pass, that the mind prefers one tenor of conduct to another; denominates the one right and the other wrong; considers the one as the object of approbation, honour, and reward, and the other of blame, censure, and punishment?[140]

[1.] . . . sympathy, or the correspondent affection of the spectator, [is] the natural and original measure of this proper degree [of virtue possessed by an act].[141]

. . . any precise or distinct measure by which this fitness or propriety of affection can be ascertained or judged of . . . nowhere but in the sympathetic feelings of the impartial and well-informed spectator.[142]

[2.] When we approve of any character or action, the sentiments which we feel are . . . derived from four sources, which are in some respects different from one another. First, we sympathize with the motives of the agent; secondly, we enter into the gratitude of those who receive the benefit of his actions; thirdly, we observe that his conduct has been agreeable to the general rules by which those two sympathies generally act; and, last of all, when we consider such actions, as making a part of a system of behaviour which tends to promote the happiness either of the individual or of the society, they appear to derive a beauty from this utility, not unlike that which we ascribe to any well-contrived machine.[143]

He has an extended analysis of conscience as based upon sympathy.

The principle by which we naturally either approve or disapprove of our own conduct, seems to be altogether the same with that by which we exercise the like judgements concerning the conduct of other people. We either approve or disapprove of the conduct of another man, according as we feel that, when we bring his case home to ourselves, we either can or cannot entirely sympathize with the sentiments and motives which directed it. And, in the same manner, we either approve or disapprove of our own conduct, according as we feel that, when we place ourselves in the situation of another man, and view, as it were, with his eyes and from his station, we either can or cannot entirely enter into and sympathize with the sentiments and motives which influenced it. We can never survey our own sentiments and motives, we can never form any judgement concerning them, unless we remove ourselves, as it were, from our own natural station, and endeavour to view them as at a certain distance from us. But we can do this in no other way than by endeavouring to view them with the eyes of other people, or as other people are likely to view them. Whatever judgements we can form concerning them, accordingly, must always bear some secret reference, either to what are, or to what, upon a certain condition, would be, or to what, we imagine, ought to be the judgement of others. We endeavour to examine our own conduct as we imagine any other fair and impartial spectator would examine it. If, upon placing ourselves in his situation, we thoroughly enter into all the passions and motives which influenced it, we approve of it, by sympathy with the approbation of this supposed equitable judge. If otherwise, we enter into his disapprobation, and condemn it.

Were it possible that a human creature could grow up to manhood in some solitary place, without any communication with his own species, he could no more think of his own character, of the propriety or demerit of his own sentiments and conduct, of the beauty or deformity of his own mind, than of the beauty or deformity of his own face.

All these are objects which he cannot easily see, which naturally he does not look at, and with regard to which he is provided with no mirror which can present them to his view. Bring him into society, and he is immediately provided with the mirror which he wanted before. It is placed in the countenance and behaviour of those he lives with, which always mark when they enter into, and when they disapprove of his sentiments; and it is here that he first views the propriety and impropriety of his own passions, the beauty and deformity of his own mind. To a man who from birth was a stranger to society, the objects of his passions, the external bodies which either pleased or hurt him, would occupy his whole attention. The passions themselves, the desires or aversions, the joys or sorrows, which those objects excited, though of all things the most immediately present to him, could scarce ever be the objects of his thoughts. The idea of them could never interest him so much as to call upon his attentive consideration. The consideration of his joy could in him excite no new joy, nor that of his sorrow any new sorrow, though the consideration of the causes of those passions might often excite both. Bring him into society, and all his own passions will immediately become the causes of new passions. He will observe that mankind approve of some of them, and are disgusted by others. He will be elevated in the one case, and cast down in the other; his desires and aversions, his joys and sorrows, will now often become the causes of new desires and new aversions, new joys and new sorrows: they will now, therefore, interest him deeply, and often call upon his most attentive consideration . . . our first moral criticisms are exercised upon the characters and conduct of other people; and we are all very forward to observe how each of these affects us. But we soon learn, that other people are equally frank with regard to our own. We become anxious to know how far we deserve their censure or applause, and whether to them we must necessarily appear those agreeable or disagreeable creatures which they represent us. We begin, upon this account, to examine our own passions and conduct, and to consider how these must appear to them, by considering how they would appear to us if in their situation. We suppose ourselves the spectators of our own behaviour, and endeavour to imagine what effect it would, in this light, produce upon us. This is the only looking-glass by which we can, in some measure, with the eyes of other people, scrutinize the propriety of our own conduct.[144]

Of course, man often rationalizes in his own favor.[145]

Mores and conscience are relative to culture.

["Custom and fashion"] have a considerable influence upon the moral sentiments of mankind, and are the chief causes of the many irregular and discordant opinions which prevail in different ages and nations concerning what is blameable or praiseworthy.[146]

However, the basic ethical principles seem to be innate in man.

. . . the general rules of morality . . . are ultimately founded upon experience of what, in particular instances, our moral faculties, our natural sense of merit and propriety, approve or disapprove of.[147]

Since our sentiments concerning beauty of every kind are so much influenced by custom and fashion, it cannot be expected that those concerning the beauty of conduct should be entirely exempted from the dominion of those principles. Their influence here, however, seems to be much less than it is everywhere else. There is, perhaps, no form of external objects, how absurd and fantastical soever, to which custom will not reconcile us, or which fashion will not render even agreeable. But the characters and conduct of a Nero, or a Claudius, are what no custom will ever reconcile us to, what no fashion will ever render agreeable; but the one will always be the object of dread and hatred—the other of scorn and derision. The principles of the imagination, upon which our sense of beauty depends, are of a very nice and delicate nature, and may easily be altered by habit and education; but the sentiments of moral approbation and disapprobation are founded on the strongest and most vigorous passions of human nature; and though they may be somewhat warpt, cannot be entirely perverted.

But though the influence of custom and fashion upon moral sentiments is not altogether so great, it is, however, perfectly similar to what it is everywhere else. When custom and fashion coincide with the natural principles of right and wrong, they heighten the delicacy of our sentiments, and increase our abhorrence for everything which approaches to evil. Those who have been educated in what is really good company, not in what is commonly called such, who have been accustomed to see nothing in the persons whom they esteemed and lived with, but justice, modesty, humanity, and good order, are more shocked with whatever seems to be inconsistent with the rules which those virtues prescribe. Those, on the contrary, who have had the misfortune to be brought up amidst violence, licentiousness, falsehood, and injustice, lose though not all sense of the impropriety of such conduct, yet all sense of its dreadful enormity, or of the vengeance and punishment due to it. . . .

Fashion, too, will sometimes give reputation to a certain degree of disorder, and, on the contrary, discountenance qualities which deserve esteem.[148]

Truly virtuous acts perpetuate the existence of the society; if the culture changed the "natural" mores too much, the society could no longer adjust adequately.

There is an obvious reason why custom should never pervert our sentiments with regard to the general style and character of conduct and behaviour, in the same degree as with regard to the propriety or unlawfulness of particular usages. There never can be any such custom. No society could subsist a moment, in which the usual strain of men's conduct and behaviour was of a piece with the horrible practice I have just now mentioned [i.e., infanticide].[149]

Like Hume, Smith discussed the effect of culture upon personality.

The objects with which men in the different professions and states of life are conversant being very different, and habituating them to very different passions, naturally form in them very different characters and manners. We expect in each rank and profession a degree of those manners which, experience has taught us, belonged to it.* . . . The different periods of life have, for the same reason, different manners assigned to them. We expect in old age that gravity and sedateness which its infirmities, its long experience, and its worn-out sensibility seem to render both natural and respectable; and we lay our account to find in youth that sensibility, that gaiety and sprightly vivacity, which ex-

---

* "The difference of natural talents in different men is, in reality, much less than we are aware of; and the very different genius which appears to distinguish men of different professions, when grown up to maturity, is not upon many occasions so much the cause, as the effect of the division of labour. The difference between the most dissimilar characters, between a philosopher and a common street porter, for example, seems to arise not so much from nature, as from habit, custom, and education. When they came into the world, and for the first six or eight years of their existence, they were, perhaps, very much alike, and neither their parents nor playfellows could perceive any remarkable difference. About that age, or soon after, they come to be employed in very different occupations. The difference of talents comes then to be taken notice of, and widens by degrees, till at last the vanity of the philosopher is willing to acknowledge scarce any resemblance. But without the disposition to truck, barter, and exchange, every man must have procured to himself every necessary and conveniency of life which he wanted. All must have had the same duties to perform, and the same work to do, and there could have been no such difference of employment as could alone give occasion to any great difference of talents."[150]

perience teaches us to expect from the lively impressions that all interesting objects are apt to make upon the tender and unpractised senses of that early period of life.[151]

The different situations of different ages and countries are apt, in the same manner, to give different characters to the generality of those who live in them, and their sentiments concerning the particular degree of each quality that is either blameable or praiseworthy, vary according to that degree which is usual in their own country and in their own times. That degree of politeness which would be highly esteemed, perhaps would be thought effeminate adulation, in Russia, would be regarded as rudeness and barbarism at the court of France. That degree of order and frugality which, in a Polish nobleman, would be considered as excessive parsimony, would be regarded as extravagance in a citizen of Amsterdam. Every age and country looks upon that degree of each quality which is commonly to be met with in those who are esteemed, among themselves, as the golden mean of that particular talent or virtue; and this varies according as their different circumstances render different qualities more or less habitual to them, their sentiments, concerning the exact propriety of character and behaviour, vary accordingly.[152]

This natural disposition to accommodate and to assimilate, as much as we can, our own sentiments, principles, and feelings, to those which we see fixed and rooted in the persons whom we are obliged to live and converse a great deal with, is the cause of the contagious effects of both good and bad company. The man who associates chiefly with the wise and the virtuous, though he may not himself become either wise or virtuous, cannot help conceiving a certain respect, at least, for wisdom and virtue; and the man who associates chiefly with the profligate and dissolute, must soon lose at least all his original abhorrence of profligacy and dissolution of manners. The similarity of family characters, which we so frequently see transmitted through several successive generations, may, perhaps, be partly owing to this disposition, to assimilate ourselves to those whom we are obliged to live and converse a great deal with. The family character, however, like the family countenance, seems to be owing not altogether to the moral but partly too to the physical connection. The family countenance is certainly altogether owing to the latter."[153]

He gave cultural interpretations of social phenomena, as, for example, in his analysis of crime.

. . . it is not so much the police that prevents the commission of crimes as the having as few persons as possible to live upon others. Nothing tends so much to corrupt mankind as dependency, while independency still increases the honesty of the people.

The establishment of commerce and manufactures, which brings about this independency, is the best police for preventing crimes. The common people have better wages in this way than in any other, and in consequence of this a general probity of manners takes place through the whole country. Nobody will be so mad as to expose himself upon the highway, when he can make better bread in an honest and industrious manner.[154]

He also studied culture from an institutional point of view, such as a section entitled, "Of the influence of commerce on manners."[155]

Smith treated the problem of cultural evolution as well. In his various books he developed hypotheses on the evolution of science, philosophy, and religion;[156] the division of labor;[157] money;[158] language;[159] and political organization.[160]

## Kames

On the whole, Henry Home, Lord Kames (1696–1782), tended toward a naturalistic approach. In his estimation, man is subject to natural law.

... constant and universal experience proves, that human actions are governed by certain inflexible laws; and that a man cannot exert his self-motive power, but in pursuance of some desire or motive.*[162]

He follows Hobbes's analysis of the problem of freedom of the will.

A man is absolutely free to act according to his own will; greater freedom than which is not conceivable. At the same time, as man is made accountable for his conduct, to his Maker, to his fellow-creatures, and to himself, he is not left to act arbitrarily; for at that rate he would be altogether unaccountable: his will is regulated by desire; and desire by what pleases or displeases him. Where we are subjected to the will of another, would it be our wish, that his will should be under no regulation? And where we are guided by our own will, would it be reasonable to wish, that it should be under no regulation, but be exerted without reason, without any motive, and contrary to common sense? Thus, with regard to human conduct, there is a chain of laws established by nature, no one link of which is left arbitrary.[163]

... man is not left loose; for tho' he is at liberty to act according to his own will, yet his will is regulated by desire, and desire by what pleases and displeases. This connection preserves the uniformity of conduct, and confines human actions within the great chain of causes and effects. By this admirable system, liberty and necessity, seemingly incompatible, are made perfectly concordant, fitting us for society, and for government both human and divine.[164]

He believed in the psychic unity of mankind.

Mankind, through all ages, have been the same.[165]

Man is a social animal.

... his nature makes him prone to society; and society is necessary to his well-being, because in a solitary state he is a helpless being, destitute of support; and, in his manifold distresses, destitute of relief.[166]

Man is indeed fitted for society. His wants prompt him to it, and his inclinations render it agreeable. Accordingly we find mankind almost every where parceled out into societies, which by accidental circumstances, have been originally formed, more or less extensive.[167]

One of the most important social sentiments is a desire for approbation.

No appetite in human nature is more universal, than that for honour or respect.[168]

No other branch of the human constitution shows more visibly our destination for society, nor tends more to our improvement, than appetite for fame or esteem: for as the whole conveniences of life are derived from mutual aid and support in society, it ought to be a capital aim to secure these conveniences, by gaining the esteem and affection of others.[169]

As did Freud later, Kames posited narcissism in the infant, which later is extended and transmuted into a love for others.

During infancy, our desires centre mostly in ourselves: every one perceives intuitively the comfort of food and raiment, of a snug dwelling, and of every convenience ... the superior pleasure that accompanies the exercise of benevolence, of friendship, and of every

* "It is a law in our nature that we never act but by the impulse of desire; which in other words, is saying, that passion, by the desire included in it, is what determines the will."[161]

social principle, is not clearly understood till it be frequently felt. To perceive the social principle in its triumphant state, a man must forget himself, and turn his thoughts upon the character and conduct of his fellow-creatures.[170]

Nevertheless, benevolence is also instinctive.

. . . man is endued with a principle of benevolence as well as of selfishness, he is prompted by his nature to desire the good of every sensible being that gives him pleasure; and the happiness of that being is the gratification of his desire.[171]

Therefore, man is both selfish and social.

. . . we are evidently formed by nature for society, and for indulging the social, as well as the selfish passions.[172]

Kames followed Shaftesbury rather than the other members of the Scotch school in assuming that the moral sense is instinctive.

The moral sense is born with us.[173]

The moral sense . . . [is] frequently discovered, even in children. It is however slow of growth, and seldom arrives at perfection without culture and experience.

The moral sense not only ripens gradually with the other internal senses . . . but from them acquires force and additional authority: a savage makes no difficulty to kill an enemy in cold blood: bloody scenes are familiar to him, and his moral sense is not sufficiently vigorous to give him compunction. The action appears in a different light to a person of delicate feelings; and accordingly, the moral sense has much more authority over those who have received a refined education, than over savages.[174]

. . . the moral sense, properly speaking, is not a principle which moves us to action. Its province is to instruct us, which of our principles of action we may indulge, and which of them we must restrain.[175]

Sympathy "is the cement of human society."[176]

. . . mutual support, the shining attribute of society, is of too great moment to be left dependent upon cool reason; it is ordered more wisely, and with greater conformity to the analogy of nature, that it should be enforced even instinctively* by the passion of sympathy.[178]

Compassion is a most valuable principle, which connects people in society by ties stronger than those of blood.[179]

. . . nature, which designed us for society, has connected us strongly together, by a participation of the joys and miseries of our fellow creatures. We have a strong sympathy with them; we partake of their afflictions; we grieve with them and for them; and, in many instances, their misfortunes affect us equally with our own . . . besides, that it is the great cement of human society, we ought to consider, that, as no state is exempt from misfortunes, mutual sympathy must greatly promote the security and happiness of mankind. And 'tis a much more comfortable situation, that the prosperity and preservation of each individual should be the care of the whole species, than that every man, as the single inhabitant of a desert island, should be left to stand or fall by himself, without prospect of regard, or assistance from others.[180]

Kames was also aware of the constraint of culture.

* " . . . how [do] we come to understand external signs, so as to refer each sign to its proper passion? . . . man is provided by nature with a sense or faculty, that lays open to him every passion by means of its external expressions."[177]

Men are governed by custom. Not one of a thousand thinks for himself; and the few who are emancipated, dare not act up to their freedom, for fear of being thought whimsical.[181]

Our opinions are greatly influenced by custom.[182]

Barbarians are slaves to custom: Polite people to fashions. The Hottentots are an instance of the former: The French of the latter.[183]

In dealing with culture, Kames was both an institutionalist and a functionalist, for, as can be seen from the foregoing quotations, he was interested in how a given biological or social phenomenon aided in maintaining the existence of the society. However, his functionalism was vitiated by his teleological approach.

Kames's evolutionism was remarkable. In regard to methodology, he used data on subhuman animals and "primitive" peoples to give him the necessary evolutionary succession. In fact, he and Westermarck made identical use of other primates in determining the evolution of human marriage.

[1. Man and other animals]

As many animals, besides man, are social, it appeared to me probable, that the social laws by which such animals are governed, might open views into the social nature of man.[184]

And as the means provided by nature for continuing the race of other animals, may probably throw light upon the oeconomy of nature with respect to man; I begin with that article, which has not engaged the attention of naturalists so much as it ought to have done. With respect to animals whose nourishment is grass, pairing would be of no use: the female feeds herself and her young at the same instant; and nothing is left for the male to do. On the other hand, all brute animals whose young require the nursing care of both parents, are directed by nature to pair; nor is that connection dissolved till the young can provide for themselves. Pairing is indispensable to wild birds that build on trees; because the male must provide food for his mate while she is hatching the eggs. And as they have commonly a numerous issue, it requires the labour of both to pick up food for themselves and for their young. Upon that account it is so ordered, that the young are sufficiently vigorous to provide for themselves, before a new brood is produced.

What I have now opened suggests the following question, Whether, according to the oeconomy above displayed, are we to presume, or not, that man is directed by nature to matrimony? If analogy can be relied on, the affirmative must be held, as there is no other creature in the known world to which pairing is so necessary. Man is an animal of long life, and is proportionally slow in growing to maturity: he is a helpless being before the age of fifteen or sixteen; and there may be in a family ten or twelve children of different births, before the eldest can shift for itself. Now in the original state of hunting and fishing, which are laborious occupations, and not always successful, a woman, suckling her infant, is not able to provide food even for herself, far less for ten or twelve voracious children. Matrimony, therefore, or pairing, is so necessary to the human race, that it must be natural and instinctive.[185]

[2. Human cultures]

In tracing the history of the criminal law, we must not hope that all its steps and changes can be drawn from the archives of any one nation. In fact, many steps were taken, and many changes made, before archives were kept, and even before writing was a common art. We must be satisfied with collecting the facts and circumstances as they may be gathered from the Laws of different countries: and if these put together make a regular system of causes and effects, we may rationally conclude, that the progress has been the same among all nations, in the capital circumstances at least; for the accidents, or the singular nature of a people, or of a government, will always produce some peculiarities.[186]

In the temperate climates of the old world, there is a great uniformity in the gradual progress of men from the savage state to the highest civilization; beginning with hunting and fishing, advancing to flocks and herds, and then to agriculture and commerce. One will be much disappointed, if he expect the same progress in America. Among the northern tribes, there is nothing that resembles the shepherd-state: they continue hunters and fishers as originally; because there is no cause so potent as to force them from that state to become shepherds. So far clear. But there is another fact of which we have no example in the old world, that seems not so easily explained: these people, without passing through the shepherd-state, have advanced to some degree of agriculture. [This he could not explain.[188]]

[With almost every aspect of culture, he attempted] to trace out its gradual progress, from its infancy among savages to its maturity among polished nations.*[190]

. . . the savage state is the infancy of man.[191]

Reasoning . . . requires two mental powers, the power of invention, and that of perceiving relations. By the former are discovered intermediate propositions, having the same relation to the fundamental proposition and to the conclusion; and that relation is verified by the latter. Both powers are necessary to the person who frames an argument, or a chain of reasoning: the latter only, to the person who judges of it. Savages are miserably deficient in both. With respect to the former, a savage may have from his nature a talent for invention; but it will stand him in little stead without a stock of ideas enabling him to select what may answer his purpose; and a savage has no opportunity to acquire such a stock. With respect to the latter, he knows little of relations. And how should he know, when both study and practice are necessary for distinguishing between relations? The understanding, at the same time, is among the illiterate obsequious to passion and prepossession; and among them the imagination acts without control, forming conclusions often no better than mere dreams.[192]

In the savage state, man is almost all body, with a very small proportion of mind. In the maturity of civil society, he is complete both in mind and body. In a state of degeneracy and voluptuousness, he has neither mind nor body.[193]

As far as his historical reconstructions are concerned, he has the following to say:

The Human Species is in every view an interesting subject, and has been in every age the chief inquiry of philosophers. The faculties of the mind have been explored, and the affections of the heart; but there is still wanting a history of the species, in its progress from the savage state to its highest civilization and improvement.[194]

Most of the subjects handled in the following sheets, admit but of probable con-

---

* "The history of mankind is a delightful subject. A rational enquirer is not less entertained than instructed, when he traces the gradual progress of manners, of laws, of arts, from their birth to their present maturity. Events and subordinate incidents are, in each of these, linked together, and connected by a regular chain of causes and effects. Law in particular becomes then only a rational study, when it is traced historically, from its first rudiments among savages, through successive changes, to its highest improvements in a civilized society."[189]

jecture*; and, with respect to such reasoning, it is often difficult to say, what degree of conviction they ought to produce. It is easy to form plausable arguments; but to form such as can stand the test of time, is not always easy.[196]

*Historical Law-Tracts* deals with the evolution of law, while *Sketches of the History of Man* gives accounts of the evolution of the following aspects of culture:

[A.] Progress of Men independent of Society.
    [1.] Progress respecting Food and Population.[197]
    [2.] Progress of Property.[198]
    [3.] Origin and Progress of Commerce.[199]
    [4.] Origin and Progress of Arts.
        [a.] Useful Arts.[200]
        [b.] Progress of Taste and of the fine Arts.[201]
    [5.] Manners.[202]
    [6.] Progress of the Female Sex [and marriage].[203]
    [7.] Progress and Effects of Luxury.[204]
[B.] Progress of Men in Society.
    [1.] Origin of National Societies.[205]
    [2.] General View of Government.[206]
    [3.] Progress of States from small to great, and from great to small.[207]
    [4.] Rise and Fall of Patriotism.[208]
    [5.] Military Branch of Government.[209]
    [6.] Principles and Progress of Reason.[210]
    [7.] Principles and Progress of Morality.[211]
    [8.] Principles and Progress of Theology.[212]

Kames usually limited himself to cultural explanations of the phenomena he investigated.

The intention of the present sketch is, to trace out such manners only as appear to proceed immediately from the nature and character of a people, whether influenced by the form of government, or depending on the degree of civilization. I am far from regretting, that manners produced by climate, by soil, and by other permanent causes, fall not under my plan: I should indeed make a sorry figure upon a subject that has been acutely discussed by the greatest genius of the present age [i.e., Montesquieu].[213]

He attempted to give an explanation for differences in the stage of cultural evolution reached by various societies.

The North-American tribes are remarkable with respect to one branch of their history, that, instead of advancing, like other nations, toward the maturity of society and government, they continue to this hour in their original state of hunting and fishing. A case so singular rouses our curiosity; and we wish to be made acquainted with the cause.[214]

. . . the only account that can or need be given, is paucity of inhabitants. Consider only the influence of custom, in rivetting men to their local situation and manners of life: once hunters, they will always be hunters, till some cause more potent than custom force them out of that state. Want of food, occasioned by rapid population, brought on the shepherd-state in the old world. That cause has not hitherto existed in North America:

---

* " . . . the common method of seeking redress of injustice done by an inferior court, is by appealing to one that is superior. . . . What was the cause of this innovation . . . by what means, and after what manner? . . . We are here left in the dark by our writers. I shall endeavour however to trace this matter the best way I can; supplying the want of positive facts by rational conjecture."[195]

the inhabitants, few in number, remain hunters and fishers, because that state affords them a competency of food.[215]

The last point to be considered is his treatment of the rise and fall of cultures.

... patriotism is the corner-stone of civil society; ... no nation ever became great and powerful without it; and, when extinguished ... the most powerful nation will totter and become a ruin.[216]

When tribes, originally small, spread wider and wider, by population, till they become neighbours, the slightest differences inflame mutual aversion, and instigate hostilities that never end. Weak tribes unite for defence against the powerful, and become insensibly one people: other tribes are swallowed up by conquest. And thus states become more and more extensive, till they be confined by natural boundaries of seas or mountains. . . .

But, at that rate, have we not reason to dread the union of all nations under one universal monarch? There are several causes that for ever will prevent a calamity so dreadful. The local situation of some countries, defended by strong natural barriers, is one of these. . . .

A second cause, is the weakness of a great state. The strength of a state doth not increase with its bulk, more than that of a man. An overgrown empire, far from being formidable to its neighbours, falls to pieces by its weight and unwieldiness. Its frontiers are not easily guarded . . . Patriotism vanishes in a great monarchy: the provinces have no mutual connection: and the distant provinces, which must be governed by bashaws, are always ripe for revolt. . . .

The chief cause is the luxury and effeminacy of a great monarchy, which leave no appetite for war, either in the sovereign or in his subjects. Great inequality of rank in an extensive kingdom, occasioned by a constant flow of riches into the capital, introduces show, expensive living, luxury, and sensuality. Riches, by affording gratification to every sensual appetite, become an idol to which all men bow the knee; and, when riches are worshipped as a passport to power as well as to pleasure, they corrupt the heart, eradicate every virtue, and foster every vice. In such dissolution of manners, contradictions are reconciled: avarice and meanness unite with vanity; dissimulation and cunning, with splendor. Where subjects are corrupted, what will the prince be, who is not taught to moderate his passions, who measures justice by appetite, and who is debilitated by corporeal pleasures? Such a prince never thinks of heading his own troops, nor of extending his dominions.[217]

Little reason then have we to apprehend the coalition of all nations into an universal monarchy. We see indeed in the history of mankind frequent instances of the progress of nations from small to great: but we also see instances no less frequent of extensive monarchies being split into many small states. Such is the course of human affairs: states are seldom stationary; but, like the sun, are either advancing to their meridian, or falling down gradually till they sink into obscurity. An empire subjected to effeminate princes, and devoid of patriotism, cannot long subsist entire.[218]

In the progress from maturity to a declining state, a nation differs widely from an individual. Old age puts an end to the latter: there are many causes that weaken the former; but old age is none of them, if it be not in a metaphorical sense. Riches, selfishness, and luxury, are the diseases that weaken prosperous nations: these diseases, following each other in a train, corrupt the heart, dethrone the moral sense, and make an anarchy in the soul: men stick at no expence to purchase pleasure; and they stick at no vice to supply that expence.[219]

## Gregory

John Gregory (1724–73) insisted that mental phenomena were subject to discoverable natural laws.

The Human Mind . . . is an object extremely fleeting, not the same in any two in-dividuals, and ever varying even in the same person . . . yet there is no reason to doubt, however fluctuating it may seem, of its being governed by laws as fixt and invariable as those of the Material System.[220]

The Imagination, like every thing in nature, is subjected to general and fixt laws, which can only be discovered by experience.[221]

He was indecisive when considering the relative importance of heredity and environment in producing the characteristics of personality, and gave evidence both *pro* and *con*.

1. In favor of heredity:

. . . many virtues as well as vices are constitutional.[222]

. . . the natural Genius or taste of the people.[223]

It is certain that, notwithstanding our promiscuous Marriages, many families are distinguished by peculiar circumstances in their character. This Family Character, like a Family Face, will often be lost in one generation and appear again in the succeeding. Without a doubt, Education, Habit, and Emulation, may contribute greatly in many cases to preserve it, but it will be generally found, that, independent of these, Nature has stamped an original impression on certain Minds, which Education may greatly alter or efface, but seldom so entirely as to prevent its traces from being seen by an accurate observer.[224]

2. In favor of environment:

There is certainly an original difference in the constitutions both of Men and of Nations; but this is not so great as at first view it seems to be. Human Nature consists of the same principles every where. In some people one principle is naturally stronger than it is in others, but exercise and proper culture will do much to supply the deficiency. The inhabitants of cold climates, having less natural warmth and sensibility of heart, enter but very faintly into those refinements of the Social Principle, in which Men of a different temper delight.[225]

All the public and social affections, in common with every Taste natural to the Human Mind, if they are not properly exericised, grow languid.[226]

Nature gives only the seeds of Taste, culture must rear them, or they will never become a considerable source of pleasure.[227]

Man has a "Social Principle."[228]

[This] principle . . . unites them into societies, and attaches them to one another by sympathy and affection. This principle is the source of the most heart-felt pleasure which we ever taste.[229]

Nature has made no individual, nor any class of people, independent of the rest of their Species, or sufficient for their own happiness.[230]

Another "principle" is that of imitation.

There is an universal principle of imitation among Mankind.[231]

Finally, Gregory gives the customary description of the stages of cultural evolution.[232]

## Robertson

William Robertson's (1721–93) basic premise was the psychic unity of mankind.

A human being, as he comes originally from the hand of nature, is every where the same. At his first appearance in the state of infancy, whether it be among the rudest savages or in the most civilized nation, we can discern no quality which marks any distinction or superiority. The capacity of improvement seems to be the same; and the talents he may afterwards acquire, as well as the virtues he may be rendered capable of exercising, depend, in a great measure, upon the state of society in which he is placed. To this state his mind naturally accommodates itself, and from it receives discipline and culture. In proportion to the wants which it accustoms a human being to feel, and the functions in which these engage him, his intellectual powers are called forth. According to the connexions which it establishes between him and the rest of his species, the affections of his heart are exerted. It is only by attending to this great principle that we can discover what is the character of man in every different period of his progress.[233]

... the human mind, even where its operations appear most wild and capricious, holds a course so regular, that in every age and country the dominion of particular passions will be attended with similar effects.[234]

Differences are the result of geographic and cultural factors. He laid stress upon the danger of oversimplification of causes.

... in inquiries concerning either the bodily or mental qualities of particular races of men, there is not a more common or more seducing error, than that of ascribing to a single cause, those characteristic peculiarities which are the effect of the combined operation of many causes.[235]

The operations of men are so complex that we must not attribute the form which they assume to the force of a single principle or cause.[236]

It is not by attending to any single cause or principle, how powerful and extensive soever its influence may appear, that we can explain the actions, or account for the character of men.[237]

[1. Geographical factors]

In every part of the earth where man exists, the power of climate operates, with decisive influence, upon his condition and character. In those countries which approach near to the extremes of heat or cold, this influence is so conspicuous as to strike every eye. Whether we consider man merely as an animal, or as being endowed with rational powers which fit him for activity and speculation, we shall find that he has uniformly attained the greatest perfection of which his nature is capable, in the temperate regions of the globe. There his constitution is most vigorous, his organs most acute, and his form most beautiful. There, too, he possesses a superior extent of capacity, greater fertility of imagination, more enterprising courage, and a sensibility of heart which gives birth to desires, not only ardent, but persevering. In this favourite situation he has displayed the utmost efforts of his genius, in literature, in policy, in commerce, in war, and in all the arts which improve or embellish life.[238]

However, the influence of the environment is inversely proportional to the degree of technological development of a society.

This powerful operation of climate is felt most sensibly by rude nations, and produces greater effects than in societies more improved. The talents of civilized men are continually exerted in rendering their own condition more comfortable; and by their ingenuity and inventions, they can in a great measure supply the defects, and guard against the inconveniences of any climate. But the improvident savage is affected by every circumstance peculiar to his situation. He takes no precaution either to mitigate or improve it. Like a plant or an animal, he is formed by the climate under which he is placed, and feels the full force of its influence.[239]

The effects of human ingenuity and labour are more extensive and considerable than even our own vanity is apt at first to imagine. When we survey the face of the habitable globe, no small part of that fertility and beauty which we ascribe to the hand of nature, is the work of man. His efforts, when continued through a succession of ages, change the appearance and improve the qualities of the earth.[240]

The labour and operations of man not only improve and embellish the earth, but render it more wholesome and friendly to life.[241]

[2. "Political and moral causes"]

Even the law of climate, more universal, perhaps, in its operation than any that affects the human species, cannot be applied, in judging of their conduct, without many exceptions.[242]

Moral and political causes . . . affect the disposition and character of individuals, as well as nations, still more powerfully than the influence of climate.[243]

[His approach was institutional.] In pointing out and explaining these causes and events, it is not necessary to observe the order of time with a chronological accuracy; it is of more importance to keep in view their mutual connexion and dependence, and to show how the operation of one event, or one cause, prepared the way for another, and augmented its influence.[244]

In every inquiry concerning the operations of men when united together in society, the first object of attention should be their mode of subsistence. Accordingly as that varies, their laws and policy must be different. The institution suited to the ideas and exigencies of tribes which subsist chiefly by fishing or hunting, and which have as yet acquired but an imperfect conception of any species of property, will be much more simple than those which must take place when the earth is cultivated with regular industry; and a right of property, not only in its productions, but in the soil itself, is completely ascertained. All the people of America, now under review, belong to the former class.[245]

1. They were divided into small independent communities. While hunting is the chief source of subsistence, a vast extent of territory is requisite for supporting a small number of people. . . . They cannot form into large communities, because it would be impossible to find subsistence; and they must drive to a distance every rival who may encroach on those domains, which they consider as their own.[246]

2. Nations which depend upon hunting are in a great measure strangers to the idea of property. . . . The forest or hunting-grounds are deemed the property of the tribe, from which it has a title to exclude every rival nation. But no individual arrogates a right to any district of these in preference to his fellow citizens.[247]

3. People in this state retain a high sense of equality and independence. Wherever the idea of property is not established, there can be no distinction among men but what arises from personal qualities.[248]

4. Among people in this state, government can assume little authority, and the sense

of civil subordination must remain very imperfect. While the idea of property is unknown, or incompletely conceived; while the spontaneous productions of the earth, as well as the fruits of industry, are considered as belonging to the public stock, there can hardly be any such subject of difference or discussion among the members of the same community, as will require the hand of authority to interpose in order to adjust it.[249]

He also showed the existence of constraint of culture and ethnocentrism.

. . . the ideas and wishes of man extend not beyond that state of society to which he is habituated. What it presents as objects of contemplation or enjoyment, fills and satisfies his mind, and he can hardly conceive any other mode of life to be pleasant, or even tolerable.[250]

For, in every stage of society, the faculties, the sentiments, and the desires of men are so accommodated to their own state, that they become standards of excellence to themselves, they affix the idea of perfection and happiness to those attainments which resemble their own, and, wherever the objects and enjoyments to which they have been accustomed are wanting, confidently pronounce a people to be barbarous and miserable. Hence the mutual contempt with which the members of communities, unequal in their degrees of improvement, regard each other.[251]

Robertson believed that evolution took place according to social laws.

. . . the disposition and manners of men are formed by their situation, and arise from the state of society in which they live. The moment that begins to vary, the character of a people must change. In proportion as it advances in improvement, their manners refine, their powers and talents are called forth. In every part of the earth, the progress of man hath been nearly the same; and we can trace him in his career from the rude simplicity of savage life, until he attains the industry, the arts, and the elegance of polished society.[252]

In order to acquire an adequate understanding of man and society, it is necessary to know how culture evolved.

In order to complete the history of the human mind, and attain to a perfect knowledge of its nature and operations, we must contemplate man in all those various situations wherein he has been placed. We must follow him in his progress through the different stages of society, as he gradually advances from the infant state of civil life towards its maturity and decline. We must observe, at each period, how the faculties of his understanding unfold; we must attend to the efforts of his active powers, watch the various movements of desire and affection, as they rise id his breast, and mark whither they tend, and with what ardour they are exerted.[253]

. . . in order to exhibit a just view of the state of Europe at the opening of the sixteenth century, it is necessary to look back and to contemplate the condition of the northern nations upon their first settlement in those countries which they occupied. It is necessary to mark the great steps by which they advanced from barbarism to refinement, and to point out those general principles and events which, by their uniform as well as extensive operation, conducted all of them to that degree of improvement in policy and in manners which they had attained at the period when Charles V. began his reign.[254]

Man in the New World was particularly important in the historical reconstruction of the evolution of culture.

In America, man appears under the rudest form in which we can conceive him to subsist. We behold communities just beginning to unite, and may examine the sentiments and actions of human beings in the infancy of social life, while they feel but imperfectly the force of its ties, and have scarcely relinquished their native liberty. That state of primeval simplicity, which was known in our continent only by the fanciful description of poets, really existed in the other.[255]

He therefore gave a picture of American ethnography and cultural evolution[256] that though valueless by modern standards because of the inadequacy of the data upon which it is based, caused Gibbon to declare that "the most original, and perhaps the most curious, portion of the history of human manners is at length rescued from the hands of sophists and declaimers."[257]

## Ferguson

Adam Ferguson (1723–1816) particularly stressed the social nature of man, which is derived from the helplessness of the human infant. This in turn results from his relative lack of instincts.

From the mere difference of result, on the part of man, compared with the other animals, an important distinction of nature may be assumed. This we commonly express in the terms, Reason and Instinct. But the line of separation here pointed out is far from being clearly marked in every instance.[258]

Among the characteristics of mind, knowledge is one of the first and most important. Considered as information of the ends we are to pursue, and the means we are to employ in obtaining them, it is to man, where mere instinct is wanting, the sole direction under which he is to act.[259]

Culture therefore provides socially acquirable behavior patterns to take the place of the absent genetically acquired ones.

. . . the arts which may be termed political, originate in the wants and defects of instinctive society.[260]

This is why human culture is so variable.

In stating the distinction of man among the animals, we remarked the indefinite varieties which the human species exhibits, in respect to condition and manner of life. While other animals of a kind or species are uniform, men are greatly diversified. Uniformity is the character of the one; variety of the other: Insomuch that men, of different ages and nations, exhibit a diversity, almost equivalent to that which takes place in the different kinds of animals.[261]

Because of the lack of instincts, the human being is helpless at birth.

. . . that the state of his infancy is more helpless, and of longer duration, than is exemplified in the case of any other species, may be ranked with the apparent comparative defects of his animal nature.[262]

The only effort of the child, or all he can do for himself, is to raise the feeble cry of distress, in which he announces at once the glad tidings of his life, and his need of assistance . . . it reaches the ear and heart of those who have means, understanding, and power, fitted to supply the relief which is wanted.[263]

. . . he is ever at the heels of his parent, and dreads being left behind as the most fatal misfortune. At every interval of separation, he longs to recover the company in which he was born.[264]

. . . he continues to apprehend, in the person of his parent, the source of every comfort of which he has any experience, or which he is any way qualified to receive.[265]

Man is consequently a social animal.

... man ... is formed for society.*[267]

Men are disposed to society.

They not only associate together, but take part with their fellow-creatures, and consider general calamities as matter of regret, general welfare as matter of joy.

This may be termed the *law of society;* and is that which qualifies the individual to be the member of a community, inclines him to contribute to the general good, and entitles him to partake in it.[268]

Man ... is ... in the highest degree, associating and political.[269]

The atmosphere of society ... is the element in which the human mind must draw the first breath of intelligence itself: or if not the vital air by which the celestial fire of moral sentiment is kindled: we cannot doubt but it is of mighty effect in exciting the flame; and that the minds of men, to use a familiar example, may be compared to those blocks of fuel which taken apart are hardly to be lighted: but if gathered unto a heap are easily kindled into a blaze.

Language is the instrument of society; and, we may presume, is not employed in any other matter but what the communications of society require; a consideration from which it should seem to follow, that man is indebted to society for every exercise of his faculties, of which language is formed to express the attainment or the use; a title under which we may fairly comprehend all the efforts of understanding or genius.†[271]

... the propensity of man to join the herd of his species, [is] a disposition, which operates even with the malevolent, and is common to all the gregarious animals.[272]

It appears from the history of mankind, that men have always acted in troops and companies.[273]

Every circumstance, in the lot of man, evinces the case of a being destined to bear an active part in the living system, to which he belongs. His very subsistence requires such a part. To obtain it, he must study the laws of natures, invent and practise a variety of arts. He is born in the society of his parents; and, for a considerable period of his life, owes, not only his well-being, but his preservation also, to their unwearied and anxious care. So soon as he is fit to act for himself, he is urged, by the most ardent and irresistible passions, to become the parent of a family in his turn; a condition in which affections are experienced, more powerful than interest or self-preservation. The company of his fellow creatures is ever required to his satisfaction or pastime. He may be unsociable, but he is not solitary; even to behave ill, he must be in society; and if he do not act from benevolence, he will act from interest to over-reach, or from ambition to command his fellow creatures, or from vanity to be admired, even by those whom he neither esteems nor loves.[274]

... nature has provided, that the individual can no where shake himself loose of his species, and that if he does not bear his part in society as a friend, he must suffer as an enemy.[275]

---

* "Societies may be referred to four general classes. Families, companies, nations, and empires.

"Families are united by affection; companies by the desire of society; nations by the desire of security; and empires by force."[266]

† " ... we have reason to consider his union with his species as the noblest part of his fortune. From this source are derived, not only the force, but the very existence of his happiest emotions; not only the better part, but almost the whole of his rational character. Send him to the desert alone, he is a plant torn from his roots: the form indeed may remain, but every faculty droops and withers; the human personage and the human character cease to exist."[270]

One expression of man's sociality is his desire for approbation.

As man is formed for society, he is justly made to enjoy or to suffer under the approbation or disapprobation of other men, as well as under his own. The complacency, therefore, of his fellow creatures, who esteem and who confide in him, or the aversion with which they reprobate or shun him, are powerful accessaries to conscience in urging its dictates.[276]

This principle of estimation . . . is known to be of sovereign influence in the government of mankind. . . . Wherever the standard of elevation and honour is erected, thither will the passions of men be pointed, and the most ardent afforts of fortitude and magnanimity be made.[277]

Man has both selfish and social tendencies.

Man, like the other animals, has certain instinctive propensities, which, prior to the perception of pleasure or pain, and prior to the experience of what is pernicious or useful, lead him to perform many functions which terminate in himself, or have a relation to his fellow creatures. He has one set of dispositions which tend to his animal preservation, and to the continuance of his race; another which lead to society, and by inlisting him on the side of one tribe or community, frequently engage him in war and contention with the rest of mankind.[278]

The interests of society, however, and of its members, are easily reconciled. If the individual owe every degree of consideration to the public, he receives, in paying that very consideration, the greatest happiness of which his nature iscapable; and the greatest blessing the public can bestow on its members, is to keep them attached to itself.[279]

Unlike most of the other members of the Scotch school, and along with Kames, he followed Shaftesbury in looking upon conscience as instinctive.

Moral approbation is comprehended in the law of estimation, and is indeed the principal fact from which we infer the reality of this law. . . .

It is, therefore, itself an ultimate fact and principle of nature, not an appearance to be explained from any other principle better known.[280]

Moral approbation is the judgement formed of characters and actions, as being excellent or just.

It is apposed to disapprobation or blame.

. . . the apprehension of excellence in himself is attended with elevation of mind. The apprehension of defect is attended with shame or remorse. The same apprehensions respecting other men are attended with complacency, veneration, love, pity, indignation, and scorn.[281]

The object of moral approbation is either some disposition of the mind, or some external action.[282]

Ferguson believed in the psychic unity of man, but because of man's lack of instincts, his desires are culturally canalized.

If in human nature there are qualities by which it is distinguished from every other part of the animal creation, this nature itself is in different climates and in different ages greatly diversified.[283]

Whoever has compared together the different conditions and manners of men, under varieties of education or fortune, will be satisfied, that mere situation does not constitute their happiness or misery; nor a diversity of external observances imply any opposition of sentiments on the subject of morality. They express their kindness and their enmity in different actions; but kindness or enmity is still the principle article of consideration in human life. They engage in different pursuits, or acquiesce in different conditions; but act from passions nearly the same.[284]

We have not any sufficient reason to believe that men, or remote ages and nations, differ from one another otherwise than by habits acquired in a different manner of life: But how differently are they affected by external causes? and what a difference do they exhibit in their choice of food, accommodations, and pleasures? The train-oil, or putrid fish, which is a feast in Labrador or Kamschatka, would be little else than poison to an European stomach.

Or if men, in situations so remote from one another, should be supposed to be of a different race; or to have incurred, from a difference of climate or situation, a change in the construction of their organs; varieties, almost equally striking, are observable, in the habits contracted in different ranks of life, by men of the same country and age. The peasant is at ease in his cottage, under a roof, and in the midst of accommodations, that would extremely discontent or displease a person accustomed to other conveniencies.[285]

As man adopts the customs of his group, he becomes subject to the constraint of culture.

Individuals, for the most part, without any authority of facts, single or multiplied, take their notion of things from report or prevailing opinion. . . .

From this source the bulk of the people derive their conceptions on the point of honour, and on the constituents of rank or distinction, whether birth, fortune, or personal qualities. From this source they derive their veneration for their religion, and their respect for the government of their country.

On these subjects, we think by contagion with other men; and remain submissive to government, or docile to religion, so long as the world continues to set the example. As we follow the herd, in forming our conceptions of what was respectable, so we are ready to follow the multitude also when such conceptions come to be questioned or rejected; and are no less vehement reformers of religion, and revolutionists in government, when the current of opinion has turned against former establishments, than we were zealous abettors while that current continued to set in a different direction.[286]

. . . men, in being repeatedly made to conceive an object in the same way, come to mistake their own habit of conception for an evidence of truth. Whence is it else, that the subjects of monarchy have one opinion respecting the obedience of political establishments, and the members of democracy a different one? Whence is it that the creed of the vulgar is so different in Asia, from what it is in Europe? . . .

There are habits of thinking peculiar to nations, to different ages, and even to individuals of the same nation and age, taken up at first without evidence, and often tenaciously retained without being questioned.[287]

It may be proved, that most of the opinions, habits, and pursuits, of men, result from the state of their society.[288]

Constraint of culture produces ethnocentrism.

Nations are frequently, by the difference of their manners and customs, mutual objects of wonder and censure, of contempt and aversion.[289]

No nation is so unfortunate as to think itself inferior to the rest of mankind: few are even willing to put up with the claim to equality. The greater part having chosen themselves, as at once, the judges and the models of what is excellent in their kind, are first in their own opinion, and give to others consideration or eminence, so far only as they approach to their own condition.[290]

Ferguson appreciated the importance of social factors in personality development.

Thinking and reasoning, we say, are the operations of some faculty; but in what manner the faculties of thought or reason remain, when they are not exerted, or by what difference in the frame they are unequal in different persons, are questions which we cannot resolve. Their operations alone discover them; when unapplied, they lie hid even from the person to whom they pertain; and their action is so much a part of their nature, that the faculty itself, in many cases, is scarcely to be distinguished from a habit acquired in its frequent exertion.

Persons who are occupied with different subjects, who act in different scenes, generally appear to have different talents, or at least to have the same faculties variously formed, and suited to different purposes. The peculiar genius of nations, as well as of individuals, may in this manner arise from the state of their fortunes.[291]

Man['s] . . . character . . . takes a stamp from his situation and the manner of life in which he is engaged.[292]

Consequently, degree of variation in personality is dependent upon the degree of social differentiation.

Mankind, when in their rude state, have a great uniformity of manners; but when civilized, they are engaged in a variety of pursuits; they tread on a larger field, and separate to a greater distance.[293]

Both *An Essay on the History of Civil Society* and *Principles of Moral and Political Science* are works in social anthropology and are based upon the premise that man is subject to natural law.

Mind, as well as body, has laws, which are exemplified in the course of nature, and which the critic collects only after the example has shown what they are.[294]

Man follows these laws blindly. .

The bulk of mankind are, like other parts of the system, subjected to the law of their nature, and, without knowing it, are led to accomplish its purpose; While they intend no more than subsistence and accommodation, or the peace of society, and the safety of their persons and their property, their faculties are brought into use, and they profit by exercise. In mutually conducting their relative interests and concerns, they acquire the habits of political life; are made to taste of their highest enjoyments, in the affections of benovolence, integrity, and elevation of mind; and, before they have deliberately considered in what the merit or felicity of their own nature consist, have already learned to perform many of its noblest functions.[295]

Though the usual interpretation Ferguson gives to social phenomena is cultural, as a result of Montesquieu's influence he gave some weight to geographic factors.

The great and striking diversities which obtain betwixt the inhabitants of climates far removed from each other, are, like the varieties of other animals in different regions, easily observed.[296]

The circumstances of the soil, and the climate, determine whether the inhabitant shall apply himself chiefly to agriculture or pasture; whether he shall fix his residence, or be moving continually about with all his possessions.[297]

He appreciated the role of diffusion, but, like modern social anthropologists, he insisted that both independently invented and diffused customs are accepted only when they harmonize with the existing culture.

Ages are generally supposed to have borrowed from those who went before them, and nations to have received their portion of learning or of art from abroad. . . .

It is known, that men improve by example and intercourse; but in the case of nations, whose members excite and direct each other, why seek from abroad the origin of arts, of which every society, having the principles in itself, only requires a favourable occasion to bring them to light. When such occasion presents itself to any people, they generally seize it; and while it continues, they improve the inventions to which it gave rise among themselves, or they willingly copy from others: but they never employ their own invention, nor look abroad, for instruction on subjects that do not lie in the way of their common pursuits; they never adopt a refinement of which they have not discovered the use.

Inventions, we frequently observe, are accidental; but it is probable, that an accident which escapes the artist in one age, may be seized by one who succeeds him, and who is better apprized of its use. Where circumstances are favourable, and where a people is intent on the objects of any art, every invention is preserved, by being brought into general practice; every model is studied, and every accident is turned to account. If nations actually borrow from their neighbours, they probably borrow only what they are nearly in a condition to have invented themselves.

Any singular practice of one country, therefore, is seldom transferred to another, till the way be prepared by the introduction of similar circumstances.[298]

In considering the evolution of culture, he paid some attention to the methodology involved.

The history of mankind is confined within a limited period, and from every quarter brings an intimation that human affairs have had a beginning. Nations, distinguished by the possession of arts, and the felicity of their political establishments, have been derived from a feeble original, and still preserve in their story the indications of a slow and gradual progress, by which this distinction was gained. The antiquities of every people, however diversified, and however disguised, contain the same information on this point.[299]

Such, therefore, appears to have been the commencement of history with all nations, and in such circumstances are we to look for the original character of mankind. The inquiry refers to a distant period, and every conclusion should build on the facts which are preserved for our use.[300]

. . . beyond the reach of such testimony, we can neither safely take, nor pretend to give, information on the subject.[301]

This is followed by a critical examination of the various kinds of data which are available.

[1. Folklore independently invented.] . . . the domestic antiquities of every nation must . . . be received with caution. They are, for the most part, the mere conjectures or the fictions of subsequent ages; and even where at first they contained some resemblance of truth, they still vary with the imagination of those by whom they are transmitted, and in every generation receive a different form. They are made to bear the stamp of the times through which they have passed in the form of tradition, not of the ages to which their pretended descriptions relate. The information they bring, is not like the light reflected from a mirror, which delineates the object from which it originally came; but, like rays that come broken and dispersed from an opaque or unpolished surface, only give the colours and features of the body from which they were last reflected.

When traditionary fables are rehearsed by the vulgar, they bear the marks of a national character. . . .

It were absurd to quote the fable of the Iliad or the Odyssey, the legends of Hercules, Theseus, or Oedipus, as authorities in matter of fact relating to the history of mankind; but they may, with great justice, be cited to ascertain what were the conceptions and sentiments of the age in which they were composed, or to characterize the genius of that people, with whose imaginations they were blended, and by whom they were fondly rehearsed and admired.

In this manner fiction may be admitted to vouch for the genius of nations, while history has nothing to offer that is entitled to credit.[302]

[2. Diffused folklore.] A mythology borrowed from abroad, a literature founded on references to a strange country, and fraught with foreign allusions, are much more confined in their use.[303]

[3. Customs of contemporary "primitive" societies.] Thucydides, notwithstanding the prejudice of his country against the name of *Barbarian*, understood that it was in the customs of barbarous nations he was to study the more ancient manners of Greece.

The Romans might have found an image of their own ancestors, in the representations they have given of ours; and if ever an Arab clan shall become a civilized nation, or any American tribe escape the poison which is administered by our traders of Europe, it may be from the relations of the present times, and the descriptions which are now given by travellers, that such a people, in after ages, may best collect the accounts of their origin. It is in their present condition that we are to behold, as in a mirror, the features of our own progenitors; and from thence we are to draw our conclusions with respect to the influence of situations, in which we have reason to believe that our fathers were placed.

What should distinguish a German or a Briton, in the habits of his mind or his body, in his manners or apprehensions, from an American, who, like him, with his bow and his dart, is left to traverse the forest; and in a like severe or variable climate, is obliged to subsist by the chase?

If, in advanced years, we would form a just notion of our progress from the cradle, we must have recourse to the nursery; and from the example of those who are still in the period of life we mean to describe, take our representation of past manners, that cannot, in any other way, be recalled.[304]

His empirical approach caused him to reject the customary speculative conjectures as to the state of nature.

Natural productions are generally formed by degrees. Vegetables are raised from a tender shoot, and animals from an infant state. The latter, being active, extend together their operations and their powers, and have a progress in what they perform, as well as in the faculties they acquire. This progress in the case of man is continued to a greater extent than in that of any other animal. Not only the individual advances from infancy to manhood, but the species itself from rudeness to civilization. Hence the supposed departure of mankind from the state of their nature; hence our conjectures and different opinions of what man must have been in the first age of his being. . . .

The desire of laying the foundation of a favourite system, or a fond expectation, perhaps, that we may be able to penetrate the secrets of nature, to the very source of existence, have, on this subject, led to many fruitless inquiries, and given rise to many wild suppositions. Among the various qualities which mankind possess, we select one of a few particulars on which to establish a theory,[305] and in framing our account of what man was in some imaginary state of nature, we overlook what he has always appeared within the reach of our own observation, and in the records of history.

In every other instance, however, the natural historian thinks himself obliged to collect facts, not to offer conjectures. When he treats of any particular species of animals, he supposes that their present dispositions and instincts are the same which they originally had, and that their present manner of life is a continuance of their first destination. He admits that his knowledge of the material system of the world consists in a collection of facts, or at most, in general tenets derived from particular observations and experiments. It is only in what related to himself, and in matters the most important and the most easily known, that he substitutes hypothesis instead of reality, and confounds the provinces of imagination and reason, of poetry and science. . . .

If both the earliest and the latest accounts collected from every quarter of the earth, represent mankind as assembled in troops and companies*; and the individual always joined by affection to one party, while he is possibly opposed to another; employed in the exercise of recollection and foresight; inclined to communicate his own sentiments, and to be made acquainted with those of others; these facts must be admitted as the foundation of all our reasoning relative to man. His mixed disposition to friendship or enmity, his reason, his use of language and articulate sounds, like the shape and the erect position of his body, are to be considered as so many attributes of his nature: they are to be retained in his description, as the wing and the paw are in that of the eagle and the lion, and as different degrees of fierceness, vigilance, timidity, or speed, have a place in the natural history of different animals.

If the question be put, What the mind of man could perform, when left to itself, and without the aid of any foreign direction? we are to look for our answer in the history of mankind. Particular experiments which have been found so useful in establishing the principles of other sciences, could probably, on this subject, teach us nothing important, or new: we are to take the history of every active being from his conduct in the situation to which he is formed, not from his appearance in any forced or uncommon condition; a wild man therefore, caught in the woods, where he had always lived apart from his species, is a singular instance, not a specimen of any general character. As the anatomy of an eye which had never received the impressions of light, or that of an ear which had never felt the impulse of sounds, would probably exhibit defects in the very structure of the organs themselves, arising from their not being applied to their proper functions; so any particular case of this sort would only show in what degree the powers of apprehension and sentiment could exist where they had not been employed, and what would be the defects and imbecilities of a heart in which the emotions that arise in society had never been felt.

Mankind are to be taken in groups, as they have always subsisted. The history of the individual is but a detail of the sentiments and the thoughts he has entertained in the view of his species: and every experiment relative to this subject should be made with entire societies, not with single men. We have every reason, however, to believe, that in the case of such an experiment made, we shall suppose, with a colony of children transplanted from the nursery, and left to form a society apart, untaught and undisciplined, we should only have the same things repeated, which, in so many different parts of the earth, have been transacted already. The members of our little society would feed and sleep, would herd together and play, would have a language of their own, would quarrel and divide, would be to one another the most important objects of the scene, and, in the ardour of their friendships and competitions, would overlook their personal danger, and suspend the

* "Mankind have always wandered or settled, agreed or quarrelled, in troops and companies."[306]

care of their self-preservation. Has not the human race been planted like the colony in question? Who has directed their course? whose instruction have they heard? or whose example have they followed?

Nature, therefore, we shall presume, having given to every animal its mode of existence, its dispositions and manner of life, has dealt equally with the human race; and the natural historian who would collect the properties of this species, may fill up every article now as well as he could have done in any former age. The attainments of the parent do not descend in the blood of his children, nor is the progress of man to be considered as a physical mutation of the species. The individual, in every age, has the same race to run from infancy to manhood, and every infant, or ignorant person, now, is a model of what man was in his original state. He enters on his career with advantages peculiar to his age; but his natural talent is probably the same. The use and application of this talent is changing, and men continue their works in progression through many ages together: they build on foundations laid by their ancestors; and in a succession of years, tend to a perfection in the application of their faculties, to which the aid of long experience is required, and to which many generations must have combined their endeavours. We observe the progress they have made; we distinctly enumerate many of its steps; we can trace them back to a distant antiquity, of which no record remains, nor any monument is preserved, to inform us what were the openings of this wonderful scene. The consequence is, that instead of attending to the character of our species, where the particulars are vouched by the surest authority, we endeavour to trace it through ages and scenes unknown; and, instead of supposing that the beginning of our story was nearly of a piece with the sequel, we think ourselves warranted to reject every circumstance of our present condition and frame, as adventitious, and foreign to our nature. The progress of mankind, from a supposed state of animal sensibility, to the attainment of reason, to the use of language, and to the habit of society, has been accordingly painted with a force of imagination, and its steps have been marked with a boldness of invention, that would tempt us to admit, among the materials of history, the suggestions of fancy, and to receive, perhaps, as the model of our nature in its original state, some of the animals whose shape has the greatest resemblance to ours. . . .we can learn nothing of his nature from the analogy of other animals. If we would know him, we must attend to himself, to the course of his life, and the tenor of his conduct. With him the society appears to be as old as the individual, and the use of the tongue as universal as that of the hand or the foot. If there was a time in which he had his acquaintance with his own species to make, and his faculties to acquire, it is a time of which we have no record, and in relation to which our opinions can serve no purpose, and are supported by no evidence. . . .

We speak of art as distinguished from nature; but art itself is natural to man. He is in some measure the artificer of his own frame, as well as of his fortune, and is destined, from the first age of his being, to invent and contrive. . . . But he does not propose to make rapid and hasty transitions; his steps are progressive and slow; and his force, like the power of a spring, silently presses on every resistance; an effect is sometimes produced before the cause is perceived; and with all his talent for projects, his work is often accomplished before the plan is devised. It appears, perhaps, equally difficult to retard or to quicken his pace. . . .

If we are asked therefore, where the state of nature is to be found? we may answer, it is here; and it matters not whether we are understood to speak in the island of Great Britain, at the Cape of Good Hope, or the Straits of Magellan. While this active being is in the train of employing his talents, and of operating on the subjects around him, all situations are equally natural. If we are told, that vice, at least, is contrary to nature; we may answer, it is worse; it is folly and wretchedness. But if nature is only opposed to art, in what situation of the human race are the footsteps of art unknown? In the condition of the savage, as well as in that of the citizen, are many proofs of human invention; and in either is not any permanent station, but a mere stage through which this travelling being is destined to pass. If the palace be unnatural, the cottage is so no less; and the highest refinements of political and moral apprehension, are not more artificial in their kind, than the first operations of sentiment and reason.

If we admit that man is susceptible of improvement, and has in himself a principle of progression, and a desire of perfection, it appears improper to say, that he has quitted the state of his nature, when he has begun to proceed; or that he finds a station for which he was not intended, while, like other animals, he only follows the disposition, and employs the powers that nature has given.

The latest efforts of human invention are but a continuation of certain devices which were practised in the earliest ages of the world, and in the rudest state of mankind.[307] What the savage projects, or observes, in the forest, are the steps which led nations, more advanced, from the architecture of the cottage to that of the palace, and conducted the human mind from the perceptions of sense, to the general conclusions of science.[308]

Ferguson gave general descriptions of what were to him the two most important stages in social evolution:

[1.] Of rude nations prior to the establishment of property.[309]

[2.] Of rude nations under the impressions of property and interest.[310]

He also described the evolution of various aspects of culture, including science,[311] religion,[312] art,[313] economy,[314] social differentiation,[315] language,[316] and political organization.[317]

His opposition to a rationalistic interpretation of cultural evolution is exemplified in his treatment of the social contract.

. . . the establishments of men, like those of every animal, are suggested by nature, and are the result of instinct, directed by the variety of situations in which mankind are placed. Those establishments arose from successive improvements that were made, without any sense of their general effect; and they bring human affairs to a state of complication, which the greatest reach of capacity with which human nature was ever adorned, could not have projected; nor even when the whole is carried into execution, can it be comprehended in its full extent.[318]

Like the winds that come we know not whence, and blow whithersoever they list, the forms of society are derived from an obscure and distant origin; they arise, long before the date of philosophy, from the instincts, not from the speculations of men. The crowd of mankind are directed, in their establishments and measures, by the circumstances in which they are placed; and seldom are turned from their way, to follow the plan of any single projector.

Every step and every movement of the multitude, even in what are termed enlightened ages, are made with equal blindness to the future; and nations stumble upon establishments, which are indeed the result of human action, but not the execution of any human design.[319]

No constitution is formed by concert, no government is copied from a plan.[320]

What this constitution may be in its earliest form, depends on a variety of circumstances in the condition of nations: it depends on the extent of the principality in its rude state; on the degree of disparity to which mankind had submitted before they begun to dispute the abuses of power: it depends likewise on what we term *accidents,* the personal character of an individual, or the events of a war.[321]

Men, in fact, while they pursue in society different objects, or separate views, procure a wide distribution of power, and by a species of chance, arrive at a posture for civil engagements, more favourable to human nature than what human wisdom could ever calmly devise.[322]

Ferguson believed in social progress.

. . . man is susceptible of improvement, and has in himself a principle of progression, and a desire of perfection.[323]

He interested himself in the factors that produce the rise and fall of cultures.

Most subjects in nature, which, from the energy of a salutary principle, are susceptible of advancement, are likewise, by the failure or abuse of that principle, susceptible of degradation and ruin. . . . Man, with whom the sources of good and of evil are more entrusted to his own management, is likewise exposed, in a much higher degree, to the extremes of comparative degradation and misery. The progress of nations in one age, to high measures of intellectual attainment and cultivated manners, is not more remarkable than the decline that sometimes ensues in their fall to extreme depravation and intellectual debility.[324]

Like Brown, he was not satisfied with the usual explanation on the basis of the organic analogy.

Such appearances have given rise to a general apprehension, that the progress of societies to what we call the heights of national greatness, is not more natural, than their return to weakness and obscurity is necessary and unavoidable. The images of youth, and of old age, are applied to nations; and communities, like single men, are supposed to have a period of life, and a length of thread, which is spun by the fates in one part uniform and strong, in another weakened and shattered by use; to be cut, when the destined aera is come, and to make way for a renewal of the emblem in the case of those who arise in succession. . . .

The image indeed is apposite, and the history of mankind renders the application familiar. But it must be obvious, that the case of nations, and that of individuals, are very different. The human frame has a general course: it has in every individual a frail contexture, and limited duration; it is worn by exercise, and exhausted by a repetition of its functions: but in a society, whose constituent members are renewed in every generation, where the race seems to enjoy perpetual youth, and accumulating advantages, we cannot, by any parity of reason, expect to find imbecilities connected with mere age and length of days.[325]

. . . a national spirit is frequently transient, not on account of any incurable distemper in the nature of mankind, but on account of their voluntary neglects and corruptions.[326]

In Ferguson's estimation, the rise and fall of a culture primarily depended upon the relative degree of virtue and vice, respectively, that existed in society.

The wealth, the aggrandizement, and power of nations, are commonly the effects of virtue; the loss of these advantages is often a consequence of vice.[327]

The institutions of men, if not calculated for the preservation of virtue, are, indeed, likely to have an end as well as a beginning: but so long as they are effectual to this purpose, they have at all times an equal principle of life, which nothing but an external force can suppress; no nation ever suffered internal decay but from the vice of its members.[328]

The strength of nations consists in the wealth, the numbers, and the character of their people.[329]

Whatever may be the natural wealth of a people, or whatever may be the limits beyond which they cannot improve on their stock, it is probable, that no nation has ever reached those limits, or has been able to postpone its misfortunes, and the effects of misconduct, until its fund of materials, and the fertility of its soil, were exhausted, or the numbers of its people were greatly reduced. The same errors in policy, and weakness of manners, which prevent the proper use of resources, likewise check their increase, or improvement.[330]

[1. Wealth.] The wealth of the state consists in the fortune of its members. . . . any immoderate increase of private expenses is a prelude to national weakness.[331]

. . . an expense, whether sustained at home or abroad, whether a waste of the present, or an anticipation of future, revenue, if it bring no proper return, is to be reckoned among the causes of national ruin.[332]

[2. Numbers.] Men will crowd where the situation is tempting, and, in a few generations, will people every country to the measure of its means of subsistence.* . . .

If the plantain, the cocoa, or the palm, were sufficient to maintain an inhabitant, the race of men in the warmer climates might become as numerous as the trees of the forest. But in many parts of the earth, from the nature of the climate, and the soil, the spontaneous produce being next to nothing, the means of subsistence are the fruits only of labour and skill. If a people, while they retain their frugality, increase their industry, and improve their arts, their numbers must grow in proportion.† Hence it is, that the cultivated fields of Europe are more peopled than the wilds of America, or the plains of Tartary.

But even the increase of mankind which attends the accumulation of wealth, has its limits. The *necessary of life,* is a vague and a relative term: it is one thing in the opinion of the savage; another in that of the polished citizen: it has a reference to the fancy, and to the habits of living. While arts improve, and riches increase; while the possessions of individuals, or their prospects of gain, come up to their opinion of what is required to settle a family, they enter on its cares with alacrity. But when the possession, however redundant, falls short of the standard, and a fortune supposed sufficient for marriage is attained with difficulty, population is checked, or begins to decline.[335]

[3. Character.] Virtue is a necessary constituent of national strength: capacity, and a vigorous understanding, are no less necessary to sustain the fortune of states. Both are improved by discipline, and by the exercises in which men are engaged.[336]

If the strength of a nation . . . consists in the men on whom it may rely, and who are fortunately or wisely combined for its preservation, it follows, that manners are as important as either numbers or wealth; and that corruption is to be accounted a principal cause of the national declension and ruin.

Whoever perceives what are the qualities of man in his excellence, may easily, by that standard, distinguish his defects or corruptions. If an intelligent, a courageous, and an affectionate mind, constitutes the perfection of his nature, remarkable failings in any of those particulars must proportionally sink or debase his character.[337]

We are now to inquire, why nations cease to be eminent; and why societies which

* " . . . it is . . . commonly observed, or admitted, that the numbers of mankind in every situation do multiply up to the means of their subsistence."[333]
† "In the progress, as well as in the result of commercial arts, mankind are enabled to subsist in growing numbers; learn to ply their resources, and to wield their strength, with superior ease and success."[334]

have drawn the attention of mankind by great examples of magnanimity, conduct, and national success, should sink from the height of their honours, and yield, in one age, the palm which they had won in a former. Many reasons will probably occur.[338]

[a.] . . . the fickleness and inconstancy of mankind, who become tired of their pursuits and exertions, even while the occasions that gave rise to those pursuits, in some measure, continue.[339]

[b.] . . . the change of situations, and the removal of objects which served to excite their spirit.

The public safety, and the relative interest of states; political establishments, the pretensions of party, commerce, and arts, are subjects which engage the attention of nations. The advantages gained in some of these particulars, determine the degree of national prosperity. The ardour and vigour with which they are pursued, is the measure of a national spirit. When those objects cease to animate, nations may be said to languish; when they are during a considerable time neglected, states must decline, and their people degenerate.[340]

The habits of a vigorous mind are formed in contending with difficulties, not in enjoying the repose of a pacific station; penetration and wisdom are the fruits of experience, not the lessons of retirement and leisure; ardour and generosity are the qualities of a mind roused and animated in the conduct of scenes that engage the heart, not the gifts of reflection or knowledge.[341]

The materials of human art are never entirely exhausted, and the applications of industry are never at an end. The national ardour is not, at any particular time, proportioned to the occasion there is for activity; nor the curiosity of the learned to the extent of subject that remains to be studied.[342]

[c.] . . . a change in the prevailing opinions relating to the constituents of honour or happiness. When mere riches, or court favour, are supposed to constitute rank; the mind is misled from the consideration of qualities on which it ought to rely. Magnanimity, courage, and the love of mankind, are sacrificed to avarice and vanity, or suppressed under a sense of dependence. The individual considers his community so far only as it can be rendered subservient to his personal advancement or profit: he states himself in competition with his fellow creatures; and, urged by the passions of emulation, of fear and jealousy, of envy and malice, he follows the maxims of an animal destined to preserve his separate existence, and to indulge his capacity or his appetite, at the expense of his species.

On this corrupt foundation, men become either rapacious, deceitful, and violent, ready to trespass on the rights of others; or servile, mercenary, and base, prepared to relinquish their own.[343]

[d.] . . . the separation of professions, while it seems to promise improvement of skill, and is actually the cause why the productions of every art become more perfect as commerce advances; yet, in its termination and ultimate effects, serves, in some measure, to break the bands of society, to substitute mere forms and rules of art in place of ingenuity, and to withdraw individuals from the common scene of occupation, on which the sentiments of the heart, and the mind, are most happily employed.[344]

[e.] . . . it is vain to expect that we can give to the multitude of a people a sense of union among themselves, without admitting hostility to those who oppose them. Could we at once, in the case of any nation, extinguish the emulation which is excited from abroad, we should probably break or weaken the bands of society at home, and close the busiest scenes of national occupations and virtues.[345]

A state of greater tranquility hath many happy effects. But if nations pursue the plan of enlargement and pacification, still their members can no longer apprehend the common ties of society, nor be engaged by affection in the cause of their country, they must err on the opposite side, and by leaving too little to agitate the spirits of men, bring on ages of languor, if not of decay.

The members of a community may, in this manner, like the inhabitants of a conquered province, be made to lose the sense of every connection, but that of kindred or neighbourhood; and have no common affairs to transact, but those of trade: connections, indeed, or transactions, in which probity and friendship may still take place; but in which the national spirit, whose ebbs and flows we are now considering, cannot be exerted.[346]

However, the decline of one culture heralds the rise of another.

. . . but while devastation and ruin appear on every side, mankind are forced anew upon those confederacies, acquire again that personal confidence and vigour, that social attachment, that use of arms, which, in former times, rendered a small tribe the seed of a great nation. . . . When human nature appears in the utmost state of corruption, it has actually begun to reform.[347]

## Millar

John Millar (1735–1801) appreciated the role of social factors in personality development.

That the dispositions and behaviour of man are liable to be influenced by the circumstances in which he is placed, and by his peculiar education and habits of life, is a proposition which few persons will be inclined to controvert.[348]

Rude and barbarous nations . . . have no such division of labour as gives rise to separate employments and professions, but are engaged, promiscuously and successively, in all those kinds of work with which they are acquainted. Having all, therefore, the same pursuits and occupations, and consequently the same objects of attention, they undergo a similar education and discipline, and acquire similar habits and ways of thinking. From the accounts of travellers and historians, we accordingly find, that however such people may happen to to be distinguished by singular institutions and whimsical customs, they discover a wonderful uniformity in the general outline of their character and manners; an uniformity no less remarkable in different nations the most remote from each other, than in the different individuals of the same tribe or nation.[349]

He mentioned a number of factors as producing the characteristics of a culture.

In searching for the causes of those peculiar systems of law and government which have appeared in the world, we must undoubtedly resort, first of all, to the differences of situation, which have suggested different views and motives of action to the inhabitants of particular countries. Of this kind, are the fertility or barrenness of the soil, the nature of its productions, the species of labour requisite for procuring subsistence, the number of individuals collected together in one community, their proficiency in arts, the advantages which they enjoy for entering into mutual transactions, and for maintaining an intimate correspondence. The variety that frequently occurs in these, and such other particulars, must have a prodigious influence upon the great body of a people; as, by giving a peculiar direction to their inclinations and pursuits, it must be productive of correspondent habits, dispositions, and ways of thinking.[350]

Among the several circumstances which may affect the gradual improvements of society, the difference of climate is one of the most remarkable.[351]

On the other hand, he showed that the geographic interpretation is faulty.

> . . . in the history of the world, we see no regular marks of that secret influence which has been ascribed to the air and climate, but, on the contrary, may commonly explain the great difference in the manners and customs of mankind from other causes, the existence of which is capable of being more clearly ascertained.

> How many nations are to be found, whose situation in point of climate is apparently similar, and, yet, whose character and political institutions are entirely opposite? Compare, in this respect, the mildness and moderation of the Chinese, with the rough manners and intolerant principles of their neighbours in Japan. What a contrast is exhibited by people at no greater distance than were the ancient Athenians and Lacedemonians? Can it be conceived that the difference between the climate of France and that of Spain, or between that of Greece and of the neighbouring provinces of the Turkish empire, will account for the different usages and manners of the present inhabitants? How is it possible to explain those national peculiarities that have been remarked in the English, the Irish, and the Scotch, from the different temperature of the weather under which they have lived?

> The different manners of people in the same country, at different periods, are no less remarkable, and afford evidence yet more satisfactory, that national character depends very little upon the immediate operation of climate. The inhabitants of Sparta are, at present, under the influence of the same physical circumstances as in the days of Leonidas. The modern Italians live in the country of the ancient Romans.[352]

Millar was an institutionalist; *The Origin of the Distinction of Ranks* is primarily an investigation of the effects of changing means of subsistence upon the evolution of marriage,[353] political organization,[354] and slavery.[355]

> The following Inquiry is intended to illustrate the natural history of mankind in several important articles. This is attempted, by pointing out the more obvious and common improvements which gradually arise in the state of society, and by showing the influence of these upon the manners, the laws, and the government of a people.[356]

His institutionalism can also be seen from the mere titles of some of his chapters in *An Historical View of the English Government:*

> The advancement of manufactures, commerce, and the arts, since the reign of William III.; and the tendency of this advancement to diffuse a spirit of liberty and independence.[357]

> How far the advancement of commerce and manufactures has contributed to the extension and diffusion of knowledge and literature.[358]

> The effects of commerce and manufactures, and of opulence and civilization upon the morals of a people.[359]

> The progress of science relative to law and government.[360]

> The grandual advancement of the fine arts—their influence upon government.[361]

Millar was also a teleological functionalist; in his own words, an analysis was only complete when "we are able to add the reasons of those particular customs which have been uniformly reported."[362]

He believed in the uniformity of cultural evolution.

> One of the most remarkable differences between man and other animals consists in that wonderful capacity for the improvement of his faculties with which he is endowed. Never satisfied with any particular attainment, he is continually impelled by his desires

rom the pursuit of one object to that of another; and his activity is called forth in the prosecution of the several arts which render his situation more easy and agreeable. This progress however is slow and gradual; at the same time that, from the uniformity of the human constitution, it is accompanied with similar appearances in different parts of the world.[363]

When we survey the present state of the globe, we find that, in many parts of it, the inhabitants are so destitute of culture, as to appear little above the condition of brute animals; and even when we peruse the remote history of polished nations, we have seldom any difficulty in tracing them to a state of the same rudeness and barbarism. There is, however, in man a disposition and capacity for improving his condition, by the exertion of which, he is carried on from one degree of advancement to another; and the similarity of his wants, as well of the faculties by which those wants are supplied, has every where produced a remarkable uniformity in the several steps of his progression. A nation of savages, who feel the want of almost every thing requisite for the support of life, must have their attention directed to a small number of objects, to the acquisition of food and cloathing or the procuring of shelter from the inclemencies of the weather; and their ideas and feelings, in conformity to their situation, must, of course, be narrow and contracted. Their first efforts are naturally calculated to increase the means of subsistence, by catching or ensnaring wild animals, or by gathering the spontaneous fruits of the earth; and the experience, acquired in the exercise of these employments, is apt, successively, to point out the methods of taming and rearing cattle, and of cultivating the ground. According as men have been successful in these great improvements, and find less difficulty in the attainment of bare necessaries, their prospects are gradually enlarged, their appetites and desires are more awakened and called forth in pursuit of the several conveniencies of life; and the various branches of manufacture, together with commerce, its inseparable attendant, and with science and literature, the natural offspring of ease and affluence,* are introduced, and brought to maturity. By such gradual advances in rendering their situation more comfortable, the most important alterations are produced in the state and condition of a people: their numbers are increased; the connections of society are extended; and men, being less oppressed with their own wants, are more at liberty to cultivate the feelings of humanity: property, the great source of distinction among individuals, is established; and the various rights of mankind, arising from their multiplied connections, are recognised and protected: the laws of a country are thereby rendered numerous; and a more complex form of government becomes necessary, for distributing justice, and for preventing the disorders which proceed from the jarring interests and passions of a large and opulent community. It is evident, at the same time, that these, and such other effects of improvement, which have so great a tendency to vary the state of mankind, and their manner of life, will be productive of suitable variations in their taste and sentiments, and in their general system of behaviour.

There is thus, in human society, a natural progress from ignorance to knowledge, and from rude, to civilized manners, the several stages of which are usually accompanied with peculiar laws and customs. Various accidental causes, indeed, have contributed to accelerate, or to retard this advancement in different countries. It has even happened that nations, being placed in such unfavourable circumstances as to render them long stationary at a particular period, have been so habituated to the peculiar manners of that age, as to retain a strong tincture of those peculiarities through every subsequent

*" . . . the refinements of taste, and the cultivation of the elegant arts, among a people, are in proportion to those improvements which multiply the comforts and conveniencies of life, and give rise to extensive affluence and luxury."[364]

revolution. This appears to have occasioned some of the chief varieties which take place in the maxims and customs of nations equally civilized.

The character and genius of a nation may, perhaps, be considered as nearly the same with that of every other in similar circumstances; but the case is very different with respect to individuals, among whom there is often a great diversity, proceeding from no fixed causes that are capable of being ascertained. Thus, in a multitude of dice thrown together at random, the result, at different times, will be nearly equal; but in one or two throws of a single die, very different numbers may often be produced. It is to be expected therefore, that, though the greater part of the political system of any country be derived from the combined influence of the whole people, a variety of peculiar institutions will sometimes take their origin from that causal interposition of particular persons, who happen to be placed at the head of a community, and to be possessed of singular abilities and views of policy. This has been regarded, by many writers, as the great source of those differences which are to be found in the laws, and government of different nations. . .

But, notwithstanding the concurring testimony of historians, concerning the great political changes introduced by the lawgivers of a remote age, there may be reason to doubt, whether the effect of their interpositions has ever been so extensive as is generally supposed. Before an individual can be invested with so much authority, and possessed of such reflection and foresight as would induce him to act in the capacity of a legislator, he must, probably, have been educated and brought up in the knowledge of those natural manners and customs, which, for ages perhaps, have prevailed among his countrymen. Under the influence of all the prejudices derived from ancient usage, he will commonly be disposed to prefer the system already established to any other, of which the effects have not been ascertained by experience; or if in any case he should venture to entertain a different opinion, he must be sensible that, from the general prepossession in favour of the ancient establishment, an attempt to overturn it, or to vary it in any considerable degree, would be a dangerous measure, extremely unpopular in itself, and likely to be attended with troublesome consequences.[365]

### Stuart

Gilbert Stuart (1742–86) was primarily an institutionalist.

It is usual to treat law, manners, and government, as if they had no connection with history, or with each other. Law and manners are commonly understood to be nothing more than collections of ordinances and matters of fact; and government is too often a foundation for mere speculation and metaphysical refinements. Yet law is only a science when observed in its spirit and history; government cannot be comprehended but by attending to the minute steps of its rise and progression; and the systems of manners which characterise man in all the periods of society which pass from rudeness to civility cannot be displayed without the discrimination of these different situations. It is in the records of history, in the scene of real life, not in the conceits and the abstractions of fancy and philosophy, that human nature is to be studied.

But, while it is in the historical manner that laws, customs, and government, are to be inquired into, it is obvious, that their dependence and connection are close and intimate. They all tend to the same point, and to the illustration of one another. It is from the consideration of them all, and in their union, that we are to explain the complicated forms of civil society, and the wisdom and accident which mingle in human affairs.

After this method, I have endeavoured to investigate my subject.[366]

Fiefs and chivalry were mutually to act upon one another. The feudal association was to direct and foster chivalry; and, from chivalry, it was to receive a support or lustre

They were plants which were destined to take root about the same period, and to sympathise in their growth, and in their decline.[367]

Because of this interdependence of customs, a given custom has a different meaning in different cultural contexts.

I am entitled to conclude, that the spirit of chivalry was not uniform any more than that of fiefs; and that, at different periods, its manners were opposite and contradictory.[368]

Another point that he made was the irrationality of social change.

It is only to those who apply to rude societies the ideas of a cultivated area, that the institutions of chivalry seem the production of an enlightened policy. They remember not the inexperience of dark ages, and the attachment of nations to their ancient usages. They consider not, that if an individual, in such times, were to arise, of a capacity to frame schemes of legislation and government, he could not reduce them to execution. He could not mould the conceptions of states to correspond to his own. It is from no pre-conceived plan, but from circumstances which exist in real life and affairs, that legislators and politicians acquire an ascendency among men. It was the actual condition of their times, not projects suggested by philosophy and speculation, that directed the conduct of Lycurgus and Solon.[369]

Confusions often lead to improvement, by demanding and pointing out a remedy.[370]

Finally, he gave the usual portrayal of the evolution of marriage[371] and law.[372]

## Monboddo

As early as 1766, James Burnett, Lord Monboddo (1714–99), expressed his interest in cultural evolution.

I project . . . a *History of Man;* in which I would propose to trace him through the several stages of his existence\*; for there is a progression of our species from a state little better than mere brutality to that most perfect state in ancient Greece, which is really amazing, and peculiar to our species.[374]

In his books he tried to show that human culture had evolved from a condition similar to that of other animals.

. . . all nations, even the most polished and civilized, of which we read in history, were originally barbarians . . . man himself was originally a wild savage animal, till he was tamed, and, as I may say, humanized, by civility and arts.[375]

. . . wherever there is a progress†, there must be a beginning‡; and the beginning in this case can be no other than the mere animal: For in tracing back the progress, where else can we stop? If we have discovered so many links of the chain, we are at liberty to suppose the rest, and conclude, that the beginning of it must hold of that common nature which connects us with the rest of the animal creation.[379]

Now, the history of man must be exceedingly imperfect without the knowledge of that original state, which is the ground-work and foundation of every other through which he has passed.[380]

How can the evolution of human culture be reconstructed?

There are not, as far as we know, any men at present to be found in the pure natural

\* "The history of manners is the most valuable. I never set a high value on any other history."[373]
† " . . . there is a progress in the *species* as well as in the *individual*."[376]
  " . . . it is evident that there is a progress in *civil* society."[377]
‡ " . . . there has been a beginning of society."[378]

state, that is, going upon all fours, and without arts of any kind.[381]

He used feral man, the orangoutang, and "primitive" man as the successive stages in cultural evolution.[382]

[1. Feral man.] What the mind of man was, while he was a quadruped, we cannot, from fact or experience, determine with any certainty, as so few example have been found of [feral] men living in that state.[383]

[2.] The Orang-Outang is, if not in the beginning, at least in one of the first stages of society, and in the progress towards a more civilized state.[384]

. . . they may be reckoned to be in the first stage of the human progression, being associated, and practising certain arts of life; but not so far advanced as to have invented the great art of language.[385]

[3.] . . . savages . . . are so much nearer the natural state of man than we, that it is from them only that we can form any idea of the *original* nature of man.[386]

. . . there have been found whole nations, not indeed altogether without arts or civility, (for that is impossible, since, according to my hypothesis, they associated together only for the purpose of carrying on some joint work), but with so little of either, that we can be at no loss to suppose a prior state, in which there were none at all.[387]

Africa, [is] a country . . . in which, if it were well searched, and the interior parts of it discovered, I am persuaded that all the several steps of the human progression might be traced, and perhaps all the varieties of the species discovered.[388]

It is by the example of those nations of North America that I propose to show what men were in the first ages of society.[389]

His approach is exhibited in his summary statements.

. . . if ever men were in that state which I call natural, it must have been in such a country and climate as Africa, where they could live without art upon the natural fruits of the earth[390] . . . If this be so, then the short history of man is, that the race having begun in those fine climates, and having, as is natural, multiplied there so much that the spontaneous productions of the earth could not support them, they migrated into other countries, where they were obliged to invent arts for their subsistence, and, with such arts, language, in process of time, would necessarily come.[391]

He was at first a quadruped . . . This first state of man I call the *animal state;* for, in that state, I consider him as a mere animal, with only the capacity of intellect, but not the use of it. And, in that state, he does not appear to be a gregarious or social animal, but of that class of animals, who do not associate, and whom we call *wild.* . . . It appears, therefore, that it is only the use of intellect, which makes man social; and it is natural that it should be so, as he is not *actually* a man till he has the exercise of that faculty. But, when he has got that, he is by nature prompted to associate with his fellow creatures, by which only could he improve his intellect, and so make some progress, in this life, towards recovery from his fallen state.

The next step of man's progress is to the herding life, when he has got so much of the use of intellect as directs him to associate with creatures of his own species. But still, I say, he is in the natural state; for he has not the use of clothes, houses, fire, nor of any strong liquor: And though the necessities of life may oblige him to kill fish or terrestrial animals, yet he has no art of fishing or hunting. His chief food was the natural fruits of the earth, such as herbs and roots; for he did not at first climb trees in order to eat their fruit.[392]

A more extended description of his theories of cultural evolution will now be given. The first stage was the "state of nature."

I mean by a state of nature . . . the original state of Man, before societies were formed, or arts invented. . . . In such a state, I say, Man had not the use of Intellect, which was then latent or dormant in him, as it is in a child among us, till it was produced by the intercourse of society, and the invention and practice of Arts. Man, therefore, in that state, could be nothing but a mere Animal*, without cloaths, houses, the use of fire, or even speech.†[395]

Man is not instinctively social, and therefore he did not live in society while in a state of nature.

. . . the political state among men is not from nature, but from institution, and . . . man, in his natural state, is a wild animal.[396]

. . . man participate[s] both of the gregarious and solitary kind . . . though they can subsist without one another's assistance, [they] yet have a strong inclination to the fellowship of their own species.

When I say so, I would not have it understood, that I believe, as Mr. Hobbes does, that man is naturally the enemy of man; and that the state of *nature* is a state of *war* of every man against every man. This is such a state as neither does exist, nor ever did exist, in any species of animals.[397]

[In fact, he praises] the good dispositions of men in the first ages of civil life.[398]

. . . men, when they were no farther advanced in the social and political life, lived together in the brutish way, copulating promiscuously, without distinction of families or races.[399]

Man, in his natural state, had not houses or clothes . . . [or] the use of fire.[400]

. . . the most natural food of Man, and what he lived upon in his primitive state, is Vegetables not prepared by fire, of which he had not then the use.[401]

. . . the first art man must have learned, was the use of his own body: And he must have begun by erecting himself, without which he could not have had the advantage of the length of his body, for attack or defence, or for the practice of the several arts of his life. Besides, it gave him the *os sublime*—enabled him to look at his native seat, the Heavens —and gave that dignity to his appearance, which was suitable for an animal that was destined to govern on this earth.

The necessary consequence, too, of the erect posture, was the use of the hands, a most useful organ, without which, as Xenophon has well observed, our reason would have availed us little in the invention and practice of arts.[402]

The first human inventions occurred through the imitation of other animals.

. . . men invented . . . arts . . . by imitation of other animals. In this way, I have derived the art from nature, the arche-type of all arts, and of every thing that is fine and beautiful among men; and I have laid the foundation of it upon that predominant quality in the human composition, by which man is so evidently distinguished from all other animals, the power of imitation.‡[404]

For we seem to set out in life without any original stock of our own, or any natural

---

*" . . . his natural state is no other than that of the mere animal."[393]
† " . . . society, and even the political life . . . may exist without language."[394]
‡ " . . . his faculty of imitation . . . is greater in him than in any other animal. . . . And, indeed, I hold that his imitative faculty has been the origin of all the arts of life."[403]

talent besides that faculty of imitation*, which nature has bestowed upon us in so high a degree, that Aristotle has denominated man, very properly, the most imitative of all animals.[406]

## From the "state of nature" man passed into the "state of society."

Having said so much of man in his natural state, I proceed to consider him in a state of civility and arts, beginning with his progress from the nature to that state. . . .

The first step in this progress must have been *associating,* or *living together in herds.*[407]

. . . by nature and instinct we have not that attachment to our species, which other animals have. . . . It was therefore some reason of convenience or necessity that first made men herd together.[408]

. . . self-defence[409] . . . joined with the want of the necessaries of life,[410] accounts for the origin of society among men.[411]

## From promiscuity there evolved marriage.

. . . if any circumstance at all is allowed to be capable of proof concerning the original state of man, this must be allowed to be proved, that men, in that state, did propagate after the manner of beasts. . . .

It appears, therefore, that the first step towards civility, and the first act of government and legislation among men, was the institution of marriage; and, as it is of human institution, so, like other human institutions, it has assumed different forms, in different nations.[412]

## Then society was formed.

. . . men, before they were civilised, lived in herds, and copulated promiscuously. . . . But this life must have produced much disorder among animals of so many passions and appetites as men. It was therefore very natural, that some should separate from the herd, taking with them one or more females and their children. And thus was constituted the family society, in which I believe men lived for several ages before civil society was instituted. . . .

That detached families should, for the purpose of carrying on any joint work, and of providing for the necessaries of life, or from some other motive of convenience, unite together and form a little state, must I think in process of time necessarily have happened. . . . More families would naturally join the few that had first associated, and for the same reasons: And thus at last a great number of families would be associated, which would make a regular polity, and form of government of absolute necessity. And thus did Government first begin.[413]

## The evolution of shelter is treated.

At first, men sheltered themselves from the injuries of the weather by thickets, rocks, and caves: Or, where nature did not furnish them that protection, they dug caverns in rocks, or lodged in the hollows of trees; and it was not till later times that men erected, above ground, those artificial coverings from the weather, which we call *houses*.[414]

## Subsistence developed from food-gathering to hunting, herding, and agriculture.

At first, I am persuaded, men lived upon the herbs and roots which the earth produced. . . . But when men increased very much in number, which they certainly did in the first ages of society, the natural fruits of the earth could not maintain them. And therefore . . .

* " . . . all our learning at first is from imitation. Children among us do certainly learn in that way; and what is commonly said I believe to be true, that men learned at first to build from the swallow, or any other bird that makes such an artificial nest; from the spider to weave; and from the birds to sing."[405]

then, and not till then, they took to hunting and fishing. . . .

That man, before he took to agriculture, lived upon the natural fruits of the earth, and by hunting and fishing, is well known.[415]

After all these aspects of culture had been evolved, man invented language, the basis of the third stage, the "state of civility and arts."

Thus far, therefore, man is advanced from the solitary savage, so as not only to be gregarious, but even political, in Aristotle's sense of the word. But he is still far removed from that state of civility, which is absolutely necessary for the invention and cultivation of arts and sciences, by which only he can make any progress in this life, towards regaining the state from which he has fallen. For that purpose, a regular polity must be formed, and properly carried on. Now, this cannot be done without language. . . . Language, therefore, may be said to be the foundation of all arts and sciences; For it is only by communication among men, which language bestows upon them, that any art worth mentioning, or science, can be invented or cultivated.[416]

I maintain, that the faculty of speech* is not the gift of nature to man, but, like many others, is acquired by him; that not only there must have been society before language was invented, but that it must have subsisted a considerable time, and other arts have been invented, before this most difficult one was found out; which appears to me of so difficult invention, that it is not easy to account how it could at all have been invented.†[420]

There are four ways by which men could communicate together, before the invention of speech: *First, Inarticulate* cries, expressive of sentiments and passions; *2dly, Gestures,* and the expression of the countenance; *3dly, Imitative sounds,* by which audible things may be expressed; and, *lastly, Painting,* by which visible objects may be represented. The first two are common to us with the brutes; the two last are peculiar to man.[421]

It is . . . inarticulate cries only that must have given rise to language; and, as every thing of art must be founded on nature, it appears at first sight very probable, that language should be nothing but an improvement or refinement upon the natural cries of the animal.[422]

[He then gives a summary of] the progress of language among savages. First, we have a number of wild men not associated, or at least not living in so close an intercourse of society as is necessary for the invention of language, and therefore without the use of speech. . . . Next, we have a people that had learned a little articulation, but not so much as to communicate their thoughts to one another, without the help of the natural language of signs. The next step is to what may be called a language, very rude and imperfect

---

* "By language I mean *the expression of the conceptions of* the mind by articulate sounds."[417]

† " . . . there is no natural language belonging to man, except what belongs to other animals; and all that can be truly said of man is, that he has the capacity of acquiring the faculty of speech, as well as many other faculties, which he has added to his nature."[418]

"In the preceding . . . we have placed man in a state of society and of political union, carrying on, of common consent, and with joint labour, some work necessary for defence, or the support of life. In this situation, and this only, could language have been invented. But more was necessary for the invention of so difficult an art. And, in the *first* place, The proper organs of pronunciation were indispensably required. These are given to some few animals besides man; but I belive they are in none so perfect. . . .

"*2dly,* They must have been a very long time in this political state; so long at least as to have improved into an art the business they were carrying on. . . .

"*3dly,* Another thing absolutely required, as preparatory to the invention of a language, is, that men should previously have formed ideas to be expressed by language: For it is impossible to conceive a language of proper names only without general terms. . . .

"*Lastly,* It appears to me to have required an extraordinary degree of sagacity, to invent so artificial a thing as speech."[419]

indeed, but such as is sufficient for communication, with little or no help from action or gesture. . . . And, last of all, comes the language of art.[423]

We are now to inquire in what country or countries such an art was invented.[424]

Egypt was, of all the countries we have heard of, the most proper for the invention of language.[425]

Religion and government are considered next.

. . . two things . . . are of absolute necessity for constituting and carrying on a regular polity. . . . *Religion* and *Government*.[426]

[Religion developed as a result of an] idea of an invisible and immaterial principle acting upon body, and in that way conducting the operations of nature, and influencing the affairs of human life.[427]

It is government that constitutes a civil society, and makes man, of a solitary and gregarious animal, a *Political* animal. . . . Government, therefore, is of absolute necessity in the civilised life.[428]

. . . rhetoric . . . is coeval with civil society and government; for, in the first ages of society, government was carried on by public speaking; as governments of single men, by arbitrary will, were not then known. For though, in the first ages of society, there were men of superior abilities, both of mind and body, and who therefore were destined by God and nature to govern their fellow-creatures, it was by council and persuasion that they governed; nor indeed could they govern otherwise in those early ages. Accordingly we find, that among all the barbarous nations, which have any kind of established government, public speaking is very much practised, and is really an art.[429]

Of course, the rate of cultural evolution is not uniform in all societies.

. . . it is to be observed, that this progress did not go on at the same time among all the inhabitants of the different parts of the earth; on the contrary, we are sure from history, that some nations were in a high state of civility, while others were no better than mere animals: But what I say is, that all nations must be supposed to have been, at some time or another, in that state, in which we know that some have been, and some are at this day.[430]

Besides the racial differences spoken of in the section on physical anthropology, Monboddo believed that other factors influenced the speech of cultural evolution.

. . . the human mind . . . will lie dormant . . . a very long time; and . . . it will be only excited by the necessities of human life, and the social intercourse required to supply these necessities.[431]

. . . the rational soul . . . I take to be of our own acquisition, and the fruit of industry, like any art or science, not the gift of nature.[432]

In the first ages of civil life, a Man cannot be far removed from a Brute; for he must be ignorant of all those arts and sciences which improve our understanding so much, and may indeed be said to create it, or, at least, to bring it into exertion, and call it forth from the latent state in which it was before. It is evident, therefore, that the intelligence of men in civil life must depend upon the progress they have made in arts; so that, if they have made little or no progress, they must appear to be very stupid and brutish.[433]

Another thing to be observed is the country and climate in which those savages live; for, if the climate be mild, and the country abounding in all the natural fruits of the earth, and not so overstocked with inhabitants, but that they may all live at their ease, the consequence will be, that the people of such a country will have little spirit or understanding, and will be a dull, sluggish, unwarlike people. This was the case of the inhabitants of the islands of the West Indies.* . . . But the inhabitants of Canada, and other parts of North America, were a people altogether different; for, living in a country and climate where men could not subsist without the invention and practice of the arts of hunting and fishing, nor without much toil and labour and great indurance of the injuries of weather, and being also engaged in frequent wars with one another, a noble race of men was formed, such as would have done honour to any age or country in the world.[435]

## Dunbar

James Dunbar (d. 1798) began his *Essays on the History of Mankind in Rude and Cultivated Ages*[436] with a discussion of man's sociality.

. . . in the interval from infancy to manhood, we may remark this gradual opening of the human faculties. First of all, those of sense appear, grow up spontaneously, or require but little culture. Next in order, the propensities of the heart display their force; a fellow-feeling with others unfolds itself gradually on the appearance of proper objects; for man becomes sociable long before he is a rational being. Last in the train, the powers of intellect begin to blossom, are reared up by culture, and demand an intercourse of minds.[437]

There is a general observation strongly applicable, in all ages, to human nature: the appearance of proper objects is essential to the exertion of its powers. . . . This much is certain, a mutual intercourse gradually opens latent powers; and the extension of this intercourse is generally attended with new exertions of intellect. Withdraw this intercourse, and what is man! . . . Society then is the theatre on which our genius expands with freedom. It is essential to the origin of all our ideas of natural and moral beauty. It is the prime mover of all our inventive powers. Every effort, beyond what is merely animal, has a reference to a community; and the solitary savage, who traverses the desert, is scarce raised so far by nature above other animals, as he is sunk by fortune beneath the standard of his own race.[438]

In addition, he advocated the gregarious theory of social development.

Society . . . had another origin than mutual dependence and mutual wants. It is not, if I may say so, the sickly daughter of calamity, nor even the production of an aspiring understanding, but the free and legitimate offspring of the human heart.[439]

The principles of union are, in the order of things, prior to the principles of hostility.[440]

Even pride, the passion which divides mankind, was originally a principle of union.[441]

Upon the whole, we may pronounce that interested intercourse in the animal kingdom, is greater in appearance than in reality; that the concourse of a tribe is often accidental; that all regular oeconomy is under the direction of instinct; and that in all the freer combinations, the society is held together by the tie of affection or conscious delight, more than by fear, or mutual wants, or any necessary call of nature.[442]

It is indeed strange that any observer should omit this obvious comment on human life, That to be the object of love, of esteem, and of respect, is in itself far more desirable than all the consequences with regard to external ease and security that can be derived from that fountain.[443]

* " . . those Savages . . . who live in a country and climate where Nature is so bountiful as to give them every thing necessary for their subsistence, without art, and with little or no labour, such as the Caribs and other inhabitants of the West Indian Islands . . . have little use of Intellect of any kind."[434]

On the whole, he tended to believe in the psychic unity of man, with differences culturally determined.

So various are the causes which concur to the full establishment of regular and well-constituted government; that no evidence decisive of the relative capacity of any people could be derived from the commencement of their civil aera. Even after the first movements have been successfully made, there are a thousand disasters, which may annoy a political consitution, in its infancy or early youth, and not suffer its principles to ripen into perfection. Circumstances in no degree affecting the genius of a people, are often sufficient to circumscribe their progress; and consistently with the full strength and vigour of the human powers, the reign of ignorance and simplicity may endure for ages.

Although great attainments indeed imply great talents, the want of talent is not implied in disappointment.[444]

A certain cast of genius and character adheres to every condition. Different degrees of refinement and civility characterise the various orders of citizens; and the dignity or meanness annexed to the sphere in which they move, is, by no violent transition of imagination, transferred to their immediate, and even to remote descendents, and regarded as appendages of posterity.[445]

A cultivated and polished nation may, in some respects, be regarded as a standing family. . . . Nations . . . as well as families, may have some inheritance to boast; and the progeny of savages or barbarians may be distinguishable, both in outward and inward form, from the progeny of a cultivated people.[446]

But the genius of man is so flexible, so open to impressions from without, so susceptible of early culture, that between hereditary, innate, and acquired propensities, it is hard to draw the line of distinction. It were necessary that the natives of one country should be bred up, and educated, from their earliest infancy, among the natives of another, in order to make fair experiments with regard to original talents.[447]

The existence of . . . varieties in the [morphological] description of man is conformable to history, and to experience, and is in part deducible from analogy and philosophic theory. But such varieties . . . afford no criterion by which to ascertain the endowments of the understanding among tribes or nations.[448]

Thus we may observe mankind, essentially the same, yet in different regions of the globe, varying continually from a fixed standard; breathing at first, if I may use the expression, unequal proportions of aetherial spirit; excelling in the rational, in the moral, or in the animal powers; born with a superior fitness for refinement, for arts, for civil culture; or cast in a rougher mould, and by native temper more indocible and wild. Yet all the capital distinctions in individuals, families or tribes, flow from causes subsequent to birth; from education, example, forms of government; from the order of internal laws, from the maxims and genius of religion, from the lights of science and philosophy.[449]

The factors that determine the characteristics of a culture are considered.

The mechanical springs of life rest not on the energy of one cause, but on the combination of many, possessing often opposite and qualifying powers. It were improper therefore to expatiate on the intensity of one principle, without attending to others which serve to heighten or to mitigate its force. One writer magnifies the power of climate; another, the effects of aliment; a third, the efficacy of labour or rest, and the peculiar influence of certain modes of life. But these circumstances are relative to each other, and it is the result of the combination with which we are alone concerned.[450]

The means of subsistence, the subject of art, the incitements to industry, the scene of its operations, so diversified in the several districts of the earth, must affect proportionably the course of affairs. And in circumstances so dissimilar, it would be strange, if the conduct of the actors were governed precisely by the same laws, or every where attended with the same success.

The genius of mankind, far from being equal, must have been as various as the situations in which they are placed, did we observe all nations exalted to an equal pitch of civility, or of eminence in arts and sciences.[451]

The fate of nations often depends on circumstances apparently the most trivial. The genius, the life, perhaps the temporary humour of a single man may, on some occasions, fix the political arrangements that affect the essential interests of one half of the globe.[452]

The series of events, once begun, is governed more perhaps by moral than by physical causes: and this propensity of genius and temper may owe its original to the primary direction of the sciences, and their early alliance with theology and civil government.[453]

Under the influence of Montesquieu, Dunbar laid stress on geographical factors but at the end of his discussion confessed that they are modified by the technology of a society.

Climate . . . may be regarded either as a natural principle, acting with powerful energy, or with irresistible impulse, on the fabric of our being; or it may be regarded merely as a local circumstance leading to a variety of action in the oeconomy of civil life.[454]

[1.] The existence of . . . varieties [which may be the result of geographic factors] in the [morphological] description of man is conformable to history, and to experience, and is in part deducible from analogy and philosophic theory. But such varieties . . . afford no criterion by which to ascertain the endowments of the understanding among tribes or nations.

[2.] Local circumstances have been pointed out as of various import; as dissuasives from, or as incentives to action, as occasions of success or disapointment to national enterprize, and as more or less auspicious to the origin and progress of arts and sciences.[455]

. . . there are at least some distinctions among mankind infallibly regulated by a local standard.

In some climates of the world, the body arrives soon at maturity, and hastens to a dissolution with proportionable celerity. In other climates a longer period is allowed both for its progress and decline.[456]

. . . in all ages of the world, the term of our existence, though depending on a multiplicity of causes, seems to have had some reference to climate; and in general to have increased with the latitude. Strength and vigour of body, till we arrive at the limit of the Polar circle, are found to increase in a similar progression.[457]

Geographical relation therefore will always be, in some degree, instrumental in retarding or accelerating, in every country, the progress of civil life.[458]

Soil and climate seem to act with a gradation of influence on vegetable, animal, and intellectual nature. . . . Man, therefore, by his rank in the creation, is more exempted from mechanical domination than the classes below him.[459]

The action of the elements on his frame is not more conspicuous, than his reciprocal action on those very elements which are permitted to annoy his being. He has a range allowed to him in the creation peculiar to himself alone; and he seems to have had delegated to him a certain portion of the government of the natural world. Revolutions, indeed, are brought about in various regions by the universal laws of motion, uncontrouled, and uncontroulable by any human power. But, under certain limitations, soil and climate are subject to his dominion; and the natural history of the terraqueous globe varies with the civil history of nations.[460]

Thus much we may with certainty affirm, that soil and climate, if not altogether foreign to the mind, are, like the mind, susceptible of improvement, and variable, in a high degree, with the progress of the civil arts.[461]

Upon the whole, we observe local advantages . . . to be of least relative moment in the most flourishing stage of the arts and sciences.[462]

As usual, his methodology in tracing cultural evolution was based on unilinearity and consisted of the use of data on subhuman animals and "primitive" man.

In some parts of our constitution, it cannot be denied, we resemble the other animals. If therefore a time was when those parts chiefly or alone were exercised, our objects, and pursuits, and habits of living must have been nearly similar.[463]

The history . . . of some of the South Sea isles, which the late voyages of discovery have tended to disclose, enables us to glance at society in some of its earlier forms.[464]

He also mentioned the use of survivals.

After a language has arrived at considerable refinement, there may be remarked in provincial phrase, or in the variety of its dialects, the characteristics of primitive barbarism . . . For, in the progress of a state, the lower ranks often fall back; or at least not moving forward in exact proportion with their superior, their language, like their manners, remains long nearly stationary. The vulgar, accordingly, of the same country, almost as widely differ in their vocabulary from the more polished, as the more barbarous differ in theirs from the more polished nations; or as the same language differs from itself in its successive stages.[465]

He gives the following general description of cultural evolution.

What pity is it, that, the transactions of this early period being consigned to eternal oblivion, history is necessarily defective in opening the scene of man!

Consistently, however, with present appearances, and with the memorials of antiquity, the following stages, it is pretended, may have arisen successively to the species.

First, Man may have subsisted, in some sort, like other animals, in a separate and individual state, before the date of language, or the commencement of any regular intercourse.

Secondly, He may be contemplated in a higher stage; a proficient in language, and a member of that artless community which consists with equality, with freedom, and independence.

Last of all, by slow and imperceptible transitions, he subsists and flourishes under the protection and discipline of civil government.[466]

He gave long descriptions of the evolution of society[467] and language;[468] his account of the origin of religion is brief:

In ages of ignorance and simplicity, mankind are so prone to credulity and admiration; that these propensities, prior to reasoning, seem to lead savages into the acknowledgement and adoration of invisible powers, and to introduce, in every country, the rude elements of popular superstition.[469]

He was in advance of most cultural evolutionists in appreciating the role of diffusion in modifying the evolutionary process in the history of a culture and in the development of civilization.

The computation indeed supposes no intercourse between the civilized and the barbarous nations. By reason of that intercourse the chance of extending civility rises, no doubt, in an eminent degree. Hence, with regard to countries possessing intercourse, the progress may be exceedingly rapid. But in the other, and sequestered corners of the globe, calculation determines that there is a growing chance against the appearance of a cultivated or polished nation. And, if we reason from actual experience, it is far more probable that, in any barbarous land, the civil arts will owe their original to foreign operations, either hostile or commercial, than to interior efforts.[470]

## Beattie

To James Beattie (1735–1803), man was subject to natural laws.

The human body, like every other corporeal system, must be subject to the physical laws of nature; and the soul of man, liable to be affected by everything that essentially affects the body, must be subject, in a certain degree, to the influences of soil and climate, food and drink, and other modes of living.[471]

There are no innate racial differences; geography and culture determine the characteristics of a group.

[After discussing the geographic and cultural factors that influence man,[472] he concludes:] By these and the like considerations, that superiority, which has hitherto distinguished the inhabitants of Europe, and of the adjoining countries, may be accounted for, without supposing the rest of mankind of an inferior species. Were two brothers of equal genius to be brought up, the one in the metropolis of England, with every advantage of education and company, the other in St Kilda, without any of those advantages; it is probable they would differ no less in accomplishment and general character, than African or American savages differ from Europeans.[473]

Man is instinctively social.

Among the inferior animals, the union of the sexes is temporary and casual; the passions that prompt to it being periodical, and the young soon able to provide for themselves. But human infants being, of all animals, the most helpless, stand most in need of education and parental care. . . . It is therefore natural that he, even in savage life, should have a certain degree of attachment to his child, and its mother, and do what he can to assist and defend them. Hence, it seems reasonable to suppose, that marriage, under one form or other, would take place, even where not many laws had been established with regard to it: and this is in fact the case. Exceptions may perhaps be found, among the worst sort of savages: but those are not considerable enough to affect the present argument. In civilized nations, the matrimonial union must appear a matter of very great importance; being, indeed, the ground-work, not only of all decency and domestic virtue, but of all good government and regular society.*[475]

There is in our nature a tendency to participate in the pains and pleasures of others; so that their good is in some degree our good, and their evil our evil: the natural effect of which is, to unite more closely to one another, by prompting them, even for their own sake, to relieve distress and promote happiness. This participation of the joys and sorrows of others may be termed sympathy, or fellow-feeling.[476]

* " . . . family . . . is the foundation of all civil society."[474]

He had a feeling for the dynamics of culture.

All human institutions are liable to change. The feudal system soon became a different thing from what it had been originally.[477]

In most societies cultural evolution went through four stages: hunting, fishing, and food-gathering; herding; agriculture; and commerce.

. . . it has been supposed by some authors, that the progress of human society, from rudeness to refinement, consists of four periods or stages: that, in the first, men lived by hunting or fishing, or on such fruits and plants as the earth produces without culture; in the second, by pasturage; in the third, by both these, in conjunction with agriculture; and, in the fourth, by all these, in conjunction with commerce, which gives rise to arts and sciences, and every other elegance of life. In some countries, particularly our own, this may have happened, but could not in all: some being so barren as not to admit of agriculture; many so peculiarly situated, as to be incapable of commerce with the rest of the world; and some so destitute of territory, and so beset with the sea, as to oblige the natives, from the beginning, to live by fishing, or practise commerce.[478]

To this development was related the evolution of property.

Property in food, being at all times necessary, must take place even in the rudest forms of society. That would probably be appropriated first which is most easily come at, as the fruit of trees and bushes, and other vegetables; then perhaps men would think of preying on beasts, and fishes, and fowls; and in many countries this must have been their first provision, and consequently, hunting, fishing, and fowling, their first employments. Afterwards, finding that a provision of animal food might be secured for some length of time, by bringing the more tractable animals together, and keeping them in flocks and herds, men would betake themselves to pasturage in countries where it was practicable. And this we learn, from the history of the patriarchs, to have been one of their earliest vocations.

In a good soil and climate, the digging of the ground, and the rearing of useful herbs, would no doubt be practised in the beginning of society, both as a recreation and as a profitable art. But agriculture, in a more enlarged sense of the word, as it depends on several others arts, especially those of working in wood and metal, could hardly take place, till after those arts were invented. And the appropriation of land, or territory, except for the purpose of self-defence, in order to keep enemies at a distance, would hardly be thought of till after the establishment of agriculture.[479]

Political organization most probably originated through social contract.

Civil government, or policy . . . is human society moulded into a certain form by human art.[480]

The origin of government is a subject which may be said to comprehend answers to these two questions.—First, For what reasons, and by what steps is it probable, that men, not subject to government, would think of it, and submit themselves to it? Secondly, What may reasonably be presumed to have been the actual origin of government among men, according to the best lights that may be had from history, tradition, or conjecture? —With respect to the first question, it is to be observed, that, before the institution of government, men would live in what is called the state of nature, perfectly independent, equal, and free. But some would have more strength, more activity, and more wisdom, than others; and it may be presumed, that they who were conscious of their own weakness in these particulars, would look up for advice and assistance to those who were able to assist and advise them; and would thus, gradually and voluntarily, confer on them some sort of authority, or lawful pre-eminence. Hence one motive to political union, arising from the diversity of human characters, and from our natural admiration of superior abilities. . . .

Another motive to political union would arise from the inconveniences of the natural state; in which men, being fallible, must often mistake their rights, and disagree about them. When this happens in the political state, the law decides the matter, and the power of government enforces the decision. But in the state of nature, man would have nothing but his own strength and caution to defend him from injury; and of course, when injured, would retaliate, which would hardly fail to produce more retaliation, and more injury, and so end in confusion. . . . Of this evil the obvious and the only remedy is government, or political subordination.

But men being wicked as well as fallible, the evils of the natural state must be greater than I have hitherto supposed. We see them injure one another in spite of the sanctions of both divine and human law. Remove these, and they would be still more injurious. . . . In short, we may presume the disorders incident to the natural state would be so great, that if it were to be at all, it could not be at any long continuance. . . . Hence the necessity of men's divesting themselves of the freedom of the natural state, uniting in society, appointing a sovereignty, entrusting it with certain powers for the public good, and supporting it in the exercise of those powers. And all the members of a political body, thus uniting their strength, and acting in one direction, are able to repel injury, and defend one another, much more effectually, than it is possible to do in the state of nature. . . .

The independence and equality of men in the natural state, being alienable rights, may be parted with, for valuable considerations. Men quitting that state, in order to establish policy, would accordingly part with them and either expressly or tacitly enter into a mutual agreement. . . . Observe . . . that the foregoing, and some of the following reasonings, are purely *hypothetical;* that is, founded on the *supposition* of what rational beings would probably do, if they were to make a transition from the state of nature to that of policy. But these reasonings are not on that account chimerical: for they do in fact lead us to discover the end, the utility, and the fundamental principles of government. Geometry may be considered as a hypothetical science; but it is not for that reason the less useful. The geometer does not inquire, whether there be in nature mathematical lines, circles, or right-angled triangles; but on the *supposition* that there are or may be, he proves that such and such must be their properties. I do not inquire, whether men ever made such a transition, as is here supposed, from the natural to the civil state; but *supposing* them to make it, and to make it rationally, and of choice, I say, that they would probably be determined by the views and motives above specified. . . .

Of the *actual origin* of government, the second thing proposed to be considered, history gives little information. . . .

That, in the first ages of the world, government may have arisen from parental authority, is very probable. . . . But, to prevent mistakes on this subject, it is necessary to remark, that the authority of a parent is very different, both in kind and degree, from that of a sovereign. . . . If therefore parents have in the early ages become the sovereign of their descendents by any *just* title, it must have been, not merely by virtue of their parental authority, but by the consent of their descendents, expressly or tacitly given for that purpose.

Many governments have been founded in conquest.[481]

Beattie derived language from gestures.

We speak, in order to make our thoughts known to others. Now thoughts themselves are not visible, nor can they be perceived by any outward sense. If, therefore, I make my thoughts perceptible to another man, it must be by means of signs, which he and I understand in the same sense. The signs that express human thought, so as to make it known to others, are of two sorts, natural and artificial.

The natural signs of thought are those outward appearances in the eyes, complexion, features, gesture, and voice, which accompany certain emotions of the mind, and which, being common to all men, are universally understood. . . . Compared with the multitude of our thoughts, these natural signs are but few, and therefore insufficient for the purposes of speech. Hence artificial signs have been universally adopted, which derive their meaning from human contrivance, and are not understood except by those who have been taught the use of them.

These artificial signs may be divided into visible and audible. The former are used by dumb men; by ships that sail in company; and sometimes by people at land, who, by means of fire and other signals, communicate intelligence from one place to another: but for the ordinary purposes of life such contrivances would be inconvenient and insufficient. And therefore audible signs, performed by the human voice, are in all nations used in order to communicate thought. For the human voice has an endless variety of expression, and is in all its varieties easily managed, and distinctly perceptible by the human ear, in darkness as well as in light.[482]

## Stewart

Dugald Stewart (1753–1828) gave a methodological analysis of the historical reconstructions of the Scotch school.

When, in such a period of society as that in which we live, we compare our intellectual acquirements, our opinions, manners, and institutions, with those which prevail among rude tribes, it cannot fail to occur to us as an interesting question, by what gradual steps the transition has been made from the first simple efforts of uncultivated nature, to a state of things so wonderfully artificial and complicated. . . . On most of these subjects very little information is to be expected from history; for long before that stage of society when men begin to think of recording their transactions, many of the most important steps of their progress have been made. A few insulated facts may perhaps be collected from the casual observations of travellers, who have viewed the arrangements of rude nations; but nothing, it is evident, can be obtained in this way, which approaches to a regular and connected detail of human improvement.

In this want of direct evidence, we are under a necessity of supplying the place of fact by conjecture; and when we are unable to ascertain how men have actually conducted themselves upon particular occasions, of considering in what manner they are likely to have proceeded, from the principles of their nature, and the circumstances of their external situation. In such enquiries, the detached facts which travels and voyages afford us, may frequently serve as land-marks to our speculations; and sometimes our conclusions *a priori,* may tend to confirm the credibility of facts, which, on a superficial point of view, appeared to be doubtful or incredible. . . .

To this species of philosophical investigation, which has no appropriated name in our language, I shall take the liberty of giving the title of *Theoretic* or *Conjectural History;* an expression which coincides pretty nearly in its meaning with that of *Natural History,* as employed by Mr. HUME, and with what some French writers have called *Histoire Raisonnée.*[483]

# NOTES

## NOTES TO CHAPTER I

1. II Tim. 3:16.
2. Rom. (*ca.* 56) 1:20. The dates for the New Testament texts are those of E. J. Goodspeed, *An Introduction to the New Testament* (Chicago, 1937).
3. I Cor. (*ca.* 54) 4:1; 11:9; II Cor. (*ca.* 55) 11:3; Rom. 9:20–21.
4. I Cor. 15:38–40.
5. Gal. 3:29.
6. *Ibid.* (*ca.* 53) 5:17.
7. Rom. 10:12.
8. Gal. (*ca.* 53) 3:28; cf. *ibid.,* 3:26; I Cor. 12:13; Rom. 2:11; Col. (*ca.* 60) 3:11.
9. *Acts* 14:15; 15:18; 17:24.
10. 1:1–3.
11. 3:5.
12. Mark (*ca.* 65) 10:6; cf. Matt. (*ca.* 80) 19:4; Luke 3:38.
13. I Tim. (*ca.* 150) 2:13.
14. Jude 10.
15. Acts 17:26; *vide ibid.,* 15:9; 17:28; cf. Eph. (*ca.* 93) 6:9.
16. *De civitate dei* (413–26), ed. E. Hoffmann (*Corpus Scriptorum Ecclesiasticorum Latinorum,* 40) (Vienna, 1898–1900), 12. 22; cf. *ibid.,* 12. 27; 13. 14; tr. M. Dods (Edinburgh, 1871).
17. *Ibid.,* 16. 9.
18. *Ibid.,* 12. 10; cf. *ibid.,* 12. 13; for his arguments against the antiquity of the earth and man, *vide ibid.,* 12. 10–12.
19. *Ibid.,* 12. 22.
20. *Idem.*
21. *Etymologiae,* ed. W. M. Lindsay (Oxford, 1911), 9. 2. 105; tr. E. Brehaut (New York, 1912).
22. *Ibid.,* 14. 5. 14.
23. *Summa theologica* 1. 46. 1; in *Opera ommia* (Rome, 1882——), IV-XII, tr. English Dominican Fathers, (2d ed., London, 1920–25).
24. *Ibid.,* 1. 46. 2.
25. *Ibid.,* 1. 44. 1.
26. *Ibid.,* 1. 91. 2.
27. *Ibid.,* 1. 91. 1.
28. *Ibid.,* 1. 93. 1.
29. *Ibid.,* 1. 92. 1.
30. *Ibid.,* 1. 92. 4; *vide biid.,* 1. 92. 2–3.
31. *Ibid.,* 1. 102. 4.
32. *Ibid.,* 1. 102. 1.
33. *Ibid.,* 1. 71. 1.
34. *SCG,* 2. 68.
35. *Summa theologica* 1. 76. 1.
36. *Ibid.,* 1. 50.
37. *Ibid.,* 1. 72. 1.
38. *Ibid.,* 1. 76. 1.
39. *Ibid.,* 1. 76. 1.
40. *Ibid.,* 2. 1. 13. 2.
41. *Ibid.,* 1. 78. 1.

42.  *Ibid.*, 1. 77. 4.

43.  *Ibid.*, 1. 91. 3.

44.  *De philosophia mundi* 1. 23; in *Patrologia Latina* 172 (*Paris*, 1854), cols. 39–102.

45.  *Gesta Danorum,* ed. J. Olrik and H. Raeder (Copenhagen, 1931——), praef. 3; tr. O. Elton (London, 1894).

46.  Florence, 1823.

47.  *Citez de Jherusalem* (*ca.* 1220), tr. C.R. Conder (*Palestine Pilgrims Text Society,* 6. 2) (London, 1888), 2. 26.

48.  Ed. W. Heraeus, (2d ed., Heidelberg, 1921).

49.  In *Itinera Hierosolymitana, saeculi IV–VIII,* ed. P. Geyer *Corpus Scriptorum Ecclesiasticorum Latinorum,* 39) (Vienna, 1898), pp. 157–218.

50.  Tr. A. Stewart, *PPTS,* 6. 1) (London, 1897), pp. 27–36.

51.  Caps. 12–13; in *Peregrintatores medii aevi quatuor,* ed. J.C.M. Laurent (2d ed.; Leipzig, 1873), pp. 1–100.

52.  In *Thesaurus Monumentorum Ecclesiasticorum et Historicorum,* ed. H. Canisius (Antwerp, 1725), IV, 331–57.

53.  Ed. F. Deycks (*Bibliothek des litterarischen Vereins in Stuttgart,* 25), Stuttgart, 25.

54.  *Ibid.*, prol.; tr. A. Stewart (London, 1895).

55.  Ed. J. P. Migne, in *Patrologia Graeca,* 88 (Paris, 1964), cols. 9–476.

56.  *Etymologiae* 14: 3–6; 15:1.

57.  *Cosmographia* (*ca.* 650), in *Ravennatis anonymi Cosmographia et Guidonis Geographica,* ed. M. Pinder and G. Parthey (Berlin, 1860), pp. 1–445.

58.  *Otia imperialia* (*ca.* 1200), 2j in *Scriptores Rerum Brunsvicensium,* ed. G. W. Leibniz (Hanover, 1707–11), I, pp. 881–1004; II, pp. 751–84.

59.  *Liber floridus* (*ca.* 1100); there is a synopsis by J. de Saint Genois in *Patrologia Latina,* 163 (Paris, 1854), cols. 1003–32.

60.  *Imago mundi* (*ca.* 1100), ed. J. P. Migne, *Patrologia Latina,* 172 (Paris, 1854), cols. 115–88.

61.  *Geographica* (1119), in Pinder and Parthey, pp. 447–556.

62.  Ed. F. Heidlauf (*Deutsche Texte des Mittelalters,* 28), (Berlin, 1915).

63.  *L'Image du monde* (*ca.* 1245), ed. O. H. Prior (Paris, 1913).

64.  Ed. P. Hamelius (*Early English Text Society* [or. ser.], 153–54) (London, 1919–23).

65.  Ed. J. H. Bridges (Oxford and London, 1897–1900), I, 303–76; II, 367–71, 383–84, 385, 387–92.

66.  *Ibid.,* I, 376; tr. R. B. Burke, Philadelphia, 1928. For example, he mentions Ruysbroek a number of times: *ibid.,* I, 268, 303, 305, 322; II, 368, 383–84, 387–88.

67.  J. K. Wright, *The Geographical Lore of the Time of the Crusades* ("American Geographical Society Research Series," 15) (New York, 1925), pp. 292–93. On the cosmopolitanism of the Europeans as a result of the Crusades, *vide* J. W. Thompson, *An Economic and Social History of the Middle Ages* (New York, 1928), pp. 433–35.

68.  *Vide* E. Dreesbach, "Die Bewohner des Orients," *Der Orient in der altfranzösischen Kreuzzugsliteratur* (Breslau, 1901, Ph. D. diss.), pp. 36–49.

69.  *Historia rerum in partibus transmarinis gestarum* (1170–83), ed. J. P. Migne, *PL,* 201) (Paris, 1855), cols. 209–892.

70.  *La conquête de Constantinople* (ca. 1216), ed. P. Lauer, (Paris, 1924); esp. chap. 65.

71.  *La conquête de Constantinople,* ed. E. Faral, (Paris, 1938——).

72.  *Historia Iherosolomitana* (*ca.* 1230), in *Gesta dei per Francos,* ed. J. Bongars (Hanover, 1611), I, 1047–1124.

73.  *Histoire de Saint Louis* (1309), ed. N. de Wailly (Paris, 1874).

74.  E. Power, "The opening of the land routes to Cathay," pp. 124–27, 139; in *Travel and Travellers of the Middle Ages,* ed. A. P. Newton (London, 1926), pp. 124–58.

75.  Ed. A. d'Avezac-Macaya, in Société de Géographie, Paris, *Recueil de Voyages et de Mémoires* (Paris, 1824–64), IV, 397–779.

76.  Ed. F. X. Michel and T. Wright, in *ibid.,* IV, 205–396.

77.  In E. Breschneider, *Mediaeval Researches from Eastern Asiatic Sources* (London, 1910), I, 164–72.

78.  Tr. H. Yule, rev. H. Cordier (3d ed.; London, 1903); also H. Cordier, *Ser Marco Polo* (New York, 1920).

79.  Ed. G. F. Pagnini della Ventura, in *Delle decima e delle antre gravezze* (Florence, 1765–66), III.

80.  Tr. E. A. Peers, London [1926]; esp. 88. 2–5.

81.  *Ibid.,* pp. 16–17.

82.  Ed. M. J. de la Espada, *Boletin de la Sociedad Geográfica de Madrid,* 2 (1877), 7–66, 97–141, 185–210.

83. *Liber peregrinacionis* (*ca.* 1301), in *Peregrinatores medii aevi quatuor,* ed. J. C. M. Laurent (2d ed.; Leipzig, 1873), pp. 101–41; *Epistolae* (*ca.* 1295–1300), ed. R. Röhricht, *Archives de l'Orient latin,* 2 (1884) (doc.), 285–96.

84. *Epistolae* (1305–6), in *Annales Minorum,* ed. L. Wadding *et al.* (Rome, 1731–1886), VI, 69–72, 91–92.

85. *Epistola* (1321), in *ibid.,* VI, 359–61.

86. *Epistolae* (1326), in *ibid.,* VII, 53–54.

87. *Descriptio orientalium partium* (1330), ed. and tr. H. Yule, rev. H. Cordier (*Hakluyt Society Publications* [ser. 2], 33), London, 1913.

88. *Livre de l'estat du Grant Caan* (*ca.* 1330), ed.——Jacquet, *Journal Asiatique* (ser. 2), 6 (1830), 57–72.

89. *Epistola* (1338), *Annales Minorum,* VII, 256–57.

90. *Chronicon* (*ca.* 1355), ed. J. Emler, in *Fontes Rerum Bohemicarum* 3 (Prague, 1882), 485–604.

91. E.g., pseudo-Beda Venerabilis, "De linguis gentium," *Opera omnia* (Cologne, 1612), II, 235.

92. *Etymologiae* 9. 1. 1.

93. *Ibid.,* 9. 1. 3.

94. *Ibid.,* 9. 1. 11.

95. *Ibid.,* o. 1. 14.

96. *Paradiso* (13—), 26. 133–36; in *Opere,* ed. E. Moore.

97. *Ibid.,* 26. 124–26.

98. *Vide De vulgari eloquentia* (1304) 1. 10, 14, 19; in *Opere.*

99. *Ibid.,* 1. 1–19; tr. A. G. F. Howell (London, 1904).

100. *Ibid.,* 1. 15.

101. *Ibid.,* 1. 16.

102. I Cor. (*ca.* 54), 15:44; cf. *ibid.,* 3:1–4; 5:3; II Cor. (*ca.* 55) 7:1; Rom. (*ca.* 56) 7:14; Phil. (*ca.* 59), 3: 3; Col. (*ca.* 60) 2: 5.

103. Rom. 6:12.

104. Phil. 3:21.

105. Rom. 7:25; cf. *ibid.,* 8:1–16; Gal. (*ca.* 53) 5:19–23; I Cor. 1:29.

106. Rom. 7:18.

107. I Cor. 7:1–9, 25–40.

108. Cal. 5:16–17.

109. Rom. 6:12; cf. Gal. 4:13–14; 5:13:24; Rom. 7:22–24.

110. Phil. 2:21.

111. Rom. 11:36.

112. I Thess. (50) 2:18.

113. Vol. 1:16.

114. Rom. 9:22–23.

115. *Ibid.,* 11:11.

116. Phil. 2:13; cf. I Cor. 4:7.

117. Gal. 6:7–8; cf. I Thess. 4:14–17; II Thess. (*ca.* 50) 1:7–10; I Cor. 3:8, 15; 15:44–55; II. Cor. 5 : 1–10; Rom. 2:5–6, 9.

118. Rom. 2:12–15.

119. I Cor. 9:20–21.

120. Gal. 3:23.

121. I Cor. 11:14–15.

122. *Ibid.,* 12:4–31; Rom. 12:4–8.

123. Luke (*ca.* 90) 12:19–20; Heb. (*ca.* 95), 12:9; 13:17; I (Peter *ca.* 95), 4:6; Gospel of John (*ca.* 110), 3:6.

124. Matt. (*ca.* 80) 10:28; Acts (*ca.* 90), 2:31; I Peter 1:24; 3:4.

125. Mark (*ca.* 65) 15:37; Matt. 27:50; Luke 23:46; Acts 5:5, 10; 12:15; Gospel of John 19:30.

126. Matt. 26:41; I Peter 1:6–7; 2:11; James (early 2d cent.) 1:12–15.

127. Mark 8:36–37; Matt. 16:26; Luke 9:25; I Peter 2:10, 18; James 1:12–15; Gospel of John 3:15; 6:63; I Epistle of John (*ca.* 110) 2:15–17; Jude (*ca.* 125) 19, 23; II Tim. (*ca.* 150) 2:22; Titus (*ca.* 150), 2:12; II Peter (end 2d cent.) 1:4. On chastity, *vide* I Tim. 4:3; Rev. (*ca.* 95) 14:4.

128. Eph. (*ca.* 93) 5:39; II Tim. 3:2.

129. Tim. 3:3.

130. Matt. 10:29; cf. Acts 15:17; 21:14; Rev. 6:2–9; 11:6; 16:9.

131. I Peter 2:13–14.

132. *Ibid.,* 3:22.

133. Gospel of John 3:27.

134. I Tim. 6:10.

135. Mark 13:8, 24:27; Matt. 24:6–8, 29–31; 25:31–46; Luke 21:9–27; Acts 24:15; Gospel of John 3:16–21, 36; 5:24–29; 12:47; I Epistle of John 3:8–10; II Tim. 4:1

136. Rev. 3:12; 11:8; 14:8; 16:9; 17:5, 18; 18:1–24; 18:2; 21:2–3, 9–27; 22:1–5.

137. Luke 16:16–17.

138. Heb. 7:16.

139. *Ibid.,* 10:16.

140. I Tim. 1:8–10.

141. Eph. 4:4–16.

142. *De testimonio animae* (197), 5; in *Opera,* I, 134–43.

143. De Corone (211) 5–6; in *Opera omnia,* ed. J. P. Migne (PL, 1–2) (Paris, 1844), II, cols. 73–102; tr. ed., A.C. Cox (Buffalo, 1885).

144. *De Anima (ca.* 210) 30; in *Opera,* ed. A. Reifferscheid and G. Wissowa *CSEL,* 20, 47) (Vienna, 1890——), I, 289–396.

145. *Contra Celsum* 5. 40; in *Werke,* ed. P. Koetschau *et al.* (Leipzig, 1899——), I–II; tr. F. Crombie, Buffalo.

146. Cyprian (200?–258) *Ad Demetrianum* 8; in *Opera omnia,* ed. W. Hartel (*CSEL,* 3) (Vienna, 1868–71), III, pt. 3, pp. 349–70.

147. Minucius Felix (fl. *ca.* 240), Octavius (*ca.* 240), ed. J. P. Waltzing (Leipzig, 1912), 6.

148. Lactantius (250?–325?), *Divinarum institutionum* (*ca.* 310), ed. S. Brandt and G. Laubmann (*CESL,* 19, 27) (Vienna, 1890–95), 5. 15; cf. 5. 16.

149. Ambrosius (340?–397) *De officiis (ca.* 391) 3. 3. 15–19; in *Opera omnia* (PL, 14–17) (Paris, 1845), II, 1, cols. 23–184.

150. *Quaestiones veteris et novi testamenti* 35; in Augustine *Opera omnia* (PL, 32–47) (Paris, 1841–77), III, pt. 2, cols. 2205–2416.

151. *Ibid.,* 91.

152. *De civitate dei* 2. 2.

153. *Ibid.,* 5. 11.

154. *Ibid.,* 4. 33; cf. 2. 23; 4. 2; 5. 19, 21–22, 25.

155. *Ibid.,* 5. 13. On the virtues of the Romans, *vide ibid.,* 5. 12, 15.

156. *Ibid.,* 5. 16.

157. *Ibid.,* 5. 19.

158. *Ibid.,* 5. 23; cf. 1. 1; 4. 1; 5. 23.

159. *Ibid.,* 12. 22; cf. 12. 23, 28; 14. 1.

160. *Ibid.,* 19. 15.

161. *Contra Faustum* (400), ed. J. Zycha 19. 2; in *CSEL,* XXV, pp. 249–797; tr. R. Stothert (Buffalo, 1887).

162. *Confessiones* (400), ed. P. Knoll; tr. J. G. Pickington (Buffalo, 1886), 1. 16. 25; in *CSEL,* 33; (Vienna, 1896).

163. *Ibid.,* 4. 10. 15.

164. *De civitate dei* 10. 14; cf. *ibid.,* 12. 14, 20–21.

165. *Ibid.,* 22. 30.

166. Ed. K. Zangemeister (*CSEL,* 5), (Vienna, 1882).

167. *Ibid.,* 1. prol.; tr. I. W. Raymond (New York, 1936).

168. *Ibid.,* 2. 1.

169. *Ibid.,* 7. 2; cf. *ibid.,* 2. 1.

170. *Ibid.,* 1. 1.

171. *Ibid.,* 2. 1.

172. *Ibid.,* 2. 3.

173. *Etymologiae* 1. 41. 1.

174. *Ibid.,* 1. 42. 1–2.

175. *Ibid.,* 5 2. 1.

176. *Ibid.,* 5. 3. 1–4.

177. *Ibid.,* 5. 4. 1.

178. *Idem.*

179. *Ibid.,* 5. 5. 1.

180. *Ibid.,* 5. 6. 1.

181. *Ibid.,* 5. 20. 1.

182. *Chronica* (1147——), ed. A. Hofmeister (2d ed.; Hanover, 1912), 7. prol.; tr. C. C. Mierow (New York, 1928).

183. *Ibid.,* 3. prol.

184.  *Ibid.,* 1. 2.
185.  *Ibid.,* 1. 4.
186.  *Ibid.,* 1. 4.
187.  *Ibid.,* 2. prol.
188.  *Ibid.,* 2. 16.
189.  *Ibid.,* 3. prol.
190.  *Ibid.,* 5. prol.
191.  *Ibid.,* 8. prol.
192.  *Ibid.,* 8. 16.
193.  *Ibid.,* 3. 45.
194.  Ed. C. C. I. Webb (Oxford, 1909).
195.  *Ibid.,* 8. 17; tr. J. Dickinson (New York, 1927).
196.  *Ibid.,* 4. 7.
197.  *Ibid.,* 8. 17.
198.  *Ibid.,* 5. 6.
199.  *Ibid.,* 8. 18.
200.  *Ibid.,* 5. 2; the analogy is carried through in *Ibid.,* 5–6.
201.  *Ibid.,* 4. 1.
202.  *Ibid.,* 4. 4.
203.  *Ibid.,* 6. 20.
204.  *Summa theologica,* 1. 91. 1; 1. 99. 1; 1. 101. 1–2.
205.  *De regno* (*ca.* 1260) 1. 1; in *Opuscula omnia,* ed. P. Mandonnet (Paris, 1927), I, 312–487; tr. G. B. Phelan (Toronto, 1935).
206.  *ST* 2. 1. 81. 1.
207.  *De regno* 1. 1.
208.  *ST* 2. 2. 104. 5; *vide De regno* 1. 3–12.
209.  *Summa contra gentiles* 3. 81; in *Opera omnia,* XIII–XV; tr. English Dominican Fathers (London, 1924–29).
210.  *ST* 1. 96. 3.
211.  *Summa* 1. 103. 3.; cf. *ibid.,* 1. 96. 4; 2. 1. 105, 1; *De regno* 1. 6; *Contra gentiles* 4. 76.
212.  *ST* 1. 96. 4.
213.  *De regno* 1. 6.
214.  *De regno* 1. 12; cf. *ibid.,* 1. 13–14; *Contra gentiles* 3. 76–83; 4. 58; *Summa* 2. 1. 81. 1; 2. 1. 90. 2; 3. 8. 1–2.
215.  *Summa* 2. 1. 93. 1; cf. *ibid.,* 1. 22. 2; 1. 103; 2. 1. 91. 1; 2. 1. 93. 3; *Contra gentiles* 3. 76–83; *De regno* 1. 12.
216.  *De regno* 2. 1–4.
217.  *Summa* 2. 1. 90. 1.
218.  *Ibid.,* 2. 1. 91. 1; cf. *ibid.,* 2. 1. 93; 2. 2. 57. 2.
219.  *Ibid.,* 2. 1. 91. 5; cf. *ibid.,* 2. 1. 98, 106–7.
220.  *Ibid.,* 2. 1. 91. 2; cf. *ibid.,* 2. 1. 94.
221.  *Ibid.,* 2. 1. 90. 4.
222.  *Ibid.,* 2. 1. 91. 4.
223.  *Ibid.,* 2. 1. 91. 3; cf. *ibid.,* 2. 1. 95. 97.
224.  *Ibid.,* 2. 1. 95. 2.
225.  *Ibid.,* 2. : 1. 95. 4.
226.  *Ibid.,* 2. 2. 57. 3.
227.  *Idem.*
228.  *Ibid.,* 2. 1. 90. 3; cf. *ibid.,* 2. 2. 57. 2.
229.  *Ibid.,* 2. 1. 95. 2.
230.  *Ibid.,* 2. 1. 93. 3; cf. *ibid.,* 2. 1. 90. 1–2; 2. 1. 92. 1; 2. 1. 93. 3; 2. 1. 95. 2; 2. 1. 96. 4; 2. 2. 57. 2.
231.  *De vulgari eloquentia* 1. 17.
232.  *De monarchia* (*ca.* 1310) 1. 6–7; in *Opere,* tr. P. H. Wicksteed (London, 1904).
233.  *Ibid.,* 1. 14.
234.  *Tractaus de origine, natura, jure et mutationibus monetarum* (*ca.* 1360), 19; in *idem* and N. Copernicus, *Monete cudende ratio,* ed. M. L. Wolowski (Paris, 1864), pp. lxxxviii–cxxxix; tr. T. W. Balch (Philadelphia, 1908).
235.  *Complete Works,* ed. W. W. Skeat (2d ed.; Oxford, 1894–1900).
236.  *Ibid.,* 4. 202. 1408.
237.  T. Walsingham, *Historia anglicana,* ed. H. T. Riley (*Rerum Britannicarum medii aevi scriptores,* 28) (London, 1863–64), II, 32.

238. Version of J. Froissart, *Chroniaue;*, ed. S. Luce *et al.* (*Société de l'Histoire de France, Publications*) (*Paris*, 1869—), 2. 212; tr. T. Johnes, ed. J. Lord, New York, n.d.; cf. Walsingham, *op. cit.*, II, 32–33.

239. Walsingham, *op. cit.*, II, 33–34.

240. Pseudo-Knighton, in H. Knighton, *Chronicon monachi leycestrensis,* ed. J. R. Lumby (*RBMAS,* 92) (London, 1889–95), II, 139–40.

241. *Ibid.,* II, 170.

242. E.g., Petrus Crassus (fl. 1084), "Defensio Heinrici IV regis" (1084), ed. L. von Heineman, 4; in *Libelli de lite* (*Monumenta Germania Historica*) (Hanover, 1891—), I, 433–53; William of Ockham (d. 1349?), *Opera politica,* ed. J. G. Sikes *et al.* (Manchester, 1940—).

243. "Letter to the Emperor Anastasius, 494," 2; in *Epistolae romanorum pontificum genuinae,* ed. A. Thiel (Braunsberg, 1868), pp. 349–58.

244. "Tractatus" (495) 4. 11; in *ibid.,* pp. 510–607; tr. A. B. Cavanagh, Washington, D.C., 1934.

245. "Letter to Hermann of Metz, Aug. 25, 1076," *Register,* ed. E. Caspar (*MGH,* Epistolae selectae, 2) (Berlin, 1920–23) 4. 2; tr. E. Emerton, New York, 1932; cf. "Letter to the German princes, Jan. 1077," R, 4. 12.

246. "Letter to Hermann of Metz, March 15, 1081," R, 8. 21.

247. R, 2. 55a.

248. 12.

249. "First excommunication of Henry IV, Feb. 14–20, 1076," R, 3. 10a.

250. "Second excommunication of Henry IV, March 7, 1080," R, 7. 14a.

251. "Letter to Henry IV, Sep. 1075," R, 3. 7.

252. "Letter to Hermann of Metz, March 15, 1081."

253. *De consideratione* 1. 6. 7; in *Opera omnia* (*PL,* 182–85) (Paris, 1879), I, cols. 727–808; tr. G. Lewis (Oxford, 1908).

254. *Ibid.,* 4. 3. 7; cf. "Letter to Pope Eugenius" (1146), *Epistolae* 256; in *Opera omnia,* I, cols. 67–715.

255. "Letter to King Conrad" (1146), *Epistolae* 244; tr. S. J. Eales (London, n.d).

256. "Letter to Duke Courad" (1131), *Epistolae* 97; "Letter to the Emperor Lothaire" (*ca.* 1135), *ibid.,* 139; "Letter to Louis" (1138), *ibid.,* 170; "Letter to Count Henry" (1152), *ibid.,* 279.

257. "Letter to the Romans" (1146), *ibid.,* 243.

258. Policraticus 4. 1; 5. 6; 6. 25; 8. 18.

259. *Ibid.,* 5. 4; cf. *ibid.,* 4. 3, 6; 5. 2.

260. "Letter to Acerbius, Nov. 1198," c. 377a-b; in *Opera,* ed. J. P. Migne (*PL,* 214–17) (Paris, 1855), I, cols. 377–78; tr. O. J. Thatcher and E. H. McNeal (New York, 1905).

261. *De regno* 1. 14.

262. *Summa,* 2. 2. 60. 6.

263. *Ibid.,* 1. 15.

264. In *Les Registres de Boniface VIII,* ed G. Digard *et al.* (*Bibliothèque des Écoles Françaises d'Athenes et de Rome* [ser. 2], 4) (Paris, 1884——), No. 5382.

265. *Unum sanctam;* tr. H. K. Mann (London, 1932).

266. *De monarchia,* 1. 2.

267. *Ibid.,* 1. 3.

268. *Ibid.,* 1. 4.

269. *Ibid.,* 1. 15.

270. *Ibid.,* 2. 13.

271. *Ibid.,* 3. 1.

272. *Ibid.,* 3. 16.

273. *Ibid.,* 3. 13.

274. *Ibid.,* 3. 16.

275. "Privilegium maius" (*ca.* 964), ed. L. Weiland; in *Constitutiones et acta publica imperatorum et regum MGH* [Leges], Sect. 4) (Hanover, 1893——), I, 667–74.

276. Manegold of Lautenbach, *Liber ad Gebehardum,* pp. 391–92; *vide ibid.,* pp. 356, 392–93; tr. M. S. Stead (London, 1914).

277. "Ad Gebhardum" (*ca.* 1090), ed. K. Francke, 30; in *Libelli de lite,* I, 300–431.

278. *Defensor pacis* (1324), ed. C. W. Previté-Orton (Cambridge, 1928), 1. 4. 1; tr. F. W. Coker (New York, 1914).

279. *Ibid.,* 1. 4. 3.

280. *Ibid.,* 1. 4. 4.

281. *Ibid.,* 1. 4. 5.

282. *Ibid.,* 1. 12. 7.

283. *Ibid.,* 1. 12. 3.

284. *Ibid.,* 1. 12. 5.

285. *Apocalypse of Baruch* (*post* 70), 85. 10.
286. *II Esdras* (*ca.* 95), 5. 53–55.
287. *Ibid.* (*ca.* 120), 14. 10; *vide ibid.,* 14. 16.
288. "De mortalitate" (252) 25; in *Opera omnia,* ed. W. Hartel (*CSEL,* 3) (Vienna, 1868–71), pp. 295–314; tr. E. Wallis (Buffalo, 1886).
289. "Ad Demetrianum" (252) 3; in *Opera omnia,* pp. 349–70; tr. Wallis.
290. R. L. Poole, *Studies in Chronology and History,* ed. A. L. Poole (Oxford, 1934), pp. 228–30.
291. John of Salisbury, *Metalogicus* 3. 4 (p. 131); in *Opera omnia,* ed. J. A. Giles (Oxford, 1848), V, 1–207.
292. *The Farie Quene* (1590–1609) 3. 8. 30; in *Poetical Works,* ed. J. C. Smith and E. de Selincourt (London, 1912), pp. 1–413.
293. *Ibid.,* 3. 8. 31; *vide ibid.,* 3. 8. 29–33; 5. introd. 1–10.
294. *Ibid.,* 5. introd. 4.
295. *Ibid.,* 5. introd. 6.
296. *Il libro del cortegiano* (1528), ed. V. Cian (Florence, 1894), 2. 1–3.

## NOTES TO CHAPTER II

1. W. Schickard, *Tarich* (Tübingen, 1628), pp. 175–76.
2. E. Delacroix, *Journal,* ed. A. Joubin (Paris, 1932), I, 274.
3. *Notebooks,* ed. and tr. E. MacCurdy (New York, 1938), II. 282.
4. *Ibid.,* I, 201.
5. *Ibid.,* p. 202.
6. *Ibid.,* p. 199.
7. *Ibid.,* p. 200.
8. *Ibid.,* p. 129.
10. *Ibid.,* II. 240.
11. *De symmetrica* (1528), Paris, 1557.
12. Zurich, 1551–58.
13. Gesner, *op. cit.,* I, 957–81.
14. Paris, 1552.
15. Wotton, *op. cit.,* 4.
16. *Antoniana margarita,* Medina del Campo, 1554; *Apologia,* Medina del Campo, 1555.
17. *Quod animalia bruta saepe ratione utantur melius homine,* ed. G. H. Ribow (Helmstedt, 1728), p. 7.
18. T. Amory, *The Life and Opinions of John Buncle* (London, 1904), pp. 420–21.
19. *Tabulae anatomicae* (1538), ed. M. Holl and K. Sudhoff) (Leipzig, 1920); *De humani corporis fabrica* (1543), (2d ed., Basel, 1555).
20. In *De humani corporis* there are the following illustrations: the skull of a man resting on that of a dog, pp. 46, 59; the sacrum and coccyx of man, monkey, and dog, pp. 98–99.
21. *Ibid.,* p. 23.
22. *L'Histoire de la nature des oyseaux* (Paris, 1555), pp. 38–33.
23. *Essais* (1580), III, 147; in *Œuvres complètes,* ed. J. Plattard (Paris, 1931——), I–VI; tr. E. J. Trechmann (London, 1927).
24. *Ibid.,* III, 148–49.
25. *Ibid.,* p. 282.
26. *Ibid.,* p. 168.
27. *Ibid.,* p. 172.
28. *Ibid.,* p. 223; *vide ibid.,* pp. 293–97.
29. *Ibid.,* p. 171.
30. *Ibid.,* pp. 184, 187–215; V, 59.
31. *Ibid.,* I, 142; *vide ibid.,* III, 216–17.
32. *Ibid.,* III, 175; *vide ibid.,* III, 176.
33. *Ibid.,* pp. 176–77.
34. *Ibid.,* p. 183.
35. *Ibid.,* p. 265.
36. *Ibid.,* pp. 223–403.
37. *Ibid.,* p. 223.
38. *Ibid.,* p. 66; *vide ibid.,* pp. 66–67.
39. *Ibid.,* p. 180.
40. *Ibid.,* pp. 181–82; on the language of gesture, *vide ibid.,* pp. 174–75.

41. *Ibid.*, p. 173.

42. *Ibid.*, pp. 182–83.

43. *De ascensione mentis in deum* (1617), *Opera omnia,* ed. J. Fèvre (Paris, 1870–74), VIII, 237–313.

44. *Philosophia magna,* pp. 75–76, 93; in *Samtliche Werke,* ed. K. Sudhoff and W. Matteissen (Munich, 1922–33) (Abt. 1), XIV, 1–375.

45. *Das Buch von der Gebärung* (1520), p. 247; in *Werke* (Abt. 1), I, 241–83.

46. *Astronomia magna* (1537–38), p. 35; in *Werke* (Abt. 1), XII, pp. 1–144.

47. *Ibid.*, p. 114.

48. *Weiteres zur Astronomia magna,* p. 469; in *Werke* (Abt. 1), XII, 445–507.

49. Pseudo-Paracelsus, *Liber Azoth,* p. 593; in Paracelsus, *Werke* (Abt. 1), XIV, 547–95.

50. *De immenso et innumerabilibus* (1590), 7. 18; in *Opera latine,* ed. F. Fiorentino *et al.* (Naples, 1879–91), I, pt. 1, pp. 191–398; I, 2, pp. 1–318.

51. *De immenso,* 7. 18.

52. *De monade numero et figura* (1590), 4 (p. 363); in *Opera latine,* I, pt. 2, pp. 319–473.

53. *Les six livres de la republique* (1576) (n.p., 1608), pp. 698–99; tr. R. Knolles, London, 1606.

54. *Ibid.*, pp. 699–700.

55. J. Burckhardt, "Die Ruinenstadt Rom," *Die Kultur der Renaissance in Italien,* ed. W. Goetz (15th ed.; Leipzig, 1926), 3. 2.

56. *Itinerarium,* ed. L. Mehus (Florence, 1742); *La Roma antica,* ed. C. Huelsen, Rome, 1907.

57. *Musaeum metallicum* (Bonn, 1648), 4. 1. 11.

58. *De rerum fossilium, lapidum et gemmarum* (1565), 3; in *De omni rerum fossilium genere,* ed. C. Gesner (Zurich, 1565–66), No. 8.

59. J. Evans, *The Ancient Stone Implements, Weapons and Ornaments, of Great Britain* (2d ed.; London, 1897), pp. 56–60.

60. Rome, 1574.

61. Quot. in *Matériaux pour l'Histoire primitive et naturelle de l'homme,* 10 (1875), 49–57.

62. Rev. ed.; London, 1607.

63. Ed. J. Calmette and G. Durville (Paris, 1924–25).

64. *English Works,* ed. W. E. Campbell and A. W. Reed (London, 1931——) .

65. Ed. J. le Laboureur (Paris, 1659).

66. *Britannia* (1586) (London, 1607); *Remains concerning Britain* (1605) (London, 1870).

67. J. A. Symonds, "The revival of learning," *Renaissance in Italy* (New York, 1935), p. 2; Sandys, *History of Classical Scholarship,* II, 1–276.

68. Bertrandon de la Brocquière 15th cent.), *Le voyage d'Outremer* (ca. 1438), ed. C. Schefer (*Recueil de Voyages et de Documents pour servir a l'Histoire de la Géographie,* 12) (Paris, 1892); Felix Fabri (1441?–1502), *Evagatorium in Terrae Sanctae* (1484), ed. C. D. Hassler (*Bibliothek des literarischen Vereins in Stuttgart,* 2–4) (Stuttgart, 1843–49); Pietro Casola (1427–1507), *Viaggio a Cerusalemme* (ca. 1495) (Milan, 1855).

69. Ruy Gonzalez de Clavijo (d. 1412), *Historia del Gran Tamorlan* (1406) (Cronicas de los reyes de Espana, 3. 2), (2d ed., Madrid, 1782); Caterino Zeno (15th cent.) *Viaggio in Persia* (ca. 1475), in G. B. Ramusio, *Delle navigationi et viaggi* (Venice, 1606–13), II, 219v–233v; Ambrogio Contarini (d. 1499), *Travels in Persia* (ca. 1477), tr. S. A. Roy, *Hakluyt Society Publications* (ser. 1), 49. 1 (1873), pp. 105–73: Ogier Ghislain de Busbecq (1522–92), *De legationis Turcicae* (1555–62), *Omnia quae extant* (Leyden, 1633), pp. 12–392.

70. Johannes Schiltberger (b. 1380?), *Reisebuch* (ca. 1427), ed. V. Langmantel (*Bibl. lit. Ver. Stuttgart,* 172 (Tübingen, 1885); Nicolo di Conti (d. ca. 1469), *Viaggi in Persia e Giava* (ca. 1445), ed. M. Longhena, Milan, 1929; Antonio Malfante (d. 1450), "Letter to Giovanni Mariono, 1447," ed. C. de la Roncière, *Bullétin de Comité des Travaux Historiques et Scientifiques, La Section de Gégraphie,* 23 (1918), 1–28; Alvise Cadamosto (1432–88), *Voyages* (ca. 1460–68), tr. G. R. Crone, *Hakluyt Soc. Publ.* (ser. 2), 80 (1937), pp. 1–84; Giosofat Barbaro 1413–94), *Travels to Tana and Persia* (1487), tr. W. Thomas, *ibid.* (ser. 1), 49. 1 (1873), pp. 1–101; *idem,* "Letter to P. Barocci, May 23, 1491," tr. W. Thomas, *ibid.,* pp. 102–3; Andrew Boorde (1490?–1549), *The Fyrst Boke of the introduction of Knowledge* (ca. 1547), ed. F. J. Furnivall, *Early Eng. Text Soc.* (extra ser.), 10 (1870), 111–222.

71. A. Gukovsky and O. Trachtenberg, *History of Feudalism,* tr. I. Zvaritch (Moscow, 1935), pp. 151–52.

72. Pierr Bontier (fl. 1404) and Jean le Verrier (fl. 1404) *Le Canarien* (ca. 1404), ed. G. Gravier, Rouen, 1874; also the earlier account compiled by Giovanni Boccaccio, *De Canaria et de insulis reliquis ultra Hispaniam in oceano noviter repertis,* in *Monumenti de Boccaccio,* ed. S. Ciampi (2d ed. Milan, 1830), pp. 55–63.

73. *The Chronicle of the Discovery and Conquest of Guinea* (1453), tr. C. R. Beazley and E. Prestage (HSP [ser. 1], 95, 100), London, 1896–99.

74. *De prima inventione Guineae* (1482), ed. J. A. Schmeller, *Abhandlungen der königlich bayerischen Akademie der Wissenschaften* (philos.-philol.), 4 (1847), pt. 3, No. 2.

75. *A Journal of the First Voyage of Vasco da Gama* (1497-99), ed. and tr. E. G. Ravenstein (*HSP* [ser. 1], 99) (London, 1898).

76. *Four Voyages* (1492-1504), ed. andttr. C. Jane (*HSP* [ser. 2], 65, 70), (London, 1930-33).

77. *The Great Age of Discovery,* ed. A. P. Newton (London, 1932).

78. *Delle navigatione et viaggi* (Venice, 1550-65).

79. *The Decades of the Newe Worlde or West India* (London, 1955).

80. *The Principal Navigations Voyages Traffiques and Discoveries of the English Nation* (1589) (*HSP* [extra ser.], 1-12) (Glasgow, 1903-5).

81. Landshut, 1524.

82. *Ibid.,* pp. 65-69.

83. Venice, 1528.

84. Tübingen, 1534,

85. Basle, 1550.

86. Venice, 1596.

87. *Franco-Gallia* (1573) (Frankfurt, 1665), 4 (p. 47); tr. R. Molsworth (London, 1711).

88. Zurich, 1555.

89. Frankfurt, 1603.

90. Frankfurt, 1603.

91. *Essais,* VI, 61.

92. *Ibid.,* III, 314-15.

93. *Franco-Gallia* (1573) (Frankfurt, 1665), 2 (pp. 24-25); tr. R. Molesworth (London, 1711).

94. *De natura legis naturae* (*ca.* 1462), 1. 4; in *Works,* ed. T. Dortescue, Lord Clermont (London, 1869), I, 59-372; tr. C. Fortescue, *idem.*

95. *Ibid.,* 1. 31.

96. *Ibid.,* 1. 29.

97. *De laudibus legum Angliae* (*ca.* 1470), 16; in *Works,* I, 373-442; tr. F. Gregor, *idem.*

98. *De natura,* 1. 5.

99. *De laudibus,* 15.

100. *The Governance of England* (1476), ed. C. Plummer (Oxford, 1885), 1.

101. *Ibid.,* 2; *vide De laudibus,* 9-13.

102. Ed. J. H. Lupton (Oxford, 1895).

103. *Ibid.,* pp. 44-47, 51-56, 58; somewhat modernized.

104. *Ibid.,* p. 304.

105. *Ibid.,* pp. 92-93.

106. *Ibid.,* p. 238.

107. *On Education* (1531), tr. F. Watson (Cambridge, 1913), pref.

108. *De subventione pauperum* (1526), tr. M. M. Sherwood (*Studies in Social Work,* 11) (New York, 1917), 2. 1.

109. *Ibid.,* 2. 10.

110. *On Education,* 1. 5.

111. *Ibid.,* 1. 1.

112. *Ibid.,* 1. 2.

113. *Gargantua et Pantagruel* (1532-64), P. 6-8; G. 14-15, 18-20, 23-24; 5. prol., 19-23; in *Œuvres,* ed. C. Marty-Laveaux (Paris, 1870-1903), I-III, 228; *Epistre du Lymosin, Œuvres,* III, 273-80; *La cresme philosophalle, ibid.,* pp. 281-85.

114. P. 29-30, 34; G. prol., 39-42, 45, 52; 3. 15, 19, 22, 29-30, 48; 4. 48-53, 64; 5. 1-6, 9.

115. P. 32, 46, 50; 3. 1.

116. P. 1; tr. T. Urquhart and P. Motteux, London, 1928.

117. 3. 8.

118. 3. 3.

119. 3. 29.

120. P. 9.

121. 3. 44.

122. 3. 48.

123. G. 10.

124. G. 1.

125. 5. 30.

126. *Pantagrueline prognostication,* pref.; in *Œuvres,* III, 229-52; tr. P. Motteux (London, 1951).

127. *La cena de le ceneri* (1684), pp. 31–32; in *Opere italiane*, ed. G. Gentile (2d ed., Bari, 1925–27), I, 1–131.

128.  *Essais*, VI, 46; *vide ibid.*, II, 24–25.

129.  *Ibid.*, V, 199.

130.  *Ibid.*, III, 269.

131.  *Ibid.*, IV, 83.

132.  *Ibid.*, p. 50.

133.  *Ibid.*, VI, 47–48; cf. *ibid.*, II, 18.

134.  *Ibid.*, VI, 65; *vide ibid.*, pp. 65–66; *Journal du voyage en Italie* (1580–81), ed.——de Querlon (Rome, 1774).

135.  P. Villey, *Les sources et evolution des Essais de Montaigne* (*Bibliothéque de la Fondation Thiers*, 14), (Paris, 1908); *idem, Les livres d'histoire moderne utilisés par Montaigne* (Paris, 1908).

136.  *Essais*, VI, 156.

137.  *Ibid.*, III, 368.

138.  *Ibid.*, I, 62.

139.  *Ibid.*, VI, 203.

140.  *Ibid.*, I, 153; *vide ibid.*, I, 18–19, 150, 153, 154–59, 160–61, 165; II, 63, 119–20, 121, 123, 212–13; III, 46–47, 86, 217–19, 368–73; V, 106–7; VI, 59, 156, 202.

141.  *Journal*, I, 176.

142.  *Ibid.*, p. 100.

143.  *Ibid.*, I, 154.

144.  *Ibid.*, p. 153.

145.  *Ibid.*, p. 159; *vide ibid.*, p. 160.

146.  *Ibid.*, II, 92; cf. *ibid.*, I, 29.

147.  *Ibid.*, I, 161.

148.  *Essais*, I, 162; *vide ibid.*, I, 162–64; II, 105–6; III, 372.

149.  *Ibid.*, III, 216; *vide ibid.*, pp. 216–17.

150.  *Ibid.*, IV, 82; cf. *ibid.*, I, 29.

151.  *Ibid.*, IV, 137.

152.  *Ibid.*, III, 142; *vide ibid.*, II, 98–99.

153.  *Ibid.*, II, 99.

154.  *Ibid.*, III, 156.

155.  *Ibid.*, I, 159–60.

156.  *Ibid.*, p. 150.

157.  *Ibid.*, p. 161.

158.  *Ibid.*. II, 119.

159.  *Ibid.*, IV, 47.

160.  *ibid.*, V, 214–15; *vide ibid.*, V, 97; VI, **190.**

161.  *Ibid.*, VI, 138.

162.  *Ibid.*, III, 244–45.

163.  *Ibid.*, p. 161.

164.  *Ibid.*, I, 159; cf. *ibid.*, VI, 188–89.

165.  *Ibid.*, IV, 84.

166.  *Ibid.*, III, 366–67; *vide ibid.*, pp. 365–**66.**

167.  *Ibid.*, p. 286; cf. *ibid.*, I, 56.

168.  *Ibid.*, III, 257; *vide ibid.*, V, 204–5; VI, 123–25, **135.**

169.  *Ibid.*, III, 304–5.

170.  *Ibid.*, p. 353.

171.  *Ibid.*, VI, 203.

172.  For his political generalizations, *vide* esp. 1. 5, 6, 9, 24, 43, 45, **47;** 2. 34.

173.  *Ibid.*, IV, 162.

174.  *Ibid.*, III, 194.

175.  *Ibid.*, II, 51.

176.  *Ibid.*, VI, 179.

177.  *Ibid.*, p. 187.

178.  *Ibid.*, 3. 11.

179.  *Ibid.*, III, 354.

180.  *Ibid.*, V, 204.

181.  *Ibid.*, p. 28.

182.  *Ibid.*, IV, 235.

183.  *Ibid.*, III, 122.

184. *Ibid.*, p. 253.
185. *Ibid.*, p. 274.
186. *Ibid.*, I, 74–75.
187. *Ibid.*, III, 309–11, 315–17.
188. *Ibid.*, pp. 272–73, 323–26.
189. *Ibid.*, I, 143.
190. *Ibid.*, 1. 21; III, 230–31.
191. *Ibid.*, III, 320–22, 349.
192. *Ibid.*, p. 347.
193. *Ibid.*, IV, 58; VI, 242–43, 247, 251–52.
194. *Ibid.*, V, 210.
195. *Ibid.*, VI, 70.
196. *Ibid.*, III, 293; *vide ibid.*, III, 79–80; IV, 47.
197. *Ibid.*, VI, 165–66.
198. *Ibid.*, II, 62.
199. *Ibid.*, VI, 94; cf. *ibid.*, pp. 66–67.
200. *Ibid.*, p. 23.
201. *Ibid.*, III, 146.
202. *Ibid.*, II. 136.
203. *Ibid.*, III, 348.
204. *Ibid.*, p. 159.
205. *Ibid.*, pp. 79–80.
206. *Ibid.*, pp. 98–99.
207. *Ibid.*, p. 349.
208. *Ibid.*, IV, 204.
209. *Ibid.*, II, 12.
210. *Ibid.*, VI, 206.
211. *Ibid.*, p. 99.
212. *Ibid.*, V, 36–37.
213. *Ibid.*, VI, 174.
214. *Ibid.*, I, 64; *vide ibid.*, II, 104.
215. *Ibid.*, III, 360–61.
216. *Ibid.*, I, 165; cf. *ibid.*, IV, 82.
217. *Ibid.*, I, 44.
218. *Ibid.*, IV, 97.
219. *Ibid.*, I, 92.
220. *Ibid.*, III, 79.
221. *Ibid.*, p. 367.
222. *Ibid.*, p. 368.
223. *Ibid.*, V, 16.
224. *Ibid.*, I, 71.
225. *Ibid.*, VI, 191.
226. *Ibid.*, p. 80.
227. *Ibid.*, VI, 181.
228. *Ibid.*, II, 94–98, 99–101, 103–5; V, 179–89.
229. *Ibid.*, II, 92–94; *vide ibid.*, II, 94; III, 231, 240–41; V, 179–80; VI, 156–57, 181.
230. *Ibid.*, I, 191.
231. *Ibid.*, II, 240.
232. *Ibid.*, p. 217.
233. *Ibid.*, V, 177; *vide ibid.*, V, 178–79.
234. *Ibid.*, VI, 138.
235. *Ibid.*, p. 8.
236. *Ibid.*, IV, 117–18.
237. *Ibid.*, III, 77.
238. *Ibid.*, p. 357.
239. *Ibid.*, pp. 357–60.
240. *De controversis christianae fidei adversus sui temporis haereticos* (1586–93), 5. 3. 5; in *Opera omnai*, ed. J. Fèvre (Paris, 1870–74), I–VI; tr. K. E. Murphy (New York, 1928).
241. *Idem.*
242. *Ibid.*, 5. 3. 7.
243. *Ibid.*, 5. 3. 6.

244. *Ibid.*, 5. 3. 9.

245. *Ibid.*, 5. 3. 6.

246. *De jure belli* (1588–89) *Classics of International Law,* 16) (Oxford, 1933), 1. 15 (p. 107); tr. J. C. Rolfe (Oxford, 1933).

247. *Ibid.*, 1. 15 (p. 109).

248. *Ibid.*, 1. 15 (pp. 110–11).

249. *Ibid.*, 3. 13 (p. 586).

250. *Ibid.*, 1. 12 (p. 92); *vide ibid.*, 1. 3 (p. 26).

251. *Ibid.*, 1. 25 (p. 202).

252. *Ibid.*, 1. 1 (pp. 10–11, 13).

253. *Ibid.*, 1. 1 (p. 10).

254. *Ibid.*, 1. 9 p. 65); cf. *ibid.*, 1. 1 (p. 11).

255. *De legationibus* (1585) (*CIL.*, 12) (New York, 1924), 2. 18 (p. 121); tr. G. J. Laing (New York, 1924).

256. *Ibid.*, 1. 1 (pp. 13–14).

257. *Ibid.*, 3. 9 (p. 541).

258. *De jure belli,* 1. 25 (p. 202).

259. *Ibid.*, 1. 3 (p. 27).

260. *Ibid.*, 2. 22 (p. 431).

261. *Ibid.*, 3. 9 (pp. 539–40).

262. *Ibid.*, 3. 9 (p. 539).

263. *The Quintescence of Wit,* tr. R. Hichcock (London, 1590), p. (viii).

264. *Ibid.*, pp. (vii-viii).

265. *Ibid.*, p. (v).

266. H. Hallam, *Introduction to the Literature of Europe* (New York, 1866), I, 246.

267. *Mémoires,* 2. 6 (I, 129); tr. A. R. Scobie (London, n.d).

268. *Discorsi sopra la prima deca di Tito Livio* (1519), 1. 10; in *Opere,* ed. A. Panella (Milan, 1938–39), II, 97–470; tr. C. E. Detmold (Boston, 1882).

269. *Istorie fiorentine,* proem; in *Opere,* I, 43–516; tr. Detmold.

270. *Discorsi,* 1. 39; cf. *ibid.*, 1. intr.

271. *Ibid.*, 3. 43. For a characterization of the French, vide "De natura gallorum," *Opere,* I, 737–38.

272. P. Villari, *Nicolò Machiavelli,* ed. M. Scherillo (4th ed.; Milan, 1927), II, 74; tr. L. Villari (London, 1892).

273. *Discorsi,* 1. 3.

274. *Il principe* (1513), 15; in *Opere,* II, 7–96; tr. Detmold.

275. *Discorsi,* 3. 46.

276. *Ibid.*, 2. 5.

277. *Ibid.*, 2. intr.

278. *Ibid.*, 1. 6.

279. *Ibid.*, 3. 1.

280. *Istorie,* 5. 1.

281. *Discorsi,* 2. intr.

282. *Istorie,* 3. 1.

283. *Discorsi,* 2. intr.

284. *Ibid.*, 1. 1–2.

285. *Les six livres de la republique* (1576) (n. p, 1608), pp. 68–69; tr. R. Knolles (London, 1606).

286. *Ibid.*, p. 663.

287. *Ibid.*, p. 666.

288. *Idem.*

289. *Ibid.*, pp. 677–78.

290. *Ibid.*, pp. 698–99.

291. *Ibid.*, pp. 696–97.

292. *Ibid.*, p. 675.

293. *Ibid.*, p. 697.

294. *Ibid.*, pp. 699–700.

295. *Ibid.*, p. 698.

296. *Ibid.*, p. 702.

297. *De jure et officiis bellicis et disciplina militari* (1582), ed. J. Westlake (*Classics of International Law,* 2) (Washington, 1912), epist. ded.; tr. J. P. Bate, Washington, 1912.

298. *Ibid.*, 2. 3; *vide ibid.*, 2. 3–13.

299. *Ibid.*, 1. 5. 16.

300. *Della ragion di stato, and Delle cause della grandezza e magnificenza delle citta,* ed. C. Morandi *Classici del pensiero politico,* 2) (Bologna, 1930).

301. *Ibid.,* p. 317; *vide ibid.,* pp. 317–25; tr. T. Hawkins (London 1635).

302. *Ibid.,* p. 325; *vide ibid.,* pp. 325–35.

303. *Ibid.,* p. 339.

304. *Ibid.,* p. 343.

305. *Ibid.,* p. 346.

306. *Ibid.,* p. 349.

307. *Ibid.,* p. 350.

308. *Idem.*

309. *Ibid.,* p. 352.

310. *Ibid.,* p. 355.

311. *Ibid.,* p. 357.

312. *Ibid.,* p. 358.

313. *Ibid.,* p. 376.

314. *Ibid.,* p. 379.

315. *Ibid.,* pp. 381–82.

316. *Monete cudende ratio* (1526), p. 56; in *Oresme and Copernicus, op. cit.,* pp. 1–79; tr. T. W. Balch, Philadelphia, 1908.

317. Ed. E. Lamond (Cambridge, 1893), pp. 32–33, 79, 86–87, 106.

318. *Ibid.,* p. 71; cf. *ibid.,* p. 60.

319. *Ibid.,* pp. 47–48.

320. *De re metallica* (1556) (Basel, 1657), pp. 12–13; tr. H. C. and L. H. Hoover (London, 1912.)

321. "Letter to Queen Elizabeth, 1558," p. 484; in J. W. Burgon, *The Life and Times of Sir Thomas Gersham* (London, 1839), I, 483–86.

322. " Political Allegory Relating to the Meeting of Pope Paul II and the Emperor Frederick III" (Venice, *ca.* 1470); in A. M. Hind, *Early Italian Engraving* (London, 1938—), 399.

323. *Vide* Hind, *ibid.,* 400; W. L. Schreiber, *Handbuch der Holz-und Metallschnitt des XV, Jahrhunderts* (Leipzig, 1926–30), 1956–58.

324. *Vide* Montaigne, *Essais,* III, 158–59.

325. *A Short Treatise of Politike Power* (1556) (n.p., 1639), p. 11; *vide ibid.,* p. 6.

326. *Ibid.,* p. 49.

327. *Ibid.,* p. 50.

328. *Franco-Gallia* (1573) (Frankfurt, 1665), 1 (p. 9); tr. R. Molesworth, London, 1711.

329. *Ibid.,* praef.

330. *De jure regni apud Scotos* (1579), p. 58; in *Opere omnia,* ed. T. Ruddiman (Leyden, 1725), I, pt. a, 1–62.

331. Tr. anonymous, ed. H. J. Laski, London, 1924.

332. *Ibid.,* p. 66.

333. *Ibid.,* p. 67.

334. *Ibid.,* p. 87.

335. *Ibid.,* p. 98.

336. *Ibid.* p. 118.

337. *Ibid.,* p. 122.

338. *Ibid.,* p. 139.

339. *Ibid.,* p. 140.

340. *Ibid.,* p. 141.

341. *Ibid.,* p. 143.

342. *Ibid.,* p. 199.

343. *Of the Laws of Ecclesiastical Polity* (1594), ed. J. Keble, rev. R. W. Church and F. Paget (7th ed.; Oxford, 1888), 1. 8. 2.

344. *Ibid.,* 1. 10. 1.

345. *Ibid.,* 1. 10. 2.

346. *Ibid.,* 1. 10. 6.

347. *Ibid.,* 1. 10. 3.

348. *Ibid.,* 1. 10. 4.

349. *Discours de la servitude volontaire,* p. 28; in *Œuvres complètes,* ed. L. Feugère (Paris, 1846), pp. 1–77; tr. H. Kurz (New York, 1942).

350. *Ibid.,* p. 12.

351. *Ibid.,* pp. 26–27.

352. *Ibid.,* p. 30.

353. *Ibid.,* pp. 33–34.
354. *Ibid.,* pp. 40–41.
355. *Ibid.,* pp. 34–35; *vide ibid.,* pp. 25–26.
356. *Ibid.,* pp. 41–42.
357. *Ibid.,* p. 46.

## NOTES TO CHAPTER III

1. "Of vicissitude of things," *Essays* (1596), ed. W. A. Wright (London, 1926), p. 232,
2. *De admirandis naturae reginae deaque mortalium arcanis* (Paris, 1616), 35; tr. T. Bendyshe (London, 1863–64).
3. *Apologia pro Galileo* (Frankfurt, 1622), p. 51; tr. G. McColley, Northampton, 1937.
4. *City of the Sun* (1623), tr. T. W. Halliday, p. 315; in *Ideal Empires and Republics* (New York, 1901), pp. 273–317.
5. (Amsterdam), 1655.
6. *Ibid.,* proem.; tr. Anonymous (London, 1655–56).
7. *Ibid.,* pt. 1; pt. 2, 1:1–3; 5.
8. *Ibid.,* pt. 1, p. 29.
9. *Ibid.,* pt. 1, pp. 29–30; *vide ibid.,* pt. 2, 3:5–7; 4:13.
10. *Ibid.,* pt. 2, pp. 233–34; *vide ibid.,* pt. 2, 3:8–11.
11. For his biblical criticism, *vide ibid.,* pt. 2, 4:1–2.
12. *Ibid.,* pt. 2, p. 193.
13. *Ibid.,* pt. 2, p. 195; cf. *ibid.,* pt. 2, pp. 195–96, 198; and 4:13.
14. *Ibid.,* pt. 2, pp. 198–99; *vide ibid.,* pt. 2, 4:3–9.
15. *Ibid.,* pt. 2, pp. 245–46; *vide ibid.,* pt. 2, 4:10–12.
16. *Ibid.,* pt. 2, 4. 13.
17. *Ibid.,* pt. 2, p. 139; *vide ibid.,* pt. 1; pt. 2, 2:1–6, 10–11; 3. 1–3.
18. L. P., *Two Essays, Sent in a Letter from Oxford, to a Nobleman in London* (1695), pp. 297–98; in *Somers Tracts, Third Series* (London, 1751), III, 291–308.
19. *Ibid.,* pp. 298, 300.
20. *Ibid.,* pp. 298–300.
21. *Ibid.,* p. 300.
22. *Ibid.,* pp. 298, 300–1.
23. *Ibid.,* p. 300.
24. *Ibid.,* pp. 295, 306–8.
25. *Ibid.,* pp. 301–2.
26. *The Primitive Origination of Mankind* (London, 1677), p. 347.
27. *Ibid.,* p. 291.
28. *Ibid.,* p. 266.
29. *The Sacred Theory of the Earth* (1681–89) (7th ed.; London, 1759), I, 5.
30. *Ibid.,* p. 44.
31. *Ibid.,* p. 43.
32. *Ibid.,* p. 50; *vide ibid.,* I, pp. 50–54.
33. *Ibid.,* p. 52.
34. *Ibid.,* p. 276.
35. *Ibid.,* p. 308.
36. *Ibid.,* p. 238.
37. "Cogitationes privatae" (1620), p. 219; in *Œuvres,* ed. C. Adam and P. Tannery (Paris, 1897–1909), X, 213–56; *vide Discours de la methode* (1637), 5; in *Œuvres,* VI, 1–78; *Objectiones et responsio* (16—), 3, resp. 1; in *Œuvres,* VII, 91–561; *Les passions de l'ame* (1649), 1:6–16; in *Œuvres,* XI, 291–497; *Principiae philosophiae,* 4. 189–97; in *Œuvres,* VIII, No. 1.
38. *L'Homme,* pp. 130 ff.; in *Œuvres,* XI, 119–215.
39. *DM,* pp. 57–58.
40. *Ibid.,* p. 58.
41. *Les estats et empires de la lune,* p. 91; in *Œuvres libertines,* ed. F. Lachèvre (Paris, 1921), I, 5–99; tr. R. Aldington (London, n.d.).
42. *Ibid.,* pp. 95–96.
43. *Ibid.,* pp. 15, 58.
44. *Les estats et empires du soleil,* pp. 130–32; in *Œuvres,* I, 100–199; tr. R. Aldington (London, n.d.).
45. *Lune,* p. 35.
46. *Soleil,* p. 164; *vide ibid.,* p. 164; *L,* p. 89.

47. *S*, pp. 129–30, 140, 166–67.

48. *Ibid.*, p. 148.

49. *L*, pp. 32–33, 38, 44–45, 52–54, 57–60, 73.

50. *S*, pp. 150–52, 157–60, 161–62, 164.

51. *S*, p. 196.

52. *L*, p. 13.

53. *A Philosophical Discourse concerning Speech* (1668), tr. anonymous (London, 1668), pp. (xvii–xviii); *vide ibid.*, pp. 11–27, 69–87.

54. *Ibid.*, "Rorarius," n. E.

55. *Dictionaire historique et critique* (1696), ed. A. J. Q. Beuchot (Paris, 1820–24), "Rorarius," n. E; tr. Anonymous, London, 1734–38, 2d ed. *Vide ibid.*, "Charron," "Pereira," "Rorarius," "Sennert."

56. A. O. Lovejoy, *The Great Chain of Being* (Cambridge, Mass., 1936), p. 52.

57. *Ibid.*, p. 59.

58. *De la sagesse* (1601), ed. A. Duval (Paris, 1827), I, 205; tr. G. Stanhope, (2d ed.; London, 1707).

59. *Ibid.*, I, 29–32; cf. *ibid.*, pp. 208–9, 215–16.

60. *Papers*, ed. Marquis of Lansdowne (London, 1927), II, 23–24; *vide ibid.*, pp. 25–26, 178–79.

61. *Ibid.*, pp. 219–20.

62. *Ibid.*, p. 223.

63. *Ibid.*, p. 155.

64. *Ibid.*, I, 155–56.

65. *Ibid.*, II, 26–29; cf. *ibid.*, p. 32.

66. *Ibid.*, p. 40.

67. *Ibid.*, I, 153.

68. *Ibid.*, II, 30–31.

69. *Nouveaux essais sur l'entendement* (1704), p. 49; in *Philosophischen Schriften*, ed. C. J. Gerhardt (Berlin, 1875–90), V, 39–509; tr. A. G. Langley (New York, 1896).

70. Though many of Leibniz' works were written after 1700, his main ideas were formulated before then and are distinctively characteristic of the 17th century.

71. "Letter to an unknown correspondent, Oct. 16, 1707," in G. E. Guhrauer, *Leibnitz* (Breslau, 1846), I, Anmerk., 32–33; tr. Langley; cf. "Letter to A. Arnauld, Sept. 1687," pp. 113, 117, 120–22; in *Phil. Schrift.*, II, 111–29; "Système nouveau de la nature et de la communication des substances" (1695), 2; in *Phil. Schrift.*, IV, 471 ff.; "De ipsa natura," 12; in *Phil. Schrift.*, IV, 504–16; "Letter to Queen Charlotte of Prussia," p. 506; in *Phil. Schrift.*, VI, 409–508; "Letter to Lady Masham, May 1704," p. 339; in *Phil. Schrift.*, III, 338–43; *Nouveaux essais*, pp. 59–60, 64, 103, 126–27, 455–56, 457–58; "Considerations sur les principes de vie, et sur les natures plastiques," pp. 542–43; in *Phil. Schrift.*, VI, 539–55; "Letter to R. C. Wagner, June 4, 1710," pp. 530–31; in *Phil. Schrift.*, VII, 528–32; *La monadologie* (1714), 14; in *Phil. Schrift.*, VI, 607–23.

72. *NE*, p. 254.

73. *NE*, p. 286.

74. "Draft of a letter to A. Arnauld" (1686), p. 73; in *Phil. Schrift.*, II, 68–73; tr. G. R. Montgomery (2d ed.; Chicago, 1931).

75. "Letter to A. Arnauld, April 30, 1687," p. 92; in *Phil. Schrift.*, II, 9–102.

76. *NE*, p. 324.

77. *La monadologie*, 19; tr. R. Latta, Oxford, 1898.

78. *NE*, p. 195.

79. *NE*, p. 329.

80. *Ibid.*, p. 126.

81. "Letter to Electress Sophia of Hanover, Feb. 6, 1706," p. 568; in *Phil. Schrift.*, VII, 565–70; tr. H. W. Carr (London, 1929).

82. *Ibid.*, p. 121.

83. *Ibid.*, p. 127.

84. "Draft of a letter to A. Arnauld," p. 72.

85. *Principes de la nature et de la grâce* (1714), 4; in *Phil. Schrift.*, VI, 598–606; tr. Latta.

86. *Monad.*, 26.

87. *NE*, p. 376; *vide ibid.*, 5, pp. 44, 129–31, 293, 306; "Letter to Lady Masham," p. 339; "Consid. sur les princ. de vie," pp. 542–43; "Letter to Wagner," pp. 530–31; *Monad.*, 82–84; *Principes de la nature et de la grâce*, 4–6, 14.

88. *NE*, p. 381.

89. "Letter to A. Arnauld, Nov. 28/Dec. 8, 1686," p. 75; in *Phil. Schrift.*, II, 73–81.

90. (On the souls of animals), p. 330; in *Phil. Scrift.*, VII, 328–32; tr. Latta.

91. *NE*, p. 65.

92. "Letter N. Remond, July 1714," p. 623; in *Phil. Schrift.*, III, 618–24; tr. H. W. Carr (London, 1930).

93. *Monad.*, 30.

94. *PNG*, 5.

95. *NE*, p. 252.

96. *Ibid.*, p. 159.

97. *Monad.*, 28.

98. *Historia animalium* (1612), ed. J. Cyprian (Frankfurt, 1712), I, 128–32.

99. *Synopsis methodica animalium quadrupedum et serpentini generis* (London, 1693), pp. 148–61.

100. "Of animals," p. 158; in J. Wilkins, *An Essay towards a Real Character, and a Philosophical Language* (London, 1668), pp. 121–68.

101. *Idem.*

102. *Loc. cit.*

103. Amsterdam, 1632), 10.

104. *Ibid.*, 7. 12–13, 35.

105. *De locutione et eius instrumenti* (1601), *Opera omnia anatomica et physiologica*, ed. B. S. Albini (Leyden, 1738), pp. 306–18; *De larynge vocis instrumento* (1615), *Opera*, pp. 268–305.

106. *De brutorum loquela* (1603), *Opera*, pp. 319–31.

107. *De vocis auditusque organis historia anatomica*, Ferrara, 1600–1601.

108. *De anima brutorum* (Oxford, 1672), 1.

109. *Ibid.*, p. 96; tr. S. Pordage, London, 1683.

110. *Orang-Outang, sive Homo sylvestris* (London, 1699), pref.

111. *Ibid.*, p. 2; *vide ibid.*, pp. 92–95.

112. *Ibid.*, p. 91.

113. "Nouvelle division de la terre, par les differentes especes ou races d'hommes qui l'habitent," *Journal des Sçavans*, 12 (1684) (pp. 148–55), pp. 148–51; tr. T. Bendyshe (London, 1863–64).

114. *Ibid.*, pp. 151–55.

115. *De gemmis et lapidibus* (Leyden, 1647), 2. 24.

116. *Note overo memorie del museo* (1656) (2d ed.; Verona, 1672), 2. 50.

117. *Scota illustrata* (Edinburgh, 1684), 2. 4. 2. 7.

118. *Gemmarum et lapidum historia* (1609), ed. A. Tollius (3d ed.; Leyden, 1647), 2. 168, 261–63.

119. *The Antiquities of Warwickshire* (London, 1656), p. 778.

120. Paris, 1666–1793.

121. *Marmora arundelliana* (1624), *Opera*, ed. D. Wilkins (London, 1726), II, cols. 1439–1586.

122. *Abrege echronologique ou extraict de l'histoire de France* (Paris, 1667–68), I, pp. 25–29, 76–85, *et passim.*

123. Cologne, 1691.

124. Ed. J. Britten (*Publications of the Folk-Lore Society,* 4), London, 1881.

125. *Jani anglorum* (1610), *Opera omnia*, ed. D. Wilkins (London, 1726), II, cols. 961–1031; *England's Epinomis* (1610), *Opera*, III, cols. 3–46; *The Duello* (1610), *Opera*, III, cols. 47–83; *Titles of Honour* (1614), *Oopera*, III, cols. 85–1058; *Analecton anglobritannicon* (1615), *Opera*, II, cols. 861–960; *The History of Tythes* (1618), *Opera*, III, cols. 1062–1344.

126. *De successionibus* (1631–38), *Opera*, II, cols. 1–200; *De anno civili* (1644), *Opera*, I, cols. 1–63; *Uxor ebraica* (1646), *Opera*, II, cols. 529–860; *De synedriis* (1650–55), *Opera*, I, cols. 758–1892.

127. *De diis syris* (1617), *Opera*, II, cols. 201–407.

128. Sandys, *op. cit.*, II, pp. 277–370.

129. E. Heawood, *A History of Geographical Discovery in the Seventeenth and Eighteenth Centuries* (Cambridge, 1912).

130. (*HSP* [extra ser.], 14–33), Glasgow, 1905–7.

131. Leyden, 1625.

132. Leyden, 1631.

133. Frankfurt, 1673.

134. *Introductionis in universam geographiam*, ed. J. Vorstius (Leyden, 1629).

135. *Microcosmos* (1622) (8th ed.; Oxford, 1639).

136. *Les estats, empires, et principautez du monde* (Paris, 1614), pref.; tr. E. Grimestone (London, 1615).

137. *Vide Enquiries Touching the Diversity of Languages and Religions*, ed. R. Brerewood (London, 1635), pp. 99–102.

138. *Ibid.*, pp. 96–97.

139. *Pilgrimage* (1613) (4th ed.; London, 1626), p. 44.

140. *De origine gentium Americanarum* ([Paris?], 1642), pp. 5–8; tr. E. Goldsmid (Edinburgh, 1884).

141. *Ibid.*, pp. 8–11.

142. *Ibid.*, pp. 12–13.

143. *Ibid.*, pp. 11–12.

144. *Op. cit.*, p. 182.

145. *Ibid.*, p. 189.

146. *Ibid.*, p. 203.

147. *Ibid.*, pp. 196–97.

148. "Discourse of carriages" (1685), p. 157; in *Philosophical Experiments and Observations*, ed. W. Derham (London, 1726), pp. 150–67.

149. "The translator to the reader," p. [vi]; in Garcilaso de la Vega, *The Royal Commentaries of Peru* (London, 1688), pp. [v-viii].

150. "An essay upon the ancient and modern learning" (1692), pp. 454–55; in *Works* (London, 1814), III, 444–86.

151. *Vide ibid.*, pp. 452–54.

152. *Ibid.*, pp. 456–57.

153. *Leviathan* (1651) (Oxford, 1909), p. 499.

154. "Diatriba de europaeorum linguis," *Opuscula varia* (Paris, 1610), pp. 119–22.

155. *Enquiries*, pp. 21–22.

156. *Ibid.*, p. 51.

157. *Ibid.*, pp. 56–57.

158. *De hellenistica* (Leipzig, 1643), 2. 2–3.

159. *Ibid.*, pp. 384–90.

160. *Ibid.*, pp. 394–96.

161. *A Treatise of Taxes and Contributions* (1662), p. 76; in *Econ. Writ.*, I, 1–97.

162. *The Political Anatomy of Ireland*, p. 206; in *Economic Writings*, ed. C. H. Hull (Cambridge, 1899), I, 121–231.

163. "De origine mundi," 19. 7–12; in *Institutionum peripateticarum* (1646) (2d ed.; London, 1647), append.; tr. Anonymous (London, 1656).

164. *An Essay towards a Real Character, and a Philosophical Language* (London, 1668). p. 2.

165. Ed. E. Lye (Oxford, 1743).

166. *Quatuor d. n. Jesu Christi Evangeliorum, versiones perantiquae duae, Gothica scil. et Anglo-Saxonica* (Dortrecht, 1665), II, 1–31.

167. *Institutiones grammaticae anglo-saxonicae et moesogothicae*, Oxford, 1689; *Linguarum veterum septentrionalium thesaurus* (Oxford, 1703–5).

168. *Grammaire générale* (1660), Brussels, 1676, 3d ed.

169. *Discours de la methode* (1637), p. 6; in *Œuvres*, ed. C. Adam and P. Tannery (Paris, 1897–1909), VI, 1–78; tr. E. S. Haldane and G. R. T. Ross (Cambridge, 1911–12).

170. *Ibid.*, p. 10.

171. *Ibid.*, p. 16.

172. *Ibid.*, 5 (pp. 45–57); *Objectiones et respensio*, 3, resp., 1; in *Œuvres*, VII, 91–561; *Les passions de l'ame* (1649), 1. 1–16; in *Œuvres*, XI, 291–497; *Principiae philosophiae*, 4. 189–97; in *Œuvres*, VIII, No. 1; *L'Homme*, pp. 130 ff.; in *Œuvres*, XI, 119–215.

173. I. V. Pavlov, *Conditioned Reflexes*, tr. G. V. Anrep (Oxford, 1927), p. 4.

174. *Discours*, p. 12.

175. *Discours sur l'histoire universelle* (1681), 3. 8 (p. 267); in *Œuvres complètes*, ed. Priests of the Immaculate Conception of St. Dizier (Nancy, 1862–63), IV, 94–358; tr. R. Spencer, London, 1731.

176. *Idem.*

177. *Idem.*

178. *Ibid.*, 3. 1 (p. 231).

179. *Ibid.*, 3. 2 (p. 232).

180. *Ibid.*, 3. 2 (p. 233).

181. "Icon animorum," p. 376; *vide ibid.*, pp. 376–79; in *Euphormionis lusinini* (1603)? (Oxford, 1634), pp. 358–553; tr. T. May, London, 1633.

182. *Ibid.*, p. 377.

183. *Ibid.*, p. 379.

184. *Ibid.*, pp. 379–80.

185. *Ibid.*, p. 380.

186. *Ibid.*, p. 383.

187. *Idem.*

188. *Ibid.*, 4–9.

189. *Ibid.*, p. 472.

190. *Ibid.*, p. 474.

191. *Ibid.,* 10–12.
192. *Ibid.,* p. 508; *vide ibid.,* 13–16.
193. *Ibid.,* p. 529.
194. *City of the Sun,* p. 282.
195. *Ibid.,* p. 285.
196. *Ibid.,* pp. 293–94.
197. *Ibid.,* p. 281.
198. *Praeadamitae,* pt. 2, pp. 29, 31.
199. *Ibid.,* pt. 2, pp. 176–77.
200. *Ibid.,* pt. 2, pp. 177–78.
201. *Sacred Theory,* I, 52.
202. *Ibid.,* p. 44.
203. *Ibid.,* p. 309.
204. *Ibid.,* pp. 311–12.
205. *Ibid.,* p. 313.
206. *Primitive Origination,* p. 212.
207. "An essay upon the original and nature of government" (1672), pp. 1–2; in *Works,* I, 1–30; cf. "Of heroic virtue" (1692), pp. 400–401; in *Works,* III, 313–405; "Of poetry" (1692), pp. 438–41; in *Works,* III, 406–43.
208. "Orig. and nat. govt.," p. 5.
209. *Ibid.,* p. 20.
210. *Observation upon the United Provinces of the Netherlands* (1673), pp. 133–34; in *Works,* I, 31–202.
211. *Ibid.,* pp. 164–65; *vide ibid.,* chap. 4.
212. *Ibid.,* p. 134.
213. "Anc. and mod. learning," pp. 459–60.
214. *Ibid.,* p. 448.
215. *Ibid.,* pp. 463–64; *vide ibid.,* pp. 463–73; "Some thoughts upon reviewing the essay of ancient and modern learning," pp. 499–504; in *Works,* III, 487–518.
216. "Anc. and mod. learning," p. 465.
217. *Ibid.,* pp. 473–74.
218. "Of heroic virtue" (1692), pp. 321–22; in *Works,* III, 313–405.
219. *Ibid.,* p. 324.
220. *Vide ibid.,* pp. 325–97.
221. *Ibid.,* p. 357.
222. "Upon the garden of Epicurus" (1685), p. 203; in *Works,* III, 202–45.
223. "Of heroic virtue," pp. 315–16.
224. "Of popular discontents," p. 38– in *Works,* III, 29–65.
225. "Orig. and nat. govt.," pp. 11–15.
226. *De la sagesse* (1601), ed. A. Duval (Paris, 1827), II,62; tr. G. Stanhope (2d ed.; London, 1707).
227. *Ibid.,* I, 123; cf. *ibid.,* pp. 151; II, 196.
228. *Ibid.,* pp. 141–42.
229. *Ibid.,* p. 132; cf. *ibid.,* II, 201–3.
236. *Ibid.,* III, 76–77.
231. *Ibid.,* I, 11–12.
232. *Ibid.,* pp. 14–18.
233. *Ibid.,* pp. 321–22.
234. *Ibid.,* pp. 322–23; *vide ibid.,* pp. 131, 323–33.
235. *Ibid.,* p. 104.
236. *Ibid.,* p. 106.
237. *Ibid.,* pp. 104–6.
238. *Ibid.,* pp. 333–35; *vide ibid.,* pp. 334–37.
239. *Ibid.,* p. 338; *vide ibid.,* pp. 339– 402.
240. *Ibid.,* pp. 402–3; *vide ibid.,* pp. 403–16.
241. *Ibid.,* p. 417; *vide ibid.,* pp. 418–39.
242. *Ibid.,* p. 42.
243. *Ibid.,* p. 43.
244. ed. I. Dyke (London, 1630).
245. *Ibid.,* p. 12.
246. *Ibid.,* p. 12; *vide ibid.,* 2.
247. *Ibid.,* p. 38.
248. *Idem; vide ibid.,* 3–22.

249. *Ibid.*, p. 280; *vide ibid.*, 23–35.
250. *Ibid.*, p. 324.
251. *Ibid.*, p. 38.
252. *Ibid.*, p. 324.
253. *Idem.*
254. *Ibid.*, p. 2.
255. *Ibid.*, pp. 12–13.
256. *La Faussete des vertus humaines,* (Paris, 1678), Pref.; tr. W. Beauvoir (London, 1706).
257. *Ibid.*, pref.
258. *Les pensées,* 100; *vide ibid.*, 11, 16, 100, 238, 455–57, 477, 492; in *Œuvres,* ed. L. Brunschvicg and P. Boutroux (Parix, 1904–14), XII-XIV; tr. W. F. Trotter (New York, 1941).
259. *Ibid.*, 451–54.
260. *Discours sur les passions de l'amour,* p. 127; in *Œuvres,* III, 103–42; tr. O. W. Wight (New York, 1864); cf. *Pensées,* 147–48, 150–51, 153, 400, 404.
261. *P,* 339.
262. *Ibid.*, 344; *vide ibid.*, 339–47.
263. *Ibid.*, 439–40.
264. *Ibid.*, 274; *vide ibid.*, 99, 252, 274–77, 412–13, 417, 467.
265. *Discours,* p. 133.
266. *P,* 89.
267. *Ibid.*, 95.
268. *Ibid.*, 92.
269. *Ibid.*, 93.
270. *Ibid.*, 97.
271. *Ibid.*, 252; *vide ibid.*, 230, 324–25.
272. *Discours,* p. 125.
273. *P,* 309; *vide ibid.*, 294. 312.
274. "Fragment de préface sur le traité du vide" (1647), pp. 137–41; in *Œuvres,* II, 127–45; tr. Wight.
275. *P,* 354.
276. *Ibid.*, 505.
277. *Ibid.*, 162.
278. *Ibid.*, 176.
279. "Discours sur la condition des grands" (1659), pp. 365–66; in *Œuvres,* IX, 359–73; tr. Wight.
280. *Œuvres,* 304; cf. *ibid.*, 299, 303.
281. *The Vanity of Dogmatizing* (London, 1661), p. 119; *Scepsis scientifica* (London, 1665), p. 88; *vide VD,* pp. 119–20; *SS,* p. 88.
282. *Plus ultra* (London, 1668), pp. 115–16; *vide ibid.*, pp. 116–17.
283. *VD,* pp. 125–32; *vide SS,* pp. 93–97; *Essays on Several Important Subjects* (London, 1676), p. 24.
284. *VD,* p. 123; *vide SS,* p. 90.
285. *VD,* p. 141; *SS,* pp. 104–5; *ESIS,* p. 26.
286. *VD,* p. 240; *vide SS,* p. 176.
287. *Lux orientalis* (1662), ed. J. Collins (London, 1682), p. 146.
288. *Réflexions ou sentences et maximes morales* (1665), 563; cf. *ibid.*, 1–4, 39, 81, 115; in *Œuvres,* ed. D. L. Gilbert (Paris, 1868–83), I, 23–267; tr. F. G. Stevens (London, 1940).
289. *Ibid.*, 102.
290. *Ibid.*, 460.
291. *Ibid.*, 295; cf. *ibid.*, 43, 103, 404.
292. "De la société," *Reflexions diverses*; in *Œuvres,* I, 267–348.
293. *Refl.*, p. 31.
294. *Ibid.*, 615.
295. *Ibid.*, 342.
296. *Ibid.*, 43.
297. *Ibid.*, 153.
298. *Ibid.*, 629.
299. *Pensées diverses sur la comète* (1682), ed. A. Prat (*Société des textes français modernes* (ser. 1), 16, 20) (Paris, 1911–12), 166; tr. Anonymous (London, 1708).
300. *Ibid.*, 46.
301. *Ibid.*, 100.
302. *Ibid.*, 84.
303. *Ibid.*, 138.
304. *Ibid.*, 136.

305. *Ibid.,* 143.

306. *Ibid.,* 171.

307. *Ibid.,* 135; cf. *ibid.,* 144, 176.

308. *Ibid.,* 136.

309. *Ibid.,* 176.

310. *Ibid.,* 4–8, 100; *Dictionnaire historique et critique* (1696), ed. J. A. Q. Beuchot (Paris, 1820–24).

311. "Of studies," *Essays.*

312. "Of seditions and troubles," *E; vide* esp. "Of the true greatnesse of kingdomes and estates," *E; The Histoire of the Raigne of King Henry the Seventh* (1662), *Works,* ed. J. Spedding *et al.* (London, 1857–74), VI, 3–263.

313. "Of followers and frends," *E.*

314. "Of boldnesse," *E.*

315. "Of seditions and troubles," *E.*

316. "Of custome and education," *E.*

317. *Idem.*

318. "Of frendship," *E.;* cf. "Of praise," *E.*

319. *De sapientia veterum* (1609), 26; in *Works,* VI, 605–764.

320. "Of frendship."

321. "Of goodnesse and goodnesse of nature," *E.*

322. "Of love," *E.*

323. "Of vicissitude of things," *E.*

324. *De augmentis scientiarum* (1623), p. 458; in *Works,* I, pp. 413–837.

325. *Novum organum* (1620), ed. T. Fowler (2d ed.; Oxford, 1889), 1 : 84; tr. ed. J. Spedding (London, 1858).

326. "Of vicissitude of things."

327. "Of seditions and troubles"; cf. "Of vicissitude of things," p. 236.

328. "Of seditions and troubles."

329. *Considérations politiques sur les coups d'estat,* [Paris], 1667.

330. *Teutscher Fürsten-Stat* (1655) (3d ed.; Frankfurt, 1665), Vorrede, 1.

331. *Ibid.,* Vorr., 2.

332. *Teutscher Fürsten-Staat* (1665), ed. A. S. von Biechling (Jena, 1737), 1. 4. 1.

333. *Ibid.,* 1. 4. 2.

334. *Ibid.,* 1. 4. 3.

335. Leipzig, 1685.

336. *Ibid.,* p. 243; tr. A. W. Small, Chicago, 1909.

337. *Oceana* (1656), ed. S. B. Liljegren (*Skrifter utgivna av Vetenskaps-Societeten i Lund,* 4) (Heidelberg, 1924), p. 175.

338. Harrington was particularly an admirer of Machiavelli; *vide ibid.,* pp. 12–13, 30, 118, 133, 135.

339. "The examination of James Harrington, taken in the Tower of London," *Works* (pp. xxviii–xxxi), p. xxx.

340. *Ibid.,* p. 118.

341. "A system of politics," 10. 23; in *The Oceana and Other Works* (London, 1771), pp. 465–82.

342. "Political aphorisms," 5; *Works,* pp. 483–90.

343. *Ibid.,* 39.

344. *Oceana,* p. 41.

345. *Ibid.,* pp. 9–10.

346. "The prerogative of popular government," 1 : 3; in *Works,* pp. 213–57; "The art of lawgiving," 1. pref.; in *Works,* pp. 359–438; "Valerius and Publicola," p. 446; in *Works,* pp. 445–64; "A system of politics," 3.

347. *Ibid.,* p. 169.

348. *Oceana,* pp. 14–15.

349. *Ibid.,* p. 16.

350. *Ibid.,* p. 50.

351. *Ibid.,* p. 53.

352. "A system of politics," 4. 15.

353. *Oceana,* p. 68.

354. *Ibid.,* p. 24.

355. *Ibid.,* p. 55.

356. *A Discourse of Trade* (London, 1621), pp. 1–2; cf. *ibid.,* pp. 7, 27.

357. *A New Discourse of Trade* (1665) (5th ed.; Glasgow, 1751), p. 44.

358. *Ibid.,* p. 108.

359. *Ibid.,* pp. 42–43.

360. *Ibid.,* pp. 43–44.

361. *Verbum sapienti,* p. 114; in *Econ. Writ.,* I, 99–120.

362. *A Treatise of Taxes and Contributions* (1662), p. 48; in *Economic Writings,* ed. C. H. Hull (Cambridge, 1899), I, 1–97.

363. *The Political Anatomy of Ireland,* p. 133; in *Econ. Writ.,* I, 121–231. He made schedules of anthropological interest; *vide* "Fundamentall questions," *Papers,* II, 39–42; "Quaeries concerning the nature of the natives of Pensilvania," *Papers,* II, 115–19.

364. *PA,* p. 260; *vide Another Essay in Political Arithmetick* (1683), p. 473; in *Econ. Writ.,* II, 451–78. On the evolution of the division of labor, *vide Papers,* I, 212–13.

365. *Political Arithmetick* (1676), pp. 255–56; in *Econ. Writ.,* I, 232–313.

366. *TTC,* p. 42.

367. *Observations upon the Dublin-Bills of Mortality* (1683), p. 491; in *Econ. Writ.,* II, 479–91.

368. *TTC,* pp. 41–42.

369. *Papers,* I, 208.

370. *PA,* p. 250.

371. *Idem.*

372. *Ibid.,* p. 255; cf. *ibid.,* p. 297.

373. *PAI,* pp. 201–2.

374. *Another Essay,* p. 475.

375. *TTC,* p. 37.

376. *PA,* p. 261.

377. *Ibid.,* pp. 262–63.

378. *TTC,* pp. 22–23.

379. *Papers,* I, 209.

380. *TTC,* p. 42.

381. *A Discourse of Trade* (1690), ed. J. H. Hollander (*Reprint of Economic Tracts,* 2) (Baltimore, 1905), p. 14.

382. *Ibid.,* pp. 25–26.

383. *Ibid.,* pp. 13–14.

384. *Ibid.,* p. 33.

385. *Ibid.,* p. 31.

386. *Discourses upon Trade* (1691), ed. J. H. Hollander (*Repr. Econ. Tracts,* 8) (Baltimore, 1907), p. 34; cf. *ibid.,* pp. 18, 21.

387. *Teutscher Fürsten-Staat,* ed. von Biechling, 1. Vorb. 3–4.

388. *Ibid.,* 1. Vorb. 6.

389. *Ibid.,* 1. 1.

390. *Ibid.,* 1. 2.

391. *Ibid.,* 1. 3.

392. *Ibid.,* 1. 4.

393. In Petty, *Econ. Writ.,* II, 314–435.

394. Whether Graunt or Petty was the author has been a matter of some dispute. For the latest pros and cons, *vide.* C. H. Hull, "The authorship of the Natural and Political Observations upon the Bills of Mortality," in Petty, *Econ. Writ.,* I, xxxix–liv; Marquis of Landsowne, "Petty and the disputed authorship of the Observations on the London Bills of Mortality," in Petty, *Papers,* II, 271–84.

395. *Observations,* p. 352.

396. *Ibid.,* p. 355.

397. *Ibid.,* p. 369.

398. *Ibid.,* p. 372.

399. *Ibid.,* p. 375.

400. *Ibid.,* p. 374.

401. Anonymous, "An extract of two essays in political arithmetick . . . by Sr. William Petty . . . ," *Philsophical Transactions of the Royal Society,* 16 (1686–87), p. 152.

402. *Papers,* I, 105; cf. *ibid.,* II, 226.

403. *Observations upon the Dublin-Bills,* p. 481.

404. Hull, "Introduction," pp. lxiii–lxiv; in Petty, *Econ. Writ.,* I, xiii–xci; Petty, *Papers,* II, 168.

405. *A Treatise of Ireland,* p. 554; in *Econ. Writ.,* II, 545–621.

406. T. Birch, *The History of the Royal Society of London* (London, 1757), IV, p. 193.

407. *PA,* pref. (pp. 244–45.)

408. *TTC,* pp. 53–53.

409. *PAI,* pref. (pp. 129–30).

410. *Two Tracts,* ed. G. E. Barnett (*Repr. Econ. Tracts*), Baltimore, 1936.

411. "Of the use of political arithmetic" (1698), p. 128; in *Political and Commercial Works,* ed. C. Whitworth (London, 1771), I, 127–49.

412. *Ibid.,* p. 135.

413. "An estimate of the degree of the mortality of mankind," *Phil. Transac.,* 17 (1963), No. 196, pp. 596–610; "Some further considerations on the Breslaw bills of mortality," *ibid.,* No. 198, pp. 654–56. He also has some remarks on statistics in: "Letter to Robert Hooke, May 19/29, 1681," p. 52; in *Correspondence and Papers,* ed. E. F. MacPike (*History of Science Society Publications* [new ser. 2]) (Oxford, 1932), pp. 49–52; "Letter to Caspar Neumann, 1693," p. 89; in *ibid.,* pp. 88–89.

414. "Further considerations," p. 655.

415. *Pilgrimage* (1613) (4th ed.; London, 1626), p. 41.

416. *Apologie* (1627) (2d ed.; Oxford, 1630), ep. ded.

417. *Ibid.,* pref.

418. *Idem.*

419. *Ibid.,* 3. 6. 2 (p. 230); *vide ibid., loc. cit.*

420. *Ibid.,* 4. 1. 1 (p. 290); *vide ibid., loc. cit.*

421. *A Discourse concerning a New Planet* (1640), p. 146; in *Mathematical and Philosophical Works* (London, 1708), pp. 137–274.

422. "Naturam non pati senium" (1645), 33–36; in *Works,* ed. F. A. Patterson (New York, 1931–38), I, pt. 1, pp. 260–67; tr. C. Knapp, New York, 1931.

423. *Ibid.,* 60–61.

424. *Ibid.,* 65–69.

425. "Essay on satire" (1693), p. 13; in *Works,* ed. W. Scott, rev. G. Saintsbury (Edinburgh, 1883–93), XIII, 1–123; *vide Essay of Dramatic Poesy* (1668), in *Works,* XV, 273–377.

426. *Reflections upon Ancient and Modern Learning* (1694) (3d ed.; London, 1705), p. xii.

427. *Ibid.,* p.v.

428. *De veritate* (1624) (n.p., 1656, 3d ed.), pp. 52–53. tr. M. H. Carré (Bristol, 1937). However, this evolutionary scheme seems merely to be a modification of the scholastic conception of the powers of the soul; *vide ibid.,* pp. 54, 57, 77, 84–85, 114–17, 120–21, 126, 223–24.

429. *Ibid.,* p. 56.

430. *Ibid.,* p. 51.

431. *Ibid.,* p. 54.

432. *Ibid.,* p. 69.

433. *Ib'd.,* p. 72; cf. *ibid.,* pp. 56–57.

434. *Ibid.,* p. 77.

435. *Ibid.,* p. 66; cf. *ibid.,* pp. 3, 9, 48, 49, 51, 53, 60–61, 67, 123.

436. *De veritate,* pp. 53–54.

437. *Ibid.,* pp. 49–50.

438. *Ibid.,* p. 55.

439. *Ibid.,* p. 50.

440. For a good description of the state of mind produced by conflicting dogmas, *vide* Thomas Amory (1691?–1788), *The Life and Opinions of John Buncle* (1756), ed. E. A. Baker (London, 1904), pp. 11–12.

441. *De religione gentilum* (Amsterdam, 1663), p. 2; cf. *ibid.,* p. 186; tr. W. Lewis (London, 1705); *De veritate,* pp. 265–88.

442. *De rel.,* p. 185.

443. *Ibid.,* p. 228.

444. *Op. cit.*

445. Samuel Purchas (1577?–1626), *Pilgrimage* (1613) (4th ed.; London, 1626); Alexander Ross (1590–1654), *A View of All Religions in the World* (1653) (4th ed.; London, 1672); William Turner (1653–1701) *The History of All Religions* (London, 1695).

446. *NE,* p. 128.

447. *Ibid.,* p. 68; cf. *ibid.,* pp. 89–90, 280–81.

448. *Ibid.,* p. 91.

449. *Ibid.,* p. 92.

450. *Ibid.,* p. 85.

451. *Ibid.,* p. 87.

452. *Ibid.,* p. 235.

453. *Ibid.,* p. 89.

454. *Ibid.,* p. 253.

455. *Ibid.,* p. 85.

456. "De justitia," p. 36, *Mittheilungen aus ungedruckte Schriften,* ed. G. Mollat (rev. ed.; Leipzig, 1893), pp. 35–40; tr. Latta.

457. "Definitiones ethicae," *Opera philosophica,* ed. J. E. Erdmann (Berlin, 1839–40), II, 670; tr. Duncan; *vide* "Letter to Nicaise, Aug. 1697," p. 577; in *Phil. Schrift.,* II, 573–80; "Letter to Nicaise, May 4/14, 1698," p. 581; in *Phil. Schrift.,* II, 580–83; *NE,* pp. 149–50.

458. "Juris et aequi elementa," p. 28; in *Mittheilungen,* pp. 19–34; tr. Latta.

459. *Codicis juris gentium diplomatici praefatio,* p. 470; in *Hist. pol. Schrift.,* VI, 457–92; tr. P. Latta.

460. "Letter to Nicaise, Aug. 1697," pp. 577–78.

461. "Le portrait du prince," p. 461; in *Historisch-politische und staatswissenschaftliche Schriften,* ed. O. Klopp (Hanover, 1864–84), IV. 459–88; tr. Latta.

462. *NE,* p. 80.

463. *NE,* pp. 452–53.

464. Hallam, *Literature of Europe,* II, 174.

465. *De jure belli ac pacis* (1625) (*Classics of International Law,* 3) (Washington, 1913), prol. 1; tr. F. W. Kelsey *et al.* (Oxford, 1925).

466. *Ibid.,* prol. 28.

467. *Ibid.,* prol. 30.

468. *Ibid.,* 1. 1. 12. 1.

469. *Ibid.,* prol. 53.

470. *Ibid.,* prol. 39–40; cf. *ibid.,* 2. 20. 41–43.

471. *Ibid.,* prol. 46.

472. *Ibid.,* 1. 1. 10. 1–2.

473. *Ibid.,* 1. 1. 10. 5.

474. *Ibid.,* 2. 3. 10. 3.

475. *Ibid.,* prol. 16.

476. *Ibid.,* prol. 19.

477. *Ibid.,* prol. 14.

478. *Ibid.,* prol. 6–9.

479. *Ibid.,* 1. 1. 13.

480. *Ibid.,* 1. 1. 14. 1.

481. *Idem.*

482. *Ibid.,* prol. 15.

483. *Ibid.,* prol. 16.

484. *Ibid.,* 1. 1. 14. 1.

485. *Idem.*

486. *Ibid.,* prol. 17.

487. *Ibid.,* 1. 1. 14. 2.

488. *Ibid.,* prol. 12.

489. *Ibid.,* 1. 1. 15. 1–2.

490. *Ibid.,* 1. 1. 15. 2; *vide ibid.,* prol. 48, 50. 1. 1. 17.

491. *Ibid.,* 1. 1. 16. 1.

492. *Ibid.,* 2. 2. 2.

493. *Ibid.,* 4. 1. 1.

494. *Ibid.,* 4. 2. 4; cf. *ibid.,* 4. 2. 5.

495. *De jure naturae et gentium* (1672) (*Class. Int. Law,* 17) (Oxford, 1934), pp. [vii-viii]; tr. C. H. and W. A. Oldfather (Oxford, 1934).

496. *Ibid.,* 2. 3. 9.

497. *Ibid.,* 2. 2. 1; cf. *ibid.,* 2. 2. 4.

498. *Ibid.,* 2. 2. 2.

499. *Ibid.,* 2. 2. 3; cf. *ibid.,* 3. 2.

500. *Idem.*

501. *Ibid.,* 2. 2. 4.

502. *Ibid.,* 2. 2. 5.

503. *Ibid.,* 2. 2. 7; *vide ibid.,* 2. 2. 8–10.

504. *Ibid.,* 2. 2. 9; cf. *ibid.,* 2. 2. 11; 2. 3. 1, 14–15.

505. *Ibid.,* 2. 2. 12; cf. *ibid.,* 7. 1. 8–11.

506. *Ibid.,* 7. 1. 7; cf. *ibid.,* 7. 2. 1.

507. *Ibid.,* 7. 2. 3.

508. *Ibid.,* 7. 2. 7–8.

509. *Ibid.,* 7. 1. 3.

510. *Ibid.,* 4. 4. 5.

511.  *Ibid.*, 4. 4. 6.

512.  *De legibus naturae* (London, 1672), prol. 1; tr. J. Towers (London, 1750).

513.  *Ibid.*, 2. 2.

514.  *Ibid.*, 2. 4.

515.  *Ibid.*, 2. 11.

516.  *Ibid.*, 2. 21; *vide ibid.*, 2. 17–21.

517.  *Ibid.*, 2. 28.

518.  *Ibid.*, 2. 29.

519.  *Ibid.*, prol. 14.

520.  *Ibid.*, 1. 6.

521.  *Ibid.*, 2. 20.

522.  *Ibid.*, 5. 8.

522.  *Ibid.*, 5. 8.

523.  *Ibid.*, 5. 10.

524.  *Ibid.*, 8. 13.

525.  *Ibid.*, 5. 1.

526.  *Ibid.*, prol. 6.

527.  *Ibid.*, 6. 2.

528.  *Ibid.*, 1. 1.

529.  *Ibid.*, 5. 1; *vide ibid.*, prol. 9; 5. 4, 24–40, 55.

530.  *Ibid.*, 6. 4.

531.  *The Convocation Book of* 1606, ed. W. Sancroft (*Library of Anglo-Catholic Theology,* 29) (Oxford, 1844), 1, chap. 2.

532.  *Ibid.*, 1, chap. 6.

533.  *Patriarcha* (1680), 1. 3; in J. Locke, *Two Treatises on Civil Government,* ed. H. Morley (London, 1884), pp. 9–73.

534.  *Ibid.*, 1. 7.

535.  *Ibid.*, 1. 8.

536.  *Leviathan,* p. 556; cf. his diatribe against the Long Parliament in *Behemoth* (*ca* 1668), ed. F. Tönnies (London, 1889).

537.  *Philosophical Rudiments concerning Government and Society* (1642), 1651), 1. 2; in *English Works,* ed. W. Molesworth (London, 1839–45), II.

538.  *Ibid.*, p. 2n.

539.  *Ibid.*, 1. 2.

540.  *L,* p. 75; cf. *Behemoth,* p. 29; *Decameron physiologicum* (1678), p. 73; in *Eng. Works,* VII, 69–177.

541.  *Ibid.*, p. 164.

542.  *L,* p. 96.

543.  *Ibid.*, pp. 96–97; cf. *PRCGS,* 1–6; *De corpore policitco* (1640, 1650), *Eng. Works,* IV, 77–228.

544.  *L,* pp. 97–98.

545.  *Ibid.*, p. 77.

546.  *L,* p. 128.

547.  *Ibid.*, p. 98.

548.  *Ibid.*, p. 205.

549.  *Ibid.*, p. 99; *vide PRCGS,* 2–3; *DCP,* 2–4. For a list of these laws of nature, *ibid.*, 100–120.

550.  *PRCGS,* 3. 29.

551.  *Elements of Philosophy* (1655, 1565), 1. 1. 9; in *Eng. Works,* I.

552.  *Ibid.*, pp. 131–32.

553.  *Ibid.*, p. 126.

554.  *A Dialogue between a Philosopher and a Student of the Common Laws of England* (*ca.* 1666), p. 147; in *Eng. Works,* VI, 1–160.

555.  *Ibid.*, p. 154.

556.  *PRCGS,* 9. 3.

557.  *EP,* 1. 1. 1; cf. *L,* p. 519.

558.  *L,* pp. 519–20.

559.  *EP,* 1. 1. 7.

560.  *L,* p. 1 : 6.

561.  *Ibid.*, p. 80

562.  *Ibid.*, p. 81; *vide ibid.*, 1 : 12.

563.  *Ibid.*, p. 8.

564.  *Ibid.*, p. 171.

565.  *Ibid.*, p. 184.

566. *Ibid.*, p. 188.
567. *Ibid.*, p. 193.
568. *Ibid.*, p. 194.
569. *Ibid.*, p. 246.
570. *Ibid.*, p. 247.
571. *Ibid.*, p. 249.
572. *Ibid.*, 2. 29; cf. *PRCGS*, 12; *DCP*, 2. 8.
573. *Ibid.*, p. 257.
574. *EP*, 4. 25. 13.
575. *Of Liberty and Necessity* (1646), p. 240; in *Eng. Works*, IV, 229–78; *vide ibid.*, pp. 263, 273; *L*, pp. 99, 162; *Questions concerning Liberty, Necessity, and Chance* (1656), pp. 38–39; in *Eng. Works.*, V.
576. *OLN*, p. 260.
577. *Ibid.*, p. 274.
578. *L*, p. 160.
579. *Ibid.*, 3. 33.
580. *Tractatus politicus*, 1 : 1–2, 4; in *Opera*, ed. J. van Vloten and J. P. N. Land (The Hague, 1882–83), I, 279–366; tr. A. H. Gosset (London, 1883); cf. *ibid.*, 7.2; *Ethica*, 3. intr.; in *Opera*, I, 37–278.
581. *Ethica*, 2. ax. 2.
582. *Ibid.*, 2. prop. 38. corol.; tr. W. H. White and A. H. Stirling (4th ed.; London, 1927).
583. *Ibid.*, 2. prop. 40. schol; cf. *ibid.*, 2. prop. 44. corol. 2. dem.
584. *Ibid.*, 4. prop. 35. schol.
585. *TR*, 6. 1.
586. *E*, 3. prop. 11. schol.
587. *Ibid.*, 4. prop. 4; cf. *ibid.*, 4. prop. 57. schol.; 4. append. 1, 6–7 5. prop. 10. schol.; *Tractatus theologicopoliticus* (1670), p. 421; in *Opera*, I, 367–630.
588. *E*, 1. prop. 32; cf. *ibid.*, 2. prop. 35. schol.; 2. prop. 48; 3. prop. 2. schol.; 4. pref.
589. *TTP*, p. 429, tr. R. H. M. Elwes (London, 1883).
590. *Ibid.*, 7–10.
591. *Ibid.*, p. 488.
592. *Ibid.*, p. 536; cf. *ibid.*, p. 527.
593. *Ibid.*, pp. 401–2.
594. *Ibid.*, p. 400.
595. *Ibid.*, p. 375.
596. *TP*, 5. 2.
597. *Ibid.*, 8. 12.
598. *TTP*, p. 436; *vide ibid.*, p. 579; *TP*, 2. 7; 3. 3, 18; 7. 4, 17; 8. 2; 9. 14.
599. *TTP*, p. 553; cf. *ibid.*, pp. 552–53, 593; *TP*, 2. 3, 5.
600. *TTP*, p. 553; *vide TP*, 2. 8, 18–23.
601. *TTR*, pp. 625–26; cf. *E*, 4. prop. 37. schol. 2.
602. *TP*, 5. 2.
603. *E*, 4. prop. 35. schol.
604. *TP*, 3. 11.
605. *TTP*, pp. 409–10.
606. *E*, 4. append. 28; cf. *TP*, 2. 15.
607. *TTP*, p. 436.
608. *TP*, 6. 1.
609. *E*, 4. append. 14; cf. *ibid.*, 12.
610. *TTP*, p. 411.
611. *Ibid.*, p. 436.
612. *Ibid.*, p. 605; cf. *E*, 4. prop. 37. schol. 2.
613. *TP*, 1. 7.
614. *TTP*, p. 604; cf. *E*, 4. prop. 37. schol. 2.
615. *TTP*, pp. 554–56; cf. *E*, 4. prop. 37. schol. 2; *TP*, 2. 9–10, **12, 16**.
616. *TTP*, p. 562; cf. *E*, 4. prop. 37. schol. 2.
617. *TTP*, p. 593; cf. *E*, 4. prop. 37. schol. 2; *TP*, 2. 18–23.
618. *TP*, 2. 23.
619. *Ibid.*, 7. 19.
620. *Ibid.*, 7. 25.
621. *TTP*, p. 584; cf. *E*, 4. prop. 37. schol. 2.
622. *TTP*, pp. 369–70; cf. *E*, 1. append; 3. prop. 50. schol.
623. *TTP*, p. 443; cf. *ibid.*, pp. 446–47.

624. *Ibid.,* p. 386.

625. *TP,* 7. 27.

626. *TTP,* p. 420; cf. *ibid.,* p. 523.

627. *TP,* 5. 2–3.

628. *TTP,* p. 410.

629. *TTP,* pp. 580–81.

630. *Ibid.,* p. 409.

631. *Table Talk,* ed. F. Pollock (London, 1927), pp. 36–37.

632. *Ibid.,* p. 61.

633. *Ibid.,* p. 69.

634. *Ibid.,* p. 137.

635. *England's Epinomis* (1610), cols. 5–6; in *Opera omnia,* ed. D. Wilkins (London, 1726), III, cols. 3–46.

636. *Titles of Honour* (1614), cols. 109–10; in *Opera,* III, cols. 85–1058.

637. *Ibid.,* col. 110.

638. *Angli pro populo anglicano defensio, prima* (1651), p. 550; in *Works,* ed. F. A. Patterson *et al.* (New York, 1931–40), VII; tr. S. L. Wolff (New York, 1932).

639. *Defensio prima,* p. 34.

640. *Ibid.,* p. 268.

641. *Ibid.,* p. 394.

642. *Ibid.,* p. 174.

643. *The Tenure of Kings and Magistrates* (1649), pp. 8–9; in *Works,* V, 1–59.

644. *Ibid.,* pp. 270–72; *vide ibid.,* pp. 76, 168, 358–62; *Tenure,* p. 10.

645. *Tenure,* p. 14.

646. *Two Treatises on Civil Government* (1690), ed. H. Morley (London, 1884), 2. 2. 4.

647. *Ibid.,* 2. 7. 77.

648. *Ibid.,* 2. 7. 81–83.

649. *Ibid.,* 2. 7. 85.

650. *Ibid.,* 2. 8. 95; *vide ibid.,* 2. 7. 87–89; 2. 8. 96–122.

651. *Ibid.,* 2. 8. 102. 108–9; *An Essay,* ed. A. C. Frazer (Oxford, 1894), 1. 2, 9. 12; 1. 3, 8, 15, 17.

652. *Essay,* 1. 2. 21.

653. *Ibid.,* 1, 2. 9–10.

654. *Ibid.,* 1, 3. 12; *vide ibid.,* 1, 2. 22–26.

655. *Treatises,* 2. 5. 49.

654. *Ibid.,* 2. 5. 41.

657. *Discourses concerning Government* (1698), ed. J. Toland (2d ed.; London, 1704), 1. 9.

658. *Ibid.,* 2. 1; *vide ibid.,* 1. 1, 6, 9–10; 2. 5, 20.

659. *Ibid.,* 2. 32; *vide ibid.,* 1. 11, 16, 20.

660. *Ibid.,* 1. 10.

## NOTES TO CHAPTER IV

1. J. B. Black, *The Art of History* (New York, 1962), p. 23.

2. *Elementa physiologiae corporis humari* (Lausanne, 1757–66), 10. 1. 1–5; "De cerebro avium et piscium" (1766), *Opera minora* (Lausanne, 1762–68), III, pp. 191–217.

3. "Mémoire sur les différences de la situation du grand trou occipital dans l'homme et dans les animaux," *Memoires de l'Academie des Sciences,* 1764, pp. 568–75.

4. *A Philosophical Account of the Works of Nature* (London, 1721), p. 95.

5. *Ibid.,* p. 117.

6. *Ibid.,* pp. 167–68.

7. *Ibid.,* p. 169.

8. 1st ed.; Leyden, 1735.

9. *Ibid.,* f. [6v].

10. *Iter lapponieum* (1732), p. 122; in *Skrifter,* ed. Kungliga Svenska Vetenskapsakademien (Uppsala, 1905——), V; tr. C. Troilius, rev. J. E. Smith (London, 1811).

11. *Idem.*

12. 2d ed.; Stockholm, 1740.

13. *Ibid.,* p. 34.

14. *Ibid.,* p. 65.

15. 6th ed.; Stockholm, 1748.

16. *Ibid.*, p. 3.

17. 10th ed.; Stockholm, 1758–59.

18. *Fauna Suecica* (Leyden, 1746), p. 1.

19. *IL*, p. 181.

20. *SN* (10th ed.), pp. 20–32. The last edition published in his lifetime gives an identical classification: *SN* (12th ed.; Stockhom, 1766–68), I, 28–47.

21. *IL*, p. 15.

22. *Ibid.*, p. 123.

23. *Ibid.*, pp. 120–23.

24. *Ibid.*, p. 123.

25. *IL*, p. 18.

26. "Oratio de memorabilibus in insectis" (1739), p. 361; in *Amoentates academicae,* ed. C. von Linné and J. C. Schreber (Leyden, Stockholm, and Erlangen, 1749–90), II (2d ed.), 356–77; tr. Bendyshe (London, 1863–64).

27. "Deliciae naturae" (1772), p. 66; in *Amoen. acad.,* X, 66–99; tr. Bendyshe.

28. *Reflections on the Study of Nature* (1754), tr. J. E. Smith (Dublin, 1786), pp. 12–13.

29. *FS*, pp. [iv-v]; tr. T. Bendyshe (London, 1863–64).

30. "Letter to J. G. Gmelin, Feb. 14, 1747," p. 55; in J. G. Gmelin, *Reliquias,* ed. W. H. T. Pleininger (Stuttgart, 1861), pp. 54–56; tr. E. L. Greene (Washington, 1909).

31. "De sexu plantatum" (1760), pp. 104–5; in *Amoen. acad.,* X, 100–131; tr. J. E. Smith (Dublin, 1786).

32. *SN* (1st ed.), observ, regna III nat., 1.

33. *Ibid.,* observ. regnum vegit., 14.

34. " Oratio de telluris habitabilis incremento" (1743), 7–9; in *Amoen. acad.,* II (2d ed.), pp. 402–30; tr. Bendyshe.

35. *RSN*, p. 2; cf. *ibid.,* p. 18.

36. *Ibid.,* p. 3.

37. *Ibid.,* p. 11; vide *Findamenta botanica* (1736) (Halle, 1747), 132; "Programma quo ad audiendam orationem aditialem M. Joannis Lastbohm invitavit" (1759), pp. 41, 44; in *Amoen. acad.,* X, 41–48; "Delicae naturae," pp. 88, 97.

38. *Vide* E. L. Greene, "Linnaeus as an evolutionist," *Proceedings of the Washington Academy of Sciences,* 9 (1909), 17–26.

39. *Fundamenta botanica* (1736) (Halle, 1747), 162; tr. Bendyshe.

40. "De sexu plantarum," pp. 127–28; cf. *ibid.,* pp. 125–28.

41. *Ibid.,* p. 129.

42. "Curiositas naturalis" (1748), p. 440; in *Amoen. acad.,* I, 429–53; tr. Bendyshe (London, 1863–64).

43. "Anthropomorpha" (1760), p. 64; in *Amoen. acad.,* VI, 63–76; tr. Bendyshe (London, 1863–64).

44. *Ibid.,* p. 66.

45. *Ibid.,* p. 68.

46. *Ibid.,* p. 76.

47. *Idem.*

48. Buffon *et al., Histoire naturelle* (1749–1804) (Brusscls, 1828–30), VI, 3; *vide ibid.,* pp. 3–4; tr. W. Smellie (3d ed.; London, 1791).

49. *Ibid.,* X, 50.

50. *Ibid.,* p. 48.

51. *Ibid.,* p. 43; cf. *ibid.,* p. 45.

52. *Ibid.,* p. 42. For his description of the apes, *vide ibid.,* pp. 42–43, 55–85.

53. *Ibid.,* p. 42.

54. *Ibid.,* p. 61.

55. *Idem.*

56. *Ibid.,* V. 3–4.

57. *Ibid.,* p. 5; *vide ibid.,* V, 1–6; VI, 7–24; X. 51–64.

58. *Ibid.,* V, 4.

59. *Ibid.,* VI, 7.

60. *Ibid.,* X, 51.

61. *Idem.*

62. *Ibid.,* X, 53.

63. *Ibid.,* VI, 28.

64. *Ibid.,* p. 34; *vide ibid.,* pp. 28–34.

65. *Ibid.,* V, 5.

66. *Ibid.*, p. 114.
67. *Ibid.*, pp. 114–213.
68. *Ibid.*, VIII, 346.
69. *Ibid.*, p. 344.
70. *Ibid.*, V, 140; cf. *ibid.*, pp. 139–40.
71. *Ibid.*, pp. 166–67.
72. *Ibid.*, IX, 1.
73. *Ibid.*, VIII, 346.
74. *Ibid.*, V. 167.
75. *Ibid.*, p. 162.
76. *Tabula affinitatum animalium* (Strassburg, 1783), 2. 3–5.
77. Leyden, 1777.
78. 3d ed.; London, 1793,
79. *Ibid.*, I, vi.
80. *Ibid.*, pp. iii-iv.
81. *Ibid*, pp. 178–226.
82. *Ibid.*, p. 178 n.
83. *De generis humani varietate nativa* (1770) (3d ed.; Gottingen, 1795), pp. x-xiv; *Handbuch der Natur-geschichte* (1779) (12th ed.; Gottingen, 1830, 1. 4; *Beyträge zur Naturgeschichte* (1790–1811) (Göttingen, 1806–11; I, 2d ed.), append. 1.
84. *DGHVN* (3d ed.), p. xv; *vide HN*, 4. 54.
85. *DGHVN* (3d ed.), 1. 2; tr. T. Bendyshe (London, 1865), *vide HN*, pp. 54–55.
86. *DGHVN* (3d ed.), 1. 3; *vide ibid.*, 1. 4–11; *DGHVN* (1st ed., reprint; Göttingen, 1776), pp. 19–25. For other differences, *vide DGHVN* (3d ed.), 1. 12.
87. *DGHVN* (3d ed.), 1. 13.
88. *Ibid.*, 1. 14–15.
89. *DGHVN* (1st ed.), pp. 32–33; tr. T. Bendyshe (London, 1865).
90. *Ibid.*, 1. 16.
91. Vide *BN*, 1. 9.
92. *DGHVN* (1st ed.), p. 20–21.
93. *Ibid.*, p. 27.
94. *HN*, p. 55; tr. R. T. Gore (London, 1825).
95. *BN*, 2. 10; *vide ibid.*, 1. 8; tr. T. Bendyshe (London, 1865).
96. *DGHVN* (3d ed.), 1. 17; cf. *DGHVN* (1st ed.), p. 29.
97. *DGHVN* (1st ed.), pp. 19–20.
98. *HN*, 3. 33–34; *vide ibid.*, 3. 37.
99. *DGHVN* (1st ed.), pp. 22.
100. *HN*, 3. 25.
101. *DGHVN* (3d ed.), 1. 18.
102. *DGHVN* (1st ed.), pp. 28–29.
103. *Ibid.*, 1. 19.
104. *Ibid.*, 1. 20–21.
105. Vide *DGHVN* (3d ed.), 4. 80; *HN*, pp. 55–56.
106. *DGHVN* (1st ed.), pp. 40–42.
107. Vide *Abbildungen naturhistorischer Gegenstände* (Göttingen, [1797]–1810), 3, 51.
108. *Vide ibid.*, 1.
109. *Vide ibid.*, 5.
110. *Vide ibid.*, 2.
111. *Vide ibid.*, 4.
112. *DGHVN* (1781, 2d ed.); in *Anthropological Treatises*, tr. T. Bendyshe (London, 1865), pp. 109–10 n.; vide *DGHVN* (3d ed.), 4. 80–89; *HN*, pp. 56–57; *BN*, 1. 12.
113. *BN*, 1. 12.
114. *HN*, pp. 57–58; cf. "Spicilegium observationum de generis humani varietate nativa," *Göttingische gelehrte Anzeigen* (1833), pt. 3 (pp. 1761–63), p. 1761.
115. *BN*, 1. 13; *vide idem.*
116. *DGHVN* (3d ed.), 4. 90; cf. *DGHVN* (1st ed.), pp. 39–40; *BN*, 1. 12.
117. *HN*, p. 55.
118. *DGHVN* (3d ed.), 2. 33; vide *HN*, 2. 8–15.
119. *DGHVN* (3d ed.), 2. 23.
120. *DGHVN* (1st ed.), p. 7; *DGHVN* (3d ed.), 2. 34; *HN*, 2. 16.
121. *DGHVN* (3d ed.), 2. 35; *HN*, 2. 16.

122. *DGHVN* (1st ed.), p. 8; *DGHVN* (3d ed.), 2. 36; *HN,* 2. 16.

123. *DGHVN* (1st ed.), p. 9; *DGHVN* (3d ed.), 2. 37.

124. *DGHVN* (3d ed.), 2. 38.

125. *Ibid.,* 2. 39; vide *BN,* 1. 1–7.

126. *DGHVN* (1st ed.), pp. 42–73; *DGHVN* (3d ed.), 3. 41–79.

127. Bordeaux, 1710.

128. *Ibid.,* pp. 23–24; tr. S. Whatley (2d ed.; London, 1743).

129. *Ibid.,* p. 44; *vide ibid.,* pp. 40–44.

130. *Ibid.,* p. 39.

131. *Ibid.,* pp. 31–33.

132. *De hominibus orbis nostri incolis* (1721), concl.; in *Opusculorum historico-critico-literariorum* (Hamburg, 1738), pp. 407–62; tr. T. Bendyshe (London, 1863–64).

133. *Ibid.,* 5. 8.

134. *A Voyage to Guinea, Brasil, and the West-Indies* (London, 1735), p. 39.

135. *Navy-Surgeon* (1732) (London, 1734), append., pp. 23–24.

136. *La spectacle de la nature* (1732–35) (Paris, 1752–55), I, epist.

137. *Amusement philosophique sur le langage des bestes* (Paris, 1739), p. 6; tr. Anonymous (2d ed.; London, 1740).

138. *Ibid.,* p. 63.

139. *Ibid.,* p. 22; cf. p. 16

140. *Ibid.,* p. 4.

141. *AMPLB,* pp. 64–65, 67.

142. *Ibid.,* pp. 67–69.

143. *Ibid.,* p. 69.

144. *Ibid.,* pp. 74–79.

145. *Ibid.,* p. 126.

146. *Ibid.,* p. 145.

147. *Ibid.,* p. 104.

148. *Ibid.,* pp. 149–50.

149. *Ibid.,* pp. 150–52.

150. *Ibid.,* pp. 127–28.

151. *Telliamed* (Basle, 1749), p. 394; tr. Anonymous (Baltimore, 1797).

152. *Ibid.,* p. 388.

153. *Ibid.,* p. 384.

154. *Ibid.,* pp. 330–50.

155. *Ibid.,* p. 364.

156. *The Natural History of Barbados* (London, 1750), p. 14.

157. *Ibid.,* p. 16.

158. *Ibid.,* pp. 9–11.

159. *Sketches of the History of Man* (1774) (Edinburgh, 1789), I, 5.

160. *Elements of Criticism* (1762) (11th ed.; London, 1839), pp. 13–14; *vide ibid.,* p. 145; *SHM,* I, 5–6; II, 108–10; IV, 3–10.

161. *SHM,* I, 79 n.

162. *Ibid.,* p. 75; *vide ibid.,* prel. disc.

163. *Ibid.,* III, 141.

164. *Ibid.,* p. 146; *vide ibid.,* pp. 146–48; cf. *ibid.,* I, 75–77.

165. *Ibid.,* I, 64–65.

166. *Ibid.,* p. 30; *vide ibid.,* I, 30–50; III, 152–53.

167. *A Survey of the Wisdom of God* (1763) (rev. ed.; London, 1809), 2. 6. 8.

168. *Ibid.,* 1. 4. 14; *vide ibid.,* 5. 4. 11.

169. *Ibid.,* 5. 4. 11; *vide idem.*

170. *Ibid.,* 2. 1. 1; *vide ibid.,* 2. 1. 1–3.

171. *Ibid.,* 2. 1. 9; *vide ibid.,* 2. 6. 3.

172. "Deux discours sur l'analogie qu'il y a entre la structure du corps humaine et celle de quadru-pèdes, des oiseaux et des poissons" (1779), in *Œuvres* (Paris, 1803), III, 325–70.

173. *Ibid.,* p. 336; tr. T. Cogan, London, 1821, new ed.

174. "De l'orang-outang, et de quelques autres especes de singes" (17—), *Œuvres,* I, 1–196.

175. "Account of the organs of speech of the orang-outang," pp. 155–56; in *Philosophical Transactions of the Royal Society,* 69 (1779), pp. 139–59.

176. *Works on the Connexion between the Science of Anatomy and the Arts of Drawing, Painting, Statuary,* &c. (1791), tr. T. Cogan (new ed., London, 1821), 1. 3. (p. 32).

177. *Ibid.,* 1. 1 (p. 16).

178. *WCSAADPS,* 1. 1 (p. 17).

179. *Ibid.,* 1. 1 (p. 14).

180. *Ibid.,* intr. (p. 8).

181. *Vide ibid.,* plates 1–3.

182. *Ibid.,* 1. 3 (p. 33).

183. *Ibid.,* 1. 3 (p. 42); *vide ibid.,* intr. 1. 3–4.

184. *Ibid.,* 1. 5.

185. *Ibid.,* 1 : 6 (p. 59); *vide ibid.,* 1. 2; "Verhandeling over het bestier van kinderen," 2; in *Verhande-lingen de Hollandsche Maatschappij der Wetenschappen te Haarlem,* 7 (1763), pt. 2, pp. 357–464; "De l'origine et de la couleur des Nègres" (1764), *Œuvres,* II, 451–76.

186. *WCSAADPS,* 2. 2.

187. *Philosophical Miscellanies on Various Subjects* (1754), tr. Anonymous (London, 1759), pp. 100–102.

188. *Institutes of Moral Philosophy* (1772) (new ed.; Basle, 1800), 1. 1. 2.

189. *Ibid.,* 1. 1. 12.

190. *Ibid.,* 1. 1. 4; after Buffon.

191. *A Comparative View of the State and Faculties of Man with those of the Animal World* (1765) (6th ed.; London, 1774), I, 9–16.

192. *Ibid.,* I, 109.

193. *Ibid.,* p. 24.

194. *Ibid.,* pp. 20–21.

196. *Ibid.,* p. 166.

197. *Ibid.,* II, 1.

198. *Ibid.,* p. 143.

199. *An History of the Earth and Animated Nature* (1774) (London, 1853), 2. 1. 15 (I, 260 b).

200. *Ibid.,* 2. 8 (I, 474 a-b); *vide ibid.,* 2. 8.

201. *Ibid.,* 2. 1. 1 (I, 184 b).

202. *Ibid.,* 2. 1. 11 (I, 232 a); *vide idem.* (I, 237 a–238 b).

203. *Ibid.,* 2. 1. 11 (I, 232 a n.).

204. *Ibid.,* 2. 1. 11 (I, 238 b).

205. *Ibid.,* 2. 1. 11 (I, 232 a–236 b).

206. *Ibid.,* 2. 1. 5 (I, 202 b).

207. *Ibid.,* 2. 1. 5 (I, 203 a).

208. *Yhe History of America* (1777), I, 269–70; in *Works* (Chiswick, 1824), VIII-X.

209. *The History of Scotland* (1759), I, 13; in *Works,* I-III.

210. *Ibid.,* I, 273–74.

211. *Ibid.,* pp. 275–76.

212. *HA,* I, 277–78.

213. *Ibid.,* I, 278.

214. *Ibid.,* pp. 282–83.

215. *Essays and Observations,* ed. R. Owen (London, 1861), I, 1–2.

216. *Observations and Reflections on Geology* (London, 1859), p. lvii.

217. *Ibid.,* p. iii.

218. "Letter to John Hunter, Feb. 24, 1785," in Hunter, *ORG,* pp. lii-liii.

219. *Ibid.,* p. liv.

220. *Œ,* I, 37.

221. *Ibid.,* II, 1.

222. *EO,* II, 1.

223. *Ibid.,* I, 43; *vide ibid.,* II, 6–35.

224. *Ibid.,* p. 276.

225. *Ibid.,* p. 278.

226. *Ibid.,* pp. 39–40.

227. *Treatise on the Natural History and Diseases of the Human Teeth* (1771–78), p. 53; in *Works,* ed. J. F. Palmer (London, 1837), II, vii-lll.

228. *EO,* I, 2–3.

229. *Ibid.,* I, 49–51.

230. *Ibid.,* p. 278.

231. *Of the Origin and Progress of Language* (1773–92) (2d ed.; Edinburgh, 1774–92; I, III), I, 175.

232. *Antient Metaphysics* (Edinburgh, 1779–99), I, 100; *vide ibid.,* pp. 85–87.

233. *Ibid.,* I, 84–85; *vide ibid.,* II, 50–62, 65–66, 133–38, 205–11; III, 5–6, 17–22, 25; IV, 2–3; VI, 7, 34–37; *OPL,* I, 176–83.

234. *OPL,* I, 136; *vide ibid.,* pp. 58–78, 135–38, 146–50, 168–70, 184, 410–11; *AM,* I, 85, 98–104, 134–38; II, 79–80, 87–89, 92–110; III, 2, 337–59; IV, 12–20; V, 227–33.

235. "Letter to James Harris, Dec. 31, 1772" p. 73; in W. Knight, *Lord Monboddo* (London, 1900), pp. 71–74.

236. *Vide OPL,* I, 41.

237. *Vide AM,* III, 222.

238. *OPL,* I, i.

239. *Ibid.,* p. iv.

240. *Ibid.,* 165; *vide ibid.,* p. 198.

241. *OPL,* I, 17–25.

242. *Ibid.,* I, 188; *vide ibid.,* pp. 188, 270–361, 426; *AM,* III, 40–43, 359–67; IV, 26–33.

243. "Letter to Linnaeus," p. 556; in *A Selection of the Correspondence of Linnaeus, and Other Naturalists,* ed. and tr. J. E. Smith (London, 1821), II, 554–57.

244. *OPL,* I, 409.

245. "Letter to John Pringle, June 16, 1773," p. 85; in Knight, *LM,* pp. 82–88.

246. *OPL,* I, 300; *vide ibid.,* pp. 300–01; *AM,* III, 222, 239–41.

247. *AM,* I, 493–94.

248. *Ibid.,* II, 351–52 n.

249. *The History of Jamaica* (London, 1774), II, 351–52.

250. *Ibid.,* p. 375 n.

251. *Ibid.,* pp. 261–62.

252. *Ibid.,* pp. 353–54; *vide ibid.,* pp. 353–56.

253. *Ibid.,* p. 375; *vide ibid.,* pp. 375–78.

254. *Ibid.,* p. 356; *vide. ibid.,* p. 372.

255. *Ibid.,* p. 356.

256. *Ibid.,* pp. 356–57, following Buffon; *vide. ibid.,* pp. 357–58.

257. *Ibid.,* p. 358.

258. *Ibid.,* pp. 362–68.

259. *Ibid.,* pp. 359–64.

260. *Ibid.,* p. 360.

261. *Ibid.,* p. 363.

262. *Ibid.,* p. 365.

263. *Vide ibid.,* pp. 369–72.

264. *Ibid.,* pp. 374–75.

265. *Disputatio inauguralis quaedam de hominum varitetatibus et harum causis exponens* (1775), p. 364; in J. F. Blumenbach, *Anthropological Treatises,* tr. T. Bendyshe (London, 1865), pp. 357–94.

266. *Ibid.,* p. 365.

267. *Ibid.,* p. 366.

268. *Ibid.,* p. 366.

269. *Ibid.,* p. 367.

270. *Ibid.,* p. 370.

271. *Ibid.,* p. 377.

272. *Ibid.,* p. 378; *vide ibid.,* pp. 378–82.

273. *Ibid.,* p. 382.

274. *Ibid.,* pp. 382–86.

275. *Ibid.,* p. 389.

276. *Ibid.,* pp. 390–92.

277. *Ibid.,* pp. 392–93; *vide ibid.,* p. 393.

278. *Ibid.,* pp. 393–94.

279. *Ideen zur Philosophie der Geschichte der Menschheit* (1784–91), p. 26; cf. *ibid.,* pp. 51–52, 54, 60, 161, 367–69, 371–72; in *Werke,* ed. H. Meyer *et al.* (*Deutsche National-Literatur,* 74–77) (Stuttgart, 1889–94), IV; tr. T. Churchill (2d ed.; London, 1803), with slight modifications.

280. *Ibid.,* p. 67.

281. *Ibid.,* p. 75.

282. *Ibid.,* p. 103.

283. *Ibid.,* p. 75; *vide ibid.,* 2. 2–4, 7.

284. *Ibid.,* p. 109.

285. *Ibid.,* pp. 115, 125–27, 139–40.

286. *Ibid.,* p. 99; cf. *ibid.,* pp. 99, 105, 113

287. *Ibid.,* p. 100; cf. *ibid.,* pp. 137–40.

288. *Ibid.,* pp. 131–32.

289.  *Ibid.,* p. 132.

290.  *Ibid.,* p. 136.

291.  *Ibid.,* p. 135.

292.  *Ibid.,* pp. 143, 145.

293.  *Ibid.,* p. 359.

294.  *Ibid.,* p. 375.

295.  *Ibid.,* p. 199.

296.  *Ibid.,* 6.

297.  *Ibid.,* p. 241; *vide ibid.,* 7. 1.

298.  *Ibid.,* p. 203.

299.  *Ibid.,* p. 375.

300.  *Ibid.,* p. 376; *vide ibid.,* 10. 2–7.

301.  *Ideen,* 4. 1, 3. [Refers to Herder, n. 279, above].

302.  *An Essay on the Causes of the Variety of Complexion and Figure in the Human Species* (1787) (2d ed.; New Brunswick, N.J., 1810) p. 4.

303.  *Ibid.,* p. 14.

304.  *Ibid.,* p. 35.

305.  *Ibid.,* pp. 263–64.

306.  *Ibid.,* pp. 268–69; *vide ibid.,* pp. 191–94.

307.  *Ibid.,* p. 29.

308.  "Aphorismen" (1807) p, 311; in *Briefe von und an Goethe,* ed. F. W. Riemer (Leizpiz, 1846), pp. 275–361; tr. C. Thomas (new ed.; New York, 1929).

309.  "Letter to C. von Knebel, Nov. 17, 1784," p. 380; in *Sämtlichen Werke* (Munich and Berlin, 1909–25), IV, 380–81.

310.  "Letter to C. F. Zelter, June 9, 1831," p. 144; in *Sämt. Werke,* XLIII, 143–44; tr. A. D. Coleridge (London, 1887).

311.  *Dichtung und Wahrheit* (18—), II, 312; in *Sämt. Werke,* XXIV, 138–399; XXV, 60–136; tr. M. S. Smith (London, 1908).

312.  "Letter to J. G. von Herder," *Sämt. Werke; vide Dem Menschen wie den Tieren ist ein Zwischenknochen der obern Kinnlade* (1784, 1820), *Sämt. Werke,* XXXIII, 401–32.

313.  "Letter to Charlotte von Stein, July 10, 1786," tr. Thomas.

314.  *Sämt. Werke,* VI, 340–77; vide "Zur Metamorphose der Pflanzen," *Sämt. Werke,* XXX, 487–517; XXXVII, 165–71; XLIII, 74–93.

315.  *Uber einen aufzustellenden Typus zu Erleichterung der vergleichenden Anatomie* (1796), p. 71; in *Werke,* ed. G. von Loeper *et al.* (Weimar, 1887–1919) (Abt. 2), VIII, 70–77; tr. Thomas.

316.  *Italiänische Reise,* I (1816), p. 273; in *Sämt. Werke,* XXIX, 228–376; tr. A. J. W. Morrison (London, 1885).

317.  "Der Verfasser teilt die Geschichte seiner botanischen Studien mit," (1830), p. 70; in *Sämt. Werke,* XLIII, 57–74; tr. Thomas.

318.  *IR,* I, 237; *vide ibid.,* pp. 237–38.

319.  *Kritik der Urtheilskraft* (1790), pp. 418–19; in *Gesammelte Schriften,* ed. Pressischen Akademie der Wissenschaften (Berlin 1902—), V, 165–485; tr. J. H. Bernard (2d ed.; London, 1914).

320.  *Elements of Moral Science* (1790–93) (3d ed.; Edinburgh, 1817), I, 10–11.

321.  *The Temple of Nature* (London, 1803), 1. 309–14.

322.  *TN,* 2. 135–58.

323.  *Ibid.,* add. note, 10.

324.  *Ibid.,* p. 119.

325.  *Ibid.,* add. notes, p. 39.

326.  *Zoonomia* (1794–96) (3d ed.; London, 1801), 1. 14. 8.

327.  *TN,* p. 91.

328.  *Ibid.,* 1. 39. 4. 8 (II, 237; *vide* pp. 237–40).

329.  *TN,* p. 26.

330.  *Z,* 1. 39. 4. 8 (II, 240).

331.  *Z.,* 1. 39. 4. 8 (II, 244).

332.  *Ibid.,* 1. 39. 4. 8 (II, 245–46).

333.  *Vide Z,* 1. 14. 8; 1. 39. 4. 8.

334.  *TN,* pp. 53–54; on the use of the hand in man, *vide Z,* 1. 16. 6.

335.  *TN,* p. 19.

336.  *TN,* pp. 12–13.

337.  *Ibid.,* pp. 5–6.

338.  *Z,* 1. 16. 3.

339.  *TN,* 3. 117–26.

340.  *Ibid.,* 1. 16.6 (I, 198–99).

341.  *Ibid.,* p. 92; *vide Z,* 1. 16. 6.

342.  *TN,* p. 120.

343.  *Ibid.,* p. 117; cf. *Z,* 1. 16. 17.

344.  *An Account of the Regular Gradation in Man* (London, 1799), p. 10.

345.  *Ibid.,* p. 1.

346.  *Ibid.,* p. 35; *vide ibid.,* p. 12.

347.  *Ibid.,* p. 39; *vide ibid.,* pp. 14–15.

348.  *Ibid.,* p. 125.

349.  *Ibid.,* p. 80.

350.  *Ibid.,* plate 2.

351.  *Ibid.,* p. 52.

352.  *Ibid.,* pp. 45–46.

353.  *Ibid.,* p. 131.

354.  *Ibid.,* p. 133.

355.  *Ibid.,* p. 135.

356.  *Ibid.,* p. 138.

357.  *Ibid.,* pp. 134–35.

358.  *Specimens of the Ancient Sculpture and Painting Now Remaining in this Kingdom* (London, 1780–87); *The Ancient Architecture of England* (London, 1795–1814); *Specimen of Gothic Arthitecture and Ancient Buildings in England* (London, 1824).

359.  London and Oxford, 1770—.

360.  "Reale Accademia Ercolanese di Archeologia," *Dissertationis isagogicae ad Herculanensium voluminum* (Naples, 1797); *idem, Herculanensium voluminum quae supersunt* (Naples, 1793–1855).

361.  *Antichità Romane de' tempi della repubblica, e de' primi imperatori* (Rome, 1748); *Vedute di Roma* (Rome, 1748–78).

362.  London, 1769–1915.

363.  Königsberg, 1717–20; quot. in *Matériaux pour l'histoire primitive et naturelle de l'homme,* 10 (1875), 297–307.

364.  "Sur les pretendues pierres de foudre" (1734), *Histoire et Memoires des Académie des Inscriptions et Belles–Lettres* (ser. 1), 12 (1734–37), 163–69.

365.  *L'Antiquité expliquée* (1719) (Paris, 1722–24, 2d ed.), V, pt. 2, pp. 194–96; tr. D. Humphreys (London, 1721–25); cf. J. C. Iselin, "Letter to B. de Montfaucon, May 12, 1718," *ibid.,* pp. 198–201.

366.  Anonymous, "Letter to an unknown correspondent, Jan. 15, 1726," p. 172; in Alexander Gordon, *Itinerarium septentrionale* (London, 1726), pp. 169–73.

367.  *Idem,* "Letter to an unknown correspondent, Feb. 8, 1725/26," p. 174; in Gordon, *IS,* pp. 174–76.

368.  *Histoire naturelle,* II, 20.

369.  The article is dated "1776," which is obviously a typographical error, since Lyttelton died in 1768, and the volume in which it appears contains papers dated from 1763 to 1772.

370.  "Some observations on stone hatchets," *Archaeologia,* 2 (1763–72), pp. 118–23.

371.  *Nenia Britannica* (1786–93) (London, 1793), p. 150.

372.  *Ibid.,* p. 154, n. 3; cf. *ibid.,* p. 158; *idem,* n. 3.

373.  *Description des zoolithes,* French tr. J. F. Isenflamm (Nuremberg, 1774), esp. pp. 18–20.

374.  "Account of flint weapons discovered at Hoxne in Suffolk" (1797), *Archaeologia,* 13 (1808, 2d ed.), 204–5.

375.  *Itiherarium curiosum* (London, 1724); *Stonehenge* (London, 1740); *Abury* (London, 1743).

376.  London, [1787?].

377.  *Ibid.,* p. 39.

378.  *Ibid.,* p. 65.

379.  Heawood, *History of Geographical Discovery.*

380.  Sandys, *History of Classical Scholarship,* II, 371–466; III, 1–46.

381.  Ed. H. B. Wheatley (London, 1886).

382.  *A Select Collection of English Songs* (1783), ed. T. Park (London, 1813); *Northern Garlands* (1784–93), ed. J. Haslewood (London, 1810); *Ancient Songs* (1790), ed. W. C. Hazlitt (London, 1877); *Pieces of Ancient Popular Poetry* (1791), ed. E. Goldsmid (Edinburgh, 1884); *Scottish Songs* (London, 1794); *Robin Hood* (London, 1795); *Ancient English.*

383.  "Das romische Karnival," in *Italiänische Reise,* III, 117–44; in *Werke* (Munich & Berlin, 1909–25), XLII, 1–179.

384.  "Sankt Rochus-Fest zu Bingen," in *Werke,* XXIX, 38–61.

385. *IR*, III, 147; tr. C. Nisbet (London, 1885).

386. C. Thomas, *Goethe* (new ed.; New York), p. 37. *Metrical Romances* (1802), ed. E. Goldsmid (Edinburgh, 1884–86); *The Caledonian Muse* (London, 1821).

387. "Letter to J. G. Herder, 1771," p. 2; in *Werke*, ed. G. von Loeper *et al.* (Weimar, 1887–1919) (ser. 4), II, pp. 1–3; tr. E. Bell (London, 1889).

388. "Sankt Rochus-Fest," pp. 55–56.

389. *Ibid.*, p. 52.

390. *Observations on the Popular Antiquities of Great Britain* (1777), ed. H. Ellis (London, 1901–3), I, vii.

391. *Archaeologia Britannica* (Oxford, 1707); *Parochialia*, ed. R. H. Morris (*Archaeologia Cambrensis* [ser. 6] suppl., 1909–11) (London, 1909–11).

392. Paris, 1701–63.

393. Paris, 1666–1793.

394. London, 1731–1907.

395. The more important material is collected in *The Gentleman's Magazine Library*, ed. G. L. Gomme, Boston [1883–84].

396. London and Oxford, 1770——.

397. London, 1775–84.

398. Calcutta, 1788–1839.

399. London, 1927.

400. *The State of the Prisons in England and Wales* (1777) (4th ed.; London, 1792); *An Account of the principal Lazarettos in Europe* (1789), ed. J. Aiken (2d ed.; London, 1791).

401. T. Carlyle, *Latter-Day Pamphlets*, p. 63; in *Works*, ed. H. D. Traill (New York, 1896–1901), XX.

402. *SPEW*, p. 1.

403. *Ibid.*, p. 469.

404. London, 1797.

405. *Ibid.*, pp. ii-iv.

406. *Ibid.*, I, i.

407. *Ibid.*, pp. i-ii.

408. *Ibid.*, p. xviii.

409. *Ibid.*, p. vii.

410. *Ibid.*, p. x.

411. *Conformité des coûtumes des indiens orientaux, avec celles des juifs & des autres peuples de l'antiquité* (Brussels, 1704), p. [vi]; tr. J. Toland (London, 1705).

412. Ed. J. Conduitt (London, 1728).

413. *Ibid.*, p. 160.

414. *Idem.*

415. *Ibid.*, pp. 160–61.

416. *Ibid.*, pp. 161–62. 225.

417. *Ibid.*, pp. 209–10.

418. *Ibid.*, p. 168.

419. *Histoire du ciel* (1739) (2d ed.; Paris, 1740), 1. 1. 1; tr. J. B. de Freval (London, 1743).

420. *Fauna suecica*, p. 1.

421. *Remains of Japhet* (London, 1767), p. 225.

422. *Ibid.*, pp. 220–21; *vide ibid.*, pp. 218–20, 229–34.

423. *Ibid.*, p. 225.

424. *Ibid.*, p. 226; *vide ibid.*, pp. 226–29, 231–32, 234–40.

425. *Antient Metaphysics*, III, iii; *vide ibid.*, pp. iii-xx; IV, 128–49, 257–63, 280–402; *Origin and Progress of Language*, I, 629–30, 654, 657, 660, 665, 678; II, 243; III, 436.

426. *Ideen zur Philosophie der Geschichte der Menschheit* (1784–91), p. 40; in *Werke*, ed. H. Meyer *et al.* (*Deutsche National-Literatur*, 74–77) (Stuttgart, 1889–94), IV; tr. T. Churchill (2d ed.; London, 1803).

427. *Ibid.*, 10. 3–4; cf. *ibid.*, pp. 39–42.

428. *Ibid.*, pp. 376–77.

429. *Ibid.*, pp. 377–78.

430. *Ibid.*, pp. 378–79.

431. *Ibid.*, pp. 379–80.

432. *Ibid.*, pp. 380–81.

433. *Ibid.*, pp. 381–82.

434. *Ibid.*, 10. 4.

435. *Ibid.*, pp. 381–82.

436. *Anniversary Discourses* (1784–94), *Works*, ed. A. M. Jones (London, 1807), III, 1–252; "On the

gods of Greece, Italy, and India," *Works*, III, 319–97; "On the antiquity of the Indian zodiack," *Works,* IV, 71–92.

437. "On the gods," p. 319; cf. *AD*, pp. 89–90.

438. "On the gods," p. 386.

439. *Ibid.*, pp. 320–22.

440. *AD*, p. 212.

441. "On the gods," pp. 341–42.

442. *AD*, pp. 191–96.

443. *Ibid.*, pp. 185–89, 191–97, 201–3; cf. *ibid.*, p. 209; "On the gods"; "Note to Mr. Vansittart's paper on the Afghans being descended from the Jews," *Works*, IV, 70; "On the antiquity of the Indian zodiack."

444. "The lunar year of the Hindus," *Works*, IV, 126–65; "On the musical modes of the Hindus," *Works*, IV, 166–210; "On the Indian game of chess," *Works*, IV, 323–33.

445. *A Grammar of the Persian Language, Works*, V, 163–446.

446. "On the mystical poetry of the Persians and Hindus," *Works*, IV, 211–35; *Poeseos Asiaticae Commentariorum, Works*, VI; *An Essay on the Poetry of the Eastern Nations, Works*, X, 329–60; *Traité sur la poësie orientale, Works*, XII, 173–270; *Dissertation sur la litterature orientale, Works*, XII, 271–310.

447. "Charges to the Grand Jury, at Calcutta," *Works*, VII, 1–71; *Institutes of Hindu Law, Works*, VII, 73–399; VIII, 1–158; *The Mahomedan Law of Succession to the Property of Intestates, Works*, VIII, 159–96; *Al sirajiyyah, Works*, VIII, 197–321; *An Essay on the Law of Bailments, Works*, VIII, 323–458.

448. *Works*, IV, 269–313.

449. *Ibid.*, p. 269.

450. *AD*, p. 50.

451. *Ibid.*, p. 214.

452. *Nouveaux essais sur l'entendement* (1704), pp. 257–58; in *Philosophischen Schriften*, ed. C. J. Gerhardt (Berlin, 1875–90), V, 39–509; tr. A G. Langley (New York, 1896).

453. *Ibid.*, pp. 260–62.

454. *Ibid.*, pp. 259–60.

455. *Ibid.*, p. 264.

456. *Ibid.*, p. 313.

457. *Ibid.*, p. 317.

458. *Ibid.*, pp. 264–65.

459. William Cowper (1731–1800), "Retirement," 691–94.

460. *Remains of Japhet*, p. viii.

461. *Ibid.*, p. xii; *vide ibid.*, chap. 9.

462. *Ibid.*, p. xx; cf. *ibid.*, p. 245.

463. *Ibid.*, pp. 245–46.

464. *Ibid.*, p. 247.

465. *Ibid.*, pp. 247–48.

466. *Ibid.*, p. 249.

467. *Idem.*

368. *Ibid.*, p. 250.

469. *Ibid.*, pp. 250–51.

470. *Ibid.*, pp. 252–60.

471. *Ibid.*, opp. p. 317.

472. *Ibid.*, pp. 317–20.

473. *Ibid.*, p. 340.

474. *Ibid.*, p. 335.

475. *Ibid.*, p. 338.

476. *Ibid.*, p. 260.

477. "Remarks on the Sumatran languages" (1781), *Archaeologia*, 6 (1783) (pp. 154–58), p. 157; *vide A Grammar of the Malayan Languages* (London, 1812); "On the Polynesian or East-Insular languages," *Miscellaneous Works* (London, 1834), No. 1.

478. *Origin and Progress of Language*, I, 665; *vide ibid.*, I, 645, 657, 660, 665, 678; V, 185.

479. *Ibid.*, I, 616–17; *vide ibid.*, pp. 601, 673–76.

480. *Ibid.*, p. 596 n.

481. *Ibid.*, p. 605.

482. *Vide ibid.*, II, 514; IV, 72.

483. *Ibid.*, I, 602, following Saumaise; *vide ibid.*, I, 601–12.

484. *Ibid.*, II, 438; *vide ibid.*, pp. 437–39.

485. *Ibid.*, p. 531.

486. *Ibid.,* IV, 25.

487. *Ibid.,* p. 25 n.

488. "Letter to William Jones, June 20, 1789," pp. 269–70; in Knight, *Monboddo,* pp. 269–71; *vide Antient Metaphysics,* IV, 321–32.

489. *Anniversary Discourses,* p. 34; cf. *ibid.,* pp. 85, 115, 119, 185–86.

490. *AD,* p. 166; cf. *ibid.,* p. 186; "Note to Vansittart's paper."

491. "Extracts from the common-place books, memoranda, etc.," pp. 518–20; in *Miscellaneous Works,* ed. J. Holroyd, Lord Sheffield (new ed.; London, 1814), V, 489–535.

492. "Philology," 18; in *Encylopaedia Britannica* (3d ed., Edinburgh, 1797), XIV, 485–569.

493. *Ibid.,* 231–32.

494. *Ibid.,* 233–35.

495. *Ibid.,* 40.

496. *Ibid.,* 58.

497. *Ibid.,* 106.

498. *Ibid.,* 82.

499. *Ibid.,* 109.

500. *The Diversions of Purley* (1786–1805), ed. R. Taylor (London, 1840), p. 14; *vide ibid.,* 1. 1.

501. *Ibid.,* p. 170.

502. *Ibid.,* pp. 23–24.

503. *Ibid.,* p. 217.

504. *A Letter to John Dunning* (1778), p. 698; in *ibid.,* pp. 685–734; *vide DP,* pp. 76–77.

505. *DP,* p. 51.

506. *Ibid.,* pp. 402–4.

507. *Elements of Moral Science,* I, 22.

508. *Archaeologia Britannica,* Oxford, 1707.

509. *Glossarium Suigothicum,* Uppsala, 1769.

510. "On the origin of the English language" (1776), *Archaeologia,* 5 (1789) (pp. 306–17), 307; *vide* "Some further remarks on the origin of the English language" (1778), *ibid.,* 5 (1789), 379–89; "Observations on the derivation of the English language," 9 (1789), 332–61.

511. St. Petersburg, 1786–87.

512. St. Petersburg, 1790–91.

## NOTES TO CHAPTER V

1. "The origin and force of prejudices," p. 1; in *Letters to Serena* (London, 1704), pp. 1–18.

2. *Ibid.,* pp. 3–4.

3. *Ibid.,* pp. 9–10.

4. *Ibid.,* p. 12.

5. *Ibid.,* pp. 12–13.

6. *Ibid.,* p. 14.

7. "The origins of idolatry, and reasons of heathenism," pp. 72–73; *vide ibid.,* pp. 81–83, 93–94; in *LS,* pp. 69–130; cf. "A specimen of Celtic religion and learning," pp. 40–41, 83.

8. "Origins of idolatry," pp. 53–54; cf. *ibid.,* p. 77.

9. *Ibid.,* p. 72; *vide ibid.,* pp. 101–3, 109–12.

10. *Characteristics* (1699–1711), ed. J.M. Robertson (New York, 1900), II, 5.

11. *Ibid.,* I, 260.

12. *Ibid.,* II, 77; *vide ibid.,* pp. 81–82.

13. *Ibid.,* I, 74–75; *vide ibid.,* II, 75–77, 79–84.

14. *Ibid.,* I, 73–74.

15. *Ibid.,* pp. 74–75, 83, 280–81.

16. *Ibid.,* pp. 72–73.

17. *Ibid.,* p. 75; *vide ibid.,* II, 244–46.

18. *Ibid.,* I, 72.

19. *Ibid.,* p. 311.

20. *Ibid.,* p. 71.

21. *Ibid.,* p. 77; *vide ibid.,* pp. 77–81.

22. *Ibid.,* p. 297.

23. "Letter to J. Stanhope, Nov. 7, 1709," p. 414; in *Life, Unpublished Letters, and Philosophical Regimen,* ed. B. Rand (London, 1900), pp. 413–17.

24. *C,* I, 81; *vide ibid.,* pp. 294–95, 298–99, 309–11, 315

25. *Ibid.,* I, 280–81; *vide ibid.,* II, 293–95.

26. *Ibid.,* I, 262.

27. *Ibid.,* pp. 305–09.

28. *Ibid.,* p. 258.

29. *Ibid.,* p. 260; *vide ibid.,* pp. 258–60.

30. *An Inquiry into the Original of Our Ideas of Beauty and Virtue* (London, 1725), pp. 99–276.

31. *Ibid.,* Introd.

32. *Ibid.,* 2:2; cf. *ibid.,* 1:1–8.

33. *Ibid.,* 1:1.

34. *Ibid.,* 7:2.

35. *Ibid.,* 1:8.

36. *Ibid.,* 4:3.

37. *Ibid.,* 2:9.

38. *Ibid.,* 5:1.

39. *Ibid.,* 2:9.

40. *Ibid.,* 7:3.

41. *Ibid.,* 5:5.

42. *Fifteen Sermons Preached at the Rolls Chapel* (1726), pref. 17–21, 24; in *Works,* ed. J. H. Bernard (London, 1900), I, 1–200.

43. *Ibid.,* 5. 1; *vide ibid.,* pref. 35, 38; 1. 6; 3. 8–9; 11.

44. *Ibid.,* 1. 7 n.

45. *Ibid.,* 1. 4; *vide ibid.,* 1. 6; 3. 8–9; 11.

46. *Vide ibid.,* 1. 6 n., 12; 2. 2, 8; 3. 7; 5. 1–2; 6. 2.

47. *Ibid.,* 1. 5–10.

48. *Ibid.,* 1. 15.

49. "Concerning the fundamental principle of virtue or morality" (1731), p. 285; in *British Moralists,* ed. L.A. Selby-Bigge (Oxford, 1897), II, 267–85.

50. *Ibid.,* p. 285.

51. *Ibid.,* p. 283.

52. *Ibid.,* pp. 280–81.

53. in *Metaphysical Tracts,* ed. S. Parr (London, 1837), II, 43–170.

54. *Ibid.,* 1. 1.

55. *Ibid.,* 1. 2.

56. *Ibid.,* 4. 13.

57. *Ibid.,* 1. 3.

58. *Ibid.,* 2. 12.

59. *Ibid.,* 1. 5.

60. *Ibid.,* 1. 6.

61. *Ibid.,* 2. 18.

62. *Ibid.,* 1. 8.

63. *Ibid.,* 2. 37.

64. *Ibid.,* 2. 42–43.

65. *Ibid.,* 4. 41.

66. *The Fable of the Bees* (1705–29), ed. F. B. Kaye (Oxford, 1924), II, 22–23.

67. *Ibid.,* p. 110.

68. *Ibid.,* p. 164; cf. *ibid.,* p. 261.

69. *Ibid.,* I, 333; II, 79–80, 108, 139, 348; *An Enquiry into the Origin of Honour* (London, 1732), p. 31.

70. *Free Thoughts on Religion, the Church, and National Happiness* (London, 1720) p. 91; *vide ibid.,* pp. 89–91.

71. *FB,* I, 39; cf. *EOH,* pp. 4–5.

72. *FB,* II, 108.

73. *Ibid.,* pp. 79–80; cf. *ibid.,* p. 139.

74. *EOH,* p. 31.

75. *FTRCNH,* p. 19.

76. *FB,* I, 333.

77. *Ibid.,* pp. 336–43.

78. *Ibid.,* pp. 41–57, 63–80; II, 177–83, 253.

79. *Ibid.,* II, p. 121.

80. *Ibid.,* p. 174.

81. *Ibid.,* p. 121.

82. *Ibid.,* p. 91.

83. *Ibid.,* I, 281.

84. *Ibid.*, p. 75.
85. *Ibid.*, II, 137; cf. *ibid.*, pp. 89, 91, 347.
86. *EOH*, p. 30.
87. *FB*, I, 200.
88. *Ibid.*, II, 223–24.
89. *Ibid.*, p. 178.
90. *Ibid.*, I, 41.
91. *Ibid.*, p. 253.
92. *Ibid.*, p. 76.
93. *Ibid.*, II, 129–30; cf. *EOH*, pp. 3–13.
94. *FB*, II, 134–36.
95. *Ibid.*, p. 131.
96. *Ibid.*, I, 124.
97. *Ibid.*, II, 333.
98. *Ibid.*, p. 64.
99. *Ibid.*, p. 89.
100. *Ibid.*, I, 124.
101. *Ibid.*, p. 64; *vide EOH*, pp. 41–42, 92.
102. *FB*, II, 95.
103. *Ibid.*, I, 316.
104. *Ibid.*, p. 68.
105. *Ibid.*, II, 64–65.
106. *Ibid.*, p. 90; cf. *ibid.*, I, 209–10, 214, 334, 336; II, 92, 96–97.
107. *Ibid.*, I, 347.
108. *Ibid.*, II, 184–85.
109. *Ibid.*, pp. 176–77.
110. *Ibid.*, pp. 183–84.
111. *Ibid.*, p. 186.
112. *Ibid.*, I, 286.
113. *Ibid.*, II, 188–89.
114. *Ibid.*, pp. 189–90.
115. *Ibid.*, p. 190; cf. *ibid.*, p. 269.
116. *Ibid.*, p. 190.
117. *Ibid.*, II, 191–92.
118. *Ibid.*, pp. 204–5.
119. *Ibid.*, I, 56.
120. *Ibid.*, II, 200–2; cf. *ibid.*, p. 280.
121. *Ibid.*, pp. 280–81; cf. *EOH*, pp. x–xi.
122. *FB*, II, 231.
123. *Ibid.*, p. 153.
124. *Ibid.*, p. 214.
125. *Ibid.*, I, 275.
126. *Ibid.*, p. 229.
127. *Ibid.*, II, 110.
128. *Ibid.*, pp. 75–76.
129. *Ibid.*, p. 90.
130. *Ibid.*, p. 155.
131. *Ibid.*, I, 173.
132. *Ibid.*, p. 330; *vide ibid.*, I, 327, 330–31; II, 95, 149, 151.
133. *Ibid.*, II, 247.
134. *Ibid.*, pp. 149–50.
135. *Ibid.*, I, 177.
136. *Ibid.*, II, 174.
137. *Ibid.*, p. 191.
138. *Ibid.*, I, 358.
139. *Ibid.*, p. 358.
140. *Ibid.*, p. 270.
141. *Ibid.*, II, 281.
142. *Ibid.*, p. 203.
143. *Ibid.*, I, 68.
144. *Ibid.*, p. 69; cf. *ibid.*, pp. 71–72.

145.  *Ibid.*, II, 78.
146.  *Ibid.*, pp. 321–22.
147.  *EOH,* p. 41; *vide ibid.,* pp. 23–25, 27–29, 39–41.
148.  *FB,* I, 169–70.
149.  *Ibid.*, II, 138–39.
150.  *Ibid.*, p. 128.
151.  *Ibid.*, I, 344.
152.  *Ibid.*, p. 221.
153.  *Ibid.*, II, 349–50.
154.  *Ibid.*, p. 230.
155.  *Ibid.*, p. 231.
156.  *Ibid.*, p. 261.
157.  *Ibid.*, p. 272.
158.  *FTRCNH,* p. 311; cf. *ibid.,* pp. 306–7.
159.  *Ibid.*, I, 286.
160.  *Ibid.*, II, 46.
161.  *Ibid.*, pp. 266–67.
162.  *FB,* I, 348.
163.  *EOH,* pp. 27–28; *vide ibid.,* pp. 23–25, 27–29, 39–41.
164.  *Vide ibid.,* I, 41–51, 71, 145, 198, 208–09, 220; II, 78–79, 218;  *EOH,* pp. 15, 60–61, 235–36.
165.  *FB,* II, 268–69.
166.  *Ibid.*, pp. 283–84.
167.  *Ibid.*, pp. 318, 320.
168.  *Ibid.*, p. 106; *vide ibid.,* I, 3–4, 183–85, 229, 231, 325, 366, 369.
169.  *Ibid.*, I, 1, subtitle; cf. *ibid.,* pp. 4, 7, 17–37, 86–123, 223–28, 369. For qualifications, *vide ibid.,* I, 248–51; *EOH,* p. ii.
170.  *FB,* I, 25.
171.  *Ibid.*, p. 169.
172.  *Ibid.*, p. 171.
173.  *Ibid.*, II, 241.
174.  *Ibid.*, pp. 207–10; cf. *EOH,* pp. 21–22.
175.  *FB,* II, pp. 284–90.
176.  *Ibid.*, p. 260; *vide ibid.,* II, 245–63.
177.  *An Essay upon Government* (London, 1716), pp. 21–22.
178.  *Ibid.*, p. 6.
179.  *Ibid.*, pp. 10–11.
180.  *La spectacle de la nature* (1732–35) (Paris, 1752–55),  VI, 1; tr. S. Humphreys and J. B. de Freval (London, 1740–48).
181.  *Ed.* E. A. Baker, London, [1904].
182.  *Ibid.*, p. 374; *vide ibid.,* p. 124.
183.  *Ibid.*, pp. 4–5.
184.  *Ibid.*, p. 10.
185.  *Ibid.*, pp. 63–69.
186.  *Ibid.*, p. 29; *vide ibid.,* pp. 16–19, 27–31.
187.  *Ibid.*, p. 8.
188.  *Fragments,* p. 190; in *Works,* ed. D. Mallet (London, 1754), Vol. V.
189.  *Ibid.*, pp. 177–78.
190.  *Letters on the Study and Use of History,* pp. 274–75; in *Works,* II, 257–502.
191.  *Ibid.*, p. 178.
192.  *Ibid.*, p. 290.
193.  *F,* p. 104; cf. *ibid.,* pp. 153–56, 201.
194.  "Of the true use of retirement and study," pp. 511–12; in *Works,* II, 509–27.
195.  *F,* p. 196.
196.  *LSUH,* p. 269.
197.  *F,* p. 109.
198.  *Ibid.*, p. 110; *vide ibid.,* pp. 130–31, 158–59.
199.  *Ibid.*, p. 158.
200.  *Ibid.*, p. 196.
201.  *LSUH,* p. 264.
202.  *Ibid.*, p. 80.
203.  *F,* p. 82.

204.  *Ibid.,* pp. 81–82; cf. *ibid.,* p. 106.
205.  *Ibid.,* pp. 51–52.
206.  *Ibid.,* pp. 53–55.
207.  *Ibid.,* p. 58.
208.  *Ibid.,* pp. 59–60.
209.  *LSUH,* p. 293.
210.  *Ibid.,* pp. 316–17.
211.  *F,* p. 126.
212.  *Ibid.,* p. 114.
213.  *Ibid.,* p. 105.
214.  *Ibid.,* p. 112.
215.  *Ibid.,* p. 108.
216.  *Ibid.,* p. 113.
217.  *Ibid.,* p. 114.
218.  *Idem.*
219.  *Ibid.,* p. 115.
220.  *Ibid.,* p. 118.
221.  *Ibid.,* p. 121.
222.  *Ibid.,* p. 125.
223.  *LSUH,* p. 339.
224.  *"Letters or Essays Addressed to Mr. Pope,* IV, 235–36; in Works, III, 309 ff., IV.
225.  *LSUH,* p. 283.
226.  *Ibid.,* pp. 359–60.
227.  *Ibid.,* p. 266.
228.  *Ibid.,* p. 287.
229.  *Ibid.,* p. 268.
230.  *Ibid.,* pp. 266–67.
231.  *Ibid.,* p. 274.
232.  "Of the true use of retirement," p. 510.
233.  *Ibid.,* p. 512.
234.  *Ibid.,* pp. 273–74.
235.  *Ibid.,* p. 275; cf. *ibid.,* pp. 345–46.
236.  *Ibid.,* p. 279.
237.  *LSUH,* p. 335; *vide ibid.,* pp. 343–44.
238.  *An Essay on Man* (1732–34), 1 : 207–32; in *Poetical Works,* ed. A. W. Ward (London, 1895), pp. 191–226.
239.  *Ibid.,* 1. 237–46.
240.  *Ibid.,* 2. 236.
241.  *Ibid.,* 2. 53–54; *vide ibid.,* 2 : 54. 80.
242.  *Ibid.,* 2. 87–88.
243.  *Ibid.,* 3. 7–26.
244.  *Ibid.,* 3. 109–14.
245.  *Ibid.,* 2. 249–54.
246.  *Ibid.,* 4. 39–46.
247.  *Ibid.,* 3. 121–50.
248.  *Ibid.,* 3. 200–94.
249.  *Ibid.,* 3. 311–18.
250–252.  [Notes missing from ms.]
253.  Lachesis Lapponica, "A Tour in Lapland" tr. J.E. Smith (London, 1811), pp. 131–32.
254.  *Ibid.,* 1, p. 222.
255.  *Ibid.,* X, 51.
256.  *Idem.*
257.  *Ibid.,* V, 154.
258.  *Histoire naturelle,* V, 154.
259.  *Ibid.,* p. 6.
260.  *Ibid.,* X, 52.
261.  *Ibid.,* pp. 52–53.
262.  *Ibid.,* p. 53.
263.  *Ibid.,* VI, 54.
264.  *Ibid.,* II, 20–21.
265.  *Ibid.,* pp. 21–24.

266.  *Ibid.*, 20–21; *vide idem.*
267.  *Ibid.*, p. 27.
268.  *Ibid.*, V, 154.
269.  *Ibid.*, p. 120.
270.  *Ibid.*, p. 139.
271.  *Ibid.*, pp. 153–54.
272.  *Ibid.*, VI, 428–29; *vide idem.*
273.  *Works,* ed. E. Gosse (New York, 1885), I, 71–80.
274.  *Ideen,* p. 83. [Refers to Herder, *Ideen zur Philosophie der Geschichte der Menschheit*].
275.  *Ibid.*, p. 637.
276.  *Ibid.*, p. 606; cf. *ibid.*, p. 629.
277.  *Ibid.*, p. 20.
278.  *Ibid.*, p. 24.
279.  *Ibid.*, p. 30.
280.  *Ibid.*, p. 608.
281.  *Ibid.*, p. 275.
282.  *Ibid.*, pp. 543–44; cf. *ibid.*, pp. 8–9.
283.  *Ibid.*, pp. 544–45.
284.  *Ibid.*, pp. 857–58.
285.  *Ibid.*, p. 598.
286.  *Ibid.*, p. 599.
287.  *Ibid.*, p. 596.
288.  *Ibid.*, pp. 291–92.
289.  *Ibid.*, p. 329.
290.  *Ibid.*, p. 30.
291.  *Ibid.*, p. 275.
292.  *Vide ibid.*, 7. 3, and pp. 39–42, 60, 288.
293.  *Ibid.*, p. 254.
294.  *Ibid.*, p. 259; *vide ibid.*, 7 4.
295.  *Ibid.*, pp. 267–68.
296.  *Idem; vide ibid.*, 8. 1.
297.  *Ibid.*, p. 282; *vide ibid.*, 8. 2.
298.  *Ibid.*, p. 292; *vide ibid.*, 8. 3.
299.  *Ibid.*, p. 300; *vide ibid.*, 8. 4.
300.  *Ibid.*, p. 313; *vide ibid.*, 8. 5.
301.  *Ibid.*, p. 351.
302.  *Ibid.*, p. 290.
303.  *Ibid.*, p. 307.
304.  *Ibid.*, p. 301.
305.  *Ibid.*, p. 149; cf. *ibid.*, pp. 331–32.
306.  *Ibid.*, p. 326.
307.  *Ibid.*, p. 152.
308.  *Ibid.*, p. 347.
309.  *Ibid.*, p. 324.
310.  *Ibid.*, p. 325.
311.  *Ibid.*, p. 329.
312.  *Ibid.*, p. 326.
313.  *Ibid.*, p. 324.
314.  *Ibid.*, pp. 323–24.
315.  *Ibid.*, p. 289.
316.  *Ibid.*, p. 287.
317.  *Ibid.*, p. 257.
318.  *Ibid.*, p. 30.
319.  *Ibid.*, pp. 144–45.
320.  *Ibid.*, pp. 333–34.
321.  *Ibid.*, p. 331.
322.  *Ibid.*, p. 359; cf. *ibid.*, pp. 134, 139–40.
323.  *Ibid.*, p. 338.
324.  *Ibid.*, p. 331.
325.  *Ibid.*, p. 332.
326.  *Ibid.*, p. 334.

327.   *Ibid.,* p. 341.
328.   *Ibid.,* p. 342.
329.   *Ibid.,* p. 340.
330.   *Ibid.,* p. 333.
331.   *Ibid.,* pp. 338–39.
332.   *Ibid.,* p. 639.
333.   *Ibid.,* p. 544.
334.   *Ibid.,* pp. 5–6.
335.   *Ibid.,* p. 325.
336.   *Ibid.,* pp. 326–27.
337.   *Ibid.,* p. 577; *vide ibid.,* 14. 4.
338.   *Ibid.,* p. 819.
340.   *Ibid.,* p. 170.
341.   *Ibid.,* p. 444.
342.   *Ibid.,* p. 330; cf. *ibid.,* p. 331.
343.   *Ibid.,* p. 340.
344.   *Ibid.,* p. 625; *vide* 4, esp. pp. 148–57.
345.   *Ibid.,* p. 629.
346.   *Ibid.,* p. 630.
347.   *Ibid.,* p. 631.
348.   *Ibid.,* p. 632.
349.   *Ibid.,* p. 633.
350.   *Ibid.,* p. 633.
351.   *Ibid.,* p. 635.
352.   *Ibid.,* p. 636.
353.   *Ibid.,* p. 859.
354.   *Italiänische Reise,* III, (18—), p. 55; in *Werke,* XLII, 1–179; tr. C. Nisbet (London, 1885).
355.   *Wilhelm Meisters Lehrjahre,* p. 358; in *Werke,* VIII; tr. T. Carlyle (London, 1897–98).
356.   J. P. Eckermann, *Gespräche mit Goethe,* ed. L. Geiger (Leipzig, [1902]), p. 61; tr. J. Oxenford (New ed. ; London, 1874).
357.   *Tag- und Jahres-Hefte* (18—), p. 379; in *Werke,* XXXVIII, 196–467; tr. C. Nisbet (London, 1894).
358.   " Letter to C. F. Zelter, Feb. 15, 1830," p. 190; in *Werke,* XLII, 189–91.
359.   "Letter to Zelter, June 28, 1831," p. 153; in *Werke,* XLIII, 152–54.
360.   "Maximen und Reflexionen," p. 41; in *Werke,* XLV, 37–102; tr. T. B. Saunders (London, 1908).
361.   "Letter to F. Schiller, March 18, 1801," pp. 25–26; in *Werke,* XIV, 25–26; tr. L. D. Schmitz (London, 1877–79).
362.   "Letter to Zelter, March 29, 1827," p. 169; in *Werke,* XXXIX, 169–72.
363.   Eckermann, *GG,* p. 123.
364.   "Letter to Zelter, Feb. 23, 1832," p. 15; in *Werke,* XLIV, 14–15.
365.   *Kunst und Altertum am Rhein und Main,* p. 425; in *Werke,* XXVIII, 363–432; tr. L. D. Schmitz (London, 1882).
366.   *Dichtung und Wahrheit,* II, 310.
367.   Eckermann, *GG,* p. 239.
368.   "Antik und Modern", pp. 288–89; in *Werke,* XXXI, 288–94; tr. ed. J. E. Spingarn (New York, 1921).
369.   *Ibid.,* p. 291.
370.   *Ibid.,* pp. 171–72.
371.   "Literarischer Sansculottismus," p. 188; in *Werke,* IX, 187–91; tr. ed. Spingarn.
372.   *DW,* I, 140.
373.   Eckermann, *GG,* p. 618.
374.   *Ibid.,* p. 123.
375.   *IR,* III, p. 12.
376.   Eckermann, *GG,* p. 155.
377.   "Literarischer Sansculottismus," p. 188; vide Eckermann, *GG,* pp. 506–7.
378.   "Die Natur," p. 289; in Werke, VI, 288–90; tr. Saunders.
379.   *Ibid.,* p. 290.
380.   *DW,* II, 90.
381.   "Sankt Rochus-Fest zu Bingen," p. 57.
382.   "Studien zur Weltliteratur" (18—), p. 496; in *Werke,* XL, 493–97; tr. ed. Spingarn.
383.   Eckermann, *GG,* p. 266. For a geographic interpretation of some aspects of culture, vide *Italiänische Reise,* II, 369–71; in *Werke,* XXX, 232–380.

384. *KARM*, p. 416.
385. *IR*, I, p. 365.
386. *TJH*, p. 382.
387. Eckermann, *GG*, p. 134.
388. "Letter to F. Schiller, April 1801," p. 32; in *Werke*, XIV, 32–34.
389. "Review of A. Duval, *Le Tasse*" (18—), p. 375; in *Werke*, XXXIX, 372–75; tr. ed. Spingarn.
390. "Maximen und Reflexionen," p. 60; in *Werke*, XLV, 37–102.
391. Eckermann, *GG*, pp. 545–46.
392. *Ibid.*, 136.
393. "Belagerung von Mainz 1793," pp. 345–46; in *Werke*, XXXIV, 345–76; tr. R. Farie and L.D. Schmitz (London, 1882).
394. *TJH*, p. 223.
395. Eckermann, *GG*, pp. 476–77.
396. *IR*, II, p. 269.
397. *Temple of Nature*, 1. 5–8; cf. *ibid.*, 1. 219–22.
398. *Ibid.*, 3. 206.
399. *Ibid.*, add. notes, p. 39.
400. *Ibid.*, 2. 244–47, 250.
401. *Ibid.*, 2. 91–94; *vide ibid.*, add. note 9.
402. *Ibid.*, 2. 103–10.
403. *Ibid.*, 3. 461–71, 478–84; *vide Zoonomia*, 1. 22. 3. 3.
404. *Z*, 1. 22.
405. *TN*, 3. 334.
406. *Ibid.*, 3. 279–92.
407. *Ibid.*, 1. 22. 3. 2; *vide ibid.*, 1. 32. 3.1.
408. *Ibid.*, p. 111.
409. *Ibid.*, p. 106.
410. *Ibid.*, p. 109; cf. *Z*, 1. 32. 3. 1.
411. *Z*, 1. 22. 3. 2–5.
412. *TN*, pp. 122–23.
413. *Ibid.*, p. 112; cf. *Z*, 1. 16. 7.
414. *The Botanic Garden* (London, 1789–91), pt. 1, p. 30.
415. *Ibid.*, pt. 1, 1. 209–16.
416. *TN*, pref.
417. *Z*, 1. 16. 9.
418. *TN*, p. 71.
419. *Ibid.*, 1. 16. 11–16.
420. *Ibid.*, 1. 16. 8.
421. *Ibid.*, p. 114.
422. *Vide ibid.*, add. note 14.
423. *Vide ibid.*, add. note 15.
424. *Ibid.*, 3. 335–82; *vide ibid.*, add. notes, pp. 104–6.
425. *Ibid.*, 3. 395–402.
426. *Ibid.*, p. 8; cf. *ibid.*, p. 15.
427. *Ibid.*, 4. 265–72.
428. *Ibid.*, p. 117.
429. *BG*, pt. 1, p. 8.
430. *TN*, p. 54.
431. *Ibid.*, 4. 369–74.
432. *An Enquiry concerning Political Justice* (London, 1793), I, 12.
433. *Ibid.*, p. 18.
434. *Ibid.*, p. 58.
435. *Ibid.*, p. 19.
436. *Ibid.*, p. 290.
437. *Ibid.*, pp. 59–60.
438. *Ibid.*, p. 110.
439. *Ibid.*, p. 79.
440. *Ibid.*, pp. 45–46.
441. *Ibid.*, p. 3.
442. *Ibid.*, p. 71.
443. *Ibid.*, p. 72.

444. *Ibid.*, p. 73.

445. *Idem.*

446. *Ibid.*, I, p. 50.

447. *Medical Inquiries and Observations* (5th ed.; Philadelphia, 1818), I, 93–124.

448. *Ibid.*, pp. 106–14, 116.

449. London, 1731.

450. *Ibid.*, p. 4.

451. *Ibid.*, pp. 39–40.

452. *The Citizen of the World, or Letters from a Chinese Philosopher Residing in London to His Friends in the East* (from the *Public Ledger,* 1760–1761), 2 vols., 1762.

453. *Ibid.*, 3.

454. Ed. H. Barckhausen *(Société des textes français modernes)* (Paris, 1932).

455. *Œuvres complètes* (Paris, 1877–85), XXI, 31–93.

456. *Complete Works,* ed. J. Bigelow (New York, 1887–88), IX, 25–33.

457. *Ibid.*, p. 25.

458. "Observations concerning the increase of mankind and the peopling of countries" (1751), p. 234; in *Complete Works,* II, 223–34.

459. *An Inquiry into the Principles of Political Oeconomy* (1767), I, 4; in *Works,* ed. J. Steuart Denham (London, 1805), I–IV.

460. *Answers to M. des Vignolles' Dissertation upon Sir Isaac Newton's Chronology,* p. 323; in *Works,* VI, 319–58.

461. *Critical Remarks . . . upon . . . Mirabaud,* p. 68; in *Works,* VI, 43–82.

462. *Observations on Dr. Beattie's Essay on . . . Truth,* p. 20; in *Works,* VI, 1–39.

463. *Ibid.*, I, 7–8.

464. *Ibid.*, p. 10; *vide ibid.*, pp. 10–64.

465. *Ibid.*, p. 3.

466. *IPPO,* I, 13.

467. *Ibid.*, p. 19.

468. *Ibid.*, p. 14.

469. *Ibid.*, pp. 11–12.

470. *Ibid.*, p. 11.

471. *CRM,* pp. 68–69.

472. *IPPO,* I, 23.

473. *Ibid.*, p. 31; *vide ibid.*, 1. 3–5.

474. Desiderius Erasmus (d. 1536), *Enchiridion,* 4; in *Opera omnia,* ed. J. Le Clerc (Leyden, 1703–6), Vol. V, cols. 1–66; tr. Anonymous (London, 1905); *vide Moriae encomium* (1511); in Opera, IV, cols. 381 ff.

475. *A Letter from Rome* (1729), p. 8; in *Miscellaneous Works* (London, 1752), III, 1–132.

476. *Ibid.*, p. 119.

477. *Some Remarks on a Reply to the Defence of the Letter to Dr. Waterland* (1732), p. 295; in *Misc. Works,* II, 243–96.

478. *A Defence of the Letter to Dr. Waterland* (1731), pp. 213–14; in *Misc. Works,* II, 179–241; *vide ibid.*, pp. 192–96, 210–16, 224–37; *A Letter to Dr. Waterland* (1731), pp. 151–57; in Misc. Works, II, 135–77.

479. *SRR DLW,* p. 295.

480. *LW,* p. 164; for qualification, *vide SRR DLW,* pp. 287–88.

481. *DLW,* p. 203; *vide ibid.*, pp. 209–10.

482. *SRR DLW,* p. 287; *vide DLW,* p. 189; "Essay on the allegorical and literal interpretation of the creation and the fall of man," pp. 125–27; in *Misc. Works,* II, 121–34.

483. *LW,* p. 162.

484. *DLW,* pp. 238–39; *vide ibid,* pp. 239–40; *LW,* pp. 160–62.

485. *A Free Inquiry into the Miraculous Powers* (1749), pp. 1–2; in *Misc. Works,* I, i–188.

486. *Ibid.*, p. 21; *vide ibid.*, pp. 17–22.

487. *Ibid.*, p. 22; *vide ibid.*, pp. 176–79.

488. *Ibid.*, pp. 23–46.

489. *Ibid.*, pp. 46–47; *vide ibid.*, pp. 22–58.

490. *Ibid.*, p. 186.

491. *Ibid.*, pp. 57–58; *vide ibid.*, pp. 68–71, 172, 179–81.

492. *Ibid.*, pp. 58–154.

493. *An Introductory Discourse* (1747), p. lxi; in *Misc. Works,* I, xxvii–xcv; for qualification, *vide ibid.*, p. lxii; "A preface to an intended answer to all the objections made against the Free Inquiry," p. 382; in *Misc. Works,* I, 371–83.

494. *FIMP,* pp. 186–87.

495. *Vide ID,* pp. lxxxvi–lxxxvii; *FIMP,* pp. xxv–xxvi, 156.

496. "Reflections on the variations, or inconsistencies, which are found among the four evangelists in their different accounts of the same facts," pp. 74–75; in *Misc. Works,* II, 21–75.

497. *Autobiographies,* ed. J. Murray (2d ed.; London, 1897), p. 57 : cf. *ibid.,* pp. 121–224.

498. *Ibid.,* p. 59; cf. *ibid.,* p. 122.

499. *Essai sur l'étude de la littérature* (1761), 47; in *Miscellaneous Works,* IV, 1–93; tr. Anomymous (London, 1764).

500. *Ibid.,* 58.

501. *Critical Observations on the Design of the Sixth Book of the "Aeneid"* (1770), p. 483; in *Misc. Works,* IV, 467–514.

502. [Reference omitted from ms.]

503. "An examination f Mallet's *Introduction to the History of Denmark"* (1764), p. 231; in *Misc. Works,* III, 231–38.

504. *Vide A Vindication of Some Passages in the XVth and XVIth Chapters of the History of the Decline and Fall of the Roman Empire* (1779), *Misc. Works,* IV, 515–648.

505. *HDFR E,* II, 32.

506. *A,* p. 311.

507. *Vide* esp. *HDFRE,* II, 69–70.

508. *A History of the Decline and Fall of the Roman Empire* (1776–88), ed. J. B. Bury (9th ed., London, 1925), II, 2; *vide ibid.,* pp. 2–54.

509. "Remarks on Blackstone's *Commentaries"* (1770), p. 546; in *Misc. Works,* V, 545–47.

510. *HDFR E,* II, 122.

511. *E EL,* 11.

512. *Ibid.,* p. 81.

513. *Ibid.,* 48.

514. *Ibid.,* 49.

515. *E EL,* 54–55.

516. *Ibid.,* 79–80.

517. *HDFR E,* III, 186.

518. *Ibid.,* I, 56; *vide ibid.,* pp. 56–58.

519. *Ibid.,* pp. 193–94.

520. *Ibid.,* IV, 166.

521. *Ibid.,* III, 186–87.

522. *Ibid.,* III, 480.

523. *Ibid.,* IV, 161–62.

524. *A (ca.* 1789), p. 285.

525. *Ibid.,* p. 62; *vide ibid.,* pp. 162–63.

526. *Ibid.,* VI, 108–9.

527. *Ibid.,* p. 107.

528. "An address, [etc.]" (1793), pp. 559–60; in *Misc. Works,* III, 559–612.

529. "Index expurgatorius" *(ca.* 1768), pp. 568–69; in *Misc. Works,* V, 548–79.

530. *A,* p. 118.

531. "Letter on the government of Berne," pp. 5–6; in *Misc. Works,* II, 1–32.

532. *Antiquities of the House of Brunswick* (1790), p. 368; in *Misc. Works,* III, 351–558.

533. *E EL,* 66–78; *A,* pp. 173–74.

534. *HDFR E,* IV, 168.

535. *Ibid.,* p. 168 n.

536. *HDFR E,* IV, 167 n.

537. *Ibid.,* pp. 167–69.

538. *The Dissonance of the Four Generally Received Evangelists* (1792) (2d ed.; Gloucester, 1805), p. 18.

539. *Christianity as Old as the Creation* (1730) (London, 1731), pp. 7–8.

540. *Ibid.,* p. 4.

541. *Ibid.,* p. 11.

542. *Ibid.,* p. 52; *vide ibid.,* pp. 5–6.

543. *Ibid.,* p. 2.

544. *Ibid.,* p. 50.

545. *Ibid.,* p. 371.

546. *Ibid.,* 41.

547. *Commentaries on the Laws of England* (1765–69), ed. T. M. Cooley and J. D. Andrews (Chicago, 1899), 39–40.

548. *Ibid.*, I, 43.
549. *Ibid.*, 47–48.
550. *Ibid.*, II, 2–15.
551. *Discours sur l'origine et les fondements de l'inégalité parmi les hommes* (1755), p. 134; in *Political Writings*, ed. C. E. Vaughan (Cambridge, 1915), I, 118–220; tr. Anonymous (New York, n.d.)
552. *Ibid.*, p. 194.
553. *Contrat social* (1762), 3. 8; in *Pol. Writ.*, II, 1–134; tr. Anonymous (New York, n.d.)
554. *Ibid.*, 2. 3.
555. *Emile* (1762), p. 242; in *Œuvres completes* (Paris, 1909–12), II; tr. B. Foxley (London, 1911).
556. *Si le rétablissment des sciences et des arts a contribué a épurer les mœurs* (1750), p. 6; in *Œuvres complète*, I, 1–20; tr. Anonymous (New York, n.d.). *Vide ibid.*, pp. 13–14; DOFIH, pp. 202, 206.
557. *De l'économie politique* (1755), p. 251; in *Pol. Writ.*, I, 228–80; tr. Anonymous (New York, n.d.).
558. *SRSACEM*, p. 3.
559. *DOFIH*, p. 136; cf. *CS*, 1. 4.
560. *DOFIH*, p. 140.
561. *Idem.*
562. *Ibid.*, p. 166.
563. *Ibid.*, p. 135.
564. *Ibid.*, p. 141.
565. *Ibid.*, pp. 142–43.
566. *Ibid.*, p. 186.
567. *E*, p. 4.
568. *Ibid.*, p. 24.
569. *Ibid.*, p. 30.
570. *Ibid.*, p. 34.
571. *Ibid.*, p. 44.
572. *Ibid.*, p. 45.
573. *DOFIH*, pp. 148–51.
574. *Ibid.*, p. 159.
575. *Ibid.*, p. 158.
576. *Ibid.*, pp. 159–63, 174–**75.**
577. *Ibid.*, p. 138.
578. *Ibid.*, p. 217.
579. *E*, p. 193.
580. Cf. *ibid.*, pp. 160–61.
581. *Ibid.*, pp. 161–63.
582. *DOFIH*, p. 154.
583. *Ibid.*, pp. 165–66.
584. *Ibid.*, p. 168.
585. *Ibid.*, pp. 155–56.
586. *Ibid.*, p. 153.
587. *E*, p. 77.
588. *CS*, 1. 2.
589. *E*, p. 104.
590. *Ibid.*, p. 227.
591. *EP*, pp. 244–45.
592. *DOFIH*, pp. 169–84.
593. *CS*, 1. 6.
594. *DOFIH*, p. 188; cf. *CS*, 1. 1. On the different forms of government, *vide DOFIH*, pp. 189–90; *CS*, 3. 2–7.
595. *CS*, 2. 6.
596. *Ibid.*, 1. 8.
597. *DOFIH*, p. 196.
598. *EP*, p. 238.
599. *CS*, 2. 8.
600. *Ibid.*, 3. 11.
601. *Ibid.*, 2. 10.
602. *Ibid.*, 3. 10.
603. *Ibid.*, 3. 11.
604. *Ibid.*, 3. 9.

605. *DOFIH,* pp. 166–67.

606. *Ibid.,* pp. 165–66.

607. *CS,* 3. 8; *vide ibid.,* 2. 11; 3. 15.

608. *Rights of Man* (1791–92), I, 67; in *Life and Works,* ed. W. M. Van der Weyde (New Rochelle, 1925), VI–VII, 1–114.

609. *Ibid.,* I, 70.

610. *Ibid.,* p. 240.

611. *Ibid.,* p. 242.

612. *Ibid.,* p. 239.

613. *Ibid.,* p. 74.

614. *Ibid.,* p. 247.

615. *Common Sense* (1776), p. 150; in *Life and Works,* II, 92–82.

616. *Ibid.,* pp. 97–101.

617. *Ibid.,* pp. 107–8.

618. *RM,* I, 250.

619. *Ibid.,* pp. 114–16.

620. *RM,* I, 265.

621. *Staatswirthschaft* (1755) (2d ed.; Leipzig, 1758), I, xi; tr. A. W. Small (Chicago, 1909).

622. "Abhandlung von den Mitterln, die Erkenntniss in denen Oeconomischen und Camberalwissen-schaften dem gemeinen Wesen recht nützlich zu machen," p. 223; in *Gesammlete Politische und Finanz-schriften* (Copenhagen and Leipzig, 1761–64), III, 219–48; tr. A. W. Small (Chicago, 1909).

623. *S,* I, xix–xx; *vide ibid.,* 1. 21–22, 26–30.

624. "Abhandlung von dem Wesen des Adels, und dessen Verhältniss gegenden Staat, und insonder-heit gegen die Commercien," p. 147; in *Ges. Pol. Fin.,* I, 147–92.

625. *S,* I, xxxi.

626. *Ibid.,* 1. 75.

627. *Die Natur und das Wesen der Staaten* (Berlin, 1760), 1. 1.

628. *Ibid.,* 1. 3.

629. *Ibid.*

630. *Ibid.,* 1. 2.

631. *Ibid.,* 1. 3.

632. *Ibid.,* 1. 4.

633. *Ibid.,* 1. 5.

634. *Ibid.,* 1. 6.

635. *S,* 1. 5; *vide NWS,* 1. 7–18.

636. *NWS,* 1. 4.

637. *Grundsätze der Polizey, Handlung, und Finanz* (1765) (5th ed., Vienna, 1787), 1. 1.

638. *Ibid.,* 1. 1 n.

639. *Ibid.,* 1. 26.

640. *Ibid.,* 1. 2.

641. *Ibid.,* 1. 27.

642. *The History of the Corruptions of Christianity* (1782), p. 489; in *Theological and Miscellaneous Works,* ed. J. T. Rutt (London, 1817–32), V.

643. *Ibid.,* p. 483.

644. *Course of Lectures on the Theory of Language, and Universal Grammar* (1762), p. 121; in *Theol. Misc. Works,* XXIII, 119–252.

645. *Theol. Misc. Works,* XXIV.

646. *Ibid.,* p. 26.

647. *Ibid.,* p. 27; *vide ibid.,* pp. 27–54.

648. *Ibid.,* p. 34.

649. *Ibid.,* p. 35.

650. *Idem.*

651. *Ibid.,* p. 34.

652. *Ibid.,* p. 36.

653. *Ibid.,* p. 208.

654. *Idem.*

655. *Ibid.,* p. 338.

656. *Ibid.,* p. 54; *vide ibid.,* pp. 54–98.

657. *Ibid.,* p. 55.

658. *HCC,* p. 481.

659. *Ibid.,* p. 8.

660.  *Ibid.,* p. 482.
661.  *Ibid.,* p. 63.
662.  *L HGP,* p. 77.
663.  *Idem; vide ibid.,* pp. 77–81.
664.  *Ibid.,* p. 82; *vide ibid.,* pp. 82–84.
665.  *Ibid.,* p. 299.
666.  *Ibid.,* pp. 402–3.
667.  *Ibid.,* p. 99; *vide ibid.,* pp. 98–127.
668.  *Ibid.,* pp. 100–101.
669.  *Ibid.,* p. 111.
670.  *Ibid.,* pp. 127–200.
671.  *Ibid.,* pp. 220–85, 403–15.
672.  *Ibid.,* pp. 285–300.
673.  *Ibid.,* pp. 300–403.
674.  *Ibid.,* p. 313.
675.  *CLTLUG,* p. 145; *vide ibid.,* pp. 145–51.
676.  *Ibid.,* p. 129.
677.  *Ibid.,* p. 131.
678.  *Leçons d'histoire* (1795), pp. 58–60; in *Œuvres* (2d ed.; Paris, 1825–26), VII, 1–135; tr. Anonymous (London, 1818).
679.  *Les ruines* (1791), pp. 26–27; *vide ibid.,* 3; in *Œuvres,* I, 1–243; tr. J. Barlow (New York, 1890).
680.  *Ibid.,* p. 28.
681.  *La loi naturelle* (1793), p. 260; in *Œuvres,* I, 245–307; tr. J. Barlow (New York, 1890).
682.  *LN,* pp. 263–66; *vide ibid.,* 4.
683.  *Ibid.,* p. 293.
684.  *R,* p. 159.
685.  *Ibid.,* p. 161.
686.  "Response au docteur Priestley" (1799), p. 361; in *Œuvres,* I, 353–70.
687.  *L H,* p. 133.
688.  *Tableau du climat et du sol des Etats-Unis* (1803), p. 413; in *Œuvres completes,* ed. A. Bossange (Paris, 1821), VII; tr. C. B. Brown (Philadelphia, 1804).
689.  *R,* p. 20.
690.  *Ibid.,* 6–11, 22.
691.  *Ibid.,* p. 36.
692.  *Ibid.,* pp. 56–57.
693.  *Ibid.,* p. 78.
694.  *Ibid.,* p. 82.
695.  *Recherches nouvelles sur l'histoire anciennce,* I, 61–240; in *Œuvres complètes,* ed. A. Bossange (Paris, 1821), IV–V; tr. W. Corbet (London, 1819).
696.  *TCS EU,* p. 456.
697.  *Ibid.,* pp. 468–69.
698.  *Questions de statistique a l'usage des voyages, Œeuvres,* VII, 375–96.
699.  Ed. H. Higgs (London, 1931).
700.  *Ibid.,* pp. 86, 90; *vide ibid.,* 1. 15.
701.  *An Estimate of the Comparative Strength of Great-Britain* (1782) (rev. ed.; London, 1802), pp. 1–2.
702.  "Observations concerning the increase of mankind and the peopling of countries" (1751), pp. 223–25; in *Works,* II, 223–34.
703.  *Ibid.,* p. 225.
704.  *Ibid.,* p. 231.
705.  *A Dissertation on the Numbers of Mankind* (1753) (2d. ed.; Edinburgh, 1809), pp. 12–13; *vide ibid.,* pp. 15–20.
706.  *Ibid.,* p. 15.
707.  *Ibid.,* p. 24; *vide ibid.,* pp. 31–32, 162–63, 334–38.
708.  *An Essay on the Principle of Population* (1798), ed. G. T. Bettany (London, 1890), p. 2.
709.  *Idem.*
710.  *Ibid.,* p. 3.
711.  *Ibid.,* p. 127.
712.  *Ibid.,* pp. 4, 6.
713.  *Ibid.,* p. 14; *vide ibid.,* pp. 295–96.
714.  *Ibid.,* pp. 7–9.
715.  *Ibid.,* p. 296.

716.  *Ibid.*, pp. 293–94.
717.  *Ibid.*, p. xxxvii.
718.  *Physico-Theology* (1713) (London, 1798), I, 264–67.
719.  *Die göttliche Ordnung* (1741), ed. C. J. Baumann (4th ed.; Berlin, 1775–76), 12.


## NOTES TO CHAPTER VI

1.  *The Battle of the Books* (1704), p. 181; in *Prose Works,* ed. T. Scott (London, 1902–11), I, 155–87.
2.  *Two Letters on the Savage State* (London, 1792), pp. xii–xiii.
3.  *Ibid.*, pp. viii–ix.
4.  *Ibid.*, p. 48.
5.  *Ibid.*, p. 40; *vide ibid.*, pp. 40–47.
6.  *Ibid.*, pp. 151–52.
7.  *Ibid.*, pp. 92–93.
8.  *Ibid.*, p. 154.
9.  *Ibid.*, p. 121.
10.  "Mythology," 2–5, 7–8; in *Encyclopaedia Britannica* (3d ed., Edinburgh, 1797), XII, 599–609.
11.  "A discourse upon comedy" (1702), p. 330; in *Complete Works,* ed. C. Stonehill (Bloomsbury, 1930), II, 326–43.
12.  *The Advancement and Reformation of Modern Poetry* (1701), 1. 1–15; in *Critical Works,* ed. E. N. Hooker (Baltimore, 1939—), I, 197–278.
13.  *Reflections . . . upon . . . an Essay upon Criticism* (1711), p. 407; in *Crit. Works,* I, 396–419.
14.  *Plan de deux discours sur l'histoire universelle* (*ca.* 1751), p. 313; in *Œuvres,* ed. G. Schelle (Paris, 1913–23), I, 275–323; tr. M. DeGrange, Hanover, N.H., 1929.
15.  *Ibid.*, pp. 315–16.
16.  *Tableau philosophique des progres successifs de l'esprit humain* (1750), p. 231; in *Œuvres,* I, 214–35; tr. M. De Grange, Hanover, N.H., 1929.
17.  *Ibid.*, p. 223.
18.  *Ibid.*, pp. 214–19.
19.  *Oeuvres,* II, 533–601.
20.  *Ibid.*, 53; tr. Anonymous (New York, 1898).
21.  *Ibid.*, 54.
22.  *Ibid.*, 2.
23.  *Ibid.*, 3.
24.  *Ibid.*, 4.
25.  *Ibid.*, 9.
26.  *Ibid.*, 21.
27.  *Ibid.*, 10; *vide ibid.*, 11–13.
28.  *Tableau,* pp. 220–21.
29.  *Ibid.*, p. 236; tr. J. S. Schapiro (New York, 1934).
30.  *Sur l'instruction publique* (1791–92), p. 183; in *Œuvres,* VII, 167–437.
31.  *Rapport et projet de décret sur l'organisation générale de l'instruction publique* (1792), p. 450; in *Œuvres,* VII, 449–573; tr. F. de la Fontainerie (New York, 1932).
32.  *Ibid.*, p. 475.
33.  *Equisse d'un tableau historique des progrès de l'esprit humain* (1793–94), pp. 11–13; in *Œuvres,* ed. A. Condorcet O'Connor and M. F. Arago (2d ed.; Paris, 1847–49), VI; tr. Anonymous (Baltimore, 1802).
34.  *Ibid.*, p. 24.
35.  *Equisse,* pp. 25–30; *vide ibid.*, pp. 289–381.
36.  *Ibid.*, pp. 31–37.
37.  *Ibid.*, pp. 39–41, 43; *vide ibid.*, pp. 39–59.
38.  *Ibid.*, p. 60; *vide ibid.*, pp. 60–78, 383–471.
39.  *Ibid.*, p. 79; *vide ibid.*, pp. 79–108, 473–513.
40.  *Ibid.*, p. 109; *vide ibid.*, pp. 109–24.
41.  *Ibid.*, p. 125; *vide ibid.*, pp. 125–37.
42.  *Ibid.*, p. 138; *vide ibid.*, pp. 138–70.
43.  *Ibid.*, p. 171; *vide ibid.*, pp. 171–235.
44.  *Ibid.*, p. 236; *vide ibid.*, pp. 236–76, 515–96.
45.  *The Divine Legation of Moses Demonstrated* (1738–41), I, 203; in *Works* (London, 1811), I–VI.
46.  *Ibid.*, I, 203–05.
47.  *Ibid.*, IV, 133; *vide ibid.*, pp. 133–40.

48. *Ibid.*, pp. 116–17; *vide ibid.*, 4. 4. 1.
49. *Ibid.*, p. 120; *vide ibid.*, 4. 4. 2.
50. *Ibid.*, p. 123; *vide ibid.*, pp. 123–30.
51. *Ibid.*, p. 130.
52. *Ibid.*, p. 131.
53. *La logique* (1780), p. 8; in *Œuvres* (Paris, 1798), XXII; tr. J. Neef (Philadelphia, 1809).
54. *Ibid.*, pp. 110–15; *vide Histoire ancienne* (1775), 3. 27; in *Œuvres*, IX–XIV.
55. *Essai sur l'origine des connoissances humaines* (1746), 2. 1. intr.; in *Œuvres*, I; tr. T. Nugent (London, 1756).
56. *Ibid.*, 2. 1. 1. 1; *vide ibid.*, 1. 2. 4. 36.
57. *Ibid.*, 2. 1. 1. 2–9; *vide ibid.*, 2. 1. 2–3, 9–12.
58. *Ibid.*, 1. 2. 4. 40.
59. *Ibid.*, 1. 2. 4. 43.
60. *Ibid.*, 1. 2. 4. title; *vide idem.*
61. *Ibid.*, 1. 4. 1. 6.
62. *Ibid.*, 1. 2. 3. 34.
63. *Ibid.*, 1. 2. 4. 35.
64. *Ibid.*, 1. 4. 1. title.
65. *Ibid.*, 1. 4. 1. 9.
66. *Traité des sensations* (1754), 4. 6. 4; in *Œuvres*, III, pp. 1–440; tr. G. Carr (Los Angeles, 1930).
67. *Ibid.*, 1. 4. 1. 1. introd.
68. *Ibid.*, 1. 4. 1. 1.
69. *Ibid.*, 1. 4. 1. 5.
70. *EOCH*, 1. 4. 1. 6.
71. *Ibid.*, 1. 4. 1. 11.
72. *L*, pp. 118–21.
73. *EOCH*, 3. 9–10.
74. *Ibid.*, 1. 11; 2. 1. 8, 14
75. *Ibid.*, 2. 1. 5.
76. *Ibid.*, 2. 1. 1 .10–12.
77. *Ibid.*, 2. 1. 4.
78. *Ibid.*, 1. 8, 12; *TS*, 4. 4.
79. *EOCH*, 2. 1. 13 (after Warburton).
80. *HA*, 1. 1–7; "De lois," in *HA*, II, 386–526.
81. *EOCH*, 2. 1. 15. 145.
82. *Idem.*
83. *Ibid.*, 2. 1. 15. 142.
84. *Ibid.*, 2. 1. 15. 143.
85. *Ibid.*, 2. 1. 15. 143; *vide ibid.*, 2. 1. 15. 146–50.
86. *Ibid.*, 2. 1. 15. 151–52.
87. Monboddo, *Origin and Progress of Language*, I, 469–70.
88. *Hermes* (1751), pp. 407–08; *vide ibid.*, 3. 5; in *Works*, ed. Earl of Malmesbury (London, 1803), II.
89. *Ibid.*, p. 1.
90. *Ibid.*, p. 329.
91. *Voyages dans l'Amérique septentrionale* (1786) (2d ed.; Paris, 1788–91), II, 142; tr. G. Grieve (London, 1787).
92. *Ibid.*, p. 264.
93. *Ibid.*, pp. 138–39.
94. *Ibid.*, pp. 134–35; cf. *ibid.*, pp. 135–42, 264–65.
95. *Ibid.*, p. 174.
96. *Ibid.*, p. 264.
97. *Ibid.*, p. 145.
98. *Ibid.*, p. 147.
99. *De la félicité publique* (1772) (New ed.; Paris, 1822) I, 22; tr. Anonymous (London, 1774).
100. *Ibid.*, I, 26.
101. *Ibid.*, p. 56.
102. *Ibid.*, p. 23.
103. *VAS*, II, 281.
104. *Ibid.*, I, 385.
105. *FP*, II, 223.
106. *Ibid.*, I, 162.

107.  *VAS*, II, 275–76.

108.  *FP*, II, 86.

109.  *Ibid.*, pp. 109.

110.  *Ibid.*, pp. 70–71; cf. *ibid.*, pp. 81, 120.

111.  *Ibid.*, pp. 120–21.

112.  *Ibid.*, p. 181.

113.  *Ibid.*, pp. 181–87.

114.  *Die Erziehung des Menschengeschlechts* (1780), 1–3; in *Werke,* ed. K. Lachmann and F. Muncker (3d ed.; Stuttgart, 1886–1924), XIII, 413–36; tr. F. W. Robertson (3d ed.; London, 1881).

115.  *Ibid.*, 82–84.

116.  *Zum ewigen Frieden* (1795), pp. 348–49; in *Gesammelte Schriften,* VIII, 341–86; tr. W. Hastie (Edinburgh, 1891).

117.  *Über den Gemeinspruch: Das mag in der Theorie richtig sein, taugt aber nicht für die Praxis* (1793), p. 297; cf. pp. 289, 295, 299, 302; in *Ges. Schr.,* VIII, 273–313; tr. W. Hastie (Edinburgh, 1891).

118.  *Idee zu einer allgemeinen Geschichte in weltbürglicher Absicht* (1784), p. 17; in *Ges. Schr.,* VIII, 15–31; tr. W. Hastie (Edinburgh, 1891).

119.  *Ibid.*, p. 18.

120.  *Idem.*

121.  *Idem.*

122.  *Ibid.*, p. 19.

123.  *Ibid.*, p. 20.

124.  *Ibid.*, p. 22.

125.  *Ibid.*, p. 23.

126.  *Ibid.*, p. 24.

127.  *Ibid.*, p. 27.

128.  *Ibid.*, p. 29.

129.  *Ibid.*, p. 30.

130.  *Gemeinspruch,* pp. 308–9; cf. *ibid.*, pp. 310–11; *Idee,* pp. 29–30.

131.  Black, *Art of History,* pp. 34–35.

132.  *Œuvres completes* (Paris, 1877–85), XI–XIII, 1–184.

133.  "Introduction de l'abrégé de l'histoire universelle" (1753), p. 51; in *Œuvres,* XXIV, 51–52.

134.  *Essai,* I, 157; tr. T. Smollet and W. F. Fleming (New York, 1901).

135.  *Œuvres,* XIV–XV, 1–142.

136.  *Ibid.*, I, 155; tr. Smollet and Fleming (New York, 1901).

137.  *Remarques pour servir de supplément a l'essai sur les mœurs et l'esprit des nations* (1763), p. 547; in *Œuvres.,* XXIV, 543–86.

138.  *Ibid.*, p. 548.

139.  *Remarques,* p. 573.

140.  "A M. de —, professeur en historie" (1753), p. 29; in *Œuvres.,* XXIV, 29–34.

141.  *Ibid.*, p. 551.

142.  *Ibid.*, p. 554.

143.  "Commentaire sur L'Esprit des lois" (1777), pp. 442–57; in *Œuvres,* XXX, 405–64.

144.  *Essai,* III, 178.

145.  S.v. "Histoire," p. 349, *Dictionnaire philosophique* (17—), III, 346–70; in *Œuvres,* XVII–XX; tr. Smollet and Fleming (New York, 1901).

146.  *Essai,* III, 182.

147.  "Letter to Frederick the Great, Oct. 1737," p. 322; in *Œuvres,* XXXIV, 320–34.

148.  S.v. "Ideé," p. 397, *DP,* III, 394–400.

149.  *Essai,* III, 169.

150.  S.v. "Liberté," *DP,* III, 580–82.

151.  *Essai,* II, 258.

152.  S.v. "Chaine ou génération des événements," p. 127, *DP,* II, 125–27.

153.  "Pöeme sur le désastre de Lisbonne" (1756), p. 472 n.; in *Œuvres,* IX, 465–80; tr. Smollet and Fleming (New York, 1901).

154.  S.v. "Lois," p. 614, *DP,* III.

155.  S.v. "Histoire," p. 354, *DP.*

156.  *Histoire de Charles XII* (1731), p. 132; in *Œuvres,* XVI, 111–368; tr. Smollet and Fleming (New York, 1901).

157.  *Idem.*

158.  S.v. "Histoire," p. 353, *DP.*

159.  *Essai,* I, 161.

160.   *Ibid.*, pp. 19–21.
161.   *Ibid.*, pp. 21–22.
162.   *Ibid.*, pp. 23–24.
163.   S.v. "Dieu," p. 357, *DP,* II; *vide Essai,* I, 10–15.
164.   *Essai,* I, 4.
165.   *Charles XII,* p. 133.
166.   "Was heisst und zu welchem Ende studiert man Universalgeschichte?" (1789), pp. 6–7; in *Samtliche Werke,* ed. E. von der Hellen (Stuttgart, 1904–5), X, pt. 1, pp. 1–19; tr. ed. C. J. Hempel (Philadelphia, 1861). For his description of primitive man, *vide* "Etwas über die ersten Menschengesellschaft nach dem Leitfaden der mosaischen Urkunde" (1790), *Sämt. Werke,* X, pt. 2, pp. 195–212.
167   "Was heisst," p. 18; *vide ibid.*, pp. 14–17.
168.   *Ibid.*, p. 18.
169.   *Ibid.*, p. 15.
170.   *Ibid.*, p. 29.
171.   *Ibid.*, p. 33.
172.   *Über die ästhetische Erziehung des Menschen* (1793–94), p. 92; in *Sämtliche Werke,* ed. E. von der Hellen (Stuttgart, 1904–5), XII, 3–120; tr. Anonymous (London, n.d.).
173.   *Ibid.*, pp. 117–18.
174.   "Moral attraction" (1713), pp. 186–89; in *Works,* ed. A. C. Fraser (Oxford, 1901), IV, 186–90.
175.   *Alciphron* (1732), p. 66; in *Works,* II, 1–368.
176.   *Ibid.*, p. 67.
177.   *Ibid.*, p. 129.
178.   *Ibid.*, p. 130.
179.   *Ibid.*, pp. 34–35.
180.   *Dei delitti e delle pene* (1764), ed. R. Palmarocchi (*Bibliotheca romanica,* 128–29) (Strassburg, n.d.), p. 70; tr. J. A. Farrer (London, 1880).
181.   *Ibid.*, pp. 99–100.
182.   *Ibid.*, p. 97.
183.   *Ibid.*, p. 70.
184.   *Ibid.*, p. 22.
185.   *Ibid.*, p. 19.
186.   *Ibid.*, pp. 52–53.
187.   *Ibid.*, p. 70.
188.   "An Essay upon the Constitution of the Roman Government," pp. 99–100; in *Works,* ed. I. Sergeant (London, 1726), I, 1–148.
189.   *Ibid.*, p. 19.
190.   *Ibid.*, p. 63.
191.   *Ibid.*, pp. 71–73; cf. *ibid.*, pp. 80–81, 83.
192.   *Ibid.*, p. 100.
193.   *Ibid.*, p. 133; *vide ibid.*, pp. 133–48.
194.   *Op. cit.*, pp. 55–56; *vide ibid.*, pp. 57–64.
195.   *Ibid.*, p. 132.
196.   *Essai politique sur le commerce* (Amsterdam, 1735), p. 28; tr. D. Bindon (Dublin, 1738).
197.   *Ibid.*, p. 103.
198.   *Ibid.*, p. 109.
199.   *Ibid.*, p. 9.
200.   *Ibid.*, p. 43.
201.   *Money and Trade* (1705), pp. 4–10; in *Œuvres complètes,* ed. P. Harsin (Paris, 1934), I, 2–165.
202.   *Ibid.*, p. 152.
203.   *An Essay upon Money and Coins* (London, 1757–58), I, 15.
204.   *Ibid.*, I, 31.
205.   *Ibid.*, pp. 34–36.

## NOTES TO CHAPTER VII

1.   *Emile,* p. 430.
2.   *Considérations sur les causes de la grandeur des romains et de leur décadence* (1734), p. 118; in *Œuvres complètes,* ed. E. Laboulaye (Paris, 1875–79), II, 101–326; tr. Anonymous (3d ed.; London, 1759).
3.   *Ibid.*, p. 273.
4.   *De l'esprit de lois* (1748), pref.; in *Œuvres,* III–VI; tr. T. Nugent (Cincinnati, 1873).
5.   *Ibid.*, 1. 1.

6. *Ibid.*, 1. 2.
7. *Ibid.*, 1. 3.
8. *Idem.*
9. *Ibid.*, 2–7.
10. *Ibid.*, 9.
11. *Ibid.*, 10.
12. *Ibid.*, 11.
13. *Ibid.*, 12.
14. *Ibid.*, 13.
15. *Ibid.*, 14–17.
16. *Ibid.*, 14. 2.
17. *Ibid.*, 14. 10.
18. *Ibid.*, 18.
19. *Ibid.*, 18. 1.
20. *Ibid.*, 18 : 4.
21. *Ibid.*, 18. 8.
22. *Ibid.*, 18. 10.
23. *Ibid.*, 18. 11.
24. *Ibid.*, 19.
25. *Ibid.*, 19. 27.
26. *Ibid.*, 19. 4.
27. *Ibid.*, avert.
28. *Ibid.*, 19. 14.
29. *Considerations*, p. 117.
30. *EL*, pref.
31. *Considerations*, p. 218.
32. *EL*, 20–21.
33. *Ibid.*, 20. 1.
34. *Ibid.*, 22.
35. *Considerations*, pp. 183–84.
36. *EL*, 23.
37. *Ibid.*, 24–25.
38. *Considerations*, pp. 116–117.
39. *Ibid.*, p. 189.
40. *Ibid.*, pp. 191–92.
41. *EL*, 3. 3.
42. *Remarks on the Influence of Climate* (London, 1781), pp. 1–2.
43. *Ibid.*, pp. iv–vi.
44. *Ibid.*, p. 257.
45. *Ibid.*, p. 258; *vide ibid.*, 6. 1.
46. *Ibid.*, pp. 321–22; *vide ibid.*, 6. 2.
47. *Ibid.*, p. 352; *vide ibid.*, 6. 3.
48. *Ibid.*, p. 404; *vide ibid.*, 6. 4.
49. *An Estimate of the Manners and Principles of the Times* (1757) (6th ed.; London, 1757–58), I, 3.
50. *Ibid.*, I, 11–12.
51. *Ibid.*, p. 13.
52. *Ibid.*, pp. 209–10.
53. *Ibid.*, pp. 213–15.
54. *Thoughts on Civil Liberty* (Newcastle, 1765), p. 9.
55. *A Dissertation on . . Poetry and Music* (London, 1763), p. 241.
56. *TCL*, p. 108.
57. *Ibid.*, p. 113; *vide ibid.*, pp. 108–13.
58. *DPM*, p. 54; *The History of the Rise and Progress of Poetry* (Newcastle, 1764), p. 50.
59. *DPM*, p. 245; *HRPP*, p. 267.
60. *DPM*, p. 25.
61. "Letter to David Garrick, Oct. 6, 1761," p. 132; in *The Private Correspondence of David Garrick*, ed. J. Boaden (London, 1831–32), I, 131–32.
62. *DPM*, p. 26; *vide HRPP*, pp. 9–10.
63. *DPM*, pp. 27–28; *vide HRPP*, pp. 11–12.
64. *HRPP*, pp. 24–38; *DPM*, pp. 36–49.
65. *DPM*, pp. 138–41; *vide HRPP*, pp. 164–69.

66.  *HRPP*, pp. 190–91.

67.  *HRPP*, pp. 196–97; cf. *DPM*, p. 155.

68.  *DPM*, p. 56; *HRPP*, p. 53.

69.  *DPM*, p. 50; *HRPP*, p. 44.

70.  *DPM*, p. 54; *HRPP*, p. 51.

71.  *DPM*, pp. 106–7; cf. *HRPP*, pp. 107–8.

72.  *Geschichte der Kunst der Alterthums* (1764), I, i; in *Werke*, ed. K. L. Fernow *et al.* (Dresden, 1808–20), III–VI; tr. G. H. Lodge (Boston, 1849–73).

73.  *Ibid.*, 1. 1. 4.

74.  *Ibid.*, 1. 1. 1.

75.  *Ibid.*, 1. 1. 4.

76.  *Ibid.*, 1. 1. 5–6.

77.  *Ibid.*, 4. 1. 4.

78.  *Recherches philosophiques sur les Egyptiens et les Chinois* (1774), I, v; in *Œuvres philosophiques* (Paris, 1795), IV–V; tr. J. Thomson (London, 1795).

79.  *Recherches philosophiques sur les Grecs* (1788), I, 3; *vide ibid.*, I, 1; in *Œuvres*, VI–VII; tr. J. Thomson (London, 1793).

80.  *Ibid.*, I, i.

81.  *Histoire philosophique et politique des etablissemens et du commerce dans les deux indes* (1771) (New ed.; Paris, 1820), 1–2; tr. J. O. Justamond (London, 1783).

82.  *Ibid.*, I, 4.

83.  *Ibid.*, X, 253–54.

84.  *Ibid.*, pp. 1–2.

85.  *Ibid.*, p. 17.

86.  *Ibid.*, p. 19.

87.  *Ibid.*, p. 231.

88.  *Ideen über die Politik, den Verkehr, und den Handel der vornehmsten Völker der alten Welt* (1793–1812), II, pt. 1, p. 495; in *Historische Werke* (Göttingen, 1821–30), X–XV; tr. G. Bancroft *et al.* (London, 1846–50).

89.  *Handbuch der Geschichte des europäischen Staatensystems und seiner Colonieen* (1809), I, pt. 1, pp. vi–viii; in *Werke*, VIII–IX; tr. Bancroft *et al.* (London, 1846–50).

90.  *Ideen*, III, pt. 1, p. 57 [Refers to Heeren, n. 88, above].

91.  *Ibid.*, p. 318.

92.  *Ibid.*, p. 59.

93.  *vide* esp. "Griechen," in *ibid.*; *Entwickelung der politischen Folgen der Reformation für Europa* (1802), *Werke*, I, 1–104; "Etwas über die Folgen der Reformation für die Philosophie" (1817–19), *Werke*, I, 105–12.

94.  *Ideen*, III, pt. 1, p. 88 [Refers to Heeren, n. 88, above].

95.  *Ibid.*, p. 236.

96.  *Ibid.*, p. 349.

97.  *Ibid.*, p. 395.

98.  *EPFR E*, pp. 7–8.

99.  *Ideen*, I, pt. 1, p. 500.

100.  *Ibid.*, p. 71.

101.  *Ibid.*, II, pt. 1, p. 487; *vide ibid.*, pp. 462–64.

102.  *Ibid.*, I, pt. 1, p. 4.

103.  *Ibid.*, II, pt. 1, p. 305.

104.  *Ibid.*, p. 352.

105.  *Ibid.*, I, pt. 1, pp. 4–5.

106.  *Ibid.*, pp. 5–6; *vide ibid.*, pp. 4–18.

107.  *Ibid.*, I, pt. 1, pp. 3–4.

108.  *EPFR E*, p. 17.

109.  *Ideen*, III, pt. 1, p. 270 [Refers to Heeren, n. 88, above].

110.  *Ibid.*, p. 197.

111.  *Ibid.*, p. 19.

112.  *Ibid.*, III, pt. 1, pp. 270–71.

113.  *Ibid.*, pp. 4–7.

114.  *Vide* esp.: England: *Versuch einer historischen Entwickelung der Entstehung und des Wachstums der brittischen Continental-Interesse* pp. 115–16; in *Werke*, I, pp. 113–364. Africa: *Ideen*, II, pt. 1, pp. 11, 333. Egypt: *Ibid.*, pp. 95, 373–74. Greece: *Ibid.*, III, pt. 1, pp. 48–49.

115.  *Ibid.*, pp. 7–8.

116. *Ibid.,* II, pt. 1, p. 333.
117. *Ibid.,* I, pt. 1, pp. 58–59.
118. *Ibid.,* pt. 2, pp. 24–25.
119. *Ibid.,* pt. 1, p. 28.
120. *Ibid.,* p. 83.
121. *Uber die Enstehung, die Ausbildung und den praktischen Einfluss der politischen Theorien,* p. 410; in *Werke,* I, 365–451.
122. *Ideen,* II, pt. 1, p. 492 [Refers to Heeren, n. 88, above].
123. *The Theory of Moral Sentiments* (1759) (London, 1853), p. 321.
124. *The Wealth of Nations* (1776), ed. E. Cannan (New York, 1937), p. 14.
125. *Ibid.,* p. 508; *vide ibid.,* pp. 421, 423, 594–95.
126. *TMS,* p. 321.
127. *Ibid.,* pp. 322–23.
128. *Ibid.,* p. 328.
129. *Ibid.,* pp. 323–24.
130. *Ibid.,* p. 334; *vide ibid.,* 6. 2. 2.
131. *Ibid.,* p. 345; *vide ibid.,* 6. 2. 3.
132. *WN,* p. 14.
133. *Lectures* (1763), ed. E. Cannan (Oxford, 1896), pp. 73–74.
134. *TMS,* p. 124.
135. *Ibid.,* p. 170.
136. *Ibid.,* p. 56.
137. *Ibid.,* pp. 70–71, 80.
138. *Ibid.,* pp. 3–5.
139. *Ibid.,* p. 7.
140. *Ibid.,* pp. 391–92.
141. *Ibid.,* p. 448; *vide ibid.,* 7. 2.
142. *Ibid.,* p. 429.
143. *Ibid.,* pp. 479–80; *vide ibid.,* 7. 3.
144. *Ibid.,* pp. 161–64; *vide ibid.,* 2. 2. 2–3; 3. 2–3.
145. *Ibid.,* 3. 4.
146. *Ibid.,* p. 281; *vide ibid.,* 5. 1–2.
147. *Ibid.,* p. 224; *vide ibid.,* p. 290; cf. *ibid.,* p. 233.
148. *Ibid.,* pp. 290–91.
149. *Ibid.,* pp. 305–6.
150. *WN,* pp. 15–16; *vide L,* pp. 170–71, *WN,* pp. 734–735.
151. *Ibid.,* p. 292; *vide ibid.,* pp. 293–96.
152. *TMS,* pp. 296–97; *vide ibid.,* pp. 297–302.
153. *Ibid.,* p. 329.
154. *L,* pp. 155–56.
155. *Ibid.,* pp. 253–59; *vide WN,* pp. 127, 435, 734–36.
156. *Essays on Philosophical Subjects,* ed. J. Black and J. Hutton (London, 1795), pp. 1–129.
157. *WN,* pp. 13, 15; *L,* pp. 168–71.
158. *WN,* pp. 22–28.
159. "Considerations concerning the first formation of languages" (1761), in *TMS,* pp. 505–38.
160. *TMS.* pp. 73, 331–32; *WN,* 5. 1. 2; *L,* pp. 9–53, 148–49.
161. *Elements of the Criticism* (1762) (11th ed.; London, 1839), p. 76; *vide SHM,* IV, 53.
162. *Sketches of the History of Man* (1774) (Edinburgh, 1789), IV, 99.
163. *Ibid.,* pp. 101–2.
164. *SHM,* IV, 107.
165. *The Art of Thinking* (1761) (new ed.; Glasgow, 1819), p. 13; *vide SHM,* I, 64–65.
166. *EC,* p. 195; *vide Essays on the Principles of Morality and Natural Religion* (Edinburgh, 1751), p. 67; *Historical Law-Tracts* (Edinburgh, 1758), I, 124; *SHM,* 2. 1; I, 79 n.
167. *Essays on Several Subjects Concerning British Antiquities* (1747) (3d ed.; Edinburgh, 1763), p. 194.
168. *Ibid.,* p. 66.
169. *EC,* p. 81.
170. *Ibid.,* p. 78 n.; *vide ibid.,* p. 16.
171. *Ibid.,* p. 77; *vide ibid.,* p. 16 n.; cf. *SHM,* II, 190.
172. *EPMNR,* p. 87; *vide EC,* pp. 14–16; *SHM,* 3. 2. 1. 3–4.
173. *SHM,* I, p. 196; *vide AT,* p. 15; *EC,* 25; *SHM,* 3. 2. 1. 2; III, 223; IV, 53, 61.
174. *SHM,* IV, 128–29; *vide ibid.,* I, 196–97; IV, 1. 19; *EPMNR,* pp. 139–42.

175. *EPMNR*, p. 76; *vide EC*, p. 42.
176. *EPMNR*, p. 24.
177. *EC*, pp. 192–93; *vide ibid.*, 15.
178. *EC*, p. 195.
179. *EPMNR*, p. 25.
180. *EPMNR*, pp. 16–17; *vide EC*, pp. 195–97.
181. *AT*, p. 19; *vide EC*, 14.
182. *AT*, p. 19.
183. *Ibid.*, p. 89.
184. *SHM*, II, 158.
185. *Ibid.*, pp. 9–11.
186. *HLT*, I, 36–37; vide *SHM*, II, 71.
187. *SHM*, III, 158–59.
188. *Ibid.*, pp. 159–61.
189. *HLT*, I, v.
190. *Ibid.*, IV, 127.
191. *Ibid.*, p. 19; *vide ibid.*, p. 130.
192. *Ibid.*, III, 222.
193. *Ibid.*, II, 154; *vide EPMNR*, pp. 139–42.
194. *SHM*, I, 1.
195. *HLT*, I, 383–85.
196. *Ibid.*, p. vi.
197. *Ibid.*, 1. 1.
198. *Ibid.*, 1. 2.
199. *Ibid.*, 1. 3.
200. *Ibid.*, 1. 4. 1.
201. *Ibid.*, 1. 4. 2.
202. *Ibid.*, 1. 5.
203. *Ibid.*, 1. 6.
204. *Ibid.*, 1. 7.
205. *Ibid.*, 2. 1; *ESSCBA*, pp. 193–216.
206. *SHM*, 2. 2–3.
207. *Ibid.*, 2. 4–5.
208. *Ibid.*, 2. 7.
209. *Ibid.*, 2. 9.
210. *Ibid.*, 3. 1.
211. *Ibid.*, 3. 2.
212. *Ibid.*, 3. 3.
213. *SHM*, I, 315; but *vide ibid.*, I, 496–501.
214. *Ibid.*, III, 149.
215. *Ibid.*, p. 150; *vide ibid.*, III, 152, 158.
216. *Ibid.*, II, 155.
217. *Ibid.*, pp. 260–64.
218. *Ibid.*, pp. 269–70.
219. *Ibid.*, IV, 131–32.
220. *A Comparative View of the State and Faculties of Man with those of the Animal World* (1765) (6th ed.; London, 1774), I, pp. 6–7.
221. *Ibid.*, II, 98.
222. *Ibid.*, p. 151.
223. *Ibid.*, p. 102.
224. *Ibid.*, I, 27–28.
225. *Ibi.*, pp. 160–61.
226. *Ibid.*, p. 131.
277. *Ibid.*, II, 3.
228. *Ibid.*, I, 160.
229. *Ibid.*, p. 149.
230. *Ibid.*, p. 166.
231. *Ibid.*, p. 169; *vide ibid.*, I, 169–71.
232. *Ibid.*, pp. v–xxi.
233. *The History of America* (1777), II, 83–84; in *Works* (Chiswick, 1824), VIII–X.
234. *Ibid.*, I, 275.

235. *Ibid.*, pp. 299–300.
236. *Ibid.*, II, 25–26.
237. *Ibid.*, p. 101.
238. *Ibid.*, pp. 97–98; *vide The History of Scotland* (1759), I, 23; in *Works*, I–III; *HA*, I, 300, 311; II, 21–22, 98–99; esp. the geographic description of the New World: *ibid.*, I, 256–69.
239. *HA*, II, 98.
240. *Ibid.*, I, 261.
241. *Ibid.*, p. 263.
242. *Ibid.*, II, 101.
243. *Ibid.*, p. 100; *bide ibid.*, I, 300–2; *HS*, I, 23.
244. *The History of the Reign of the Emperor Charles V* (1769), I, 22; in Works, IV–VII; *vide ibid.*, I; *HS*, 1; *HA*, 1.
245. *HA*, II, 1.
246. *Ibid.*, pp. 13–14.
247. *Ibid.*, p. 15.
248. *Ibid.*, p. 16.
249. *Ibid.*, pp. 17–18.
250. *Ibid.*, p. 94.
251. *Ibid.*, I, 290.
252. *Ibid.*, p. 273.
253. *Ibid.*, p. 288.
254. *HR EC*, I, 12.
255. *HA*, I, 288–89.
256. *Ibid.*, 4.
257. "Letter to W. Robertson, 1777," pp. 202–3; in *Misc. Works*, II, 201–4.
258. *Principles of Moral and Political Science* (Edinburgh, 1792), I, 60.
259. *Ibid.*, p. 70; *vide ibid.*, pp. 52–53, 70–71, 122–23.
260. *Ibid.*, p. 256.
261. *Ibid.*, p. 231.
262. *Ibid.*, p. 28; *vide ibid.*, p. 239.
263. *Ibid.*, pp. 28–29.
264. *Ibid.*, p. 30.
265. *Ibid.*, p. 31.
266. *Ibid.*, 1, 1. 6.
267. *Ibid.*, II, 41.
268. *Institutes of Moral Philosophy* (1772) (New ed.; Basle, 1800), 2. 2. 2.
269. *Ibid.*, 1. 1. 6.
270. *An Essay on the History of Civil Society* (1767) (8th ed.; Philadelpha, 1819), p. 33.
271. *Ibid.*, I, 268–69; *vide ibid.*, I, 266–68.
272. *Ibid.*, II, 17.
273. *Ibid.*, 7. 1.
274. *Ibid.*, II, 59.
275. *Ibid.*, p. 329.
276. *PMPS*, II, 174.
277. *Ibid.*, I, 150; *vide IMP*, 6. 3.
278. *EHCS*, pp. 18–19; *vide ibid.*, pp. 93–94. Selfish: *ibid.*, 1 : 2; *PMPS*, I, 202, 244. Social: *EHCS*, 1. 3. 6; pp. 27, 393; *PMPS*, I, 124; II, 14–19.
279. *EHCS*, pp. 105–6; *vide ibid.*, 96–97.
280. *IMP*, 2. 3. 8.
281. *Ibid.*, 2. 3. 6.
282. *Ibid.*, 2. 3. 7.
283. *Ibid.*, p. 18.
284. *Ibid.*, p. 88; *vide PMPS*, I, 223–24.
285. *PMPS*, I, 221.
286. *Ibid.*, pp. 134–35.
287. *Ibid.*, pp. 213–14; *vide ibid.*, p. 223; II, 136–52.
288. *IMP*, 7. 1.
289. *IMP*, 1. 1. 8.
290. *EHCS*, p. 366; *vide ibid.*, p. 422; *PMPS*, I, 216–17; II, 151–52.
291. *EHCS*, pp. 46–47; *vide ibid.*, 4. 3; pp. 127, 320–22, 331, 340–42.
292. *PMPS*, I, p. 232.

292.  *EHCS*, p. 338.
294.  *Ibid.*, p. 312.
295.  *PMPS*, I, 201.
296.  *EHCS*, p. 25; *vide ibid.*, 3. 1.
297.  *Ibid.*, p. 177.
298.  *Ibid.*, pp. 304–6.
299.  *Ibid.*, p. 135.
300.  *Ibid.*, p. 137.
301.  *Ibid.*, p. 139.
302.  *Ibid.*, pp. 139–40.
303.  *Ibid.*, p. 141.
304.  *Ibid.*, pp. 146–47.
305.  For his criticisms of Hobbes and Rousseau, *vide PMPS*, I, 198–99; II, 205–6, 215–22.
306.  *EHCS*, p. 28; *vide PMPS*, I, 195–96.
307.  *Vide EHCS*, p. 303.
308.  *Ibid.*, pp. 1–15.
309.  *Ibid.*, 2. 2.
310.  *Ibid.*, 2. 3.
311.  *PMPS*, 1. 3. 11.
312.  *Ibid.*, 1. 2. 15.
313.  *EHCS*, 3. 7–8; *PMPS*, 1. 3. 12.
314.  *PMPS*, 1. 3. 9; *IMP*, 1. 1. 9.
315.  *EHCS*, 4. 1–2; pp. 272–74, 314, 331; *PMPS*, I, 244, 250, 293; II, 423–24.
316.  *PMPS*, 1. 1. 4.
317.  *EHCS*, 3. 2; p. 282; *PMPS*, 1. 3. 10; *IMP*, 1. 1. 10–11.
318.  *EHCS*, pp. 327–28.
319.  *Ibid.*, p. 222; *vide PMPS*, I, 215–22, 256–61; II, 245, 268–69, 462, 496.
320.  *EHCS*, p. 223.
321.  *Ibid.*, p. 229.
322.  *Ibid.*, p. 427.
323.  *Ibid.*, p. 14; *vide ibid.*, p. 53; *PMPS*, I, 198–99, 235, 249, 253, 281–82, 299, 302, 310, 313, 315.
324.  *PMPS*, I, 202; *vide ibid.*, I, 205–6, 282, 310, 313; *EHCS*, p. 197.
325.  *EHCS*, pp. 374–75; *vide ibid.*, p. 387.
326.  *Ibid.*, p. 403.
327.  *Ibid.*, p. 370.
328.  *Ibid.*, pp. 505–6.
329.  *Ibid.*, p. 419.
330.  *Ibid.*, p. 420.
331.  *Ibid.*, p. 421.
332.  *Ibid.*, p. 424.
333.  *PMPS*, II, 409.
334.  *Ibid.*, I, 253.
335.  *Ibid.*, pp. 256–58; *vide IMP*, 1. 1. 7.
336.  *Ibid.*, p. 405.
337.  *EHCS*, pp. 427–28.
338.  *Ibid.*, p. 378.
339.  *Idem.*
340.  *Ibid.*, pp. 378–79; *vide ibid.*, 5. 2–3; p. 429; *PMPS*, I, 94.
341.  *EHCS*, p. 462.
342.  *Ibid.*, p. 388.
343.  *Ibid.*, pp. 429–30.
344.  *Ibid.*, p. 392.
345.  *Ibid.*, p. 45; *vide ibid.*, 1. 4.
346.  *Ibid.*, p. 395.
347.  *Ibid.*, p. 505.
348.  *An Historical View of the English Government* (1787) (4th ed.; London, 1818), IV, 174.
349.  *Ibid.*, IV, 363.
350.  *The Origin of the Distinction of Ranks* (1771) (3d ed.; London, 1781), pp. 2–3.
351.  *Ibid.*, p. 9; *vide ibid.*, p. 9–12.
352.  *Ibid.*, pp. 12–14.
353.  *Ibid.*, 1–2.

354. *Ibid.,* 3–5.
355. *Ibid.,* 6.
356. *Ibid.,* p. 14.
357. *HV EG,* IV, 102–37.
358. *Ibid.,* pp. 138–61.
359. *Ibid.,* pp. 174–265.
360. *Ibid.,* pp. 266–310.
361. *Ibid.,* pp. 311–75.
362. *ODR,* p. 16.
363. *Ibid.,* p. 106.
364. *HVEG,* IV, 313.
365. *ODR,* pp. 3–8.
366. *A View of Society in Europe* (Dublin, 1778), pp. iii–iv.
367. *Ibid.,* p. 40.
368. *Ibid.,* p. 154.
369. *Ibid.,* pp. 58–59.
370. *Ibid.,* p. 136.
371. *Ibid.,* pp. 18–19.
372. *Ibid.,* pp. 41–42.
373. Quot.: J. Boswell, *Journal of a Tour to the Hebrides,* ed. F. A. Pottle and C. H. Bennett (New York, 1936), p. 55.
374. "Letter to James Harris, March 26, 1766," p. 50; in W. Knight, *Lord Monboddo* (London, 1900), pp. 48–50.
375. *Of the Origin and Progress of Language* (1773–92) (Edinburgh, 1774–92; I, III, 2d ed.; II, 1809 ed.), I, 144.
376. *Antient Metaphysics* (Edinburgh, 1779–99), III, 377.
377. *OPL,* I, 361.
378. *Idem.*
379. *Ibid.,* I, 146.
380. *Ibid.,* p. ii.
381. *Am,* III, 105.
382. *Ibid.,* IV, 25–34.
383. *Ibid.,* p. 54.
384. *OPL,* I, 361.
385. *Ibid.,* p. 269.
386. *Ibid.,* p. 152.
387. *Ibid.,* p. 237.
388. *Ibid.,* p. 253; *vide ibid.,* p. v.
389. *AM,* III, p. 206.
390. *vide OPL,* I, 390–91.
391. *Ibid.,* p. 359.
392. *AM,* V, 3–4.
393. *OPL,* I, 429; *vide ibid.,* pp. 2, 171–74, 184–85, 367, 433.
394. *Ibid.,* 426; *vide ibid.,* pp. 416–17, 420–21, 426–27, 677; *AM,* III, 52–57.
395. *Ibid.,* III, 26–27.
396. *OPL,* I, 367.
397. *Ibid.,* pp. 221–22; *vide ibid.,* pp. 223–35.
398. *AM,* IV, 58–59; *vide ibid.,* pp. 55–59.
399. *Ibid.,* 63; *vide OPL,* I, 240, 244, 246, 248, 445–54.
400. *AM,* III, 89; *vide ibid.,* IV, 45.
401. *Ibid.,* III, 94.
402. *AM,* IV, 35–36.
403. *AM,* III, 219; *vide OPL,* IV, 187.
404. *OPL,* I, 497.
405. *OPL,* I, 208.
406. *Ibid.,* pp. 208–9.
407. *AM,* IV, 61.
408. *Ibid.,* pp. 62–63.
409. *Vide OPL,* 2. 10.
410. *Vide ibid.,* 2. 8–9.
411. *Ibid.,* I, 405.

412. *Ibid.,* pp. 449–50; *vide ibid.,* pp. 450–55.
413. *AM,* IV, 176–77; *vide OPL,* I, 362–67, 442.
414. *AM,* V, 18; *vide ibid.,* IV, 43–44.
415. *Ibid.,* IV, 39–40; *vide OPL,* I, 393–95.
416. *AM,* IV, 64.
417. *OPL,* I, 5; *vide ibid.,* p. 8.
418. *Ibid.,* pp. 345–46.
419. *Ibid.,* pp. 456–59.
420. *OPL,* I, 12; *vide ibid.,* I; II, 176–77, 186–87; "Letter to John Pringle, June 16, 1772," p. 83; in Knight, *Lord Monoboddo,* pp. 82–88; *AM,* III, 40; IV, 41–42, 64, 106–27, 264–79.
421. *Ibid.,* p. 461; *vide ibid.,* 3. 2.
422. *Ibid.,* p. 475; *vide ibid.,* 3. 4–6.
423. *Ibid.,* pp. 256–57; *vide ibid.,* II, 5–6.
425. *AM,* IV, 128.
426. *Ibid.,* p. 136; *vide ibid.,* pp. 128–36; *OPL,* I, pp. 578–79, 586, 624–25, 660, 665.
427. *AM,* IV, 150.
428. *Ibid.,* p. 152; *vide ibid.,* pp. 150–72, 365–70, 374–78.
424. *Ibid.,* p. 175.
429. *OPL,* VI, iii–iv; *vide AM,* IV, 179–83.
430. *AM,* III, 28; cf. *ibid.,* pp. 68–69.
431. *OPL,* I, 438.
432. *Ibid.,* p. 437.
433. *AM,* III, 205.
434. *AM,* II, 157.
435. *Ibid.,* p. 206.
436. London, 1780.
437. *Ibid.,* p. 16.
438. *Ibid.,* pp. 3–6.
439. *Essays,* p. 17.
440. *Ibid.,* p. 26.
441. *Ibid.,* p. 30.
442. *Ibid.,* pp. 12–13.
443. *Ibid.,* p. 33.
444. *Ibid.,* p. 174; *vide ibid.,* pp. 172–81.
445. *Ibid.,* p. 405; *vide ibid.,* pp. 405–8, 411–15.
446. *Ibid.,* pp. 419–20; *vide ibid.,* pp. 420–21.
447. *Ibid.,* p. 425; *vide ibid.,* pp. 425–31.
448. *Ibid.,* p. 319; *vide ibid.,* pp. 319–22.
449. *Ibid.,* pp. 432–33.
456. *Ibid.,* pp. 351–52.
451. *Ibid.,* pp. 208–9.
452. *Ibid.,* p. 279.
453. *Ibid.,* p. 225.
454. *Ibid.,* pp. 207–8.
455. *Ibid.,* p. 303; *vide ibid.,* pp. 207–301.
456. *Ibid.,* p. 315.
457. *Ibid.,* p. 317.
458. *Ibid.,* p. 300.
459. *Ibid.,* p. 324; *vide ibid.,* pp. 325–28.
460. *Ibid.,* pp. 336–37; *vide ibid.,* pp. 337–46.
461. *Ibid.,* p. 342.
462. *Ibid.,* p. 300.
463. *Ibid.,* p. 14.
464. *Ibid.,* p. 26.
465. *Ibid.,* p. 119.
466. *Ibid.,* pp. 2–3.
467. *Ibid.,* pp. 3–32.
468. *Ibid.,* pp. 59–139.
469. *Ibid.,* pp. 196–97.
470. *Ibid.,* pp. 178–79.
471. *Elements of Moral Science* (1790–93) (3d ed.; Edinburgh, 1817), II, 66.

472. *Ibid.,* pp. 40–47, 55–69.
473. *Ibid.,* p. 69.
474. *Ibid.,* p. 1.
475. *Ibid.,* pp. 1–2.
476. *Ibid.,* I, 126.
477. *Ibid.,* II, 111.
478. *Ibid.,* pp. 96–97.
479. *Ibid.,* pp. 93–94.
480. *Ibid.,* p. 147.
481. *Ibid.,* pp. 149–60.
482. *Ibid.,* I, 11–13.
483. "Account of the life and writings of Adam Smith" (1794), pp. 33–34; in *Collected Works,* ed. W. Hamilton (2d ed.; Edinburgh, 1877), X, 3–98.

# ANALYTICAL GUIDE

# ANALYTICAL INDEX

Prepared by Miriam P. Arnett

THE Analytical Guide on the preceding page summarizes the coverage and organization of *Readings in Early Anthropology*. All of the entries in this Guide appear as headings in the book itself, in the same order, and the Guide gives (in italics) the page number on which each subdivision begins.

The index that follows refers the reader in the usual way to the pages on which references appear in the text or notes; page numbers appear in italics. In addition, for each author quoted in the text, the index refers the reader to the appropriate main part and subdivision of the Analytical Guide; these references are given in roman numerals and letters preceding the page reference numbers. In this way, the reader will be able readily to determine for each author cited the chronological period and general subject of his work.

Dr. Slotkin generally gives full bibliographic references for works cited, sometimes in the text, more often in the Notes that appear at the end of the text, and a separate bibliography would have been voluminous and unnecessarily repetitive. However, the notes annotating the major works cited are listed for each author in the index, to aid the reader in compiling bibliographic information.